DATE DUE

MY 29 01			
AP 20 '04			
MY 9 07			

DEMCO 38-296

The Origins of Japan's
Medieval World

The Origins of Japan's Medieval World

Courtiers, Clerics,
Warriors, and Peasants
in the Fourteenth Century

EDITED BY

Jeffrey P. Mass

Stanford University Press

STANFORD, CALIFORNIA   1997

Stanford University Press
Stanford, California
© 1997 by the Board of Trustees of the
Leland Stanford Junior University
Printed in the United States of America

CIP data are at the end of the book

To Sir Christopher Zeeman,
Friend of Japanese Studies,
and Principal Emeritus of
Hertford College

Preface

ON THE FIRST of September 1994, some sixteen Japanese medievalists from around the world gathered in a medieval site in Oxford for the purpose of taking a new look at Japan in the fourteenth century. The sponsor of our conference was Hertford College, whose origins actually predate the fourteenth century, to the year, indeed, that followed the second Mongol Invasion of Japan (1282). Thus when "Hart Hall" was young, Go-Daigo and Takauji had not even been born! Inspired, uniquely, by such surroundings, we met in a room that dated from the age of Nobunaga. Under the gaze of scholars from centuries past, and amidst shelves filled with centuries-old tomes, we proceeded to fill portions of our own medieval canvas, as we sought to understand Japan after the fall of Kamakura.

The planning for this conference seems almost as old as its venue and subject matter; it originated in long-ago conversations at the Association for Asian Studies annual meeting. A first concrete step was taken in 1990, when the Medieval Academy of America invited me to organize a panel of Japanese medievalists for the purpose of introducing our field at their yearly convention. The title of this book dates from that occasion, when I and four former students embarked on what we hoped would be a breakthrough experience. Andrew Goble, Thomas Keirstead, Joan Piggott, and Hitomi Tonomura were my copanelists, gathering in Vancouver for the great event. At the appointed hour, we took our places behind a microphone in a cavernous room with hundreds of seats—and spoke to an audience of no more than a dozen. However, we cheered ourselves by realizing that we were on to a good idea, which we might develop into something more ambitious. Four years later we convened our expanded group in Oxford, thanks to the generosity of Hertford College.

The conference was to be international, balanced by discipline, seniority, and country of origin. To explore anything as grand as the origins of a medieval world seemed to require a world view! As it happened, the two senior figures I most wanted were unable to attend—John Whitney Hall, owing to his debilitating illness, and H. Paul Varley, who was about to take up his new post in Hawaii (though Varley gallantly contributed a paper). The absence of Hall was especially disappointing, since we had hoped to draw inspiration from him yet again. At any rate, when we drank the opening toast to our absent mentor, the College's claret never tasted better.

Others who were invited but could not attend were Barbara Ruch, Suzanne Gay, and Thomas Keirstead—all scholars of the fourteenth century, and, in Ruch's case, a specialist on popular culture, which we could not compensate for. Kozo Yamamura was also unable to attend, leaving us without an expert on the economy for a period whose developments in this sphere were so obviously central. But the papers we did have moved easily between disciplines (history, religion, and literature), and the one by Goble drew heavily on the visual arts. Moreover, historians dealt with intellectual currents and not merely institutions, and religionists dealt with the entrenched establishment and not just Zen. Though the papers, in some cases, were only introductions to their rich subjects, their authors (as well as the field) can now build on these beginnings.

Beginnings were very much on our minds, as witness the number of young scholars making their professional debuts. At the time of the conference, Mikael Adolphson, Thomas Conlan, and Thomas Nelson were all working on their dissertations, and their papers, printed here, are their first major publications. Yet it also seemed essential to have seniority well represented, and Seno Seiichirō (Waseda) and Ōyama Kyōhei (Kyoto) were thus invited from Japan. Seno was my original teacher of old documents a quarter-century ago, and Ōyama has been teacher-adviser to three of my students (Goble, Adolphson, and Conlan). Moreover, Kondō Shigekazu, a younger scholar, joined us from Tōdai, and exhibited a special warmth that none of us will forget. The presence of the three medievalists from Japan gave our conference a greater depth, even as we sought to set our own agenda. The absence of a common vocabulary among the different disciplines was a reminder of just how much distance still separates us.

Other participants in Oxford were Richard Bowring and Noel Pinnington, from Cambridge, who provided important ballast on the side of literature. Though they did not deliver papers, they were active in the conference in every other way. Also attending were Neil McMullin, from Toronto, and Carl Steenstrup, from Munich, with each contributing richly to our discussions. Several Japanese colleagues from Oxford joined us for the opening ceremonies, and Professor Christopher Zeeman, the Principal of Hertford, hosted the initial dinner. I have sought to express our gratitude to Professor Zeeman and to the College by dedicating this volume of papers to him.

Needless to say, numerous persons deserve my special thanks. Professor Zeeman helped to shepherd my application through the College's Japan Appeal Committee. Left with the task of actually bringing a membership together, I consulted Cappy Hurst, Andrew Goble, Martin Collcutt, and various others. As the conference itself approached, James McMullen, of Oxford, became a major player, listening to my worries about late papers. In Japan, Bruce Batten served as a coordinator for the Japanese participants, along with Haruko Wakabayashi. Peter Baker, the College Bursar, became a confidant, helping me with the budget and with local arrangements. Paul Coones, Fellow of Hertford, arranged the use of the "Nobunaga Room," succumbing to my plea that only the College's oldest would do. The staff at Hertford, too many to name, were outstanding, from the butler, to the porter, to the catering manager, to the scouts who unfailingly made up the beds.

My two "young assisters" also deserve special mention—Haruko Wakabayashi, who provided summaries of the Japanese papers, and Thomas Nelson, who doubled (and tripled) as copyist, chauffeur, and guide. On our final morning, a lovely Sunday, it was he who carried the tour flag for our Japanese group as we wandered among Oxford's most beautiful colleges. As the gargoyles looked down and we walked from cloister to cloister, we savored our final medieval experience together.

The Humanities Center at Stanford has provided me with a "detached" office and time off, and Stanford's Japan Fund and Center for East Asian Studies provided support for a research assistant and an indexer. Andrew Goble obtained permission to use the portrait of Go-Daigo that adorns the jacket, and Arnie Olds prepared the map. Finally, I am grateful to Nathaniel Bolin, who prepared the Bibliography and typed the final text, and made himself, in the process, a world authority on macrons.

J.P.M.

Contents

Editor's Note   xiii

Contributors   xv

Introduction   I
JEFFREY P. MASS

PART ONE

I   Of Hierarchy and Authority at the End of Kamakura   17
    JEFFREY P. MASS

2   Largesse and the Limits of Loyalty in the Fourteenth Century   39
    THOMAS CONLAN

3   The Kikuchi and Their Enemies in the 1330s   65
    SENO SEIICHIRŌ

4   Bakufu and Shugo Under the Early Ashikaga   78
    THOMAS NELSON

5   Peasants, Elites, and Villages in the Fourteenth Century   91
    KRISTINA KADE TROOST

PART TWO

6   Visions of an Emperor   113
    ANDREW GOBLE

7   Re-envisioning Women in the Post-Kamakura Age   138
    HITOMI TONOMURA

8   Warrior Control over the Imperial Anthology   170
    ROBERT N. HUEY

9   Cultural Life of the Warrior Elite in the Fourteenth Century   192
H. PAUL VARLEY

10   The Warrior as Ideal for a New Age   209
G. CAMERON HURST III

PART THREE

11   Enryakuji—An Old Power in a New Era   237
MIKAEL ADOLPHSON

12   Musō Soseki   261
MARTIN COLLCUTT

13   Kokan Shiren and the Sectarian Uses of History   295
CARL BIELEFELDT

PART FOUR

14   Ashikaga Takauji and the Fourteenth-Century Dynastic
Schism in Early Tokugawa Thought   321
I. J. MCMULLEN

15   The Fourteenth Century in Twentieth-Century Perspective   345
ŌYAMA KYŌHEI

Notes   369
Bibliography   451
Index   477

Editor's Note

M Y CONCERN in helping to prepare these papers for publication
has been to ensure clarity of presentation before anything else. That
has meant a concentration on the text—on readability, organization, and
trenchancy as the highest values. Yet consistency, at some level, is also important, from the meanings of Japanese terms, to the romanization of emperors' names (Godaigo or Go-Daigo), to matters of capitalization, to the
techniques for rendering Japanese dates (era names or not). Concerning
the last, the contributors from Britain had to be gently reminded that the
month precedes the day at Stanford University Press, emulating the style
of Japanese documents themselves (thus 12/24, not 24/12).

The Notes were another matter, and it has been part of my education
to realize that scholars in other disciplines have their own techniques, and
that there remains little consensus even among fellow historians. Acknowledging that I had no right to occupy the high ground alone, I decided to
allow a limited decentralization, reflecting a familiar theme of the fourteenth century itself. I have sought internal consistency in the papers and
nothing more, saving a stab at something slightly more ambitious for the
Bibliography.

Contributors

MIKAEL ADOLPHSON received his Ph.D. from Stanford in 1996, and is Assistant Professor of History at the University of Oklahoma. The title of his dissertation is "Monks, Courtiers, and Warriors in Premodern Japan: The Secular Power of Enryakuji in the Heian and Kamakura Eras."

CARL BIELEFELDT is Associate Professor of Religious Studies at Stanford University, and the author of *Dōgen's Manuals of Zen Meditation* (Berkeley: University of California Press, 1988).

MARTIN COLLCUTT is Professor of East Asian Studies at Princeton University, and the author of *Five Mountains: The Rinzai Zen Monastic Institution in Medieval Japan* (Cambridge, Mass.: Harvard University Press, 1981), among other studies.

THOMAS CONLAN is a Ph.D. candidate at Stanford University, and is writing his dissertation on medieval warfare in Japan.

ANDREW GOBLE is Associate Professor of History at the University of Oregon, and is the author of *Kenmu: Go-Daigo's Revolution* (Cambridge, Mass.: Harvard University Press, 1997).

ROBERT N. HUEY is Associate Professor of Japanese Literature at the University of Hawaii, and the author of *Kyōgoku Tamekane: Poetry and Politics in Late Kamakura Japan* (Stanford, Calif.: Stanford University Press, 1989).

G. CAMERON HURST is Professor of Asian Studies at the University of Pennsylvania, and the author of *Armed Martial Arts of Japan: Swordmanship and Archery* (New Haven, Conn.: Yale University Press, forthcoming), among other studies.

JEFFREY P. MASS is Yamato Ichihashi Professor of Japanese History and Civilization at Stanford University, and Visiting Professor of Japanese at Hertford College, Oxford University. He is the author of the forthcoming *Yoritomo's Japan: The Foundations of Dual Government at the End of the Twelfth Century*, among other studies.

I. J. MCMULLEN is Fellow and Tutor in Japanese at Pembroke College, Oxford University, and the author of *Genji Gaidan: The Origins of Kumazawa Banzan's Commentary on the Tale of Genji* (Oxford: Ithaca Press, 1992), among other studies.

THOMAS NELSON is a candidate for the D. Phil. at Oxford University, and is a Lecturer at the University of Stirling in Scotland. His dissertation is on the warrior houses of northern Kyushu during the twelfth to fourteenth centuries.

ŌYAMA KYŌHEI is Professor Emeritus of Japanese History at Kyoto University, and the author of "Medieval Shōen," in the *Cambridge History of Japan*, vol. 3 (Cambridge: Cambridge University Press, 1990): 89–127, among numerous other studies.

SENO SEIICHIRŌ is Professor of Japanese History at Waseda University, and the editor and compiler of *Nanbokuchō ibun—Kyushu hen*, 7 vols. (Tokyo: Tōkyōdō shuppan, 1985–92), among numerous other studies.

HITOMI TONOMURA is Associate Professor of History at the University of Michigan, and the author of *Community and Commerce in Late Medieval Japan: The Corporate Villages of Tokuchin-ho* (Stanford, Calif.: Stanford University Press, 1992).

KRISTINA KADE TROOST is East Asian Librarian and Adjunct Assistant Professor of History at Duke University. Her dissertation is entitled "Common Property and Community Formation: Self-Governing Villages in Late Medieval Japan."

H. PAUL VARLEY is Sen Sōshitsu XV Professor of Japanese Cultural History at the University of Hawaii, and the author of *Warriors of Japan as Portrayed in the War Tales* (Honolulu: University of Hawaii Press, 1994), among other studies.

The Origins of Japan's
Medieval World

The provinces of Japan in the 1330s

The Provinces of Japan in the 1330s

Introduction

JEFFREY P. MASS

THE FOURTEENTH CENTURY in Japanese history has been known variously, evoking that era's unusual complexity. Following its initial third, known universally as the "late Kamakura" (Kamakura *makki*), confusion of a high order sets in. The brief episode of the Kenmu Regime (Kenmu *seiken*) was once regularly referred to as the "Restoration" (Kenmu no chukō), emphasizing a powerful thematic message. Similarly, the Age of the Northern and Southern Courts (Nanbokuchō, 1336–92), which we now regularly encounter, was once pared in half and known as the Age of Yoshino. As recalled by Professor Seno from his days as a schoolboy, textbooks of that era insisted on the Southern Court at Yoshino, with the Northern "emperors" an illegitimate line of usurpers.[1] Finally, bypassing altogether this once-important stress on the imperial center, the Muromachi is now preferred over the Ashikaga, though the choices here are mostly matters of taste — similar (place and family) to the interchangeable Edo and Tokugawa.

Scholars today seem untouched by these old controversies.[2] That is, to call the era Nanbokuchō on one page is not inconsistent with calling it Ashikaga on another; we are no longer making choices between the respective courts, or making choices, indeed, between courtiers and warriors. The problems of interpretation clearly lie elsewhere, with characterizations no longer tied to a selection of names. Instead, the place of the fourteenth century in the larger flow of Japanese history is uppermost, which means juxtaposing it with what preceded and followed it. As expressed in the title of this book, the origins of Japan's medieval experience merit being pushed forward, to the end rather than the beginning of the Kamakura age.

Several specific motivations influenced the choice of the fourteenth century for collaborative study. First, the trajectory of my own research was now moving in that direction, having been devoted almost exclusively to what came before it. Second, the fourteenth century was now attracting the interest of younger scholars, who were choosing it as the general context for their Ph.D. theses. For historians especially, the "comfortable predictability" of the Kamakura age now made it seem less a time of change than the post-Kamakura. And third, a full-scale conference in the West devoted to that era had never been held, despite its obvious interest and importance.

There was also, at least for a few of us, the memory of a twenty-year-old book review written by Nagahara Keiji in which he chided us for using the title "Medieval Japan" for a collection of essays whose subject matter began in the eighth century and whose first five chapters dealt with the Nara and Heian periods.[3] In truth, we had given no thought whatever to the implications of that title, satisfied, at the time, simply to celebrate the attention we were now giving to a new subject (the eighth to sixteenth centuries). The papers, and the professional commitment, were what was important; the title was little more than a statement of a pioneering purpose. Those of us who participated in that first multiauthor project on the pre-Tokugawa were simply working to promote the emergence of a new field. But a generation of research and writing has now passed, and it has seemed appropriate to turn to the long-postponed question of what it was that did, after all, make Japan "medieval."

Unfortunately, we underestimated the intransigence of this formidable problem, even as we did our best to approach it at the conference. Our final session was a stimulating discussion of whether to use the title of the conference for the book that was to follow. In the end, we had too little time in which to resolve this thorny problem, leaving me with neither an endorsement nor a rejection. After considering a number of possible alternatives, I decided to keep the original title, drawing on the papers in their revised form. Though the title may not reflect a mature consensus, it does introduce the debate on periodization, and the papers, on this question, can speak for themselves.

My own preliminary thinking might usefully be summarized here, with my remarks limited to those best suited to institutional history. As I now believe, what was new in the 1180s was introduced into a context that was very old yet still vibrant, whereas what was new in the 1330s had broken free of the constraints of that framework. No one, in the 1330s, could have predicted much of the future. Thus, the start of the medieval period was synonymous with the erosion of reasonable certainty, which was itself a result of the loosening of the past's informing assumptions. At such a juncture, the center came to be occupied by persons previously external to it, who might compete relatively unhandicapped by the circumstances of their birth. At the same time, the hinterland was no longer assumed to be in a condition of natural indenture to the center: it now had the potential to begin to forge its own destiny. The start of the medieval, then, involved a merging of the worlds of the courtiers and the warriors, followed by an inversion of their relative positions, and a decline in the momentarily enhanced status of the center itself. The age of Kamakura had witnessed none of these conditions and had been an era best characterized by the separation into jurisdictional spheres. Japan's bold experiment with two authority systems ended in the 1330s.

These remarks represent an elaboration of the views that I posed initially in my letter of invitation to attend the Oxford conference. The invitation laid out the basic argument with these observations: "The encasement of the past began to break up only in the fourteenth century, [when] the Heian-based social hierarchy started to turn over. . . . The rules changed, new behavior was everywhere, the past was only one of several competing influences. After the better part of a millennium, the spell cast by courtiers was finally broken." Not unexpectedly, the traditional periodization remained a tenacious presence for many who chose to attend, even as some participants began to consider their own new criteria for assessing the transition to the medieval. Thus, for example, for Conlan it was the unprecedented condition of sustained warfare, which exerted an utterly transforming effect on the country's warriors, whereas for Troost it was the settling down of peasants into nucleated villages, accompanied by a new aggressiveness to set the terms for their own lives and livelihoods. Or again, for Goble, it was the onset of a kind of intellectual "millennium" in the early 1330s under the leadership of Go-Daigo and then Ashikaga Takauji, who merit being considered Japan's first medieval men. For Tonomura, the origins of the medieval were linked to a descent by women into a hitherto unknown condition of subservience; for Hurst, they were associated with the warriors becoming the moralists and principal spokesmen of their age. For Adolphson, the nub of the transition lies in the collapse of the joint defense of the polity by the central and provincial elites; for Bielefeldt, the transition lies in the emergence of a new sectarianism, as revealed in the first partisan Buddhist histories. The criteria, as so formulated, are obviously in an early stage of development, yet they oblige us to consider seriously a basic change in our conceptualization: Japan in the Kamakura period was still trying to retain its ancient framework, and the transition between different epochs occurred in the fourteenth century, not in the twelfth. The transition is the common subject of the papers contained in this book.[4]

IN MY OWN CONTRIBUTION (Chap. 1), I have sought to make my views on the chronological positioning question as explicit as possible, and have thus adopted a methodology that is simple and straightforward. Delving headlong into the fourteenth century, looking for new insights, I encountered an extraordinary mix of new underminings of *shōen* and *shiki* (estates and estate rights)—that system of organization expressed by a hierarchy of named entitlements, which had been dominated since mid-Heian times by courtiers and clerics. Most surprising, these underminings were not merely the products of a more aggressive level of criminality by warriors, but rather took the form also of new kinds of transactions between new and old partners. Persons at different social levels were now starting to accumulate identical sources of income, as the nomenclature of *shiki* ceased to be class-specific, and as relationships became more easily rooted in power-based contexts. The *shōen* as the ultimate paradigm of Japan's traditional social order was in the process of being transformed, with changes now expressed by the couplings and decouplings of a new age.

In fact, the argument here might have seemed familiar even to contemporaries, who would have interpreted the advancing chaos as the product of a failure to "rectify names" and to uphold social status. Of course such a diagnosis would have implied its own remedy, involving exhortations to the heart and to the conscience. However, the criteria of eligibility were now being bypassed by too many people, with the scaffolding of social boundary markers becoming rungs on a ladder that could now, for the first time, actually be climbed. As the erosion of the traditional entitlement system became well advanced, the stability of the society was progressively undone.

In the course of my treatment, I introduce such subjects as the violence that bred coercion now at the expense of justice; the uncapping of language and the search for new scapegoats; the property market that made the era one of notaries and adjusters; and the martially inexperienced managers who, only in the 1330s, were called on to become professional fighters. The removal of the insulating cover of the country's "dual polity" now gave local strongmen their first chance to achieve some real history.

The essay by Thomas Conlan shows how we have been taken in by some of our field's oldest assumptions. As openers, he reverses the conventional wisdom of an era of "turncoats and mediocrities" by arguing that treachery would not be reviled unless the society genuinely valued loyalty, and that success, after all, would have been incompatible with mediocrity.[5] In an era in which the rules were unbound as never before, only the nimble of foot could hope to prosper, with constancy and loyalty now deemed impractical. In fact, *chūsetsu* (hitherto, "loyalty") conveyed the cynical notion of "service for sale," leaving loyalty to those residing at the bottom of the warrior ladder. Men who were loyal were those who had no other choices, with autonomy the road to advancement by the upwardly mobile and the ambitious. In Conlan's perfectly rendered phrase, "Instead of transcending personal interest, *chūsetsu* was synonymous with it."

These remarks on loyalty are only to set the stage for the rest of his paper, for Conlan then shifts to an analysis of Takauji's remarkable success. Along with his genius for flexible planning, Takauji pushed himself to become his era's most generous man. He obtained land for the purpose of giving it away, and in so doing, he succeeded in buying the *chūsetsu* of the greatest men of his age, as he took control of the realm by creating a lordship over its leading figures. Conlan's paper is the first study in English to tackle the complexities of building such a system, in the new free-for-all environment of the fourteenth century.

Seno Seiichirō's study of the leading families of Kyushu in the 1330s provides a concrete example of the *chūsetsu*-type options and hazards that were facing the major players. With the realm seemingly adrift at this unprecedented juncture, decisions became subject to a reading of prevailing winds. In fact, even Takauji stood perilously close to being destroyed on a Kyushu battlefield in 1336, an incident, described by Seno, that conveys an effective point. For had a single, critical battle gone the other way, the chapter headings in our history books would all be different. Here we have the essence of the 1330s environment.

Seno's essay is a perfect follow-on to the arena of hard choices presented by Conlan. But as Seno reminds us, pragmatism had to compete with hatred, which was not the simple opposite of devotion. Loyalty may have been for sale, but only by those who could overcome their old animosities. In the case of Kyushu, the house of Kikuchi made the wrong turn, a product of its long-standing hatred for its rivals, all of whom were now allying with Takauji. As a result, the potential of the Kikuchi was seriously impaired, and the family ceased to be a dominant local power.

The paper by Thomas Nelson provides further insights into an environment in which policy decisions were the result of trial and error, with flexibility the great asset of the Ashikaga hegemons. As Nelson demonstrates, the *shugo* post now became a far less uniform entity than its Kamakura predecessor, as Takauji sought to strengthen or weaken it depending on circumstances. In a sense, Nelson likens Takauji to a master chess player, even as much of the competition was with his own men. At the same time, Nelson compares the Ashikaga kindred with that of the Hōjō who preceded them, arguing that Takauji's vaunted house organization was indebted to earlier models.

In another area, Nelson underscores our sense of the provinces becoming increasingly different from one another, requiring individualized attention by the Ashikaga leadership. As local power relations changed, the internal boundaries of provinces came to be redrawn in various ways, and administrative systems were adjusted according to need. The historian's notion of *shugo*, "one to a province," is a major casualty here, obliging us to seek a more complicated matrix of overlapping policies.

The countryside, its people, and its economy are the subjects of Kristina Kade Troost's paper on rural Japan in the fourteenth century. Beginning with a discussion of the growth of population and expansion of the arable, she enumerates the forms of agricultural intensification during that general era, allowing us to see beyond such simple concepts as double-cropping. Students of the medieval need to emulate contemporaries in their quest for greater knowledge of the physical environment—of the advantage, for example, of saucer ponds over valley ponds, and of the uses to which different technologies might be put. Troost reveals a world of mostly old knowledge now given new applications, which resulted in a countryside with a changing face. As she informs us, a large percentage of current village names actually date from the fourteenth century—a product of the social transformations occurring at that time.

Troost elaborates on the rise of independent smallholders, and the appearance, only now, of the nucleated village. She provides a sense of people settling down, living in houses intended to last, and defining their permanent places of residence by encircling them with walls and moats. She goes on to identify the core elements of an emerging village self-government, emphasizing not only a broadening of political participation but also an increase in military and judicial powers, as well as in collectively owned property. As Troost explains, this phenomenon developed mostly from a growing awareness that villagers were now capable of assuming such responsibilities. On this point, she joins an emerging consensus of scholarly opinion that elites and nonelites together were now seeking mutual advantage. Peasants in the fourteenth century never had it so good, as they acquired their own voices at the bargaining table.[6]

For some years now, Andrew Goble has been consulting the voices of his informants, the contemporaries who knew, or knew about, the emperor Go-Daigo. But now Goble has gone further by claiming to have had a visual sighting—Go-Daigo lives(!), as depicted, for posterity, in various portraits. After observing that the vengeful spirit of the emperor was thought to have survived his death in 1339, Goble undertakes to keep the embalming fluid flowing freely, by reflecting on the living legacy of this extraordinary man. As he observes, Go-Daigo had the ultimate "fresh start" mentality required by his age, which allowed him to be the great originator and tinkerer of his times. Nothing save his own centrality was to be considered sacred, and even that, he realized, might be at risk unless he removed the dangers.

For Goble, then, the era was one of reinvention in which the new and old would require dosages of remixing, until the "pivot of the realm"—the emperor himself—was fully restored. That the age marked a true ending of the classical world was clear, moreover, to contemporaries—to an extent, as depicted by Goble, that seems remarkable. For the imperial institution itself was now a topic of discussion, with its survival no longer a matter simply of its divine beginnings. In other words, an "end of history" was actually debated at this time, with restless intellectuals like the former emperor Hanazono at the forefront. Fueled by such ruminations, Go-Daigo set about to create a first chapter in a new volume of history, a chapter that he fully intended to be followed by a second. Unfortunately for him, the actual author of that second chapter was Takauji, even as much of its inspiration derived from Go-Daigo.

The paper by Hitomi Tonomura deals with the deteriorating condition of women in the fourteenth century. Tonomura sets out to achieve two major goals. First, she uses the final aristocratic diary written by a woman as a "metaphor for the close of the age of the female voice." And second, she takes us through a rehearsal of the sequence of marriage forms, recapitulating—and questioning—the pioneering historian of that subject, Takamure Itsue. On both counts, Tonomura has immeasurably advanced our understanding of women in these times and has given us our most informed treatment in English of each subject.

The poignant life of Tonomura's diarist, Hino Meishi (d. 1358, the same year as Takauji), underlines the transition to a new age, in which the subjective voice of female authors comes to be stilled, to be replaced by writing that "exclusively described men's lives and transmitted men's ideas and orders." This shift is unmistakable, and it extends our understanding of the fourteenth century as a watershed. But it is Tonomura's treatment of marriage that allows her to make her strongest statement, positing the indenture of women as a further criterion for marking the origins of the medieval. As she puts it, aptly invoking Michel Foucault, here was a "dense transfer point for power relations."

As Tonomura suggests, "Marriage in premodern Japan never resembled its medieval Western counterpart." She then goes on to describe the transition from a fundamentally sexual relationship without ceremony, to a highly elaborate, highly public melding of two houses. Using Takamure's schematized sequence of stages, she emphasizes the importance of the removal of the woman's body from the place of her natal family, to a patri-local site in which the groom's family enjoyed new leverage. Juxtaposing the silence of Kamakura sources with the ostentation of later materials on the subject of marriage, Tonomura strengthens her point by showing how warrior authorities reacted to this change. They did so by acknowledging wives now as the possessions of their husbands. The onset of the medieval thus becomes synonomous with the progressive commodification of women.

Robert Huey uses the history of imperial anthology production to highlight his own way of assessing the shift to the medieval. He points out that the selection of poets to be represented in each new collection was profoundly political, so that the makeup of the literary canon was a reflection of the balance of power in Kyoto during each generation. Huey notes a beginning involvement by the Bakufu before the end of Kamakura, though one that was consistent with the growing interaction of the two capitals. As in other spheres, the rivalry between the two imperial branches now increasingly required an external referee. After 1336, conditions came to favor a rapid acceleration toward control of the process by Takauji, though the anthologies remained styled as imperial compilations. The perception of their continuing importance is revealed by the sponsorship of a competing collection by the rival Southern Court.

On the related question of whether a warrior flavor came to dominate the poetry itself, Huey's view, much like the problem, rests on nuance and degree. The battlefield and society's dislocation became legitimate themes, but alongside, rather than in place of, the moon, flowers, and snow. However, when the initiative for a new anthology passed explicitly to a warrior leader for the first time (Takauji, in 1356), the occasion, and the circumstances, had now changed. The inducement was no longer one of celebrating a shift between imperial factions; rather, it was one of commemorating Ashikaga victories.

H. Paul Varley in his essay tells a story of the sparks that came flying once warriors, heady with victory, took over the broadways of Kyoto. The well-known theme of *basara* ("extravagance") has long been associated with the fourteenth century, but here we are given vivid portraits of individual practitioners. The most illustrious was Sasaki Dōyo, a *shugo* who was also a trickster and consummate trendsetter. Drawing heavily on the *Taiheiki*, Varley recounts the most famous anecdotes for which Dōyo's life is so memorable, and helps us to draw closer to the new elite of those times.

If the flamboyant behavior itself constitutes its own most vivid evocation, Varley's treatment of related subjects (fads, furnishings, feasts, etc.), contributes to a more fully rounded picture. Much of what was new socially in that era proved to have real staying power, making Dōyo, in a sense, a kind of Renaissance figure—a theater-going, art-collecting, tea-drinking epicurean, who was fortunate, given his fancies, to have lived when he did. It is hard to imagine him prospering under Japan's first Bakufu, by contrast with the Ashikaga so stodgy, humorless, and restraining. On the other hand, the somewhat more refined tastes of the succeeding Kitayama epoch might not have suited him well either.

If Dōyo was the quintessential sensualist of his era, warriors were increasingly concerned with reconciling their new place in society intellectually. G. Cameron Hurst III profiles the cerebral warrior, a subject that is satisfyingly rich and many-sided. He begins by comparing the legal formularies (*shikimoku*) of the first two shogunates, and shows how they represented different mind sets, and, therefore, times. Whereas the Formulary of 1232 was concerned with fitting the warriors into the ancient order, its counterpart of a century later acknowledged a much more dangerous world; the warriors now bore responsibilities commensurate with their new status as society's captains, requiring them to cultivate their skills as both sage and soldier. It had fallen to the country's fighting men to govern high and low.

As Hurst makes clear, a handful of individual warriors now presumed to record compendia of advice (*kakun*), which were targeted for the soldier-statesmen, the new men of the hour. By comparing the topics and emphases in the most prominent of these manuals, Hurst shows that there was a mix of views at the time, albeit within a fairly narrow framework. Typically, Takauji, one of these authors, seems unusually prescient and aware, the first to encourage a true balance of the civil and military (*bun* and *bu*), but wary, simultaneously, of warriors residing in Kyoto.[7] Other writers adjusted this balance variously, with Shiba Yoshimasa stressing virtue and cultivation, and Nitta Yoshisada extolling the martial values. Assessing Yoshisada is in fact problematical. If warriors were only now learning their trade for the first time (as several of our papers argue), his exhortations to prepare for the battlefield would have been timely and practical.

Hurst's final major subject, the ancient practices (*kojitsu*) of the fighting men, is a gloss on precisely this kind of potential contradiction. For the "old ways" seemed to emphasize many of the wrong things. In particular, at a time when swordsmanship was replacing archery as the indispensable skill, the *kojitsu* manuals remained rapturously attached to the bow; it seemed not to matter that mastery of that great tradition was increasingly irrelevant. Hurst notes the many anomalies between ideals and this new kind of reality, stressing a nostalgic dimension to the era's writings.

Clearly, the instructional tone of warrior manuals seemed to derive little from the mysteries of religion. However, that did not mean that organized Buddhism had ceased to be a significant influence. The paper by Mikael Adolphson elaborates two subjects: the condition of long-established temples like Enryakuji in an age of Ashikaga-sponsored Zen, and the applicability to the Nanbokuchō of Kuroda Toshio's thesis of shared power among the elites (*kenmon taisei*). Beginning with John Hall, all historians writing in English on the Heian and Kamakura periods have been indebted to Kuroda's notion of courtiers, clerics, and warriors sharing national governance. Before Kuroda, Japan's military age was seen to have begun in the 1180s, when its courtier age ended, with the next century and a half marking a decline into feudalism. Japanese history, without Kuroda's thesis, relied, implausibly, on a few great turning points.[8] The questions posed by Adolphson are more difficult, however: first, the degree to which the shared governance ever fully included the temples, and second, the extent to which Kuroda's thesis retains its utility for the fourteenth century. It is fair to say that Adolphson harbors reservations about both.[9]

He also notes a significant realignment of the religious world into old and new factions in the 1330s. After centuries of competition among themselves, the "establishment" temples now made peace with one another and targeted a new enemy: the cluster of Zen institutions that were prospering under Ashikaga patronage. Meanwhile, the Ashikaga developed policies designed to weaken the autonomy of temples like Enryakuji, succeeding to the point of eroding much of their independence. As described by Adolphson, the Ashikaga were now impinging on their capacity for self-governance. Like much else, then, we note here a marked departure from the conditions of the previous century. The country's first true rulership by warriors was effectively foreclosing the interactive governance of the Kamakura era.

In the context of such extraordinary new possibilities, the fourteenth century witnessed the appearance of a number of major historical figures. Beginning with Go-Daigo and several royal contemporaries of rare achievement, there were also Takauji and Tadayoshi, not to mention Masashige, Yoshisada, and Dōyo, among various others. In the realm of religion too the era seemed to produce giants, with perhaps none better known (then and now) than Musō Soseki. The paper by Martin Collcutt sketches the life and times of this remarkable figure, the many facets of whose character tantalize but still mystify us. Thus we follow Musō on his peripatetic journeys from temple to temple, seemingly not wanting (and certainly not waiting) to make his mark anywhere. Yet gradually Musō begins to emerge as the consultant of princes and generals, achieving a level of eminence that promotes him to the very pinnacle in the 1330s. Thus the question for Collcutt is one of assessing the career against the environment. Musō emerges from this exercise as a kind of quintessential product of his times, a man prepared to change patrons as often as required. As we have already seen, success in the fourteenth century required loose-fitting garments, and Musō's absence of personal attachments obviously served him well. That is, he offered his ample mix of *chūsetsu* to potential bidders, and then waited for these buyers to join the queue.

Along the way, Musō also contributed greatly to the success of Rinzai Zen, with the opening of the Tenryuji in 1345 one of the milestone events. Whereas both Adolphson and Collcutt see it as representing a triumph for the new religion, their perspectives, reflecting their topics, are actually quite different—a tale of the twilight for Adolphson, who is describing the Enryakuji; but one of the sunrise for Collcutt, who is depicting the ascent of Zen. Differing perspectives are also at work in the treatments of the Rinsenji, another Zen temple. Thus, whereas Collcutt refers to it as Musō's refuge from a troubled world, I depict it as showing that such refuges were now illusory. In my account, the attack from all directions on Rinsenji's estate holdings underscores the collapse of the ancient order. At any rate, such overlapping coverage by different authors, with their own vantage points, is potentially valuable.

The essay contributed by Carl Bielefeldt draws us further into the religious and intellectual world of Buddhism. Bielefeldt begins by elaborating the problems modern scholars have had of recreating the chronologies of the standard sectarian divisions: there were schools of thought before there were identifiable sects, and founders who were discovered only by their successors. This observation resonates well with the work done by Kamakura historians, who find in their thousands of temple-related documents virtually no references to affiliations by sect. Instead, temples belonged to hierarchies centered in or near Kyoto or Nara, and they were held together less by beliefs than by the expediences of patronage. Thus the concept of formal sects developed only slowly, requiring a new, more exclusive way of conceptualizing what would have been characterized hitherto as merely different study preferences. One of the objectives of Bielefeldt's essay is to show how a few capacious minds in the thirteenth and fourteenth centuries began to anticipate a new form of cleaving within the Buddhist world.

One of these figures was Gyōnen, the first person, according to Bielefeldt, to produce a history of Buddhism organized around a notion of evolving schools; teachers, places, and events deferred to the clusters that were now recognized as separate orthodox teachings. But it was Kokan Shiren, a leading Zen prelate of the fourteenth century, who wrote the first fully mature history of Buddhism; he derived much of his stimulus from Zen's awareness of its own distinct historical tradition, and that differentness implied the same for other schools. Ignoring the gloomy prognostications of *mappō*-induced pessimism, and demonstrating little concern for doctrinal debating points, Shiren produced a work dedicated to recovering the past, but a past that had its own Zen-driven agenda. As Bielefeldt remarks, it was a testament to the reality that times had changed, and that the multiple strands of the Buddhist legacy were about to be reordered. History and current conditions required it.

The final two papers are more consciously historiographical in nature, beginning with I. J. McMullen's reconstruction of the seventeenth-century's memory of the fourteenth. In particular, McMullen looks at the divergent assessments of the early Ashikaga through the writings of two influential Confucian authors of the early Tokugawa. He shows that the inherent interest in the Nanbokuchō derived from its seeming recapitulation of many of the central issues of the later day, that is, questions involving legitimacy, class relationships, and the nature of power. Of course the debates of the seventeenth century were filtered through Confucian lenses, which were further refracted by the complex historiography of China. Asami Keisai represented the interpretive tradition of the ancients, with its emphasis on a growing discrepancy between names and status, which revealed itself, in the era of Go-Daigo, by the treachery of Takauji. Keisai's commitment to a loyalism built around the line of Go-Daigo led him to condemn the disruptive, social-climbing Takauji. What followed was an era of blatant Ashikaga misrule.

By contrast, Yamaga Sokō had little patience with explanations that demonized the ambitions of individuals, though he also found neo-Confucianism's stress on self-cultivation superficial. The judgment of history rested on the effectiveness of its leading figures, and on this point Takauji was the man of the hour. Possessed of a combination of military prowess and governmental decisiveness, he rescued Japan from its inefficiencies and self-indulgences, and was thus a proper link to the Tokugawa present. Sokō's realism and secular understandings of his own world were bolstered by his impressive reading of Japanese history.

In the twentieth century, there have been numerous impressive readings of the fourteenth century. The paper by Ōyama Kyōhei seeks to survey some of the best. In fact, the omission of certain major figures from his account is a mark of the richness of this field in Japan, and of the long-standing and continuing attraction of the Nanbokuchō era itself. Though Professor Ōyama generously offered to expand his coverage to include some of the missing names, comprehensiveness, in such an exercise, is obviously always elusive.[10]

What Ōyama has given us is a series of portraits of individuals and of schools, beginning with the pioneering figures of early this century. He has sought, where possible, to trace intellectual lineages, though he is very much aware of the problem of overlapping careers and influences. Historians are not like dominoes, to be lined up neatly in rows. Nevertheless, the essence of historiography is to seek to identify antecedents and clusters, and Ōyama has delineated the major schools and their leading figures. As he notes, only in the 1930s was there a paralyzing rigidity, whose emphasis on imperial legitimacy led to the "Age of Yoshino." On the other hand, the liberating experience of 1945 yielded great historians like Matsumoto Shinpachirō, who evolved a periodization that closely anticipates ours.

Moreover, even some of the seeds of current trends can be traced to earlier figures, though the topics, as Ōyama admits, are now unprecedently broad. With an emphasis no longer on the linear or on elites, "the people," though never neglected, have been repositioned to center stage. As a by-product, the stage itself has now been widened to accommodate a much larger gallery of historians, with populists joining the older legalists and Marxists. Nonagricultural persons now rub elbows with peasants and proprietors, and the free (and the free-wheeling) sit beside the oppressed; the menus of contemporary historians are making us fat. On the other hand, the notion of multiple experiences in the fourteenth century has been a reminder that digesting it all is not getting any easier.

The approach of the twenty-first century gives us an opportunity for brief reflection. In this age of skepticism about what we can know, we must remember that what we do know can only begin with original traces; the problem is one of reconciling the todays and tomorrows faced by Go-Daigo and Takauji, with the yesterdays of our own retrieval efforts. In spite of the obstacles, the papers in this volume have sought to narrow the gap that separates us from those inventive and practical spirits of the fourteenth century.

PART ONE

CHAPTER I

Of Hierarchy and Authority at the End of Kamakura

JEFFREY P. MASS

THE INNOVATIONS that became institutions during the opening phase of the Kamakura period were designed to stabilize a society whose moorings, after all, had been only moderately unsettled. In spite of the unprecedented scope and violence of the Genpei War (1180–85), its consequences fell somewhat short of being truly revolutionary. That is, rather than warriors now taking over pieces of the countryside in their own names, the Kamakura Bakufu, under its leader Yoritomo, took steps to foreclose precisely that possibility. With winners in the recent war now needing to be held back, Yoritomo commenced his search for a new kind of stasis.

The leadership of the nascent Bakufu had to acknowledge that some things had changed. On the one hand, if warrior ambitions were indeed to be curtailed, a restraining hand from Kamakura would have to be made standard. On the other hand, the legitimate aspirations of warriors would need to be sympathetically handled, lest the Bakufu find itself at odds with too many of its own men. In the end, Yoritomo elected to introduce a pair of organizing principles into the provinces of a kind that had never before been attempted.

First, he acknowledged the key members of his winning coalition as a permanent clientage, granting them their first ever status unrelated to

Kyoto: the families of Kamakura would be known as *gokenin*, or members of a new brotherhood of Minamoto "housemen." Not only would this body exist wholly apart from imperial authority, but also it would be capable of perpetuating itself from one generation to the next. The Minamoto had never before been recognized as a legitimate entity, and had always to be reconstituted by successive leaders.[1]

And second, the men whose collective energies had made Yoritomo's chieftainship possible were given a place in the established economic order, one that would be uniquely identified with Kamakura. Thus, Yoritomo appointed his followers to managerial authorities known as *jitō shiki*, which were to be located within estates (*shōen*) owned by capital-based proprietors. In other words, the most deserving members of the winning coalition were to be rewarded but also restrained, by making them *jitō* who owed estate services. Moreover, the titles of ownership (*ryōke shiki*) were to be placed permanently beyond their reach, perpetuating a division of society by class and function. In effect, the top and the middle of the social hierarchy had not yet been intermixed; nobles and priests were still alone at the summit and fighting men still dominated the middle. However, the "top of the middle" was now controlled by the new *jitō*, who were recognized as a warrior elite, having been appointed, and therefore honored, by Kamakura.

But as the *jitō* soon learned, even their managerships were now made subject to their own good behavior, monitored by the Bakufu, which had assigned them. And thus the military character of the new "warrior" authority was allowed to drop away, a product, fleetingly, of the war years. In its place, the reasoned and the judicial now became paramount, banishing forever the arbitrary and the coercive. As the leadership now realized, if *jitō* were to be prevented from using indiscriminate force, Kamakura would need to impose on itself institutions and controls.

From as early as the mid-1180s, the Bakufu began to direct its energies toward the mediation of disputes. Governance became a matter mostly of hearing and then responding to grievances. In this world, no *jitō* would be so strong as to be capable of avoiding being named a defendant, yet no *jitō* would be so weak that he could not, in different circumstances, also be a plaintiff. In fact, this potential for role reversal proved to be one of the system's most enduring features, obliging all who wished to change something to argue their positions in court. Might could never be seen to have prevailed.

In practice, both capitals had to commit themselves to just and peaceful settlements. Inevitably, the two authorities came to rely on many of the same methods and beliefs, and they found themselves defending what they now shared in common. Each of the capitals thus developed effective systems of justice, with their tribunals working to sustain the single hierarchy of statuses that segmented yet integrated them. The hierarchy itself was conceived of as a scaffolding of offices known as *shiki*, which were rights and responsibilities packaged as "named entitlements," heritable and transferable within limits. Holders of particular *shiki* essentially could only replicate themselves, by accumulating or divesting within the same social class or even family. In this way, *shiki* levels were intended to correspond to the natural divisions of society, a condition that the respective tribunals would work tirelessly to defend. But just as important, *shiki* connected people who occupied different rungs on individual ladders, giving them responsibilities to those above and below them. The landed estate that mutually supported them was to be their joint enterprise—at the same time that it was the mandate of both capitals to ensure a commitment to separate but interdependent worlds.[2]

These conditions lasted until about 1300, and they represent one of several sets of criteria that support the revised periodization proposed in this book. In such a view, most of the Kamakura age becomes less an opening than a closing phase; it marked less the beginning of a new, warrior-dominated age than the final stage, before unraveling, of a lengthy classical epoch. In this construction, the advances of warriors are eclipsed by the tenacity of courtiers, leaving us to ponder why the Kamakura age was unable to bring about the end of its Heian predecessor.

When the decline of the old world finally did begin in earnest, it was marked by changes at all levels of the society. What had always seemed sacrosanct and standard now became unreliable and unpredictable, prodded by an unprecedented upsurge of violence. *Shiki*, the society's shock absorbers, now succumbed to usages never before seen, and a wave of experimentation shook confidences everywhere. After the better part of a millennium in which change had been mostly controlled, new situations were now undermining old certainties.

For most Japanese, the new environment, we can only imagine, must have seemed unsettling in the extreme, with the decline in security, variously defined, the dominant new reality. As a consequence, the two capitals came to be importuned to use the authority that, ironically, they were now losing. In turn, the vitality of the country's justice was now being sapped, and the voices of those with grievances took on a new stridency and urgency. A new vocabulary of rage now followed, with accounts of murder and mayhem its primary vehicles. Emotions that were raw burst into popular discourse, as petitions superseded judgments as the era's most evocative records.[3]

With old boundaries, of all kinds, now being violated, principles that were once important came to be sacrificed. The jurisdictional divisions that formed the basis of the dual polity now became confused under the onslaught of too many wrongdoers crossing too many "borders." The traditional criteria for accepting cases no longer worked. Even worse, a proliferation of the tribunals themselves now occurred, including an array of retired emperors presiding over their own chambers, and a newly revived Central Police Office (Kebiishi-chō) and Records Office (Kirokujo). To a considerable degree, the pursuit of justice now became indistinguishable from the search for patronage and protection, with both rendered equally as the quest for "results," or *seibai*.[4]

At all events, we need to introduce some of the novelties and surprises of this new age, which distinguish it so markedly from its more ordered predecessor. The sense of privilege that once fixed people in their places forever was now eroding to a point in which challenges could no longer be denied on the basis of their being simply unimaginable.

SOME OF THE NEWER JUXTAPOSITIONS

Before the two capitals became effectively branches of the same authority, the emphasis was on separation and on boundaries. *Shiki* captured these divisions well by segmenting people according to standards of birth and eligibility. But now in the fourteenth century we encounter startling new inversions and mergings—from a warrior's appointment as a *ryōke* by Kamakura, to the same warrior's confirmation as a *shugo* (provincial constable) by Kyoto;[5] from a warrior's serving as a *ryōke* and a *jitō* in one estate, to a temple's serving as a *ryōke* and *jitō* in another;[6] and, finally, from a suit brought by a *jitō* against his own deputy, to a suit brought by a *ryōke* against his.[7] A century earlier the right to appoint a deputy would have assumed the power to judge and discipline him, and no higher authority could have intruded upon that power. But now in the fourteenth century a new order appeared, as when a proprietor called on the Bakufu to apprehend a non-*gokenin* who was none other than *his own* managerial appointee.[8]

As the nomenclature of the *shiki* system became less a reflection of a holder's status, it now stood in danger of losing much of its awe and power. The relaxation of eligibility requirements was only one part of this phenomenon; another was the trivialization that resulted from generations of partible inheritance. As a cohort of "fractional" *jitō* now came to reside in adjoining units, the significance of being a title holder was correspondingly diminished.[9] Moreover, not only were there groupings of persons now in possession of what was once a sought-after entity, but also there were persons who were combining these sherds with other fragments of income. As such titles came to be collected into new amalgams of identity, the specificity—and therefore the power—of their constituent elements began to fade.[10]

A final pressure on the *shiki* system was the conversion of these entitlements into piecemeal commodities for sale or endowment (*kishin*). In other words, paralleling the fragmentation of *shiki* through partible inheritance, the lands and rights once conceived of as integrated offices now began to be splintered and traded away. Buyers were no longer judged by eligibility in genealogical terms, but instead were, in practice, judged by their ability to pay. Moreover, much of what the Bakufu had earlier prohibited was now being facilitated and legitimated under its own writ. Thus, Kamakura was not only now involved in the hearing of commodities suits, it was also guaranteeing many of the sales transactions that it was still publicly condemning.[11] In this respect, Kamakura was no different from the sources of justice and patronage in Kyoto, all of whom were parties (along with locals) to the emergence of a thriving commerce in blackmarket *shiki*.

The maturation of this development in the period under review has profoundly affected our understanding of the *shiki* themselves. Once thought to be "infinitely divisible" during the era of their formation,[12] they did not really become so until nearly 200 years later. Thus, the chaos that their emergence seemed to forecast immediately was delayed until the *shiki* themselves ceased to be class signifiers. In the early fourteenth century these packages of social meaning and fixity began to succumb to conditions that were driven by debt and by profit. It is a subject upon which it will be useful to elaborate.

In 1297, the Bakufu unleashed a wave of so-called "debt-cancellation decrees" (*ontokusei*), which were designed to slow the pace of buying and selling. Pawn tickets that were expired could now be redeemed and even sales voided, thereby curtailing, it was hoped, some of the frenzy of the marketplace. Speculators would now, accordingly, be denied, leading to a reduction of impoverishment by *gokenin*, and to a strengthening of the traditional economic order. Those who could count on receiving their full pay packages would be better able to discharge their regular duties.[13]

In a number of instances sales transactions came to be invalidated,[14] improving some family economies in the short term but also creating the conditions for much wider confusion. A variety of would-be patrons now rushed to issue cancellation orders of their own, exacting a price, naturally, for their services; to pawn or sell and to redeem without repayment now seemed possible. At the same time, the new climate of irresponsibility fed by these *ontokusei* edicts began to drive serious buyers and sellers toward fresh strategies. The objective was how to get around the restrictions hampering land transactions. Very quickly, the sale deeds of this period had new clauses inserted in them, underlining the inviolability of sales and transfers. That is, invalidations were now waived by good-faith sellers in advance, voiding subsequent cancellations preemptively. In the language of the day, any "Court or Bakufu invalidation" (*kuge buke ontokusei*) that might be issued was to have no power to upset the transaction being conducted.[15] And to be sure that the buyer understood fully that he would not lose his purchase price, he was guaranteed "his money back," or even more, in writing.[16]

The significance of these provisions lay in their challenge, however implicitly, to the *shiki* system. In effect, the top-down flow of patronage that had underlain the age-old hegemony of high status was now being questioned by persons from the middle of the hierarchy. As those who wished or needed to sell obviously realized, buyers required an environment in which their purchases would be safe. Contracts had to be made secure from official meddling. The result was a new approach to protection of one's resources, with contingencies anticipated and interference enjoined. The sentiment contributed to an assault on privilege more generally.

On the other hand, buyers and sellers might still find themselves needing a patron. The possibility that a courtroom would be required was still real. In particular, the heirs and relatives of sellers might feel their interests compromised unfairly. As a result, they engaged in violations against properties already sold, and also lodged claims that were little more than petitions for "cancellations." For this reason, sale deeds often included yet another kind of waiver, precluding descendants and relatives from any future challenges.[17] For buyers and sellers, then, the sources of potential trouble were the invalidations that made doing business precarious, and the persons who might profit from such disruptive actions. However, the most powerful image remains that of the denunciation of the *ontokusei* edicts themselves. In their indictment of a form of meddling that only persons at or near the summit could engage in, they represent a level of querying that was demonstrably new.

In other ways, too, sale deeds represented a challenge to the top-down organization of authority. In particular, the deeds might be disingenuous on what was being sold. Though lower-level *shiki* seem to have been disposable without any disguise,[18] *shiki* higher up were harder to sell openly.[19] The authorities who had assigned them were frequently quick to object, since transfers created a gulf between those authorities and current holders.[20] Presumably for that reason, the easier course to take was to split *shiki* into tiny slivers, declaring them to be lawfully owned, but not bothering to specify their origins. At any rate, the overwhelming majority of sale deeds fail to cite any connection to *shiki*.

Transfers by sale had of course been around for a long time. So, for that matter, had the transfers known by historians as commendations (*kishin*). In the eleventh and twelfth centuries, such endowments had been central to the growth of *shōen*. In the classic model, a local figure commended his "private holdings" (*shiryō*) to a central noble or cleric, thereby splitting the ownership into proprietary and managerial levels. Significantly, however, the property, now labeled a *shōen*, was registered in the name of the proprietor, who proceeded to grant the commender a managerial or custodial title. It is the tale, writ large, of the divisions by status and influence that constitute the very essence of the growth of the *shiki* system.[21]

Local-to-central commendations did not cease during the early decades of the Kamakura age, though their pace was slower than either earlier or later. It was not until near the end of the century that a new round of endowments again became fully identifiable. Not surprisingly, however, the overall context was largely changed. New *shōen* appear to have been only marginally involved, and new *shiki*, specifically named, were infrequent. Moreover, persons of all classes were now engaging in the practice, with their motivations correspondingly harder to categorize. One thing of course was entirely clear—that donations, which were couched as "pious acts," would not have been subject to *ontokusei*. In fact, there were fewer rules overall controlling the issuance of commendation deeds (*kishinjō*), making the act simply part of the larger disintegrative process we have been observing.

As mentioned, commendations now came from all directions, including those from a "higher" to a "lower" level. That is, courtiers and clerics now issued *kishinjō*,[22] as did the shogun, the Hōjō, and the Bakufu more generally.[23] Moreover, *kishinjō* were issued by persons explicitly signing themselves as "proprietors" (*ryōke*)[24]—the very figures who were the commendees of two centuries earlier. Finally, the recipients of almost all commendations were now religious institutions, narrowing (compared with the past) the scope for such endowments. The temples and shrines themselves obviously pursued these donations vigorously, producing a corpus of new documentation that confirmed the terms and conditions of the transfers of ownership. But few of these records seem integral to the historical mainstream of particular *shōen*.

The best explanation for the new arrangements and the new inducements relates to the new mix of what constituted advantage. The motivation of the religious institutions was obvious: with many of their *shōen* under attack locally, they were seeking to pick up an accumulation of dues, small properties, and other benefits. As we shall see, the range of what was now being commended was vast. For the donors, however, the motivations, as noted, were more complex. Among Kyoto families, patronage was no longer the hierarchical process of earlier times, when those of the highest ranks were the most valued commendees, since it was they who were the system's ultimate guarantors. But now even the imperial family had to buy influence and connections, with a multiplicity of competing royals engaged in the same pursuit. Thus when aristocrats made donations to temples and shrines, they were targeting institutions with which they hoped to strike, or to deepen, special arrangements.

At the same time, the motivations of commenders in the provinces were now less predictable. In particular, refuge from civil governors was no longer the standard inducement for much of anything; the attempt to shield one's interests behind the wall of a *shōen*'s immunities was a practice that belonged essentially to earlier times. Instead, donations to strictly local institutions now often made more sense, since connections closer to home were more compelling than those with the center.[25] Moreover, on the infrequent occasions when a commender did seek a *shiki* in return, it was more likely, commensurate with his status, to be only a minor one, such as a hereditary right to cultivate (*sakunin shiki*) as recompense for paddy donated to the Tōji.[26] In fact, even the old desire to secure one's heirs might now, quite deliberately, be turned on its head. For instance, donors now stipulated that the endowments they were enacting were to foreclose on any possible claims by their descendants.[27]

The question thus arises as to why such commenders elected to endow rather than to sell. Though sales and commendations were in some ways similar, buyers were almost exclusively persons whose payments then concluded the relationship; exchanges involved money for property. The nature of the exchange in commendations was more ambiguous, with donors seeking a connection with a religious institution that might endure. To be the benefactor of a temple was within reach of many persons, but without any particular need to surrender full rights.[28] At the same time, commendations, done out of piety, might evade the strictures, and certainly the invalidations, of *ontokusei*. Donors enjoyed greater discretion than sellers.

We should note, finally, that the commodities donated ranged from cash, to lands, to whole *shiki*. Thus, in one instance, cash was pledged to a local temple in the amount of five *kanmon* annually, a donation that by its very nature forged a continuing relationship.[29] At the other end of the spectrum, the shogun and the Hōjō now "commended" *jitō* titles to shrines and temples, much as they once granted them, by appointment, to *gokenin*.[30] Meanwhile, the holders of other *shiki* were now potential donors, in addition to being investees, legatees, and testators. Thus, in 1330, the manager-priest of an estate in Izumi commended his hereditary *gesu* and *kumon* titles to a local shrine. In other words, this donor was relinquishing what his ancestor may have received at the time of his own commendation.[31] In between, measurable pieces of almost anything of value might be donated, with the only common denominator their status as owned property. As we have seen, ownership itself was now variously achieved.

Moreover, an unknown number of commenders were now demonstrably *jitō*, though outright endowments of their titles are all but unseen. Instead, holders donated portions of their legacies to temples and shrines, for all the same reasons as non-*jitō*.[32] An episode of 1326 brings these strands together, emphasizing what appears to be a freedom of action. In this tale, a widow had inherited a *jitō* post from her late husband, some of whose parts she then molded, "out of piety," into a commendation to a temple. In doing so, however, she warned against her own offspring who might behave as "wicked children" (*akushi*), branding them, in advance, as despoilers in waiting.[33] Though the precise context of her donation cannot be known, the widow's capacity for self-indulgence seems to emerge.

THE NEW ORBIT OF BLAME

During the heyday of Kamakura, the *shiki* system functioned as the principal buttress of law and order. Attempts by individuals to exceed the limits of their entitlements triggered much of the era's judicial activity, which was handled by the tribunals of the two capitals. However, by the start of the fourteenth century, the bottom of society was now bothering the middle and the top in new ways, and was also showing itself to be immune from judicial sanctions. At the same time, there were also unprecedented lateral pressures.

The phenomenon of *akutō*, or bandit gangs, best exemplifies these various new developments.[34] Indeed, their evocation of social flux is very much to the point here. In particular, *akutō* had the potential to entice different parts of the provincial hierarchy onto the side of lawlessness, including *jitō* and, in a few cases, even *shugo*,[35] though the rank and file tended to be drawn from the *hyakushō*, or "yeomanry."[36] Moreover, since not everyone in a troubled area was, or would have remained, the member of an *akutō*, conditions were frequently highly fluid, with victims and victimizers often the same people at different times. The following pair of situations might therefore be considered typical—from one estate in which *hyakushō* expelled the resident official (*gesudai*), to another in which the complainants were the untitled themselves.[37]

Exhibiting organizational patterns that were not strictly or necessarily top-down, *akutō* proved highly unpredictable. Thus if lawlessness was blamed earlier on one person who was named as a defendant, accountability was now diffused among the many. It was a situation that was incompatible with the traditional conception of justice in Japan, with lengthy lists of miscreants replacing the responsible figure in the dock. It was at this time that "wanted posters," containing full and partial names, became commonplace,[38] and in turn served to encourage a drift toward a new kind of solution. Increasingly, a reliance on the use of force replaced traditional justice. Such force, like the criminal activity it was designed to suppress, promoted collective action by men drawn from the region.

As a substitute for the coercive power of the old *shōen*-based hierarchies, men referred to as *jitō gokenin*[39] were now mustered on a provincial or supraprovincial basis.[40] In effect, they were invited to leave their estates to engage in police actions against persons who might simultaneously have been leaving theirs. That is, *akutō* now came to embrace "locals from other domains" (*tashō no tomogara*),[41] people who hitherto would have had few opportunities to collaborate. To the extent then that both sides were now joined in these territorial ventures, the *shōen*-based character of *shiki* experienced a further challenge. Until only recently, *jitō* had spent their entire lives in a campaign to usurp their own estates, by gaining an active sway over local hierarchies.[42] But now in the environment of the post-1300 era, the seeds of new forms of collective action were clearly taking root.

Nor was established authority in much of a position to meet the new challenge. Petitions seeking redress reached new levels of intensity, and even the imperial family was now reviling outlaws—and enemies—as *akutō*.[43] The Bakufu, for its part, ordered its men to suppress banditry, though there is little to indicate effective results. In particular, the age-old strategy of depriving incorrigible criminals of their inherited status was now losing much of its cogency in the face of obvious defiance.

On the other hand, though parts of the country seemed to some degree in crisis,[44] there was no overall resignation in deference to a new situation. No *akutō* anywhere were seeking to replace the *shōen* with something new, even as they undermined estates through campaigns of terror. If local governance was under siege it was not being reconfigured. Nevertheless, the *shōen* as the ultimate paradigm of a stable social order was no longer a didactic model to itself. Petitioners sought new categories of blame.

To underline a growing sense of what must have seemed inexplicable, complainants now enriched the language with a new vocabulary, which effectively captured the rising frustration. *Akutō* were thus accused of having committed "iniquitous deeds" (*akugyō*);[45] the term appears repeatedly in numerous documents. At the center of such accusations was the willful destruction of life and property, typified, in one case, by the burning of a thousand homes, a crime described as "widespread and wanton" (*ran'aku*).[46] Indeed, the violations themselves exceeded a mere flouting of the law, since they represented, in their flagrancy, a breaching of the accepted standards of morality. They were acts that were unprecedentedly evil, committed by persons whose behavior took them beyond the pale.

In an era of "evil deeds" there now emerged "evil language," with "misrepresentation" and "slander" evoked by the ubiquitous term *aku-kuchi* (lit. "bad-mouthing").[47] In a world in which memory of the past still provided much of the footing for the present, nothing could be more unsettling than the manipulation of oral and written expression. Thus litigants were accused of perjury, eliciting rebuttals that charged slander—with both acts rendered equally as *aku-kuchi*.[48] At the same time, although there had always been forgeries, now, in the new circumstances, there were forgers (*bōshonin*), which was another way of impeaching opponents for bearing false witness.[49] Rivals were no longer merely in violation of the customs of local areas, but were now, in addition, the instruments of a capricious misuse of the courts. They were charged by their opponents with calumny and falsehood, crimes that were captured by such terms as *kyoso* ("mendacious charges") and *ranchin* ("spurious defense").[50] The word *moaku* ("ferocious evil") represents a further gloss on a level of frustration that was obviously deepening.[51]

Pretense was another dimension of this kind of manipulation—exaggerations involving oneself instead of an opponent. Persons pretending to hold *shiki* were hardly a novelty, but now they were more difficult to detect, especially since such posturings might have some long-ago basis in fact.[52] Both the patronized and their patrons exacerbated the problem by allowing holdings to be alienated beyond their natural hierarchies, which then encouraged new involvements by extraneous authorities. Thus when sellers and commenders warned posterity not to hide behind the influence of others, they were really warning against confusions of precisely this sort.[53]

The fear of interference by the powerful was now given vivid new expression. In numerous documents we encounter warnings against misuses of the authority (*i*) of shrines and temples (*shaji*), the ranking families (*kenmon*), and the military (*bu*).[54] On the one hand, these points of reference served to confirm the status of the traditional sources of patronage. But on the other, they indicated a new willingness to confuse lines of authority. Support came increasingly from where you could find it.

From a different angle, those perceived to be powerful might also now be closer to ground level. For more than a century, the *jitō* had been the most feared presence locally. After 1300, however, a torrent of new invective came to be directed toward the deputies of *jitō*, acknowledging them, on many estates, as the dominant figures in residence. Since such a trend held the potential of weakening accountability overall, these deputies (*jitōdai*), with increasing frequency, were now themselves called to answer charges in writing, and were summoned to trial in their own names.[55] Moreover, they could now, on their own, initiate legal actions, and could also enter into formal compromise accords (*wayo*) with estate authorities.[56] During an age in which so many *jitō* titles were being fragmented into little more than tiny sources of income, it made little sense to do other than to identify, and then recognize, de facto power.[57]

To militate against the possibility of a deputy *jitō*'s becoming the natural center of an *akutō* therefore required a disposition to acknowledge them.[58] In fact, higher authority more generally and not merely the Bakufu needed to do so—as occurred when the emperor received a complaint and then issued an edict in the matter of a *jitōdai*. And even though the emperor here was seeking to prod the Bakufu into investigating, he was encouraging a sequence of involvements that would have been unlikely earlier. The highest authorities were now concerning themselves with persons of virtually no status.[59]

New practices and contradictory behavior often went hand in hand. To a large extent, much depended on which side of an issue one happened to be on. For example, a seller who wished to be free to alienate to unrelated persons might be the same person who admonished his heirs not to sell or bequeath to others. That is, a willingness, even eagerness, to take advantage of opportunities was tempered by rising apprehensions for the next generation. Thus fathers railed against adopted heirs, female heirs, and even plural heirs, placing these relationships at the core of their own orbits of blame.[60] Meanwhile, subdividing and repeated parceling were especially stigmatized, a call for sanity amidst patchwork holdings everywhere. A heightened sense of worry made these decades a time of contingency planning, and a deed was no longer a deed without the small print.

With status no longer flowing so automatically from *shiki*-holding, men of the provinces now began to seek substitutes. Formal membership in Kamakura's band acquired a new currency, denied in the past to other than descendants of original *gokenin*. But eligibility on the basis of distant achievements now seemed less persuasive than more recent history, leading to the prying open of a long-closed subject; yet another category of exclusivity was about to be questioned. The continuing threat from the Mongols provided the main impetus here, causing Kamakura to invite capable locals to join the defense effort.[61] When documents acknowledging their service were then supplied to them by *shugo*,[62] a willing class of new recruits seemed to be at hand. Here were men prepared to offer dues and military service in return for being allowed to call themselves *gokenin*.

In fact, *gokenin* status was now becoming more integral to a warrior's identity than whether he was a partial *jitō* on a miniscule plot of land. The two terms, always separate, now fused into one, with the emphasis in *jitō gokenin* starting to favor the latter. Moreover, whereas the holding of a *jitō* post continued to presume obligations to estate owners, *gokenin* status was now interpreted as a license to use force. Thus whereas *gokenin* who broke laws a century earlier might have sought to style themselves as *jitō*,[63] now *jitō* who did the same called themselves *gokenin*.[64] For its part, Kamakura was in any event distributing far fewer *jitō* posts, and appointment documents, once so commonplace, were now decidedly rare.[65] The Bakufu was rewarding men from around the country by recognizing them as now residing within its own orbit.

In view of this new emphasis on the present, it is ironic, but perhaps revealing, that the past could still be perceived by some as a refuge.[66] Indeed, numerous petitioners were now presenting long histories, supplemented by genealogies, which itself constituted a largely new development. These *keizu* are of interest for several reasons, not least because they were the first produced by warrior houses in any real numbers.[67] Their purpose was to present abbreviated versions of family histories, as interpreted, naturally, by their current sponsors. That meant positing prestigious beginnings, whether they existed or not; and papering over conflicts and discontinuities along the way. The *keizu* thus produced were often rich artifacts of the imagination, open to criticism both then and now. Yet the timing of their appearance cannot be mere coincidence, so that we must look for simultaneous developments elsewhere. After more than a century of fierce court battles among siblings seeking to break the bonds of family,[68] genealogies may have constituted part of an effort the other way. The beginnings of the replacement of partible inheritance by single heirship at this time might have helped to restore the notion of "kindred" to respectability. A common history, and a long one, would have made sense to some.

Genealogies were current concoctions that potentially distorted and conflated. But there were also genuinely old records that achieved a new currency, though these were used less by provincials than by members of the central establishment. Warriors, surely, would have possessed few documents that dated from the period before the 1180s.[69] At any rate, huge packets of paper, containing items hundreds of years old, now came to be submitted to judges and patrons. To cite only a few examples, a petition by Kōyasan, with seventeen documents appended, had its oldest dating from the year of its own founding, 816.[70] Similarly, a suit brought by Tōdaiji cited a *shōen*, which the temple claimed as its exclusive possession (*ichien no jiryō*) since the age of its own founder, the emperor Shōmu.[71] Finally, this marshaling of evidence from the very earliest time possible might even reach to the supposed beginnings of Japan itself, as in the claim of a status unchanged since the age of Emperor Jinmu, precisely 1,959 years earlier.[72] At the behest of families and institutions whose origins obviously predated those of provincial rivals, conditions in antiquity could thus be postured as the norm, with subsequent challenges and distortions the cause of the present chaos. By inference, Japan needed to have its clock put back.

Yet that clock, during these decades, was having its mainspring removed forever, mostly for the reasons that we have encountered here but also owing to the compromises now entered into by estate owners themselves. These agreements, known as *wayo*, were designed to improve conditions by restructuring them, in effect, dividing responsibilities between proprietors and managers in new ways. By doing so, the owners were acknowledging that courtroom verdicts were no longer sufficiently efficacious, and that concessions of unprecedented kinds (physical divisions of estates, etc.)

would be required.[73] For our purposes, the transfer by proprietors of so much authority to persons not of their own class marked the beginnings of a surrender of the control of local history itself. To this point, rural governance had never been able to conceive of itself as other than a delegation from above, with the destinies of local areas intertwined with destinies centrally. But now after 1300 and the onset of a thousand small fractures, the stresses to the unity of the façade were becoming more obvious.

THE CRUCIBLE OF THE 1330S

Were one to rely on the rhetoric heard in the courtrooms of c. 1330, one might easily conclude that conditions had reached the point of desperation and that the scaffolding of legitimate land rights was facing ruin. Among the numerous expressions of this sentiment, none may be quite as vivid as a lament from the Rinsenji, a newly founded Zen temple in Kyoto.[74] Issued in the form of a petition, the document enumerates a list of revenue shortfalls from the temple's holdings, but it also makes clear that the problems have individual explanations. Guilt, as we shall see, is variously ascribed.

The document contains an inventory of estates from the legacy (*iseki*) of a son of Go-Daigo, and is a call at its end for "justice," or *seibai*.[75] The estates involved were dispersed across a total of sixteen provinces, from Hitachi and Sagami in the Bakufu's heartland, to Bingo and Sanuki to the west of the capital. Three levels of *shiki* holders were identified in each estate (the patron, the proprietor, and the *jitō*, if there was one), along with the annual rent totals owed from each domain. The condition of those rents was then recorded for each estate, though the violators, contrary to expectation, were not always *jitō*. For instance, in one domain, in Izumi Province, it was an *akutō* that was accused, whereas in another, in Awa Province, it was the patron (*honke*). In short, the violations were specific to different levels within individual hierarchies, though the main issue (and the point of the appeal) was the fate of the rents.

When we look at the cases in which *jitō* were the persons accused, we are reminded of the extraordinary range of possibilities that might now involve these managers. For example, a *jitō* in Kaga Province had agreed to pay the proprietor 360 *kan* annually, in return for which the *jitō* would enjoy total local control. Yet in spite of the attractiveness of this so-called "receivership" (*ukesho*), he was still, according to the indictment, underpaying. In a second case, the estate, in Sanuki, had been divided (*chūbun*), by lawful covenant, between the *jitō* and proprietor. However, the *jitō*, upon the pretext of the previous year's "disorder" (*doran*), had siphoned rents from the sector that was not his.[76] In a final example, a *jitō*, of Kii, was cited for rent theft for "more than ten years," with a debt that had now reached 200 *kan*.

Though the situations of these individual violators were different, the thieves were all cited as *jitō*. Even the man with a seeming ownership over half an estate was designated this way, with the *shōen* referred to as a "land divided between a *ryōke* and *jitō*" (*ryōke jitō chūbun no chi*). In other words, the status of the two "owners" seems not to have changed, suggesting the difficulty of conceiving of true parity. In fact, the full implications of the *jitō*-as-owner had hardly been tested, and proprietors were loath to acknowledge or discuss what they had surrendered. Thus, it was they more than the *jitō* who continued to claim possession of the *shōen*'s name, as in the registers that continued to list their landed holdings.

Earlier we noted the parcelization of *jitō* rights, in contradistinction to the "successes" of the *jitō* described here. To the extent that the concept was expanding beyond easy definition, much of its original appeal may have been dissipating. At any rate, we know that it would soon come to be subsumed under a new post-*shiki* category of "men of the province" (*kokujin*), which also included other managerial titles. Moreover, a similar kind of generalizing process was occurring at the top of the hierarchy as well, with the statuses of proprietor (*ryōke*) and patron (*honke*) starting to be conflated. Though at one time they were the preserve of the "higher" and the "highest" nobility, respectively, they were now being combined and shorn of their individual prestige requirements. As we can see from the Rinsenji document, *honke* could now be accused of crimes rather than existing to prevent them; and they could also have their status at the top contested. In short, rivalries within the capital might now be referred to as "*honke* disruptions" (*honke no iran*), in contradistinction to those occurring outside it, which were "*jitō* disturbances" (*jitō no ōbō*). From the point of view of the petitioner, the wealth of the temple was now being squeezed from all sides.

At no point in the Rinsenji petition-inventory is there any reference to the Kamakura Bakufu, and accordingly we cannot identify the anticipated judicial venue(s). The references to guilty *jitō* may have made such explicitness unnecessary, though the naming of *honke* as defendants obviously points toward Kyoto.[77] Nor do we know whether the named defendants had opinions of their own, to the extent of feeling wrongfully or exaggeratedly accused. Ambiguities in such matters were the very reason for lawsuits, and the temple's tale of betrayal may have masked partial guilt of its own. In other words, none of the main actors may have been playing true to his original role, turning these events into a drama of their times. Thus the patrons would no longer have been the guarantors of anything important, and the proprietor would have been little more than an extorter of rents. The *jitō*, the one-time rent collectors, stole and intimidated. Put differently, to the extent that overlapping interests had replaced the mutual shareholding of the past, the *shiki* system, as ladder and cushion, was becoming an anachronism.

Other sources from this period provide other perspectives, and opportunism and despair could readily be combined: the *jitō* who stole may have been deeply in debt, and the *gokenin* who terrorized may have been the object of terror from his own kin. For every emergent strongman there were others obviously falling into dependence. Under a parallel scenario, not all courtiers and clerics could have been hapless victims, though the numbers they cite tend to make grim reading. For example, though Tōdaiji may have exaggerated the totals to a degree, the decline of a certain revenue source—from 4,000 to 50 *chō*—is striking.[78] Yet if some of the luxuries of such temples may have been at risk, the survival of the institutions themselves certainly was not, and the buoyancy of the newer centers may have been countervailing.[79] At any rate, a sense of mounting crisis was unmistakable, which seemed to call for new ideas and renewed energy. As it happened, a small group of extraordinary men appeared on the national scene in the 1330s, each seeking to ride the currents in some new direction.[80]

BEFORE THE 1330S, men who enjoyed military status could exploit it without having to prove much on the battlefield. Their obligations as *gokenin* rarely involved personal risk; and the era was one of incidents more than warfare. Japan's age of armed engagements was a product not of this epoch but of the next. It was only in the 1330s that politics came to be influenced by the ability to deliver force—at the very moment that the Bakufu's monopoly of coercion ultimately failed it.

The convergence of the two spheres of the dual polity helps to explain what otherwise might seem anomalous. That is, as Kyoto and Kamakura became progressively intertwined, their potential to win the support of military followers also converged. Thus, when a handful of courtiers posed as generals and began proffering rewards, they found that they were under little handicap in the competition for men. No warriors then living had ever enjoyed what was suddenly on offer—the luxury of a choice of military allegiances.

In fact, to a degree not actually realized until the events of 1331–33, the country was experimenting with a new performance-based matrix of values. Though the role reversals involving *shiki* constituted a harbinger of things to come, the exigencies of the moment forced a more conscious reappraisal. In particular, as provincials now discovered that they were in demand as warriors, they realized that they might put their services up for sale. They might now become professional fighting men by diverting their skills to a new venue—away from the paddy and practice fields, and over, instead, to the battlefield. The stakes were especially high for the economies of local areas, since the managers of *shōen* were about to be encouraged to leave their estates; the deployment of armies was to be given higher priority. In this climate, courtiers and clerics joined local elites in thinking about and actually preparing for war.

It is striking that men from utterly different backgrounds now had the potential to emerge as military leaders, epitomized, most eloquently, by Prince Morinaga and Kusunoki Masashige. The former was a son of the emperor Go-Daigo, the latter a low-ranking warrior from Kawachi near Kyoto.[81] The prince, in particular, played a role that proved pivotal, issuing a vast number of calls to military service. By succeeding in this endeavor beyond all reasonable expectations, he proved not only that courtiers could be commanders but also that warriors were not necessarily synonymous with the "men of Kamakura."

In the runup to the Bakufu's destruction in the fifth month of 1333, both the Hōjō and Prince Morinaga began to engage in a competition of military patronage. Both sides directed their appeals to warriors and religious institutions alike. Moreover, both called on men to gather up their relatives and appear for service—either as members of the Bakufu's "Loyalist Force" (Kantō *gunsei*) or as members of the "Imperial Army" (*kanpei*).[82] Like Yoritomo 150 years before him, the prince did not shrink from recruiting those who had initially chosen the other side,[83] and he also showed himself adept at attuning his message. Thus, for example, when he sought the support of the priests of the Kumedadera, he pledged no misbehavior by his forces on their lands.[84] Similarly, when he appealed for the backing of a certain warrior from the west, he invited him to join a crusade against the "Barbarians of the East" (*azuma no i*). He then embellished that invitation by promising a *jitō* post.[85] For that matter, the prince now began to condemn the twelfth-century founder of the Hōjō house, thereby allowing him to target all his (Tokimasa's) descendants. Those descendants, properly excoriated, were then vilified as the quintessential Eastern Barbarians.[86] The Bakufu, for its part, could only appeal in the opposite direction, calling, defensively, for nonalignment with the prince. Moreover, when Kamakura made such overtures to shrines and temples,[87] it created at least the potential for a mixed message. That is, by admitting that class affinities were not the sole basis for a choice of loyalties, it allowed the prince to enlarge his appeal to include warriors.

In the meantime, Go-Daigo, following his escape from exile, began, like his son and his enemies, to distribute perquisites to warriors and temples without distinction. Moreover, by electing to build much of his program around *jitō shiki*,[88] he fragmented, in an instant, the Bakufu's monopoly authority over that title. The emperor also moved to personalize his foe by citing the Hōjō chieftain by name. Condemning "the former governor of Sagami Taira Takatoki" for "violating the Imperial Will," he castigated him for "usurping the provinces" and "causing anguish to the people."[89] Both the emperor and the prince now declared Takatoki an enemy of the state, a man who would therefore have to be destroyed.[90]

When an edict bearing this message came to be circulated, it found its way to the home province (Shimotsuke) of the Ashikaga.[91] Though ostensibly still loyal to the Bakufu at this stage, Takauji, the Ashikaga head, seems quickly to have decided to jockey for position. By seeking support in and out of his home province, he in fact began to loom on the horizon as a new patron. For instance, he moved to confirm the holdings of the illustrious Shimazu in Echizen, and then promised, on his own authority, to punish violators.[92] When he added temples and shrines to his declared safety net,[93] he was announcing his intention to be a national player.

But the voices being heard were not merely those of the recruiters. In fact, a chorus of sanctimony now exploded from the rank and file—never had Japan seen so much merit. Men whose recorded statements would have been limited to their wills and to their courtroom protestations, now, with the collapse of the Bakufu, became champions of their own virtue. Yūki Munehiro was probably typical. After enumerating the family members who had joined him in the campaign to destroy Takatoki, he solemnly declared his family's steadfastness "in Kyoto, in Kamakura, and in Ōshū [the north]."[94] For that matter, warriors were now recording their mere arrivals for service, before they had performed any deeds at all.[95] Converging from different directions and seeming to speak all at once, they represented a diverse interest group that did not want to get left out.[96]

Significantly, temples were just as likely as warriors to expound on their contributions to the cause, with both emphasizing sacrifice and hardship.

Thus the congregation (*shuto*) of the Taizanji in Harima listed its encounters and its war dead, extolling its heroic deeds on myriad battlefields.[97] Meanwhile, other temples were simply recording what it was that they wanted.[98] For Takauji and the other commanders, the flow of supplicants now became continuous, to the point that we can all but imagine ourselves as eyewitnesses. The camps of a handful of national figures were receiving visitors almost daily, with the tally sheets they brought with them the basis for the preferments they now sought. As a certain Takama Yukihide obviously realized in this context, nine battles participated in were better than one.[99]

If much of our evidence seems to underscore the new competition for military patronage, Go-Daigo, in the capital, was thinking about unity. By imperial edict, he was prohibiting violations by warriors and nonwarriors alike (*bushi-kōotsunin*),[100] and also authorizing "civil and military governors" (*kokushi shugonin*) to execute his orders.[101] Moreover, he was accelerating his rewards program so as to embrace all *shiki*, including, as we know, *shugo* and *jitō*. Thus, for example, he appointed a *shugo* to Hida Province in the Chūbu, and followed that by assigning *jitō* posts to the latter's kinsman.[102] In other cases, he invested individual priests, and even whole congregations, with *jitō* titles,[103] but he also condemned misbehavior by *jitō* and canceled their offices. For instance, after admonishing the *jitō* in the habitually troubled estates of Tara and Ōyama, he moved, two months later, to dismiss them outright, and then followed that by transferring their powers to the proprietor.[104] At a stroke, he thereby nullified the divided authority that had characterized the two estates, and that had characterized the now defunct old order.[105] In another case, therefore, Go-Daigo combined *ryōke* and *jitō* titles into a single award, bridging the gulf traditionally symbolized by these two offices.[106] To an extent, he was moving to curtail the need for the nomenclature itself, a strategy that now led in new directions.

From this juncture, the emperor started to make awards in which *no shiki* were specified, such as to the Kobayakawa, in Aki and Iyo provinces.[107] Previously, the reputation of that family had flowed from its *jitō* posts, which had been granted under the authority of the Kamakura Bakufu.[108] But now confirmations and awards over what were called simply possessions (*chigyō no chi*) became a regular form of imperial largesse; a cluster of these, for example, was granted on a single day in the eighth month.[109] Yet Go-Daigo did not overturn things for no reason; he appointed an aristocratic Kujō to an altogether appropriate *ryōke shiki*, and he also prohibited a *jitō*'s infractions on another Kujō estate.[110] Similarly, he accepted a warrior's request for a confirmation in remote Mutsu,[111] and he elected to leave many warriors in place in different parts of the country.[112] In making such decisions, the emperor seems to have been guided by the current situation, which allowed him to ignore prior associations with Kamakura.

Go-Daigo sought above all to pursue a practical rewards policy that enabled him to embrace old and new configurations. *Shiki* could be awarded in traditional or nontraditional ways, even to the extent of not using them at all. Similarly, the emperor devised a set of punitive policies that might, or might not, rely on earlier jurisdictions: he could condemn "local residents" (*domin*) directly for their wrongdoing, as in one case,[113] and censure specific *shiki* holders in others.[114] Conversely, however, there now emerged provincial figures who felt freed from the old strictures, men who might respond to the jurisdictions of the past by ignoring them. In other words, with the unanticipated collapse of the Kamakura Bakufu in 1333, the stabilizing supports of the dual polity had been dealt a devastating blow.

Of course, the problems of place and identity still had to be confronted by individuals, with some striking results. In particular, we are surprised to find the continuing currency of the term *gokenin*, even after the destruction of the Bakufu. Clearly, the constituent elements of the Kamakura system had not been destroyed—only, as it were, the sum of its parts. The rank and file who were identified with the regime were obviously still present, and so was the term connoting their historic connection to it. Even a choice of loyalties the other way did not really break that tie, since the *gokenin* who fought against the Bakufu had targeted the Hōjō; Takatoki's status was now mocked variously.[115] Meanwhile, the purgers saw themselves as upholding a distinguished tradition, whose Minamoto origins were obvious by definition, and which pointed, conveniently, toward the Ashikaga. *Gokenin* arriving at the camp of Takauji were thus eager to invoke that status, distinguished only by their province of origin.[116] In search of a new network of support, they presented the only calling card they shared in common.

In other ways, too, the traditions of the past were made separable from the just-deposed Hōjō. Nowhere was this truer than in the area of justice. For someone like Takauji to presume to inherit responsibilities of governance was to obligate him to provide a forum for the mediation of disputes. Sentiments like the following could be expressed by a complainant, as he recorded his petition in the seventh month: in his own words, "Just at the moment that we had a suit pending with the Kantō [i.e., Kama-kura], the Kantō came to be destroyed."[117] Here indeed was someone who was already looking forward to a revived Bakufu.

If we discount the brief episode of the Taira a century and half earlier, Japan had never experienced the collapse of an established government. The sense of national trauma could only have been overwhelming, pro-voking a host of new questions that could not possibly be answered. The caretakers of the moment were truly on the spot. As we have seen, *shiki* as the society's stablizers had started coming undone on their own, but now they were having their original meanings deliberately scuttled. A general evisceration of the concept was in progress, as we see from a final, con-cluding example.

Thus, what could it have meant when a proprietary title (*ryōke shiki*) was divided into fractional portions, only *one* of which was still held by the original temple owner?[118] In short, what were the implications for the protected summit of the old hierarchy when ownership, the final rampart, could be reduced to mere shares? Put differently, was not the spell cast by courtiers at last being broken when titles no longer expressed an objecti-fied world of consensus privilege? And when that stage was reached, were not men from the provinces finally in a position to challenge the only con-dition they had ever known—that of being apprenticed subordinates to absentee interests?

CHAPTER 2

Largesse and the Limits of Loyalty in the Fourteenth Century

THOMAS CONLAN

IT WOULD SEEM to have been a misjudgment. On the twenty-sixth day of the eighth month of 1375, Imagawa Ryōshun, shortly after storming an enemy castle, invited Shōni Fuyusuke to a banquet, whereupon he had the hapless Fuyusuke hacked to death in the midst of festivities. Imagawa Ryōshun justified his callous deed by claiming that Fuyusuke's duplicity and disloyalty demanded drastic punishment. The Shimazu and Ōtomo, Imagawa allies, disagreed: the former defected to the opposing Southern Court while the latter wavered, persuaded to maintain wary allegiance only after being liberally compensated.[1] Even though Ryōshun had been on the verge of annihilating the Kikuchi and other Kyushu supporters of the Southern Court, his offensive collapsed after Fuyusuke's death.

The dissolution of Ryōshun's army is perplexing, since victory and lucrative rewards had seemed at hand; the enervated forces of the Southern Court faced imminent defeat. Instead, the latter's beleaguered forces were rejuvenated by defectors from the Imagawa. This turn of events raises a significant issue. If the warriors of the fourteenth century were as unscrupulous and aggrandizing as they have long been imagined, why would they abandon their own best interest? In fact, the disintegration of the Imagawa army may have been a consequence of Ryōshun's demand for unconditional loyalty.

Nearly all narratives of this epoch have the same underlying assumption: "Loyalty was the highest value . . . [in] an age when disloyalty was commonplace. From Ashikaga Takauji until Tokugawa Ieyasu, *gekokujō*, the overthrow of lords by their vassals, was one of the most salient features of political life."[2] Or, as proclaimed by James Murdoch in his well-known indictment of the era, the fourteenth century was "a golden age, not merely of turncoats, but of mediocrities."[3] Yet it is possible that this emphasis on treachery is misplaced, for, as we shall see, the disjunction between loyalty and disloyalty was not as clear as it would initially seem.

Murdoch is hardly alone in portraying fourteenth-century warriors as rebellious, disloyal men. For example, Peter Arnesen describes how Mōri Motoharu, an Aki warrior who had repeatedly fought for Ashikaga Takauji, "rebelled" against Takauji's *shugo* in 1350, but later fought for the Ashikaga in the 1360s.[4] Arnesen admits some bafflement by the ease of Mōri's "treason" and his subsequent reinstatement, an anomaly that goes to the heart of the problem here. How could it be that rebellion and treason, among the most egregious offenses of the modern era, seemed to evoke hardly a shrug in the fourteenth century? The existence of carefully preserved documents addressed to the same man but emanating from both the Ashikaga Bakufu and the Southern Court—incontestable proof that he was a "turncoat"—throws doubt on the notion that stigma adhered to those whose loyalty shifted. Moreover, warriors who repeatedly switched sides suffered little ill-consequence and may even have been generously rewarded, revealing either an enormous toleration for cynicism on behalf of the fourteenth-century Japanese, or a system of obligation in which loyalty was limited.

As I should like to argue, words such as "treason" or "loyalty" should be used with caution, for they imply the existence of a coherent and widely recognized ethos of encompassing devotion to a political or institutional entity that is capable of transcending personal interest; such an ethos seems absent in fourteenth-century Japan. The term *chūsetsu*—generally defined as "loyalty"—appears in a bewildering variety of circumstances, most of which are only tenuously related to abstract loyalty. One can find references to *kitō chūsetsu*, or *chūsetsu* through prayer; *chūsetsu* for divine matters and festivities; and even the *chūsetsu* of upright temple administration.[5] Warriors were rewarded for "battle *chūsetsu*," "wound *chūsetsu*," the *chūsetsu* of dismembering an opponent, the *chūsetsu* of taking prisoners, the *chūsetsu* of arriving at an encampment, the *chūsetsu* of causing others to surrender, the *chūsetsu* of defecting, and the *chūsetsu* of building an arrow storehouse.[6] Descendants of warriors who had been killed would write of their father's "loyal service" (*chūkin*); fathers who lost their sons could receive praise and *jitō shiki* for their son's *chūsetsu*; and a few enterprising sorts could receive nearly simultaneous recognition for *chūsetsu* by both the Northern and Southern courts.[7] At times, *chūsetsu* meshes with our sense of loyalty: Nomoto Tsujūmaru boasted of his undivided (*muni*) *chūsetsu* for the Ashikaga, and Shōni Sadatsune proclaimed, shortly before his suicide: "I have exhausted *chūsetsu* for my lord. Let not my descendants be divided."[8] Although Sadatsune believed suicide to be the ultimate manifestation of *chūsetsu*, a Hōjō retainer proclaimed, "If we turn back safely, preserving our lives for battles to come, we will always be remembered as men who understood the meaning of loyalty (*chūgi*)."[9] The one common denominator is that *chūsetsu* refers to tangible, meritorious services worthy of compensation, such as prayers for victory, participation in battle, temple administration, or the construction of fortifications. The term *chūsetsu* is less an abstraction than a description of services rendered.

The meaning of the term *chūsetsu* is critical in comprehending the nature of military service in fourteenth-century Japan. If *chūsetsu* is conceived of as "loyalty," then one would assume that military service was obligatory; in other words, a warrior was ideally bound to fight for some lord, and his failure to do so would constitute treachery. If we understand *chūsetsu* as being roughly analogous to "service," however, then the autonomy of those rendering it should be seen as normative; warriors who rendered *chūsetsu* labored under no encompassing obligation. *Chūsetsu*, predicated upon the receipt of adequate remuneration, constituted a narrowly defined commitment to fight or provide some other service, which cannot be equated with unconditional obedience; instead of transcending personal interest, *chūsetsu* was synonymous with it.

Of course, not all those who fought were recognized for their service (*chūsetsu*). Indeed, all who fought and killed were not, in fourteenth-century parlance, even warriors. Some received little recognition for their exploits and were barely distinguishable from common laborers. Others, hereditary warriors, had their acts of merit subsumed into the rewards of still others. Finally, some men received recognition for their personal exploits and the actions of their followers. Thus, instead of reifying the diverse body of men who fought into a single analytic category, they should be judged according to their social position and concurrent obligations.

Warrior actions were embedded in a social matrix; the particulars of each man's social situation delineated the parameters of possible—or socially acceptable—behavior, which shaped their general actions and ambitions. Hereditary followers, secure with name and lineage, remained remarkably loyal to their lord and strove for his success, for they prospered as he did. By contrast, autonomous warriors jealously preserved their privileged status and homelands, resisting service under the command of socially distant, prestigious men of Ashikaga, Nitta, or imperial lineage.

No single system of lordship could encompass such disparate warrior interests. Those who aspired to regional lordship—a lordship over land—attempted to amass lands and increase their bands of hereditary followers. In contrast to these regional magnates, national hegemons achieved the support of autonomous warriors through confirmations, grants of land rights, and other gifts: they constructed, in short, lordships over men. A hegemonic lord was obliged to keep his supporters content through the magnanimous distribution of rewards. If he failed to offer adequate compensation, or if his promises were unreliable, then his followers would desert him. In other words, land grants were offered in exchange for service (*chūsetsu*); no further obligation was entailed. Land was merely a conduit that linked a hegemon's promises and legitimating authority to the interests of autonomous, free-spirited warriors. He who offered the most reliable compensation secured the support and conditional allegiance of autonomous warriors. Only when such a system of lordship is understood are we in a position to judge whether the fourteenth century was an age of "turncoats and mediocrities."

HEREDITARY WARRIORS

All who fought were not equal. *Akusō*—"evil priests"—and *nobushi*—literally "those who lie in the fields"—fought and died but were not generally considered to be warriors. Only those of warrior lineage could fight and receive recognition; these men took pride in being born to a warrior house (*yumiya no ie*).[10] Hereditary warrior obligations differed, however, between "insiders," or *miuchi*, who maintained strong ties to a lord, and autonomous "outsiders," or *tozama*. In other words, *tozama* and *miuchi* labored under different obligations and expectations.

The distinction between *miuchi* and *tozama* appears with deceptive clarity in the *Sata Mirensho*, a law primer of the early fourteenth century: "*Tozama* are *jitō gokenin* who serve the Shogun's house. *Miuchi* are vassals (*miuchi-hōkōnin*) of the Lord of Sagami [the Hōjō]."[11] According to the *Sata Mirensho*, a warrior's relationship with the Kamakura Bakufu determined his status as either *tozama* or *miuchi*.

One might assume that the categories of *tozama* and *miuchi* would disappear with the Hōjō and the Kamakura Bakufu, but this did not occur. In fact, belying the *Sata Mirensho*'s political definition, these terms had gradually become social categories.[12] In other words, a warrior's identity as a *miuchi* or *tozama* had become sufficiently divorced from political allegiance and enshrined as a hereditary right, which would retain significance apart from the existence of any political entity. For example, approximately two decades after the destruction of the Kamakura regime, a *miuchi* of Ashikaga Yoshiakira, Myō no Shimotsuke, indignantly refused an overture from Ashikaga Tadafuyu, whom he denounced for "sending a messenger who makes no distinction between *miuchi* and *tozama*."[13] Believing himself to be a *miuchi* of the Ashikaga shogun, Myō no Shimotsuke could not countenance receiving rewards from another lord. Conversely, no leader could override the pervasive belief that *miuchi* lacked autonomy in determining allegiances and that they were thereby ineligible to receive significant rewards from anyone other than their lord.[14]

Miuchi who shifted allegiances independently of their lord were castigated as traitors. Thus, one Ashikaga houseman (*kerai no mono*) who had fought valiantly for the Nitta was, upon his capture, summarily executed.[15] In a variation, the treachery of a *miuchi* of the Shōni house proved to be the catalyst for his own lord's suicide.[16] Or again, it was declared to be entirely "the punishment of heaven" that a retainer who had stripped off and hidden for his own use the armor of his dead Hōjō lords (*shu*) should be captured and ignominiously executed.[17] A *miuchi* who was willful enough to rebel, but too weak to succeed, could expect to be severely punished because his behavior transgressed the bounds of social acceptability.

Striking examples of *miuchi* loyalty frequently appear. The powerful *tozama* Utsunomiya Kintsuna joined Ashikaga Takauji's forces upon the defeat of the Southern Court's Nitta Yoshisada. Unaware of this development, two *miuchi* bands (*tō*) of Utsunomiya warriors, the Ki and Sei, marched with Kitabatake Akiie of the Southern Court to the capital. However, "when they heard that Utsunomiya [Kintsuna] had joined [Ashikaga Takauji's] forces, they all took their leave [and] . . . went up to the Capital."[18] These two bands of fighting men, after "galloping toward their lord (*shu no moto*),"[19] built forts and subsequently bore the brunt of Akiie's offensive.[20] *Miuchi* followed the lead of their lord even when his choice entailed grave personal sacrifice.

Miuchi who abandoned their lord merited strict censure, but this did not preclude the possibility of some achieving autonomy. A *miuchi* had to be resourceful in order to switch allegiances independently of his *tozama* lord. For example, one Haga hyōe nyūmon Zenka barricaded himself in a castle with an infant son of his Utsunomiya lord (*shu*) and joined an opposing military alliance. Although a contemporary chronicle decried Haga's behavior as "disturbing the relations between lord and follower (*shujū no reigi o midare*)," he legitimated his de facto autonomy by acting in the name of his lord's son.[21] Zenka's actions generated enough ambiguity of social position to allow for his success, but he could not openly behave like a *tozama*. Perhaps a generation or more needed to pass before the autonomy of such *miuchi* became hereditarily enshrined and the descendants of a *miuchi* became widely accepted as *tozama*.

In fact, most *miuchi* remained *miuchi*, even though their lord, or focus of loyalty, might shift. For instance, when Hosokawa Kiyouji was destroyed by the forces of the Ashikaga Bakufu, many of his *miuchi* transferred their allegiance and became followers of Hosokawa Yoriyuki.[22] Only a few of Kiyouji's most powerful *miuchi* used the opportunity to achieve independence, among them the ignoble Hayami Shirō.[23] Formerly a *miuchi* of Kiyouji, he turned over a strategic castle to Ashikaga forces and thereby severed his *miuchi* relation with the Hosokawa while securing his autonomy. In the process he ensured the destruction of Kiyouji.[24]

The only *miuchi* who could achieve independence were those who controlled substantial lands and followers. Those of little means reaped benefits directly from their *miuchi* status by participating in distant military campaigns and by sharing the rewards that accrued to their lord. That meant that unless internal dissension weakened that lord severely, the lord could normally crush the rebellion of a *miuchi* who should have had to overcome military inferiority and the stigma of treachery. For most *miuchi*, the advantages of service and protection outweighed the drawbacks of dependence.

The stability of a *tozama*'s band of *miuchi* depended on the extent of the lands they controlled. *Miuchi* who administered or were entrusted with extensive lands could behave, or at least attempt to behave, as *tozama*. In other words, *miuchi* loyalty was contingent upon the maintenance of social distance between *miuchi* and *tozama*, which was predicated upon a disparity of directly controlled resources. Those with few—if any—lands were the most loyal, whereas those with significant holdings tended to be unreliable. When the distinction between *tozama* and *miuchi* collapsed in all but name, a volatile situation developed, which frequently led to the disintegration of ties of dependence.

Two distinct strata existed among *miuchi*: those who were individually bound to their lord, and those whose obligation stemmed from corporate membership. The latter organizations, composed of men of vastly inferior social position, generally had little choice but to remain loyal. Although occasionally the term "warrior bands" has been used to describe the relationship between a lord and his followers, this term obscures the multiplicity of subservient relations. *Miuchi* belonging to corporate organizations had no direct relation with their lord; instead, the entire corporate entity was treated roughly as if it were an individual *miuchi*.

Most *miuchi* organizations consisted of either warrior bands (*tō*) or military units known as *ikki*. For example, sixty-seven obscure warriors signed an oath and formed the Kadochigai *ikki* sometime during the first decade of the Nanbokuchō era.[25] Their individual landholdings were minuscule; indeed, their collective landholdings were far from substantial. Each member sacrificed individual freedom in order to belong to a group with collective responsibility. Thus, for instance, one clause in the oath contained a provision that progeny who were orphaned should be raised by other *ikki* members.[26]

One apparent irony is that although the principle of subservience to a magnate remained unquestioned, *miuchi* organizations as a whole retained limited autonomy in determining how to fight. Although one clause of the Kadochigai *ikki* oath contains the acknowledgment that regional peace and stability were based on the prowess of their Ōtomo lords, another states as follows: "Concerning military service: the core group (*shūchū*) shall decide what is appropriate . . . but this shall not violate the [wishes] of the majority (*tabun no gi*)."[27] Inasmuch as these warrior bands (*tō*) and *ikki* were unlikely to rebel, their limited autonomy posed no threat to their lord. Moreover, the social distance between *ikki* participants and local magnates enabled the former to behave with more latitude than was generally possible for individually bound *miuchi*. At the same time, *ikki* might collectively be granted rewards, for example, *jitō shiki*, as in the case of awards by Ashikaga Takauji and Yoshimitsu to the Kadochigai *ikki*, nearly thirty years apart.[28]

As should be evident, such corporate *miuchi* were not ephemeral organizations. The Kadochigai *ikki* survived for at least thirty years. Furthermore, the Ki and Sei bands (*tō*) who fought loyally for the Utsunomiya from the 1330s through the 1350s had also participated in an attack against the Andō of Tsugaru in 1323.[29] Thus *miuchi* organizations, which might have come into being in the late Kamakura age, were clearly capable of surviving an extended period of political turmoil. By contrast, other less comprehensive allegiances were prone to disintegration. In an age of in-stability, then, assemblages of *miuchi* were a bastion of support for *tozama* and an important source of stability for the dependent warriors them-selves, who were able to enjoy in the process a degree of autonomy.

Like most social designations, *tozama* status is more identifiable than it is definable; some men were *tozama* while others were not. Autonomy in war, or "freedom of movement" (*kyoshū no jiyū*), each a cherished desire of nearly all warriors, represents more a function than a defining feature.[30] The equation of *tozama* and *gokenin* in the *Sata Mirensho* is singularly un-helpful since both suffered from the same inherent ambiguities. Although the authors of that law primer bravely attempted to distinguish *gokenin* from non-*gokenin*, their claim that the former were men "whose ancestors held ownership of land since time immemorial . . . and received a Bakufu *kudashibumi* [edict of confirmation]"[31] while the latter were not, cannot be sustained. In fact, many hereditary landowners, particularly those of west-ern Japan, received no such edicts, even though their forebears had ap-peared on *gokenin* registers. Nevertheless, the hereditary aspect of *gokenin* status was solely determined by genealogies and hereditarily transmitted documents.

Although genealogies might be fabricated and embellished, this did not undermine their role as a principal vehicle of social classification. An investigation of the veracity of a warrior's hereditary rights, or genealogi-cal claims, was well-nigh impossible; merely to accuse a warrior of being a non-*gokenin* constituted slander.[32] One should not, however, overesti-mate the autogenesis of *gokenin* or *tozama* status, since men of manifestly inferior social rank, such as hereditary *miuchi*, could be recognized as a *gokenin* (*tozama*) only with difficulty. Instead, the way to expand the num-ber of *gokenin* was through the prosperity of their families. All landholding members descended from a family of *gokenin* status could use this desig-nation for themselves. The determining factor of such status was simply a man's plausible, genealogically justifiable claim that he was a *gokenin*.

Central authorities failed to realize the degree to which *gokenin* status had become an autogenic social designation, free of any iron-clad asso-ciation to any political entity. Emperor Go-Daigo, for example, sought to abolish the position of *gokenin* after the destruction of the Kamakura Bakufu, based on his perception of a link between the two.[33] *Gokenin* re-sisted less out of any visceral loyalty to the defunct Kamakura regime than out of a realization that Go-Daigo was seeking to establish the Court as the sole arbiter of social status. *Gokenin* complaints that they were now indistinguishable from commoners (*bonmin*) and little better than "slaves and servants" indicates that many were keenly aware of the significance of their social space and the threat its elimination posed.[34] Attempts to abolish *gokenin* status, in addition to being tantamount to a personal insult, jeopardized *tozama* power and authority by creating a pervasive state of social ambiguity. *Tozama* resisted and continued to refer to themselves as *gokenin* in documents addressed to the Kenmu regime, and subsequently to the Ashikaga Bakufu and to the Southern Court.[35]

Documents relating to the Nejime family of southern Kyushu illustrate that *tozama* status was linked to autonomy in war; only *tozama* were individually recognized in battle. Nejime Kiyonari, the head or *sōryō* of the Nejime, received documents that ordered him to mobilize the Nejime family (*ichizoku*).[36] Kiyonari was responsible for followers and family members who fought for him, and he received credit for their actions and compensation for their loss.[37] Nejime Kiyotane, a *gokenin* cousin of Kiyonari, was wounded at the very engagement where Kiyonari fought, but his wounds are not recorded in the latter's petition for reward (*gunchūjō*). Instead, Kiyotane submitted his own petition.[38] Separate petitions and recognition merely imply autonomy, not disunity. Kiyotane could fight where and when he pleased, whereas Nejime *miuchi*, both relatives and hereditary followers, could not.

The autonomy of *tozama* was manifest in their method of military mobilization and rewards. Military commanders requested *tozama* service through orders of mobilization (*saisokujō*). A formal request to fight ipso facto implies conditional obligation; true loyalty is not contingent upon invitation. An oath written in 1336 also expresses the fundamental autonomy of the Nejime *tozama*. All who signed, landholders of *gokenin* status, promised "as a clan (*ichimon*) . . . to act in complete accord (*ichimi dōshin*) concerning everything." Furthermore, the signers vowed: "Let there be no differences of opinion (*igi*). Everything shall be discussed at the council (*shūgi*). If some disobey this purport, they shall suffer the punishment of all of the middling, small, and great gods of the country of Japan in Heaven, Earth, and Hell."[39] Formal unity among Nejime *tozama* was forged through an oath, indicating the voluntary nature of this agreement and alliance. By contrast, Nejime *miuchi* labored under informal and unconditional obligations, which required no oath; those truly obligated to fight remain largely unrecorded in documentary sources.

Occasionally the distinction between *tozama* and *miuchi* seems vague. When *miuchi* were entrusted with substantial lands or castles by their *tozama* lord, tension arose from the inherent ambiguities of a nominally landless retainer's control of land holdings, a hallmark, after all, of *tozama* status. *Miuchi* who viewed such a possession as a delegation of a *tozama*'s authority tended to scorn offers of outside rewards, though there were always those who opted the other way—particularly when a lord was otherwise preoccupied. The ambiguous position of a landholding *miuchi* made social mobility a possibility, even though attempts to change one's status entailed great risk.

Although the categories of *miuchi* and *tozama* maintained a degree of permeability—landed *miuchi* could, with luck and skill, achieve *tozama* status, while a weakened *tozama* could become the *miuchi* of a particularly influential man—expectations regarding warrior behavior remained constant throughout the fourteenth century. A question thus emerges as to how one might organize a force of autonomous warriors. A social system that allowed *tozama* to maintain their privileges obviously posed problems for would-be regional or national hegemons. Among these aspiring lords, some sought to create a regional authority over land, while others sought to construct an interregional lordship over men.

THE LIMITS OF LANDED LORDSHIP

Prior to the onset of protracted warfare in the 1330s, no stable method of regional lordship existed. The only extant pattern of lordship, that of a landholding *tozama* and his *miuchi* followers, became inherently unstable as the *tozama*'s power increased and his *miuchi* also became landholders. No mechanism existed for incorporating landed *miuchi* or, for that matter, *tozama*, into an institutionalized system of regional control or military organization.

Tozama were loath to serve under any figure of similar social status.[40] The Kōno, a powerful *tozama* family which had been established in Iyo Province for centuries, could not readily mobilize other *tozama*. In the sixth month of 1336, Ashikaga Tadayoshi ordered the Kōno to lead "the Kōno family (*ichizoku*) and the *jitō gokenin* of Iyo Province."[41] Judging from the frequent reiteration of this order, the Kōno were singularly unsuccessful. Some orders of mobilization (*saisokujō*) contained injunctions such as: "Lead the *jitō gokenin* . . . of Iyo Province. . . . Those who do not follow [your command] should be identified in order to be punished";[42] others cajoled and admonished: "the *jitō gokenin* of Iyo Province should follow Kōno Tsushima Nyūdō. . . . Those who render *chūsetsu* shall be duly noted and rewarded for their valor. . . . [Those remaining in Iyo] will be punished."[43] In fact, the Kōno were unable even to lead their own collateral lineages.[44] Instead, Southern Court forces, composed of Iyo *tozama*, kept the Kōno on the defensive and even managed to capture and occupy the main Kōno castle.[45] Ashikaga Tadayoshi eventually dispatched the *taishō* Hosokawa Yoriharu to help subdue the "rebels" of Iyo in 1342.[46]

Hosokawa Yoriharu was more successful than the Kōno because *tozama*, or *jitō gokenin*, were more amenable to serving under him. Kobayakawa Ujihira of Aki Province, for example, fought under Yoriharu's command.[47] *Tozama* refused to serve under the Kōno in spite of Kōno Michimori's appointment as *shugo* of Iyo Province in 1350.[48] Even as late as 1380, it was still necessary for Ashikaga Yoshimitsu to issue the following proclamation: "*Jitō gokenin*, those exercising administrative authority over homelands (*honshoryō azukaridokoro satanin*), and *myoshū* shall obey the commands of the *shugo* and render *chūsetsu*."[49] Ashikaga Bakufu authority and prestige constituted an important bulwark for Kōno efforts to mobilize *tozama* warriors; their own power and prestige were otherwise insufficient.

The power of local warrior lordship paled in comparison with the power that was wielded by upstart warriors of Ashikaga blood. Much of the success of Ashikaga collaterals stemmed from the fact that they, more than magnates such as the Kōno, could readily ensure that *tozama* would receive rewards.[50] The Isshiki, Shibukawa, Shiba, Momonoi, Kira, Hosokawa, Niki, and Imagawa, little more than weak *gokenin* possessing minuscule landholdings in Mikawa Province during the Kamakura period, suddenly became leaders of great armies as the Ashikaga amassed power and prestige.[51] Ancient local warrior families such as the Kōno could not compete with these former *gokenin* from one of the Ashikaga base areas.

Social stratification also profoundly influenced institutional developments. Ashikaga collaterals were appointed military commanders — *taishō* — who could mobilize *tozama* from several provinces. *Shugo* offices were less powerful.[52] During the first two decades of the Nanbokuchō period *shugo* were unable to readily mobilize *tozama* from their appointed provinces.[53] Even when a powerful *tozama*, such as Kōno Michimori, was appointed *shugo* of his native province, he remained unable to call up other *tozama*. When men who had served as *taishō* were concurrently appointed *shugo*, however, the office of *shugo* became virtually indistinguishable from that of *taishō*. This institutional amalgamation arose from the prominence of personality vis-à-vis position. *Tozama* were more concerned with the social status of a military leader than with his office; Ashikaga collaterals exercised power regardless of whether they were *taishō* or *shugo*. By contrast, the office of *shugo* was coveted by *tozama*, since it enabled them to distinguish themselves from other *tozama*.

Tozama, or *jitō gokenin*, who did not become the *miuchi* of powerful men remained amenable to serving under Ashikaga collaterals who now occupied a status superior to that of *tozama*. For the *tozama* themselves, service under collaterals (be they *shugo* or *taishō*) in no way compromised their autonomy, or lessened their status vis-à-vis other *tozama*. By contrast, service under the command of *tozama*, even those appointed *shugo*, was fundamentally undesirable for *tozama*. For example, the *tozama* Kutsuki Yoriuji willingly fought under the command of Ashikaga collaterals such as the Imagawa in 1336, the Ishibashi in 1339, and Hosokawa Akiuji in 1347, but resisted serving under the command of Sasaki Dōyo, a non-Ashikaga magnate and *shugo* of Ōmi Province, in 1338.[54]

The power of Ashikaga *taishō* could be ephemeral. Armies composed of *tozama*, while vigorous for a few weeks, might suffer from inherent instability, and could, if defeated or stalemated, disintegrate with astounding rapidity.[55] Ashikaga collaterals had to rely upon other means, namely, the creation of a local band of *miuchi*, to amass power and build a regional lordship. Some were successful, others were not. After the Kannō Disturbance of 1350–51, several lineages of the Ashikaga *ichimon* were destroyed or severely weakened.[56] On the other hand, the Hosokawa had no notable historical base in Shikoku but were able quickly to recruit or absorb a number of Shikoku warriors as *miuchi*. This was a relatively easy task for the Hosokawa because warriors of no great means preferred serving under a *taishō* as opposed to under a *tozama*. Correspondingly, *miuchi* of the Hosokawa occupied a superior social and political position compared with *miuchi* of local *tozama*. Those who linked their fortunes to a rising lord amassed derivative power, prestige, and quite possibly an opportunity for autonomy.

Social equality created a situation inimical to the creation of a local lordship. *Tozama* who amassed a degree of local power or prestigious titles incurred the hostility of other *tozama*. Furthermore, any *tozama* who expanded his local sphere of influence was forced to entrust castles and other lands to subordinates, thereby providing them with an opportunity to achieve autonomy. In short, local magnates labored under severe difficulties when attempting to dominate a particular area. By comparison, Ashikaga collaterals dispatched to localities occupied a position of manifest social superiority to local *tozama* and easily forged a fairly strong, if somewhat brittle, basis of regional support.

Considerations of lineage, status, and personality influenced the nature of lordship a magnate might attempt, and the relative ease (or difficulty) he would experience in achieving his goals. Those who sought to dispossess neighboring warriors generated the concerted opposition of local *tozama*, which ultimately crippled their attempts at regional consolidation. Of course, the creation of a regional lordship was not impossible; it was merely a labored, piecemeal process most effectively accomplished over a span of several decades. *Taishō* who held powers of gift giving had a significant advantage over their indigenous *tozama* competitors because they occupied a clearly superior social status. Their largesse generated goodwill and prestige, which, if they so chose, could be more readily transformed into a landed lordship. During the fourteenth century, however, the ephemeral qualities of prestige, awe, and reliability generated by magnanimous rewards were a sufficient basis for attracting *tozama* support.

Those *tozama* magnates who were most successful, such as the Ōuchi, took advantage of the turmoil of the Kannō era to usurp hegemonic powers of largesse. Ōuchi Hiroyo first used the disturbances of the 1350s to occupy (*ōryō*) shrine lands.[57] More remarkably, in 1352, the Ōuchi started granting small amounts of land to followers.[58] Ōuchi documents increased dramatically in scope and frequency during the ensuing decades. Disputes were adjudicated, indicative of the establishment of a local judicial apparatus, lands and *jitō shiki* were granted or entrusted to warriors for the sake of provisions, transfers of *jitō shiki* were confirmed, warriors were recommended to the Bakufu to receive rewards, and even *tozama* holdings were confirmed.[59] In addition, the Ōuchi issued prohibitions for temples and undertook an extensive campaign of shrine rebuilding.[60] Through these myriad efforts the Ōuchi attempted to increase the social distance between themselves and other *tozama* by adopting a munificent policy of local patronage and largesse.[61] *Tozama* remained unwilling to serve under him, however. For example, when Ōuchi Yoshihiro crossed into Kyushu in 1375, he led only 300 family members and *miuchi*.[62] By contrast, Imagawa Ryōshun's army exceeded 4,000 men.[63]

Ashikaga collaterals, such as Imagawa Ryōshun, led armies composed of *tozama* drawn from northern Kyushu and western Japan, but they could maintain a force for only a brief period of time. Indeed, even before his murder of Shōni Fuyusuke in 1375, Imagawa Ryōshun's problems were considerable. According to a petition by Mōri Motoharu of Aki Province:

The *jitō gokenin* of the two provinces of Bingo and Aki either sent a representative (*daikan*) or arrived late or returned to their provinces. Only Motoharu alone, bringing his sons served together [with Imagawa forces] since the very beginning [of this campaign] four years ago. In various encampments in various areas, not once have I been negligent. My service (*chūsetsu*) has been outstanding.[64]

Motoharu depicted his *chūsetsu* of remaining in Kyushu as truly exceptional; *jitō gokenin* acted as they pleased, joining and departing Ryōshun's army according to whim. After Ryōshun's debacle of 1375, Ashikaga Yoshimitsu dispatched his younger brother to lead *jitō gokenin* from Tōtōmi, Suruga, Bingo, and Aki provinces to Kyushu to aid the beleaguered remnants of the Imagawa army.[65] Only a younger brother of the Ashikaga shogun had the prestige to lead a force of *tozama* drawn from such diverse areas.

Nearly all documented rewards were granted to fickle *tozama* and not to their *miuchi* counterparts. This apparent irony, that those who were least reliable received the most rewards, indicates that national, hegemonic lordship operated according to a different set of norms from regional lordship. National leadership, in other words, did not entail obligatory *tozama* subservience. Hegemonic lordship was based on land grants, not land per se. The act of granting lands and other rewards to disinterested *tozama* enabled a hegemon to create a reservoir of symbolic capital, which then formed the cornerstone of his political power. In order to rule the realm, one first had to give it away.

LAND, LARGESSE, AND LORDSHIP

One might be inclined to conclude, after reading the above survey, that Murdoch was essentially correct—it was an age of turncoats, if not, perhaps, mediocrities. *Tozama* warriors apparently exemplify men of mean scruple, demanding excessive rewards and offering niggardly service. Kitabatake Chikafusa certainly believed so, stating: "These days a popular saying has it that if a warrior should enter into a single battle or suffer the loss of a vassal he will demand that 'My reward should be all of Japan; half the country will not be enough!' Of course, no one is really apt to make such an absurd demand, yet the saying is a first step to disorder."[66] Chikafusa's criticism is founded on the belief that warriors should not be too boastful of their services or demand compensation.

Kitabatake Chikafusa posits the root of disorder in the failure of warriors to serve their "lords." He laments: "Today . . . there are only people who, in all matters, disdain their lords and trumpet their own merits." [67] And yet, as should be evident, *tozama* had no lord or focus of obligation that transcended narrow self-interest. A social context in which *tozama* autonomy was normative indicates, *pace* Chikafusa, that the onus of responsibility rested not on *tozama* warriors but on the competing regimes to secure support through largesse in granting rewards. Instead of grants of land that guaranteed obligation, it was service (*chūsetsu*) that demanded adequate compensation.

Needless to say, this view is pregnant with ramifications. Confirmations and land grants bestowed upon autonomous warriors forged social bonds but did not entail additional obligations of military service. A regime whose promises were generous and reliable established credibility and accumulated power in the form of symbolic capital directly proportionate to its largesse.[68] This symbolic capital enabled Ashikaga shoguns and collateral *taishō* to formalize their superior status by means of their monopoly of the distribution of rewards. This largesse not only generated confidence among the *tozama*, it also guaranteed them a free hand in controlling their lands. The resultant division between *tozama* and those of Ashikaga blood allowed the latter to construct and lead large armies. The seeming selflessness of refusing to amass lands themselves enabled Ashikaga collaterals to command men whose wealth might have been greater than their own. Lords of men, not land, ruled the realm.[69]

"Then was then; now is now—rewards are lord!" [70] This slogan, bandied about in the fourteenth century, is less a cynical commentary on warriors—as it might initially seem—than a metonymic recognition of the centrality of rewards for lordship. Of course, rewards came in many guises. A character from one's own name could be bestowed upon a deserving warrior; battle flags could be given; swords could be granted to valorous warriors; homelands (*honryō*) could be confirmed; new land rights, or *shiki*, could be granted; and finally, lands and revenues could be provisionally entrusted to warriors for the sake of military provisions.[71] Regardless of the form of rewards (*on*), largesse was an essential component of hegemonic lordship.

Although neither the *Baishōron* nor the *Taiheiki* is a model of historical objectivity, both reveal that magnanimity was the hallmark of an ideal leader. Ashikaga Takauji received extravagant praise for his generosity: "Ruling the realm was his prime motive, so he placated bitter enemies by confirming their homelands (*honryō*) and bestowed grand rewards on those who had performed acts of merit (*chūkō*)."[72] Go-Daigo, on the other hand, was admonished for his parsimony:

> Since the great disturbance of Genkō (1331–33), all the soldiers (*shisotsu*) of the realm joined the imperial army (*kagun*) in order to receive rewards (*shō*) for military merit (*gunkō*). . . . These countless warriors hoped for a token of appreciation for their exploits after peace had returned to the realm. Nevertheless, only nobles and rank officials (*hikan*) have been granted rewards (*onshō*). Each warrior, resentful that his acts of merit (*chūkō*) have received no recognition, discards his petitions (*mōshijō*), abandons his suits . . . and returns, alienated, to his home province.[73]

In fact, Go-Daigo was more magnanimous than the *Taiheiki* would lead us to believe. Two days after returning to the capital in triumph in 1333, for example, he confirmed the holdings of the rival imperial lineage.[74] Since the right to bestow and to confirm implied superior authority, such generosity served to reinforce his supremacy.[75]

On the other hand, he was not able to grant bountiful rewards to all who aided his cause. His dismissal of Akamatsu Enshin as *shugo* of Harima Province, for instance, stems from the latter's willful disregard of imperial orders; Enshin had continued to despoil proprietary lands.[76] For Go-Daigo, the protection of land rights and his own imperial prerogatives superseded the need to reward men such as Akamatsu Enshin. However, the tenacity of the *Taiheiki* critique suggests that generous compensation of military exploits was widely recognized as an integral component of national lordship.

Go-Daigo's Kenmu regime only rewarded those who directly participated in battle; merely reporting for duty was considered obligatory.[77] In contrast, the Ashikaga praised warriors for arriving at an encampment.[78] From the very beginning, the Ashikaga seem to have had lower expectations regarding their followers' obligations. Or, phrased positively, they provided compensation for a wider variety of military services than did Go-Daigo.

Ashikaga promises of rewards exceeded the narrow bounds of legality, but this did not infringe upon their legitimacy. During the heady days immediately after the destruction of the Hōjō, Ashikaga Takauji and his brother Tadayoshi confirmed landholdings and granted rewards from hereditary Ashikaga and Nitta lands, even though they had no official authority to distribute the latter.[79] Promises were honored even when lands had been mistakenly granted; warriors were simply promised other lands. For example, Ōi Kishirō Takatsuna and eight other men interfered (*ōbō*) with the administration of Zōta-no-shō in Sanuki Province on the basis of their having been promised the *ryōke shiki* as a reward for military valor. However, since the proprietor of this land, Daisō Shōbō of Zuishin'in, was a staunch supporter of the Ashikaga-sponsored Northern Court, Ashikaga Tadayoshi ruled that his manager continue to exercise control of the estate. For his part, Takatsuna would be in line to receive (*yodatsu*) other lands.[80] The promise of a reward was more important than the lands that composed it.

Lands became appropriable (*kessho*) when the proprietor aided a competing political entity, which essentially destabilized the validity of all land rights. As land rights became insecure, the need for a protector or guarantor increased; established rights per se paled in significance to rights established through contemporary edicts of confirmation. The confirmations or rewards of lands that were most valued were those that were issued by a hegemon who had a reputation for reliability. In other words, the more prestigious and reliable the edict, the easier it was for a local to maintain (or seize) landed holdings. All lands could be declared appropriable. *Kessho* claims originated from local areas, with central authorities frequently relying on oaths to determine their veracity.[81] Of course, the potential for abuse was considerable. For example, the perfidious Miyoshi Michihide took advantage of Yamanouchi Michitada's absence—Michitada was fighting in Kyushu under the direction of Imagawa Ryōshun in 1375—and labeled as *kessho* the hereditary lands (*honryō*) of the Yamanouchi, the Jibi Estate. After receiving an edict (*kudashibumi*) legitimating his claim, Michihide proceeded to enter forcibly (*rannyū*) and plunder the *shōen*.[82] However, the plot failed owing to Imagawa Ryōshun's staunch support for Yamanouchi Michitada.

A warrior's hereditary homelands (*honryō*) were held dearly; *tozama* invested much honor in their maintenance. According to one *tozama*, "[the act of] granting one's homelands to another is an affront to warrior honor (*yumiya no menmoku*)."[83] A hegemonic lord who unwittingly awarded a *tozama*'s hereditary lands to another would revoke his grant and arrange for a different reward. For example, a certain Shimazu Suō Gorō Saburō Tadakane complained that his hereditary lands had been mistakenly rewarded to the "military forces of Shirahata Castle." In due course, these lands were restored.[84] Conversely, a hegemon who confiscated a *tozama*'s

homelands secured his lasting enmity, creating, in the process, an impla-
cable foe. Again, according to the *Baishōron*'s panegyric, Ashikaga Takauji
"placated bitter enemies by confirming their homelands." [85] In other words,
a lordship of largesse entailed leniency toward the defeated; their rights to
homelands were largely respected. *Tozama* tenaciously attempted to maintain their lands. Similarly, this right of innate ownership, contingent on
force alone, provided a formidable barrier to those attempting to create a
lordship over land. Those leaders most cognizant of these attitudes toward
the land, as well as of the latent power of *tozama*, were those who were
ultimately most successful.

Lordship was predicated upon the ability to procure rewards for allies
and followers. This is most evident during the Kannō era (1350–52) when
warfare erupted, precipitated by a dispute between the Kō brothers—Ashikaga retainers—and Ashikaga Tadayoshi. Ashikaga Takauji fought with
the Kō brothers against his younger brother Tadayoshi, but suffered a
string of defeats. Peace was restored on the twenty-seventh day of the second month of 1351 after the two Kō brothers had been ambushed and
killed.[86] According to the *Entairyaku*, "The Shogun, through tremendous
effort, secured rewards for forty-three warriors." [87] He achieved this feat
even though he had been worsted in battle by his brother. Furthermore,
Takauji extracted an oath from Tadayoshi to honor his rewards. This concession was significant because Tadayoshi had already declared the lands of
the forty-three appropriable—*kessho*—and had actually rewarded them to
his followers.[88] Tadayoshi's "victory" thus enhanced Takauji's power and
prestige by underscoring his authority as the ultimate giver of gifts, the
proof for which came almost immediately: when Hosokawa Akiuji arrived
in the capital at the head of an army drawn from Shikoku, he requested
an audience with Takauji but was rebuffed, for the shogun "had no desire
to meet a man who had surrendered (*kōsannin*)." [89] In other words, once
the indefatigable Takauji had established primacy in granting rewards, he
could punish those who fought against him by claiming such a pretext, and
indeed even move to declare Akiuji's lands potentially appropriable. From
another angle, Takauji's promise, more binding than Tadayoshi's, ensured
the supremacy of his authority. Those who fought with him invariably
benefited; those who fought for Tadayoshi were less sure of adequate compensation. It should come as no surprise that when warfare resumed a few
months later, Takauji easily defeated his brother.[90]

Hegemonic lords amassed considerable power even though they knew
next to nothing about the lay of the land. For example, Ashikaga Tadafuyu,

an illegitimate son of Takauji, dominated northern Kyushu and western Japan during the 1350s and 1360s. However, when he promised a certain Yasutomi Yasushige a particular site as a reward, he mistakenly identified the province![91] In order to avoid such misunderstandings, Tadafuyu often issued *uragaki ando*, in which he simply confirmed a petition that had been submitted to him by adding a brief notation to the reverse side.[92] In other words, Tadafuyu responded to *tozama* requests by granting whatever they desired. Tadafuyu's grants of land would be revoked, however, if the original owner elected to join his forces. As we have seen, hereditary homelands were inviolable *in all circumstances*. As Tadafuyu stated: "If the original owner of [previously rewarded] lands allies himself with [our] forces, then [his lands shall be returned and] other lands shall be exchanged for rewards."[93] Tadafuyu's leniency ensured that he would develop no mortal enemies. However, unfortunately for him, a great number of western warriors, impressed by his generosity, flocked to his banner, thus creating an untenable situation. Those who had previously served with Tadafuyu lost their rewards, for all lands were now returned to their original owners. The hapless Yasutomi Yasushige lamented: "Although I was rewarded various lands for military merit (*gunkō no chi*), I have become virtually landless (*musoku*) since the original owners (*honshu*) have joined our forces. This turn of events is unbearable (*nankan no shidai nari*)."[94] Tadafuyu became a victim of his own success. Because nearly every local warrior joined his forces, appropriable lands became virtually nonexistent. Tadafuyu exhausted his supply of "gifts." As his promises became less dependable, his forces withered.

Tadafuyu's initial military strength contrasts sharply with the legendary tribulations of Isshiki Dōyū.[95] Although Dōyū granted *jitō shiki* to some warriors, he confiscated land from others.[96] In 1337, he threatened Ryūzōji Rokurō Ietane as follows: "Those who do not report (*fusan no tomogara*) [to the Isshiki] will have all appeals for rewards (*onshō soshō*) ignored; those [who report but] render no military service (*gunchū*) shall have one fifth of their lands (*shoryō*) confiscated."[97] Isshiki Dōyū eventually confiscated Ryūzōji homelands and granted them to Imagawa Tsuneyori. This action naturally earned him the lasting enmity of the Ryūzōji, one of whose numbers, Iemasa, excoriated Dōyū as being "unprincipled (*mudō*)" for such effrontery.[98] Although Ryūzōji remained nominally allied to the Isshiki, they quickly joined Ashikaga Tadafuyu with the hope of receiving confirmation of their homelands. Typically, Tadafuyu obliged with an *uragaki ando* to Ryūzōji Ietane in 1350.[99]

Isshiki Dōyū, by penalizing warriors who fought neither for nor against him, ultimately hindered his ability to mobilize forces. A comparison between Isshiki Dōyū and Ashikaga Tadafuyu reveals that magnanimity and largesse allowed a hegemon to gain the support of *tozama* warriors, while punitive measures spawned deep-seated grudges by warriors who felt unfairly treated. Isshiki Dōyū acted too much like a regional magnate, attempting to build a base of lands, and not enough like a "gift-giving" supraregional hegemon. By confiscating lands of warriors who arrived in encampments but refused to fight, Isshiki Dōyū seemed arbitrary and unreasonable to *tozama*. Tadafuyu's failure stemmed from the opposite flaw—his promises exceeded the bounds of reliability.

Kitabatake Chikafusa's relations with the Ishikawa family of Mutsu Province illustrate that Southern Court leaders were cognizant of the importance of rewards but less aware of the significance of homeland rights to *tozama* warriors. Even though the Ishikawa had participated in Nitta Yoshisada's sack of Kamakura in 1333, the Governor of Mutsu under the new Kenmu regime, Kitabatake Akiie, granted Ishikawa lands to Yūki Munehiro in 1334.[100] By contrast, Ashikaga Takauji confirmed the landholdings (*hon chigyō*) of one Ishikawa collateral, Ishikawa Kabata Gorō Tarō, in 1335, even as he neglected that family's main line.[101] In the event, both Ishikawa Kabata Gorō Tarō and the other Ishikawa warriors fought for Takauji, participating in both the epic battle of Minatogawa and the attack on Mount Hiei in 1336.[102]

Because their neighbors, the Yūki, were staunchly allied with the Southern Court, the Ishikawa came under intense pressure to defect. Kitabatake Chikafusa tempted them: "The Ishikawa have generally been enemies (*onteki*), but those who, regretting their past actions, join our forces will have their homelands (*honryō*) confirmed; later merit (*kō*) will be subsequently rewarded."[103] The Ishikawa responded by asking for the very homelands that had been granted to the Yūki in 1334. This incensed Kitabatake Chikafusa, who berated them as follows:

It has been customary for those who regret their prior inaction [i.e., those who refuse to respond to a call to arms] to have only one half or one third of their landholdings (*shoryō*) confirmed. Confirmation of [all] your homelands (*honryō*) exceeds the bounds of benevolent rule (*zensei*). In recent years, you have been deeply [tainted] with [association with] the enemy (*onteki*); now, prior to joining our forces you present a list of desired lands. Is that not an insult to warriors (*yumiya no chijoku*)? . . . How can [people] who tend to have the outlook of a merchant (*shōnin*) be of use to the Court? Nevertheless, as previously promised, your homelands (*honryō*) shall be confirmed; later acts of service shall be correspondingly rewarded.[104]

Kitabatake Chikafusa had no qualms about enticing warriors for tangible acts of merit. He could not countenance the invalidation of earlier decrees; a reward was a reward. Lands granted to the Yūki could not be returned to the Ishikawa. Instead of finding other suitable lands to compensate the Ishikawa (or the Yūki), as Takauji might have done, Chikafusa castigated the Ishikawa as having "the outlook of a merchant" for daring to request additional lands before joining his forces. The impasse between Kitabatake Chikafusa and the Ishikawa stemmed from the perhaps inevitable uncertainty regarding the delineation of a family's homelands. From the Ishikawa's perspective, homelands constituted the full extent of their holdings—all the lands under their control prior to 1334. For Kitabatake Chikafusa, however, Ishikawa homelands were composed solely of current holdings. The Ishikawa demanded the full restoration of their homelands in order to rehabilitate their warrior honor (*yumiya no menmoku*), but to Kitabatake Chikafusa the desire for pre-1334 homelands was an unreasonable request (and reward) for surrendering. Because Kitabatake Chikafusa failed to recognize the importance of homelands to a *tozama* like the Ishikawa, the latter remained an enemy of both the Southern Court and the usurper of "their" lands, the Yūki.

For his own part, Yūki Chikatomo abandoned the Southern Court cause in 1343, after receiving the enticing offer from Ashikaga Takauji that, "there shall be no disturbances regarding holdings (*chigyō*) [awarded] prior to Kenmu 2 (1335)."[105] With this edict, Takauji was able to keep his promise to Ishikawa Gorō Tarō, yet also entice the Yūki by allowing them to maintain their ex-Ishikawa lands.[106] Moreover, once the Yūki allied themselves with the Ashikaga, the hapless mainline of the Ishikawa had no choice but grudgingly to support the Southern Court.[107] But the Ishikawa lost out in the competition over lands; they suffered the ignominy of losing their homelands and subsequently disappeared from the historical record. The Yūki, however, increased their holdings, showing that some *tozama* prospered at the expense of others. One can also surmise that the most effective manipulator of this system was Ashikaga Takauji; he was able to preserve the value of his promises, keep his partisans satisfied, and also expand his base of support. In contrast to Kitabatake Chikafusa, who pontificated profusely but only grudgingly granted rewards, Takauji's promises carried great weight and his largesse was unsurpassed.

Yūki Chikatomo timed his transfer of allegiance well and profited accordingly. The Ishikawa were not so fortunate, but still presumably received a confirmation of their homelands as delineated by the Southern Court. According to the customary "law of surrender (*kōsan no hō*)," however, a warrior would be confirmed with only half his lands.[108] Or, to be more precise, "according to the set rule, half of the homelands (*honryō*) of those who had surrendered (*kōsannin*) were returned."[109] This "set rule" seems to have been observed more in the breach than in reality. Powerful *tozama* rarely suffered such ignominy. For example, Aso Koresumi, distressed by the liberal treatment of his father-in-law, Aso Koretoki, complained: "It is a set rule that those who surrender (*kōsannin*) should have only half [their holdings] confirmed. . . . How can [Koretoki] possibly wish for a full confirmation (*ichien ando*)?"[110] Koretoki maintained a powerful local *tozama* lordship; even after briefly dallying with the Ashikaga forces he received full confirmation of his lands from the Southern Court.[111] For those who realized that they had allied themselves to a losing cause, the confirmation of homelands was a welcome compensation.

How can one account for the difference between warriors who lost half their lands and those who suffered not at all? Timing was crucial. One warrior's comment after another had surrendered in the field proves illuminating: "I have never heard of such a thing! Norinaga, if you had intended to surrender (lit. become a *kōnin*), you should have done it when the Shogun [Takauji] . . . invited you to join his forces with a communiqué (*migyōsho*)! After burning your expressly delivered communiqué, [why did] you come here to surrender? It is too much for words."[112] In other words, a *tozama* responding to a request for service could switch sides and suffer no punishment. Those who arrived at an encampment with a request to join allied forces were actually eligible for further rewards. If defeated in battle, however, a warrior had to hand over his weapons and unstring his bow, as was the customary practice for the act of surrender (*kōsan no hō*).[113] Thus the most powerful warriors possessed ample opportunities to transfer loyalties independently of defeat in battle. Those unfortunate enough to suffer defeat were in a position of such weakness that the loss of some of their lands became inevitable.

This distinction was lost on some. Imagine a warrior's consternation if instead of receiving rewards for service he had only half his lands confirmed! Such was the unhappy lot of Sōma Tanehira. He expressed indignation in 1348 because he had been confirmed with only one-half of his holding in spite of the service (*chūsetsu*) rendered on his behalf by his son, who helped attack the Southern Court fortress of Reisan. To add insult to injury, according to Tanehira, his younger brother had fought at the same battle and received a full confirmation of lands.[114] Sōma Tanehira asserted that such a difference in treatment was incomprehensible. He failed to mention, however, that during 1336–37 he fought for the Southern Court.[115] Tanehira seems to have waited too long to switch sides. Five years after Yūki Chikatomo had defected, Southern Court supporters were hardpressed by Ashikaga armies. In all probability, Tanehira had not received an invitation to fight, but, on the other hand, he had not surrendered his weapons in accordance with the custom of *kōsan no hō*. Surrender could be an ambiguous process.

The attitude of Sōma Tanehira and of the Aso indicates that although familial unity existed as an ideal, personal concerns were paramount. Upset that his brother was rewarded far more than he, Tanehira's primary concern was not familial welfare. The Ishikawa's divisions likewise stemmed from divided interests: Ishikawa Kabata Gorō Tarō staunchly supported the Ashikaga, while the main line, whose lands had been granted the Yūki, fought with whoever opposed the Yūki. Families with united interests fought together; as interests diverged, so did loyalties.

The success of interregional hegemons depended upon weaving as many competing strands of *tozama* self-interest into a fabric of guarded satisfaction. Popularity and military power were inexorably linked; by legitimating *tozama* rights, a regime was able to establish a degree of support commensurate with its ability to protect promised rights and rewards. A lack of foresight or flexibility in resolving the myriad of *tozama* claims weakened a hegemon's basis of support; a failure to honor one's promises ensured that the laboriously intertwined interests would unravel. Those who overtly attempted to aggrandize lands incited the opposition of *tozama* who were determined to retain holdings that were theirs by right. Only a hegemonic lord keenly aware of the interests of his men and of his own fragile basis of support could devote himself to providing adequate compensation for his followers; his edicts of confirmation secured and legitimated *tozama* rights in an unstable age of competing claims. Successful leaders ensured that *tozama* self-interest and their own interests were one. By balancing the myriad of *tozama* desires and respecting as many rights as possible, a hegemon cobbled together a coalition of disparate warriors even as his position remained precarious. The fourteenth-century political terrain was unforgiving of missteps, and profoundly ill-suited for mediocrities.

CONCLUSION

Individual warriors exhibited conflicting attitudes, which were inexorably linked to the particulars of their social and political position. Commoners who fought, although ineligible for rewards, could achieve *miuchi* status for some notable act. *Miuchi* were ideally bound to their *tozama* lord and only attempted to act independently when, in addition to securing enough lands and followers of their own, an opportunity arose for them to seek to achieve autonomy. *Miuchi* who were without extensive holdings tended to remain loyal, for their interests were in fact indistinguishable from those of their *tozama* lord. Finally, *tozama* exhibited autonomy in war and fought according to personal and narrowly defined family interests, not out of a sense of allegiance to any "lord."

During the Age of the Northern and Southern Courts, political stability hinged upon social stratification. Of course, some men took advantage of the inherent instability of the age to obfuscate their social position. Thus, some *miuchi* attempted to attain *tozama* prerogatives, while other *tozama* struggled to establish a regional lordship. Those who were less fortunate clung to the privileges of their increasingly precarious social position, and either attempted to quash upstart *miuchi*, or, fearful of losing their status, refused to serve under *tozama* magnates. It remains eminently clear, however, that armies and polities were most effectively led by men who were socially distant from their compatriots.

The crucial divide in fourteenth-century lordship was between those who could offer grants to followers, and those who could not. The former were national or supraregional hegemons; the latter provincial magnates. Supraregional hegemons' powers were great, if unstable. Some, such as Ashikaga Tadafuyu or a few Ashikaga collaterals, precipitously descended into obscurity. Others, such as the Hosokawa, were gradually able to attract locals as *miuchi*, and eventually established a landed lordship. Ashikaga Takauji proved the most successful of all by guaranteeing his promises and by providing the most generous and comprehensive compensation. By contrast, those, like Go-Daigo or Isshiki Dōyū, who aspired to a national or regional authority, could not countenance such a diffusion of power and accordingly received less *tozama* support.

During the first two decades of the Nanbokuchō period, only members of the Ashikaga kindred and a few closely related *shugo* maintained the ability to lead armies drawn from several provinces.[116] Only after the turmoil of the Kannō Disturbance (1350–51) were a handful of *tozama* magnates, such as the Ōuchi, able to grant gifts or confirmations. In spite of this, the power of most *tozama* magnates remained limited, even in the case of *shugo* like the Kōno of Iyo. Inasmuch as hegemons were able to harness the dissatisfaction of less fortunate *tozama* (while also liberally rewarding their more prosperous counterparts), they succeeded in displacing or dominating those who, for their own part, had attempted to become regional magnates.

Military leaders could only mobilize *tozama* after respecting their homelands, and after promising adequate remuneration for those who chose to participate in battle. Hegemons, lords of men, compensated *tozama* instead of competing with them, and thereby accumulated symbolic capital, which was the foundation of their lordships. In the process, they found themselves bound to keep their promises, and also to forgive *tozama* lapses of loyalty. In short, the warriors of the fourteenth century have been unfairly castigated as "turncoats," since in fact they owed service to none.

When Imagawa Ryōshun killed Shōni Fuyusuke he seemed, in this sense, to have behaved unreasonably and excessively, for Fuyusuke's behavior had been neither egregious nor particularly unusual (though the same obviously could not be said for Ryōshun's cowardly act). And yet, although his forces disintegrated in 1375, the indomitable Imagawa was able to regroup and eventually to dominate most of Kyushu. Ryōshun's ultimate success indicates that the locus of power had already begun to shift toward regional magnates, which meant, conversely, that *tozama* autonomy was now becoming precarious. A remarkable oath, signed in 1392 by the Shibuya, a *tozama* of southern Kyushu, makes this point:

> Concerning those allied with the Shimazu: at all times . . . we shall protect the Shogun (*shogun-ke*). When we are not in accord with the [Shimazu] *shugo*, we shall, of course, all follow the wishes of the *Kubō* [Imagawa Ryōshun]. . . . There must be no dissension. The members of this *ikki* must be in accord. [If we] are lacking in right (*ri*), we will lose [the right of] service (*chū*). [Thus,] in order for our sons and grandsons to remain able to render military service (*guneki*), and also to remain able [to maintain our] landed holdings (*chigyōbun*), we shall rely together upon the *Kubō*, who will determine the merit (*rihi*) [of all matters].[117]

It was at this stage that the many were starting to become the *miuchi* of the few. *Tozama* such as the Shibuya preserved their autonomy from the Shimazu by subordinating themselves to a supraregional figure like Imagawa Ryōshun. Although service in an *ikki* organization was not particularly desirable to a *tozama*, it was preferable to *miuchi* status vis-à-vis a regional magnate. But this is a story more of the fifteenth century than of the fourteenth. The age of limited loyalty was coming to a close. Perhaps, in the end, Imagawa Ryōshun's assassination of Shōni Fuyusuke was not such a grave misjudgment after all.

CHAPTER 3

The Kikuchi and Their
Enemies in the 1330s

SENO SEIICHIRŌ

IN THE POLITICAL LIFE of Japan, 1336 was a year of great choices and of huge discord. Marching east from Kyushu, Ashikaga Takauji defeated Nitta Yoshisada and Kusunoki Masashige at Minatogawa (1336/5/25), thus allowing his triumphant reentry into Kyoto, and also prompting Go-Daigo's flight to the Enryakuji on Mount Hiei. Though a compromise subsequently permitted Go-Daigo to return to the capital, the settlement proved only fleeting and the emperor now took refuge in the mountains of Yoshino. In national terms, 1336 marked the decisive break between what became the Northern and Southern courts, ushering in a lengthy era of civil strife.

Kyushu like other regions was affected by these momentous events. Yet Kyushu was also in the eye of the storm in 1336, with events occurring there that influenced both the regional and the national pictures. Alliances were made and broken during that year of great uncertainty, when families with long histories found themselves no longer sure which way to turn; insights into the future were hard to come by. The experiences of the Kikuchi of northern Kyushu are a useful lens through which to highlight the dramatically heightened importance of the battlefield in sorting such things out. At Tatarahama in 1336, the fate of none other than Ashikaga Takauji hung in the balance, underscoring the extraordinary fluidity of the 1330s.

THE PRELUDE TO THE EVENTS OF 1336 IN KYUSHU

The Kikuchi family was based in that region of Higo Province bearing their name, and there are a number of conflicting theories about their origins.[1] Of these the most plausible argues that they were a local magnate family who had held the post of district head (*gunshi*) in Kikuchi-gun on a hereditary basis. In the middle of the eleventh century, they entered the service of Fujiwara Takaie, the regional governor for Kyushu (Dazai *gon no sochi*), who had been sent down from Kyoto. Thereafter, they had been able to use their new-found influence within the Kyushu commandery (*Dazaifu*) to become local warriors of some importance.

At the end of the twelfth century events far away in eastern Japan led to the establishment of Japan's first military government, the Kamakura Bakufu, which, during the initial stages at least, ran in tandem with the old imperial administration. The wars surrounding the birth of this new regime saw the Kikuchi clan coalesce into a powerful warrior league, or *bushidan*. In 1181/2, their leader, Kikuchi Takanao, joined with Ogata Koreyoshi of Bungo, another important local warrior, in rebellion against the Taira, which converted them into *de facto* allies of Minamoto Yoritomo, founder of the Bakufu. This rising was, however, crushed by Haruda Tanenao.[2] Then, perversely, as the fighting drew to a close and the Taira star waned, the Kikuchi chose to align themselves with their erstwhile enemies and, together with other leading Kyushu warriors including the Haruda, Yamaga, and Itai, suffered a crushing defeat at the hands of the now triumphant Bakufu.[3] The battle took place off the coast of Kyushu, at Dannoura, and it saw the emergence of Minamoto Yoritomo as Japan's unquestioned military leader. His forces were drawn largely from the east, while, in their dying moments, the Taira had relied almost exclusively on warriors from Kyushu. The new military regime, therefore, tilted decidedly toward the east and against the west, a fact that was to have profound consequences for the island's future.

Among those most affected were the Kikuchi. Their decision to return to the Taira fold at the last moment had a distinctly negative effect on their position as warriors throughout the Kamakura era. Although they were soon rehabilitated as *gokenin*, or direct vassals of the Kamakura regime, their ill-fortune was compounded in 1221 in consequence of their being on guard duty in Kyoto when the retired emperor Go-Toba chose to launch his attack on the Bakufu in Kamakura. The Kikuchi had no choice but to join Go-Toba's side in the Jōkyū War, for which the Bakufu subsequently stripped them of a number of their holdings. Later they performed loyally in resisting the Mongols, but their previous record precluded any chance of their achieving high office under the Bakufu. Thus the whole Kamakura age was marked by deep frustration for the Kikuchi, who could never hope to realize their full potential. By contrast, the Shōni, Ōtomo, and Shimazu, all of whom originated in the east, monopolized most of the important posts within the Bakufu's command chain in Kyushu, most particularly that of *shugo*, or provincial military governor.

In spite of all this, however, the Kikuchi were able to overcome many of the obstacles placed in their path, and, by the end of the Kamakura era, were on their way to wielding de facto powers rivaling those of the three great *shugo* families. Be that as it may, as long as the Kamakura Bakufu survived, they could hardly hope to supplant any of these three houses. This essential point of difference between the Kikuchi and the three *shugo* was brought into sharp focus by the events surrounding the collapse of the Bakufu in 1333, and most especially by the assault on the Chinzei Tandai, the Bakufu's local representative based in Hakata. The main point at issue was the degree of change that each party regarded as desirable. During the Kamakura period, these differences had always existed, but they had never burst into anything approaching open conflict.

Meanwhile, Go-Daigo, who had been emperor since 1318, had long been dreaming of reestablishing direct imperial rule (*tennō shinsei*). In pursuit of this aim, he had for some time been moving in the direction of using military force. He was able to capitalize on the seething changes that beset society at all levels. It was this latter that provided the backdrop to the Bakufu's inevitable demise. The Kamakura regime successfully fended off two direct challenges from Go-Daigo, but the final collapse, when it came, was unstoppable. The Kikuchi themselves represented one of these currents of change in their ambition to realize their dream of becoming true regional lords. Go-Daigo's resort to arms ignited local forces across the land who, like the Kikuchi, were eager to advance themselves. In Kyushu, the emperor himself sent out imperial commands (*rinji*) to such groups, and his son and local representative, Prince Kaneyoshi, did essentially the same thing. There seems little doubt that such documents would have found their way to the Shōni, Ōtomo, and Shimazu, as well as to other families, such as the Kikuchi. In the meantime, the Bakufu's representative in Kyushu (its Chinzei Tandai), Hōjō Hidetoki, was well aware of the state of affairs nationally and of the hostile activities close by. He accordingly ordered the local *gokenin* to make their way to Hakata to defend his own headquarters.

The *Hakata Nikki*[4] states that Kikuchi Ikejirō nyūdō Jakua (Taketoki) of Higo Province was one of the warriors who answered this call to arms, arriving in Hakata on 1333/2/11. However, it also reports that when he presented himself at the Tandai's residence the next day, he was reprimanded for his lateness by Hiroda Shinsaemon no jō Hisayoshi, who, as vassal commander (*samuraidokoro*), was responsible for confirming the arrival of warriors for service. This incident provides an indication that the Kikuchis' loyalty was already in doubt. The *Taiheiki*, for its part, offers the following commentary. Shōni nyūdō Myōe (Sadatsune), Ōtomo nyūdō Gukan (Sadamune), and Kikuchi nyūdō Jakua (Taketoki) had informed Go-Daigo, then in Hōki Province, that they would join his cause, which was acknowledged by the emperor with a brocade banner and the relevant edicts (*rinji*). The three chieftains kept this plan to themselves, but the Tandai, it seems, had some inkling of their intentions; he thus ordered the Kikuchi to Hakata, apparently as a test. Taketoki, suspecting that the plot had been uncovered, made his way to Hakata, but with the intention of launching a preemptive strike. According to the *Taiheiki*, he was raising forces from the moment he set off from Higo Province, though this is contradicted by the *Hakata Nikki*, which takes the position that Taketoki's defection was prompted by the reprimand from the *samuraidokoro* on the occasion of his arrival.

The *Hakata Nikki* then continues by giving the following version of events. Taketoki was now only too well aware of the fact that he was not well thought of in official circles, and he therefore started fires in Hakata on the thirteenth day and sent messengers to Shōni Sadatsune and Ōtomo Sadamune bidding them to gather their forces. Sadatsune's answer was to have two of Taketoki's messengers killed and their heads sent to the Chinzei Tandai. Sadamune, however, advised the Kikuchi to terminate their military preparations and, for his part, made no move to join them. The *Taiheiki* gives the following explanation for the refusal of the Shōni and Ōtomo to respond to the Kikuchis' call to arms: "Saying it was not yet possible to tell what would become of the realm, the Ōtomo did not give him [Kikuchi Taketoshi] a clear answer. Furthermore, the Shōni, having heard that the Rokuhara Tandai had lately enjoyed a spate of military success in Kyoto, thought he would make good his earlier fault [in supporting Go-Daigo]."

The Shōni and Ōtomo thus judged the Kikuchis' move to be premature, leaving Taketoki to face the Chinzei Tandai alone. The outcome was inevitable. Taketoki, his son Yoritaka, his younger brother Kakushō, and all the members (*wakatō*) in their band fell in battle.

The *Hakata Nikki* gives a somewhat different version of events:

So the heads of Kikuchi nyūdō, his son Saburo, Jakua's younger brother Kakusho, and the *wakato* were hung up in the place where warriors practice shooting dogs from horses. Jakua's, Saburo's, and Kakusho's [heads] were displayed separately. In the evening they were taken down and placed in the residence where they remained for about ten days. Then they were nailed to a board and a sign said that they were the heads of the rebels, Kikuchi Taro nyūdō Jakua, his son Saburō, and Jakua's younger brother, Jirō Saburō nyūdō Kakusho.

The deep humiliation of the Kikuchi had been exposed for all to see and it would not be stretching the imagination to conclude that they would have blamed their fate on the treachery of the Shōni and the Ōtomo.

The *Taiheiki* carries on by saying that Hidetoki, the Tandai, had actually resolved to commit suicide owing to the ferocity of the Kikuchi assault, but that the tide of the battle turned in his favor with the arrival of 6,000 Shōni and Ōtomo horsemen. According to this source, the Kikuchi forces under Taketoki were actually killed by the Shōni and Ōtomo.

Of course not everything the *Taiheiki* says can be taken at face value, but there can be little doubt that the great antipathy the whole Kikuchi clan harbored toward the Shōni and Ōtomo was the direct result of these events. It seems, moreover, that this hatred was passed down and helped to sustain the Kikuchi in their sixty-year struggle against the Ashikaga Bakufu. Indeed, if, at this time, the three great families had been able to work together, the whole history of Kyushu might have been different—though looked at with the benefit of hindsight, such cooperation seems impossible. After all, local forces had traditionally allied themselves with the central authority in their struggles with their peers, meaning that the continued existence of the Tandai was necessary if the Shōni and Ōtomo were to overcome the Kikuchi. By the same argument, the Kikuchi failed to establish regional supremacy in Kyushu precisely because they were seeking to do so without the support of central authority. There are no instances of local forces in Kyushu establishing a position of dominance without the backing of the central government. That government, in turn, adopted the old policy of divide and rule, leading to a melding of interests between agents of the center and certain local warriors.

At any rate, the Tandai ordered the *shugo* of Higo to mop up the surviving Kikuchi forces which had fled back to the province. The *shugo* burned down the residence of the Aso Shrine head and reduced the Kuraoka fortress where he and the Kikuchi had taken shelter. From this we can conclude readily that it was the Tandai's aim to destroy the Kikuchi once and for all.

As we have noted, the Shōni and Ōtomo had felt the attack by the

Kikuchi on the Tandai to have been premature; they had thus sided with the Bakufu. They were accordingly caught by surprise when Takauji destroyed the regime's headquarters in Kyoto, which dramatically altered the whole complexion of events. On 1333/5/25, barely two months after Kikuchi Taketoki's death, they joined with the Shimazu and the other Kyushu *gokenin* in an attack on the Chinzei Tandai. This time Hidetoki did indeed commit suicide, and with him vanished the Bakufu's presence on the island. According to the *Taiheiki*, it had been Shōni Sadatsune, who, upon hearing of the destruction of the Rokuhara headquarters, now realized his error and sought to make amends by destroying the Chinzei Tandai. He sent messengers to the Kikuchi and the Ōtomo asking for their cooperation. However, it had been barely two months since Sadatsune's betrayal of Kikuchi Taketoki, and therefore the latter's clan made no move to respond to the Shōni's invitation. The Ōtomo, who were under no such moral injunction, easily switched sides and responded favorably to the Shōni's appeal. The Kikuchi, for their part, were repeating their own history by failing, as they had in 1185, to anticipate what was happening around them. This time, though, their error was based on personal enmity. Nor can it be supposed that this fact was lost upon the Kikuchi themselves. During the Nanbokuchō era, the prime motivation behind their actions was rooted in their indelible hatred for the Shōni and Ōtomo.

THE ATTACK BY THE KIKUCHI
ON SHŌNI SADATSUNE

During the three years of the Kenmu Shinsei, the Shōni, Ōtomo, and Shimazu were all rewarded for their roles in the destruction of the Chinzei Tandai and were in the process of establishing a position of political primacy on the island. In an edict (*rinji*) dated 1333/8/28, Go-Daigo rewarded Ōtomo Sadamune with Okinohama in Hakata, the site of the Chinzei Tandai's residence.[5] In 1334, Shimazu Sadahisa likewise received a *rinji* authorizing him to take charge of the defense of Kyushu from foreign invasion, and giving him jurisdiction over Satsuma and Hyuga.[6] In 1334/7, Shōni Sadatsune and Ōtomo Sadamune led the *gokenin* of Kyushu in the suppression of a revolt by two Hōjō partisans, Kiku Takamasa and Itoda Sadayoshi.[7] However, there is no evidence of their receiving any cooperation or assistance from the Kikuchi at this time. In the midst of all this, a succession of local warriors was making its way to Kyoto either to have existing lands confirmed or to demand reward for services rendered.

Among them were Ōtomo Sadamune, Shōni Yorihisa, and, interestingly, Kikuchi Takeshige. Meanwhile Shōni Sadatsune remained at the Dazaifu where he strengthened his primacy over the whole island. In 1335/1, he destroyed a revolt led by two surviving Hōjō warriors, crushing them at Sagari Castle, the administrative center of Nagato Province.[8]

Then, in 1335/11, the Kenmu Shinsei was rent asunder by the defection of Ashikaga Takauji. Nitta Yoshisada was immediately dispatched to the east to destroy Takauji, and among the forces he took with him were those of Kikuchi Takeshige, Ōtomo Sadanori, and Shimazu Sadahisa. On the eleventh day of the following month, this army was defeated by Takauji and his younger brother, Tadayoshi, at the battle of Hakone Takenoshita. The following day, this defeat turned into a rout, when, at the battle of Sanoyama in Izu Province, Ōtomo Sadanori and his force of over 300 horsemen defected to Takauji.[9] Yoshisada was forced to withdraw to Kyoto but Kikuchi Takeshige remained loyal to him. In other words, here was another instance in which the Kikuchi had been betrayed by the Ōtomo.

The main document form used in recruiting forces at this time was the *gunzei saisokujō*, and Go-Daigo sent off a whole flurry of these to the various families in Kyushu. A number of these documents survive, including those sent to warriors in at least six Chinzei provinces.[10] Undoubtedly there were many more which have either been lost or were destroyed deliberately during the Nanbokuchō Wars. By contrast, Ashikaga Takauji simply sent his instructions to Shōni Yorihisa, Ōtomo Ujiyasu, and his lieutenant, Sadanori, ordering them to muster the *gokenin* in the various provinces where they were *shugo*.[11]

Among several others, Kimotsuki Kaneshige and Ito Sukehiro of Hyūga as well as Kikuchi Taketoshi rallied to Go-Daigo's order.[12] With his elder brother Takeshige now in Kyoto, Taketoshi had remained in Higo where the arrival of the emperor's recruitment call allowed him to vent his full fury at the Shōni and Ōtomo. Remembering their betrayal of his father, Taketoshi mustered his forces at Kikuchi Castle and then struck north to attack Shōni Sadatsune at Dazaifu. Sadatsune responded by sending Aki Sadamoto and Takuma Sadamasa, who defeated Taketoshi on the final day of the year. The Shōni army then pursued the defeated forces into Higo and attacked Kikuchi Castle itself. The castle fell on 1336/1/8, though Taketoshi was able to escape.[13]

Meanwhile, in Kyoto, the triumphant Ashikaga army had just suffered a reversal by being defeated by the Nitta and Kusunoki. Taketoshi attempted to capitalize on this chance by raising forces in Higo again and by attacking the Dazaifu.[14] In turn, Takauji accepted the advice of the Shōni, Ōtomo, and Shimazu that they all return to Kyushu gathering forces along the way. On the twelfth day of the second month, Takauji himself set sail from Hyōgo aboard the Ōtomo chief's boat. The *Baishōron* gives the following account of this event: "Between 5 and 7 p.m. on the same day, it had not been decided who should board which ship, and a great throng were all squabbling to be first." The *Taiheiki* states: "Soon [Takauji] boarded the Ōtomo chief's ship. His troops, seeing this, shouted that the shogun was fleeing to Kyushu. They threw what was close at hand onto the ships shouting that they would be too late to board. There were barely three hundred ships in all." From both these quotations, it is clear that Takauji's embarkation was anything but orderly. He called in at Muro-notsu in Harima Province where the forces that had been unable to join him earlier now boarded ship. He also used the occasion to appoint various military commanders to the provinces of Shikoku and western Honshu.

When Takauji arrived at Tomo in Bungo Province, a monk appeared bearing an order (*inzen*) from the retired emperor Kogon, which Takauji had earlier insisted that he issue. In fact, from the moment he had mustered his forces, Takauji had feared being named an enemy of the Court. Though, initially, he had hoped to establish his power through his relationship with Go-Daigo, he now strove to acquire the legitimacy for his military actions by way of an *inzen* from the retired emperor Kogon. Of the Jimyōin line, Kogon was naturally opposed to Go-Daigo, who was of the rival Daikakuji branch. At all events, once he had acquired this document, the Nanbokuchō Wars entered a new stage. The *Baishōron* comments: "With this their courage rose, and he said that he could not now be called an enemy of the Court. It is excellent indeed that the commanders of the land may now be told to hoist the brocade banner."[15]

Almost immediately, Takauji began to spread word of his having received the *inzen* and, upon such a pretext, he summoned local warriors to battle. His most important source of support came from the Shōni, who since Kamakura times had exercised immense influence over the fighting men of Kyushu.

However, the *inzen* now pitted Takauji against Kikuchi Taketoshi, who was bent on blood revenge against the Shōni. Nevertheless, the advantage lay with Takauji, who was now steadily gathering men to his colors. Late in the second month, Shōni Sadatsune's son and heir, Yorihisa, went out to greet Takauji with over 500 horsemen. This was timely assistance indeed, but it left Uchiyama Castle in Dazaifu unprotected, where Sadatsune himself remained. Taketoshi, ever alert, advanced into Chikugo intent on attacking his old enemy, though Sadatsune sought to counter this threat by going out to meet his adversary. A ferocious clash between the two forces occurred on the twenty-seventh in Kōzuma-gun (Chikugo), in which the Shōni army was defeated and forced to retreat to Uchiyama Castle.[16] Taketoshi pursued it and took the fort two days later. Shōni Sadatsune then committed suicide. According to the *Baishōron*, even the military equipment that had been set up around the castle in preparation for Takauji's arrival was now left in ashes. Also, save for those members of Shōni who had gone to greet Takauji, some 500 family members and retainers now took their own lives.[17]

Sadatsune's defeat and death had a profound effect on the attitude of local warriors. It was also a development of considerable consequence to Takauji, who was just then hoping to revive his fortunes. The news was immediately carried to Sadatsune's heir, Yorihisa, who was in Chikuzen with the Ashikaga leader, though he kept the information secret fearing its effect on morale in Takauji's army.

Sadatsune's death meant that Taketoshi had gone some way toward realizing his dream of vengeance. It also served, of course, to make the Shōni the sworn enemies of the Kikuchi. The deaths of Taketoki in 1333 and Sadatsune in 1336 both have a claim to be considered as the starting point for the Nanbokuchō Wars in Kyushu.

THE SIGNIFICANCE OF THE BATTLE OF TATARAHAMA

The *Baishōron* states that on the first day of the third month, Shōni Yorihisa led the Bakufu's forces out of Ashiya and, between 5:00 and 7:00 P.M., entered the residence of Ujinori, the chief priest of the Munakata Shrine. Ujinori, it goes on, presented Takauji and Tadayoshi with armor and horses. Takauji, who had heard of Sadatsune's suicide, was extremely disheartened, the more so since Taketoshi's forces were massing around Hakata for a final, decisive assault on the Ashikaga army. Takauji summoned Yorihisa to discuss strategy. Yorihisa told him: "Because they had come here to meet you, all my forces were absent from the recent battle in Dazaifu and it was for this reason that we were defeated. At tomorrow's battle, the local stalwarts (*kokujin*) will certainly come over to your side. There is no doubt that I alone could smite him [i.e., Taketoshi]."

Yorihisa's proud words were underpinned by the long dominance of his family in Kyushu. Not only had the Shōni been, since Kamakura times, the *shugo* of some five provinces (Chikuzen, Buzen, Hizen, Tsushima, and Oki), but also they held the top regional post in the old imperial command chain, that of Dazai Shōni, a title they had adopted as their surname. By comparison, the Kikuchi were no more than ordinary local warriors. During the Kamakura period, they had never achieved a position of primacy vis-à-vis their peers. However, during this new era it had become customary for warriors to choose sides on the basis of current power relations. Old relationships and obligations simply did not enter into their reckoning. The *Baishōron* makes the following comment concerning the evident weakness of Takauji's forces: "The men who accompanied him from the Kantō were prepared to die for him. However, they discarded their horses in Hyōgo and it was not certain that they would catch up with him on foot."

On the second day of the third month, Takauji moved his forces forward and made camp on a small hill overlooking the Tatara River. The Kikuchi army pitched its tents facing them from the other side. According to the *Baishōron*, whereas the Kikuchi commanded some 60,000 horsemen, the Ashikaga had only a tiny contingent—the 100 or so men they had brought with them from Kyoto along with a total of some 500 Shōni. The *Taiheiki*'s figures are similar, with 40–50,000 Kikuchi horsemen facing 300 to 500 Ashikaga. Though the totals are obviously not believable, at least we can credit the Kikuchi's huge numerical advantage. At the same time, however, the *Baishōron* leaves the impression that the Kikuchi army had been cobbled together and was devoid of any unity. At all events, when the two armies encountered each other a fierce melee ensued. At one stage, conditions looked bad for Takauji's side when Tadayoshi's encampment nearly fell, but then, just as Yorihisa had predicted, elements of the Kikuchi began to desert to the Ashikaga side. According to the *Taiheiki*, a certain contingent of Kikuchi did not make any effort to fight, but rather rolled up their battle flags, took off their helmets, and defected to the enemy. By nightfall on the first day of battle, the Kikuchi army had completely disintegrated. Taketoshi fled to Chikugo and thence back to his home base in Higo. The defeated Kikuchi army dispersed, each element fleeing to its home region.

Between nine and eleven o'clock in the evening on that historic day, Tadayoshi entered the Dazaifu, which was the Shōnis' home base. Takauji lodged at the Hakozaki Temple and presented a sword to the Hakozaki Shrine. By virtue of his victory at Tatarahama, Takauji had survived the greatest crisis of his career. But the point needs to be made that his fate had rested on the rivalries of the main warriors in Kyushu. Divided into two hostile camps between the Shōni and the Kikuchi, in the end it had been the Kikuchi who had been devastatingly defeated.

Why the Kikuchi should have attacked Takauji is, in fact, uncertain. Traditionally explained in terms of the favors shown them by Go-Daigo, there is actually no evidence to suggest that the emperor had favored the Kikuchi any more than he did the Shōni, Ōtomo, or Shimazu. Similarly, those who have stressed their consistent devotion to the Southern Court in subsequent decades simply fail to account for their ill-fated assault on Takauji at Tatarahama. "Loyalty to the imperial cause" is insufficient—a kind of rationalization to lend legitimacy to a failed but noble effort. In fact, the Kikuchi's motivation was not inspired by any such concept as loyalty; rather, it came from the same considerations as had guided them before—namely, their desire to end the supremacy of the triumvirate in Kyushu, who had maintained their position of primacy even after 1333. Their support for Takauji meant that the Kikuchi would necessarily become Southern Court "loyalists." Seen from this perspective, the Battle of Tatarahama was to be of huge significance in determining the course of Kyushu history during the Nanbokuchō Wars.

ASHIKAGA TAKAUJI'S STRATAGEMS FOR RULING KYUSHU

Takauji, victorious at Tatarahama, quit his quarters at Hakozaki the following day (the third). He moved to Dazaifu where he now ordered the warriors of Kyushu to crush the Kikuchi and their supporters.[18] These local forces had been waiting to see what course events would take, but they now responded to Takauji's summons and rallied to his side.[19] He then began dispatching commanders to various parts of the island. Nikki Yoshinaga was sent to attack Kikuchi Castle;[20] others were directed to lay siege to Kusu Castle in Bungo and to fortresses in Chikugo, Higo, and Hyūga.[21]

Remaining behind at Dazaifu, Takauji now rewarded the warriors who had served him at Tatarahama. The *Baishōron* records that Shōni Yorihisa was acknowledged first. For his part, Ōtomo Ujiyasu received the *jitō shiki* for Yamamoto-no-shō, Chida-no-shō, and the lands of the Takemiya Shrine, all in Higo,[22] while Shimazu Sadahisa was given Kawanabe-gun in Satsuma and Hon-no-shō in Ōsumi.[23] Others who had performed meritoriously received their rewards in turn,[24] and the temples and shrines of Kyushu were given lands and ordered to pray for the peace of the realm and the future prosperity and military success of the Ashikaga.[25]

At the same time, Takauji was now steadily laying plans for his own return to Kyoto.[26] On the twelfth day of the third month, he ordered Nejime Kiyonari of Ōsumi to report on the numbers of sailors and helmsmen who could be recruited along the bays and inlets of that province;[27] the chief priest of the Takeo Shrine in Hizen was instructed to supply a horse, saddle, bow, arrows, a shield, and a foot soldier.[28] Takauji informed the Iwashimizu Hachiman Shrine that he would leave Dazaifu on the twenty-eighth of the month,[29] though the date was put back until he, the Ōtomo, and the Shōni and their combined forces set sail on the third day of the fourth month.[30] It was barely one month since his defeat of the Kikuchi at Tatarahama. However, inasmuch as there were still hostile forces in Kyushu, he left behind Isshiki Dōyū to deal with these and to administer the island.[31] One of the main reasons that the wars there lasted so long and developed in such a complicated manner flowed directly from the activities of this Ashikaga deputy.

In fact, no sooner had news of Takauji's departure reached Kikuchi Taketoshi than he raised an army and launched a widespread guerrilla campaign against the forces of Isshiki Dōyū in Chikugo. He also succeeded in impeding the Bakufu's local administration in Kyushu.

In 1336, the fighting was still concentrated in three areas: the area between Taketoshi and Dōyū in Chikugo and Higo; an area in the southwest (Hyūga, Ōsumi, and Satsuma) involving the Kimotsuki, Itō, and Mashido against the Hatakeyama and Shimazu Sadahisa; and the area of Bungo, where Isshiki Yoriyuki was conducting a seven-month siege of Kusu Castle, which fell finally on 10/13.

The fighting around Kusu Castle was an internal family matter over who within the Ōtomo clan should be house head. By contrast, the decision of the Kimotsuki, Itō, and Mashido to align themselves with Go-Daigo's field commanders[32] was aimed at undercutting the *shugo* placed above them (Shimazu Sadahisa). Finally, the Kikuchi drew their resolve, as they had always done, by venting their hostility against the Ōtomo and Shōni. Thus in 1336 the war in Kyushu had not gone much beyond the stage of traditional rivalries. It can be argued further that the Ashikaga had not yet achieved a position in which they could rise above this conflict rather than being a party to it. Conversely, those who were not in a position to enjoy the support of the Ashikaga had little choice but to declare for Go-Daigo—ostensibly on the grounds of loyalty to the imperial cause. Their actions were not prompted by any love of the emperor; that indeed was only a mask for the realization of their own ambitions.

CONCLUSION

The origins of the Nanbokuchō Wars in Kyushu can be traced to the betrayal of the Kikuchi by the Shōni and Ōtomo over their planned attack on Hōjō Hidetoki, the Chinzei Tandai. Even though the families of Kyushu were of like mind about destroying the Tandai, their true aims in doing so emerged in their squabble over the timing of the assault. All were hoping to use central authority as a means of establishing their own local power, which could only occur if the Bakufu was swept away completely. However, in their haste to exploit the center for their own private purposes, they ended by aligning with the Ashikaga, who sought to rule Kyushu by causing its families to divide among themselves. True independence could only have come by ending the Bakufu concept itself. In the event, the Shōni and the Ōtomo committed their initial error when they opposed the Kikuchis' first attack on the Tandai. As a consequence, the warrior houses of Kyushu now split into hostile camps, igniting the fuse that led to the explosion of war on the island.

In 1336, these families might still have swept away central authority, then tentatively being reconstructed in the form of the new Muromachi Bakufu. Their best chance came with the Battle of Tatarahama. Once again, however, the Shōni, Ōtomo, and Shimazu committed the same mistake, by using the power of the Bakufu against their local rivals, the Kikuchi. Had they been wiser, they might have sought to destroy the Ashikaga, and then followed that by moving to crush the Kikuchi.

That Takauji was able to weather the crises that beset him in 1336 was owing, then, to the continued adherence of the three great *shugo* houses. Later, he would be able to restore central authority in Kyushu by leaving Isshiki Dōyū as his agent on the island, and hastening back to retake the capital.

CHAPTER 4

Bakufu and *Shugo*
Under the Early Ashikaga

THOMAS NELSON

THE *shugo* of the Nanbokuchō period (1333–92) have usually been seen in a different light from their Kamakura-period (1185–1333) predecessors in that, for the first time, greater emphasis is placed upon their role as independent regional magnates than on their position as local deputies of the central military command, or Bakufu. From this point onward, they are viewed not as officials or administrators but as harbingers of a new polity formed from a loose collection of semiindependent domains, or *ryōkoku*, owing varying degrees of allegiance to a weak central regime based in Kyoto. This change in approach is not entirely unreasonable. The growing authority of the great *shugo* houses and the new powers that they acquired are indeed among the most important political developments of the age. The tendency has thus overwhelmingly been to see the Nanbokuchō-period *shugo* as an intermediate figure between the truly independent regional *shugo-daimyō* of the later Muromachi and Sengoku periods and his more subservient Kamakura-era predecessor. In practice, there has been very little effort to study the *shugo* from 1333 to 1400 as a figure in his own right.

The approach of Western scholars differs only in detail from the analysis offered by most Japanese specialists, who likewise stress the importance of the Nanbokuchō-period *shugo* as an intermediary figure. Satō Shin'ichi has argued that the Hōjō regents, who dominated the Kamakura Bakufu, made a desperate attempt to swim against the tide of history, which favored the rise of local forces, and strove instead to build up a highly centralized, authoritarian administration. The reaction that this provoked led directly to the collapse of their regime.[1] In a somewhat different light, Matsumoto Shinpachirō, writing in the 1950s, saw the same period as representing the final stage in the disintegration of the original court-centered polity. The establishment of the Muromachi Bakufu in 1336 thus became the triumph of the periphery over the center.[2]

Such views can only be maintained, however, if a series of important contradictions are first addressed. One of the supposed manifestations of Hōjō absolutism was that family's placement of its own members (*ichi-mon/ichizoku*) in *shugo* posts across the land. It is illogical then to argue that the Kamakura regime fell because of its absolutist tendencies, and not make the same criticisms of its successor, which, while apparently championing local interests against an overbearing center, pursued exactly the same policies with regard to the placement of its own *ichimon shugo*. Although some families, such as the Takeda of Kai and the Chūjō of Owari, who had been stripped of their *shugo* posts by the Hōjō were reha-bilitated by the Muromachi Bakufu, most ex-Hōjō *shugo* titles passed into the hands of the new Ashikaga regime. Even more significantly, the Ashi-kaga, whose influence in the Kamakura period was confined to eastern Japan, were able to effect these policies in areas where traditionally they had had no presence. The enormous influence of the Hōjō on the atti-tudes of their Ashikaga successors was not lost upon Satō Shin'ichi, who makes reference to it, but then does not discuss the subject further.[3] In particular, all but the most recent scholarship fails to address two funda-mental questions: how were the Ashikaga able to intrude their own family members (*ichimon*) as *shugo* into local areas, and how did these new *shugo* then bolster their strength? After all, if the Ashikaga had no means of con-trolling their own *ichimon* appointees, then their presence in the provinces would have been of no more use to them than the simple recognition of the rights of powerful unrelated, or *tozama*, houses.

One key to answering these questions comes from an analysis of the "Murodomari no gungi," in which the first shogun, Takauji, outlined his initial *shugo* placements.[4] The circumstances surrounding the issuance of this document are roughly as follows. In late 1335, Takauji rebelled against Emperor Go-Daigo, who had made a brief attempt to reestablish direct imperial rule after overthrowing the Kamakura Bakufu in 1333. However, having suffered a number of military reverses in central Japan, Takauji retreated to Kyushu, there to regroup and prepare a counterattack.[5] To prevent Go-Daigo's allies from launching a preemptive strike, Takauji established a defense line in Shikoku and western Honshu and assigned a number of *kunitaishō*, or supraprovincial military commanders, to that perimeter. For example, the chief of the Hosokawa clan was given authority over the whole of the island of Shikoku. The Hosokawa were related to the Ashikaga main line, but had traditionally served them in a variety of administrative functions and had not established themselves as an independent family with extensive land rights. The Imagawa had a similar relationship to the Ashikaga and were given control of Bingo Province.

In areas where the dominant local family was too strong to be ignored, Takauji might recognize its position, but simultaneously place either a clansmen or a close ally alongside it. For example, Bizen had a *tozama shugo* called Matsuda Moritomo, but the Bakufu gave Ishibashi Kazuyoshi, an Ashikaga relative, joint powers of military command. Similarly, in Suō, Takauji recognized the position of Ōuchi Nagahiro, leader of the dominant local clan, but also dispatched Oshima Yoshimasa, a close associate, to assist him. Only once was this pattern broken. Akamatsu Enshin, a *tozama* lord, was given sole command of the warriors who declared for the Ashikaga cause in Harima Province. This anomaly is explicable, however, in that the Akamatsu seem to have enjoyed such a close relationship with Takauji as to have been very nearly honorary kinsmen (*ichimon*).

The "Murodomari no gungi" set the tone of the Bakufu's *shugo* policy for years to come. Within it may be discerned a number of basic patterns. By dividing *shugo* posts and assigning supraprovincial command powers to its clansmen and closest allies among the *tozama*, the Bakufu was able to begin a program of intruding its own appointees into local politics. By redrawing boundaries and tailoring the institution of the *shugo* to Japan's jigsaw-like political map, and by splitting the very office of *shugo* and assigning different powers to different commanders, the Ashikaga made the institution a far less uniform entity than it had ever been. The "Murodomari no gungi" contains some of the earliest references to the *kunitaisho* and to the concept of the *bungun shugo* (split *shugo* posts), both of which were to become characteristic of the era.[6]

In many ways, the "Murodomari no gungi" heralded a new and more truly medieval state. The Kamakura regime had always respected ancient jurisdictional boundaries and had derived much of its power from local warriors serving in the court's provincial headquarters (*kokuga*). By contrast, the Ashikaga relied on the military might that local magnates could bring to bear at a given time and place, regardless of whether it violated traditional boundaries. Thus, the emerging regime corresponds to Heinrich Mitteis's definition of a medieval polity, in which a kaleidoscope of power centers was in constant flux, with each owing greater or lesser loyalty to the central authority. Such a regime cannot be described as a bureaucratic entity, but must be viewed in terms of the processes at work within it at any one time.

Although the "Murodomari no gungi" gives some inkling as to the means by which the Bakufu intruded its officers into provincial *shugo* posts, it does not address one of the fundamental questions posed earlier— that is, why Ashikaga clansmen should have been more reliable than other warriors as agents of Bakufu rule. After all, one of the major themes addressed by historians has been the lack of a strong group ethos among related warriors. The *shoshi*, or collateral branches of a clan, often sought independence from the main line, and might even petition the Bakufu to recognize their autonomy. Satō Shin'ichi has argued that *shoshi* tended to align themselves with antiestablishment movements (e.g., the Kō brothers in the 1340s), while the central figure of the clan, the *sōryō*, tended to favor the established order.[7]

In fact, however, contemporary warriors did have a strong sense of clan in spite of its evident shortcomings and their own misgivings about subordinating themselves to it. The virulence of the opposition of some *shoshi* to their clan patriarchs reflects not only the flaws in the system but also the fact that it was a fundamental part of warrior life. Thus, the Bakufu tended to seek to recruit military forces by ordering the *sōryō* to muster his clan membership (*ichizoku*). On other occasions, members who had long been economically independent of the main line would retain their old clan surname along with the new family name they might have adopted. In that context, the decision of the Ashikaga to use their own family members as agents of their rule in the provinces is to liken them to the other military houses of the period.

Although the status of the various collateral branches of the Ashikaga house tended to change over time, there is, nevertheless, a loose correlation between their position within the original clan and the tasks they were assigned in the early years of the Nanbokuchō period. For example, the post of *Kantō Kubō*, the Bakufu's plenipotentiary commander in the east, would be taken over by a junior branch of the main line. High-ranking collaterals were given major posts, while the lesser lineages continued to serve in the administrative capacity that had been their role in the old Ashikaga household organization. Only three families were able to fill the leading post of *kanrei*: the Shiba and the Hatakeyama, both of high status, and the Hosokawa, who had achieved that status during the time of Yoriyuki. As is well known, it was Hosokawa Yoriyuki who oversaw the maturation of that office during the minority of Yoshimitsu, the third shogun.

Evidence that these divisions remained important throughout the Nanbokuchō era may be drawn from an anecdote in the *Taiheiki*. In 1362/7, Shiba Yoshimasa took over the post of *shitsuji*, or "chief administrator," which had previously been held by Hosokawa Kiyouji. Yoshimasa, a younger son of Takatsune who was head of the Shiba clan, was then a thirteen-year-old boy. Both Takatsune and an older son, Ujiyori, had been proposed for the post, but they rejected it on the grounds that they were too high ranking. The position had, they argued, been held by lesser lineages such as the Hosokawa, or by hereditary retainers of the main line, such as the Kō.[8]

That the Muromachi Bakufu was, in its initial stages, something of a clan enterprise can be seen additionally by comparing the Ashikaga with the Minamoto and the Hōjō. Minamoto Yoritomo established Japan's first military government by creating direct ties of vassalage between himself and a large percentage of the nation's warriors, now known as *gokenin*. With such support from non-kin, he was able to view his own relatives more as a threat than as potential collaborators and he systematically eliminated his brothers and cousins. By contrast, the Hōjō were of low rank, with lineage less important in their family organization. Thus, when Yoshitoki, the Hōjō head, died in 1224, his successor, Yasutoki, felt freer to distribute among his siblings the greater part of their late father's legacy. This may have reflected Yasutoki's own lack of prestige vis-à-vis other family members. Since the beginning of the Kamakura period, there had been three generations of Hōjō in charge of the affairs of state, and the main line of the family alone had spawned some thirty male members, many of whom had adopted surnames in their own right. And it was thus that Yasutoki set out to arrest this fragmentation by sharing his inheritance with his own brethren. He also set up the office of *karei*, or house administrator, to which he appointed Bitō Kagetsuna, a trusted servant of the Hōjō main line, in 1224. The Bitō were themselves a warrior house of some distinction, and their office, whose role was to administer the Hōjō family lands, soon came to be known as the *uchikanrei*. The *miuchibito*, who served under the *uchikanrei*, acted as a kind of secretariat to the Hōjō and their chief, the *tokusō*.[9]

The first test for this new family structure came in 1263, when Hōjō Tokiyori was succeeded as *tokusō* by a thirteen-year-old boy, Tokimune. Tokimune had an elder brother, Tokisuke, but thanks to his mother's higher status, it had long been decided that he should be the future clan patriarch. Although he gained an influential ally when he was married to Adachi Yasumori's daughter in 1261, it is nonetheless noteworthy, given the potential for division, that the transition to minority rule should have proceeded as smoothly as it did.

This does not mean to say, however, that the Hōjō were not affected by the divisions that afflicted other warrior clans. In particular, the *tokusō*'s brother, Tokisuke, remained a rallying point for discontent, which finally burst to the surface in the Nigatsu-no-Ran of 1272. Tokimune moved pre-emptively to strike down Tokisuke's allies in both Kyoto and Kamakura. In the east, the main threat came from the Nagoya (Nagoe), who were Hōjō collaterals. In particular, this threat was embodied in Nagoya Noritoki, who was younger brother to two warriors who had been punished earlier in the Kangen Incident of 1246. In Kyoto, Tokisuke had been appointed one of the two Rokuhara deputies (Tandai). Both men were killed by troops serving Tokimune.[10]

The factional feuds within the Hōjō clan mirrored the situation in the Ashikaga family, where power was initially divided between Takauji, who held the post of shogun, and Tadayoshi, his younger brother, who was placed in charge of the bureaucracy. Indeed, the division of authority as expressed by this early dyarchy produced such irreconcilable differences that the two parties took up arms in the Kannō Disturbance of 1351–52. Though this has long been appreciated, greater attention is now being paid to the changing pattern of alliances following the defeat of Tadayoshi's faction.[11] Without minimizing the continuing existence of the Southern Court, most of the serious political disputes that now ensued can be traced, indeed, to divisions within the Ashikaga alliances.

Clustering around Takauji were the old service families such as the Kō, together with the more minor clansmen who had not acquired an independent landed base under the previous regime.[12] Takauji also found support among a small group of *tozama* with whom he had established close personal relations, most especially Sasaki Dōyo and Akamatsu Enshin. By contrast, Tadayoshi drew his support largely from those, such as the Shiba, of high rank, as well as from a group of more independent-minded *tozama*, in particular the Yamana.[13] It is hard to say why the old service families should have tended to support the shogun while the higher-ranking clansmen usually opted to support his brother. Perhaps it was merely that senior *ichimon* and independent-minded *tozama*, who had status in their own right, preferred to see the Bakufu as a kind of *shugo* federation and so opposed Takauji, who, as nominal head of the Bakufu, was the symbol, in their eyes, of central authority. Conversely, minor service families were more likely to owe their increased prominence to Takauji.[14]

But, typical of the day, the victorious faction of 1351–52 was soon rent by internal disputes of its own, which led first to the destruction of Niki Yoshinaga, and then to the fall of Hosokawa Kiyouji. A conflict between the two men led to a rebellion by the former and a successful attack on him by the latter. But the victor of the moment, Kiyouji, now himself almost immediately fell from favor, the victim of personal animosities from other members of the Takauji faction. Indeed, it is possible to see how anxious Takauji and his son, Yoshiakira, were to stop such disputes by noting their rush to placate the two men.[15] In the end, however, it was Kiyouji's aggressive attitude toward his patrons that damned him. He had held Shikoku since the 1330s and was possessed of a superb military record, but he frequently opposed the will of the new shogun, Yoshiakira, who had appointed him "chief administrator" (*shitsuji*). He seems to have begun to wield excessive powers within the Bakufu, and there are some who believe that it was he, and not Hosokawa Yoriyuki, who was the principal architect of the *kanrei* system. A clash with Sasaki Dōyo over the *shugo* post of Kaga Province led to his defection to the Southern Court in 1361/9, and he was killed by warriors serving Yoriyuki ten months later.[16]

The victory of the Takauji faction, centered around Sasaki Dōyo and later Hosokawa Yoriyuki, launched the latter's career as regent to the young shogun Yoshimitsu. However, the forces that had once gathered around Tadayoshi proved to be only temporarily in eclipse and succeeded in ousting Yoriyuki as *kanrei* in 1379. In the wake of that development, the old Tadayoshi faction (Shibukawa, Shiba, and Yamana) now came to be joined by former associates of the first shogun, families such as the Akamatsu and Kyōgoku.[17]

If the Bakufu is best characterized as a collection of Ashikaga-related *shugo* backed up by a small core of reliable *tozama*, how did it conduct actual governance? In particular, what was the nature of its interaction with the *shugo*? On these questions, it has long been argued that the powers of the *shugo* were defined, in Kamakura times, by the *taibon sankajō*, or "three great crimes." According to this definition, the *shugos'* duties consisted of mustering troops for guard duty and war, and punishing the crimes of rebellion and murder. Recently, however, this view has been challenged by Nitta Ichirō and others,[18] who have shown that the term *taibon sankajō* appears only once in Kamakura-period records, and that the more normal expression was simply *sankajō* by itself. Furthermore, since one of these "three articles" referred to the mustering of troops and not to a crime, the legal jurisdiction of the *shugo* really covered just two felonies. The third crime, that of brigandage and piracy, was appended as a supplement to the *Goseibai Shikimoku*.

In the early years of the Nanbokuchō era, the *shugo's* legal jurisdiction was extended beyond the *sankajō* to include *karita rōzeki*, or the illegal harvesting of crops. In addition, he was given a set of wholly new prerogatives: the right to use *shisetsu*, or local agents, to enforce land transfers; the right to bestow half the rent from land in time of war to provision troops (*hanzei*); and the right to requisition one-half to two-thirds of the rice rent during a military emergency (*hyōrōmai*). Thus, by this juncture, the prerogatives of the *shugo* fell into three categories—criminal, military, and judicial. Of these, the raising of troops and the allocating of land rights speak directly to the role of the *shugo* in Bakufu policy.

Of course, the very concept of clearly defined areas of authority would no doubt have seemed alien at the time, with power having meaning only insofar as it was enforceable. This meant that jurisdictional boundaries were extremely fluid. The Bakufu might wield powers that in theory belonged to the *shugo*, and vice versa. Indeed, the holder of rights might even come from an unexpected source, for example, the traditional aristocracy. Thus, in southern Iyo and southern Ise, the dominant interests were so-called *kuge daimyō*. In Iyo, the Saionji were able to establish themselves on the Uwa Estate in the wake of the Kannō Disturbance, where they cooperated with the forces of the Southern Court. In Ise, the Kitabatake, another group of Southern Court partisans, were able to build up a substantial on-site landed base. The positions of both families were recognized by the Northern Court after its adversary, the Southern Court, gave up its struggle.[19]

On other occasions, the Bakufu was forced to bow to the will of local warriors, who would not accept its candidate for the *shugo* post. In 1351, Yamana Tokiuji, the *shugo* of Wakasa, joined Tadayoshi when the latter fled Kyoto. Takauji thereupon sent in Otaka Shigenari to replace him, but Shigenari's agent was expelled by resident warriors. By contrast, when fighting erupted in Etchu between locals and representatives of the *shugo* in 1377, the former were defeated and driven out.[20]

AMIDST THIS MAELSTROM of local power politics, the authority to command troops in a given province was the *shugo's* first and most important right. In this area, the Bakufu employed a number of techniques to ensure that Ashikaga-related *shugo* enjoyed prerogatives greater than those acknowledged for outsiders (*tozama*). The methods it used may be divided into two categories. As the "Murodomari no gungi" makes plain, the Muromachi Bakufu, from its inception, either appointed more than one military commander to a province or recognized a *shugo* but gave overall command to supraprovincial *taishō*.

Thus the powers of the *shugo* might be cut back in terms of territory or the power to muster and reward troops. The earliest known example of such a divided *shugo* post comes in 1336/2 when two districts in Tanba Province were placed under the control of Uesugi Tomosada, who was the *shugo* of neighboring Tango.[21] Although the practice, albeit unrecorded, may have dated from the Kamakura era, it only became common during the Nanbokuchō period, with the life span of these "*bungun shugo-shiki*" ranging from a few years to two centuries. By withdrawing strategic areas from the control of a particular *shugo*, the Bakufu was seeking to limit his power while enhancing that of a rival.

Though it represented a major retreat from the age-old practice of relying on provincial boundaries, the Bakufu's policy of dividing *shugo* jurisdictions accorded it a new form of leverage. If a *tozama* was strong and had to have his position recognized, the Bakufu might still limit him to but a portion of the province. The institution of *bungun shugo* needed to be adaptable, leading to a range of diverse experiences. In Owari Province, for example, the ruling Toki family was rent by a serious internal dispute culminating in the Mino Disturbance of 1390. Though Toki Mitsuyori survived the affair and retained control of the *shugo* post, the Bakufu immediately transferred important areas to neighboring *shugo*. Chita-gun went to Isshiki Akinori of Mikawa, while Kaito and Kaisai-gun were passed to the Yamana.[22]

On other occasions, a *shugo* post might be divided along jurisdictional as well as geographical lines, as, for example, in Ōmi, which from the 1330s was split between the two branches of the Sasaki family, the Rokkaku and the Kyōgoku, to which Sasaki Dōyo belonged. Although the

Rokkaku held the title of *shugo* to the whole province, they had untrammeled powers in only seven districts out of twelve. In the remaining five they had to share authority with the Kyōgoku. In these latter, both families had responsibility for tax and rent collection, but only the Kyōgoku could bestow *hanzei* rights or command military forces.[23]

Still elsewhere, the Bakufu might leave a family in nominal possession of a *shugo* post, but allow neighboring families to pare down their landed base. The Shōni of northern Kyushu are the most notable victims of this latter tactic, punished by the Bakufu after they sided with the Southern Court. Specifically, the Ōtomo of Bungo and the Ōuchi of Suō and Nagato were granted vital landholdings in the Shōni's home province of Chikuzen. Following the assassination of their chief by Imagawa Ryōshun, the Shōni were progressively weakened, and by the early years of the fifteenth century they were no longer Kyushu's dominant family.[24]

Alternatively, the Bakufu might limit a *shugo*'s right to muster and reward warriors. Warriors were summoned to battle when their commander issued them with a recruitment order (*gunzei saisokujō*). The standard such order of the Kamakura era was issued by the *shugo* to the *gokenin*, but many of those from the beginning of the Nanbokuchō are subtly different. Major *shugo* houses are seen limiting their call to arms to their own clansmen, while the other warriors served under the colors of an Ashikaga commander (*taishō*). The Ashikaga were well placed to exploit the natural cleavages between the *shugo* and the lesser warriors of the province. In addition, the right to make private land awards for loyal service was not one that the *shugo* gained immediately, and rewards at first could only be issued by the shogun. Under those circumstances, warriors hoping to be compensated had to serve with an accredited commander.[25]

Restricting the freedom of the *tozama shugo* to issue testaments of military valor (*kanjō*) provided another means by which the Bakufu could favor its own kinsmen at their expense. *Shugo* might issue *kanjō* either to acknowledge a warrior's valor in battle, or to initiate reward procedures with the Bakufu. This latter category of document may be subdivided further with the first type merely promising that a report would be made and the second pledging that steps would be taken to ensure that a reward was forthcoming. Only Ashikaga clansmen could issue this second type.[26]

As mentioned above, the *shugo* were accorded a package of new powers concerning the allocation of property, which included the privilege of assigning "half-rights" (*hanzei*) and "commissariat rice" (*hyōrōmai*). According to Prescott Wintersteen, the development of these powers can be traced largely through a series of laws that illustrates the Bakufu's step-by-step acceptance of warrior-centered domains, in place of the old provincial estate system. Beginning in 1337 with a censure of those who failed to return fields that had been seized "for emergency purposes," it proceeded to acknowledge the new status quo, making it law finally in 1368. In that year, the Bakufu recognized the division of all lands (*hanzei*) in the central provinces between *shugo* and the traditional proprietary elite.[27]

In fact, a new view of the importance of the 1368 edict has been developed by Murai Shōsuke, who likens it to a Kamakura-style *tokusei* edict intended to protect the traditional rights of religious institutions.[28] Rather than stressing the new privileges of warriors, he emphasizes a defense of old interests. At the same time, however, Murai underlines the importance not merely of the laws themselves but also of the methods by which they were applied. Whereas earlier *tokusei* edicts had been enforced by special commissioners appointed by Kamakura, enforcement was now placed in the hands of the *shugo*. Thus, it was the *shugo* who decided when the law should be applied and to whom. In this regard, the appointment of special enforcement agents (*shisetsu*) needs to be elaborated.

In the wake of the growing disorder following the Mongol Wars, there occurred an increasing number of references to a crime known as *gechi ihai*, or failure to obey a Bakufu order. The leadership in Kamakura confronted this problem by introducing an element of coercion into its judicial system. It began to appoint enforcement officers under a variety of titles, including *ryōshi* and *ontsukai* as well as *shisetsu*. The punishment these officers meted out normally involved the seizure of part or all of the transgressor's property.

The studies of how this system operated in the later Kamakura period have inevitably concentrated on the powerful Yuasa family, who served the Hōjō *shugo* as *ryōshi* and *ontsukai* in the province of Kii and for whom the surviving records are particularly complete.[29] The fact that the Bakufu chose to rely on this family to carry out its orders in Kii shows how much local power the Yuasa could wield. In most cases two *ontsukai* were appointed, one from the Yuasa and one a direct representative of the Hōjō, although on a few occasions both were drawn from the ranks of the Yuasa. Their responsibilities included the issuing of summonses, the carrying out of investigations, the transmission of orders, and the forwarding of apprehended criminals to the Bakufu's Rokuhara headquarters in Kyoto. On rare occasions, the Yuasa chief was given the title of *kunijōshi*, indicating that his remit extended over the entire province. During the Kamakura period, such province-wide appointments are recorded for only Kii and Bungo. In the case of Bungo, the powers of the *shisetsu* could actually match those of the *shugo* in dealing with lawbreakers. In 1300/11/26, for example, Shimazu Hisatsune received an order stating that he and the *shugo* were to exercise joint responsibility for suppressing major crimes, whereas sixteen years earlier, the *shisetsu* and *shugo* were jointly charged with suppressing night attack, banditry, piracy, *akutō* activities, and gambling.[30]

If *kunijōshi* were rare during the Kamakura period, they were appointed quite extensively by the Kenmu regime. According to Andrew Goble and Yamaguchi Takamasa,[31] they provided the government of Go-Daigo with a third pillar of regional administration in addition to the *shugo* and the civil governor (though neither scholar makes reference to the existence of comparable officers in the years before or after). In fact, the most powerful of the *ontsukai*, the *kunijōshi*, cannot be identified with certainty following the demise of the Kenmu regime, although important local warriors were occasionally assigned to carry out similar roles. In 1341, for example, the Bakufu jointly appointed the *shugo* of Bingo and a local warrior called Sugiwara Mitsufusa to investigate a dispute between a temple and another warrior over the ownership of land. Mitsufusa reported back that those responsible for the alleged outrages had fled during the deputy *shugo*'s inquiry.[32]

Many of the early examples of the Muromachi Bakufu's using *shisetsu/ontsukai* come from the provinces where the Ashikaga had taken over from the Hōjō as *shugo*. This is natural when one considers that the Ashikaga had no long-standing presence in these areas and relied on the cooperation of leading local families. But other generalizations are hard to make, and variations seemed to be common. In Kii, for example, the Ashikaga *shugo* does not seem to have adopted the preexisting system, perhaps because the Yuasa had declared their adherence to the Southern Court. Or again, in Kaga Province, the Tokashi, who had often served the Hōjō as enforcers, were themselves made *shugo* and, as a consequence, did not need to employ special agents from other clans. In Bingo and Harima, by contrast, the position of the new *tozama shugo* was far less secure, leading to the extensive use of enforcers by Bakufu and *shugo* alike. Matsui Teruaki has shown that in Aki, enforcers acted on the instructions of the *shugo* only 20 percent of the time, with the Bakufu appointing the non-*shugo* Kobayakawa for another 20 percent.[33] Significantly, the Kobayakawa would one day become important members of the shogun's personal army (the Hōkōshū), indicating their growing capacity to assert themselves independently of the *shugo*. In Bingo Province, on the other hand, the *shugo* achieved control of the *shisetsu* more quickly, with almost half dispatched on his exclusive orders.

AS INDICATED HERE, modern writing on the fourteenth-century *shugo* contains a major contradiction. The Hōjō are deemed to have fallen because of their absolutist tendencies as manifested by their placement of clansmen in *shugo* posts across Japan. These policies went against the trend of the times, which favored the rise of local forces. In turn, the Ashikaga rode this wave of discontent by being more responsive to local warriors, a major element of which was the greater independence they allowed the *shugo*. But such an argument fails to account for the fact that the Ashikaga were just as zealous as the Hōjō in appointing their own kinsmen as *shugo*. Why did they seek to do this and what was the level of their success? In the end, how does the Ashikaga policy affect our understanding of the *shugo* institution itself?

The Muromachi Bakufu, like its Hōjō predecessor, constituted a warrior coalition with families of greater and lesser loyalty making up the whole. Indeed, the wars of the era reflect divisions within the ruling group much more than they do a rivalry between the Northern and Southern courts. For this reason, the defeat of Tadayoshi's faction and its replacement by Takauji's clique of mainly lower-ranking clansmen and ex-service families was of greater moment in terms of the balance of power than the shifting alliances surrounding the two courts. For similar reasons, the fall from grace of Hosokawa Yoriyuki in 1379 owing to the defection of one-time supporters of Takauji marked a more important turning point than the reconciliation of the courts thirteen years later.

If the Bakufu's efforts to control *itself* thus constituted its primary challenge, this would explain why its leadership sought to appoint reliable clansmen as its regional representatives. In the initial stages, it was able to appoint kin as military commanders over whole blocs of provinces, and then to give them greater powers to raise and to reward forces. In addition, it violated provincial boundaries and divided the jurisdiction of *shugo* in order both to intrude its own family members locally and to pare down the power of established *tozama*. In time, however, the *shugo* acquired the right to enfeoff local warriors on their own territory, and also to appoint *shisetsu* to ensure that judgments and land transfers were carried out. As these powers slowly drifted away from the Bakufu and over to the *shugo*, the stage was set, as it were, for the next century, characterized, as we know, by the emergence of *daimyō*.

CHAPTER 5

Peasants, Elites, and Villages in the Fourteenth Century

KRISTINA KADE TROOST

D EMARCATING HISTORICAL turning points, while a historian's specialty, is an uncertain enterprise. Yet the fourteenth century seems to have marked a new direction for villages in the economically advanced areas of central Japan. The gulf that separated rural society in 1250 from that of 1450 spanned economic, political, and social organization, agricultural technology and development, and, as well, the physical configuration of the village.[1]

If we choose to see the fourteenth century as a turning point for villages in central Japan, this does not mean that new forms were fully matured or older forms extinguished. Rather, enough characteristics of the semi-autonomous village community emerged in this era to suggest a trend. These new forms of social, political, and geographical organization matured in the Muromachi and Sengoku eras and continued to characterize rural Japan through much of the Tokugawa age.

What are the discernible changes in the fourteenth century? First, and perhaps most basic, was the intensification of agriculture; it had a revolutionary impact on people and social organization. Based on the implementation and spread of a variety of technologies known in the preceding period, but not widely practiced, the cultivation of fields stabilized, and yields per acre rose.[2] As a result, population grew, social organization changed, and commerce expanded; in the exercise of power and the removal of warrior elites from agriculture, the effects were felt beyond the confines of rural society.

Two of the defining characteristics of the village community in the Muromachi and Sengoku eras were closely linked to the agricultural changes: the participation of smallholders in village control of irrigation and common land and the close physical proximity of the residents themselves. The formation of nucleated villages made control of behavior possible and also promoted a sense of exclusivity by defining and limiting membership. Combined with the withdrawal of central authority and new pressures on communal resources, the growth of nucleated villages was associated with the emergence of the semiautonomous community in the Muromachi era. The medieval village was no longer simply a place to live in but a unit based on common ownership of property, the political participation of large and small landholders, and the community's control of military force.[3]

POPULATION GROWTH AND AGRICULTURAL CHANGE

In spite of the havoc associated with the wars between the courts, the fourteenth century seems to have been a relatively beneficent one for farmers.[4] Famines and epidemics were comparatively infrequent, and the relative scarcity of peasant revolts, by comparison with the fifteenth century, suggests a lack of grievances as well as the requisite social organization for coordinating mass violence. A variety of evidence suggests a growing population after about 1200. Two major famines linked with epidemics occurred in 1230–31 and 1256–58, but their impact seems not to have been pronounced, and after 1277, there was nearly a century without a major epidemic or famine. Then, after two bad years in 1360–61, another sixty years passed before the numerous famines of the early fifteenth century.[5]

By 1300, there was evidence of a growing, settled population, though most of the measures here are rather imprecise. Evidence suggests that cultivated land increased by an annual rate of 0.17 percent,[6] and that the cultivation of fields previously in and out of use was stabilized.[7] The evidence is anecdotal: places referred to as "plains" in Wakasa Province in the Heian period had become villages with farmland by the Nanbokuchō.[8] Tokuchinho in Ōmi was developed in the late Heian–early Kamakura eras with the building of two irrigation networks,[9] and new villages were formed by migrants in Nitta-no-shō in Kōzuke, Hine-no-shō in Izumi, and Yano-no-shō in Harima. The timing probably varied by area, but the descendants of early medieval vagrants had become residents by the fourteenth and fifteenth centuries.[10]

Another piece of evidence in this puzzle comes from archaeological excavations of villages, which suggest that the preponderance of present-day villages were settled in the fourteenth century or later.[11] For example, in examining the remains of forty-five villages in Ōmi, Okamoto Takenori found that 80 percent of the villages established between the tenth and thirteenth centuries were extinct by 1300, while those established in the fourteenth century and later coincide with present-day villages.[12] Amino Yoshihiko, too, has argued that three-quarters of Japanese villages appeared in Muromachi times.[13]

Rules governing migration are revealing and suggest significant changes in population and cultivated land between Heian and Muromachi times. There were many regulations from the Heian period that welcomed migrants (*rōnin*) from other provinces. Evidently, there was more land than people who might farm it, in contrast to the fifteenth century when villages became increasingly closed to outsiders. Two laws from Imabori in Ōmi mirror the change: in 1403, the village proclaimed that newcomers without land (*mōto*) could be seated in the shrine association after they paid their dues, albeit three places lower than what was appropriate to their age.[14] Regulations issued in 1460 and strengthened in 1489, however, limited membership and controlled the ability of outsiders to enter Imabori.[15] A perception of diminishing resources in the fifteenth century was one among several contributing causes here.

Population growth combined with expansion of the arable made the fourteenth century a turning point for agriculture in central Japan. A variety of labor-intensive and capital-intensive techniques were developed at this time, including improvements in irrigation, fertilizer, seed beds, and weeding, along with the conversion of dry fields to paddy and the maturation of raised fields and double-cropping.

A basic form of intensification in the Kamakura and Muromachi periods involved the conversion of dry fields into paddy.[16] For example, 20 percent of new paddy in Yano-no-shō in Harima in 1299 had been so converted;[17] the increase was even larger in Hine Estate in Izumi.[18] Imabori began to convert dry fields into paddy in the late fourteenth century, and built small-scale irrigation ditches and ponds that served as reservoirs of water for irrigation during the dry months.[19]

Another form of intensification, raised fields (*shimahata*), contributed to gains in productivity by leveling the soil for a designated area. Beginning in the thirteenth century, raised fields were made on the flood plains of rivers where small differences in topography caused high fields to suffer from drought in some years, and low fields to suffer from waterlogging in others.[20] Both problems led to fields being withdrawn from cultivation. However, by lowering some paddy and using the soil to create adjacent dry fields, it was possible to introduce a kind of checkerboard pattern, thereby stabilizing both. Naturally, such efforts were highly labor intensive,[21] and were thus predicated on available labor and the anticipated value of the improvement.

The third form of intensification, the growing of two crops in one year on the same land, developed first on dry fields in Heian times, and by the sixteenth century was practiced on 20 to 30 percent of paddy in central and western Japan.[22] There was even some evidence of triple-cropping: a Korean envoy to Japan in 1420 commented on the Japanese ability to sow seeds three times on one field in one year after his visit to Amagasaki in Settsu.[23] At any rate, double-cropping was widely practiced on dry fields by at least the late twelfth century,[24] with beans and sesame seeds in the summer, and wheat and safflower in the winter (millet, rushes for mats, mulberry, and vegetables were also grown). Later on, cotton, tea, and oil-producing plants were added.[25]

Although dry field double-cropping was routine enough to lead to double dues in the twelfth century, the earliest reference to double-cropping on paddy appears in a dispute of 1118 in Ise over the right to plant paddy after the rice had been harvested. Before then, the removal of markers after the rice harvest permitted grazing or the planting of a different crop, especially by peasants with insufficient land.[26] Kawane Yoshiyasu, extrapolating from the dispute in Ise, has argued that double-cropping arose out of communal patterns of land use rather than as a result of some new technology. Later, after double-cropping became widely practiced, there was an effort to make low, damp fields dry.[27]

Double-cropping of paddy required drainable paddy, sufficient irrigation, and fertilizer, and was aided by the introduction of new varieties of rice. Although there was some artificially irrigated, drainable paddy in the ancient period, much of paddy land was naturally irrigated and of low yield. To improve these conditions, peasants began to dam the top of valleys and create ponds, and records of such spring-fed enclosures relying on the natural topography of hillsides for walls are extensive for the period 1300–1450.[28]

In addition to ponds built in mountain valleys as reservoirs to catch runoff, a new form of pond began to appear in the fourteenth century. Saucer ponds were square or rectangular shallow reservoirs with artificial walls, built on high spots on a plain. They collected runoff water from spring rains, rivers, and deeper valley ponds, and were full from the third to the sixth month.[29] This water was then distributed during the rice-growing season, and by the end of the tenth month, the saucer ponds were dry. Their function was to keep rice paddies watered during the growing season, and their shallow depth of two to four meters made their water warmer than that of the deeper, valley ponds. Such warmer water was beneficial for rice growing, serving to produce higher yields. At the same time, however, saucer ponds required more advanced technology and a greater input of labor, underlining once again the connection with population growth.

In his examination of the Yamato basin, Kinda Akihiro found that five deep valley ponds out of twenty-two ponds probably predated the fourteenth century, but that beginning in the fourteenth century, shallow valley ponds or saucer ponds became predominant.[30] On the basis of such evidence, the fourteenth century represented a turning point in agricultural practices, with labor plentiful enough and land scarce enough for intensification to be more practical than the opening of new fields. In other words, the spread of double-cropping, achieved by making wet fields dry and by irrigating dry fields, was the era's hallmark. Largely piecemeal in its execution, it led to a major rise in productivity and supported an increasing population. Though not revolutionary in technology, agricultural intensification was revolutionary in its impact.

In fact, the necessary technology had been mostly known in the eighth century.[31] Fertilizers remained the same as well—green manure, ashes, and excrement—but they came to be more widely and frequently applied. Growing several varieties of rice had also been practiced in the ancient period; in the fourteenth century, however, the use of early, middle, and late varieties became routine. As for irrigation, water pipes were first seen in Chimori-no-shō, an early Todaiji *shōen*, and were used not only to carry water from ponds and rivers to ditches but also at the crossings of ditches. Likewise, dry field farming techniques were practiced in the ancient period, although both less extensively and less intensively.

But despite these technological continuities, there was a qualitative difference to fourteenth-century agriculture. Ester Boserup has argued that the crucial date in agricultural development was not when new technology was introduced, but rather when conditions became ripe for its large-scale diffusion.[32] Thus, for example, though the waterwheel was introduced from China in the early ninth century, its first recorded use appears in a twelfth-century poem about a place near modern Otsu.[33] By the fourteenth century, there are numerous references to different types of waterwheels—man-powered, animal-powered, and water-powered.[34]

Waterwheels allowed peasants to raise water from rivers to higher ground and thereby to irrigate fields without easy access. Even though only a limited area could be irrigated directly from the river, waterwheels could be combined with irrigation canals to divert water in much greater volume. Dikes, which had been known earlier, only came to be successfully employed in the Kamakura era.[35]

COMMON LAND OR "THE MOUNTAINS AND THE FIELDS"

Common property developed in Japan as individuals and institutions established boundaries and claimed exclusive rights over what had previously been open-access land.[36] In the eighth and ninth centuries, many nobles, temples, and shrines claimed undeveloped land—whether mountain or pasture—as private property.[37] Claims of ownership of open-access land and efforts to restrict or regulate peasant use resulted in the incorporation of undeveloped land within the estate system by the twelfth century. Regulation largely relied on farmer-managers (myōshu) and involved the collection of user fees.[38] The payment of dues rather than village membership determined use.

Despite the assertion of private property rights, boundaries remained vague, users were only roughly defined, and use was not significantly limited because sufficient waste land was available. In the late Kamakura, increased competition over water and unfarmed land led to disputes among villages and between villages and proprietary lords,[39] and resulted in narrower definitions of access rights and village assumption of managerial prerogatives.

Regulation based on custom proved insufficient in managing communally used resources, and so, beginning in the mid-fourteenth century, villages acted to limit use to community members and to prevent cheating. Communally used resources became common property under collective control, and laws were written that circumscribed individual rights in order to protect these resources for the collectivity.

CHANGES IN SOCIAL STRUCTURE

Behind village management of communally used resources were changes in rural social structure stemming from agricultural intensification. Farmers stand as the intervening variable between changes in land-use patterns and the development of the village community. By fostering the small farmer, the intensification of agriculture had a ripple effect throughout rural society. By 1300, the organization of rural society had changed markedly from that around 1100. Small independent farmers appeared on land registers and on petitions, whereas 200 years earlier, *myōshu*, a select group of peasants with responsibility for overseeing cultivation and collecting dues, had played the dominant role. At the same time, local warriors were abandoning the direct management of their farming enterprises, and proprietary lords—the owners of *shōen*—were withdrawing from direct assignment of tenancy fields (*isshikiden*) to peasants.[40] Conditions were thus propitious for major change.

But it was rising yields that were the primary cause of the independence of small cultivators.[41] Such increases made small operations correspondingly more viable, causing peasants not to shrink from the higher inputs of labor that were now required.[42] *Kajishi*, a surtax on land that appeared in the late thirteenth century, was crucial here.[43] A right to income separate from ownership and cultivation, its size might equal or surpass the dues that were paid to proprietary lords.[44] Moreover, peasants might sell these *kajishi* but still retain their rights to work the land. Cultivators were not tied to holders of *kajishi* in any kind of dependent relationship.[45]

The spread of iron tools, even to poor peasants, also contributed to rising productivity, allowing household servants and branches to open new fields. Improvements in iron smelting occurred in the fourteenth century, leading to the diffusion of iron implements much more broadly. By the fifteenth century, iron tools became widely affordable,[46] and smallholders came to possess iron grub hoes, sickles, axes, and hatchets.[47]

Kuroda Hideo's study of Hatsukura-no-shō on the Oi River in Tōtōmi from the twelfth to the mid-fifteenth century illustrates the important role new fields played in providing a base for the establishment of smallholders.[48] Over 60 percent of the development was small scale: 403 out of 634 new fields for one village in 1443 were less than two *tan* in size. The richest and poorest peasants carved out most of the development, and few of those with midsize holdings had any new fields. New fields were central to the livelihood of the poorest peasants who lived on the lands they created.[49]

Another development that contributed to the independence of small-holders was a rise in the stability of their tenures. Fields that had been subject in the past to regular reassignment by proprietary lords became the objects of continuous cultivation by the small peasants who worked them.[50] A sense of personal identity and attachment correspondingly grew.

At any rate, the independence of small cultivators was central to the emergence of the village community. Spatially, politically, and socially, the organization of rural society in central Japan differed significantly in 1400 from what had existed 200 years earlier. Nor was this change only transitory; many of the new institutions continued into the Tokugawa era.

NUCLEATED VILLAGES

The most immediate outcome of the independence of smallholders and full cultivation of the arable was a change in settlement patterns.[51] Nara and Heian Japan had been characterized by isolated farmhouses and small-scale, scattered clusters around *myōshu* or managers' homesteads, mostly outside of present-day villages. Beginning in Yamato in the thirteenth century and spreading throughout central Japan thereafter, concentrated, compact settlements developed, which have continued to the present day.[52]

Houseland in the eleventh century was untaxed, predominately outside the control of the state and proprietary lords, and located on high ground that could not be made into productive paddy. Houseland, arable, and waste were all intermixed, without clear definition. Houses were usually widely separated; it was rare for more than ten houses to be in one square *chō*. Houses themselves were transitory. Built with wooden pillars buried in the ground, they needed to be rebuilt every ten to twenty years. Often, their location changed in the process. Okamoto's survey of Ōmi found that only a handful were repeatedly rebuilt in the same location. Classifying houses by size, he found that small houses of less than three *tsubo* were almost never rebuilt in the same location, whereas large houses of fifteen to forty *tsubo* tended to be rebuilt in the same place.[53] In short, agricultural and architectural technology combined with the tax system's emphasis on people rather than land to facilitate moving.

Eventually, the cultivation of fields stabilized, making movement less practical, and helping to define houseland, arable, and waste. In a sense, settled villages reflected the separation of residence from the arable. House lots now became standardized at one *tan*, and whereas solitary homesteads had once been surrounded by fields, the newly independent small cultivators now tended to cluster together. This clustering in nucleated villages also separated warriors from the village community, a condition further extended by the decision of warriors essentially to withdraw from farming.

The change from dispersed to agglomerated villages occurred fairly widely during this period, leading to villages surrounded by moats and walls and to a growing number of buildings within limited spaces.[54] Kinda traces this transformation in Ikeda-no-shō in Yamato.[55] In 1186, house lots varied in size and were scattered over eight *tsubo*; two were especially widely separated from the other twelve. Four were a standard one *tan* in size while others were smaller—60 *bu*, 120 *bu*, 180 *bu*. Kinda argues that the irregular house lots in 1186 were probably descended from house lots a century earlier, whereas the same-size lots represented a new form. Of course, in other villages irregularity remained the norm. In Otogi-no-shō in Yamato, for example, there were homesteads located in nineteen places across five *tsubo* in the late thirteenth century.[56] Population increase played only a small role. The population of Wakatsuki-no-shō grew from twenty to thirty-seven homesteads between the late Heian and 1306–7, but the houses remained scattered in several hamlets.[57] Nucleation was driven first and foremost by social and economic change.

Encircling a village with moats and walls was the final stage in this process. Such moats began to appear in the mid-fourteenth century and were concentrated in the Kinai—173 cases have been documented in Yamato.[58] As defenses, they were related to the growth of autonomous villages and the frequent warfare of the Sengoku era, but they also irrigated nearby fields and served as reservoirs by trapping rainwater and runoff. They were thus related to the agricultural changes of the fourteenth century. At the same time, moats also had social and political roles, serving to define the members of the village. In this vein, Fukuda Ajio contrasts the patrilineal groupings that tied rural populations together in most of Asia to the geographical bonds of Japan.[59] Thus, not only were villages nucleated in character, but their memberships resided within strict geographical boundaries. A regulation of Imabori that forbade the building of residences east of the moat vividly illustrates this association.[60]

But there was more to it than simply villagers living in close proximity. The corporateness facilitated dealing with outsiders and was not an act of altruism. In response to increased competition over natural resources and the spread of commerce in the fourteenth century, peasants mobilized, engaged in disputes, and spoke collectively; village-wide involvement increased their chances of success. Later, the continuing need for managerial efficiency fostered the formation of self-governing organizations whose interests extended beyond communally held property.

As already noted, proprietary lords encouraged villages to take control of their own affairs,[61] and the village could not have accomplished such an aim without support and protection. In this way, semiautonomous villages arose in central Japan, but their proprietors continued to receive income from them and were not displaced by warriors. Rather than viewing village government as emerging from a power vacuum, I would emphasize an assumption of responsibility within the context of proprietary support. In other words, being actively involved in estate management was not a primary interest for owners; revenue was. Some proprietary lords even took the initiative themselves rather than waiting for a village to actively seek it.[62] Behind such thinking was a notion that villages were more reliable as tax payers than warriors were as tax contractors.

SHRINE ASSOCIATIONS

The vehicle for the development of village governmental organizations was the village shrine association (*miyaza*). Established to conduct religious festivals and oversee the village shrine, it provided an organizational framework by being a village-level rather than an estate-wide institution. Local religious practices thus facilitated a shifting of the primary unit of activity downward.

In central Japan, village shrine associations developed in the thirteenth and fourteenth centuries. They then spread to western Japan in the late Muromachi era and to all of Japan during the Tokugawa period.[63] Their primary function was to see that funds were raised for festivals, materials prepared, ceremonies conducted, and the populace banqueted afterward. Thomas Smith has argued that in Edo times "*miyaza* appeared only where the structure of privilege was relatively insecure and required exceptionally elaborate institutional support."[64] Using this logic, it seems reasonable to argue that their original creation was a response to the emergence of independent peasants with small and medium-size holdings. Villages needed to define who would participate in religious ceremonies and in what capacities.

Membership was not to be all inclusive, however, since villages varied greatly in their social and economic structures. Some villages were dominated by warrior-peasants and large landholders, with participation probably limited to such individuals. Sometimes small holders were included.

Likewise, ranking within the association was sometimes family- or status-based and sometimes age-based. In short, membership in shrine associations was coterminous with the political community, and, like it, varied in inclusiveness and organization. Leadership, too, was identical with that of the village political order.

An examination of shrine organizations for four semiautonomous villages reveals that they, like many others in central Japan, were all founded in the late thirteenth or fourteenth centuries. Where information exists, the shrine organizations may significantly postdate the founding of the shrines; for instance, Ōshima Jinja was founded in 967 and Okutsushima Jinja in 806, but the first records of the shrine association date from the 1260s.[65] In some, the formation of a political community and the establishment of a shrine organization seem to have been closely intertwined.[66] In others, such as Higashimura in Kokawa-no-shō in the fourteenth century, a shrine association with limited membership expanded its membership as it mobilized the peasant community toward a common goal. In many villages, the shrine association became the nucleus of village government, with shrine elders being political as well as religious leaders. Serving as a festival leader and joining the adult men in the shrine association were often closely linked, and in an era when religion was pervasive, such cooperation served to reinforce the political ends of the shrine association and the role of village leaders. Certainly as villages mobilized to gain collective ends—to protect common land, fishing grounds, or trade routes, to acquire territory, to fight for tax reduction, to resist local warriors, and to build ponds—they needed the support of their own communities. In turn, this led to the emergence of institutions of self-government.

VILLAGE GOVERNMENT

Three features define Muromachi villages: political participation by descendants of both former *myōshu* and smallholders, village-owned property, and the possession of military and judicial powers held previously by proprietary lords. The first two features, closely tied, appeared almost simultaneously, and the third was the outgrowth of the second.

Beginning around 1300, peasants as a whole (*sōbyakushō*) began to appear as petitioners. In 1314, for instance, twenty-four residents of Yugeno-shima signed a petition protesting the actions of Tōji's agent. Nine were old *myōshu*, three were newlly created *myōshu*, and eight of the remainder were cultivators.[67] Petitions and oaths from Okujima and Kamikuze-no-shō provide similar examples.[68] In effect, peasants of different status, bound only by geography, joined together to present a united show of force. For example, in Okujima ninety-seven peasants signed an oath protesting damage to the shrine's fishing maze, a group action quite unlike that of a dispute of thirty-six years earlier, where only a privileged few—myōshu all—affixed their signatures.[69]

Jointly with the widening of political participation came an expanded concept of community. The widening of political participation is apparent in references to decisions "as a group" (shūgi no jo); soon, if not simultaneously, the term "community of the whole" (sō) also appeared. Closely associated with these developments was the commendation of property to the village shrine.

Village-owned property first appeared in the fourteenth century and was acquired through commendation and purchase. Proprietary lords commended land or its income to the support of shrines early on, but later the donations started to come from peasants. The first of these latter occurred almost simultaneously with episodes affecting the village as a whole, for example, in Okujima during the 1340s.[70] In Higashimura, the village bought land in 1342 on which to build a pond, and in the next year a commendation to the shrine and a local temple was made by residents.[71]

The prices paid to purchase land were sometimes high. Higashimura paid nine times the going rate to buy the land for its pond,[72] and Suganoura bought two parcels of forest for 10 and 19.5 kanmon, respectively.[73] Imabori overpaid for privately held dry fields and forest in the midst of its woods, seemingly attempting to create a single block of jointly owned woodland.[74]

The amounts of land were sometimes sizable. In Imazaike, for instance, village-owned land made up about 20 percent of the total. The village was the largest landholder, and cultivation rights to the best fields, which were used for vegetables, represented a sizable proportion of its holdings.[75] In Imabori, too, the village probably held about 20 percent of the fields.[76]

All this naturally required management. For one thing, the villages had to oversee the collection of dues,[77] and in Imabori they were to be paid at the hermitage regardless of status.[78] For another, many villages had laws regarding who could use the land and specifying penalties for misuse. In addition, the village might appoint cultivators, confiscate rights for malfeasance, and reduce dues in years of drought or water damage.[79] A similar comprehensive prerogative affected Ōshima Shrine's fishing mazes,[80] and an Imabori law of 1460 denied cultivators the right to claim village land as their own in consequence of their having paid dues on it for a long time.[81] In Okujima and Imabori, the acquisition of shrine land built an economic base which facilitated many activities such as lending money or rice to villagers or building irrigation facilities.

Management together with income led to an expansion in the activities of the shrine association, moving matters beyond religion to village governance. In particular, the regulation of misbehavior regarding shrine land led to a growing concern with the enforcement of regulations. By the fifteenth century, such villages as Imabori, Suganoura, and Higashimura had taken over many of the political and judicial functions previously exercised by proprietary officials.

POLITICAL FUNCTIONS

In the Heian and Kamakura periods, dues had been assigned to and collected from *myō*. In the fourteenth century a shift toward individuals began to take place. For example, in Kamikuze-no-shō, the change occurred between 1324 and 1357.[82] Elsewhere the shift came slightly later. Thus it was not until the 1430s and 1440s that Kokawadera and Enryakuji got around to surveying their respective estates, establishing individual cultivators as taxpayers and villages as primary units of taxation.

While many villages became geopolitical units on which taxes were assessed, a few villages assumed the additional responsibility for their collection and payment (*jigeuke*), displacing the proprietary agent. The best-known example is Suganoura, which conducted its own surveys and paid twenty *koku* and twenty *kanmon* on the fields of Hisashi and Morokawa for over 200 years, irrespective of external conditions. The process began in the 1340s with the allocation of taxes to the village rather than to *myō*, and was closely associated with the first appearance of the "community of the whole."[83] In less than a century, Suganoura had assumed collective responsibility for payment, and receipts were addressed to the village under phrases such as "paid, Suganoura *gohyakushō chū*," or "paid, *sō gohyakushō*," or "*sōshō* paid."[84] Concurrently, Suganoura's holdings of shrine land began to grow; in effect, when the village became the intermediary between cultivators and proprietary lord, it received land for money lent to cover unpaid taxes.[85]

The peasant role in determining to whom to pay taxes, together with their actual collection, shows growing collaboration with proprietary lords. In fact, rather than referring to the withdrawal of lords from active management, it would be more accurate to point to village initiative, leaving only a few areas for proprietary authority.[86] The shift of administrative responsibilities to local figures was a widespread trend during this era, whether to warriors like the Kawashima with ties to the shogun, to peasant-warriors like those in Kamikuze, or to villages like Imabori and Suganoura.[87]

Villages gained proprietary powers and authority in four ways: purchase, commendation, lawsuits, and usurpation. Suganoura bought forest lands and the right to levy taxes from its *kumon*, a *shōen* official,[88] and two local officials commended a fishing maze to Okunoshima's shrine.[89] Okujima also had mountain fields donated to it by local managers.[90]

The power of petition was also frequently invoked. For example, Okujima appealed to its proprietor against certain actions by *shōen* officials; Yugenoshima, petitioning Tōji, engaged in a protracted lawsuit with a manager; and Suganoura used a lawsuit to try to exclude a local constable.

Finally, villages sought to initiate change through mass demonstrations and the use of force. In one such incident, the peasants of Kamikuze demanded one hundred *koku* in relief as the result of heavy rains and flooding in 1437. Tōji, however, was intransigent, agreeing only to a ten-*koku* reduction, which led to a march on the temple by sixty peasants. Tōji doubled its offer, but peasants threatened to abandon their lands and flee. After a month of agitation, the temple finally agreed to a 60 *koku* reduction that included a graded system of eleven increments.[91] In another case, Carole Ann Ryavec has described the differences between local and proprietary notions of justice and its enforcement in Hine-no-shō, and concludes that by 1500 the "proprietor lacked any authority to act for or against individual peasants in their disputes."[92]

Yet antagonisms were balanced by mutual advantage; all sides used each other for their own ends. Indeed, the rivalries between warriors and proprietary lords and within the warrior class gave the peasantry much of its room for maneuver. Thus, peasants were often successful in their petitions against managers whom the lords, for their own reasons, wished to curtail. For instance, in 1350 and 1370, the Okujima peasants successfully complained to Enryakuji about the illegal actions of the resident manager, his agent, and a nearby overseer.[93] In addition, peasants were able to use warriors against each other. A dispute between Suganoura and Ōura shows this on a large scale with both sides seeking to take advantage of local rivalries.[94] Imabori used this principle with a different twist. Peasants in Imabori and other villages in Tokuchinho established ties with multiple warriors; thus seven peasants from Imazaike were linked with five warriors, while five from Imabori were linked with two.[95] As a result, warriors found it difficult to dominate individual villagers.

Moreover, the peasantry continued to rely on the patronage of proprietary lords in the conduct of a village's external affairs. For example, through their ties to the emperor and their status as suppliers of certain traditional goods, the residents of Suganoura gained protection of fishing rights and exemption from harbor taxes. These benefits were significant enough to allow the tie to continue long after the decline of imperial power. At any rate, the presence of several actors provided the peasants with options, even though the outcomes were not always successful; the peasants of Yugenoshima failed, for instance, to persuade Tōji to replace its agent.[96] An additional variable centered on geography. Thus two similar villages in Izumi had different experiences, with the location of a warrior homestead the key factor. In the case in which that homestead was across a river, the peasants largely controlled their own affairs.[97]

Peasants, then, were not helpless bystanders but active participants; sometimes they demonstrated savvy and a potential for manipulation. Changes in tactics were a part of their arsenal, and Hitomi Tonomura has cited "their ingenuity in cultivating relationships, in adjusting to changing times, and in redefining themselves mythologically."[98] In Suganoura, peasants made choices about which dues to pay in order to maintain ties to certain proprietary lords. For their part, these lords might be willing to forgo new surveys and possible increases in revenue in order to avoid risks. Frequently they found that working through a village governing organization was their best guarantee of the continued flow of taxes.

The peasants, in fact, gained by assuming responsibility for these taxes. Like peasants elsewhere, they did not oppose the concept but rather its potential for arbitrariness. They thus sought to place any flexibility in their own hands. As one example, in exchange for paying the dues of delinquent cultivators, villages acquired control over the right to assign fields to their residents. They also used their knowledge and control of the local situation to negotiate actual reductions, for example, a halving by Suganoura of the dues from certain fields in 1470–71.[99]

While peasants moved to exclude proprietary lords and their agents as well as local warriors from active involvement, not all functions performed by higher authority were easily dispensed with. Patronage remained important, since villagers continued to need spokesmen in the wider world. In fact, conditions often dictated the need for more than one proprietary lord or warrior—for example, in the ongoing search for access to certain essential resources. Both this complexity and the sponsorlike character of the lord-village relationship would diminish in the Tokugawa era when villages were less able to use competition between elites to enhance their own ends, and lords came to serve more as lawgivers, enforcers, and tax collectors than as sponsors. This shift from a many-stranded to a single-stranded relationship also characterized the shift from a manorial to an early modern economy in Europe.

JUDICIAL FUNCTIONS

The assumption by villages of judicial functions from provincial and proprietary authorities was more limited than that in the political and economic spheres. The exercise of justice included the pursuit, capture, and trial of criminals and the confiscation of their property—that is, the roles of policeman, judge, and jailor were one.[100] Although both police and judicial authority had originally been considered regular functions of the state, they were gradually taken over by the proprietors of the estates, who in turn delegated them to a variety of representatives.[101]

After 1185, with the growth of military power, the right to exercise justice involving elite warriors was claimed by the shogun. At provincial and local levels, officials might receive confiscated property and certain administrative rights, and therefore justice proved to be economically valuable; the rights themselves were often split between proprietary lords and warriors when estates were divided. For example, the splitting of Yugenoshima-no-shō between Tōji and the *jitō* included "jurisdiction" (*kendan*).[102] Thus, while villages wrote laws concerning property and assumed other responsibilities for internal affairs, prosecutions, especially for capital crimes, were rare.

The laws just referred to covered a wide spectrum but tended to center on matters that villagers shared in common: there were laws about fighting, gambling, dogs, wills, and house building,[103] but even more dealt with the village assembly and communal property. Yet both communal and private property were protected, as in the case, experienced by many villages, of cattle eating crops.[104] Imabori specified that the punishments were to be the same for damage to woodland regardless of ownership.

The frequency of references to common property, however, undoubtedly underlines the difficulties in managing it.[105] Indeed, villages needed clear and powerful enforcement mechanisms to check the temptation to cheat on the rules of access. Imabori relied on heavy fines and on social sanctions—in particular, the loss of membership in the shrine association.[106]

Villages controlled water use with particular strictness, since water was in many instances insufficient. Robert Wade has noted a correlation between village government and water scarcity in southern India in which villages with low supplies preferred formal rules and community control.[107] Higashimura was concerned that no one alter the current route of water flow,[108] whereas Imabori wrote laws regarding turning up the soil where the water left the fields.[109] Outsiders naturally posed a problem for collective management, leading to a number of different strategies. Thus, Suganoura prohibited the sale of fields in Hisashi and Morokawa to outsiders,[110] while Okujima regulated access to mountain fields, limiting it to community membership.[111] On the other hand, the theft of food or grain was considered a capital crime, and therefore might be prosecuted by these very outsiders. The rules governing theft were especially severe, with death the punishment for as little as three *mon* in value.[112] This condition made it desirable for a village to prosecute its own cases, but unless someone was caught in the act, there could be a challenge, leaving the door open for proprietary interference. As a result, some villages sought to prohibit the involvement of higher authority, calling on the community to resist. Suganoura stated its position affirmatively: "No entry to the *shugo*; this is a place with the right to exercise justice."[113]

To strengthen their cases, villages were concerned that justice be properly executed, rather than being based on personal jealousies. Thus, Suganoura and Imabori wrote laws requiring that those accused of crimes should be seen, questioned, and punished by the villagers as a whole (*sōshō*). Suganoura specifically enjoined anyone from using the power of the *sōshō* to levy a fine on a person who "is your enemy."[114] Imabori, too, was concerned that the entire village participate in the prosecution of its criminals and in the upholding of its laws.

Villages differed from warriors in how they handled criminals' possessions. Though confiscation was practiced, homes and cultivation rights were preserved when possible. This allowed for continuity between generations, which would have been a matter of concern to neighbors and kin, if not to warrior lords or other outsiders. Though the case is drawn from slightly later, an incident involving a stolen sword led to the following judgment: "The criminal had an eight-year-old son. I ordered that the household headship be held in trust for him and protected against

seizure by others. However, all his property was divided among my commissioners." [115] Apparently, the villagers had persuaded the outside prose-
cutor that the family headship included the continuing responsibility for
tax payment. [116]

In Suganoura, a village that was unusual for the degree of its judicial autonomy, the position was expressed forthrightly: "The house and fields of
someone in Suganoura who does something contrary to law and receives
capital punishment or is banished from the area should be left alone, if
there are children who succeed him." [117] From this and other evidence, it
would seem that peasants in general tried to protect cultivator rights and
did not extend automatic punishment to kin. But it was in cases of capital
crimes that the potential for differing priorities might erupt into conflict.
The melding of interests between villages and higher authority could not
always be extended indefinitely.

Most of the village laws that dealt with individual behavior or village-
wide concerns date from the late fifteenth or sixteenth centuries. It is
difficult to know if they reflected earlier practice that might need to be recorded to ensure compliance. They clearly represented the maturation of
the village community, which had begun to emerge so dramatically in the
fourteenth century.

CONCLUSION

Charting changes in rural society is a challenge. Documentary evidence is
limited, because only spotty records survive and even changes that strike
us as revolutionary in retrospect were undoubtedly gradual enough that
little comment was required. [118] Yet while much of the change may have
been slow and cumulative, the case can be made for a turning point
in the fourteenth century. Triggered by agricultural changes reflected in
pond building and the increased use of fertilizers, waterwheels, and weeding, five developments can be identified with that era: (1) yields doubled,
which led to the appearance of *kajishi*; (2) small cultivators became independent, which was reflected in taxation that was based on individuals
rather than on *myō*; (3) shrine associations emerged and promoted a spirit
of community among villagers; (4) conflicts over water and mountain land
increased, leading to the appearance of peasant petitions with multiple signatures; and (5) nucleated villages appeared. In the century and a half that
followed, villages began to clarify rules of membership, restrict access to
mountain land and water, enact laws, collect taxes, and keep records.

The documentary record so generated was a product of decisions that were now made by groups. By contrast, villages that remained under warrior dominance tended to leave much less detailed records. This discrepancy helps to account for the unevenness of the surviving local archive. Though documents from on high continue to abound, it is those that were generated within the village that provide us with our most intimate views of ground level.[119]

As this chapter has shown, warriors did live in the countryside, even in central Japan, and remained engaged in agriculture at some level. Yet many absented themselves from the village for significant periods of time beginning in the fourteenth century, foreshadowing their movement into castle towns during the Tokugawa period. The gradual removal of warriors from villages was predicated on the agricultural and social changes of the fourteenth century—the increase in yields and the nucleation of villages. A new, geographically coherent unit of local administration based on residence and land-use patterns emerged first in central Japan and later spread throughout much of the archipelago. Village assumption of responsibility for the administration of internal affairs was an important legacy for early modern government.

PART TWO

CHAPTER 6

Visions of an Emperor

ANDREW GOBLE

THE KENMU REVOLUTION—defined here as the activities of the emperor Go-Daigo (1288–1339) in the 1320s and 1330s, and as a decades-long repudiation of prior political, economic, and social assumptions—marks a clear period of rupture. It was an acknowledgment that what we might term the Heian-Kamakura order of life had failed, and an attempt by a wide range of actors to construct a new world whose shape would reflect fourteenth-century realities.

There is general agreement on the many changes coursing through Japanese society from the mid-thirteenth century, which provided the essential backdrop for the Kenmu Revolution. But there has been less agreement on how to interpret some of the essential elements in that revolution—or even to acknowledge that there was, in fact, a revolution. Rather, interpretative stances have tended to focus on such notions as a (failed) restoration anomalously coincident with longer-term changes (e.g., the rise of the warrior class), which were nonetheless catalyzed to their natural fruition by that restoration.

I have argued at length elsewhere[1] that these interpretive stances are inherently misleading and should be abandoned. In particular I have argued that efforts to interpret Go-Daigo and the Kenmu Revolution that do not acknowledge that they were integral to, and in fact propelled, the changes that shaped the medieval period, give us a misleading sense of the dynamics of the medieval age. Such approaches tend to focus on narrative structures and on problem-definitions that explain not so much known results as how to articulate threads of continuity; in so doing, discontinuities are missed, and the disruptions that made (and make) it necessary for some to seek continuity are played down. Several examples of this could be adduced, but let me note the recent discussion of medieval views of sovereignty by Imatani Akira and Itō Kiyoshi.[2] In taking up such issues as kingship and Ashikaga Yoshimitsu (1358–1408) or the (admittedly vexed) issue of why the imperial family continued as an imperial family, both authors assume some form of ideological unity and agreement on definitions that antedate the period in question. While both recognize that the problematization of sovereignty we note for the late fourteenth century was not unrelated to Go-Daigo and Kenmu, they adhere to an outmoded conceptualization of imperial continuity which elides significant breakpoints: neither addresses the range of thought on the issue of sovereignty in Go-Daigo's time, neither fully comprehends the extent to which the debate itself was initiated by Go-Daigo and his actions, and neither gives a nuanced sense of how contemporaries and successors sought to address Go-Daigo's legacy. That is, to make the point strongly, they have failed to see why there was a debate over medieval sovereignty.

This essay will approach some of these issues, and also give some sense of the medieval world view that, breaking with the past, embraced the need to dissect inherited ideologies that were seen as inadequate to the times.

THE SPIRIT OF THE TIMES

Around the spring of the fifth year of Rekiō [1342] epidemic raged through house after house in the capital, the number of those who died from illness uncountable. Along with the fears that this was no ordinary occurrence, night after night people saw in their dreams a blazing light that resembled an Imperial carriage issuing forth from the Imperial tomb at Yoshino and flying up over the capital, and all trembled with the knowledge that this could only be the vengeful spirit of the former sovereign [Go-Daigo].[3]

Shortly thereafter such suspicions seemed confirmed. Ashikaga Tadayoshi (1306–52) was suddenly stricken with a serious illness, becoming wildly delirious. Nothing—not prayers, the fervent offerings of the Bureau of Divination, or the ministrations of the court's hereditary physicians— seemed to ameliorate Tadayoshi's condition. Perhaps he would die, and a ready analogy sprang to the lips of many: his death would portend exactly the same worldly end for the Ashikaga as had that of Shigemori (1138–79)[4] for the Heike. Go-Daigo's cause, in other words, would soon triumph, owing in no small part to his continuing activities from beyond the grave.

Suitably distressed by the ramifications of Tadayoshi's death, retired emperor Kōgon (1313–64) prayed fervently to heavenly powers to save him: surely the gods and buddhas understood the bond of sovereign and minister in a dual court-military polity, and the need to remember the great legacy of Minamoto Yoritomo (1147–99) that had effected this. Fortunately, Tadayoshi recovered three days later (and lived for nearly another decade before being fatally poisoned by his brother Takauji, 1305–58). For some, Tadayoshi's recovery was as significant an event as when, during the founding of the Chou dynasty, the affliction of King Wu responded to the prayers to Heaven of his full brother Kungtan, which was construed as clear proof that Wu enjoyed Heaven's Charge. The precedent was obviously a weighty one. But others were somewhat more skeptical, suggesting that the recovery was already under way and that Kōgon had simply timed his prayers well.

Nonetheless, the episode confirmed that Go-Daigo's vengeful spirit was quite capable of inflicting suffering on those who had usurped his regime and treated him badly. A source from 1340 had already pointed to this concern, by noting that when a blazing light (i.e., vengeful spirit) had appeared before Takauji it had been decreed that the late Go-Daigo was to be worshiped in accordance with precedents laid down originally for Emperor Sutoku (1119–64).[5] Go-Daigo's continued existence as a vengeful spirit was thus a devastating commentary on both the Ashikaga and Kōgon's Northern Court, which were seeking to portray themselves as legitimate parties in the ongoing Kenmu revolution.

The Ashikaga continued to be exercised by the problem of dealing with Go-Daigo. Tadayoshi was apparently sufficiently disturbed by the prevalence of references to Go-Daigo's spirit that he ordered an entire chapter of the *Taiheiki* destroyed, as well as other entries suppressed.[6] Takauji, long troubled by the ideological implications of his revolt against the reigning emperor, had begun his own expiatory effort to ameliorate the imperial spirit virtually from the moment of Go-Daigo's death in 1339. In particular, he prevailed upon the eminent Zen prelate Musō Soseki (1275–1351) to become the founding abbot of a new temple, Tenryūji (Temple of the Heavenly Dragon), whose principal purpose was to pray for the salvation (and thus pacification) of Go-Daigo's soul.

Tenryūji was not the only religious institution used by the Ashikaga to ameliorate Go-Daigo's soul; and its construction served as a touchstone for many interests, motivations, and enmities.[7] Among them was Takauji's well-known concern about Go-Daigo's vengeful spirit. The compilers of the *Taiheiki*, for example, who were hostile to Tenryūji, vehemently denied any relation between the founding of Tenryūji and talk of vengeful spirits. But on the other hand, the compilers of Tenryūji's Chronicle of Construction (*Tenryūji zōei kiroku*) were in no doubt about either Takauji's fears or his motivation in pressing Musō to accept the charge. Now, Musō himself did not fully share Takauji's reasoning (since he did not believe in vengeful spirits), but he was certainly concerned with the implications of the way in which Go-Daigo had been treated, and convinced of the need to repose his soul.[8]

Musō had been intellectually and personally quite close to Go-Daigo, and Go-Daigo had proved to be a generous patron. In mid-1333 Go-Daigo impressed upon Musō his own sense that, with the realm now unified under his own leadership, it was a propitious time for the reglorification of the inseparable Dharma of the Sovereign and the Dharma of the Buddha (*ōbō buppō*).[9] In 1334 Musō presided over Go-Daigo's baptism into Zen. Nevertheless, there is little evidence to suggest that Musō shared Go-Daigo's vision of Kenmu, or even that he had a particular stance on what Go-Daigo was trying to effect in that enterprise. But Musō did have views on the shape of the post–Go-Daigo realm, of the relationship between sovereign and Buddhism, and of the relationship between the imperial family and the military oligarchy (i.e., the Ashikaga).

Musō was no political naïf, and was close to many prominent political figures of his age. He spent some time with Ashikaga Tadayoshi discussing the matter of the position of the imperial house vis-à-vis the warrior estate, part of those discussions ending up in Musō's noted *Muchū mondō* (Dialogues in a Dream).[10] In this effort to recreate an ideology that justified the Ashikaga's hold over the imperial house in Kyoto, the imperial family emerges as an important but dependent part of the polity, reliant upon the support of the military estate. Both, however, were interdependent with the Law of the Buddha, which was to be on an equal footing with secular power. In short, there was no place for any ideology like that of Go-Daigo, which emphasized that the imperial family was supreme, soverign, and self-legitimating.[11]

Elsewhere, however, Musō was highly critical of the Ashikaga, and these views tell us much more about his efforts to find an appropriate place for

Go-Daigo.[12] Musō, while acknowledging that the military estate was an integral part of the polity, nevertheless felt that it should assist the imperial family, leading to a unity of sovereign and minister. Musō felt that his former disciple had been treated unjustly and that Go-Daigo's loss of power was unrelated to any personal, moral, or political failing; the prevailing disorder was the direct fault of the Ashikaga and, by implication, of Kōgon and the opposing imperial line. Musō was not shy in stating his views, even presenting them to Kōgon in public. The problem, then, was how to heal the terrible rupture that had been brought about by the assault on Go-Daigo, the legitimate embodiment of the political order.

Musō's preferred solution was to address the issue of Go-Daigo's unassuaged soul. By positioning this Son of Heaven in a cosmology that would be understood by the former pupil, it would be possible to effect a posthumous reconciliation. For Musō the dedication of Tenryūji and the worship of the late emperor would ensure that Go-Daigo's soul would achieve full enlightenment, and thus repose, in the ultimate reality of the Flower Garland Dharma-realm (*Kegon hokkai*) of the Buddha, in which was found the perfect unity of all existences. The merit accruing therefrom would, according to Musō, lead to five specific benefits: the nonarising of disorder, the permanent endurance of the imperial rank, the rejoicing of the populace, the flourishing of the shogunal family, and the mutual flourishing and growth of *ōbō* and *buppō*.[13] This merit would heal ideological rupture and undergird a new polity in which the Ashikaga, the imperial family, and Buddhism would be joined. Those five benefits were in the event not to be realized (at least not equally). Yet the weight attached to their achievement reflects Musō's fervent belief that no stability would be forthcoming until Go-Daigo was properly positioned, properly worshiped, and properly understood.

Others, too, shared that belief. Yet their vision of Go-Daigo was quite different, and expressed in other ways. We shall commence our view with a look at some portraits, images that quite literally reflect the fourteenth-century's brush with Go-Daigo.

IMAGES OF THE PAST

Until recently the rich tradition of painting, portraiture, and sculpture bequeathed from medieval Japan has been largely the province of students of art and religion, "documents" that have rarely been used by historians to enlarge the human context. By the same token, and with some instructive exceptions,[14] they have not always been considered with respect to the cultural and social context within which they were produced, or considered as guides to the broader cultural and intellectual life of the times. Yet artistic production was an integral part of medieval culture. Indeed, it was one of the primary vehicles by which the religious and political elite formed an image for itself and for posterity.

Motives for production and the medium of presentation varied considerably. In some instances where the record was that of a life and the social impact of that life—such as in the scroll paintings of eminent figures like Hōnen (1133–1212)[15] or Ippen (1237–89),[16] or a portrait of Myōe (1173–1232)[17]—the production reflected a mixture of pride, propaganda, and piety. In other cases a group of people might collaborate, and strengthen their familial and political bonds, by commissioning a set of religious paintings to honor a figure important to them all, as with the collective effort that produced a set of the Eight Shingon Patriarchs as a memorial to Saionji Sadako (1196–1302) in 1315.[18] Yet others might individually commission or execute by their own hand paintings of important Buddhist figures, as with the two pictures of Monjusri produced by the priest Monkan (1278–1357, one of Go-Daigo's prime religious confidantes) in memory of his mother in 1334.[19] Other paintings of Buddhist figures might be produced in order to receive some divine assistance in a particular endeavor, as with the Bakufu official Iga Kanemitsu's dedication of a sculpture of Monjusri in support of Go-Daigo's move against the Bakufu in 1324.[20]

Representation of individual personages through painting or sculpture was a major genre. These portrayals could be produced during the person's lifetime or (generally fairly soon) after death. Irrespective of how widely the existence of any image was known (to say that they were "in circulation" or readily viewable would be grossly misleading), such representations were designed to leave a perpetual image, to portray the person in a way that would make a statement about the person's life. With religious figures, the task was in one sense an easy one, since that was the arena of activity for which they wished to be remembered, a sentiment shared by disciples and successors. We might note in this regard the genre of paintings of Zen teachers (chinso), which included such figures as Musō Soseki,[21] Shūhō Myōchō (1282–1337),[22] and Kokan Shiren (1278–1346).[23] Yet for others, such as members of the Kamakura warrior class, the images, while reflecting how they wished to be remembered, do not tell us, in the end, much about "warriors." We may cite any number of images of Hōjō regents (painting of Tokimune,[24] sculpture of Tokiyori),[25] of members of the Kanesawa family,[26] and of power-brokers such as Uesugi Shigefusa[27] or of members of the Andō family (whose portraits were inscribed by the noted Chinese priest Mingji Chujun/Minki Soshun),[28] and find no association with a warrior background but rather an association with cultural traditions of the civil aristocracy or of religious achievement. Indeed, without an identifying label for one of the most well known paintings of all, that of Minamoto Yoritomo, one might easily mistake him for an anonymous courtier, never realizing that one of the rewards for political achievement was to be painted in the image of a courtier.[29] It is not until after the era of Go-Daigo, in fact, that we begin to encounter portraits of warriors *qua* warriors.[30] For that matter, numerous portraits of aristocrats and imperial family members tend to stress their religiosity while declining to provide the viewer with a sense of what it was that justified the portrait in the first place. Nor do they tell us what an aristocrat or imperial house family member "was." This is not to suggest that the portraits say nothing about them as people, but rather that they attest to canons of normative representation. Most notably, these images studiously avoid allusions to power and influence, the very elements that made them worthy of representation in the first place.

While there were diverse motivations behind the production of an image, the crucial point is that the fact of the image was a statement about the person's position in society. In this context, the manner of the portrayal—for example, age of the subject, clothing style and appurtenances, and the presence (and identity of its author) of an inscription—provide important clues about the person whose life is represented.

We can, accordingly, assume that the five known portraits of Go-Daigo (all posthumous, three near contemporary and readily accessible for examination)[31] will help us to appreciate how he was seen and perhaps how he saw himself. Yet although the production of these images was not in itself inherently unusual, Go-Daigo was unquestionably a unique subject, one not amenable to easy interpretation, and distinctly different from his imperial peers. We shall look first at Go-Daigo as part of a group, and then at portraits of him as an individual figure.

A FACE IN THE CROWD

In the *Tenshi sekkan miei*,[32] a scroll of twenty-one Imperial portraits put together in the second half of the fourteenth century, Go-Daigo appears as one of nineteen (of a possible twenty-three)[33] emperors covering the reigns from Toba (r. 1107–23) to Go-Daigo (r. 1318–39) himself. Bringing the number to twenty-one are the "emeritus" emperor Go-Takakura (emeritus 1221–23), and the current fourth sovereign of the Northern Court Go-Kōgon (r. 1352–71). Though the seated postures are almost identical, each face and expression is individual. The pattern, color, and type of the clothing are distinct: three are in religious garb; twelve are in a variety of casual court garb; three are in casual imperial garb (ohiki nōshi); and the remaining three, including Go-Daigo, are wearing working imperial garb. Yet even allowing that these last six had been portrayed in clothes reserved only for emperors (probably because there had not been opportunities to remember them otherwise),[34] and that all were portrayed only because they were imperials, there is little in portrayal or background to suggest much about what emperors did, or even how they saw themselves.

But the paintings do make a statement. Aligned together in order of succession (except for Go-Kōgon), they suggest an essential continuity of the imperial line, and, with the inclusion of emeritus Go-Takakura, an acknowledgment that within the imperial family the fact of succession rather than the direction of succession was of paramount importance. On the other hand, that statement was fraught with its own problems. The inclusion of Go-Kōgon argues that the locus of legitimate succession did not lie with Go-Daigo's line, even though the inclusion of Go-Daigo makes it clear that he himself was a legitimate emperor; yet none of the four combined emperors from either the Southern and Northern courts after Go-Daigo and prior to Go-Kōgon is depicted.[35] We can understand Go-Kōgon's reluctance to celebrate Go-Daigo's son and immediate successor, Go-Murakami, who was still reigning at the time; but this does not explain the absence of Go-Kōgon's Northern predecessors. If the Northern branch was legitimate—presumably this was the formal position of Go-Kōgon and the Northern Court—then why not bridge the gap and include earlier sovereigns? Or was there some doubt on the matter of just where the imperial family stood? To get some direction on this, let us move slightly beyond these Imperial portraits.

The Son of Heaven portraits were but one scroll in a set of three, the other two being those of thirty imperial regents and eighty ministers of state, respectively. As with the Imperial portraits, the time frame and frame of reference for this aristocratic oligarchy are the reigns from Toba to Go-Daigo, a clear statement of the importance of reigns in defining legitimacy of the oligarchy as a whole. Unspoken (or unseen) was that the imperials were of only one family, while regents and ministers of state (including

Minamoto Sanetomo, 1192–1219, Kamakura's third shogun) might spring from many. Yet by the same token, the fact that all the regents and ministers of state are, without exception, dressed in formal robes of office, and that the styles of clothing and colors in each category are identical, leaves little doubt that there were other levels of continuity besides the imperial. Moreover, we are given a striking visual reminder that the authority for governing was supposed to lie only in the hands of the aristocracy. Emperors may move through stages of life (as of course did all members of the aristocracy), but they were temporary incumbents of an imperial rank that served as a symbolic capstone for hereditary aristocrats who are constant embodiments of the state. The portraits taken together affirm, even stress, a satisfactory order of the world that many fourteenth-century aristocrats looked to as a model for their polity.

One of the often-adduced examples is that of Kitabatake Chikafusa (1293–1354) who, in his tour de force the *Jinnō shōtōki* (Chronicle of the Legitimate Descent of Divine Sovereigns)[36] left no doubt about the proper order of society and the crucial importance of the aristocracy as advisers to imperials; and in a detailed study of ranks and appointments, the *Shoku-genshō* (Treatise on the Origins of Posts),[37] he gave those arguments further constitutional body. Another work, which enjoyed greater currency among contemporaries, was the massive genealogical compendium *Sonpi bunmyaku* (Bloodlines of Noble and Base) of Tōin Kinsada (1340–99).[38] This compilation leaves no doubt that records of descent ipso facto explain why continuity was of such crucial import, and Kinsada's selections also tell us that the military families of the realm (who had obviously kept their own family genealogies, records just as important as land confirmations and the like) were now to be considered part of the oligarchy. True, the genealogical privileging connoted by "noble" and "base" differentiates rather than joins seamlessly, yet the two are together as never before. *Sonpi bunmyaku*, which could not have been compiled without the cooperation of the warrior class, should be seen as a work of history (even the extirpated and formerly reviled Hōjō are well preserved here, their place in the oligarchy enshrined permanently) as much as it is a genealogical reference tool. Thus *Sonpi bunmyaku* is an attempt to deal with the post–Go-Daigo world and to create an ideology of social and political jointness; it affirms that an old order continued (as did the Ashikaga in their efforts to preserve a sphere for the old imperial system)[39] while simultaneously recognizing that court and military must coexist.[40]

But while continuity and coexistence are (understandably) central concerns after Go-Daigo, the *Tenshi sekkan miei* scrolls, commissioned by an emperor who inserted a vacuum between himself and Go-Daigo, suggest something that these other works did not wish to acknowledge explicitly, even as their appearance was underlain by that very concern. Namely, that with Go-Daigo there had been a break, there had been a world of which Go-Daigo had been the last representative, there had been a world for which there was no future after Go-Daigo.

Go-Daigo in the *Tenshi sekkan miei* is thus more than just one portrait among many. Clad in an unadorned imperial green robe (the color second in the chromatic hierarchy to the preeminent red-brown color that denoted an emperor), Go-Daigo is literally sitting at the end of something, looking back. But he is not nostalgic: he does not appear in the least concerned, his face betrays neither a trace of worry nor a lack of confidence. We see a full, strong visage, that of a mature adult, adorned by a strikingly luxuriant beard that easily outclasses those of any other figures known to us;[41] a wry smile dances on the lips, raised and arched eyebrows reflect a general bemusement, and the eyes gaze knowingly at the world. Go-Daigo too may have seen an ending with himself; but as other portraits suggest clearly, he also saw a beginning.

A SINGULAR IMAGE

Two other near-contemporary portraits of Go-Daigo, recently the subject of fine analysis by Kuroda Hideo, are housed in Kyoto's Daitokuji[42] and in Fujisawa's Shōjōkōji.[43] Though they (and the portrait in the *Tenshi sekkan miei*) were painted by different persons under different auspices,[44] the facial similarity of all three suggests they were painted by, or at the direction of, someone who had personal knowledge of the imperial visage. We note a strong, confident gaze; a slightly fleshy appearance; whitish flesh, light vermilion around neck, ears, and cheeks; black hair, pronounced beard and eyebrows, with traces of gray in beard and hair. They depict Go-Daigo in his later years, and unmistakably as the Son of Heaven. Indeed, unlike many other imperials, and certainly unlike his contemporaries Go-Uda (1267–1324, his father)[45] and Hanazono (1297–1348, his immediate predecessor),[46] we have no images of him at notably different ages or in clothing that suggests different stages of life. As noted earlier, it is true that since Go-Daigo never entered holy orders or abdicated, the possibility of portraying him at a retired stage of life was nonexistent; but it might have been possible to portray him in "casual" garb, or even at an earlier age.

Neither was done, so we can only assume that the decisions of different people to remember Go-Daigo exclusively as an adult emperor were conscious and purposeful. Let us look at each.

Daitokuji. The Daitokuji portrait, perhaps painted not too long after death, was partly intended to assuage Go-Daigo's soul (*tsuizen kuyō*; a major concern, we recall, of the Ashikaga and of Musō Soseki). As such, it represents the emperor in a way that the soul would recognize as a fitting image. Behind Go-Daigo is a largely obscured Imperial sleeping platform (*michōdai*); this locates Go-Daigo in his private quarters in the Seiryōden building within the imperial compound. In front of the dais are the traditional *Koma inu* (Korean dog) shrine guardians, painted in different colors, A with the open mouth to the right and UN with the closed mouth to the left; their function in this context is to ward off evil spirits while the emperor is in a vulnerable state of repose. Go-Daigo is seated on a brownish and white checked mat which is placed on two tatami mats, the *ungenberi* green color being used exclusively for emperors. He is clad in the *ohiki nōshi* daily robes which could be worn only by emperors; the torso robe is white with sewn silver design of hollyhocks, the trousers vermilion. In his right hand he is holding a fan. These elements together all affirm that the person portrayed is an emperor.

Other elements, however, make a direct statement about how Go-Daigo defined emperorship. On the mat to Go-Daigo's left is a large sword—perhaps the one that he requested from Izumo Grand Shrine during his return from exile in 1333[47]—an item unusual not simply because "objects" do not normally clutter portraits, but because of the message that this is an emperor who wields weapons as he rules, whose authority is backed by armed might as much as it is by status. Other elements provide a complementary message, that Go-Daigo is also to be remembered as a lawgiver and wielder of the pen. Immediately to his front lies an ink box (black lacquer, decorated with golden sprigs of chrysanthemum) containing inkstone and writing brush ready to write an imperial decree, perhaps as a result of consultation and discussion with an adviser (often identified as Madenokōji Nobufusa, fl. 1258–1336) sitting in the foreground, face slightly averted from the imperial visage.

This portrait, held in a major Zen temple patronized by both Go-Daigo and the Ashikaga, is that of a ruling emperor at home with the tools of governance; it is an image that accords with our general view of Go-Daigo. He died as an emperor, and after death has returned to his rightful and permanent place in the imperial palace. However, visible attempts to retouch the painting (a not very good attempt to paint out the sword, and a more successful effort to erase a small table or stand positioned between Go-Daigo and his adviser) raise a less well known issue, that of Go-Daigo's association with one of the most important cultural figures in Japanese history, Shōtoku taishi (574–622).

The Daitokuji portrait draws heavily on a well-known painting genre of Shōtoku taishi in the Seiryōden lecturing on the Queen Srimala sutra to some assembled advisers (or, in one variant, a single adviser).[48] The overall composition of the two paintings, the location in the Seiryōden, and the emphasis on the regnal and instructional functions of the two figures are too similar for this to be simply a matter of coincidence. Not only was Go-Daigo familiar with aspects of the devotional art of the Shōtoku taishi cult popular in his time, but Go-Daigo and Shōtoku taishi are the only pre-Meiji members of the imperial family ever to be depicted "in action" with an audience. A further link between the two figures is provided by Go-Daigo's sword. While not evident in the "Queen Srimala" painting, another genre of Shōtoku taishi portraits from the thirteenth and fourteenth centuries, held in places like Shitennōji (whose treasures Go-Daigo is known to have viewed) portray him as a lawgiver and statesman, clad in robes of office, clasping baton of rank, and with a sword prominently attached to his belt.[49] It was extremely rare for emperors to be in any way associated with swords, and indeed the only pre-Meiji figures depicted with them were Shōtoku taishi, Go-Daigo, and, intriguingly, Daigo (885–930).[50]

Obviously some contemporaries saw a close connection between the two figures. Yet that link was so powerful and so unsettling that whoever commissioned the work felt it necessary to try and eradicate the telling references (echoes of Tadayoshi and the *Taiheiki* here) of the sword and the small table that would make the Shōtoku analogy abundantly apparent, remind the viewer of Go-Daigo's activist rule, and of course implicate the Ashikaga and the Northern Court in the basest acts of *lèse-majesté*. Much needs to be studied about the cultural symbolism of Shōtoku taishi in medieval Japan, but there is no doubt of its political potency: it can hardly be accidental that the Ashikaga statement of good government and conduct of 1336, the *Kenmu shikimoku*,[51] consists of seventeen articles, just like Shōtoku taishi's hallowed constitution of 604. Presumably the Ashikaga did not wish Go-Daigo to be competing with them here as well. But such editorial discretion did not control all production. Another portrait produced under different auspices makes the symbolism of the Daitokuji portrait, already powerful, pale by comparison.

Shōjōkōji. The Shōjōkōji portrait[52] is an even more complex work of reinforcing and overlapping symbolism. It positions Go-Daigo literally at the center of the universe, and as the incarnation of the fount of knowledge and authority that is second only to Heaven, the Buddha, and Amaterasu ōmikami. It is a large claim, well beyond the portrayal of any other emperor in Japanese history. Some of the items of garb and decoration appear in slightly abbreviated or variant form, but as Kuroda has demonstrated, what is intended to be portrayed can be elaborated.

Go-Daigo is seated on an apricot-colored, lotus-shaped mat bordered by a thick vermilion strip; the mat is placed on green brocade half-tatami matting that is itself placed on a ceremonial imperial dais; the dais is decorated around the vertical border by (on each side) a set of three variously colored lions, painted against white cloud "roundels," which are, respectively, charging, crouching, and standing. Go-Daigo wears a daily-use court crown that is topped by a golden four-sided ceremonial crown (itself topped by a red orb) from which hang twelve golden tassels. His main garment is a red-brown robe (the color of an emperor's daytime wear) decorated with patterns of clouds and dragons, with stylized sun and moon on the shoulders. Over this is draped a Buddhist cloak that has patches of red, green, and blue on a white background; this is bordered and divided by strips of green decorated by serried vermilion chrysanthemums. Hanging down from under the cloak at front are four ribbons, two red outer ones and two blue inner ones, each tipped by a small golden bell. In his hands he holds implements of Shingon esoteric Buddhism: in the right hand a three-pronged Diamond Pestle (*Kongō goko sho*), in his left hand a three-pronged Diamond Bell (*Kongō goko rei*). In the foreground are the two Koma inu, A and UN, flanking the dais. At the top of the picture are three banners inscribed with the names of deities: in the center and raised above the others is Amaterasu ōmikami (progenitress of the imperial family), to his right Kasuga Daimyōjin (tutelary deity of the Fujiwara),[53] and to his left Hachiman Daibosatsu (tutelary deity of the Minamoto and the warrior class as a whole). What messages are being conveyed here?

Go-Daigo's clothing, and the twelve-tassel ceremonial crown that normally could be worn (albeit with caution, since it is a notably unstable headpiece) only by a Son of Heaven, leave no doubt that the subject is emperor and Son of Heaven.[54] But the crown is of further interest: the only other member of the imperial family portrayed wearing such a crown is Shōtoku taishi, firstly in the "Queen Srimala" portrait, and, secondly and far more strikingly, on a statue dating from the twelfth century.[55] We can only assume that Go-Daigo's crown was modeled on that of Shōtoku taishi; and since Shōtoku, despite never having attained the rank, was graced with an emperor's crown in order to emphasize the preeminence of his imperialness, we can infer that Go-Daigo's crown is meant to convey a similar message.[56]

Go-Daigo is also represented as a divinity, a particularly noteworthy point since, notwithstanding traditional ideologies of divine imperial descent, no known image of any other emperor makes such an overt claim. But, as we know from portraits of Toyotomi Hideyoshi and Tokugawa Ieyasu,[57] the Koma inu in the foreground imply that the subject has been deified; the three divinity banners—with Kasuga *daimyōjin* and Hachiman *daibosatsu* subordinate to Amaterasu ōmikami—indicate that Go-Daigo enjoys their collective protection, and also that when worshiping them one is worshiping Go-Daigo, a living god.

The dais upon which Go-Daigo is seated is the lion dais used by Buddhas, bodhisattvas, and high-ranking priests; the eight-petaled lotus mat (the seat of a Buddha or bodhisattva) and the three-pronged Diamond Pestle in the right hand both symbolize that Go-Daigo has received enlightenment in this very existence. Moreover, the Diamond Pestle, and the Three-pronged Diamond Bell in the left hand, along with the posture of the arms, indicate that Go-Daigo is an avatar of Kongō satta,[58] venerated in esoteric Buddhism as the second of the bodhisattvas, one who as a human had received secret ordination directly from the preeminent Buddha Dainichi nyorai. But there are further references in this already rich image: an allusion to Aizen myōō, whose original form is Kongō satta, whom Go-Daigo had earlier enlisted as a powerful accomplice in his endeavors;[59] and the posture and esoteric associations lead to an easy identification with Kōbō daishi (774–835), who is in turn a transformation body of Shōtoku taishi, with both also regarded as transformation bodies of Nyōirin Kannon.[60]

Finally is the ultimate message that Go-Daigo has transcended all emperors, Buddhas, and gods save only the ultimate progenitors. Go-Daigo is the legitimate successor to the founding divinity of the imperial family, Amaterasu, whose original trace is Dainichi nyōrai, symbolized here by the red sun orb atop Go-Daigo's crown. Below these two and fusing them as they are fused is Go-Daigo the avatar of Kongō satta; that is, we have a double image of Amaterasu the ancestral divinity of the imperial house with Go-Daigo ranking second, and of the chief Shingon divinity Dainichi nyōrai fused with the second most important, Kongō satta.

In short, the Shōjōkōji portrait portrays Go-Daigo, the Son of Heaven and Kongō satta, second in the universe only to Dainichi nyōrai and Ama-terasu ōmikami, a deity in his own right situated at the center of sover-eignty, of the Buddhist dharma, and of the gods.

ILLUSTRATING GO-DAIGO'S VISION

These portraits are suffused with the most extraordinary and potent sym-bolism. The claims about emperorship are overt and staggering. Though there had never been any shortage of generic imperial ideology about de-scent from the gods, being a Son of Heaven, or ideas of Buddhist mon-archy, given that few other imperials had ever bothered to elaborate the notion of sovereignty, or even their own qualifications for emperorship,[61] almost any statement by an emperor on such matters would have been bound to stand out. Still, nothing quite prepares us for the intensity of appropriation and identification that is evident here. Indeed the claims are even stronger than the confident assertions that Go-Daigo made in an amazing letter to the Bakufu in 1324 in the wake of his failed plot against it:

> I am the Lord of this entire country. All below are in receipt of the favors of the Court. To constrict [me] is equivalent to dwelling in the shade and snapping off the foliage, or to drawing water from a stream and forgetting the source. It is furthermore akin to bearing a great burden and treading in a valley, or embracing danger and climbing a peak. Though a Crown may be old, it is upon One's head [lit. neck]. Though a Sovereign may be foolish, it is [he] who is the Lord who steps on the surpassing traces of the Golden Wheel. Though the shoes may be new they tread on the ground; furthermore the shogun, even though he may be loyal and sincere toward the Court, is an underling.[62] . . . The superior are above and the inferior below. This law has yet to startle Heaven. By [its] grace, for numerous generations since the founding of Japan, Imperial reigns have followed one upon the other. This is a wise pattern which cannot but be acknowledged. Furthermore, all in all, this is in accord with what is ordained by Heaven. . . . Lao Tsu stated that "the rain dragon receives water and thence becomes its god. The sagacious Lord receives wisdom and thence stands in the Imperial rank." Therefore I have ac-quired wisdom; it is impossible for me to be ignorant with respect to propriety.[63]

Go-Daigo has left no posthumous comment on whether the pictures in fact represented him accurately, so it is no doubt possible to ponder whether they reveal more about the artists, and the manner in which Go-Daigo was worshiped as a deity after his death, than about Go-Daigo's self-image—although such imperial visions would be no less valuable. Yet there is other evidence to suggest that these portraits articulate Go-Daigo's perspective faithfully.

Go-Daigo's view that with him there would be a new beginning, a fresh start, shows itself in a variety of statements, actions, and policies. His fascination with origins was evident in his choice of era names from the outset of his reign in 1318. It culminated in 1334 with an unusual direct borrowing of a Chinese era name. The choice, Kenmu or Building the Military, was the first era name of the Later Han dynasty, the only case in Chinese history where a ruling dynasty regained its position after being overthrown. Kenmu thus implied continuity, legitimacy, and also the fact that a ruling house had reconstituted itself with a new founding and a new line.[64] Go-Daigo did in fact create a new ruling group in the imperial family with himself as the imperial progenitor, centered around his second cohort of children sired in the 1320s. He also abolished the *insei* system by which former emperors had been eligible to exercise political power in retirement; he divested the rival Jimyōin line and rivals within his own branch of eligibility for the imperial rank, thus creating a clear and undivided program of succession to replace the chaos that had reigned in this area for the preceding six decades; and, as demonstrated by the short shrift he gave to assertions by Tōdaiji that it enjoyed an unassailable special position since it had been so recognized by Emperor Shōmu (the object of cult worship over the preceding centuries),[65] Go-Daigo believed that the actions of previous emperors were in no way binding upon him. Go-Daigo, in other words, was supreme among emperors.

This sense of primacy, that his actions and pronouncements would be the ultimate basis for legitimation, is summed up in a celebrated statement from mid-1333: "The practices and precedents of the present are merely modifications of things which were themselves 'new practices.' My 'new practices' shall be precedents for the future."[66] This was no casual claim, and it underlay actions in a number of areas. One example, and the most literal expression of the desire to create new precedents, was Go-Daigo's authorship of the *Kenmu nenchū gyōji* and the *Nitchū gyōji*.[67] These detailed and, for most people, arcane manuals on ceremony (procedures, celebrations, appointments) represent an effort to cut through an accumulated and increasingly chaotic body of lore and tradition that symbolized just how much imperial activity had ceased to be defined by the interests of emperors. Go-Daigo's "reinvention" of ceremony—indeed, his works are the only ones in the genre not written by hereditary specialists—and the downgrading of even time-honored procedures of the ancient *ritsuryō* state, were thus an effort to establish a new framework for ceremonial life that pivoted around the imperial personage.

A more visible expression of the urge to establish new precedent involved revalidation of the basis of claims to legitimate authority. One such area was recertification of the most revered documents bearing on the legitimacy of religious tradition. A prime example of this was copying out in his own hand Kōbō daishi's document of 826 that had been granted to his disciple Shinga (801–79). Possession of this document was thereafter the prime evidence that a chief priest (*zasu*) of the Daigoji esoteric lineage was in the line of legitimate succession.[68] For emperors even to see this document was unusual. For Go-Daigo to make his copy, invalidate any other copy, and thus presume to recertify the legitimacy of the founder of the Shingon tradition, Kōbō daishi, was extraordinary. Yet according to Monkan, the recipient of the new Go-Daigo copy, Go-Daigo considered himself an incarnation of Kōbō daishi,[69] and so perhaps a self-legitimation confirming the supremacy of his current incarnation seems less unusual. In a similar vein, Go-Daigo reaffirmed, adding his vermilion Imperial handprint, a Kōbō daishi document for Mount Kōya. Continuing this incarnate program, subsequent to perusing the copy in Shōtoku taishi's own hand of the founding chronicle of Shitennōji, Go-Daigo wrote out his own copy and certified it, again, with a vermilion handprint.[70] In Go-Daigo we see unified continuity, new beginnings, and absolute legitimacy.

Another area of recertification was that of land rights. Go-Daigo's prerogatives (and the possibility of his retribution) had been recognized immediately after the fall of the Kamakura Bakufu as holders of rights at many levels of the landowning hierarchy petitioned Go-Daigo for reconfirmations.[71] The pleas from those at the top levels (such as aristocratic families and religious institutions) were unprecedented, for they implicitly acknowledged that Go-Daigo was invested with both de facto and de jure authority to rule a priori on the legal validity of any document upon which ownership of land rights was based. Of greater immediate impact, however, were two decrees from mid-1333. These asserted that no rights claimed by warriors would be deemed valid unless they had been explicitly reconfirmed by documents issued by the new regime (an initial insistence on documents signed personally by Go-Daigo was later modified to allow validation by delegated authority). This policy was influenced by the need to assert authority in confused conditions (the Kamakura Bakufu having just been bloodily extirpated) and a wish to provide restitution to those whose rights had been usurped by Kamakura; but underlying those concerns was the more fundamental desire to emphasize that there were to be no sources of legitimacy past or present superior to Go-Daigo.

In sum, Go-Daigo acted on the assumption that he was the progenitor of a new world. That assumption was certainly bold. However, since his vision did not, ultimately, prevail, Go-Daigo has often been regarded as somewhat bizarrely outside the current of his time, not to mention outside the traditions and theories of sovereignty that underlie the imperial house. But is this a reasonable representation?

PERSPECTIVES ON SOVEREIGNTY

Go-Daigo's Daitokuji and Shōjōkōji portraits make strong claims about his status—Son of Heaven, descendant of the Gods, a living Buddha, incarnation of Shōtoku taishi. Yet the claims in themselves are not extreme. Simply by virtue of becoming emperor Go-Daigo was a descendant of the Gods and he was the Son of Heaven. The claim to being a Buddha is less easy to prove; but though it is a rare achievement, it was regarded as an attainable quest, and others were known to have realized similar goals: Kujō Michiie had attained Buddhahood in this very existence,[72] and Hanazono's endeavors had enabled him to attain a high order of esoteric knowledge as well as the Zen goal of *satori*.[73] Go-Daigo's recorded esoteric program of baptisms, initiation into the highest mysteries, and participation in the most efficacious of rites would have qualified him for great progress; and substantial indirect evidence suggests that he pursued, under the guidance of Monkan, Tantric rites of the Tachikawa sect that had a specific timed regimen for achieving Buddhahood.[74] Thus it would not be beyond credence that Go-Daigo had been able to achieve Buddhahood. As to Shōtoku taishi, that two portraits painted under different auspices should both allude to this suggests something more than a casual association. Certainly it is a powerful claim not made lightly, but others before him—Emperor Shōmu (701–56), Kōbō daishi, and Fujiwara Michinaga (966–1027)—had been so identified, thus making it not at all impossible that Go-Daigo too, given his impact on the world, might be so regarded. For Go-Daigo to identify with a powerful cultural and political icon—as he did also when he selected his own posthumous name to honor Emperor Daigo[75]—who was lauded for an outstanding and morally worthy impact on the world may reflect an extraordinarily potent self-image. But, again, the assertion itself does not strain credulity.

We can thus acknowledge that some basic claims were valid. But what of Go-Daigo's other assertions regarding sovereignty, the imperial house, and a change in dynasty?

In Go-Daigo's day there was, contrary to the image we are usually given, strikingly little agreement even on some basic questions. The variety of perspectives that we can identify suggests two things: first, the general lack of a hegemonic ideology; second, that the general failure of existing political institutions had engendered a crisis of ideology and a concomitant reevaluation (even rejection) of informing assumptions about the polity. In order to get some sense of whether Go-Daigo's views (which, as with anyone else, were of course ultimately the product of his own intellectual processes) were as outré as they have sometimes been portrayed, we can usefully examine the views of some contemporaries on such things as the continuity of the imperial line, historical factors affecting change in Japan, and the basis of legitimacy.

One work brought to Go-Daigo's attention was Kokan Shiren's study of Buddhism in Japan, the *Genkō shakusho*.[76] Shiren presented it to Go-Daigo, whom he lauded as the emperor "who renews the supreme harmony of En[gi] and Ten[ryaku]," [77] in the eighth month of 1322. The work stresses that one of Japan's special characteristics is the existence of native gods (*kami*), who undergird both Buddhism and sovereigns. Shiren's arguments, at least regarding the gods and the sacred regalia (mirror, sword, and jewel) of sovereignty, are not vastly dissimilar from those of the well-studied ideologue Chikafusa some twenty years later ("We regard the original regalia as vital to the very existence of our country and as the seed-bed of its virtue").[78] Both emphasize the importance of the regalia, though when Chikafusa wrote the issue was of immediate practical relevance, Go-Daigo after all having claimed that he never relinquished the originals to the Ashikaga-supported Northern Court. But the need to emphasize the special qualities of Japan's sovereignty leads Shiren into some interesting comparative ground:

> The three regalia are Heaven-made and natural: they come from Heaven and were first bestowed by Amaterasu ōmikami in her heavenly palace. . . . In the time of the three emperors China originally had the Hsia cauldrons, but these were lost when Ch'in snatched the empire from Chou. Since the time of Han a sword [from Han Kao-tsu] and seal [from Ch'in-shih Huang-ti] have constituted the two national regalia (*kokuki*), both of which, with the cauldrons having been lost, have come to be such because of human artifice. China is called a great country, but even though the land is vast, all the tallies for receiving the charge are artificial (*jinkō*) and are not heaven-made. Even though our country is small it was founded by the divine [gods opened the basis] and it has the spirit which transmits the regalia. One ought not in the same day speak [of the two cases]. Further, as to sword and seal, the two courts do not await [them/the same thing]. And

what is it to link them? Rather, in what ways would the fate (*un*) of the Son of Heaven (*tenshi*) be the same? Thus even though Shina transmits seal and sword there have been several tens of surnames [acceding to emperorship] how much so is this because the treasured regalia are human artifacts. Our country is of one seed. Is not the thread continuous and without limit because of the heaven-made and natural regalia? Accordingly it is said that even after a thousand and ten thousand generations there will not be the fear of [sovereignty] being snatched away. How would these heaven-made sacred regalia become the plaything of another clan or a different lineage?[79]

That is, Japan and the imperial house can rest assured that the imperial line will endure. But Shiren and Chikafusa (or for that matter Watarai Ieyuki, author of the *Ruijū jingi hongen*)[80] were not the only voices who thought about Japan and China.

For Chūgan Engetsu (1300–1375),[81] a Zen priest who returned from several years' study in China in 1332, the issues of sovereignty and origins of legitimacy that stared everyone in the face in the wake of Go-Daigo's spectacular triumph the following year demanded attention. To Engetsu, a violently decisive change of such massive dimensions connoted nothing less than a change of dynasty, the succession of a ruler who enjoyed Heaven's mandate, and the rightful destruction of the unworthy who had temporarily usurped it.[82] Accordingly, Engetsu presented Go-Daigo with a Memorial to the Son of Heaven[83] that proffered advice on policies appropriate to this epochal juncture. In it Engetsu compared the change not to some unbroken line of Japanese history or to *kami* forces operating in their correct fashion, but to the transitions from Shang to Chou and Ch'in to Han, and suggested that Go-Daigo could build as enduring a state as the founders of the Han, T'ang, and Sung dynasties, those morally outstanding sovereigns who had rightfully succeeded to the Mandate of Heaven. Laudatory praise was rarely eschewed by those seeking imperial favor, but Engetsu took his arguments one step further: the Japanese imperial line drew its legitimacy from two sources: the Chou dynasty and a line of sovereigns descended from the gods ("His Majesty, His illustriousness inherited from Chou Wen, His virtue received from Jinmu, is to revive the kingly and abolish the hegemonic"). Although we are no stranger to claims of historical resonance with the Chou dynasty in this period—recall the analogy noted by the *Taiheiki* for Tadayoshi's recovery from illness—this is exceptional; yet we are also reminded of some implicit assumptions in Shiren's idea of legitimacy in the Chinese tradition.

Engetsu's proposals were sometimes a little radical for his readers, and

in fact another work, about which little is known, seems to have been confiscated and destroyed by order of Go-Daigo. But Engetsu, also the author
of the noted treatise *Chūshōshi* (Master of the Centered and Correct),[84]
clearly belonged to a widely accepted world of ideas that explicitly incorporated "Chinese" notions of change and sovereignty as much as they did
"Japanese" notions. This was considered not in the least unusual. Thus,
if Engetsu could find Chinese models to underlie the Japanese experience
and the position of the imperial house, was it possible to go further and
argue that *kami* protection and divine descent were not in fact a sure guarantee for the imperial house, that the imperial line could indeed come to
an end? One affirmative answer to this was provided by Go-Daigo's contemporary, former emperor Hanazono.

Hanazono first addressed the issue in 1324 when, having read Ban Biao's
seminal essay on the *Mandate of Kings*, he expressed serious doubts about
one of Ban Biao's basic arguments, namely, that the ruler inherits the right
to rule from the founding ancestor of his house.[85] In his 1330 essay "Admonitions to the Crown Prince" (*Kaitaishi sho*) he went a step further;
rejecting "common wisdom," he informed Crown Prince Kazuhito (later
Emperor Kōgon) that there was no inherent reason why the imperial line
could not come to an end:[86]

Simply you take the claim that you are of the lineage of past sovereigns and
arrogantly hope for that time when you will attain to the weighty appointment
over the myriad affairs. . . . This is akin to throwing out a net and waiting for the
fish to trap themselves, or not doing any cultivating and hoping that the grains
will ripen. Attaining this [rank?], how is it not difficult? Even if one were to hold
that through diligent effort one would thereby attain it, in all likelihood this is
not [the same as] making it one's own possession. It is for this reason that though
the government of Ch'in was powerful it gave way to the Han, and though Sui
Yang flourished he was destroyed by the T'ang. Notwithstanding, foolish flatterers
hold that in our country the Imperial line is of one lineage and is not the same
as this foreign country (*gaikoku*) where the cermonial cauldron is transferred on
the basis of virtue and where people contend for sovereignty [chase the deer] on
the basis of raw power; thus even though [an emperor's] virtue may be miniscule
there is not as in neighboring countries (*rinkoku*) the danger of [people] waiting
for the time to pounce, and thus even though the government be disordered there
is no fear that those of a different family will snatch it by violence. The reason for
this is the assistance of the legacy of the Imperial ancestors, a far superior tradition than that of other countries (*yokoku*). . . . The lack of knowledge of court
gentlemen and ladies, that they listen to these words and all of them think them
appropriate. Ignorantly they think this, and they are deeply in error.

Hanazono's views—rejecting the tenet that continuity through the imperial institution is a notable and unique characteristic of Japan, arguing that divine descent is a poor ideology of political legitimation, and believing that the imperial institution could cease to exist—are not ones generally associated with members of the imperial family or its apologists. Nonetheless, Hanazono's observations, made in part because he wanted to avoid the extinction of the imperial family, accord remarkably well with Go-Daigo's historical understanding. Times had indeed changed; informing assumptions about the social order and structure of power were being challenged across the board, and clear-eyed assessment was in order. For Go-Daigo this meant that the imperial institution must be given a fresh start, and an ideology articulated by a member of the imperial family that reflected an awareness of social changes in the fourteenth century.

Overall, Go-Daigo, unlike most, was aware both of the general intellectual environment and of the range and type of arguments that were being put forward. Given the multiplicity of viewpoints on even the most fundamental of questions (which means, in effect, that there was no standard ideology), Go-Daigo's efforts to address the future thus make eminent sense. What things did he envisage?

GO-DAIGO'S VISION OF THE FUTURE

Go-Daigo's sense of his time was that the existing polity had come to a dead end and that a different approach was required. With respect to the imperial family—or, more specifically, to Go-Daigo and his imperial line—Go-Daigo's vision is fairly clear. Yet it is important to note that this vision also contained within it a sense that, as with Hanazono, the existing imperial family could well be eliminated. Thus, a new Imperium, a medieval sovereignty that consciously broke with the past, could not simply come into existence by decree, but had to take account of social and political change.

Throughout the Kenmu Revolution Go-Daigo introduced a number of policy initiatives. For example, while retaining the notion and social status of the aristocracy, he capitalized upon the aristocracy's loss of control over its sources of income and its ongoing generational fragmentation: he tried to reorient its privileges into benefices dependent upon the imperial gift, and to divest it of automatic access to power and station. Go-Daigo did not eliminate the aristocracy, any more than he eliminated inconvenient sections of the imperial family, but he did supersede it. In not dissimilar fashion, he tried to reorient traditional privilege within the religious establishment in order to create a subsidiary accompaniment to the imperial rank. In both these areas (and, while not addressed here, in the commercial and economic realms too) Go-Daigo's efforts were far more than simply a manifestation of a desire to gain at the expense of other elements of the traditional polity; rather, he did not accept the assumptions by which these entities had for centuries enjoyed privilege.[87]

Equally to the point, Go-Daigo's vision of the future had taken account of the major medieval political phenomenon, the rising status of the warrior class. Go-Daigo's antipathy toward the Kamakura Bakufu is well known. Likewise, events were to demonstrate that he was equally opposed to the Ashikaga attempt to establish an autonomous military administration. This basic attitude has usually been construed as evidence that Go-Daigo was antagonistic toward the warrior class as a social group, with that perception forming part of a broader evaluation of Go-Daigo as acting without regard to the social changes of his century. However, the reality was somewhat different, and more nuanced.

Go-Daigo shared with the warrior class (not by any stretch of the imagination a monolithic group) a clear sense that political power in the early fourteenth century could not be effectively exercised without access to military force. His first foray against the Bakufu in 1324 had taught him this lesson, and he never forgot (as the sword in the Daitokuji portrait reveals). In acknowledging, and consistently acting upon, this reality, Go-Daigo made an immense psychological break with the traditions of imperial and aristocratic culture. Hanazono, too, had acknowledged that legitimacy (itself a vexing question in the fourteenth century) alone was no basis for asserting claims, but Go-Daigo's embrace of coercion was a major step; it was also the first truly medieval statement about the nature of sovereignty. Having made this psychological break, the issue confronting Go-Daigo was not one of how to avoid the military, but of how best to control it as an integral part of the future.

It is apparent from Go-Daigo's policies toward the warrior class[88] that he anticipated no particular ideological challenge to the notion that he as emperor possessed the legitimacy to exercise ultimate authority. For one thing, there is little evidence that warriors had taken the existence of the Kamakura Bakufu as a sign of a particular inevitable historical trend; or presented another way, the readiness with which warriors united to destroy that Bakufu in the knowledge that this could only result in the triumph of Go-Daigo's campaign to assert unified imperial authority is hardly strong evidence for arguing that warriors would be opposed to an imperial regime. For another thing, the fact that the Ashikaga took close to half a century to consolidate recognition of their claims to sovereign powers does not suggest (their assertions and hopes apart) a strong and broad-based sense that a warrior polity was inherently preferable to an imperial one.

Go-Daigo's policies reflect his recognition that in the future no central regime, even his own, would endure unless it actively harnessed the interests of warriors. Thus, and not for one moment disregarding the intense rivalries and traditional affiliations within the warrior class, we see policies that gave great discretion to warriors as much as they asserted the primacy of imperial authority. For example, Go-Daigo gave provincial constables far greater authority and greater recognition of their provincial position than had ever been the case under the Kamakura Bakufu. His policy on confirmation of land rights, acknowledging finally the primacy of actual current possession, likewise gave greater legal security than had been the case earlier, and concurrently recognized virtually all acquisitions and divisions of land made at the expense of aristocratic proprietors. In return, Go-Daigo demanded that prior claims to privilege (such as the status of former Kamakura vassals) be abandoned and that all warriors place themselves in the service of the Court when necessary. In implementing these policies Go-Daigo exhibited a fairly clear understanding both of the reality of provincialism and of the varied social circumstances in different regions of the country. (No doubt the opportunities for extended travel throughout the nation that had been thrust upon Go-Daigo and his confidants when sent into exile by the Kamakura regime played a part here.)

Go-Daigo was nonetheless unyielding on one point, his unchallenged supremacy. Hence, while he accepted that the warrior estate was part of the future, he did not accept any notion that warriors (or anyone else for that matter) should enjoy prerogatives or autonomy outside his new state. Thus he was willing to grant much regional discretion, but he also established regional commands under imperial princes that were intended to function somewhat like statelets. More than simply organizational responses to the conditions of the time (and there was not inconsiderable ferment during the Kenmu Revolution), these policies and measures suggest another aspect of Go-Daigo's vision of the future. Simply put, Go-Daigo realized that without a central polity led by an emperor who alone enjoyed ideological legitimacy, and who thus provided the only sense of national unity, the forces of regionalism would assert themselves. Amid this, no doubt, the future of the imperial family would become problematic, a fate against which Go-Daigo and his progeny (a remarkably martial cohort of imperials) were quite prepared to struggle indefinitely.[89] In the case of Prince Kaneyoshi, this even meant creating the new royal title of King of Japan in order to out-legitimize opponents and inject new ideological issues; as we know, this produced, under Ashikaga Yoshimitsu, a whole new dimension to the medieval debates over sovereignty. But at a very fundamental level Go-Daigo's vision recognized the multiple possibilities for royal symbols, and within that was entertained an unflinching possibility: if there was to be no Go-Daigo line, the fate of the imperial house otherwise was irrelevant, and political power would pass elsewhere permanently.

GO-DAIGO'S VISION encompassed his vision of himself, of what he would like a new Imperium to look like, and of what he thought society was going to look like in the future. He was quite aware that an old system was in the process of collapse, that a new history was being written, and that his age presented great opportunities. The only issue was how best to seize and shape those chances, and then find a means of surviving the transition to the new age. Ultimately, Go-Daigo was unsuccessful in his quest. Yet, in this, he exemplifies those who repudiated the assumptions of the Heian-Kamakura age and indelibly shaped the medieval period. Go-Daigo's grand visions and ideology, nonetheless, lost out not because of his claims — as we have seen, those claims and Go-Daigo's image remained potent and could not be ignored — but because of their encounter with another part of the vision, the need to control enough military might to undergird and stabilize an ideology.

CHAPTER 7

Re-envisioning Women in the Post-Kamakura Age

HITOMI TONOMURA

H OW DID WOMEN in Japan's post-Kamakura society situate themselves and give meanings to this era? This is a daunting question inasmuch as women, just as did men, lived in diverse circumstances, met varied opportunities, and negotiated different requirements. Historical sources, unevenly produced and preserved on the one hand, and reflecting the diverse reality on the other hand, offer no singular or unified interpretation. The multiplicity of representation, marked by inconsistencies and disjuncture, indeed challenges our task to recover a women-centered history, especially one that could characterize an era (the medieval age), a historian's construct that assumes a measurable degree of internal coherence.[1] Without denying these difficulties, then, I seek out the dominant trends and interrelated principles that significantly marked or altered the social relations of women and men in and after the fourteenth century. For this purpose, I shall impose an organizing framework of status categories and separately discuss aristocrats, warriors, and commoners while also considering patterns that were particular to the female sex across classes.

SUBJECTIVITY AND THE BODY OF THE ARISTOCRAT

"Make War Not Love": The Meaning of the Undiscussed

From the early years of the fourteenth century, the discursive field that follows them seems only sparsely dotted with memoirs and diaries (*nikki*) composed in the "woman's hand (*onna-de*)," a means and mode of expression that elegantly shaped the literary space that preceded it. Formulated in *hirakana*, the Japanese syllabary, the woman's hand expressed the author's subjectivity in writing far more than did men's works written (mostly) in Chinese. The tenth through fourteenth centuries marked an era that would be unmatched until modern times in the dense proliferation of consciously female creativity. Hino Meishi's memoir, the *Takemukigaki*, from the mid-fourteenth century is the last in the stream of aristocratic women's personal voices to come down to us.[2] In later medieval times, men continued to write memoirs and journals that were "less a product of quiet reflection of life at home" than they were "works inspired by some kind of [physical] transfer—whether evacuation or the mobilization for war."[3]

Unlike the "Mother of Michitsuna" or "Sei Shōnagon" (Shōnagon is her title) and many other writers who preceded her, the author of *Takemukigaki* left her full name. Although she may have been known to her contemporaries as "Takemuki (Facing the Bamboo),"[4] a name associated with her room, the full name of Hino Meishi (d. 1358) has survived. Hino was a northern line of the Fujiwara that produced a number of important scholars.[5] In the complex political maneuvers of the Restoration and anti-Restoration movement of the 1330s, some Hino men (Suketomo and Toshimoto—Meishi's uncle and a distant relative) sided with Go-Daigo and were executed by order of the Kamakura Bakufu in 1332. Meishi's father, Sukena (1285–1338), who had attained the Senior Second Rank, sided with the Northern line and managed to ride the political current long enough to flourish in the post-Restoration imperial court and in the Ashikaga Bakufu. Meishi's brother's daughter (Nariko) married shogun Ashikaga Yoshimitsu. Ashikaga shoguns—Yoshimochi, Yoshinori, Yoshimasa, and Yoshimi—all had a Hino woman as a wife. Meishi is separated by five generations from Hino Tomiko (1440–96), Ashikaga Yoshimasa's famed wife who bears the historiographical burden of having caused the Ōnin War (1467–77).

Like Lady Nijō, who wrote *Towazugatari* (The Confessions of Lady Nijō) about half a century before her,[6] Meishi served in the court of the Jimyōin line (the Northern Court) emperors. Situated in the eventful

years of the shift from what we call the Kamakura to the Nanbokuchō
period, her memoir comes in two volumes, covering 1329–33 and 1337–49,
respectively. The first volume opens with the coming-of-age ceremony of
Prince Kazuhito, and continues with Meishi's romance with and marriage
to Saionji Kinmune (1310–35), intertwined with the ups and downs in
Emperor Go-Daigo's plots, including the enthronement of Prince Kazuhito as Emperor Kōgen after Go-Daigo's arrest by the Kamakura Bakufu.
After a four-year lapse, Meishi opens her second volume with the three-
years-old ceremony of her son, Sanetoshi, moving on to his coming-of-age
ceremony at age eight, and his promotion to the position of *gonchūnagon*
(Provisional Middle Counselor), Senior Third Rank, at the memoir's end.
Though volume two also includes descriptions of her father's death, her
travels to shrines and temples, and her reflections on religious views, its
self-conscious attention to the rise of her son in his lineage and at the imperial court underlines the significance of her second career as his mother.
Meishi died in 1358 when her son was a twenty-four-year-old *gondainagon*
(Provisional Major Counselor) holding the Senior Second Rank.[7]

Meishi's memoir is an appropriate metaphor for the close of the age
of the female voice. The memoir's descriptive categories—ceremonies,
romance, religion, and so forth—shape it as a conventional female hand,
mostly a product of wealth, leisure, and relative freedom from violence
enjoyed by capital aristocrats for centuries.[8] But by means of silence, or
intentional concealment, Meishi confronts the relevance of these categories and subverts the meaning of the female hand in surroundings that
were constant only in their unpredictability, violence, and turmoil. By her
strategy of exclusion that draws a gap between her two volumes, Meishi
conspires to misrepresent the reality and invalidates the universe of possible discourse embedded in the female hand. Juxtaposition of Meishi's
writing against the dramatized narrative in a war chronicle, the *Taiheiki*,
provides a version of a more multidimensional vision of reality. The following is a rough summary of a chapter in the *Taiheiki* titled "About Lord
Kitayama's treachery," which describes the events of 1335 that are centered
around Saionji Kinmune (Lord Kitayama), Meishi's husband.[9]

THE SAIONJI FAMILY, since the time of the Jōkyū War (1221), has
been more intimate with the Bakufu than with the court.[10] But it is Kinmune's own brother (Kinshige) who accuses him of harboring a treacherous intention whose concrete consequence in fact had been revealed to
Go-Daigo in his earlier dream.

The imperial army, numbering 2,000, rushes to the Saionji family's

Kitayama mansion. Kinmune meets the troops without surprise, apparently a visible sign of admitted guilt. But his wife [that is, Meishi], maids, and servants, not knowing why this is happening, run around and most flee. Soldiers enter the mansion and begin destroying its ceiling and curtains to find Kinmune's missing collaborator. Kinmune willingly accompanies Sadahira, a man charged with this mission, in hopes of proving his innocence. But he is detained in a narrow space at Sadahira's house. His supposed conspirator, also arrested, is tortured for three days and nights, and after confessing all, is pulled out to the riverbed and executed. On the following night, the imperial council decides to banish Kinmune to Izumo. Sadahira goes to report this to Meishi. In tears, Meishi visits Kinmune and finds him sunk behind a tightly built lattice door, about to float away in his own tears. Kinmune tells his pregnant wife to raise the child with hope and care, and hands over music sheets for secret *biwa* melodies out of his charm bag. He takes a brush and writes a poem[11] on the outer piece of paper, but his falling tears dilute the ink. Meishi takes it, tears and all, as her husband's memento.

While Meishi is there in the depth of her sorrow, an official arrives to announce that Kinmune shall be handed over first to Nagatoshi who will then deliver him elsewhere in the morning. In the midst of the commotion, Meishi hides herself to watch what will happen next. One of several hundred armed men pulls Kinmune out by rope. No description can do justice to how Meishi feels while watching this. As Kinmune begins to climb into a palanquin positioned in the yard, Sadahira calls out to Nagatoshi, "Quickly." Understanding this to be an order to kill, Nagatoshi runs up to Kinmune, grabs his hair, pulls him face down, and cuts off his head. Watching this, Meishi collapses. She is helped into her palanquin by her maids and returns to the Kitayama mansion, now a deserted ruin. Meishi gives birth to a son on the one-hundredth-day anniversary of Kinmune's execution. With no proper ceremonies, paternal protection, or a wet nurse's care, the mother herself embraces and cares for the child. Before the bedding even has a chance to dry, however, Sadahira's messenger arrives, offering to take the child, if a boy, to the court to provide a wet nurse. Meishi suspects deceit and danger and has Kinmune's mother declare that the child has died. Soon the shogun's rule is revived, and it is none other than Saionji Sanetoshi, Kinmune's son, who continues the Saionji line and serves the shogunate.[12]

MEISHI'S "WOMAN'S HAND" stands structurally and thematically opposed but interrelated to the war tale's insistence on dramatizing the bloody spectacle of a dismembered aristocratic male body. Situated between her marriage and her son's three-years-old ceremony, Meishi's "intentional omission" includes the death of her husband and the birth of her son. Her silence forms a part of a discursive process on a continuum; it amplifies rather than diminishes the meaning of these events and their impact on her life and status, and on the child's future. Whether motivated by political, psychological, aesthetic, or literary considerations, Meishi's strategy of concealment symbolizes the historical forces operating far beyond the bounds of her discursive authority embedded in the "woman's hand." The undiscussable represents articulation of the female gender. Meishi maintains an illusion of elegance by excluding the execution from her discursive field; the chaos and bloodshed that would spread across society thereafter left no room for the woman's hand.[13]

The Aristocratic Woman at Work: Crossing the Categories

The epistemological break represented by Meishi's memoir did not, however, signify that aristocratic women ceased their writing activities altogether. Women in the court began keeping daily records that were more public log than personal statement, a trend illustrated by *Oyudono no ue no nikki* (Daily Records of the Honorable Lady of the Imperial Office of Housekeeping), which lists the details of imperial housekeeping in a strictly businesslike style—with no poetic grace, no subjective viewpoints, though still in *hirakana*.[14] According to Saiki Kazuma, the format and choice of subjects in *Oyudono* closely resemble those in the Palace Diary (*Denjō nikki*) that the imperial secretariat (*kurōdo*) had kept from the late ninth through mid-twelfth centuries. Several centuries later, *Oyudono* essentially revived the tradition, but with two fundamental differences: it was written by women instead of men, and in Japanese instead of Chinese.[15] Although the extant version of *Oyudono* dates from 1477 and ends in 1826, it is speculated that there had been an earlier section that was destroyed in the fires of the Ōnin War. Female officials (or, ladies-in-waiting: *nyōbō*)—with such titles as *tenji* and *shōji*—took turns recording matters such as the date, weather, visitors' names, food consumed by the emperor, and ceremonial details, for the duration of at least three and a half centuries.[16] Female officials with similar titles also issued "female palace official's pronouncements" (called *nyōbō hōsho* from the Kamakura period on; *naishi no sen*, earlier), which transmitted the imperial will in *hirakana*. Although women of various titles who were close to the emperors had been issuing these types of documents since the ninth century, the volume and functional significance of their pronouncements in the Muromachi period greatly surpassed those of earlier eras.[17]

Perhaps women's involvement in this kind of imperial task is hardly surprising, given the work of female officials, such as Meishi, who, like her father Sukena and her lover Kinmune, held a position of great responsibility in the court of the retired emperor Go-Fushimi. Meishi frequently mentions the names of these male relations along with others in her description of ceremonies and processions, allowing us to envision a gender-integrated work space (the palace) and work goals (the maintenance of imperial prestige) that were, in the first instance, class and status specific. Unlike Lady Nijō, who in *Towazugatari* records sometimes forced sexual relationships with emperors and aristocrats, Meishi does not mention any instance of sexual servitude.[18] Instead, she proudly describes the central role she held in various administrative responsibilities. Before the coming-of-age ceremony for Prince Kazuhito, Go-Fushimi's seventeen-year-old son, for example, Meishi is commissioned to reduce a large diagram of the ceremonial setup that was initially drawn by the Council of State. After some attempts, she successfully completes the task and receives much praise for her work. Her drawing is entered in Go-Fushimi's diary and, in Meishi's words, "there it remains to this day."[19]

Meishi is a more than an interested observer of political vicissitudes over 1331–33; her position and family are directly involved. For instance, she notes the movements of Emperor Go-Daigo, who was missing as of 1331/8/24, and of the "eastern barbarians" (*Azuma no ebisudomo*: i.e., warriors of the Kamakura Bakufu) then in pursuit. She notes that emperors Go-Fushimi and Hanazono, along with Prince Kazuhito, have moved to the Rokujō Palace near the Bakufu's Rokuhara headquarters.[20] The Bakufu then orders the accession of Prince Kazuhito to replace Go-Daigo, a situation that quickly demands Meishi's direct involvement.

The ceremony takes place on 1331/9/22. Meishi is concerned about the irregularity in the escort size; although there are to be forty female attendants, only thirty or so could be assembled. Her greater preoccupation, however, is with the status of the sacred regalia. Because the sacred sword and jewel are still with Go-Daigo, a substitute sword is used. When Go-Daigo's capture finally brings the regalia back to the palace, it is Meishi and two other attendants who receive them. Describing in detail the condition of the box that contains the regalia, Meishi is deeply moved by the idea that they have come down to her time since the days of the gods.

More awesome still, she takes turns with another attendant to guard them day and night.[21] The enthronement ceremony takes place on 1332/3/22. This is an event of grave significance for Meishi; she stands at the ceremony behind the new emperor, a duty of visible prestige. For this work, she is later granted the Junior Third rank.[22] On 1333/5/7, she witnesses in disbelief—though it had been anticipated—as the pro–Go-Daigo force razes the Rokuhara headquarters, and worries about the safety of the emperors and her lover.[23]

Meishi's memoir demonstrates that women bore much responsibility in running the imperial administration. Women's work, in fact, was becoming increasingly more visible in the fourteenth century and thereafter. Even though personal diaries went unwritten (or failed to survive) after Meishi's time, women in the court continued to exercise their hand in a secretarial capacity, keeping a daily log and transmitting the imperial will. In the households of the Fujiwara regents and of the shogun as well, women with such titles as *senji no tsubone* ("[Aristocratic] Women in Charge of Decrees") wrote letters and transmitted the regent's and shogun's orders.[24]

There was, then, a dramatic shift in the style and meaning of women's writing after Hino Meishi's time, when the highly literate women actively served as scribes in the country's most prestigious institutions. Women's writing no longer expressed the author's personal thoughts, feelings, and artistic creativity. Displacing female subjectivity with objective instrumentality, it exclusively described men's lives and transmitted men's ideas and orders. This situation clearly invalidates the dualistic equation that associates the public sphere with Chinese writing and maleness and the private sphere with Japanese writing and femaleness. As Wakita Haruko has remarked, a "domestic" record of the imperial family's "private household" is a "public" record, inasmuch as private matters in the imperial household —from baths and ceremonial arrangements to financial transactions and transmission of imperial communications—all embody a public quality.[25] In earlier centuries as well, Japanese imperial bureaucracy had only feebly invested itself in promoting a clear-cut separation between public and private spheres, leading to the invasive strength of familial interests in office holding and landholding. This situation, however, differed from earlier situations in that, now, the public record that had been written by men was written in Japanese and by women, the supposed guardians of the private sphere. The imperial court of the post-Kamakura era further obfuscated the idealized dichotomy between the domestic and the public upon which, according to some anthropologists, male prestige rests.[26]

Your Bed or Mine? Transferring the Body and Power

"What about you? You are afraid of the snow!" exclaims Kinmune when Meishi hesitates to leave the fireside to join the emperor and others in the East Garden where the bamboo droops under the weight of the snow.[27] This was in the eleventh month of 1331. Meishi's romance with Kinmune, then twenty-two years old, apparently began some time before then.[28] They frequently met at a neutral spot that was neither her home, his home, nor the palace (their workplace). Awoken by the chirping of birds, as the clouds in the mountain peaks began to pale, they would have to go separate ways in their carts.[29] Returning to her home in the morning, she might slip off her garments and catch some sleep. On one such morning, a palace attendant comes to summon Meishi by the emperor's order. Noting the clothes strewn about, the attendant makes remarks about Meishi's trysting while nudging her to get up. Meishi tries to ignore the messenger and pulls the covers over her head.[30]

At home on the first day of spring in 1333, Meishi receives from Kinmune a poem written on pale crimson paper soaked in fragrance, in which he pledges himself to her for every spring to come.[31] Thus Kinmune is to begin visiting Meishi openly—that is, their relationship now receives public recognition as a suprasexual relationship of reasonable durability and familial interest. Meishi expresses fears about having committed herself to the position of a wife of a man higher in rank than her own family. The political situation grows increasingly unpredictable, however, preventing Kinmune from visiting Meishi frequently.[32]

About then, with mounting anxiety, Meishi reports on the precarious position of the Rokuhara. Her father, Sukena, takes up residence in Kiyomizu and calls Meishi to move in also. In the fourth month, Kinmune steals a night to visit Meishi at her father's Kiyomizu residence. On the seventeenth day of the fifth month (1333), Ashikaga Takauji attacks Rokuhara. Amid the ensuing commotion, Meishi is housed, temporarily, in a quarter (Myōondō) of the Saionji family's Kitayama mansion. The retired emperors Go-Fushimi, Hanazono, and Kōgen return to the capital, as do Meishi's father and brother, who had taken Buddhist vows. In the middle of the sixth month, the Saionji family tells Meishi to move to the main part of the Kitayama mansion as Kinmune's official wife. Meishi returns to her natal residence for a visit. The first volume closes as she rides along the hilly roads in a palanquin that was sent from Kitayama, and anxiously contemplates what her life will be like in the future.[33]

Meishi's marriage to Kinmune, even if it occurred in an extraordinary political climate, nonetheless vividly illustrates a stage in the long pattern of transformation in Japanese marriage practices. Marriage in premodern Japan never resembled its medieval Western counterpart: "a divinely ordained institution designed by God and strengthened by Jesus for the licit expression of the sexual impulse, the procreation of children, and the mutual pursuit of salvation."[34] There was no divine power that sanctioned it, no concern for performance of sex for procreation only, nor any idea of marriage connected to salvation. But from ancient through medieval times, marriage underwent fundamental changes: to put it simply, from a primarily sexual relationship between a woman and a man to a more publicly elaborate arrangement between two houses (or lineages).[35] It also changed from an arrangement that kept the woman's body stationary (at her house) and the man's body mobile, to one that transferred the woman's body to the man's house. The transformation in marriage practice signified, above all, the reorganization of sexuality and a social reevaluation of the woman's body.

Family, including marriage relations, is a basic and deeply embedded social institution that resists quick transformation. Takamure Itsue, a pioneering women's historian, charted the transformational pattern not only in marriage but also in women's status throughout Japanese history. Her understanding of the transformation in marriage customs and their impact on women is based on the analytical distinctions she invests in three terms: *tsumadoi* (visiting a wife), *mukotori* (taking a groom or son-in-law), and *yometori* (taking a bride or daughter-in-law). In *tsumadoi*, the man visited the woman; in *mukotori*, the man lived at the woman's house; in *yometori* the woman lived at the man's house. She further divides these into a number of subcategories. Conceptualizing historical transformations along a linear axis, she has argued that marriage gradually shifted from *tsumadoi* to *mukotori*, with the crucial change to *yometori* occurring in the fourteenth century—that is, about Meishi's time. The new marriage system accommodated the intensified need on the part of the patriarchal institution to maintain private property along the patrilineal line of descent and inheritance.[36]

Takamure's work laid the foundation for all subsequent inquiry, and in so doing also has invited vigorous reexamination and reinterpretation of her categories and analyses.[37] We can question Takamure's employment of the term *mukotori*, for instance. *Mukotori* was not a mirror image of *yometori* in which the woman was incorporated into the man's line, even if she did not change her surname to his—just as Hino Meishi did not become a Saionji. In the situation described as *mukotori*, the man did not become incorporated into the woman's lineage.[38] Scholars who followed Takamure employed more precise anthropological terms to clarify changes in marital residential models—duolocal, uxorilocal, neolocal, and virilocal—as did William H. McCullough, for example.[39] In addition, Takamure's eagerness to resist and revise the previous scholarship, which had tended to ignore any *mukotori* pattern, also compelled her to name all subphases between the "pure *mukotori*" and the "pure *yometori*" stages as variations of *mukotori*, not variations of *yometori*. This scheme has in part allowed her to date the beginning of Japan's patriarchy (*kafuchōsei*) in the fourteenth century, the point marked by the switch from her *mukotori* to *yometori*. Along with McCullough, however, most scholars today see the beginning of patrilocal marriage (or *yometori*) several centuries earlier than did Takamure.[40] Japanese historians concerned with the "establishment of patriarchy" therefore typically date it in Heian and Kamakura times.

The Japanese debate over patriarchy (*kafuchōsei*) has focused more on the issue of timing than on the meaning of the term or practice. Correlating the beginning of patrilocal marriage with the beginning of patriarchy, the debate rarely has sought to provide a precise definition for the institution that is called patriarchy. Takamure's and recent scholars' attempts to give a specific date—1336, for example, for the end of a "fictional *mukotori*" phase—is, in my view, artificial and meaningless because it undermines the very notion of historical *process* as distinguished from *events*.

Despite these problems, the original classificatory categories employed by Takamure—*tsumadoi*, *mukotori*, and *yometori*—have real analytical value. Instead of considering marital *locations* in the first instance (as with the term "patrilocal," for example), Takamure's categories unambiguously register the persons—and their bodies—as the strategic focus for the operation of any marriage institution. Takamure's terms privilege the shifting meanings that came to be encoded on the body, especially the female body, within the changing spatial organization of marriage. I believe that it is this body-centered approach that enabled her to link the changing marriage institution analytically to the changing valuation of women, body, and sexuality.

For Takamure, the fourteenth century (Nanbokuchō, in her words) marked a watershed in the history of sexuality. The practice of "taking the bride" organized the appropriation of female sexuality in a new era, which demanded one-sided chastity and imprisoned bodies to beget patrilineal offspring, all for the perpetuation of the lineage's private property. Takamure's paradigm offers a way to understand a broad network of interconnected practices that began to converge upon the woman's body. In this sense, I believe that the fourteenth century—whether or not *yometori* marriage or patriarchy actually began then—can meaningfully signal a dense transfer point for power relations, in the Foucauldian meaning of the term.

We can assess Meishi's marriage to Kinmune by following her body. Initially, the marriage was a visiting (duolocal) marriage. Meishi's case varied a little from the standard duolocal model in that they met at a neutral place, probably for political reasons. The duolocal model that Heian literature often illustrates was built on the man's genuine, presumed, or imaginary, attraction to the woman. Without it, the relationship would cease. Each visit was a performance that demanded appropriate knowledge, sensitivity, and grace regarding the accepted aesthetic and poetic conventions. Meishi's description of her sexual encounters with Kinmune seems to fit the formula elegantly, even when Meishi retorts in her poem, "but I cannot be the only woman you are sleeping with," in response to his apologies for a lapse in visits. "Marriage" in a duolocal style constituted a redefinition of the ongoing sexual relationship in terms of expected durability, from the evanescent nightly sexual arrangements to one with an expectation of long-lasting and perhaps more frequent encounters.[41] This was the marriage mode that Takamure has overromanticized by concentrating on the supposed sexual freedom that it gave women. Whether or not the visited woman consistently appreciated this precarious arrangement is questionable, however, given that men often had multiple bedmates. The mother of Michitsuna, who wrote *Kagerō nikki* (The Gossamer Years), for example, expressed anger at the infrequency of her husband's visits, while his primary wife Tokihime moved into his mansion in a patrilocal *yometori* style.[42]

For Meishi, the progress from what we might call a "dating" stage to the "visiting marriage" stage promised that sexual unions would be pursued more openly at Meishi's house, though this happened infrequently for strategic reasons related to the ongoing political upheaval, at least according to his explanations. As if to follow a standard model, Meishi's marriage later changed to a patrilocal (or *yometori*) marriage in which Meishi moved into

Kinmune's Kitayama mansion.[43] Before the full transfer into the Kitayama mansion, however, Meishi first stayed for a time in a structure adjacent to it. This intermediate stage may have had a ritual function—to provide a period of modified patrilocal arrangements in order gradually to break the taboo on two female lines (the Saionji's and Hino's) sharing one hearth, a legacy of an earlier era.

The centuries that followed Meishi's time increasingly saw a regulation of marriage into an uncomplicated patrilocal arrangement that dislodged the female's body (in the literal sense of the term, *yometori*) from her natal surroundings to the house of her male sexual partner. No longer was the marriage primarily a redefinition of sexual relations between the two partners (with their parents' approval). It was, more than ever, lineages that mattered.

Takamure has noted that the transfer of the female body in the new standardized marriage practice increasingly took on a quality of public spectacle in the form of an elaborate ceremony that announced and socially sealed the arrangement. In the early Heian duolocal or matrilocal practice, marriage began with the man's sharing of rice cakes at the hearth of the woman's house after the parental (prearranged) "discovery" of the two in the daughter's bed. The ceremony was small and private, involving no outside spectator and enacted only for the marrying families.[44] Meishi mentions no ceremony of either kind in her memoir.

The custom of sealing marriage with a public ceremony evolved slowly and unevenly, as did most other changes in the marriage institution. Before the spectacle could be truly grand, the notion of patrilocal marriage had to be unambiguously instituted and fully legitimated, demanding, for example, eradication of the taboo concerning sharing of a hearth by two women in two matrilineal lines. Tōin Kinkata's granddaughter's marriage to Konoe Michitsugu in 1346, only about a decade after Meishi's marriage to Kinmune, illustrates the difficult but certain transformation toward the ideal patrilocal marriage.[45] The ceremony took place in the patrilocal mode, at the Konoe residence under the authority of Konoe Mototsugu, the groom's father. As befitted a "take-the-bride" marriage, the husband's side dispatched a palanquin to fetch the bride, Kinkata's granddaughter. The bride's palanquin, accompanied by three samurai, thirteen servants, three ox hands, a cart for the maids, and a cart for the bride's mother, proceeded to the Konoe residence. A later event demonstrates that the fathers of the two families regarded this union to be symbolically illegitimate. About two months later the bride's father and grandfather visited the

Konoe residence at the insistence of the Konoe family. There, a small sake-drinking ceremony was held. As it turned out, however, the "hosts" of the ceremony were the bride's father and grandfather, not the groom's, despite the location of the ceremony. Apparently, the initial wedding format and the marriage mode that it underscored were still somewhat unacceptable for these traditionally minded aristocrats. They symbolically reformulated the marriage with a *mukotori*-inspired cup of sake.[46]

Patrilocal marriage occurred with some thematic variations in the marital residential setup. Although Takamure has neatly organized these variations along a linear axis, it seems more likely that each family's economic or social conditions had much to do with the choice. An entry for 1481/2/11 in the diary of Kanroji Chikanaga (*Chikanaga kyōki*) demonstrates one such variation. The marriage of Motonaga, the adopted son of Chikanaga, brought the bride into a newly constructed section of his father's residence located on Karasuma Street. The entry explicitly uses the term "*yometori*," and Chikanaga often refers to the newlyweds' quarter as "the separate quarter (*ichimon betsumune*)."[47] This was an essentially patrilocal marriage, but by establishing a separate quarter in a neolocal mode, the families continued to uphold the legacy—now perhaps a habit—of the earlier *mukotori* ideal that prevented the sharing of one hearth by women of two different families. This example suggests that, at the end of the fifteenth century, a full acceptance of *yometori* marriage was still conditional on the removal of the hearth taboo, at least for these aristocrats. But for the woman, *mukotori* marriage that allowed her to stay home had been long abandoned, even if some kinks in the symbolism survived.

The slow transformation in marriage practice paralleled the gradual diminution of property rights of women in this close-knit social circle.[48] Before the fourteenth century, the highest-ranking female aristocrats held some of the biggest blocks of income in the country. From the tenth through eleventh centuries, the imperial family and the Fujiwara family, whose female members dominated the inner court, easily passed property between the two families. Thus property moved from Fujiwara Kaneie to Emperor Sanjō, then back to Fujiwara Michinaga (Kaneie's son) after Sanjō's death. In the late eleventh century, frequent conflicts that arose between the two families prompted the imperial family to shut out the Fujiwara in-laws by practicing patrilineal endogamy, using three generations of emperors (Go-Suzaku, Go-Reizei, and Go-Sanjō).[49] This coincided with the beginning of the so-called "*insei*" politics that centered around the authority of the retired emperors. Around the same time, from the eleventh through mid-twelfth centuries, the emperor's mother received the honorable title of *kokubo*, or "mother of the country," while an unmarried female member (who was not a mother at all but perhaps a sister or aunt) in the emperor's patrilineal family came to be designated as the emperor's *junbo*, something in the order of an "associate mother."[50] Blocks of property came to be passed through the hands of these "mothers," and perhaps through the hands of emperors' wives as well, as those of strategically adopted sons. To illustrate, Hachijō'in (d. 1211), a daughter of Emperor Toba and *junbo* of Emperor Nijō, held an estate composed of more than two hundred units. This strategy aimed to keep the property within the emperor's patrilineal family.

In the thirteenth century, the split within the emperor's patrilineal family between two rival brothers, Go-Fukakusa and Kameyama, gave rise to the practice of a "lifetime" bequest, with the destination after the holder's death designated by the father. Eventually most property was steered to one male heir. In the Jimyōin line, this started with the bequest given by Go-Fukakusa in 1304, and in the Daikakuji line, with the bequest given by Go-Uda in 1308. This marked the end of large-scale inheritance by women in the imperial line.

In the Fujiwara regents' line as well, the mechanism of lifetime inheritance was employed in the early thirteenth century—a century earlier than in the imperial family—with the bequest given to Senshūmon'in, daughter of Kujō Kanezane and wife of Emperor Go-Toba. This was after the Fujiwara regents' line had split into the Kujō and Konoe lines. Both the imperial and regents' lines, therefore, adopted the lifetime inheritance strategy shortly after the lineage was split into two interest groups.[51] To what extent female property-holding deteriorated thereafter in comparison with that of males is a matter that demands further exploration. It was a period of great financial distress for the entire aristocratic class that prompted, for example, Tōin Kinkazu to sell in 1483 *Entairyaku*, the diary of Tōin Kinkata, his ancestor from six generations before (d. 1359)—a true family heirloom.[52] One must wonder about the gender balance in the distribution of scarcity at that time.

As many scholars have pointed out, Takamure perhaps was overzealous in extending the time of *mukotori* marriage and idealizing its content. But Takamure's classic work has correctly pointed out that aristocratic women in post-Kamakura periods faced personal and economic conditions markedly different from those experienced by most of their female forebears of three centuries earlier. The woman's relationship to her own parents, spouse, children, and even her own body had been reformulated by the reality of physical transfer to the man's house.

Takamure developed her periodization scheme mostly by examining sources related to aristocratic families. She admits that, among warrior families, "confusion in marriage practices occurred early."[53] By the early Kamakura period, warrior-class women were already being given away to the man's family. The marriage of Yoritomo's niece (daughter of Ichijō Yoshiyasu, an aristocrat who was adopted as Yoritomo's brother) to Fujiwara Kujō Yoshitsune (aristocrat: regent Kujō Kanezane's son) illustrates the gap between the warrior class and the aristocratic class regarding what was considered proper in the early Kamakura period. Out of modesty, Yoritomo proposed to "give away" his niece to the aristocratic groom, a person of a higher social status. The regent interpreted this as the ultimate insult. Yoritomo therefore arranged to have Yoshitsune come to live at the Ichijō residence in the *mukotori* manner.[54]

The Kamakura Bakufu's chronicle, *Azuma kagami*, attaches relatively little significance to the marriages of the shogun, probably reflecting the custom of the time. Because the shoguns tended to be "imported" aristocrats from Kyoto, however, the marriage mode had to be negotiated. The entries for 1228/1/23 and 1230/1/7 casually mention, for instance, that Kujō Yoritsune, grandson of Yoshitsune, above, and the fourth shogun (r. 1226–44), visited Takegosho, the bride. An entry from 1230/12/9 describes, this time, her move to his quarters in a procession composed of only about ten samurai and two torchbearers besides her palanquin. The entry emphasizes that this was a "private ceremony (*mitsugi*)."[55] For the marriage of the sixth shogun, Prince Munetaka (r. 1252–66; Emperor Go-Saga's son, Go-Fukakusa's and Kameyama's brother), *Azuma kagami* spares considerably more space. It notes the adoption of the bride-to-be, Konoe Kanetsune's daughter, by Hōjō Tokiyori on 1260/2/5, Munetaka's entry into the bride's quarters nine days later, and finally *tokoro arawashi*—a ceremony associated with *mukotori* marriage, a month and a half later. Although the ceremony was more elaborate than the one mentioned for Yoritsune, it was not in the *yometori* style. The marrying couple was of aristocratic stock before adoption.[56]

Provincial warrior houses, such as the Imagawa, Ise, and Ogasawara, were different from the aristocrat-turned-warrior class men and women. They apparently practiced *yometori* marriage in the late Heian and Kamakura periods while aristocrats still held attachment to *mukotori* practices.[57] Even among the warrior class, however, the institution of publicly visible marriage ceremonies evolved slowly until the sixteenth century when the warlords (*daimyō*) demonstratively asserted their material strength in their unambiguously patrilocal marriage practice. A grand spectacle accompanying the marriage of Takeda Harunobu's daughter to Hōjō Ujimasa is described in an entry dated 1554/12 in a diary, *Myōhōjiki*. Clothes, gold, twelve palanquins, women, 3,000 horses along with 10,000 followers and forty-two chests, make up a partial list of items that adorned the bridal procession that was met by 5,000 persons.[58]

In this outward expression of the transfer, the woman's body became a measurable entity, symbolically enumerated in the material objects that accompanied her. Marriage became a "performed-for-an-audience" social drama in which the woman's body was a trophy for the man's conquest, not for sexual pleasure but for such external purposes as political or military alliances. The size of the spectacle doubtless depended on the strength of the house.[59] The most important actor in the arrangement was neither the groom nor the bride, but the father with the power to authorize the marriage and the subsequent family relations.

REQUIREMENTS OF THE WARRIOR SOCIETY

Economic Foundations for Military Power

The warrior class began marrying patrilocally earlier than did the aristocrats, but this marital arrangement preceded the notable decline in female property rights by several centuries. This discrepancy is not a contradiction, since much of the daughter's property in question came in the form of landed income rather than as property for personal use connected with the home. Like the aristocrats, the woman's property was also maintained separately from the property of the husband. Marriage, therefore, had little relevance to a daughter's property-holding status, except that she might gain an additional bequest from her husband.

The speed and the precise order by which the inheritance pattern altered varied greatly from one family to another. But for a period of two to three centuries, we can see a broad outline of transformation moving toward a definite goal: the consolidation of all property in the hands of one son through whom the family name would descend.[60] In the Kamakura period, the divided inheritance practice nearly guaranteed property rights to daughters, as it did to sons, and granted the recipient of either sex both the rights and the responsibilities attached to the land. This pattern, however, came to be gradually abandoned in favor of a lifetime bequest, and subsequently of a unitary inheritance mode that directed all the property to a primary son. In the Kobayakawa family, for example, a land parcel went from the husband, to his widow, to their daughter, and then to the primary son in the fourteenth century.[61] In this passage, the daughter's portion was designated as a lifetime holding; after her "use" it was to revert back to the main line headed by the primary son. Fukuo Takeichirō, who meticulously examined extant documents related to land and income transfer—including bequest, sale, and purchase—has indicated that Kamakura-period holding showed a gender ratio of seven to three between men and women. In the mid-fourteenth through early fifteenth centuries, women held 10 percent, and in the subsequent warring period, this fell to about 3 percent.[62] Generally speaking, bequests from husbands to wives came to be designated as lifetime portions earlier than did the daughters' portions.[63]

For the warrior class, land was often a concrete medium that bound a lord and a vassal with mutual obligations. In the Kamakura period, women's land rights (*shiki*) often entailed service and monetary obligations to the Bakufu. This was true to a certain extent in later years as well. Some women were involved in fulfilling the military obligations derived from their land during the chaotic era of the 1330s. Kusome of Hizen Province, for instance, dispatched in 1333 a proxy to destroy Hōjō Hidetoki at the Bakufu's Kyushu headquarters (*tandai*).[64] Women also received vassals' land in place of their dead male relatives. In 1340, an unmarried daughter of Ōtsuka Kazunari received a *jitō shiki* in place of her father.[65] When the family's resources were finally consolidated in the hands of one man, parts of these resources could be apportioned to daughters, sisters, and secondary sons as "protection" land or cash stipends. But receiving a stipend would be a far cry from having one's own land to manage and alienate to one's heir.[66]

Like memoirs by aristocratic women, documents from warrior-class women also diminish in number after the fourteenth century. This diminution reflected changes in the distribution of property-holding rights. Heian and Kamakura times had produced an abundance of documents written and signed by women of the propertied classes, including inheritance documents, sales and purchase slips, and records of suits over land rights. Among the 610 extant trial records of the Kamakura Bakufu between 1187 and 1332, approximately 15 percent were signed by women. When women's property rights, which had normally embodied the right to alienate as well as to hold, increasingly shifted to rights for the holder's lifetime only, the need to write devises to transmit land or wealth also disappeared. Kobayakawa Shigekage's daughters, for example, could enjoy land for their lifetimes in accordance with the devise dated 1363/6/29, but they had no power to write a will of their own because their lifetime holdings had a destination preestablished by their father.[67]

In post-Kamakura society, then, warrior-class women faced a new economic dependency that probably weakened the woman's already vulnerable position associated with patrilocal marriage. It is hardly surprising that the forces that shaped this conjuncture also generated a new disciplinary discourse over female sexuality.

The Female Body in a Man's Space

Patrilocal marriage arrangements imposed restrictions on the woman's body in a way that matrilocal marriage arrangements never did on the man's body. But the form of these restrictions varied from one social group to another. In the warrior class, the complete and fully integrated set of clear-cut patrilocal marriage, patrilineal inheritance, and descent systems doubtless buttressed the goals of the territorially hungry, yet moralistically astute, chiefs more effectively than had any previous system. A house (or lineage) chief with authority and organizing skills oversaw the management of human resources—including reproduction and gender relations—as he strove to realize territorial goals expressed in production, proprietary relations, and military force. From the chief's perspective, everyone under him (women and men) was to promote order and prosperity in the territory. The notion of order affected the meaning and use of the body capable of producing offspring—a valuable resource, or a potential source of trouble, in inheritance and descent systems. Because Japan's warrior society, if anything, encouraged male-male sexual relations—unlike in the West where homosexuality, along with other forms of male sexual expression, was taboo for religious and moralistic reasons—the ordering mechanism reached only those sexual relations that involved the female.[68] The concept of adultery, which had held little discursive or practical meaning in earlier marriage relationships, evolved into an issue that mattered to each warrior and warrior government.[69]

The Kamakura authorities included a provision regarding adultery in its codes (*Goseibai shikimoku*), issued in 1232.[70] The important point about the Kamakura codes, in comparison with later laws, is that they conceptually distinguished various forms of sexual relations that a woman might have with a man who was not her husband. The thirty-fourth article divided the crime of "secret embracing" (*mikkai*) into "forced (*gōkan*, i.e., rape)" and "consensual (*wakan*, i.e., adultery)." Having made the conceptual distinctions, however, the Bakufu nonetheless prescribed one punishment for both. For a man embracing another man's wife, a Bakufu's retainer and the woman involved would each have half of their fiefs confiscated.[71] The woman could be either a willing adulteress or a rape victim. She would lose half of her land either way.

The Muromachi Bakufu inherited, for the most part, the legal traditions of the Kamakura Bakufu. Provisions regarding rape or adultery, however, were omitted from its first set of codes issued on 1336/11/7. But a volatile situation arose in the aftermath of the Ōnin War, involving a samurai who had sex with the wife of a Kyoto sake brewer. The "violated" husband then revenged himself by cutting down the samurai on the street. The situation exploded into a major confrontation, since the two men were affiliated with two major rivaling warrior houses.[72] In response, the Bakufu issued a code in 1479.[73]

The change in the language of the law from Kamakura's *Goseibai Shikimoku* demonstrates even less regard for the female body as her own subject. The new discourse eliminated the conceptual distinction between coerced and consensual sexual intercourse. All was simply "secret," thus illicit, intercourse. Worse still, the new law prescribed for the wronged husband to take revenge into his own hands and to kill the wife as well, if the act of revenge took place outside his home. The wife's dead body served to explain the motive of the killing of the interloper—revenge, not murder. If the revenge took place inside the husband's home, however, the wife could remain alive; the location of the murder itself served to explain the legitimate nature of the killing. It seems that a woman would have a better chance of living if she was engaged in planned adultery at home than if she was raped outdoors by chance.

The Bakufu apparently incorporated the then widely accepted spirit and custom of revenge. For the goal of maintaining social order, it prescribed an ultimate form of injustice. It ignored the humanity of the woman entirely; at the worst, she could be violated by a rapist and, for that, be murdered by her own husband. The "adulteress" who had inspired the writing of this code was indeed cut down by her husband.

As male blood flowed plentifully on the battlefields, those at the political center attempted to help men regularize the meaning of boundaries for their territory—the land, soldiers, productive and reproductive resources.

Men lived expecting to fight and shed blood over their space. Incursion into another man's territory called for retaliation with physical force. The woman's body also signified a kind of territory. The violator would be justly punished. Sexuality was translated into property and was used in the exercise of power. The existence of the code itself, even if its application was rare, stood for a disciplinary technique that governed women's and men's sexuality. It neatly confined sex into monogamous domesticity—at least for women. For men, sexual recourse to another man's wife risked retaliation that was now backed by law, while concubines remained available and commercialized sex proliferated. In this society threatened by instability, the female body helped to define the operative boundary for the exercise and maintenance of male honor.[74]

Japanese law resembled the West's medieval secular law in its disregard for the woman's autonomous sexuality. Western law defined "rape" as a wrong committed against the man who had legal power over the woman or property that was violently seized. It imposed a penalty of death and confiscation of property against the rapist, though this was often substituted by bodily mutilation and fines.[75] Though this heavy penalty reflected the value of the damaged property to its owner (the husband), Western law at least clearly recognized the practical distinction between rape and adultery, and did not prescribe the death penalty for the rape victim.

DIVERGENT PATTERNS OF THE COMMONERS

Community and Economic Base

Around the thirteenth and fourteenth centuries, rapidly increasing agricultural and commercial productivity, a relative drop in the percentage of extraction, and the consequent accumulation of surplus in the commoners' own households greatly expanded the scale and volume of consumption, involving more women and men in commerce. This new economic base made it possible for the villages in Japan's central region to begin organizing shrine associations (*miyaza*). They were, at bottom, male-dominant institutions, although rules and regulations regarding women's participation varied from one village to another. In the village of Imabori in Ōmi Province, for example, the wives of the all-male shrine association members formed their own auxiliary wing. Little is known of its activities, however.[76] In Higashimura in Kii Province, a fourteenth-century regulation shows that daughters of villagers normally served as ceremonial heads by "prohibit[ing] even those native-born daughters of Higashimura from performing ceremonial headship (*tō nyoshō no mono*) once they have left the village and started living elsewhere."[77]

These villages around the capital began to keep records of communal organizations that aimed to promote local interests, financially and spiritually. For example, Imabori has kept close to one thousand documents beginning in the late thirteenth century. Because women had a limited role in the local shrine association and in the local merchant collectives, the majority of village documents bear the signature(s) of men. But fortunately a considerable number of women left records of land transactions and of donations of their property rights to the local shrine. Okushima-no-shō in Ōmi Province left nineteen documents that involve women in the transfer of land rights. They date from 1329 through 1478, and thirteen are from the fourteenth century. With the exception of two bequests in 1353 and 1360 in which women appear as recipients, the others are sales or commendations of rights held by women.[78] A sales slip signed by Fukumatsume, for example, shows that she sold her land in 1366, and another document testifies that Torame purchased land in 1460 and commended it to the local shrine five years later.[79]

Like their aristocratic and warrior-class sisters, then, peasant women also held property. But their property rights embodied a meaning quite different from the rights held by the aristocrats and warriors. Unlike the elites' property, in which feudal and status values were embedded, peasant property was fundamentally economic.[80] Because of this difference, the survival pattern of property held by peasant women also took a different path from that of the socially and politically charged property of the aristocratic and warrior-class women. Just when the elite women's rights were diminishing in quantity, female commoners' rights made their upward jump.

Peasant women's writings also reflect the expanding economy that was evident in the towns, where both women and men could market their specialized skills and products. In a series of *Shokunin uta awase* (Poetic contests in the voice of artisans and merchants), dating from the thirteenth through sixteenth centuries, pictorial and poetic depictions of female makers and vendors of such items as tofu, obi, rice, and sake appear alongside male makers and vendors of, for example, rope, armor, straw sandals, and cookware. The varieties of items produced and handled increase in number in the chronological order of the *uta awase* series, from twenty-four in the thirteenth-century version to 142—more than six times—in the one completed in 1500.[81]

Sex and Class

Meishi's memoir reveals that courtiers spent a great deal of their time preparing for and participating in ceremonies and festivities. These occasions often demanded the presence of female entertainers, who traveled between the world of commoners and those who lived "above the clouds." Highly accomplished in the arts of music, dance, and poetry, they occupy a small but significant position in historical records and fiction, especially because they were often desirable objects of the sexualized male gaze. It would be inappropriate to give these women an undifferentiated label of "prostitutes," inasmuch as their occupational designation and its form and social meaning changed greatly from ancient through early modern times. The dancer-visitors in Meishi's court who participated formally in the *gosechi* ceremony were called *maihime*, or "dancing maidens," presumably without sexual content. According to Fukutō Sanae, *maihime* of the ninth century sexually entertained the emperor on the evening of the dance, and subsequently entered imperial service as palace ladies. But beginning in the tenth century, they just "went home" after their artistic performance.[82] There is nothing in Meishi's memoir that suggests sexual engagement. Each of the five *maihime* in Meishi's court was sponsored by a noble, such as Meishi's father, and received gifts. It is possible that they were not commoners but rather daughters of lower-level courtiers or provincial officials.[83] Earlier records reveal a variety of names for female entertainers who visited the palace; "*yūjo*," "*asobime*," "*kugutsu*," and "*shirabyōshi*" make up a partial list. *Shirabyōshi*, for example, were oft-romanticized figures who danced to their own poetry compositions dressed in male attire. Sad stories about Giō and Hotoke, two *shirabyōshi* who received Taira Kiyomori's adoration, wealth, and whims in successive turns, enhance a chapter in the *Tale of the Heike*.[84] Kujō Kanezane writes in his *Gyokuyō* on 1191/11/21 that two *shirabyōshi* visited the court and two male courtiers joined in the dance.[85] Lady Nijō, in *Towazugatari*, also describes two *shirabyōshi* sisters, Harugiku and Wakagiku, entertaining Emperor Go-Fukakusa in 1277 during two nights of a sake-filled party. Lady Nijō exposes her understanding of these women's social position by calling them *keisei*, or "prostitute," on the second day of the party.[86]

Dancing women who came to court before Meishi's time sometimes obtained ties with the court that went beyond the artistic.[87] Their participation in public functions must have given them visibility and easy proximity to observing men. Many not only slept with, but also became legitimate wives of, aristocrats and high-ranking warriors in late Heian and Kamakura times. What surprises historians is that many of their children attained high court rank. *Shirabyōshi* Yashame's son Tokudaiji Sanemoto, for example, earned the Junior First rank, Major Counselor; and Muryō's son, Tōin Kintada, became a Senior Second rank Provisional Middle Counselor.[88]

The categories of women with such designations as *shirabyōshi* disappear from aristocratic discourse sometime before the fourteenth century, however. This development reflected a larger-scale transformation in the interconnected dynamics between the country's economy and gender relations.

The greater commercialization that advanced the economic opportunities for commoners in the fourteenth century doubtless affected the meaning of sexualized professions. A number of *uta awase* list figures of women whose trade could include partly or wholly the sale of their bodies, from *katsurame* who sold fish caught in Katsura River, to *oharame* who sold produce from the Ohara region, and *kusemai* who danced. The first two were vendors who carried their commodities to the capital and sold them on the street. The *kusemai* dancers (both men and women) traveled to festivals to perform. Taking sexual customers might be within their job description. But it is the figures of prostitutes appearing in the *shichijū-ichiban uta awase*, dating from 1500, that quintessentially symbolize the new age: *tachigimi* ("madame stander") who worked the streets and *zushigimi* ("madame person of a narrow alley") who worked from an established structure located in an alley.[89]

In the earlier period, sexuality and domesticity were only vaguely distinguished, a condition that allowed dancers to become legitimate mothers of upwardly mobile aristocratic sons.[90] Conversely, there was only a little distance between court ladies—expected to mother aristocratic offspring—and outside entertainers. Both were sexually available to male aristocrats and similarly highly accomplished in literature, the arts, and music. In the newly commercialized age, sex became a clear-cut commodity.

To Takamure Itsue, this situation signaled a separation of womanhood into two dichotomous categories—domestic-reproductive slaves for the patrilineal family and sexual slaves for the patriarch. Rendering coherence in her periodization scheme, she argues that the "taking-the-bride" mode made love hardly relevant in marriage, and severely restricted married women's sexual expressions while granting married men the freedom to purchase commercialized bodies in the rising prostitution quarters. Meanwhile, female entertainers were losing autonomy also. An eleventh-century source suggests that they were then organized into an association led by a female chief. More and more, however, they became pawns manipulated by pimps.[91] According to Amino Yoshihiko, the *zushigimi* and *tachigimi* in Kyoto paid taxes to a city police chief, the Seta family. They fell under an increasingly complex structure of control in the sixteenth century as the Seta became vassals of the Koga family and paid taxes to them. By 1536, the Hatakeyama family was also collecting revenue from these quarters and paid taxes to the Koga family.[92]

In the new historical phase, the prostitute's body served as a poignant nexus for a set of developing concepts and practices that tended to force old ambiguities into new, well-defined categories. "Prostitute" was an occupational role that stood in opposition to the reproductive role of domestic women, in a bifurcated division of female labor defined in relation to men and their perceived needs.

DEFINING THE FEMININE

Varieties of Motherhood

The second volume of Meishi's memoir describes her second career as a mother who, having lost her husband, remained in the Saionji mansion and played the significant role of *goke*, literally "after-house" or widow. She concerned herself with the succession of the Saionji family—naturally, since it would involve her son's future. After Kinmune's death, the lineage headship had gone to Kinmune's brother, Kinshige, who appears in *Taiheiki* as the informant of Kinmune's treachery. Meishi worked to steer the family's headship back to her son, Sanetoshi, while simultaneously promoting his position in the court. In 1337, after the revival of the Northern imperial line, Sanetoshi was conferred the Junior Lower Fifth rank at his three-years-old ceremony. This is an important date that, to Meishi, also signified the revival of the Saionji family in proper hands. At age fifteen, as Meishi proudly records, Sanetoshi was promoted to the Senior Third Rank, Gonchūnagon (Provisional Middle Counselor). Meishi may have written her memoir as a testimonial to her accomplishment as a mother.

Motherhood may be viewed as a universal and unchanging phenomenon. Yet its meaning and practices have varied greatly, depending on the particularities of society, class, and time. The significance of motherhood went far beyond the maternal; motherhood may, for example, be a target of social rules that establish the norms for gender relations. In Japan, explicit discourse concerning motherhood made its first appearance sometime in the eleventh century. The meaning of this particular discourse in Japan's gender history should be assessed in conjunction with a discourse on childbirth that began to spread after the fourteenth century. The reality of parturition and motherhood—two particularly feminine experiences— may form a continuum from a woman's perspective. The discourses concerning them, however, developed along two separate lines for different social and economic reasons, and they seem to impart meanings that are mutually contradictory. But they share in common an impulse to essentialize women and isolate their "feminine" traits from their person.

The new "mother" categories—"mother of the country (*kokubo*)" and "secondary or associate mother (*junbo*)"—invented for the imperial house in the eleventh century expanded the meaning of motherhood to embody a sense of abstract space and function, while also fragmenting motherhood into compartments that came to be embedded in different persons. The title "mother of the country" made the emperor's biological mother a metonymic entity since it equated the emperor's body with the country itself. The "associate mother," a title invested in an unmarried woman in the emperor's patrilineal family, was a cultural category employed for the purpose of property transmission, as explained earlier. Both "mothers" were desexualized and idealized symbols that stood apart from the woman's maternal identity.

Idealization of motherhood took a different form in the writings of Kujō Kanezane and Jien. In *Gyokuyō*, Kanezane expresses in an entry for 1181/11/28 that women are superior (*masaru*) to men because every woman is a true mother of various buddhas of the three realms. No man is a true father of various buddhas. This is because when Buddha incarnated, he necessarily stayed temporarily in the womb. Buddha did not receive his body, hair, and flesh from the father. In *Gukanshō*, Jien also focuses on the womb but emphasizes the maternal pain of delivery: human birth is a process of being born after staying in the mother's womb. The suffering of the mother is beyond description. Suffering thus, mothers give birth to human beings. Jien presents this discussion as a way to explain the reigns of ancient female emperors, Kōgyoku and Kōken, in the context of emphasizing the uniqueness of Japan as the country of gods headed by Amaterasu the mother. Jien thus displaces the political, spiritual, and ritualistic role of the female emperors with their uniquely feminine biological trait.[93]

If the titles of *kokubo* and *junbo* dissociated women from their physiology, the views of Kanezane and Jien did the opposite by emphasizing the essentially biological nature of motherhood. Although their writings do not denigrate women's maternal capacity per se, their exclusive spotlight on it leaves women's other characteristics in shadow. Their essentializing approach is oddly antithetical to the operative norms of the upper reaches of Heian society, which owed so much to women's cultural accomplishments. We may say that the writings of Kanezane and Jien introduce an element of what anthropologists have called the nature-culture dichotomy. Their position differs from the Western duality model, in that for them biology has a high place, not a low one, in their hierarchical ordering of dualistic concepts.

The law codes of the Kamakura Bakufu also paid attention to the role of mother. A number of provisions discuss material and spiritual benefits of "father and mother," a feature that presupposes the mother's economic power (including the right to alienate property to her children) and moral authority in a family. Mothers could annul an earlier bequest to a child, for example.[94] The code also essentially recognized women's freedom to become mothers—married or not—by legally endorsing the prevalent practice of adopting heirs in their name.[95] The difference between the Kamakura codes and the fourteenth-century Muromachi codes is striking in this regard. The latter no longer mention "mothers" at all, suggesting the insignificance of mothers in the family's formal relations of authority. (This is not to deny that mothers probably had considerable informal power.) The ever increasing need to consolidate the warrior house under one male chief, thus diminishing women's (and secondary sons') property rights, must have negatively affected the mother's authority over the children. In both periods, however, widows (*goke*) held substantial power and authority that had been invested in their husbands. Hino Meishi was a replacement figure for her husband with the responsibility to guard the family line, in addition to being mother of Sanetoshi.

A Room of One's Own (in Hell)

Two bloody incidents color the silent space left by the memoir's volumes and accentuate the power of rupture over the discursive coherence that the memoir seeks to achieve. Saionji Kinmune, Meishi's husband, lost his life and blood at the hands of enemy men. One hundred days later (so states *Taiheiki*), Saionji Sanetoshi, Meishi's child, traveled a bloody passage to life with the aid of supporting women.

The process of giving birth was a feminine affair. It took place in a confined space with few men present. Scrolls show women sitting and supported by several women to deliver a child.[96] Unlike the hierarchy of recent times that imposes the cultured male with medical technology over the biological female, social relations of power in the birth process in premodern Japan remained largely in women's hands. The only men present in the delivery room were priests of various religious persuasions—including yin-yang diviners, Shinto and Buddhist priests, shamans—there in order to pray for a safe birth. With its visible flow of blood and high risk of death, birth-giving remained a feminine preserve. Yet the outcome of the process had everything to do with the male, particularly his name and lineage. It was a liminal sphere of unpredictable forces that must have invited male fear.

The fourteenth century saw the Blood Bowl Sutra (*ketsubonkyō*) begin to spread among commoners, though it was known earlier among aristocrats.[97] It originally came from China and, though it consists of only 420 words, variants with differing messages have survived in Japan. The version that spread in the Muromachi period focused on parturition blood in the following way.[98]

It states that the Priest Mokuren once saw the Blood Bowl hell when he was in China. In this hell there were women with iron shackles receiving punishment. Mokuren asked why only women were being made to suffer in this manner. The chief of this hell explained: women fall into the Blood Bowl hell and suffer because the blood that women discharge at the time of childbirth touches the earth and pollutes the earth gods. If she then washes her polluted clothes in the river, they will pollute the water. If then good men and women take the water to make tea and offer it to various holy people, it will pollute the pure priests. This is a major sin. Because women commit these polluting acts, they suffer in the Blood Bowl hell. In order to avoid the Blood Bowl hell, it is necessary to do Blood Bowl rituals, form an association, and recite and copy the Blood Bowl Sutra.[99]

Pictorial representations dating from late Muromachi times depict a variety of hells, among which some were exclusively for women. In one scene, naked women with long hair wallow in a blood pond. In another scene, in contrast, women are doomed to the symbolic task of pulling up bamboo shoots in the Hell of Sterility.[100] Thus women could be condemned to one of "women's" hells whether they gave birth or could not give birth—a reflection of complex sentiments that childbirth incited in men who desired both to avoid (female) blood and to have offspring. Men had no hell that was created exclusively for them.[101]

According to Takemi Momoko, the reasons for descent into the Blood

Bowl hell changed from one period to another. While versions from the Muromachi period focus on parturition blood, the Tokugawa version lists, in addition, menstrual pollution. By the late Tokugawa period, blood accompanying childbirth fell off the list of "causes," leaving only menstrual blood. More recent scrutiny of sources by Kōdate Naomi, however, points out a mention of menstrual pollution in one Muromachi version.[102] We can conclude, then, that while the Blood Bowl Sutra was shaped to embody adjustable meanings, what particular demands it responded to requires further study. At any rate, it is undeniable that the Blood Bowl Sutra spread broadly in the centuries following the fourteenth.

The appearance and spread of the Blood Bowl Sutra probably reinforced the accepted notion regarding female blood that had been current for several centuries. Ancient Japanese society considered female blood as a source both of sacred power that fortified men and of temporary pollution. Its power was operant only for a given duration, and did not encode women as polluted beings.[103] "Procedures of the Engi Era" (Engi-shiki, 901–22) prescribed seven days of abstinence after childbirth. But a fifteenth-century regulation for the Goryō Shrines ("Goryōsha bukki ryō," 1403) established thirty days of abstinence for pollution accompanying childbirth. People experiencing secondary and tertiary contacts (those coming into contact with the woman in delivery, and those coming into contact with them) also became polluted and required cleansing.[104]

Prayer sticks bearing the Blood Bowl Sutra and dating from the fifteenth century have been unearthed in an archaeological site in Kusatsu.[105] They vividly illustrate that women indeed followed the Sutra's recommendations, and serve as evidence for the process of what Foucault would call subjectification, active self-formation that goes through various "operations on [people's] own bodies, on their own souls, on their own thoughts, on their own conduct." It is a process of self-perception that was mediated by developing social and religious values.[106]

Beyond Sexuality

Widows typically renounced this world, though Hino Meishi remained to manage worldly matters. The thirteenth century saw the establishment of several institutions to accommodate women who intended to stay celibate. Zen and Ritsu schools of Buddhism established nunneries alongside monasteries. Myōe, for example, set up Zenmyōji for women who became widowed during the Jōkyū War (1221). The purpose of these institutions was social as well as religious. As monasteries served to contain surplus aristocratic males, nunneries served to absorb surplus aristocratic females, sometimes in their infancy. The mother superior (*chōrō*) of Hokkeji in Nara, for instance, was Shōkeibō Jizen, who had served as a lady-in-waiting for Shōshi, Emperor Go-Toba's daughter. She became a nun after Shōshi's death in 1211, and by 1243, at the latest, she was one of the sixteen nuns there. They became disciples of Eison, the head of Saidaiji with which Hokkeji became affiliated.[107]

Demand for nunneries increased dramatically from the thirteenth century onward. What caused this increase? Taira Masayuki argues that the new demand reflected the growing belief that access to the woman's body should remain solely with the husband during and after his lifetime. Women usually became nuns upon the forty-ninth-day commemoration of their husbands' death.[108] Although plausible, this explanation fails to address the situation faced by women who never had a husband. Instead, or additionally, the rising instances of retirement to a nunnery may have been caused by the general trend toward attenuation of property rights among aristocratic women.[109]

Renouncing one's sexuality, at any rate, was not always voluntary; life in a nunnery was sometimes forced on the woman. A sixteen-year-old concubine of Prince Ogawamiya (younger brother of Emperor Shōkō) had been married for two years when the prince suddenly died in 1425. His father, retired Emperor Go-Komatsu, then compelled her to shave her hair and made her ineligible for remarriage.[110] Nunneries also provided space for women who had remained single and childless, as had many palace attendants (*nyōbō*). Sometimes the lack of protectors also left a woman no choice but the nunnery. This was the case with Sonkei, an older sister of Lady Nijō (author of *Towazugatari*) by a different father. Sonkei was an aristocrat who was orphaned before her sixteenth year; she had lost her mother (also Nijō's mother) first, and subsequently her father.[111]

The nunneries and monasteries—institutions built upon the principle of sex (biological) distinction without sexuality—also gender-coded their activities. The Saidaiji Ritsu school temples sponsored a variety of socially useful activities, such as the construction of bridges and roads. The nunneries associated with them assigned their nuns to the task of laundering the monks' soiled clothes.[112] The ideal of gender-based division of labor into domestic and extradomestic spheres invaded this religious sphere organized according to sex differentiations.

AFTERTHOUGHTS

Hino Meishi lived in an age that was fundamentally untidy. She herself authenticated the age by silently recognizing these social realities that resisted integration into her "woman's hand." Her writing marks the last line of defense against what was to come. In maintaining the form and subject matter befitting the "woman's hand" through the technique of exclusion, did she foresee the disappearance of the aesthetic tradition deeply embedded in her class and gender? The new forces that would invalidate the "woman's hand" destroyed the social base that supported its aesthetic values. In the *yometori* era, poetic love affairs no longer structured aristocratic women's day-to-day lives. Love affairs were practically and discursively invalidated—even in fantasy. For warrior-class women, whose marriages were increasingly part and parcel of military strategy, extramarital affairs became a source of severe punishment. The new morality that was imposed especially on women thoroughly disoriented the aesthetic sensitivity embedded in the "woman's hand."

In the changing atmosphere governed by insecurity, however, court women vitalized their role as scribes. Why did female attendants keep the ongoing record of the imperial household, *Oyudono*? In the absence of evidence, a definitive explanation is impossible. But we can consider the question from a structural standpoint, borrowing Victor Turner's four-phase model and applying it to the era of political turmoil surrounding the imperial restoration.

Turner begins with (1) an initial breach of norm-governed social relations (imperial schism), building to (2) a phase of mounting crisis (Kenmu Restoration), followed by (3) an attempt at redressive action (Nanbokuchō) and (4) either the reintegration of the disturbed social group or the social recognition and legitimization of irreparable schism (end of Nanbokuchō).[113] Japan's imperial-Bakufu symbiotic structure in the fourteenth century faced breaches of "regular" norm-governed relations in the holding of offices and land, as well as in imperial succession. These breaches led to, in the person of Go-Daigo, a crisis phase of ideological reexamination, or of "anti-structure" with a new set of ordering principles. It was a time to question and destabilize the self-evident, and heretofore unquestioned, principles that underlay the "traditional" superstructure.[114] (Meishi's memoir, in the lineage of the writing of the earlier era, fell precisely into this crisis phase, which also shook the palace's social relations and symbolism—the universe of meaning for the "woman's hand.")

The process of reexamination, however, probably exposed women's level of literacy and involvement in "public" affairs—a level that had been taken for granted, along with the more obvious male-centered ordering structures. In the redressive phase, the threatened warrior *and* aristocratic society sought to regain stability through various actions—formal and informal, economic and political, practical and ritual. Revival of the palace diary may have been one such redressive practice to discursively reinforce the durable constancy of imperial rituals and symbols. Highly literate women, who were closely and consistently engaged in processing the "public" imperial body—from food to bath to sleep, had the technique and social training to serve in this effort. Their work therefore coincided with the rapid and drastic attrition of the imperial authority and power—though not necessarily of its prestige—in the country's politics and economy.

In Hino Meishi's era, a whole range of social forces converged to form a maelstrom. The situation's very instability demanded countervailing practices that would restore a semblance of order. This meant organizing, classifying, and defining various social categories—male, female, purity, family, outcasts, and motherhood, for example. This process of reorganization directly affected gender relations, but its effect was not necessarily synchronous among different classes with different economic and social needs. Broadly speaking, once the aristocratic class—comparatively a latecomer to the new marriage practice—fully adopted patrilocal marriage, the marital residential pattern probably became standardized. The family structure grew tidier, and its rights and authority came to be situated around the principal male, who held the family's wealth and acquired an outside woman to mother his heir. The warrior society boldly outlined limits on married women's sexual autonomy, bounding the (sexual) territory possessed by each man and forcing one-sided chastity on women. Commoners, with economic requirements that differed from those of the elites, grew historically more visible in certain aspects of life.

The focus on the peculiarly feminine biological experiences, however, informed cultural understanding and powerfully reorganized social relations that affected all classes. One target was women's reproductive role that came to be seen as a source of pollution and female sufferance as well as (in the shape of "motherhood") a source of gender-based idealism disconnected from the woman's body. The most potently negative subjectification of the female sex, therefore, came from the most irreplaceable resource of that sex—the reproductive capacity that men cannot have. In post-fourteenth-century Japan, saturated with instability and unpredictability, the female body increasingly became a ground on which to attempt a new sort of social order.

> Writing down all I've gathered,
> Gathered like a fisherwoman raking
> Seaweed washed up on shore—
> Thus does this nun find consolation
> While passing aimlessly through a sad and fleeting world.
>
> I cannot prevent
> Others from seeing me as thoughtless
> After I am gone
> If my hastily written words are left behind,
> Strewn in disarray like seaweed on a beach.
>
> —Hino Meishi[115]

CHAPTER 8

Warrior Control over the Imperial Anthology

ROBERT N. HUEY

PERHAPS NOTHING speaks more clearly to the change in *waka* composition and publication practices than the fact that in the twelfth century, three imperial anthologies were ordered and compiled, in the thirteenth, the number rose to five, and in the fourteenth, it was eight (and five of those were in the first half of the century). Assuming that an imperial anthology was an attempt to establish cultural hegemony (a canon) — a proposition to be discussed later — the frequency would suggest rapid social change and the perceived need to redefine norms with virtually each new generation and shift of power.

In pursuing this notion, however, I seemingly end up at odds with the title of this volume, for the process I describe *begins* in the thirteenth century, and leads up to the middle of the fourteenth, at just about the point of departure for many of the other essays herein. The contradiction is more apparent than real. To begin with, canonical forms change glacially, even as some artists are pursuing radically different ideas. That most "medieval" of poetic forms, *renga*, actually saw widespread popularity from the late Heian period, but when does it become a mark of the "medieval"? Not until much later, when imperial *renga* anthologies are commissioned (the first being *Tsukubashū* in 1357) and it becomes canonical. This also overlaps with the shift toward warrior control over "imperial" waka anthologies.

Secondly, how we view continuity and change depends on which end of the process we are looking from. The process I trace here chronicles the end of monolithic courtly control of imperial anthologizing as warrior-aristocrats gain ever greater sway over court poetry. Yes, hints that the imperial institution was losing full authority over its anthologies can be seen as early as the thirteenth century, but it is in the fourteenth century that truly dramatic changes occur, both in the way imperial anthologies are ordered and compiled, and, to some extent, in their content.

What follows then is an overview of the thirteen imperial anthologies that were compiled in the thirteenth and fourteenth centuries, with a more detailed look at those that have remarkable histories from our standpoint, that is, anthologies that point to increasing warrior input. I shall look as much as possible at contemporary documents to get an idea of how these collections were compiled, but shall also take note of later "histories," such as *Masukagami* and *Honchō Tsugan*, which, though perhaps not totally reliable, in some cases offer the only information available. Furthermore, the story they tell is significant in that it represents what society believed took place. In addition, late Kamakura and Muromachi poetic treatises (*karon*) can also provide information about the traditional history behind a particular collection, though again, we need to be wary of their ideological baggage.

IMPERIAL ANTHOLOGIES FROM *SHINKOKINSHŪ* (1205) TO *SHINGOSHŪISHŪ* (1384)

Elsewhere, I have criticized the tendency of Robert Brower and Earl Miner to focus too much on imperial anthologies and to use them to support an evolutionary view of waka.[1] Why now make *chokusenshū* the center of this exploration of how waka changed through the Kamakura period? The key is the notion of canon. What appears in the imperial anthologies is not necessarily the "best" poetry, not even by the standards of that day.[2] Rather, by Emperor Shirakawa's reign imperial anthologies are monuments, public works projects, attempts to define what is proper in public poetry.[3] They are, in other words, the canon, with all its political ramifications. By looking at the circumstances surrounding the various *chokusenshū* of the Kamakura period and somewhat beyond, we should actually see reflected in their respective processes some of the historical forces at work. Three anthologies—*Shinchokusenshū* (1235), *Shokukokinshū* (1265), and *Fūgashū* (1346)—will receive closer attention since each reflects some noteworthy social or political shifts.

Shinkokinshū will serve as a kind of benchmark to begin the survey, for it is unquestionably a political document, but reflects probably the last purely "imperial" anthology among the twenty-one. Waka fans might take exception to characterizing *Shinkokinshū* as a political monument. Surely its compilers were striving to radically redefine the face of poetry. Surely the careful labor Go-Toba put into it was motivated by artistic concerns. Yes, and no. Of course Go-Toba had a genuine love of poetry,[4] but he no doubt also saw—as had the sponsors of *Man'yōshū* centuries earlier, and Chinese dynasts for centuries before that—that an imperial anthology was an attempt to put the mark of its sponsor on cultural affairs, on the life of the people, at least such people as made up the ruling elite. As proof that in the end *Shinkokinshū* was as political as any other anthology, consider which text is now standard. Go-Toba labored for years in Oki exile polishing and repolishing the collection, assuming that his final adamantine version would be the definitive one. But the Oki-bon is now a footnote, an asterisk in standard texts. Go-Toba lost the political struggle; Go-Toba was exiled. His vision of *Shinkokinshū* was no longer socially compelling, and history turned back to the earlier version to canonize.

In any case, during his glory years as retired emperor, Go-Toba completely dominated the process of *Shinkokinshū*'s compilation. He did a brilliant job orchestrating it, juggling all the factions at court to do so. He also raided Kamakura, bringing up, among others, one Fujiwara Masatsune, originally for his *kemari* skills. But Masatsune proceeded in the *Shinkokinshū* years to make a name for himself as a poet as well, and to establish his branch family, the Asukai, as one of Japan's premier poetry houses, a position it held at least into the seventeenth century. Go-Toba skillfully neutralized the older ruling houses while promoting new talent, so as to ensure his place at the center. It seems obvious that by 1201 or 1202, he saw the project as part of his larger vision of restoration, which of course was dashed in the Jōkyū War. The aftermath of that political disturbance had great impact on the next collection—in fact, this is where I believe the Bakufu first begins to tamper with the *chokusenshū* process.

This next anthology eventually acquired the name *Shinchokusenshū*. Scholars, and the compiler himself, Teika, agree that the person behind this project was Kujō Michiie. It was not the first time a "civilian" had tried to lay the groundwork for an imperial anthology.[5] Michiie, though, had strong connections to the Bakufu. His father was Kujō Yoshitsune (whose own father, Kanezane, has been seen, simplistically, by some historians as "pro-Bakufu," but who is better thought of as a realist who attempted to forge a relationship between the court and Bakufu in the 1180s). Michiie's mother was the daughter of Ichijō Yoshiyasu, himself married to Yori-tomo's sister. One of Michiie's sons, Yoritsune, became the fourth Kama-kura shogun. At the same time, of course, his pedigree as a Kyoto aristocrat was virtually flawless, being one of several branches of the *sekkanke* that periodically provided regents and chancellors as the political wind shifted. In fact, at the time in question here, his branch was on top.

The record, as written by Teika in his *Meigetsuki*, is quite clear about Michiie's involvement in the project. It seems Michiie first approached Teika in Kanki 2 (1230) 7/5 with the idea of doing an imperial anthology, though it is not clear whether Michiie had discussed the matter with the emperor yet. Teika is excited at the prospect, and notes that this might give him an opportunity to honor "the previous monarchs" (by which most scholars assume he meant Go-Toba and Juntoku) with poems. "The pre-vious monarchs composed so many excellent poems that one could easily fill the whole collection with them," he writes. And he adds that great anthologies of the past had so honored retired emperors. But then he im-mediately expresses concern that in the current political climate it might not be so easy, though he quickly adds that to omit poems from these ex-sovereigns would also "invite the world's scorn."[6] In other words, he is aware of the political implications, and is already considering some form of self-censorship.

In any case, owing to a series of natural disasters, the project was put on hold for two years, but finally retired emperor Go-Horikawa issued the formal order on Jōei 1 (1232) 6/13.[7] Before Teika could complete his charge, Go-Horikawa died (1234/8/6), and the next day Teika burned his draft of the project. How easily those words are printed on the page and pass by the reader! One needs to stop and consider carefully what Teika did. This was a man whose fanatical devotion to poetry was legendary, matched only by his pride in his own importance to the art. When the idea of an imperial anthology had first been broached to him in 1230, and when the actual commission was made, he expressed a profound joy at having the chance to keep his art and his family name alive. Yet when the emperor who ordered the project died, Teika matter-of-factly says: "I took the twenty rolls of my draft, which had been ordered by His Majesty (*choku*), into the south garden and burned them. There was nothing left but ashes." He felt there was no other choice since there was no precedent for the situation.[8] This decision speaks volumes not only to the power of precedent in the ultraconservative world of waka, but also to the enormous weight carried by the word *choku*.

Michiie, however, was not about to let the project end in such a way. Though Teika's *Meigetsuki* is blank for this period, we know from other sources that Michiie got hold of an earlier draft of the collection, which Teika had sometime before given to Go-Horikawa for initial approval. (The draft Teika burned must have included his revisions based on Go-Horikawa's instructions, though no record remains to prove this.) According to the *Hyakurenshō*, on 1234/11/9 Michiie and his son gave this earlier draft back to Teika, who had presumably considered the project moot. They instructed him to cut about one hundred poems and add a few others.[9] It is generally believed these cuts involved poems by Go-Toba, Juntoku, and Tsuchimikado—"losers" in the Jōkyū War. There is no evidence that Michiie had been pressured by the Bakufu to order the cuts. Probably he simply wanted to avoid giving offense to his friends in Kamakura, who would not have wanted the Go-Toba faction honored publicly. Michiie left no records of his thinking on the matter; his own diary entries in this period only make vague references to meetings with Teika over poetry matters.[10]

The evidence that Michiie's cuts involved the above-mentioned sovereigns is circumstantial, but strong. First, as mentioned earlier, when Teika first discusses the project in 1230, he makes it clear that he intends to honor his old patron, Go-Toba, with numerous poems, though the final product does not. Second, Shunzei no Musume, Teika's niece and adopted sister, writes years later to Tameie, and refers to the incident. She says there is something dark, even shady (*me mo kuretaru*) about the fact that the fine poetry of Go-Toba and Juntoku is missing from the work, and only Go-Horikawa is left to represent the then-contemporary imperial family. She also says she has heard that Teika was forced to excise some seventy imperial poems, though she does not say who made him do it or which poems were cut. She concludes that the excision was an embarrassing mistake (*katahara ita ya*).[11] Of course, her reaction to *Shinchokusenshū* may be colored by the fact that Teika, for some reason, included only eight of her poems. She had been much better represented in *Shinkokinshū*.

Whatever the actual facts, this account of Michiie's "censorship" was taken as true from very early on, and the finished product is indeed conspicuously lacking in poems by Go-Toba and Juntoku, surprising considering Teika's relationship to the two sovereigns. A little more than a century later, Ton'a (a waka scholar allied with the mainstream Nijō line of Teika's descendants) wrote in his treatise *Seiashō* (c. 1360) that wags had given *Shinchokusenshū* the nickname "the Uji River Collection" (*Ujigawashū*, a reference to the fixed expression *mononofu no yasoujigawa no* — literally, "the Uji River district, with its eighty warrior clans") because it included so many warrior poets (*bushi no ooku iritaru nari*).[12] Interestingly, though, the Nijō line itself eventually canonized *Shinchokusenshū*, even above *Shinkokinshū*.

Two measures of where a compiler stands in the factional and political disputes that swirled in every waka age are how many poems the compiler chooses from which poets, and whose poems occupy the opening pages of the first Spring book, since that section sets the tone for the entire collection. That it is hard to find a thread in Teika's choices in both these measures suggests that he was looking to protect himself on all sides. The top nine poets in the collection, in order, are Teika's friend in poetry Fujiwara Ietaka (1158–1237); Kujō Yoshitsune (1169–1206); Teika's father Shunzei (1114–1204); Saionji Kintsune (1171–1244, related by marriage to Michiie; he was a long-time ally of the Bakufu and had opposed Go-Toba in the Jōkyū War); Jien (1155–1225), of the Kujō house; the young shogun Sanetomo (1192–1219); Michiie himself; Asukai Masatsune (1170–1221); and Sagami (1000?–1061?). All but one of these poets were contemporaries of Teika's, though five of them were dead by the time of this anthology. In a roundabout way this list does in fact honor Go-Toba, since Ietaka, Yoshitsune, Shunzei, Jien, Masatsune, and Teika himself had all been part of Go-Toba's poetry circle in the feverishly active years leading up to *Shinkokinshū* (1205).

All in all it is a safe group, as indeed are the poets whose poems make up the opening of the first Spring book: in order, the late emperor Go-Horikawa, Shunzei, Ki no Tsurayuki (868–945), Anonymous, Higo (1020?–1101? — a lady in service to the *sekkanke*), Ōnakatomi Yoshinobu (921–91), Tsurayuki again, Minamoto Morotoshi (1080–1141), and Minamoto Toshiyori (1055–1129). These choices — and some of them are on the obscure side — suggest that Teika was more interested in content at this point than in pleasing this or that faction. It would seem, then, that while he responded to Michiie's pressure, he was still able to satisfy his own artistic vision in doing so.

The next anthology, *Shokugosenshū*, is not especially noteworthy, either historically or literarily. In 1248, retired emperor Go-Saga commissioned the project from Teika's son, Tameie. Though Tameie had been something of a radical in poetry (he and other innovators had collaborated in 1244 in a collection known as *Shinrokujōdai waka*, which produced some highly unorthodox waka that inspired the Kyōgoku school of half a century later), *Shokugosenshū* turned out to be a rather conservative anthology. Most noteworthy about it from our standpoint, though, is that Go-Toba (Go-Saga's grandfather) is "rehabilitated," and given prominent representation (third among all the poets), as are Tsuchimikado and Juntoku, who had also been left out of *Shinchokusenshū*. In fact, although I said earlier that *Shinkokinshū* is probably the last of the purely "imperial" anthologies, I have found no evidence that the Bakufu had any hand in *Shokugosenshū*, either. This is partly because it was occupied with its own internal problems (the so-called Hōji Gassen having taken place the previous year) and partly because Go-Saga had gained the Bakufu's trust by being cooperative in reducing the influence of the Kujō family, which the Hōjō had begun to find overly meddlesome.

As for content, Shunzei no Musume's words to Tameie, which she had intended as the highest praise, give us a pretty fair notion of the literary content of the collection, which was completed in 1251: "It lacks nothing; neither does it have too much of anything. It neither inclines to the left, nor does it bend to the right."[13] Tameie had become more and more conscious of his responsibility as head of the Mikohidari house, and the anthology honors his ancestors (the first spring poem is by Shunzei) and their patrons (Go-Toba and Tsuchimikado). For the conservative mainstream of later waka poets (starting with Tameie's eldest son, Tameuji, and continuing through the Nijō branch of the family), such "correctness" was a virtue, and they canonized *Shokugosenshū* along with *Shinchokusenshū* and Shunzei's *Senzaishū* (1187) as their "*Shinsandaishū*" (loosely, the "New Big Three").

For more inventive poets, however, such "correctness" amounted to mediocrity. Included here were some of Tameie's old fellows from the days of the *Shinrokujōdai waka*. Feeling that Tameie had compromised and that the Kyoto poetry scene was apparently in his grip, the most vocal of his critics, Shinkan,[14] turned to Kamakura for sponsorship. He moved there in 1260 and became the poetry tutor for the shogun, Munetaka Shinnō, who was actually Go-Saga's first son, though by a lesser concubine.

In the meantime, Go-Saga decided to commission another imperial anthology. His earlier effort had begun just a year after his second son, Go-Fukakusa, took the throne. This time the commission was given less than a month after his third son, Kameyama, became emperor in 1259. The timing hardly seems coincidental. The short gap between the two anthologies came close to devaluing the notion of a *chokusenshū* as a public monument. For Go-Saga it was like a private celebration.

For this new anthology, which came to be called *Shokukokinshū*, Go-Saga again asked Tameie to be the sole compiler. But anti-Tameie sentiment had grown considerably, and Shinkan, the spiritual leader of the opposition, now had an important ally in the shogun. Indeed, he went to Kamakura a year after Go-Saga had first commissioned Tameie, and it seems likely that his purpose for going there was to rally support. With Prince Munetaka urging him on, Go-Saga was persuaded in 1262 to enlarge the commission to include Shinkan, and three other poets: Fujiwara (Kujō) Motoie, Fujiwara Ieyoshi,[15] and Fujiwara (Rokujō) Yukiie.

Again, the evidence that Munetaka Shinnō exercised direct pressure on their selection is circumstantial. Nothing is mentioned in works like *Masukagami* or *Honchō Tsugan* either about the original commission or the addition of the four new compilers three years later (though all three works discuss the formal presentation and/or subsequent banquet, listing the full complement of compilers as a given).[16]

However, Tameie's descendants are much more explicit in their depiction of the occasion. The least ambiguous account is from *Genshō Waka Kuden* (c. 1294), by Tameie's second son, Genshō (1224–1303), who was alive during the events described (though that does not necessarily make his story unimpeachable): "Shinkan went east to serve as poetry teacher to Nakatsukasakyō (Prince Munetaka). He taught as he pleased, and many people followed him. When he returned to the capital, he had himself and several like-minded people appointed as compilers, claiming this had been the Prince's order." According to Genshō, when Tameie complained to Go-Saga he got no satisfactory reply, but was told, "His Majesty has so ordered simply because Kamakura has suggested it (*tada Azuma yori mōsaruru ni yorite sadameōseraruru yoshi nari*)."[17]

It bears noting that while one might characterize Munetaka's intervention as pressure from the Bakufu, he was, after all, Go-Saga's son, and not some rough warrior from the east with no understanding of the subtleties of literary life in the capital. And it is also unlikely that he would "order" his father, Go-Saga, to do anything.

Indeed, the backgrounds of the four poets the shogun Munetaka supported indicate that the dispute really was a literary one, or at least a conflict among various "schools" of poetry, rather than any serious, larger political matter. Yukiie, for example, was the last of the Rokujō poetry line, which had been a bitter rival of Tameie's Mikohidari house since the time of Tameie's grandfather Shunzei. Ieyoshi's family, too, had traditional ties with that same Rokujō house. Motoie had been snubbed by Teika at the time of the *Shinchokusenshū*, so he, also, had a long-standing dislike of Tameie.

On the other hand, Shinkan's feelings seem to have been motivated by genuine literary disagreement more than any past history of factional infighting. He is most famous for having been a strong partisan of *Man'yōshū*, though the conservative world of waka had generally favored only the more courtly approach of the later Man'yō poets, as well as some of Hitomaro's smoother tanka.[18] But Sengaku's (1203–69?) monumental work on *Man'yōshū*[19] had finally made the whole collection accessible to anyone who could read, and he was much in fashion in both Kamakura and Kyoto, lecturing for both Munetaka Shinnō and Go-Saga. Shinkan thus became interested in the Man'yō style, and the fact that some of Sengaku's poems appear in *Shokukokinshū* is presumably his doing. Tameie did not share this enthusiasm for *Man'yōshū*.

To return to the theme of court and Bakufu, however, it is noteworthy that both Shinkan and Motoie had had ties with Go-Toba. It seems that once Go-Saga came to power, connections to Go-Toba were no longer something to be hidden, and the wounds of the Jōkyū War, in Kyoto at least, had been more or less healed.[20] The connection between *Shokukokinshū* and Go-Toba went deeper. It is clear from the title of the collection and other elements associated with it that *Shinkokinshū*, Go-Toba's creation, was its model. In his account of the banquet that accompanied its completion, Go-Fukakusa draws the parallels proudly and explicitly, and the later history *Masukagami* also comments on the relationship.[21]

The resulting collection is seen as having more of Shinkan in it than of Tameie, and the tensions among the compilers are evident at every turn. The first poem, for instance, goes to Teika, but the second is by Kiyosuke (1104–1177), once head of the Rokujō clan and Shunzei's fierce rival. And in terms of numbers, Munetaka Shinnō has the most poems in the anthology.

In any case, the main line of Tameie's descendants, the Nijō house, and its partisans were as displeased as he had been that the commission for *Shokukokinshū* was shared, and to the extent that they remained at the center of court poetry for another century or so, the reputation of the collection suffered. In the above-cited passage from *Genshō Waka Kuden*, Genshō goes on to attack the collection for being excessively influenced by Shinkan's quirky tastes. And Ton'a (1289–1372), in his *Seiashō*, is similarly negative about Shinkan's role.[22] (Ton'a was not related by blood to the Nijō but he became one of their strongest champions.) The jealousy of the Nijō house with regard to their perceived position as the premier family of court poets became a theme that was to dominate the next century of poetic activity in the capital. And the whole court was soon dragged into the fray. Initially, the Bakufu remained as much as possible at the periphery of the literary dispute, though eventually it became directly involved. In the end, then, as will be discussed below, it was the inability of the court to resolve its squabbles internally that led to Bakufu intervention even at the level of imperial anthologizing.

Tameie's house did not have to share the limelight for long. In the seventh month of 1266, just months after the *Shokukokinshū* presentation banquet, Munetaka Shinnō ran afoul of the Bakufu and was forced to return to Kyoto in disgrace. His political fall left Shinkan and the anti-Mikohidari group without a powerful backer, and suspect themselves. They were quickly shunted away from the poetry center, though not out of the picture entirely.

As noted earlier, Go-Saga's decision to commission anthologies that roughly corresponded with the beginning of his two sons' reigns seems to have set a precedent. Because Go-Saga came to favor his second son, Kameyama, over his first, Go-Fukakusa, a struggle developed between the two over whose descendants should occupy the throne, and more importantly, the position of imperial family head.[23] As the dispute developed into an outright split, each side attempted to sponsor an anthology every time there was a shift in power over the next few decades, as though this represented some sort of legitimation. This pattern first became clear when Kameyama's son Go-Uda was named emperor in 1274. Within two years (and it might have been sooner if the succession had been smooth — in fact the timing of the commission can be seen as "proof" that Kameyama's side had finally consolidated its position) Kameyama commissioned another imperial anthology, which became known as *Shokushūishū*.

There being now no serious rivals to Mikohidari hegemony, the commission went to Tameie's son, Tameuji (1222–86) alone. Tameuji completed his work by 1278. The result is pretty much forgettable from a literary standpoint, but two historical points stand out.[24] First, there was a relatively high proportion of warrior (*bushi*) poets represented, according to scholars, though then, as now, the notion of what constituted a warrior was so vague as to be almost meaningless in this context. Were these real, sword-carrying warriors, or were they aristocrats who happened to live in Kamakura? Most were the latter, of course.[25] Yet it does indicate that the Mikohidari house was beginning to broaden its patron base, and several decades later, Emperor Hanazono chastised the Nijō branch of the family (especially Nijō Tameyo, Tameuji's son) for certifying would-be poets too easily, essentially pandering their poetic heritage to anyone who could pay, regardless of social class.[26]

The second consequence of *Shokushūishū* was that it brought into the open a brewing dispute among Tameie's descendants. Tameuji had included just a few poems by his niece and nephew, Tameko (1250?–1316?) and Tamekane (1254–1332), of what would come to be called the Kyōgoku branch of the family. Their father, Tamenori (1227–79), was incensed and filed a formal letter of protest with the Bureau of Poetry. Tameuji was already under attack by another of Tameie's sons, (Reizei) Tamesuke (1263–1328), over the family estate. He and Tamenori thereafter refused to enter each other's homes, and the split between the Nijō branch on one side, and the Kyōgoku and Reizei branches on the other became the dominant reality within court poetry circles.[27]

Since each side also allied itself with one or the other of the two contending imperial factions, literary matters became inextricably tied to court politics as never before. I have covered this ground exhaustively elsewhere, so will not linger on details of these rivalries except as they relate to the topic at hand.[28]

The notion that each shift of power necessarily entailed the commissioning of an imperial anthology held true at the next break, when Go-Uda of the Daikakuji line retired and Fushimi of the Jimyōin line took his place in 1287. By custom over the centuries, imperial anthologies had come to be sponsored by retired emperors rather than by sitting monarchs, but perhaps because Go-Fukakusa had not shown any particular bent for poetry, Fushimi took it upon himself to attempt the next anthology in 1293.[29] During his time as crown prince, Fushimi had grown close to Kyōgoku Tamekane, and now hoped he could involve Tamekane in the anthology's compilation. But Tamekane was not the head of the main branch of his family (the Mikohidari), and there were already tensions between him and others in his clan. Fushimi, a traditionalist regarding precedent albeit innovative in his poetic practice, could not break so thoroughly from historical practice as to name Tamekane sole compiler. Instead, he invited representatives from the major poetic houses to participate in a committee. However, his effort failed because neither he nor the Kyōgoku faction he was closely tied to had sufficient clout to persuade the rival houses to cooperate on the project. Moreover, shortly after the attempt, Tamekane was placed under house arrest for some political misstep presumably on behalf of Fushimi's Jimyōin line.

Go-Uda learned from Fushimi's mistake, and in 1301, when his bloc secured the throne and he became *chisei no kimi*[30] and felt compelled to sponsor his own imperial collection, he made no effort at all to harmonize contending parties. He simply turned the whole project over to Nijō Tameyo (1250–1338), who produced a collection, *Shingosenshū*, that favored his faction and its allies at court—a display of partisanship that suggests a leadership vacuum, one that the Ashikaga would eventually fill.

In his choice of poets, Tameyo traces a neat chronology in the collection. The top three poets are his Mikohidari progenitors in order: Teika, Tameie, and Tameuji. Powerful political patrons Saionji Sanekane (1249–1322; because of close personal and marriage ties to both imperial lines and his role as liaison between the court and the Bakufu [*Kantō no mōshitsugi*] he could affect the course of the imperial succession dispute) and Takatsukasa Mototada were also represented in the top nine. Tameyo also paid tribute to his imperial patrons, and again their chronological order matches their rank in terms of numbers of poems overall: Go-Saga, Kameyama, and Go-Uda. The only outsider in the group was Fushimi, who was seventh (tied with Go-Uda and Mototada)—a nod either to his obvious talent, or to political reality, or to both. Tameyo's father, Tameuji, is honored with the opening poem.

Reaction to the collection fell, not surprisingly, along partisan lines. Tamekane was not at all pleased, and sought the compiler out for a confrontation at Saionji Sanekane's mansion, but Tameyo fled. Tamekane was overreacting in a way. In fact, both he and his sister had nine poems in the new collection, only two fewer than the compiler himself, and more than any other poet of the Nijō house. As Inoue Muneo notes, this is all the more remarkable considering that Tamekane had just returned from exile.[31] To be sure, poets of the Kyōgoku school are more or less ignored as a group; furthermore, the Daikakuji line is extremely well represented while among Jimyōin line members only Fushimi received significant attention. So the anthology is not especially balanced, but Tamekane and Tameko actually get more coverage than one might expect.

However, more significantly for the immediate course of the imperial family squabble, Sanekane himself was disgruntled for several reasons, including the fact that one of his sons had not received his due in the anthology. He and Tamekane—who were often at serious odds—found themselves in agreement on this point.[32] Evidence suggests that Sanekane had come to favor the Kyōgoku and Jimyōin factions at this stage. For example, there is Tamekane's sudden return from exile in 1303. (Notably, though Sanekane is assumed to have been behind Tamekane's exile in the first place, he actually participated in at least one of the contests marking Tamekane's homecoming.)[33] In addition, Tamekane's selection as sole compiler of *Gyokuyōshū* would have required Sanekane's support, or at least lack of active interference.

Even the Nijō partisan Ton'a reports years later (c. 1360) that some people had had reservations about *Shingosenshū*, though he uses the pejorative *bōka* ("gossip mongerers," that is, people who like to speak ill of others) to describe them. He says that because the Tsumori family, whose daughter had married Tameyo, seemed to have had a strong hand in the collection, less charitable types in the capital had dubbed the collection "Tsumorishū."[34]

One noteworthy feature of the process, however, was that Go-Uda set up a committee called the Rensho, to which a team (including two members of the Tsumori family) was appointed to provide the assistance Tameyo needed for his task. This team supplemented the role of the Wakadokoro (Bureau of Poetry), which since Go-Toba had revived it in 1201 had been the locus of imperial anthology selection activities. By Go-Uda's day, compilers were allowed to choose their own members (*yoriudo*) for the Wakadokoro, so it is not clear why Go-Uda felt the need to set up another body to help in the work.[35]

In any case, perhaps this same Tameyo can be held responsible for finally opening the way for the Bakufu to intervene in the imperial anthology process.[36] At the point of the next succession, when Hanazono took the throne and Fushimi became once again *chisei no kimi* (1308), yet another imperial anthology seemed inevitable. This time Fushimi learned from his own previous error and Go-Uda's success, and he simply appointed his charge, Kyōgoku Tamekane, to be sole compiler of the effort. This collection would clearly cover the other half of court poetry that had been ignored by Go-Uda and Tameyo.

But Tameyo was not about to sit back quietly. Two decades earlier, his stepmother Abutsu (Tameie's last wife, and mother of Reizei Tamesuke) had appealed to the Bakufu in her dispute with the Nijō descendants over Tameie's estate. Tameyo saw himself as the legitimate family head, and as such not only the rightful heir to the tangible estate (the object of his dispute with Abutsu) but also the only one who could rightfully be asked to compile an imperial anthology, since poetry was, in his words, the "family vocation" (*kagyō*). If the Bakufu was going to be brought into the one issue, he apparently felt it also ought to have a voice in the other. When he lodged a formal protest against Tamekane's appointment as *chokusenshū* compiler, he took pains to send it both to the court and to the Bakufu. Details of the incident are outside the scope of this paper, but briefly, in 1310 Tameyo and Tamekane exchanged a series of suits and countersuits in which they attempted to settle, mainly by reference to past court practices and the issue of Tamekane's exile, whether or not Tamekane had the right to compile *Gyokuyōshū*.[37] In any case, the important point is that Tameyo *invited* the Bakufu officially to arbitrate in an area that it had not intervened in before as an institution. (It is my contention that the interventions by Michiie on behalf of the Bakufu in the case of *Shinchokusenshū* and by Munetaka Shinnō on behalf of Shinkan et al. in *Shokukokinshū* were more individual than institutional. But this time, Tameyo was making a formal plea to Kamakura.)

Tameyo may have ended up regretting his decision to involve the Bakufu, for it eventually ruled against him. Though unfortunately no formal decision or order now exists, Fukuda Hideichi has cited a letter by Tameyo that states clearly that in the fifth month of 1311, the Bakufu made a formal ruling in favor of Tamekane as sole compiler, and that Fushimi quickly issued the appropriate imperial order.[38]

By now it should come as no surprise that yet another anthology, *Shokusenzaishū*, would be commissioned by Go-Uda of the Daikakuji line shortly after his second son, Go-Daigo, ascended the throne in 1318. He chose Tamekane's rival, Tameyo, as sole compiler, and the results were dryly assessed in *Masukagami*: "Since this was the same compiler who had done *Shingosenshū*, naturally it did not differ much from that collection."[39] In this anthology, Tameyo got his revenge by refusing to include any poems by Tamekane or Tameko. Moreover, he had the temerity to change the wording of one of the poems by Fushimi's widow, Eifukumon'in, despite strong protests from her and Hanazono. The world of poetry was now as completely polarized as the court itself.

Just how fragmented things had become was soon clear. Go-Daigo, it seems, was not content to have an anthology commissioned on his behalf by his father. Just five years later he ordered yet another collection, which became *Shokugoshūishū*. That he should have done so while he was still on the throne is significant. Except for Fushimi's aborted 1293 attempt, imperial anthologies had for over two centuries been the charge of retired emperors.[40] By sponsoring an anthology, Go-Daigo, whose descendants had been left out of the Compromise of 1317 (Bunpō Wadan), seemed to be signaling his determination to remain at the center of the imperial court.[41] There is a superficial similarity with Go-Toba's situation at the beginning of the thirteenth century, though Go-Toba was far more successful at bringing together the poetic and political factions at court as he prepared *Shinkokinshū*. Go-Daigo, on the other hand, put his collection in the hands of Nijō Tamefuji (1275–1324), son of Tameyo. Tamefuji, whom Hanazono evaluated with relative generosity (in terms of moral character, if not poetic ability), died before finishing the job, and in any case Tameyo had kept a firm hand on things behind the scenes, so the result was another partisan anthology.[42]

The events surrounding Go-Daigo's failed restoration attempt, the fall of the Kamakura Bakufu, the rise of the Ashikaga, and the establishment of a rival court at Yoshino all had their effect on the world of public waka, too. In particular, reign changes were no longer automatically accompanied by a new imperial collection. Perhaps this development was simply a result of the unsettled times, but it could also be strong evidence that the emperor was becoming less and less relevant. The dispute between the junior and senior lines had now reached its logical end, with each faction turning to outside forces for support. For such interests, an imperial anthology as a declaration of cultural hegemony might have seemed a luxury, at least initially, though it was not long before those who supported this or that imperial faction began to see the value of an imperial anthology as a mark of legitimacy.

One imperial family member, however, still strove to find a significant cultural role for the imperial house. The "Compromise of 1317" had disenfranchised the heirs of both Go-Daigo and Hanazono, and the two emperors could not have reacted more differently. Go-Daigo, of course, attempted to raise an army. Hanazono, by contrast, buried himself in Confucian and Buddhist writings, partly in hopes of finding out where he and his forefathers had "gone wrong," and partly to find a way to redefine the imperial role in an age in which emperors had been stripped of real political power.[43]

It is not surprising, then, that when matters had settled a bit in the capital, Hanazono began to promote the idea of an imperial anthology, probably in late 1342 if we are to judge from the increase at that time in palace-sponsored poetry contests, which could provide materials for an anthology.[44] In addition to political motivations, he and Eifukumon'in (who died earlier in 1342) had long held a literarily partisan interest in a new anthology. Their old poetry circle had almost all died, and Tamekane had left no blood heirs to carry on the family line. On his deathbed, Fushimi had expressed his wish that the Kyōgoku style, as embodied by Tame-kane, be kept alive.[45] Hanazono claims that Fushimi's words were directed at Go-Fushimi, Fushimi's first son, who was *chisei no kimi* at the time of Fushimi's death. But Go-Fushimi did not get along with Tamekane, and in fact did nothing to obtain a pardon for him during his second exile, so it fell to Eifukumon'in and Hanazono to keep the Kyōgoku flame burning.

When the opportunity arose, however, and retired emperor Kōgon, with Hanazono's backing, set to the task, it was now necessary to get the explicit permission of the new Bakufu in Kyoto. In fact, Kōgon had to petition twice before the Bakufu finally approved.

Unfortunately, there seems to be no paper trail to delineate this process. The only hint comes from Tōin Kinkata's diary, *Entairyaku*. Kinkata (1291–1360) describes a meeting between Kōgon and Ashikaga Tadayoshi in the tenth month of 1344 in which Kōgon complained that his request for an anthology had been ignored the previous year. According to Kinkata, Tadayoshi then gave his permission to the project.[46] We do not know why Kōgon's first request was denied (or at least ignored). Opinion among scholars ranges from the suggestion that Tadayoshi simply forgot the request, all the way to the notion that he favored the Nijō house and was looking for an opportunity to support it.[47] Regardless, the fact that Kōgon could not act without Tadayoshi's assent demonstrates clearly that the imperial family had lost control over the commissioning of *chokusenshū*. Practically speaking, Ashikaga support was probably necessary from an economic standpoint as well, since recurring warfare had taken its toll, for instance, on Hanazono's ability to finance a big project like an imperial anthology.

The resulting collection, *Fūgashū*, more or less completed by 1348, broke new ground in imperial anthologies. To begin with, it was the first collection since Tameie's *Shokukokinshū* (1265) to have both Chinese and Japanese prefaces. The intervening anthologies had perhaps come so rapidly that there was insufficient time to prepare prefaces. But the Hanazono we see in his diary was a ruler who fully recognized the social and political import of an imperial anthology, and he was not about to let such a monument be published without proper prefaces. Expanding on the notion of poetry's relationship with government that is found as far back as the *Kokinshū*'s *kana* preface, Hanazono writes in his own *kana* preface: "[Waka] instructs the subject and advises the ruler. In short, it forms the basis of government."[48]

Like no imperial anthology before it, *Fūgashū* addresses the unsettled nature of its time. Even in the preface, Hanazono discusses the conditions under which the collection was produced: "Recently the dust of conflict in our land has settled, the horses on the battlefield are reined in, and the rough waves on the four seas have calmed. . . . And now, following the precedent of the Genkyū era (i.e., the time of *Shinkokinshū*), we select and collect into twenty books such poems old and new as come to our attention and suit us."[49]

But its poetry and headnotes, too, discuss warfare and its dislocations in a way that earlier anthologies would never have done.[50] Headnotes and poems like the following:

Composed when she heard that the Lieutenant of the Right Guards Koremori had died on the beach at Kumano,

Kanashiku mo	How sad
Kakaru ukime o	That such a thing
Mikumano no	Should come to pass—
Urawa no nami ni	You throw yourself into the waves
Mi o shizumekeru	Off Kumano's lovely shore!

Composed when the poet was depressed and acutely aware of the sorrows of this world, having left Kyoto and gone west during an uprising, then returned to the capital only to find all his acquaintances dead.

Sa mo koso wa	O, how this world
Arazu narinuru	Has come to be
Yo ni shi arame	So unlike it ever was—
Miyako mo tabi no	Now even in the capital
Kokochi sae suru	I'm a stranger on a journey![51]

Tsugita and Iwasa also point out that *Fūgashū* varies in other ways— medieval ways, we might say—from earlier anthologies. In the typical anthology of earlier times, the dominant images were, in order of frequency, flowers, the cuckoo (*hototogisu*), moon, and snow. In *Fūgashū*, the major images, in order, are flowers, snow, moon, and mountain hut. The growing importance of the mountain hut image is significant. Depending on the context, it can suggest a hermit sage (FGS 1827) or a courtier caught up in warfare (FGS 1753). The former is a trope with deep roots in Japanese literature (as in Kamo no Chōmei's 1212 essay *Hōjōki*, and even earlier waka references). However, the latter was new to waka and marks the anthology as truly a product of its time, since, traditionally, the waka in imperial anthologies simply did not make explicit reference to historical events.[52]

But Hanazono and Kōgon were not content to portray the court as passive victims of their circumstances. They also hoped to demonstrate that the imperial presence still had significance. Poems 2 and 3 in the anthology become here thinly veiled allegories:

Kokonoe ya	In the jeweled garden
Tamashiku niwa ni	Within the nine-fold walls
Murasaki no	A line of purple sleeves
Sode o tsuranuru	Stretches across a thousand ages—
Chiyo no hatsuharu	Another spring begins!
	—Shunzei

Tachisomuru	Shining like
Haru no hikari to	A brightening spring
Miyuru kana	That has just begun—
Hoshi o tsuranuru	An array of stars
Kumo no uebito	These dwellers in the clouds!
	—Kujō Kanazane

Expressions like "nine-fold walls," "purple sleeves," and "dwellers in the clouds" all refer to the imperial palace and its courtiers. Even in their original contexts these poems were celebrations of life at court, specifically and most significantly life at Go-Toba's court, seen from the other end of the Kamakura period as a kind of Golden Age. There is no mistaking the message here—nor the irony that Hanazono and Kōgon needed Bakufu permission to deliver it.[53] (They knew enough to honor their patron, too; among the poets in *Fūgashū*, Ashikaga Takauji is tied for sixteenth place, along with Saionji Sanekane, with a total of sixteen poems.)

Given the thesis that sponsoring an imperial anthology was one way of establishing a cultural hegemony to shore up a (perceived) political one, we would expect that the Southern Court would also attempt to sponsor a collection. Certainly the talent was there, since many of the Nijō poets who had been the backbone of the Daikakuji line's poetry circle had accompanied Go-Daigo and his court to the south. And in fact, an anthology was put together by Munenaga Shinnō (1311–89?), son of Go-Daigo and grandson of Nijō Tameyo, under the title *Shin'yōshū* (Collection of New Leaves), a surprisingly unconventional title for an anthology that was supposed to establish its sponsors' traditional right to rule.[54] Like *Fūgashū*, *Shin'yōshū* contains its share of allegories on the warfare of the times, and expressions of desire that the imperial line be reunited (under one line or the other, of course, depending on the particular anthology).[55] But it was not even begun until 1374, long after the breakaway court had settled in Yoshino. By this time, the Northern Court had compiled three anthologies and was working on its fourth.

After *Fūgashū*, the *chokusenshū* took another large step away from imperial control. To this point, even as Bakufu interference in the process had grown, the conception and planning of the anthologies had always been in the hands of the court. Though Hanazono and Kōgon had needed explicit Bakufu permission, the idea for the project had been their own, and had come largely in response to their own agenda, which included providing a mouthpiece for the Kyōgoku style.

But Ashikaga Takauji recognized the value and importance of controlling the traditional canon, and in 1356, a year after regaining the capital from armies of the Southern Court, he directed Emperor Go-Kōgon to commission yet another anthology, which was to become *Shinsenzaishū*.[56] It is hard to imagine Yoritomo or any of the Hōjō approaching the court with such a request, and if they had, it would surely have been rejected out of hand. That Takauji did so, and got what he wanted, is a clear demonstration not only of how differently he viewed the parameters of his power but also of how much conditions had changed and how weakened the court had finally become. In addition to the fact that the shogunal position had been redefined and was no longer held by an imperial prince, as it had been under the Hōjō, the shogun himself now resided in Kyoto, which put Takauji much closer to the literary world he was now seeking to influence.

Again, there is no convenient order or letter proving Takauji's intervention, but Tōin Kinkata in his diary *Entairyaku* is quite unambiguous about Takauji's role: "This imperial anthology was initiated at the direction (*mune*) of the military authorities [Takauji]."[57] Go-Kōgon quickly issued the order. The anthology does not play favorites in terms of imperial politics (Fushimi, Go-Uda, Go-Daigo, and Hanazono are among the top ten poets), though with Nijō Tamesada (1293–1360) as the compiler, Nijō poets dominated from among the poetry schools (Tameyo ranks first in numbers of poems). Takauji's name appears among the top ten, though otherwise there are no warrior-aristocrats in the top group.

It was especially important that Go-Kōgon be involved in the project as its sponsor, since Takauji and his allies had placed him on the throne without proper ceremony at a time when the Southern Court was ascendant and in possession of the imperial regalia. Perhaps it was by a kind of circular logic, since only an emperor or retired emperor could commission a *Chokusenshū*. But Takauji apparently saw the imperial anthology as an important mark of imperial legitimacy, if not quite on the same level as the imperial regalia. To that extent the court still retained its mysterious cachet.

A few years later, Takauji's son, Yoshiakira, again used Go-Kōgon and a new imperial anthology to celebrate another round of victories over the frequently resurgent Southern Court. In 1363, after returning Go-Kōgon to Kyoto from a "safekeeping" visit to Ōmi, he had the sovereign sponsor a collection that came to be called *Shinshūishū*. Nijō Tameaki (1295–1364) was named compiler but died before its completion, so the project was finished by Ton'a. Contemporary accounts make it clear that once again the idea for the collection came from the shogun, and one source, Konoe Michitsugu's *Gukanki*, says the anthology excited little public interest.[58] None of the sources contained in *Dainihon Shiryō* even names the sponsoring emperor, Go-Kōgon, the character for "choku" being the only indication that an imperial personage was involved. In the case of the previous anthology, Go-Kōgon had been prominently mentioned in most of the accounts. This omission may well indicate again how irrelevant actual emperors had become to the compiling of imperial anthologies.

In *Shinshūishū* the swing toward Nijō poetry continued, with Tamefuji, Tameyo, and Tamesada among the leading poets. There is significant warrior representation in the collection as a whole, though no warrior-aristocrat's name appears among the top ten compilers.[59]

In any case, just as past imperial successions had occasioned new imperial anthologies, so new Ashikaga shoguns wished to leave their mark on the cultural scene. In fact, Yoshiakira's son, Yoshimitsu, followed this trend by asking Emperor Go-Enyū in 1375 to order another *chokusenshū*. This project became *Shingoshūishū*, though owing to the continuing conflict in Kyoto, it was not completed and presented until nearly ten years later. The compilers were Nijō Tametō (1341–81) and Nijō Tameshige (1325–85), and it is significant that three Ashikaga shoguns—Takauji, Yoshiakira, and Yoshimitsu—are among the top ten poets. The warrior aristocracy was making its way to the front of the ranks.

The twenty-first imperial anthology was *Shinshokukokinshū*, requested by Yoshimitsu's son Ashikaga Yoshinori, and formally commissioned by Emperor Go-Hanazono from Asukai Masayo in 1433. The Nijō line had died out and Yoshinori disliked the Reizei line, so Go-Hanazono commissioned Asukai Masayo, who was ill-prepared, and received no help from the Reizei house, which could have provided useful historical materials. Medieval factionalism once again impeded an imperial collection. But by now poetic energies had turned largely to *renga*, and *Shinshokukokinshū* turned out to be the last of the imperial anthologies.

As control over the sponsorship of *chokusenshū* slipped out of imperial hands (though by definition an imperial order was still required), was there a detectable change in poetic style, and if there was, would it be fair to call it a *bushi* style? If the warrior elite appropriated the imperial anthology for themselves, did they do anything with it to propagate their own values? The problem itself is relevant, though it would require separate treatment to be handled thoroughly. But initially the answer appears to be that, as seen in the earlier *Fūgashū* examples, there were some changes in poetic topic and vocabulary, but by and large waka remained little different. There is no evidence of a unique warrior style. One would find it virtually impossible to distinguish one of Takauji's poems in an imperial anthology from the poems of a traditional courtier.

By the end of the Kamakura period, the poetic scene was fragmented in terms of style. Any poet, warrior or otherwise, had a range of styles and masters to choose from. To the extent that a particular imperial anthology in the thirteenth or fourteenth century was in the hands of a particular faction, its contents would more likely reflect that faction's bent, and it was regardless of warrior input. In fact, the warrior-sponsors themselves (the Ashikaga shoguns especially) got caught up and began to take sides in the Nijō-Reizei-Kyōgoku dispute that reverberated through the age.

In traditional anthologies, poems in the Seasonal, Love, and Miscellaneous sections were deemed the most important literarily, and the most acceptable as sources for allusive variation. In the imperial anthologies through *Shingoshūishū* (1384), the courtly tradition still held in these sections, and to the extent that new vocabulary and diction had entered these collections (and there was not much of the former) it reflected stylistic change within the courtly poetry houses and was not the result of warrior influence. Perhaps this is why the Ashikaga turned to *renga* anthologies and other artistic outlets that better expressed the new age.

THIS SURVEY of imperial anthologies from the thirteenth and fourteenth centuries has shown a steadily increasing encroachment by the Bakufu (tentative and sporadic on the part of Kamakura, aggressive on the part of the Ashikaga) on the sponsorship and compilation of these collections. This encroachment first took the form of behind-the-scenes suggestions in the thirteenth century—sometimes politically motivated (as in Michiie and *Shinchokusenshū*) and sometimes motivated by literary differences (as in shogun Prince Munetaka and *Shokukokinshū*), but always low key and indirect. By the fourteenth century, however, the Bakufu was being asked to make formal rulings, as in their confirmation of Tamekane as sole *Gyokuyōshū* compiler. And by the 1340s, Ashikaga Takauji's permission was required for *Fūgashū*. Soon, the Ashikaga shoguns were actually initiating the collections themselves, as with the last four anthologies. Clearly the establishment of the Ashikaga shogunate marked a turning point.

I have characterized this process as an attempt by the warrior aristocracy to take control of the poetic canon that had been central to Japan's cultural life since the Nara period. Yet I also maintain that the new aristocracy did not really attack the core of that cultural legacy. Though warrior poets began to appear with ever greater frequency in imperial anthologies as early as *Shinkokinshū*, their work was rarely identifiable as being the product of a soldier's mentality, or even of someone who lived outside the capital. Furthermore, the fact that four Ashikaga shoguns (Takauji, Yoshiakira, Yoshimitsu, and in the fifteenth century, Yoshinori) chose to continue exploiting the imperial collection for the cultural cachet it still held, demonstrates that while the de facto sponsorship of imperial anthologies had passed into the hands of the warrior aristocracy by the 1340s, the power of the traditional courtiers to dictate cultural values was still strong.

The last three imperial anthologies excited little interest even in their day, and waka ultimately gave way to *renga* and Nō as the popular literary activities among warrior aristocrats.[60] Yet the flowers, birds, and wind, the Waiting Woman, the moon, the sense of *aware* all still found their way into the newer arts. It was not until the assault of Saikaku and the merchant class centuries later that courtly values came to be largely supplanted in Japanese culture, and even then a reservoir remained to be tapped by nationalist scholars like Motoori Norinaga.

CHAPTER 9

Cultural Life of the Warrior Elite in the Fourteenth Century

H. PAUL VARLEY

THE PRINCIPAL DETERMINANT of cultural life among the warrior elite (*buke*) of the Muromachi period was the location of this elite—that is, members of the Ashikaga shogunal house and the shugo-daimyos and their families—in Kyoto in proximity to the imperial court and the courtier class. The Muromachi warrior elite, and indeed the warrior class as a whole, was profoundly influenced by traditional court culture. This is apparent not only in the pursuit by warriors of the classical courtier arts, such as *waka* poetry, but also in the role they played as patrons and participants in the development of the new arts of the Muromachi period, including the *nō* theater, *renga* (linked verse), and *chanoyu* (the tea ceremony).

The presence of warrior leaders in Kyoto was nothing new. From the time of the rise of a warrior class in the provinces during the Heian period, its leaders were frequently in the capital. Thus, although historians speak, for example, of Taira and Minamoto going out from Kyoto, serving in provincial posts, and settling down in the provinces, in fact many of these men continued to keep residence in the capital and in many cases to spend more time there than at their provincial bases. A prominent example is the Minamoto chieftain Yoshiie (1039–1106), victorious commander in the Later Three Years War (1083–87) in northern Honshu in the late eleventh century, who spent most of his life after the war—he died in 1106—living in Kyoto.

Warrior chieftains also became the clients of influential men at court. Minamoto leaders, for example, served as samurai—as the "claws and teeth" (*sōga*)—of the Fujiwara regents; and the Ise Taira, beginning about the early twelfth century, established a patron-client relationship with the senior retired emperor Shirakawa (r. 1072–86) that lasted for three generations of retired emperors and Ise Taira.

The putative adoption of courtier ways and the acquisition of courtier culture by the Ise Taira during their ascendancy in Kyoto under Kiyomori (1118–81) in the late twelfth century is well known. The fact that our primary source of knowledge about this process of Taira "aristocratization" is the war tale *Heike monogatari* (The Tale of the Heike) is itself significant. Until very recently the *Heike* has been regarded by the Japanese as generally reliable history, and through the centuries they have little questioned the veracity of the *Heike*'s portrayal of how the Ise Taira became aristocratized—that is, became what we may call courtier-warriors. But the principal version of the *Heike*, the Kakuichi version, was completed in 1371 and therefore was a product of the early Muromachi period, indeed of the Kitayama cultural epoch. The textual evolution of the *Heike* was an exceedingly complex process extending over at least a century and a half, and I do not wish to draw patently simple conclusions from any single version, even the great Kakuichi *Heike*. But I suggest as a hypothesis that much of the aristocratization of the Ise Taira as described in the *Heike* was a product of Muromachi tastes. I shall return to and test this hypothesis at the end of this essay in a discussion of the warrior plays of the *nō* theater. The warrior plays were almost entirely the creation of Zeami (1363–1443), one of the great recipients of elite warrior patronage in the Kitayama epoch, and nearly all the plays are based on stories from the *Heike*.

I shall speak only briefly about the cultural influence of the court on the warrior elite during the Kamakura period. Even though the elite was primarily situated in Kamakura, court influence on it was considerable. The Rokuhara magistrates (*tandai*), some of whom later became shogunal regents (*shikken*), were of course able to partake directly of court culture at its source. The shogun Sanetomo (1192–1219), although he never visited Kyoto, became an avid admirer of court life and art, devoting himself especially to the study of *waka* poetry. Sanetomo benefited in particular from the instruction in *waka* that he received by mail from Fujiwara no Teika (1162–1241).[1] Court culture was also channeled to Kamakura by the Fujiwara and princes of the blood who were brought to Kyoto to be shoguns, creating their own "courts" in the east, which became centers of courtly conduct and pursuit of the courtier arts.[2]

The Kenmu Restoration (1333–36) and the founding of the Ashikaga-Muromachi Bakufu (1336–1573) brought a decisive shift in the center of *buke* power from Kamakura to Kyoto. Such diverse records as the *Kenmu Shikimoku* (Kenmu Code), the *Nijō-Kawara Rakusho* (Nijō-Kawara Lampoons), and *Taiheiki* tell of the chaotic conditions caused by the massive influx of warriors into the imperial capital during these years. The Lampoons, which were compiled during the Kenmu Restoration, begin, for example, with the grim observation that among the "things common in the capital these days [are] night attacks, robbers, counterfeit edicts, criminals, fast horses, random fighting, [and] severed heads."[3] And *Taiheiki* observes that, whereas courtiers were steadily descending into poverty, *buke* were "increasing their wealth a hundredfold day by day."[4] We can have little doubt of the seriousness of the social disruption and breakdown in order caused by this warrior influx when we observe that the new shogun, Ashikaga Takauji (1305–58), and his advisers chose to devote the first five articles of the *Kenmu Shikimoku* to injunctions aimed at curbing what we can assume was primarily the extravagant, rambunctious, and lawless behavior of newly arrived warriors in Kyoto.

Articles 1 and 2 of the *Kenmu Shikimoku* are sumptuary decrees, inveighing against extravagance, including the wearing of finely wrought silver swords and richly elegant attire of damask and brocade that "dazzle the eyes," and against gambling and consorting with loose women.[5] The word here translated as "extravagance" is *basara*, which seems to mean extravagance or excessiveness especially in the sense of going beyond what is proper for one's status or position (*bun*). *Basara* appears frequently in fourteenth-century records, most memorably perhaps as a descriptive term for the behavior of three warrior chieftains—Sasaki Dōyo (1306–73), Kō no Moronao (d. 1351), and Toki Yoritō (d. 1342)—whose escapades are vividly recounted in *Taiheiki*.

Interestingly, the two forms of gambling mentioned in article 2 are associated with tea competitions (*cha-yoriai*; *tōcha*) and linked verse (*renga*) gatherings, at which people are said to have made wagers and to have incurred losses "beyond calculation."[6] The Nijō-Kawara Lampoons confirm the popularity of both tea competitions and *renga* poetizing in Kyoto around this time. In the case of *renga*, the Lampoons convey the sense of an artistic activity out of control; it notes that the Kyoto and Kamakura styles were intermingled, creating a phony kind of *renga* belonging to no school, *renga* and *waka* were being composed with all participants claiming to qualify as judges (there was "no one who was not a judge"), and no distinctions were recognized between hereditary and newly risen schools of verse. The situation was one of "unchecked confusion" (*jiyū rōzeki*).[7]

We can glimpse the reaction of one member of the courtier class to this *basara–jiyū rōzeki* type of behavior in the following remarks by Yoshida Kenkō (1283–1350) in *Tsurezuregusa* (Essays in Idleness), which he wrote in the early 1330s:

> The man of breeding never appears to abandon himself completely to his pleasures; even his manner of enjoyment is detached. It is the rustic boors who take all their pleasures grossly. They squirm their way through the crowd to get under the trees; they stare at the blossoms with eyes for nothing else; they drink sake and compose linked verse; and finally they heartlessly break off great branches and cart them away. When they see a spring they dip their hands and feet to cool them; if it is the snow, they jump down to leave their footprints. No matter what the sight, they are never content merely with looking at it.[8]

Kenkō refers here to *hana-no-moto* linked verse or linked verse composed by people gathered "under the blossoming cherry trees," a form of entertainment that became popular during the Kenmu Restoration and the early Muromachi period, especially among the townspeople of Kyoto and other commoners. In an earlier age, a courtier litterateur like Kenkō would hardly have taken note of activities of this sort among the lower classes. But in the social disruption of the times, he could not ignore— even if he might not understand the significance of—such activities, which no doubt occurred frequently and were quite conspicuous. *Renga*, like *nō*, performed the important function in the cultural history of this period of perpetuating the classical courtier literary and aesthetic traditions that flowed from *waka* poetry. It also was much affected—again, like *nō*—by popular tastes, such as those at work in *hana-no-moto* linked verse.

Although Yoshida Kenkō may have had little real contact with the lower classes (for example, the "rustic boors" mentioned in the passage from *Tsurezuregusa* quoted above), he appears to have become familiar with at least some members of the warrior elite who took up residence in Kyoto during the Kenmu Restoration and later. We surmise this primarily from a story in *Taiheiki* about the *basara* warrior Kō no Moronao, a leading vassal of Ashikaga Takauji who, as portrayed in *Taiheiki*, is almost a stereotype of the arrogant, ostentatious, and luxury-loving warrior chieftain in the capital during this age. Notorious as a womanizer (pursuing especially women of the court nobility), Moronao, in the *Taiheiki* story, engages Kenkō—"an eremite (*tonseisha*) skilled in letters"—to write a love letter to a court lady married to a provincial warrior named Enya Hangan. But when the lady, a great beauty slightly past her prime, refuses even to read the letter, Moronao becomes so enraged with Kenkō—rather unfairly, it must seem to us—that he forbids him ever to come near the Kō residence again.[9]

The terms *basara* and *jiyū rōzeki*, along with a third term that appears in the Nijō-Kawara Lampoons, *gekokujō* (overthrowing or surpassing one's superiors), vividly convey the chaotic, and yet vital and exciting, nature of cultural life in Kyoto from the time of the Kenmu Restoration and the establishment of the Muromachi Bakufu until at least the late fourteenth century. Prescott Wintersteen and Suzanne Gay have discussed how the Bakufu was gradually integrated into Kyoto life over a period of decades as a military, administrative, and judicial entity.[10] In this essay I wish to examine how the Bakufu—the warrior elite—entered Kyoto's cultural life and before long came to control much of it through patronage. In the process, the Ashikaga and other warrior leaders contributed both to the perpetuation of classical court culture and to the expansion of culture-art into important new realms, such as *nō*, *renga*, and *chanoyu*.

The cultural life of the Muromachi warrior elite during the mid-fourteenth century stands apart from that of the remainder of the Muromachi period precisely in the qualities conveyed by the terms *basara*, *jiyū rōzeki*, and *gekokujō*. Beginning in the late fourteenth and early fifteenth centuries, the exuberance and even "lawlessness" of earlier Muromachi warrior culture was increasingly restrained and controlled. The wild tea-judging parties and freewheeling *renga* sessions described in the Nijō-Kawara Lampoons, for example, were transformed into the "way of tea" and into a linked verse that was a serious form of versifying based on traditional courtier aesthetics. And *dengaku*, described in *Taiheiki* as a cause of the downfall of the Kamakura Bakufu,[11] was channeled, along with *sarugaku*, into the classical art of *nō*. It is striking—and perhaps ironic—that, while the elite culture of the Muromachi period thus made the transition from the extravagance and upheaval of the mid-fourteenth century to an increasingly more controlled artistic and aesthetic order from the Kitayama epoch (late fourteenth and early fifteenth centuries) on, society and politics steadily descended into the abyss of *gekokujō*.

Let us look at the career of Sasaki Dōyo, the most prominent of the *basara* warriors, as a starting point for an inquiry into the elite warrior culture of the early Muromachi period. Dōyo was born in 1306 into the Kyōgoku or junior branch of the Sasaki family of Ōmi Province, and entered the service of the Kamakura Bakufu in 1326. Joining the Hōjō leader Takatoki (1303–33) in taking Buddhist vows,[12] he assumed the name Dōyo (his original name was Takauji). In 1332 the Bakufu gave Dōyo the important assignment of escorting Emperor Go-Daigo (r. 1318–39) into exile after Go-Daigo's failed effort to rally loyalist forces to overthrow the Bakufu (Genkō Disturbance). The very next year, however, Dōyo turned against the Bakufu when he secretly transmitted an order from the exiled Go-Daigo to Ashikaga Takauji to rise up against the Hōjō.

During the Kenmu Restoration, Dōyo served as a member of the Ketsudan-sho. In 1335 he joined Takauji in his campaign to the Kantō to put down an uprising by former supporters of the Hōjō led by Takatoki's son Tokiyuki (Nakasendai Uprising). And when Takauji, flouting the orders of Go-Daigo, remained in the Kantō and subsequently fought against an army led by Nitta Yoshisada (1301–38) that Go-Daigo sent to chastise him, Sasaki Dōyo adhered to Takauji. In an age of frequent transfers of allegiance, Dōyo remained faithful to Takauji until the Ashikaga leader's death in 1358, even siding with him during the clash with his brother Tadayoshi (1306–52) from 1350 until 1352 (Kannō Disturbance) that nearly destroyed the Bakufu from within.[13]

When the Ashikaga Bakufu was established in 1336, Dōyo was appointed *shugo* of Wakasa Province and participated in the writing of the *Kenmu Shikimoku*.[14] Dōyo's role as coauthor of the *Shikimoku* was ironic inasmuch as he, at least as portrayed in *Taiheiki*, became probably the most flagrant violator of the *Shikimoku*'s sumptuary prescriptions.

Before turning to the portrayal of Sasaki Dōyo in *Taiheiki*, let me say a few words about the compilation of this war tale and its value as a historical record. Compared with the textual evolution of the early medieval war tales (*Hōgen monogatari*, *Heiji monogatari*, and *Heike monogatari*), which underwent extensive alteration and embellishment over a century and a half or more, especially at the hands of tale singers (*biwa hōshi*), the process of *Taiheiki*'s evolution was much simpler. Parts of it were written as the events they describe were occurring, and the work as a whole was most likely completed shortly after the terminal point of its story in 1372. Moreover, whereas the *Hōgen*, *Heiji*, and *Heike* have come down to us in many, divergent texts, the *Taiheiki* versions differ only slightly one from another. Although the historicity of *Taiheiki* has been sharply attacked by some scholars, others have demonstrated that important portions of it are generally reliable history.[15] I wish, in any case, to discuss passages from *Taiheiki* concerning Sasaki Dōyo and other *basara* warriors not with the intent of claiming that these passages are true in all their particulars, but to use them as indicators of trends in the cultural tastes and behavior of the early Muromachi warrior elite.

In the tenth month of 1340, according to *Taiheiki*, an expensively and ostentatiously (*basara*) attired party consisting of Sasaki Dōyo and some of his kinsmen went bird hunting in the eastern suburbs of Kyoto. On its return to the city that evening, the party passed Myōhōin Temple, whose head abbot happened to be the younger brother of the retired emperor Kōgon. Admiring the maple trees in the temple's garden—trees whose leaves were then at the height of their autumnal brilliance—members of the group ordered some servants to gather branches from them. The abbot himself was at the time viewing the trees and softly reciting poetry. When he saw the Sasaki servants tearing off branches, he called for help, and a number of monks seized the servants and soundly thrashed them.[16]

When Sasaki Dōyo learned what had happened, he was outraged, demanding to know who—no matter how socially exalted—would have the temerity to treat servants of his family in this manner. Leading some three hundred riders, Dōyo attacked Myōhōin and set it afire. Fanned by a powerful wind, the flames engulfed and destroyed not only Myōhōin but also buildings of nearby Kenninji Temple.[17]

Myōhōin was a branch of the powerful Enryakuji, and the priests of that temple demanded that the Bakufu arrest and execute Sasaki Dōyo and his son Hidetsuna. But Takauji and Tadayoshi, who treasured the services of Dōyo, refused. Only when the Enryakuji priests took the extreme measures of closing their gates and the gates of affiliated temples and shrines and of terminating various prayers and rituals that it conducted for the court and others did the Ashikaga leaders relent. But, avoiding the extreme penalty of execution, they ordered Dōyo and Hidetsuna into distant exile: Dōyo to Dewa and Hidetsuna to Mutsu.

Taiheiki says that when the day arrived for Dōyo and Hidetsuna to leave for their places of exile they were accompanied by some three hundred of their family and followers, all decked out in great finery, including quivers covered with rabbit skin. The use of rabbit skin was intended as an insult to Enryakuji, since the rabbit was the messenger animal of the Shinto shrine, the Hie Shrine, with which Enryakuji was associated (the insult was compounded by the fact that the quivers touched against the posteriors of those who wore them).[18] Sumptuous quantities of food and drink had also been prepared for the journey, and complaisant ladies were waiting at the various inns where father and son planned to stop.[19] Thus, their departure from Kyoto was more like the commencement of a pleasure excursion than the beginning of exile for criminal conduct.

This incident is one of several in *Taiheiki* that suggest an utter disregard on the part of some warrior chieftains of this age for traditional court and ecclesiastical authority and status. Another is the blatant case of lèse-majesté committed a few years later, in 1342, by Toki Yoritō of Mino Province. Returning, like Sasaki Dōyo, with a party from an outing in the Kyoto suburbs, Yoritō encountered the procession of the former emperor Kōgon. Ordered by Kōgon's aides to dismount and perform obeisance, Yoritō demanded to know whose procession he had come upon. When informed that it was the procession of the *in* (retired emperor), Yoritō retorted: "Did you say *in*? Or did you say *inu* (dog)? If it's a dog, perhaps I should shoot it!"[20] He thereupon fired arrows at Kōgon's cart. In this case, even the Ashikaga were alarmed at how far a warrior chieftain had gone in his disrespect for royalty. Tadayoshi was particularly incensed and, according to *Taiheiki*, insisted upon having Toki Yoritō executed, despite pleas for mercy from such exalted and influential people as the Zen priest Musō Soseki (1275–1351).[21]

Another striking example of Sasaki Dōyo's *basara* conduct—but also of his essential refinement and taste—can be found in the *Taiheiki* account of a series of events in 1361. These events centered on the defection to the Southern Court of a leading Bakufu commander, Hosokawa Kiyouji (d. 1362), who had served as *shitsuji* to the Ashikaga shogun. Kiyouji's defection was probably a consequence of the complex of rivalries among the Bakufu's leading commanders over grants of land and offices from the Bakufu; and, in this regard, Sasaki Dōyo was just one rival among many.[22] But *Taiheiki* suggests that Kiyouji was, in the end, prompted to defect by a social coup that Dōyo engineered against him.

Kiyouji had invited the shogun Yoshiakira (1330–67) to a poetry party at his residence on 1361/7/7 (the night of Tanabata), inviting also a number of prominent poets and stocking his residence with drink and many exotic foods. To embarrass and upstage his rival, Dōyo invited the shogun to an affair at his residence on the same night and made it known that he would have the residence sumptuously decorated and that there would be a seven-course meal and a tea-judging competition with many prizes. Compared with the rather staid party planned by Kiyouji, Dōyo's affair promised to be up to date and exciting. Accordingly, Yoshiakira, known for his love of partying and especially of imbibing, chose Dōyo's invitation over Hosokawa Kiyouji's.[23]

When Kiyouji went over to the Southern Court in 1361/11, he became a powerful advocate of the strategy of attacking and occupying Kyoto. Armies of the Southern Court had, in fact, already occupied Kyoto on three occasions—in 1352, 1353, and 1355. Kyoto had traditionally been regarded as a city difficult to defend militarily. Hence, rather than try to mount a defense against a Southern Court attack when conditions were unfavorable, the Ashikaga strategy during this period was simply to withdraw from the city, regroup, and counterattack. The Southern Court managed to hold Kyoto for only a month in 1352 and 1353 and for two months in 1355.

When Kiyouji pressed the idea of taking Kyoto for a fourth time in 1361, Kusunoki Masanori (dates not known), the leading Southern commander, objected on the grounds that occupying the city after it was taken would, as always, be difficult. But so intense was the desire of the courtiers of the Southern Court to return to the "flowery capital" that they overruled Masanori's objection. In the event, Masanori was proved all too right. He and Kiyouji led an army that captured Kyoto in 1361/12, but they were able to hold it less than a month.[24]

Taiheiki tells us that Sasaki Dōyo, forced to leave Kyoto with the shogun Yoshiakira and anticipating that one of the Southern Court commanders would take occupancy of his residence, decided to leave the residence in elegant condition. Accordingly,

[he] spread rush matting with boldly emblazoned crests on the floor of the six-bay banquet chamber (*kaisho*) and arranged everything in its proper place, from the triptych of hanging scrolls to the flower vase, incense burner, teakettle, and server. In the study (*shoin*) he placed a Buddhist verse in grass-writing by Wang Hsi-chih and an anthology by Han Yü, while in the sleeping chamber he laid silken night-garments beside a pillow of scented aloe wood. He provisioned the twelve-bay guardhouse with three poles bearing chickens, rabbits, pheasants, and swans and with a three-*koku* cask brimming with sake. Finally, he directed two *tonseisha* to remain behind, giving them precise instructions that "if someone should come to this dwelling, greet him with a cup of wine."[25]

As it happened, Kusunoki Masanori occupied Dōyo's residence, and so impressed was he with it and with his greeting that, when forced within weeks to abandon it to make way for the returning forces of the Ashikaga, he left the residence even better provisioned than he had found it. He also left a treasured suit of armor and a silver-inlaid sword as gifts for Sasaki Dōyo.[26]

This *Taiheiki* description of Sasaki Dōyo's residence, whether or not it is historically accurate, is extremely illuminating for the cultural historian. For one thing, it illustrates the *basara* taste of the period at its best. In our esteem for—even idealization of—the later trend toward aesthetic restraint and severe economy of expression and display in the arts and elite culture in general, we may be tempted to dismiss or discount the mid-fourteenth century as a time of cultural excess and confusion. Admittedly, there was, as we have observed, much excess and upheaval (*gekokujō*) in the world of elite culture during this period. But the evidence also reveals the exercise of important aesthetic sensibilities by people like Sasaki Dōyo as he is portrayed in this episode from *Taiheiki*. In addition, the account of how Dōyo arranged his residence in anticipation of its being occupied by a Southern Court commander also points toward, indeed sets the stage for, some of the most important cultural developments of the later Kitayama and Higashiyama cultural epochs.

We find in the account, for example, one of the earliest references to a *kaisho* (banquet chamber). Although the available records do not provide information sufficient for us to envisage precisely what kind of room the *kaisho* was, it clearly represented a transitional stage in the evolution of the *shoin*-style room that took concrete form in the fifteenth and sixteenth centuries. In addition to its architectural and aesthetic merits, the *kaisho-shoin* room provided an important new setting for the arts, a setting necessitated, as it were, by the powerful trend toward "situational" (*yoriai*) arts during the Muromachi period:[27] that is, pursuits such as *renga*, *chanoyu*, and flower arrangement (*rikka*) which brought people together to engage socially or collectively in both the creation and the appreciation of art.

The description of Dōyo's residence also mentions the display of various articles, including hanging scrolls, flower vase, incense burner, teakettle, and server, that were very likely—along with the "Buddhist verse in grass-writing by Wang Hsi-chih" and the "anthology by Han Yü"—*karamono* or imported "Chinese articles." As I have discussed elsewhere, the gradual development of connoisseurship in the handling and display of these Chinese articles of art and craft during the Muromachi period was not only central to the creation of *shoin* aesthetics and *chanoyu*: it exerted its influence throughout the arts and elite culture.[28]

As I also have discussed elsewhere, the *tonseisha* whom Dōyo supposedly left in charge of his residence to greet its anticipated new master from the army of the Southern Court were forerunners of the *dōbōshū* (companions) employed by the Ashikaga Bakufu from Yoshimitsu's time.[29] These men became major players in cultural and artistic developments for the remainder of the Muromachi period.

According to *Taiheiki*, Sasaki Dōyo in 1366 played almost exactly the same kind of trick on another rival commander of the Ashikaga Bakufu, Shiba Takatsune (1305–67), that he had played on Hosokawa Kiyouji five years earlier. Father of the *shitsuji* Shiba Yoshimasa (1350–1410), Takatsune had fought with the Ashikaga from the early days of Takauji's rise to national prominence in the 1330s. During his son's term as *shitsuji*, 1362–66, Takatsune exercised considerable influence in Bakufu councils, and in the process made many enemies, including Sasaki Dōyo.[30]

The opportunity for Dōyo to upstage and embarrass Takatsune socially —and culturally—presented itself when Takatsune made plans in the third month of 1366 to hold a *hana-no-moto* (beneath the flowers) party on the lawn of the shogun Yoshiakira's residence in Kyoto. Takatsune sent an especially politely worded invitation to Dōyo, presumably aware that Dōyo's presence at the affair would enhance it as a social occasion. But even as he accepted the invitation, Dōyo began laying plans to have his own *hana-no-moto* party on the same day at the Buddhist temple in Ōharano in the western suburbs of the capital. For this party Dōyo engaged "performers and masters of all the arts throughout the city, not excluding a single one." The performers and masters so engaged included *renga* poets, singers, *dengaku* and *sarugaku* actors, and *shirabyōshi* dancers.[31]

The account of Sasaki Dōyo's Ōharano party is one of the most lavish and ornately worded descriptions of an event in *Taiheiki*. The rails on the bridge leading to the temple, the account says, were covered with gold brocade; the knobs atop the posts were wrapped in gold foil; and imported rugs of damask and twill were spread across the walking planks. In the garden of the temple's main building (*hondō*), enclosures had been erected around blossoming cherry trees, and beneath the trees were huge brass vases brimming with decoratively arranged flowers. Countless incense burners, tightly aligned, emitted rare fragrances that "suffused the four directions." So wonderful were these fragrances that people believed they were in Amida's Pure Land paradise. In the shade of each tree was a curtain, and behind the curtain were chairs, trays heaped with exotic foods, and the preparations for tea-judging competitions (*tōcha*). The prizes to be given to the winners of each competition were piled high, like mountains.[32]

We may assume that Dōyo devoted particular care to the display of the flowers in the brass vases, since he was especially expert in the art of flower arrangement (*rikka*) and, indeed, even wrote a book—*Rikka Kuden Daiji*—on *rikka* etiquette. The mention of chairs in connection with *tōcha* is interesting, because the Ōharano party, if there actually was such a party, occurred on the eve (in the late fourteenth century) of the evolution of the tea ceremony (*chanoyu*). We know that, at first, chairs were used in *chanoyu*, and that this was the result of Chinese influence exerted by Zen priests who visited China during the Kamakura and Muromachi periods and were the main importers of *karamono*, including chairs. Only later did the Japanese move *chanoyu* to the floor, where it then developed in the traditional Japanese manner in accordance with "etiquette on the mats (*tatami*)."[33]

Sasaki Dōyo is one of the most flamboyant personages portrayed in *Taiheiki*, a work notable for its cast of flamboyant, obstreperous, irreverent, and iconoclastic characters. *Taiheiki* describes many warriors and courtiers in Kyoto during the chaotic days of the Kenmu Restoration and the early Muromachi period who submerged themselves in lives of luxury and conspicuous consumption. These were the principal targets, one assumes, of the sumptuary articles in the *Kenmu Shikimoku* discussed at the beginning of this essay. But Dōyo, although guilty of a grave indiscretion—indeed, of *lèse-majesté*—in the Myōhōin incident, stands apart from these other *basara* people because of his taste and artistic sensibilities. He is also distinctive because of his skillful use of culture for political purposes (e.g., the upstagings of Hosokawa Kiyouji and Shiba Takatsune).

Yet history remembers Dōyo best, I believe, for his real contributions to the development of the elite culture of the early Muromachi period. In addition to his activities in the shaping of *rikka* and *chanoyu* (at its initial, *tōcha*, stage), Dōyo was an important participant in the elevation of *renga* to a serious art during these years. He was on familiar terms with both the regent Nijō Yoshimoto (1320–88) and Kyūsei, who, as representatives of the elite and commoner levels of society, took the lead in promoting *renga*. Eighty-one of Dōyo's verses are included in *Tsukubashū* (1356), the first imperially authorized linked verse anthology, and his style of *renga* was popularly known as the "Dōyo style" (Dōyo-*fū*).[34]

The last major art in which Sasaki Dōyo played what may have been a significant role is the *nō* theater. *Nō* was created, largely by Kan'ami (1333–84) and his son Zeami (1363–1443), during the time of the third Ashikaga shogun, Yoshimitsu (1358–1408)—that is, during the Kitayama cultural epoch of the late fourteenth and early fifteenth centuries. Kan'ami and Zeami were members of a troupe of performers of *sarugaku*, whose chief rival was *dengaku*. Sasaki Dōyo appears to have favored *dengaku* and to have patronized the *dengaku* masters Itchū and Dōa.[35] At the same time, he may have been among the first to encourage Yoshimitsu to view *sarugaku*. Yoshimitsu's baptismal attendance at a *sarugaku* performance, which occurred in 1374 at the Imakumano Shrine in Kyoto, was an epochal event in cultural history because it inspired him to patronize *sarugaku* and especially Kan'ami and Zeami, whose troupe performed at Imakumano.

Creation of the *nō* theater was perhaps the finest artistic achievement of the Kitayama epoch. Since this essay is concerned with the cultural life of the warrior elite of the early Muromachi period (that is, before Yoshimitsu and the Kitayama epoch), *nō* lies beyond its scope. I wish, nevertheless, to discuss aspects of the development of *nō* both because the story of Sasaki Dōyo leads to it and because *nō*, more than any of the other arts of this age, reflects the extent to which the warrior elite of the early Muromachi period helped, through their patronage, not only to sustain the classical aesthetic and cultural traditions of the court but also to direct them into new realms of creativity.

Zeami was, without question, the towering figure in the creation and perfection of *nō*. He was also the preeminent cultural intermediary between the courtier and warrior elites of the Kitayama epoch. Zeami's role as intermediary is most strikingly seen in his relationships with two of the leading figures of the day: the linked verse master Nijō Yoshimoto, scion of a branch of the Fujiwara family and imperial regent (*kanpaku*), and the shogun Yoshimitsu. We have just noted that Yoshimitsu extended patronage to Zeami and his father, Kan'ami, after observing a performance of their *sarugaku* troupe in 1374. Yoshimitsu was evidently entranced both by the theatrical art of Kan'ami and Zeami and by the physical charms of the youthful (eleven-year-old) Zeami. Nijō Yoshimoto was also homosexually attracted to Zeami, frankly confessing that he had "lost [his] heart" to the boy and describing him in terms of an analogy drawn from *Genji monogatari* (The Tale of Genji): "In *The Tale of Genji*, Lady Murasaki is described as 'adorable with her misty, yet-unplucked eyebrows,' and this boy is just as entrancing. I should compare him to a profusion of cherry or pear blossoms in the haze of a spring dawn; this is how he captivates, with this blossoming of his appearance."[36]

One of the most puzzling questions about Zeami is how he acquired the education, including skill in *waka* and *renga* poetry, that enabled him to write plays that are regarded as among the finest Japanese literary works. A plausible guess is that he was educated by Nijō Yoshimoto and perhaps other courtiers.[37] If this guess is correct, we have the phenomenon of a person from one of the lowest levels of society (the class of professional entertainers) mingling with the bluest of blue bloods and almost literally being transformed into a courtier in terms of taste and artistic skills. The "courtier" Zeami became the playwright Zeami, who was patronized by and catered to the tastes of Yoshimitsu and others of the warrior elite.

Most of Zeami's *nō* plays are *mugen*, or "ghostly dream," plays. For the purpose of this discussion, the ghosts of these *mugen* plays may be categorized as people from the past, both real and fictional (fictional ghosts include, for example, characters from *The Tale of Genji*), who, because they are unable to abandon worldly passions, have been consigned to a netherworld between death and final salvation, usually in Amida's Pure Land (*Jōdo*).[38] Use of the ghostly dream device in the *nō* theater was an important artistic means for expressing cultural nostalgia for the past, a way of looking back to—seeking to recapture—an earlier, perceived "golden age." Although opinions differed about which time was the past's true golden age, golden age thinking, which grew in intensity throughout the Muromachi centuries, focused primarily on the mid-Heian period, the tenth and early eleventh centuries, when the Fujiwara regents were at their peak and when the court produced such literary masterpieces as *Kokinshū*, *The Tales of Ise*, and *The Tale of Genji*.

As is well known, Zeami in his plays emphasized the development of the *yūgen* aesthetic. Like all aesthetic terms, *yūgen* defies precise definition, although the usual rendering of it in English as "mystery and depth" points in the right direction, suggesting important developments in aesthetic tastes from at least *Shinkokinshū* and the early medieval age. In his critical writings on the *nō* theater, Zeami says different things about *yūgen* at different times, but perhaps his most famous discussion of the term is the one that appears in *Kakyō*, the major critique of his later years:

> In what sort of place, then, is the stage of *yūgen* actually to be found? Let us begin by examining the various classes of people on the basis of the appearance that they make in society. May we not say of the courtiers, whose behavior is distinguished and whose appearance far surpasses that of other men, that theirs is the stage of *yūgen*? From this we may see that the essence of *yūgen* lies in a true state of beauty and gentleness. Tranquillity and elegance make for *yūgen* in personal appearance. In the same way, the *yūgen* of discourse lies in a grace of language and a complete mastery of the speech of the nobility and gentry, so that even the most casual utterance will be graceful.[39]

Zeami goes on to say that the actor must aspire to *yūgen* no matter what part he plays, whether it be a character "of high or low birth, man or woman, priest, peasant, rustic, beggar, or outcast."[40] In all parts, actors should look, speak, and act like courtiers. Although we certainly cannot take these remarks as Zeami's final pronouncements on acting, it is fascinating to see how powerfully he seeks to infuse *nō* with the spirit of court-liness, *miyabi*. Indeed, in this discussion in *Kakyō* Zeami in effect equates *miyabi* with *yūgen*, which he asserts must be the standard of excellence in all acting.

The finest of *mugen* plays—for example, *Matsukaze* and *Izutsu*—are in the category of women plays (called *katsura* or "wig" plays). Here, how-ever, I want to discuss the second major category of *mugen* plays, those found in the warrior (*shura*) category, which, besides illustrating the de-velopment of *yūgen* as *miyabi*, are also of interest because of the attraction they held for the warrior elite of the Kitayama epoch in drawing warriors themselves into the *miyabi-yūgen* world of *nō*.

Zeami created and perfected the warrior category of *nō* plays. Of the sixteen warrior plays currently in the repertoires of *nō* schools, five are by Zeami and six others are attributed to him.[41] Fourteen of the sixteen ex-tant plays are based on stories from *The Tale of the Heike*. Zeami insisted that plays taken from the *Heike* must be faithful to their source,[42] and for the most part the *Heike* plays contain accurate reproductions of episodes from the great war tale.

A distinctive feature of the warrior plays is their frequent use of *katari* or "extended narratives." The *katari* typically appears in the second act of a warrior play, when the *shite*—a warrior such as Atsumori, Tadanori, or Yorimasa—recounts in detail some battle or event, often one that resulted in his defeat and death (thirteen of the sixteen extant warrior plays deal with the deaths of "loser-heroes").[43] The influence of *The Tale of the Heike*, that greatest of warrior narratives, is unmistakable in this marked usage of the *katari* in warrior plays: *katari* are like narrative sequences taken from the *Heike*. As noted earlier, the finest version of the *Heike*, the Kakuichi text, was completed in 1371 and was thus a product of the Kitayama cul-tural epoch.

The *shura* or warrior ghost in the Buddhist tradition is a frightful being who has been consigned to an existence of ceaseless strife and combat. Zeami aestheticized the *shura*, softening and humanizing him by provid-ing him—as he provided all his *nō* characters in accordance with the *yūgen* dictum discussed above—with courtly (*miyabi*) language, manners, and appearance.[44] Here we see, I believe, one of the most important phases in the merging of the *bun* and *bu* in warrior society beginning about the Kitayama epoch. In the evolving *nō* theater, which grew in popularity among all classes through the remainder of the Muromachi period, the theatergoing audiences of Japan saw a class of warriors more elegant than ferocious. In reality, the later Muromachi period, especially the *Sengoku* (provincial wars) age, 1478–1568, witnessed probably the ugliest, bloodiest, and most brutal behavior of warriors in Japanese history, at least until World War II. Yet even in that dark time, there was the civilizing ideal of warriors capable of behaving in a more noble, culturally elevated way. A well-known example of this from the literature of the *Sengoku* age appears in *Shinchō Kōki*, the war tale recounting the life of Oda Nobunaga (1534–82). Just before the Battle of Okehazama in 1560, when he decisively defeated a much larger army commanded by Imagawa Yoshimoto that had invaded his domain, Nobunaga, according to *Shinchō Kōki*, danced the *shite* part from the *kōwaka* play *Atsumori* before his assembled troops on a stage in his fortress. His dance completed, Nobunaga immediately took command of his troops and led them into bloody battle with the Imagawa.[45] As a dancer, Nobunaga had assumed the role of a famous courtier-warrior, thus displaying the *bun* side of his character. As commander at Okehazama, he became a model of the ferocious practitioner of *bu*.

Zeami's aestheticizing of the *shura* character for *nō*, it seems to me, was not entirely original. Rather, I strongly suspect that he took his cue from the Kakuichi text of the *Heike*, which served as the source for nearly all his warrior plays. One of the most significant features of the Kakuichi *Heike* is its presentation of warfare as a noble—perhaps even elegant—pursuit. The descriptions of battles convey little sense of the horror, gore, and unspeakable suffering that are inherent in all warfare. On the contrary, the greatest of the *Heike* battles—Ichinotani, Yashima, Dannoura—are substantially aestheticized to give beauty to the most primal of human activities. It is my belief that Zeami, strongly influenced by both the content and what we may even call the courtly style of the *Heike*, created the warrior category of *nō* plays in consonance with powerful aesthetic trends in the Kitayama epoch, especially those designed to appeal to the *bun-bu* tastes of the new Muromachi warrior elite.

I BEGAN THIS ESSAY with the observation that the principal determinant of cultural life among the warrior elite of the Muromachi period was its location in Kyoto in proximity to the imperial court and the courtier class. The frequency of references in *Taiheiki* and other records to constable-daimyos and other members of the warrior elite maintaining residences in Kyoto suggests that this elite was largely Kyoto-based from the beginning. From Yoshimitsu's time in the late fourteenth century, as is well known, constable-daimyos were obliged to live full-time in Kyoto and were allowed to return to their domains only with special permission.

During the middle and late fourteenth century not only did the warrior elite increasingly assert control over the military, administrative, and judicial realms of Kyoto life but also, as I have sought to illustrate, they came to dominate much of the capital's cultural world, through both patronage and participation. The warrior elite's physical entry into Kyoto during the Kenmu Restoration and the early years of the Muromachi period was quite boisterous, as warriors, flaunting their power and, in many cases, their newly acquired wealth, poured into the capital. Warriors became involved with cultural pursuits in large part because of the great expansion in socializing they brought to Kyoto life. The Bakufu took the lead in encouraging such socializing by instituting, for example, the practice of shogunal processions (*onari*) to the residences of the various constable-daimyos. These and other kinds of social visits among both warriors and courtiers required entertainment, and from the various kinds of entertainment provided there developed such arts as linked verse, *chanoyu*, and the *nō* theater. Like the *nō* theater, linked verse and *chanoyu* may in this context be regarded as "performing arts." In addition to the development of these performing arts, the Kyoto socializing promoted by the warrior elite gave impetus to the evolution of new forms of room structure, decoration, and the display of art and craft that, in the fifteenth and sixteenth centuries, were perfected as "*shoin* culture." The stories about Sasaki Dōyo and his parties as given in *Taiheiki*, although no doubt embellished and in some cases perhaps fanciful, nevertheless provide us with a general picture of how the early Muromachi warrior elite influenced cultural development in the ways just mentioned.

Sasaki Dōyo was also, as we have seen, a major figure in the aesthetic tempering that evolved around the Kitayama epoch as the arts sponsored by the warrior elite drew more and more upon classical courtier tastes. The *nō* theater, with its *yūgen* aesthetic, is perhaps the finest achievement to emerge from this tempering. And, in the warrior plays of the *nō*, which drew so heavily upon *The Tale of the Heike* (itself a product of Kitayama culture in the form of the Kakuichi text), we see an important aspect of the merging of the *bun* and the *bu* among the Muromachi warrior elite.

CHAPTER 10

The Warrior as Ideal
for a New Age

G. CAMERON HURST III

THE FOURTEENTH CENTURY boasts a number of distinguished *bushi*: Kusunoki Masashige, beloved by Japanese loyalists; Ashikaga Takauji, intrepid warrior and founder of the Muromachi Bakufu; and Ashikaga Yoshimitsu, who led the Bakufu to the height of its power. But perhaps none surpassed Imagawa Sadayo (1325–1420), better known by his priestly name, Ryōshun.

A distinguished soldier, Ryōshun secured the Bakufu's control over Kyushu in a lengthy, hard-fought campaign. Author of warrior ceremonial treatises and a critique of the *Taiheiki*, he was an avid poet and passionate participant in the fierce poetic disputes between the Nijō and Reizei schools. Ryōshun urged warrior-aristocrats to cultivate both the civil and military arts (*bunbu ryōdō*), but few achieved the balance as well as he. If anyone represents the fourteenth-century warrior as an ideal, it is Imagawa Ryōshun. The late Sir George Sansom noted that with Ryōshun, "a new model of warrior was coming into fashion." [1]

In this chapter, I explore both the fourteenth-century warrior as an ideal and the ideals of the warriors of the fourteenth century. By examining several major documents—warrior legislation (*buke-hō*), warrior codes (*buke kakun*), warrior ceremonial (*buke kojitsu*), and *Taiheiki* (The Chronicle of the Grand Pacification), I hope to capture a sense of the warrior ideal epitomized by Ryōshun.

BUKE-HŌ: THE KENMU SHIKIMOKU

All three of Japan's military regimes promulgated legislation to control their retainers, yet only the Tokugawa Bakufu stressed the military aspect of ruling in its basic legal document. The *Buke shohatto* of 1615 opened with a reference from Chinese antiquity:

The arts of peace and war, including archery and horsemanship, should be pursued single-mindedly.

From of old the rule has been to practice "the arts of peace on the left hand, and the arts of war on the right"; both must be mastered.[2]

The text is appropriate, since no other Bakufu so successfully balanced the civil and martial aspects (*bun* and *bu*) of governance. The irony is that no Bakufu was as "un-martial" in its rule as the Tokugawa.[3] Although *Buke shohatto* addressed primarily security arrangements, it did provide some moral guidance for the early modern warrior elite, under the general advocacy of a *bunbu* complementarity. Many Tokugawa thinkers, beginning with Ieyasu's close adviser Hayashi Razan, urged this balance: "To have the arts of peace, but not the arts of war, is to lack courage. To have the arts of war, but not the arts of peace, is to lack wisdom. . . . How can a man discharge the duties of his rank and position without combining the peaceful and military arts?"[4]

Almost half a millennium earlier, the Kamakura Bakufu had not perceived the need for a code until almost fifty years after its founding, when it could no longer govern its vassals through courtier and manorial law. Moreover, the need for a code was indicative of the fact that the new warrior regime had exceeded the jurisdiction initially granted it by the court. Kamakura's code, the *Jōei shikimoku* of 1232, and supplementary legislation (*tsuika-hō*), helped to bring a period of unusual peace and stability to the thirteenth century. But the *Jōei shikimoku* did not address military matters, nor did it provide much moral guidance for its vassals.

By contrast to both the Kamakura and Edo regimes, the Muromachi Bakufu enjoyed little respite during its 237-year history, a period racked by warfare, instability, piracy, and the rise to regional hegemony of the daimyo, once nominally the shogun's vassals. The Muromachi Bakufu inherited Kamakura's mantle of legitimacy by forcibly seizing it away from

Emperor Go-Daigo's Kenmu government. And, although as a Minamoto, Ashikaga Takauji might lay claim to the shogunal position, his overthrow of Go-Daigo virtually demanded a document to legitimize his rule, indeed to justify his return to a form of government Go-Daigo had sought to extirpate. His code would necessarily be different from the *Jōei shikimoku*.

The Muromachi code, the *Kenmu shikimoku*, was promulgated in late 1336, only six days after Takauji seized the imperial regalia from Go-Daigo and bestowed them upon Northern Emperor Kōmyō—and almost two years before he was appointed shogun. It was an unusual code. More of a dialogue on legislation, it was compiled by a "committee" headed by Nakahara Zeen and his younger brother Shin'e which responded to questions posed by Takauji.[5] What does the *Kenmu shikimoku* tell us about the warrior as an ideal for a new age?

The code addressed several unsettled issues facing Takauji's new regime. The introduction first debates whether the Bakufu ought to be located in Kamakura or Kyoto. Kyoto, the traditional seat of imperial government, was for political, logistic, and economic reasons the ideal location. However, Yoritomo's choice of Kamakura was a strong precedent, even if later Hōjō regents had ruled there in despotic fashion. The consensus reached—after considering positive and negative aspects of Kamakura rule and examining Chinese history—was that "the misfortune of man lies not in the bad luck of the dwelling place."[6] Kyoto was therefore deemed appropriate as the site of a new military government.

The introduction next discusses proper rule and stresses the necessity of following the "good government" (*zensei*) of the Kamakura Bakufu, especially under the early Hōjō regents. Thus the new regime proclaims itself the rightful successor to the Kamakura Bakufu. Moreover, appropriating the Confucian definition of good government as "virtue," it claims the right to "take immediate action to alleviate the suffering of the people."[7]

From the outset, then, the Muromachi Bakufu moved beyond the scope of its Kamakura predecessor, in effect rendering the *kōbu* polity[8] a dead letter and establishing warrior supremacy in the governance of Japan. The first article of the *Kenmu shikimoku* proclaims the scope of the Bakufu's authority, adopting a stance of defending the populace from the ravages of the elite:

Recently, fashion has been used as an excuse to indulge in extravagance and excess, such as the wearing of twill damask and brocade, ornamental silver swords, and elegant attire to dazzle the eyes. While the rich swell with pride, the poor are ashamed because they cannot match them. This is the major reason for the poverty of the population, and it must be severely suppressed.[9]

The new regime cast itself as the savior of the people who, according to criticism such as the *Nijō rakusho*, suffered under Go-Daigo's Kenmu government. In fact, this article sets the tone for the rest of the code: the articles are essentially moral maxims, stressing the need to suppress lawless behavior, indulgent living, and other immoral acts, to hear the suits of the poor, and to prohibit bribery. It is a "law and order" document, presenting the warrior regime as a legitimate inheritor of the Mandate of Heaven, which the discredited Kenmu government has clearly lost.

In its attempt to inculcate morality among its retainers—to establish the fourteenth-century warrior as an ideal type—the *Kenmu shikimoku* is reminiscent of Prince Shōtoku's Seventeen Article Code of the early seventh century, which also was essentially a set of moral guidelines for the elite of that era. Structuring the code in seventeen articles could hardly have been innocuous under the circumstances. It can only be seen as part of Takauji's attempt to invoke symbols of just rule to legitimize his usurpation.[10]

Thus the Ashikaga established a military regime that saw itself as a far more extensive institution than Yoritomo's. Moreover, compared with the limited violence that accompanied the founding of the Kamakura regime, the Ashikaga Bakufu faced almost a half-century of warfare, albeit fought only sporadically, after it was established. Takauji and his followers were well aware of the need for both military skill and just rule. Thus, although the focus of the *Kenmu shikimoku* lay in administrative matters and moral guidance, in its closing words, Zeen surveys the continuous warfare that engulfed them and advises prudence: "People of old said that when you live in peace, you must think of danger. Today we live in danger; must we not think of danger?"[11] There is a hint here of the first article of the *Buke shohatto*, which warns that in times of peace, it is wise to prepare for war.

The *Kenmu shikimoku* envisions as an ideal a just and moral government of warriors precisely because it is a time of violence. The precedents marshaled to justify the reestablishment of a military regime are both civilian and military: "In the past, we sought the virtuous example of the two sages of Engi and Tenryaku [i.e., Emperors Daigo and Murakami], and, more recently, we took the behavior of father and son Yoshitoki and Yasutoki as our recent teachers."[12] Chinese classics are quoted, Yao and Shun are lauded, and the seventeen articles themselves link the regime with Prince Shōtoku.

If positive resonances legitimize Ashikaga military rule, criticism of the abuses of the Kenmu government provide negative rationale justifying Takauji's usurpation. Articles referring to bribery to get lawsuits heard, to the necessity of appointing able men as *shugo*, to the need to prohibit seizing houses in Kyoto, and to demands for returning Kyoto lots to rightful owners are a few that directly indict Go-Daigo's rule.

Whether actually realized or not, just rule and moral government are at the core of the political philosophy of the new fourteenth-century warrior leaders; virtue and duty are the ideals that warrior rulers should exemplify. While silent concerning the warrior's martial prowess, the *Kenmu shikimoku* envisions an ideal warrior-administrator who should emulate virtuous rulers from the pages of Japanese and Chinese history. Though the term *bunbu* does not appear, the *Kenmu shikimoku* leaves no doubt that the fourteenth century requires a ruler who combines these elements. Written for the man of war, it proposes the arts of peace.

For example, according to the *Kenmu shikimoku*, ruling properly involves a careful cultivation of decorum (*reisetsu*): "In ruling the nation, there must be an overriding concern for etiquette (*rei*). The lord must practice his own proper conduct, the minister his. Both high and low must each preserve his station; in speech and conduct they must strenuously observe decorum (*reigi*)."[13] This article is in accord with the introductory section on government (*seitō*), in which the necessity of examining established practices (*kojitsu*) is invoked. As warriors replaced courtiers as effective rulers, it was deemed important to know precedent and observe proper etiquette. Warriors would learn courtier behavior as well as codify their own (*buke kojitsu*). Ruling correctly was a matter of form as much as of content. Doing things in the proper manner, observing punctilious etiquette, was crucial. The *Kenmu shikimoku* makes that clear.

The *Kenmu shikimoku* is a very Confucian document. If the *Jōei shikimoku* was a practical document to "define the parameters of the (Kamakura) *gokenin's* world,"[14] the *Kenmu shikimoku* is far more idealistic, seeking instead to articulate a view of military rule based upon the idea of Confucian virtuous administration.[15] One is struck by the Confucian tone of medieval works of political and ethical thought. The ideal ruler portrayed in this basic legal document of the fourteenth century is a warrior-aristocrat who is a virtuous Confucian administrator. The background of the compilers suggests that it could be little else. As members of a family long known as legal specialists, the Nakahara brothers were steeped in

Confucian texts: one (Gen'e) was a monk knowledgeable in Sung studies; another (Hino Fujinori) was from a family specializing in Confucian studies and literature.

BUSHIDŌ: WARRIOR CODES

Let me turn to fourteenth-century texts that are specifically concerned with warrior ideals and the warrior as ideal. These texts are often referred to as chronicles of *bushidō*. Many writers, following Nitobe Inazō, assume that *bushidō* was a well-defined code of warrior behavior in premodern times which then became universal—the "soul of Japan"—among prewar Japanese.[16] Rather than a single normative "code" of behavior for the warrior class, however, there were many formulations of behavioral norms for warriors in medieval and early modern Japan; and a number of these texts remain for us to examine.

In the fifteenth century, especially amid the chaos following the Ōnin War, daimyo eagerly sought to turn local warriors into direct vassals to defend or expand their territories (*ryōkoku*). Many issued house laws (*kahō*) and maxims to heirs (*kakun* or *okibumi*), which attempted to dictate warrior behavior. Warrior leaders of the fourteenth century, however, as officers of the Ashikaga Bakufu, were still tied to the crumbling, yet remarkably resilient, *shōen* system, and therefore were hampered in establishing their own domains; they wrote no house codes. But several daimyo wrote *kakun*, representing a progression from the Kamakura period, when we have just two texts by Hōjō Shigetoki.[17] These fourteenth-century *kakun* provide our best insight into the ideals of the warrior and the warrior as ideal: *Tōjiin goisho*, left by Ashikaga Takauji, Imagawa Ryōshun's *Gusoku Nakaaki seishi*, *Chikubashō* of Shiba Yoshimasa, and *Yoshisadaki*, attributed to Nitta Yoshisada.[18]

The first chronologically is Takauji's testament (1357). Although there is considerable doubt that the document was actually written by Takauji, the text is nonetheless regarded as representative of fourteenth-century warrior mentality and therefore is a valuable document even if of uncertain authorship.[19] Moreover, the ideas expressed in the testament seem consistent with what we know of Takauji.

Takauji states that his testament of twenty-one articles, was to be "transmitted to my descendants. There is no doubt that if they turn their backs on these precepts, the house will perish." The document contains what purports to be Takauji's views not only of the role of the warrior in society but also of his philosophy of governance. The ideals are fully consistent with those expressed in the *Kenmu shikimoku*.

It is perhaps not surprising, given the fact that he himself was twice a turncoat, that Takauji begins with a discussion of loyalty and the relationship between sovereign and subject. In fact, the document bristles with references to the Sovereign (*kimi*), Heaven (*ten*), the "Way of Heaven" (*tentō*), and the realm (*tenka*) (e.g., article 9: "He who holds the realm must never slack even for a moment, but must keep his eyes focused on the Way of Heaven"). But his specific formulation is instructive: the sovereign interprets (*wakimau*) matters related to Heaven, while the minister (*shin*) governs (*shiru*) matters of earth. Article 1 states:

There is Heaven, there is the Sovereign, there is the earth, and there is the minister. Therefore, the way of the loyal minister is to revere the imperial position (*ōi*) and respect virtue. If the joint path of Sovereign and subject is reversed, then there will be neither Heaven nor earth, Sovereign nor subject. We must understand that this is [tantamount to] destruction.

Article 2 continues in a similar vein:

It is said that if the Sovereign embodies Heaven and the subject is in accord with earth, then winds and rains will follow in seasonal accord; the ten rains and five winds will moisten the plants, and the subjects will take pleasure.

In China, Takauji points to the age of Shun, while in Japan he praises the Engi and Tenryaku eras. Although he urges harmony between sovereign and subject, he advises that "henceforth, for there to be harmony between Heaven and earth, [political] matters ought to proceed from the military authorities (*buke*)."

Thus Takauji (or those who affixed his name to the document) is quite careful in this testament. With liberal references to the virtues expected of Confucian rulers, he indicates that while the emperor is to be revered, the ministers—in this case, warrior aristocrats, that is, the Ashikaga—rule the land. Continuing on with hackneyed Confucian phrases about the importance of those below respecting those above and ruling in harmony with the will of Heaven, Takauji carefully specifies the role of the warrior. He constructs the general background:

Sovereign and subject, general and soldier, are all of one body; they are not at all separate bodies. If we liken the general to the trunk, then the soldiers are the limbs. The Sovereign is the heart. If the limbs are sick, the body suffers. When the body is ill, the heart suffers. How, then, can they be separate bodies? Both the limbs and the trunk are manipulated by the heart.

Takauji suggests a balance between sovereign and soldier, civil and military, which are united rather than separate entities. Yet later he concludes in article 12, that the "rise or fall of the nation lies solely in not forgetting the military element (*bu*)." Thus, while paying appropriate lip service to the imperial dignity, Takauji clearly asserts that the role of the warrior is to rule.

It is in article 12 that Takauji most specifically addresses ideals of the warriors and the warrior as ideal:

The two paths of civil and military arts (*bunbu ryōdō*) are like the two wheels of a cart; lacking one wheel, the cart will not carry any one. However, on a battlefield, the cultured man is without merit. Thus we should learn that the civil arts are the basis of ruling the nation, to be used in times of peace (*taihei*); the military arts are to be employed when the nation is at war. Thus he who would rule the realm need be concerned with the civil arts; for the lesser man who arms himself with the five weapons, learning is of no value.

Takauji thus focuses upon the complementarity of civil and martial elements in ruling the land. Yet he distinguishes between high-ranking *bushi*, especially those of the Ashikaga house, who should rule and therefore be acquainted with the civil arts, and lesser warriors who should concentrate their energies upon martial training. And his opening lines, which relegate the sovereign to dealing with matters of Heaven while placing the "subject" in the role of governing, clearly demonstrate his commitment to continuing—indeed, even expanding upon—the Kamakura military precedent.

In stressing the balance between *bun* and *bu*, Takauji is one of the first medieval leaders to seize upon this ancient Chinese ideal. It was the theme, as we shall see, of others as well. Though neither the phrase nor the concept was new to the fourteenth century, it was for the first time expressly advocated as an ideal by and for the rulers of Japan.

At several points in his document, Takauji deals with specific *bushi* behavior. Fearful that sojourning too long in the capital would strip the warrior of his martial zeal, he forbids vassals to spend more than three years in Kyoto. He also warns that desire for amassing money and dealing with merchants would dilute warriors' martial character, and he castigates the profit motive. Warrior and merchant are birds of a different feather, he says: "The hawk entering the water is artless; the cormorant in the mountain is without skill." Thus, he enjoins, "the roots of the military family names lie in *bu*." The last several articles urge great warriors to value men of virtue and wisdom, those who are loyal and valorous. The great warrior should nourish his soldiers "with the affection of a chicken sitting on its eggs."

The final article is worth quoting in its entirety: "Both Ashikaga housemen (miuchi) and outside vassals (*tozama*) . . . should make rewards clearly. They should be warm in their intimacy toward men of rank, and they should alleviate the poverty of the humble. They should love with compassion; they should not turn a small offense into a great crime. They should share welfare together." This echo of the earlier sentiments from the *Kenmu shikimoku* marks the testament as a highly Confucian document: Takauji urges his descendants, who have accepted responsibility for the realm, to equip themselves with the knowledge and virtue to rule wisely. The warrior regime is the final authority; but the basis of warrior rule must not lie solely in military might. It lies in familiarity with the civil arts, the cultivation of virtue, and the proper selection of and concern for vassals.

Of the four fourteenth-century *kakun* under consideration here, Shiba Yoshimasa's *Chikubashō* is probably the best known and also the longest.[20] Yoshimasa was born in 1350 into the Shiba clan, a branch of the Ashikaga, and he rose rapidly in the ranks of favored Bakufu officials; at thirteen he became a steward (*shitsuji*) and served on the Board of Councillors (*hyōjōshū*). As the *shugo* of Etchū Province, Yoshimasa was fated to spend much of his time at the center of Bakufu politics. He served as shogunal deputy (*kanrei*) on three different occasions and was the major force in consolidating Bakufu administrative and judicial organs under Yoshimitsu. Yoshimasa put down local warrior (*kokujin*) uprisings in his home area, joined in driving Hosokawa Yoriyuki from Kyoto in 1379, and helped pacify Ōuchi Yoshihiro's rebellion in Sakai in 1399. He became *kanrei* for the third time in 1409 and was soon actively trying to repair relations with Korea by suppressing the pirates that were raiding Korea's coastal towns.[21] Though a staunch ally of Yoshimitsu and his son, Yoshimochi, Yoshimasa reputedly protested the court's attempt to award Yoshimitsu the posthumous title of retired sovereign.

Besides the *Chikubashō*, which he wrote for his descendants during his second term as *kanrei* in 1368, Yoshimasa also composed poems sufficiently admirable to have been included in the imperial anthology *Shin goshūi wakashū*. Thus he exemplified the *bunbu* ideal in his own life.

Chikubashō is in its style totally different from Takauji's testament. *Tōjiin goisho* is written primarily in *kanbun*, with some sections using Japanese grammar; it is virtually Chinese in tone, with Confucian, even Taoist references, but no hint of Buddhist influence in spite of Takauji's personal devotion. *Chikubashō* is written mainly in *hiragana*, and uses very few Chinese characters. There are few explicit Chinese references and only minor Confucian undertones. With its strong Buddhist flavor, *Chikubashō* is a much more "Japanese" text.

Chikubashō is also more specifically concerned with the warrior. Takauji's document is more philosophical and overtly political, troubled as he must have been to legitimize his usurpation and preserve Ashikaga hegemony; Yoshimasa sets out to civilize the warrior. He assumes that a warrior will equip himself with martial skills, but he does not dwell on the point, nor is he specific about which martial skills are important, though two references clearly indicate that archery was still the primary warrior skill. In one instance he refers to warriors as *kyūzen o toru mono* ("those who draw bows"),[22] and the one sentence he does devote to martial training also has to do with archery: "Insofar as martial arts are concerned, it goes without saying that one should practice *mato, kasagake,* and *inuoumono*."[23]

Yoshimasa is mainly interested in the spiritual and cultural accomplishments that subsequent generations of Shiba warriors must develop in order to rule effectively. Since he believes that his descendants need to be prepared for all exigencies rather than react to situations on emotion, intelligence and the training of the mind are crucial to him. Throughout *Chikubashō* Yoshimasa urges the warrior to train his mind—by acquiring culture, but also by developing his mental capacity. He speaks of the development of a "true mind" (*kokoro makoto*) or a "pure mind" (*kokoro sunao*) and warns that "warriors should not be unmindful (*kokoro o awatsuka*)." Without advocating specific religious practices, Yoshimasa likens the preparedness of the mind (*yōjin*) needed by Shiba warriors to that of a Buddhist monk: "It has been said that the preparedness of the good warrior and the Buddhist monk are the same. It is regrettable if in all things one fails to pacify one's mind."

Even in the practice of his martial arts, Yoshimasa urges the warrior not to neglect his mind: "Especially, the military man should calm his mind and examine the depths of the other's mind; this could be called the first of the martial arts (*heihō*)." Indeed, Yoshimasa may be the first Japanese warrior to discuss "mind" in relation to martial training. It was a practice that would become quite common in peaceful Edo times, when Shimada Toranosuke would write: "The sword is the mind. If you wish to study the sword, first study the mind."[24]

Training in the martial arts might be urged as a means of training one's mind by Edo times, but Yoshimasa, writing much earlier, believes that it is in *bun*, in the civil arts, that such training occurs. He urges study of the arts and literature, for example, because "this world values only reputation (*meiri*)," and thus a man needs to be able to compose poetry, play music, or even participate in a *kemari* game without feelings of embarrassment. But it is not only to acquire social polish that Yoshimasa urges one to cultivate the arts. Reading *Genji monogatari*, or Sei Shōnagon's *Makura no sōshi*, Yoshimasa argues, is excellent "instruction for discerning people's behavior and judging the quality of their minds."

Throughout, Yoshimasa is also concerned with one's outward behavior, so that not just the warrior himself but his descendants of the Shiba house will be thought well of. In several places he mentions the importance of "the house" (*ie*). In his second article, Yoshimasa offers what at first glance seems a strange injunction: "Rather than following the good [seen] in others, one should imitate his own flawed parents." He explains that to follow even "stupid parents" (*orokanaru oya*) is in accord with the Way of Heaven (*tentō*); in general, he says, what parents say is in accord with the reasoning of their children. Most important, by imitating one's parents one transmits the customs of the house (*ie no fū*) and becomes a model (*hito no ato*) for one's descendants.

In this passage Yoshimasa touches on an important aspect of Muromachi warrior society: the emphasis upon the house and its traditions. In fact, he is talking about *kojitsu*, a subject to which I shall return. Here, he places more weight upon the traditions of the house than on the individual desires of the warrior himself. That is why he feels that passing on the ways of even foolish parents is more important than aping the practices of others.[25] Yoshimasa lays great stress on the warrior's concern for his house, and its traditions and its future.

Yoshimasa's theory of leadership is clear: future Shiba warriors should cultivate their minds, equip themselves with culture, and revere the Buddhas and gods so that, with "intelligence and a wise mind," these warrior leaders will be able to put others to good use. "A man ought to be employed at that with which he is familiar," he declares, and by training his mind and cultivating *bun*, a leader will acquire the ability to judge people correctly and employ them properly. Yoshimasa's conclusion is similar in spirit to Takauji's final injunction.

A third document illustrative of the ideals of fourteenth-century warriors is *Imagawa Ryōshun gusoku Nakaaki seishi* (alternately the *Imagawajō*, or *Imagawa kabegaki*) of Imagawa Ryōshun. Although this document apparently dates from just after the turn of the fifteenth century (it was likely produced in two sections, the first twenty-three articles sometime shortly after 1395 and the remainder probably in 1409),[26] it reflects the career of a man who lived largely in the fourteenth—indeed who lived through most of the century.[27]

Ryōshun was the giant of his age, looked upon as a model *bushi* to be emulated as a warrior, a politician, a noted poet, and as an author of several works of *buke kojitsu*. As Ashikaga kinsman, Ryōshun's father Norikuni joined Takauji against the Hōjō and was rewarded with the title of *shugo* of Suruga. Ryōshun spent his early years fighting for Takauji, then inherited his father's *shugo* post and began his political career under Ashikaga Yoshiakira. After being appointed Kyushu Deputy (*tandai*) in 1370, Ryōshun revived Bakufu power on the island by defeating the Kikuchi and Shimazu houses in campaigns extending over twelve years. Subsequently, he was slandered and banished to Suruga. Suspected of involvement in Ōuchi Yoshihiro's revolt, Ryōshun was attacked by Yoshimitsu's troops; by 1400 he had lost all but a portion of his holdings. Later pardoned, he returned to Kyoto where he spent the last years of his long life writing poetry, travel diaries, works of warrior ceremonial, and the *Nan-Taiheiki*.

Imagawa kabegaki is a manual of practical advice for Ryōshun's younger brother and heir Nakaaki, but its balance of Confucian virtues and martial arts brought it a wide circulation later on; it even became a text for Edo-period schoolchildren.[28] Stylistically at least, the document is very different from the *Chikubashō*. Like *Tōjiin goisho*, the first twenty-three articles are written in *kanbun*; the last section mixes *kanbun* and *kanamajiri* styles. The articles, a series of warnings for Nakaaki, are followed by a reflection, which places them in context.

Ryōshun gives his heir detailed advice about serving as *shugo*: he warns about making punishments fit the crime, enjoins against exploitation of others for personal gain, warns against flatterers, and urges Nakaaki to be frugal, fair, respectful, and compassionate. Like Yoshimasa and Takauji, he assumes that his warrior heir will practice the martial arts, but in the first article he sets the balance between *bun* and *bu*: "Without knowledge of the civil ways (*bundō*), martial ways (*budō*) will ultimately not result in victory." He stresses the administrative skills Takauji articulated and shares Yoshimasa's concerns for culture.

Ryōshun does not touch on the *bu* element again until the later section, where he again notes, "It is natural to practice mounted archery and warfare; but it is most important to carry out [this training]." Both Confucian classics and ancient Chinese military treatises, he observes, stress the importance of the civil virtues in defending the realm. Later he returns to the necessity of balancing the two: "One must never put the civil and martial arts (*bunbu ryōdō*) out of one's mind." Some have credited Ryōshun with formulating the idea itself of *bunbu ryōdō*,[29] but I am not sure we have enough evidence to make this attribution though it is certainly a product of his era.

In sum, Ryōshun admonishes Nakaaki not to neglect the Confucian virtues of humanity, righteousness, etiquette, and wisdom. He reminds his brother to be compassionate in the dispensation of rewards and punishments, and, like both Takauji and Yoshimasa, urges him to employ men wisely.

The final document to consider is *Yoshisadaki*, like the testament of Yoshisada's Genji kinsman Takauji often considered a fabrication.[30] The document is somewhat more complex than the others. It is more a work of warrior ceremonial, with most of the text devoted to details of military affairs, yet it resembles a *kakun*—an alternative title is *Nitta sachūshō Yoshisada kyōkunsho* ("injunctions")—since it also deals with ideals and values. Moreover, the text in places contradicts sources like the *Taiheiki* in its picture of Yoshisada as an intrepid but impetuous general who died at age thirty-eight at the Battle of Fujishima. In other words, except for a brief respite during Go-Daigo's Kenmu regime, Yoshisada was a man of action rather than a statesman, not a warrior-administrator like our three other *bushi* authors.

Yet *Yoshisadaki* reads in places like other Muromachi treatises on politics and ethics. In article 2, for example, Yoshisada seems consistent with Takauji, Yoshimasa, and Ryōshun: he urges generals to exercise compassion, to have an expansive heart, to reward vassals justly,[31] to regard others as one's family (*oyako no gotoku ni omoi*), and to display virtue. Most revealingly, given his own devotion to Go-Daigo, he cautions that even when the sovereign is not adequate (*kimi ga kimi tarazaru toki*), the minister must not accept the dominant ways of the world but still exercise virtue and prize wisdom.

In other articles, Yoshisada appears the paragon of prudence, advising generals to be deep thinkers and strategic planners, to select the most auspicious days to launch an attack (which he conveniently lists). He even cautions against recklessly sacrificing one's life in battle. It is these sections, which seem at odds with the *Taiheiki* image of Yoshisada, that suggest that the text is not genuine.[32]

Yet it is precisely because Yoshisada was a very different figure from those successful warrior-aristocrats like Takauji that *Yoshisadaki* is instructive. For example, the text opens with a statement that seems at first glance to be in accord with the other *kakun* authors but, as he elaborates, becomes in fact quite at odds with them: "From the past down to the present, *bun* and *bu* have been separated (*bunbu nibun ni shite*), and their virtues resemble Heaven and earth. Lacking one, the country cannot be properly governed. Courtiers place the *bun* first: these are the arts of poetry and music. The warrior way takes the *bu* as it base: these are the ways of mounted archery and warfare."

Thus Yoshisada, ever the warrior, presents an earlier view of *bun* and *bu*, one that presumes a separation of function between warrior and courtier. This idea seems fully consistent with Yoshisada's career, opposing first the Hōjō and then choosing to cooperate with Go-Daigo in a regime that sought to keep the functions separate, with *bu* subordinate to *bun*. Much of the remainder of the text is devoted to *kojitsu*, with military information for the warrior—for example, the appropriate size of weapons, battlefield strategy, preparations for a journey, and even instructions for suicide.

Yoshisadaki is representative of an earlier view, one might say a discredited view, of the warrior. While not neglecting the Confucian virtues a great warrior ought to exemplify, Yoshisada considers *bun* and *bu* separate and spends most of his time discussing the *bu* element of the equation. His advice is not for a warrior who would rule the realm but for the warrior who would exercise his talents to protect it. Yoshisada's document is the exception that proves the rule: viewed in juxtaposition to the *kakun* of the successful fourteenth-century warrior-administrators propounding a new ideal for the warrior, *Yoshisadaki* articulates an outdated view of the division of *bun* and *bu*, separately relegated to courtier and warrior, which reflected the ideals of the ancient world more than those of medieval Japan.

Thus, fourteenth-century *kakun* emphasize the necessity of the warrior to practice *bunbu ryōdō*—which will become spelled out two centuries later in the *Buke shohatto* admonishment to "practice the arts of peace on the left hand, and the arts of war on the right." This is not for all warriors, since the documents are meant for the eyes of shogunal and *shugo* successors, that is, warrior-aristocrats, who are the rulers of the great mass of warriors. But they express the ideals of warriors of the age and depict the warrior-ruler as an ideal type. Nowhere do we find deference to courtiers or emphasis on the lineage of civil aristocratic houses. Rather it is the warrior, the one who practices the martial arts to pacify the land, who must cultivate the civil arts to become master of Japan.

THE *BUNBU RYŌDŌ* IDEAL

Neither the term nor the concept *bunbu* was of course new in Muromachi times. The idea itself dates back to China's classical age, since the term is simply a compound of the names of the first two Chou rulers, Kings Wen and Wu. When Wu (1169–16 B.C.) destroyed the Yin and established the Chou dynasty, he honored his father with the posthumous name of King Wen, the wise ruler who solidified the kingdom. Thenceforth, the two were frequently mentioned in tandem, representing the civil and military requirements of government and epitomizing the ideal ruler. In his Analects, Confucius idealized the "way of Wen and Wu" (*bunbu no michi* in Japanese).

The term *wenwu* appeared with regularity in Confucian and other classical texts—*Han Fei Tzu* makes reference to the state's need for utilizing *wen* and *wu*, for example—either as a compound itself, or in several combinations.[33] The *Shu ching* and the *Wei chih* both exalt the complementarity of *wen* and *wu*; the *Hanshu* and the *T'angshu* recognize the necessity of "combining *wen* and *wu*" (Jap. *bunbu kenbi*). In his *Ti-fan* (Plan for an Emperor), written as a political testament for his successor Kao-tsung, T'ang Tai-tsung warned that neither of "the two ways of *wen* and *wu*" (Jap. *bunbu nito*) can be discarded. Later generations would regard T'ai-tsung's reign as an ideal: "His reign combined the dual virtues of *wen* and *wu*, civil order and military might, as no reign before or after."[34] The exact formulation *bunbu ryōdō* (Chin. *wenwu liangpu*) appears less frequently, but was not unknown.

Although many scholars emphasize the Chinese tendency to disparage *wu* and laud *wen*, there thus is a long tradition of respect for a balance between the two. T'ai-tsung may be the most notable example, but Howard Wechsler reminds us of a type of official "that remained common throughout the seventh century, the man who was equally at home as a court official or as a commander-in-the-field, characterized by the phrase *ju-hsiang, ch'u-chiang*."[35] During the Sung dynasty, after the execution of Yueh Fei in 1141, "the scholar officials with their ideal of the 'scholar-general' (*ju-chiang*) gained unquestioned ascendancy."[36] Writing of *wen* and *wu*, the late John King Fairbank concluded, "Almost from the beginning the government of China had been a codominion of these two functions."[37]

This Chinese ideal also found currency in Korea and Japan. Early Korean history abounds with examples of heroes the chroniclers would have us believe combine these two functions. Perhaps Wang Kŏn, founder of the *Koryŏ* dynasty in the late ninth century, most closely approaches the T'ai-tsung model;[38] but Kim Pu-sik in the twelfth century and Yi Sŏng-gye, founder of the Yi dynasty in the late fourteenth century, also fit the model well.

The concept made its way into Japan, but textual references to the complementarity are rare until the appearance of war tales dealing with the upheavals of the late Heian period. Certainly Emperor Tenmu (r. 673–86) most closely resembles the T'ai-tsung ideal. The *ju-chiang* ideal was clearly preserved by the Japanese in the Heian custom of appointing ranking ministers to serve as generals in charge of troops to suppress rebellion. But it is with the war tales (*gunki monogatari*) that both the terms and the ideal become more fully developed.

Heiji monogatari in fact opens with a reference to the concept: "Inquiring into the ways in which sovereigns in both China and Japan have praised their ministers from antiquity to the present, they have given precedence to the two paths of *bun* and *bu* (*bunbu no nidō o saki to su*)."[39] Likewise, in *Heike monogatari*, the priest Kakumei is praised as a paragon of *bun* and *bu* balance:

Kakumei was attired in a dark blue *hitatare* and a suit of armor with black leather lacing. At his waist, he wore a sword with a black lacquered hilt and scabbard; on his back, there rode a quiver containing twenty-four arrows fledged with black hawk's-wing feathers. His lacquered rattan wrapped bow was at his side; his helmet hung from his shoulder-cord. He took a small inkstone and some paper from his quiver, knelt in front of Lord Kiso, and began to write the petition. What a splendid combination of civil and martial arts (*bunbu nidō no tassha*) he seemed![40]

References to the concept appear in *Jikkinshō* and other literary works but seemingly not in warrior documents, such as those collected in *Kamakura ibun*, or in *Azuma kagami* or the *Jōei shikimoku*. Yoritomo himself took the position that *bu* is subordinate to *bun*: "The *bushi* is like the monk who defends the precepts of the Buddha . . . he is the instrument (*utsuwa*) that defends the Sovereign."[41] Although Hōjō Shigetoki in his two *kakun* does not use the term *bunbu*, certainly the thrust of his advice is for warriors to cultivate the civil arts to augment their mastery of the military arts, as Carl Steenstrup points out.[42]

We find the notion among the courtier class too. That is, if there are numerous examples of fourteenth-century warriors urging adoption of *bun* to supplement *bu*, there are also courtiers who take up the *bu* in order to succeed in medieval times. The above-mentioned Kakumei, scion of a

Confucian family who served in the Fujiwara family's Kangakuin academy before becoming a Buddhist prelate, may be the first example. But the *Taiheiki* provides ample evidence of several others. H. Paul Varley has recently written of these figures as "warrior-courtiers," specifically referring to Prince Morinaga (Moriyoshi) and Kitabatake Akiie.[43]

In Book Three of *Taiheiki*, Morinaga has a long discussion with his father, Go-Daigo (through a messenger), as he prepares for war. Go-Daigo urges him instead to return to his life as a Buddhist priest. But Morinaga argues that theirs is an age when "the two ways of *bun* and *bu*" are equally necessary for ruling the realm (*bunbu no nidō onajiku tatte osamarubeki*"). He stresses that he can return to his priestly life later, noting both Chinese and Japanese precedents for royalty changing their status in times of crisis. He cites Emperor Tenmu, who yielded the succession to his brother Prince Ōtomo and became a monk before returning to seize the throne; and Empress Kōken, who reascended the throne after once having abdicated.[44]

It is not strange that such Chinese ideals should influence Japanese leaders at this moment. Both Sung China and Japan experienced crisis at the hands of the Mongols, and neo-Confucians such as Chu Hsi had reformulated the traditional corpus of Confucian thought. Although there was a repository of Confucian knowledge already present among the Kyoto families who preserved such study,[45] newer Sung Confucian ideas arrived in Kamakura and Muromachi times, brought both by Chinese monks and by Japanese monks who had visited China once relations were restored. These so-called *jusō* ("Confucian monks") had much to do with the spread of Confucian ideas, which were especially influential at the courts of Hanazono and then of Go-Daigo, at precisely the time of the overthrow of the Kamakura regime and the initiation of Go-Daigo's Kenmu restoration.[46]

Kitabatake Chikafusa, influenced by Confucian concepts of legitimacy and loyalty,[47] is of course the best-known fourteenth-century author who espoused the complementarity of *bun* and *bu*. Chikafusa believed that only by combining the *bu* element with the *bun* could the courtier class once again wrest power from the warriors. His ideal warrior was his own son Akiie, who according to *Jinnō shōtōki*, responded to Go-Daigo's call to arms after the emperor argued: "The country is already united under the court and no distinction should be made between the military and the civil. In ancient times many princes and other members of the imperial family, as well as descendants of the great courtier families, took command of armies. These same people must once again take up arms and become the bulwark of the court."[48]

The ideal of combining the elements of *bun* and *bu* was thus by the fourteenth century familiar to members of the Japanese ruling elite, both warriors and courtiers alike. The *bunbu* complementarity not only appeared in literary texts but was now espoused by warrior-aristocrats, and even by some courtiers, in the main political texts of the day. By the mid-fourteenth century, *bunbu ryōdō* thought was well established in Japan, with the warrior-ruler now entrenched as the ideal type.

BUKE KOJITSU

I should like to turn briefly to the subject of *kojitsu*, or ceremonial, which is mentioned by virtually all warrior writers of the day. *Buke kojitsu*, literally "warrior customs," refers to correct behavior for carrying out the warriors' main functions of preserving law and order, maintaining weapons, and training in martial arts and strategy. These are matters that are addressed in the *Yoshisadaki*, for example; but during the Muromachi period the subject was extended to include *bushi* etiquette, ranging from matters of dress to the proper way of entering and leaving a bath. *Buke kojitsu* was essentially a warrior version of *yūsoku kojitsu*, or "ancient customs and practices," referring both to court ceremonial practices and to the compilation of the details of those practices. Thus, *kojitsu*, though originally an investigation of precedents for correct procedure in a certain ceremony or social situation, developed into established procedural and ritual forms of behavior.[49]

Kojitsu were extremely important in the Heian period; certain houses specialized in chronicling correct procedures to follow in the exacting round of court ceremonial (*nenjū gyōji*). These *yūsoku-ke* (families specializing in ceremonial) detailed such matters as proper dress at court functions, the proper order in which courtiers should stand, and the serving of foods at certain banquets.[50] *Yūsoku-ke* were guardians of the ritual of court life, antiquarians in some sense, except that the knowledge they possessed was believed essential to assure proper regulation of the realm. There was extreme concern for the proper way, the correct procedure in all performances.

With the rise of the *bushi* in Kamakura times, a warrior version of courtier ceremonial, called *buke kojitsu*, developed as men of the provinces showed concern for maintaining their own customs, especially military practices. *Buke kojitsu* was not yet highly developed, although certain families specializing in military practices were favored by Yoritomo and his successors. The Ki and Tomo were especially skilled in mounted archery (*kyūba*), for example, and were charged with preserving that tradition.[51]

Since military skills could obviously safeguard a warrior's life, the development of effective fighting practices was arguably even more important than the *kojitsu* of courtiers. Indeed, we hear of many skilled warriors who practiced martial arts in late Heian times and must therefore have developed methods for their transmission.[52] But since there survive no texts that actually describe martial practices, we must assume that the subject remained unrecorded and was transmitted orally. Widespread illiteracy among warriors may also have inhibited the development of a textual tradition.

Yet *kojitsu* were valued, and some must have been written down. In preparation for his journey to the capital in 1194, Minamoto Yoritomo met at Oyama Tomomasa's residence with eighteen major vassals skilled in archery "to peruse texts and discuss precedents" (*kyūki o hiran shi, senchō o aitazuneru*).[53] They examined the traditional practices (*kojitsu*) of forms of archery, in preparation for a *yabusame* performance to be held at Sumiyoshi Shrine. The purpose of studying these traditions was to establish a basic form of archery for Eastern warriors to demonstrate to the people of the capital region (*kyōgi no tomogara*).

Clearly there was already in Kamakura times an awareness of a warrior style, different from that of the Heian courtier, and Yoritomo was concerned with both fostering and preserving that awareness.[54] But the concern seems to have been largely confined to the specifics of military affairs. And if texts were compiled, they have not survived.

Yoritomo was not alone in his regard for warrior etiquette. *Azuma kagami* abounds with references to *kojitsu*. In the winter of 1203, for example, Sasaki Takatsuna rode up from Mount Kōya to join other Kamakura vassals in an attack on Enryakuji monks. When he encountered his son Shigetsuna, dressed in armor and ready for battle, "he stared at him awhile, unable even to blink. Nor could he utter a word."[55] Nothing is more important in going into battle, Takatsuna said, than one's weapons and armor. Moreover, he continued, where fighting would be on foot up the mountainside, one ought to wear light armor and carry a short bow: it was all entirely in accord with *kojitsu*. That Shigetsuna instead wore clumsy armor and carried an unwieldy bow was not only inappropriate; but "he might not be able to avoid death."

Thus from early Kamakura times, warrior ceremonial was deemed important, even if it was not yet codified. But the concern for *kojitsu* increased markedly with the onset of the Muromachi age. Once *bushi* leaders began to assume court offices and ranks, an interest developed in creating and transcribing warrior ceremonial on the one hand, and in mastering courtier protocol on the other.

Such an attitude illustrates a fundamental difference between the two warrior regimes. In the Kamakura period, efforts were made to keep warriors and courtiers separate, and warrior ceremonial was more focused upon the mastery of martial skills. This separation was unrealistic. Hōjō warriors stationed in Kyoto could hardly have kept from aping courtier behavior nor could shoguns of imperial lineage have failed to appreciate warrior customs, yet in principle there was more antagonism than accommodation between the two orders.[56] The very existence of separate courtier and warrior capitals helped to define this antagonism.

But in the fourteenth century the establishment of a new Bakufu in Kyoto, where the daily mingling of courtiers and warriors bred familiarity, inevitably produced a different attitude. The shogun and his supporters were expected to conduct themselves in a manner appropriate to the status they had achieved as warrior-aristocrats. Expectations may have been even higher, since power was seized from a ruler still widely regarded as legitimate. As reflected in the *Kenmu shikimoku* expression of a desire to follow both courtier and warrior precedents of good government, the new warrior leaders were aware that adopting the proper ritual procedures could enhance their sovereignty. As a consequence, we encounter a new emphasis on *bunbu ryōdō* as well as on warriors learning courtier etiquette.

Though the urgency was less than acute during the tenures of the first two shoguns, a heightened concern for learning courtier *kojitsu* and compiling warrior *kojitsu* began to build during Yoshimitsu's shogunate and even more so following the rapprochement between the courts. The courtier style adopted by Yoshimitsu is well documented.[57] Yet it was not simply that the shogun now received instruction in judging scent or that he now aspired to the pinnacle of the ancient court hierarchy; there was also an assumption that when warriors were invested with courtier posts they had an *obligation* to preserve the associated ritual behavior. Thus Yoshimitsu engaged Nijō Yoshimoto as an "adviser" on court ceremonial, and also consulted with Konoe Michitsugu.[58] Yoshimitsu's adoption of court ritual was a powerful tool for eliciting acquiescence in his exercise of power.

Yoshimitsu's actions were only the most conspicuous in a generalized warrior effort to imitate the precise behavior of courtiers. Since the very "performance" of governing tasks had long been highly ritualized and since the life of a courtier consisted in large part of intense cultivation of prescribed etiquette, fourteenth-century warrior-aristocrats and their successors also followed such behavior. Earlier, when warriors intervened less directly—and from a distance—in courtly affairs, there had been little necessity for such concern with ritual, but this condition changed when warriors mingled with courtiers on a daily basis. For that matter, ranking warriors seem to have incorporated the new etiquette into their everyday practices even when they were not in attendance at court.[59] It was not merely a quaint aping of courtier polish; it was a fundamental component of warrior conduct as ideal ruler. It was the *bun* element in *bunbu ryōdō* writ large.

Ashikaga Yoshimitsu himself went beyond simply imitating courtier etiquette. For one thing, as part of his campaign for acceptance as the "King of Japan," he had records compiled of major ceremonies in his life. Conceived in the form of *buke kojitsu*, the *Rokuonindono gogempukuki* and *Rokuonindono on'naoihajimeki* dealt, respectively, with Yoshimitsu's coming-of-age ceremony and his first wearing of proper court ceremonial dress.[60]

But Yoshimitsu was not satisfied to reproduce past forms for their own sake. His ambition went beyond that. Owing to his awareness of himself as representing a new fusion of courtier and warrior society, he moved to adjust ceremonial procedures and indeed to develop his own forms, which were then passed on as *kojitsu* for later generations.[61] Here we encounter an apparent incongruity: on the one hand, a concern for maintenance of proper ceremonial, but on the other, a willingness to evolve new precedents. It is a theme to which I shall return presently.

A new warrior ideal had emerged in the fourteenth century. Thrown into close association with courtiers, warriors now developed a heightened sense of their own etiquette and began to codify it as *buke kojitsu*. Having seized the Japanese equivalent of the Mandate of Heaven, they chose not simply to master the arts of war but to adhere to the practices and lessons of courtier *kojitsu*. Yoshimitsu may have been atypical in his virtual rejection of the warrior element; but such a posture may have been necessary to bridge the gap between the two orders, not to mention mending the rift between the two courts. For most warriors, the objective became *bunbu ryōdō*.

Perhaps their ideal was not too different from Chaucer's "parfit, gentil knyght."[62] The warrior in Japan was now expected to be "brave, chivalrous, cultivated, elegant, charming, pious, and well-educated."[63] In other words, he would need to pursue the cultivation of *kojitsu*.

The subject itself has received scant attention from Western scholars. Steenstrup observed in *Hōjō Shigetoki* that "urbanized *buke* upper crust . . . sought out *kojitsu* not as models for the present, but because they took a consciously antiquarian interest in the values of the past,"[64] and though he has recently modified this assessment somewhat, a streak of mindless antiquarianism is of course undeniable. The Muromachi texts themselves acknowledge this. Thus we encounter: "This may seem a strange [custom], but it is the way it has been done since the past." Or again: "This [practice] has been transmitted and recorded from earlier times. I do not know the reason."[65]

Clearly there was a degree of empty formalism. Ancient practices could become rituals whose origins and purposes were completely unknown. This was true not only of the tedious etiquette of how to sit or rise when meeting people of different rank, or the proper way of handing a bow to persons of different rank;[66] it was true even of military practices. In *Yoshisadaki*, for example, the author details the eighteen steps in donning armor and arms in preparation for battle, a procedure attributed to Hachiman-tarō Yoshiie in the eleventh century.[67] Such minutiae do seem irrelevant to performance on the battlefield.

But a closer examination of the function of *kojitsu* in medieval warrior society reveals a more profound behavioral value. All ritual is symbolic statement—codes of dress, ceremonies, and the like—and can function as a powerful support for authority.[68] Acquiring courtier customs represented not just a desire but in fact a requirement for newly ascendant warriors seeking to emulate a normative standard. Some social scientists argue that authority can only be verified by rituals and symbols,[69] and Muromachi warriors were instinctively aware of this. Yet this awareness did not lead to total cynicism, since their concern had a serious underside. Mastery of *kojitsu* was the outward demonstration of the warriors' right to rule.

In Chapter 8, Robert Huey discusses Ashikaga "cultural hegemony." That the Ashikaga shoguns should appropriate the canon via control of imperial poetic anthologies is perfectly in accord with the above analysis of *kojitsu*. In other words, Ashikaga actions in the poetic world were part of a larger effort to invoke the symbols that would legitimize their political ascendancy; they were thus eager to demonstrate their fidelity to activities considered appropriate for rulers. Ashikaga Takauji, Shiba Yoshimasa, and Imagawa Ryōshun all considered poetry composition an essential part of the warrior ideal.

Ritual behavior also fosters conservatism. Warrior concern for *kojitsu* thus derived as well from a strict awareness of the minute distinctions in rank and status of the hierarchy of feudal society. Though this top-to-bottom scaffolding was under siege, as Jeffrey Mass makes clear in Chapter 1, the *Kenmu shikimoku* still admonished, "High and low must each bear in mind their proper station." In fact, warriors in the fourteenth century were sticklers for *kojitsu*, concerned with correct behavior so that they would not be thought ill of. Part of being the "parfit, gentil knyght" involved knowing the proper protocol of each social level.

Though *kojitsu* served to preserve order by controlling behavior, it was not a transcendent order like the legal system. On the other hand, like law it could be and was revised, renewed, even partially replaced. Both law and *kojitsu* were seen as complementary, imperishable bodies of material whose purpose was to maintain a semblance of stability.[70]

Yet *kojitsu* was highly social and much influenced by contemporary fashion. Dress was perhaps the most conspicuous example here with costume a marker of inequality of status. Other examples are taste in architectural style and home furnishings, and the cultivation of cultural forms, such as an interest in tea. The body of warrior etiquette thus underwent constant revision, while never losing the ideal of preserving proper behavioral norms from the past. As T'ang T'ai-tsung retorted once when accused of violating established ritual, "Since rituals arise out of men's feelings, how can they remain permanent?"[71] *Kojitsu* were an important means of medieval warrior empowerment.

BUGEI: THE MARTIAL ARTS

The earliest Muromachi compilations of *kojitsu* are those devoted to archery, especially those compiled by the Ogasawara. In Yoshimitsu's era, for example, Ogasawara Nagahide supposedly wrote the *Kyūba mondō* (Dialogue on Mounted Archery) and collaborated with Ise Mitsutada and Imagawa Ujiyori in compiling the *Sangi ittō ōsōji* (Outline of the Unified Three Teachings), so called because it brought together the traditions of mounted archery etiquette. Indeed, the Ogasawara and the Ise became the primary repositories of warrior *kojitsu* practices in Muromachi times, when the current head of the Ogasawara family of mounted archery specialists claimed a descent from thirty generations earlier.[72]

During the Muromachi period, *inuoumono* was a popular form of mounted archery in which the warriors shot at dogs with blunted arrows. It was a grandiose affair, more a sport than a type of paramilitary training, with numerous performers, judges, and dog handlers. Nonetheless, it was regarded as a way of keeping warriors sharp for battle. *Inuoumono* was supposedly abolished in Go-Daigo's era, the result of the emperor's pity for blameless dogs who might be injured. But tradition holds that Ogasawara Sadamune submitted a memorial to Takauji requesting that he lift the ban. In his petition, Sadamune referred back to the hoary past of Emperor Jinmu and Empress Jingū when Japan had originally been pacified by bow and arrow. He argued that in times of peace martial activities should not cease, and, in particular, that warriors should be allowed to sharpen their skills through *inuoumono*.[73]

Is there anything new to be found in *kojitsu* manuals and other texts on the subject of warriors as fighting men? Obviously, the numbers of men engaged in warfare were now, in the fourteenth century, at new levels—even as we discount the inflated numbers in *Taiheiki* and other chronicles.[74] At the same time, the level of violence had now escalated beyond anything previously known. As suggested in other chapters of this book, warriors were now obliged to prepare for and actually practice warfare. Shimokawa Ushio provides the revealing statistic that whereas we can identify 1,550 sword makers for the Kamakura period, some 3,550 are recorded for the Nambokuchō and Muromachi eras.[75] Although the later period was almost a century longer, the increase in numbers is still impressive, yielding an important conclusion: that the bow was being replaced by the sword as the preferred weapon, whether wielded on horseback or on foot.

In fact, *Taiheiki* differs markedly from *Heike monogatari* in the matter of weapons. Whereas the latter reports little fighting with swords,[76] the former abounds with references to swords and techniques for using them—to cuts with names like "pear splitter," "bamboo splitter," "thunder cutter," "breast splitter," "nail cutter," and the like. Fukuma no Saburō, a resident of Inaba Province, was a Yamana vassal known for possessing a sword of some "seven *shaku* and 2 *sun*" (just over seven feet, albeit surely an exaggeration).[77] The chronicle notes that an enemy struck by the blade would have his torso or knees sliced clean off.

Battle descriptions in *Taiheiki* have swords splitting helmets "down to the cross-stitched bottom flap so that (the enemy) was cleft in two and perished." A warrior charges into battle amidst "flying sparks of fire." Whereas in *Heike* enemies are invariably "shot down," in *Taiheiki* they are far more frequently "cut down." The work is hardly alone; *Ōtomoki*, commenting on the Tatarahama Battle of 1336, records that one Betsugi Akitsura of Hōki Province was "stronger than other men; and since he had acquired the mysteries of using the sword ("*tachiuchi ni myō o etaru*"), he destroyed (his opponents) by slashing in all directions."[78] Warriors were still skilled at mounted archery—in *Taiheiki*, archery feats are common—but the sword was becoming the more important weapon.

Given the advance of the sword over archery as a warrior martial skill, why were so many *kojitsu* texts devoted to mounted archery? Concerned, as we have observed, with the recording of established customs, such texts naturally remained preoccupied with the primary skills of the warrior. In that context, both mounted and ground archery had been part of court ceremonial from Nara times.

As warriors eagerly adopted the civilian governing arts of the courtier class, the concern for compiling *kojitsu* grew—both as "busy-work for men of scholarly leanings"[79] and as an act of preservation of family martial traditions. Equestrian skills (*bajutsu*)[80] and forms of mounted archery dominated. Texts devoted to swordsmanship evolved more slowly, and only after a considerable period of specialization with the sword did it develop into something significant enough to record as *kojitsu*. Dozens of texts involving the precise etiquette of mounted archery (especially *inuoumono*) were drawn up during the Muromachi period, with the earliest appearing in the fourteenth century. As one-on-one mounted archery came to be replaced by armies of sword-wielding cavalry supported by archers and spear bearers (*ashigaru*) on foot, concern for punctilious performance of *inuoumono* might well have atrophied. Instead, it became fully integrated into warrior *kojitsu*. That such an antiquated form of mounted sport archery would remain popular with the warrior elite is consistent with the ideal of the warrior as one who masters the requisite forms of etiquette, the "parfit, gentil knyght."

The fourteenth century represents a new age in Japan. It was a chaotic age, but the chaos represented an opportunity for those who would seize it. Disorder provided the rationale for warriors to wrest control of the nation's governance away from the courtiers. The *bunbu ryōdō* amalgam and the new emphasis on *kojitsu* were a natural development as warriors sought to appropriate the symbols they would need to justify their rule. The models at hand were the civil virtues of ancient China and earlier Japan. They thus appropriated a version of Confucian statecraft and grafted it onto their experiences on the battlefield. The result was the warrior-administrator who combines *bun* and *bu*, and as long as warfare was rampant that was sufficient. The stress of course was on the acquisition of *bun* for the purposes of ruling, a condition that would not change until Tokugawa times. In that new context, shoguns and philosophers would have to encourage the *bu* element among vassals who were increasingly effete.

███████

PART THREE

CHAPTER 11

Enryakuji—An Old Power in a New Era

MIKAEL ADOLPHSON

W̶HEN ASKED to describe the relationship between the state
and religious institutions in fourteenth-century Japan, few if any
scholars would mention such traditional Buddhist temples as Enryakuji,
Tōdaiji, and Kōfukuji.[1] The discussion is far more likely to focus on the
warrior class and Zen.[2] But the old Buddhist sects, which were powerful
enough to put pressure on the government in the preceding eras, continued to exert considerable influence after the establishment of the Ashikaga Bakufu in 1336. In 1368–69, for example, monks from the Enryakuji
complex on Mount Hiei northeast of Kyoto entered the capital to protest
the privileges that the Bakufu had awarded to a Zen temple. Eventually,
the Bakufu complied with the demands by exiling two prominent Zen
monks and demolishing the gate of their temple. This conflict, known as
the Nanzenji Gate incident, was not so much a dispute over economic
privileges as it was members of the Buddhist establishment opposing the
Bakufu's attempts to promote Zen as its officially sanctioned sect. But
what rights did Enryakuji have to interfere with the warrior government's
religious policies? In other words, how are we to understand Enryakuji
and its political role in the early Muromachi state? Did the fourteenth-
century leaders regard religious institutions as a part of the state? Or were
they, as one scholar has put it, outside organizations that played "no role

in the affairs of the state?"[3] Although these questions are too vast to be answered in one short essay, I should like to focus on Enryakuji's public role and official status in the years following the establishment of the Ashikaga Bakufu. Toward this end, it will be helpful to begin with a discussion of the political role of religious institutions during the preceding era.

THE KENMON THEORY

Although the development of religious doctrines has received much attention in the West, few scholars have approached temples and shrines as sociopolitical institutions. Only recently have the pioneering works of a handful of historians given them due recognition by attempting to place religious institutions in their historical context.[4] These studies owe much to the works of the Japanese scholar Kuroda Toshio and his *kenmon* theory.

In the mid-1960s Kuroda introduced the *kenmon* theory in an attempt to describe the ruling system in Japan from the eleventh to the fifteenth centuries.[5] According to this theory, the highest authority in the state was shared by a number of private elite groups known as *kenmon* ("influential families" or "powerful lineages").[6] These elites were the leaders of three great power blocs—the court nobles (*kuge*), the warrior aristocracy (*buke*), and temples and shrines (*jisha*)—which ruled the realm together by sharing responsibilities of government and by supporting each others' privileges and status. Cooperation was a fundamental principle in the *kenmon* system of rule in spite of occasional conflicts among the blocs. In fact, Kuroda stated that the *kenmon* were mutually dependent on each other to maintain their status and wealth.[7] Put differently, one *kenmon* was never powerful enough to rule without the support of the other elites. During the twelfth century, for example, the retired emperor dominated the political scene but relied on warrior aristocrats to supply military force. A similar dependence existed between the court and the Kamakura Bakufu in the thirteenth century.[8]

Although several Western scholars have mentioned and benefited from Kuroda's theory, no thorough treatments of the theory itself and its usefulness in describing the Japanese Middle Ages have been presented in English.[9] Yet it is no exaggeration to state that a study of the sociopolitical powers of religious institutions without a discussion of the characteristics of the *kenmon* and its system of rulership would lack both historical and historiographical frames of reference. Simply put, we need to know what a *kenmon* was. What was its power based on? How did the system of *kenmon* rule evolve? The following discussion is a concise and critical appraisal of the *kenmon* theory.

Kuroda defined five criteria that characterized the *kenmon*. First, they all had their own private headquarters (*mandokoro*), which handled administrative and economic matters within the *kenmon*. Second, the headquarters issued edicts to convey orders from the head of the group. Third, each *kenmon* had a number of retainers or followers, who were loyal only to its leader. These retainers included both armed and civil personnel. Fourth, the head of each elite had complete judicial rights, that is, rights to self-rule, over their own family or lineage. Fifth, the *kenmon* also had immune control and jurisdiction (another aspect of self-rule) over their assets, which included a large number of private estates known as *shōen*. The *shōen* contained a vertical division of rights (*shiki*) that was an integral part of the *kenmon* system.[10] In fact, the terms were inseparable. The *kenmon* constituted the political elite of a socioeconomic system based on *shiki* and *shōen*. This argument is convincing since the term *kenmon* itself first appears in *shōen* documents of the mid-Heian period.[11]

In substance, the *kenmon* system was a ruling system in which a number of elites ruled through their private, or "extralegal," assets. It was the head of the most powerful *kenmon* who dominated the government. The headquarters of that elite thus assumed a more official character and issued documents to different government organs. The retainers of the *kenmon* leader also came to serve the government and received official titles. At the same time, not even the dominating *kenmon* had enough power to become an absolute ruler. He was dependent on the support of the other elites who assumed specific public responsibilities (religious, military, or administrative) in exchange for confirmation and support of both their private control of land and their own lineage. The *kenmon* system was, in other words, a ruling system in which private (or familial, to use John Hall's terminology) and official powers were combined to achieve efficient government over land and people.

The Fujiwara family was the first *kenmon* to emerge. By the tenth century, the Fujiwara leaders dominated the imperial court in Kyoto through their private wealth and resources. They had acquired tax-immune estates, a private headquarters, and retainers who were used in government matters. However, since they were still dependent on government titles to rule and to maintain their position (even within their clan), Kuroda claimed that it did not signify the beginning of *kenmon rule*.[12] The first signs of a *kenmon* system appear, according to Kuroda, late in the eleventh century when the imperial family reasserted its dominance under retired emperors. The crucial point at this junction was that rulership now took place without high government offices. Thus, rulers typically retired in order to be able to exert their power.[13] Bureaucratic titles mattered little to both the imperial family and the Fujiwara leaders at this point. In short, direct control of estates, provinces, and manpower was more important than titles as the means by which to influence or dominate the government.

, During the twelfth century the *kenmon* style of rule was further expanded as other groups were included. Religious institutions and aristocratic warriors assumed the characteristics of *kenmon*, resulting in a tripartite rulership by the mid-twelfth century. Three blocs—the court, the warrior aristocracy, and religious institutions—shared the privileges and responsibilities of government. Even though they all exhibited the typical *kenmon* characteristics, Kuroda emphasized that they had their own peculiarites.[14]

The court nobility (*kuge*), consisting of the imperial family and the capital aristocracy, held the administrative and ceremonial responsibilities of the state. Supported by their private organizations and assets, the nobles maintained their privileges by their access to government offices, and they remained the formal leaders of the state. The emperorship, however, stood above the system—in effect, the outstanding symbol of the state itself. To Kuroda, this symbolic representation of the *kenmon* system was the reason for the emperorship's exceptional survival throughout the Middle Ages. It was the emperor who made all important appointments, including the title of shogun, even as the imperial power per se may have been limited. In other words, the three power blocs all needed this figurehead in whose name they jointly ruled and individually prospered.[15]

The warrior aristocracy (*buke*) was responsible for keeping the peace and for physically protecting the state. Beginning in the mid-twelfth century, these duties were entrusted to prominent warrior leaders such as Taira no Kiyomori and Minamoto no Yoshiie. This unofficial division of responsibilities was formalized with the establishment of the warrior government in the east (the Kamakura Bakufu) in the 1180s. Kuroda saw this as a second phase and consolidation of the *kenmon* system. Although the Bakufu could easily outpower the court and its supporters in the capital area (which actually happened in the Jōkyū War of 1221), it could not eliminate the court and rule on its own. Since it lacked the administrative and bureaucratic apparatus to extend its rule over all classes in thirteenth-century Japan, its responsibility was limited to keeping the peace and to controlling the warrior class.[16] The court and the Bakufu consequently complemented each other in an overlapping rulership, which has been termed a dual polity by historians.[17]

The third member of the ruling triumvirate—the religious establishment—supplied the state and its members with spiritual protection. It also supported a vertical differentiation among the rulers and the ruled through rituals and ceremonies. Since the power of religious institutions is the subject of this study, and the religious bloc is the most controversial part of Kuroda's theory, it will be useful to explore his analysis of temples and shrines in some depth.

During the ninth century, the most popular Buddhist sects (known as the *kenmitsu* schools)[18] developed close relations with the most powerful families in the capital. However, after two centuries of patron-client relations, the larger temples became less dependent on direct and voluntary support from the capital nobility. By the eleventh century, these temples possessed private estates, vast numbers of monks, lay followers, and branch institutions, over all of which they held judicial and administrative control. Administrative duties and management of these assets were handled by the temple's own headquarters. A head abbot, often of noble or imperial birth, represented the temple and served as the channel of communication with the other elites. Even though the head abbot was a chosen leader, his leadership within the sect was not unlike that of the Fujiwara chieftain or the retired emperor. In short, these religious centers had been "*kenmon*ified."[19] At approximately the same time, a doctrine was developed that supported the interdependent relationship between the imperial court and Buddhism. Known as the *ōbō-buppō* (the Imperial Law and the Buddhist Law) concept, it conveyed the idea that the state and Buddhism were as dependent on each other as the two wings of a bird or the two wheels of a cart.[20]

Kuroda's *kenmon* conept is appealing because it treats religious institutions as political powers both in their own right and as providers of doctrine and spiritual support. Moreover, the idea of a shared rulership in late Heian and Kamakura Japan can help to explain a number of complex relationships involving elites from the three different groups. However, it can also be misleading since it labels religious institutions as a coherent power bloc on the same level as both the court and the Bakufu. Three points illustrate the problems that occur here.

First, it is difficult to imagine that the religious establishment had the same kind of power as the court or the Bakufu. Taira Masayuki, Kuroda's student and successor, adjusted his mentor's theory in this aspect. Taira has stated that religious institutions never had enough power to form an independent government on the model of the warrior aristocracy. In fact, he even claims that temples never held ultimate authority in any way. That power belonged exclusively to the secular powers.[21]

Second, if religious institutions did not have the same kind of powers as the other two power blocs, then how independent were they? Kuroda himself seems to have recognized this problem. Temples, he concluded, were "half-dependent" on the court.[22] Indeed, the sources leave little doubt that Enryakuji's ties with the court were very strong and much different from those with the Bakufu and the warrior class in general. For example, the ceremonial and religious duties of the *kenmitsu* temples—their raison d'être—were almost exclusively directed to serving the members of the imperial court.

Third, by making a separate power bloc of the religious establishment, Kuroda assumed that there was a sense of unity among the most powerful temples and shrines. This is perhaps the weakest point in the whole *kenmon* theory. While the court and the Bakufu were coherent in that they were vertically integrated and had clear apexes in their blocs, the religious establishment cannot be seen as a single hierarchy during this period. Different doctrines and sects coexisted and competed for favors from the court in a system that can most aptly be described as one of doctrinal multitude. It is therefore misleading to treat the religious establishment as a collectively active body. In short, individual temples and shrines enjoyed *kenmon* status, but they were too diversified in power and structure to be equal to the court or the Bakufu.

In spite of these flaws the *kenmon* theory has had a positive impact on the field. The notion of privately based elites that shared governmental duties is an important insight that facilitates our comprehension of the ruling structures of Heian and Kamakura Japan. To be more specific, the *kenmon* theory brought attention to three important issues. First, the concept of shared rulership opposed the traditional view that Heian and Kamakura rulership was characterized by a sequence of political elites in total control of government. Kuroda pointed out that the Fujiwara family, the retired emperors, and the Kamakura Bakufu, even during the heydays of their respective power, were never completely dominating. They were merely the *primer inter pares*—the dominating elite among other elites— who could not rule without the support of their peers. More important, the other elites were never completely eclipsed when the balance shifted to their disadvantage. The Fujiwara family, for example, continued to play an important role in the capital throughout the reign of retired emperors and during the Kamakura period.

Second, the importance of the year 1185 as a defining point in Japanese history must be reevaluated in light of the *kenmon* theory. The establishment of the Kamakura Bakufu did not, according to Kuroda, mark the transition from court rule to warrior rule, or from the ancient to the feudal era.[23] Recently, other scholars have also pointed out that there were more continuities between the Heian and Kamakura periods than were previously acknowledged. The continued authority of the imperial court and the central proprietors is one important aspect of this revision.

Third, Kuroda showed that religious institutions were not parasites who usurped authority from the imperial court. On the contrary, they were important participants in the government as providers of religious rituals for the well-being of the state and its officials. Such rituals were instrumental in creating and maintaining the social stratification that supported the court hierarchy. The ability to finance and perform lavish and often magical ceremonies augmented the status of those involved. Moreover, temples and shrines served as extensions of the state when they collected income in the provinces as its representatives and religious protectors.[24] In short, the *kenmon* theory made scholars realize that religious institutions in premodern Japan were sociopolitical institutions integral to the government and its rule.

In the end, the usefulness of Kuroda's *kenmon* theory depends on the definition of the theory itself. It contains two aspects that need to be distinguished. On the one hand, the idea of a tripartite ruling system is problematic since the religious bloc lacked the kind of cohesion and independence that Kuroda assumed. On the other hand, the *kenmon* concept is crucial in understanding Japan's Heian and Kamakura eras. The *kenmon* were individual elites, which, through their private assets, assumed a public role in the state, sharing the duties and responsibilites of government. In return, they were entitled to economic and judicial immunities, which became the trademarks of these elites.

The *kenmon* concept is thus an important element in the study of Heian and Kamakura Japan. But how useful is it in describing the fourteenth century? Kuroda stated that the *kenmon* system began to decline in that century when its economic base—the *shōen* system—began to disintegrate. This was a slow death caused by equally slow-moving socioeconomic changes on the local level. Villages as well as villagers began to question the authority of the absentee proprietors and formed horizontal alliances that resulted in more independent village units. The proprietor's control declined further as local warriors interjected themselves between the proprietor and the farming population. Subsequently, new kinds of conflicts appeared as whole regions rebelled against the old proprietors. In the end, it became increasingly difficult for the traditional elites in the central region—the imperial family, the high nobility, and religious institutions—to control and to collect dues from their estates.[25]

Other signs of the breakup of the old elite system were visible from the fourteenth century. Kuroda noted that a decline began in the belief in and use of the ōbō-buppō concept. He also noted an increase in conflicts between different temples and sects.[26] In particular, the emergence of new, populistic sects changed the religious and political context. These sects offered new, simplified ways of achieving spiritual blessing, which challenged the complex and elitist rituals of the established schools. As evidenced by the Zen monk Eisai's successful relations with Enryakuji, Zen and Tendai were not mutually exclusive, though a polemic to that effect with origins in the late twelfth century came to characterize their relationship. Apart from Eisai, Enryakuji and the rest of the Buddhist establishment managed to keep the Zen movement from gaining any considerable momentum in the capital area during the thirteenth century. However, the situation changed dramatically in the next century, when Zen became the most favored sect in Kyoto. As we shall see presently, the emergence and promotion of Rinzai Zen affected the nature of the cooperation between the religious and secular powers in the capital.

Kuroda duly noted such changes in the fourteenth century, but he still argued that the kenmon system of cooperative rule somehow survived until the Ōnin War (1467–77).[27] Unfortunately, he did not explain how such an arrangement outlasted the Kamakura Bakufu by a full 130 years. He merely stated that the balance among the kenmon changed as all the elites save for the Ashikaga Bakufu lost power.[28] Suzanne Gay has even maintained that the kenmon system survived, at least in Kyoto, into the sixteenth century.[29]

Kuroda has been much criticized for his inclusion of the Muromachi Bakufu within the kenmon system. In particular, Nagahara Keiji objected to the appropriations of a single theory for the two shogunates, which were so fundamentally different from each other.[30] He argued that Kuroda exaggerated the continuities between them, just as traditional historians had exaggerated the differences between Heian and Kamakura. To throw light on this debate, we need to compare the status of Enryakuji prior to the Muromachi era with its experiences under Ashikaga rule.

ENRYAKUJI IN THE PRE-MUROMACHI AGE

Enryakuji became one of Japan's most privileged temple soon after its foundation late in the eighth century. The founder, Saichō, and his immediate disciples received aristocratic support to establish the Tendai sect, which was intended to be outside the influence of the Office of Monastic Affairs, dominated, at the time, by competing sects in Nara. In the bypassing of this office, Enryakuji's leaders developed close contacts with the most prominent members of the imperial government. As a result, Enryakuji came to cater directly to the personal needs of the Kyoto nobility, which, for its part, donated rights to taxes and private estates to the temple. The administration of these assets and the organization of Enryakuji itself were to be entirely the private domain of the temple and its leaders. By the eleventh century, the Enryakuji complex encompassed about 3,000 residing monks, a vast number of *shōen*, and a network of branch institutions that extended to the western extremity of the main island.[31]

Although the imperial government had no direct control over Enryakuji, there were two ways in which the Kyoto nobility might influence the temple. First, the emperor retained the right to appoint the head abbot (*zasu*), though this was not a privilege that he could use arbitrarily. In fact, numerous demonstrations by monks centered on disagreements over appointments, which meant that a *zasu* could be effective only if he had the support of both the court and the clergy. Only under such conditions might he serve as a channel of communication between them, and be able to control the clergy and the temple's armed "evil monks" (*akusō*).

The second and more informal means of influence came through noble cloisters (*monzeki*) that were headed by abbots born to the most prominent families in the capital. These cloisters, although located in the outskirts of the capital, became the *de facto* centers of power within the temple organization in the Kamakura period. The position of individual abbots was based on their status as nobles, as well as on the private assets they controlled through their religious and secular ranks. In particular, sons of emperors and princes maintained their familial connections and thereby provided an informal imperial control of parts of Enryakuji.

The temple's noble contacts also assured it of a privileged status in the capital region, as did its favorable location on Mount Hiei overlooking Kyoto. Enryakuji could thus claim to be the "Temple for Pacification and Protection of the State" (*chingo kokka no dōjo*). This concept along with the many rituals its monks performed on behalf of the state supports Kuroda's idea that religious institutions were actively and legitimately involved in government affairs. Enryakuji supplied religious support to the state in return for the economic and judicial privileges reserved for the country's elites.

Together with a multitude of shrines and temples, Enryakuji thus performed religious ceremonies on behalf of their patrons as well as the state. Supported by leading members of both the imperial family and the Fujiwara, Tendai monks were especially prominent in different rituals at court, but similar rituals were also performed by other privileged temples such as Kōfukuji and Tōdaiji, which (along with elite shrines) shared the responsibility for the spiritual welfare of the state.

The privilege of performing such rituals was accompanied by a variety of benefits. Monks from the most prominent temples were promoted to the highest religious offices in the realm. Donations of land, tax rights, and funding for specific enterprises also reflected the recipient's standing with the court. In short, religious rituals, monk promotions, and economic privileges were all important indications of a temple's official status. It should come as no surprise, therefore, that religious centers jealously guarded these privileges. Even the slightest disruption of the accustomed balance resulted in protests from the disfavored side. Occasionally, these protests developed into violent conflicts with government troops or an opposing temple, sometimes with both. Although historians have blamed the temples for causing such troubles, these conflicts tended to be caused by the secular authorities who were seeking to use patronage as a way of strengthening their own positions. The following examples will suffice to illustrate this point.

In the first decade of the twelfth century Retired Emperor Shirakawa openly promoted Tōji (a Shingon temple in Kyoto) at the expense of other temples, in particular, Enryakuji. In response to this favoritism, Enryakuji monks frequently descended the mountain and entered the capital to protest. For example, in the third month of 1108 Tendai monks[32] complained to the court that a Tōji monk had been wrongfully assigned to perform an esoteric ritual in the capital. Previously, monks from the Tendai and Shingon schools had been appointed in alternate years.[33] At a court meeting on the twenty-third, the retired emperor, ignoring opposition from several court nobles and facing the threat of monk demonstrations, simply declared that he had the right to break these old customs. For this ceremony, he stated, "many Tōji monks shall be employed while Tendai monks will be used [only] occasionally." [34] Enryakuji responded by taking the appeal to the next level. On the thirtieth, after the ritual had taken place, Tendai monks left Mount Hiei to protest in the capital. Highly skilled Minamoto and Taira warriors were sent out to protect Kyoto and managed to keep the monks out of the capital proper. Yet the threat of continued troubles induced the court to promise the next appointment to Tendai, thus satisfying the monks, who returned to their temples.[35]

During the thirteenth century there were several violent and devastating conflicts between Enryakuji and Onjōji. Onjōji, located just southeast of Mount Hiei, was originally part of the Enryakuji complex but became an independent Tendai temple in 993. Thereafter the two temples were often in dispute over monk offices, estates, and religious privileges. This opposition was deepened by the court's willingness to support Onjōji in order to weaken and control Enryakuji. To mention just one recurring case in point, the Enryakuji monks protested to the court in 1239, 1264, and again in 1291 when the head abbotship of Tennōji—presumably an Enryakuji prerogative—was awarded to Onjōji instead.[36]

Although the Kamakura Bakufu intervened in religious matters in Kyoto only occasionally, it aimed at keeping the peace and maintaining the balance among the sects. It was sensitive to physical pressure, and its policies and methods were no different from those of the imperial court, as demonstrated in an interesting episode from 1308. In that year, Enryakuji complained to the court over a posthumous title that was about to be awarded to a Tōji monk. In the first month of that year a protest was directed to Retired Emperor Go-Uda who was planning to receive an esoteric initiation at Tōji. The ceremony duly took place and Go-Uda awarded the posthumous title of Grand Master (*daishi*) to the founder (Yakushin, 827–906) of the lineage that officiated at the ceremony. The Enryakuji monks appealed in response, claiming that the title had never been granted for performing merely an initiation ceremony, while also arguing that it was hundreds of years after the awardee's death; in addition, Yakushin had never traveled to China in search of the Buddhist Law, unlike the experience of the four Grand Masters.[37]

In the eighth month of 1308, the Enryakuji monks increased their pressure by closing their temple and burning down parts of Hiesha (Enryakuji's main shrine affiliate located on the eastern foot of Mount Hiei).

Go-Uda did not relent but his attempts now fell short owing to the untimely death of his son, Emperor Go-Nijō. In accordance with the prevailing custom of alternating succession between the two imperial lines,
Go-Uda was now forced to relinquish his position as retired emperor. The
new retired emperor Fushimi, reluctant to start his reign with an incident
involving Enryakuji, thus annulled the honorary title in the tenth month.
But the conflict continued to fester as Tōji, assisted by Tōdaiji, Daigoji,
and Kōyasan, now appealed to the Bakufu, which ruled in favor of the
plaintiffs. This reversal caused Enryakuji to forward a lengthy protest of
its own, arguing against the title now re-granted to Yakushin. In the end,
the pressure of monks demonstrating in Kyoto in 1312 forced the Bakufu
to resolve the dispute in Enryakuji's favor.[38]

The examples presented here should leave no doubt that temples played
an important role not only as providers of doctrines but also as political
players in the factional jockeying in the capital area. Many secular rulers
might have preferred support from one sect over another, but they tended
to be thwarted by the temples' determination to maintain a balance of
power among themselves. Thus a system of doctrinal multitude developed
into a consciously controlled religious balance among the main temples.
However, this balance came to be challenged, and then altered, after the
establishment of the Ashikaga Bakufu. Enryakuji was one of the most
sturdy defenders of the old system, and it will be of particular interest to
see how this ancient temple fared under the changed circumstances of the
post-Kamakura age.

ENRYAKUJI'S RELIGIOUS STATUS
IN THE EARLY MUROMACHI POLITY

During the fourteenth century, the leaders of the new regime promoted
Zen in an attempt to create a new religious hierarchy. Zen was a relative
newcomer with little economic and political power of its own, and with
its earlier ties to the Kamakura Bakufu,[39] it seemed a suitable doctrine to
further the interests of the Ashikaga. At the same time, the Bakufu's policies dealing with religion became a vital threat to the old Buddhist schools,
in particular, its one-sided patronage of Rinzai Zen, which threatened the
entrenched system of doctrinal multitude. As a consequence, the age-old
competition among the *kenmitsu* sects was now replaced by one between
Zen and *kenmitsu* temples.[40] Enryakuji in particular responded vehemently
to the favors now granted Zen institutions. Two incidents demonstrate

this point vividly. Though they are only two decades apart, they resulted, as we shall see, in different conclusions, reflecting two different political complexions.

In 1339, Ashikaga Takauji, his brother Tadayoshi, Retired Emperor Kōgon, and the Zen monk Musō Soseki agreed to convert an imperial palace (Kameyama) in the western part of Kyoto into a Zen monastery. *Shōen* were provided by the Bakufu to finance the reconstruction, but the temple was still not completed two years later. To increase the funding for the project, Takauji decided to send a trade mission to China and to give the profits to the temple. The enterprise was scaled down to a mere two ships because of protests from Enryakuji.[41]

The new temple, named Tenryūji, was finally completed in 1344. A memorial on the anniversary of Emperor Go-Daigo's death was planned for the next year, but once again Enryakuji protested. Since a Zen temple had never been the location of an imperial memorial service, the Enryakuji monks felt that Tendai's public role and religious status were now under threat. Such a perception is well demonstrated in the temple's appeals, issued between 1344/12 and 1345/7/20, which emphasized the tradition of state protection by the *kenmitsu* schools. As argued by Enryakuji, Tenryūji itself, which was described as little more than a private Zen hall, could scarcely, with justification, be made an imperially designated temple (*chokuganji*). In particular, Enryakuji objected to the retired emperor's visiting such a place for the purpose of attending a memorial service. Clearly, the monks stated, it was Enryakuji that had served as the protector of the state since the capital had been moved to Kyoto originally (794).[42] In the monks' own words, "the safety of the state is through Enryakuji's protection," whereas Zen, in its neglect of the *kenmitsu* temples, represented the first step in the progression toward state destruction. In support of their claim, the monks did not fail to mention that the Kamakura Bakufu, which had favored Zen, no longer existed.[43]

Although the Enryakuji monks may have been genuinely concerned with the welfare of the state, their primary concern was Tendai's status within the Muromachi polity. They felt that the *kenmitsu* schools stood to lose immensely if Zen was favored, since it was not compatible with other Buddhist doctrines. It is not likely that the monks conceived the Bakufu's policies as steps toward the creation of a new system, but they were convinced that its patronage of Zen constituted an attack on the long-entrenched multidoctrinal system.

In the eighth month of 1345 Enryakuji became more aggressive in its demands. Not only did the monks demand that Tenryūji be demolished and that Musō Soseki be exiled, but they also began to prepare to enter the capital and demonstrate. In addition, Tōdaiji and Kōfukuji were invited to join Enryakuji in the protest.[44] On the fourteenth day of that month the retired emperor now canceled his visit to Tenryūji,[45] though the Bakufu was not ready to capitulate. Rather, it threatened to depose Enryakuji's three most prominent abbots and to confiscate the private and public possessions of the monks should they enter the capital.[46] On 1345/8/29, the Bakufu leaders and a large number of prominent warriors attended a grand ceremony at Tenryūji, though without the presence of the retired emperor.[47] By doing so they displayed their new power while also rejecting Enryakuji's demands.

The Bakufu briefly controlled the capital following this incident, but internal rivalries and the Southern Court's attacks on Kyoto weakened its position considerably in the first half of the 1350s. However, the Ashikaga regained control by 1355, and the second shogun, Yoshiakira, enjoyed a steady rule in the capital until his death late in 1367. The next shogun, Yoshimitsu, was only ten years old at that time, leaving Bakufu matters in the hands of a council of warrior leaders. Such was the political situation in 1368 when Enryakuji renewed its pressure against the Bakufu's favoritism of Zen.

The incident actually began in 1367, when a novice from Onjōji was killed as he tried to force his way through a toll barrier newly constructed by Nanzenji. This Zen temple, heavily patronized by the Bakufu, had been allowed to build the toll station to finance a reconstruction of the temple's main gate. Onjōji and Enryakuji, which both had interests in Ōmi Province where the toll gate was erected, disapproved of what they judged to be unfair competition. Armed monks from Onjōji proceeded to tear down the new barrier, with fatalities occurring on both sides.[48] A week later the Bakufu decided to retaliate and dispatched warriors who destroyed three of Onjōji's own toll stations, followed up by the confiscation of a number of Onjōji estates.[49] Since the larger issue was clearly the Bakufu's extensive patronage of Zen, Onjōji now managed to get the support of Enryakuji and Kōfukuji. Facing the combined powers of three such influential temples, the Bakufu and the court made peace with them in the eighth month.[50]

The opposition between the followers of Zen and Tendai did not disappear, however. In 1368, the abbot of Nanzenji, Jōzan Sozen, wrote a polemic, the *Zoku shōbōron*, in which he stated that Zen was the only true Buddhist learning and that other sects were inferior perversions. He mocked the Tendai monks, calling them monkeys and toads.[51] In spite of such insults, the petitions from Enryakuji were more concerned with protecting the traditional rights of the *kenmitsu* schools, while also discouraging the Bakufu's patronage of Zen.[52] The Bakufu responded by claiming that Enryakuji was not the only imperial temple, that it did not know who the author of the polemic was, and that Enryakuji itself had been disloyal to the state four times since the Bakufu had moved to Kyoto.[53] The Bakufu thus avoided the issue of Zen as an exclusive state doctrine, not to mention the effects it would have on the old multidoctrinal system. For its part, Enryakuji, in its most comprehensive petition, revealed the depth of its concerns with the Ashikaga Bakufu and its religious policies: "The court and the Bakufu have honored and favored Zen. Even though Tendai has not been bestowed such [honors], this sect should not be neglected and this mountain's Buddhism should not be forsaken."[54] In fact, the sources reveal that the monks had good cause to be worried. For at the same time that the Bakufu was funding construction and repairs to Zen institutions, it was often reluctant to respond in the same way on Enryakuji's behalf.[55]

Such tactics notwithstanding, the Bakufu was neither strong enough nor unified enough to resist the pressure from Enryakuji in the Nanzenji Gate incident. Several of its warrior leaders wished to comply with some of the temple's demands and punish Jōzan, but the dominating figure at the time, Hosokawa Yoriyuki, continued to protect Nanzenji.[56] Finally, in the eleventh month of 1368, Yoriyuki gave in and exiled Jōzan while also agreeing to delete his name from the register of monks.[57]

Encouraged by their partial victory, the Enryakuji monks continued to demand that the Nanzenji gate be completely demolished. The Bakufu complied on 1369/7/19, and the gate was torn down at the end of that month.[58] The events that led to this decision included several monk demonstrations in the capital. Employing a method that the Enryakuji monks had used for centuries, they carried portable shrines as a way of putting additional spiritual pressure behind their demands.[59] Actually, some of those shrines had been damaged in the course of fighting with Bakufu troops, thereby leading the temple to insist that they be rebuilt at Bakufu expense. The warrior regime eventually agreed to build new shrines in 1372, but it delayed the actual assessment of taxes and the reconstruction until 1380.[60]

Enryakuji was defeated, then, in the Tenryūji incident, but it was ultimately victorious in the Nanzenji Gate matter. Yet the victory did not result from a change in the Ashikaga's religious policies. Rather it was a consequence of the Bakufu's own power, which was now at low tide. As noted earlier, the second shogun, Yoshiakira, died in 1367, and the third shogun, Yoshimitsu, was still too young to rule on his own. The leaders of the Bakufu were far from united, and internal struggles prevented resolute decision making. Yet the Bakufu had attempted to enforce the policies introduced by its founders. To the regime, Zen was a controllable sect and therefore to be favored over the older Buddhist schools. Consequently, Zen institutions were promoted and protected throughout the fourteenth century, and they continued to prosper as long as the Bakufu remained vigorous. Yet at the same time, Enryakuji and the other *kenmitsu* schools continued to perform religious ceremonies on behalf of the imperial court, even as their overall influence was unmistakably declining. The Bakufu was now the dominant power in the Muromachi polity.

Enryakuji and the Ashikaga Bakufu represented two fundamentally different approaches to the role of religious institutions. Whereas the former was a representative of a system of doctrinal multitude and of interdependence, the latter sought to create a single system that could be controlled by itself. In so doing, it used both new and old methods. As shown earlier, it was quite common for government leaders to support a particular sect to assure its total loyalty. By promoting Zen, however, the Bakufu not only was favoring a particular Buddhist school, but also was attacking the underlying concept of doctrinal multitude. Monks and courtiers clearly noted this unprecedented change. During the thirteenth century, it would not have been imaginable for the Bakufu to neglect the established Buddhist schools. The Tenryūji and Nanzenji Gate incidents, then, were less conflicts between the older schools and Zen than they were a defense by the former of their traditional rights vis-à-vis the Bakufu.

ECONOMIC PRIVILEGES AND JUDICIAL IMMUNITY

In addition to its diminished religious importance, Enryakuji also faced challenges to its economic privileges. Like all central proprietors during the fourteenth century, the temple experienced increasing problems in securing income from its estates. Moreover, Enryakuji's ability as a *kenmon* patron to control and protect guilds now began to decline. Contrary to the change in its religious status, however, these problems were caused not by the Bakufu but by local persons who started to question the authority of the traditional elites. The term *gekokujō* ("the lower overthrowing the higher"), a contemporaneous concept for describing sociopolitical changes, may thus also be applied to describe the period's economic challenges.

By using its judicial immunity Enryakuji served as a patron of trade and of merchant guilds (*za*). These *za* developed as groups of producers came together under a proprietor for whom they provided products and services. The first *za* appear in documents as early as the eleventh century, but they became widespread when commerce and specialization developed outside the confines of *shōen* during the Kamakura era. In the 1280s, the Enryakuji complex (including its branches) controlled some 80 percent of the sake brewers and moneylenders (often coexisting in the same house) in Kyoto. The temple provided protection, which included the lending out of manpower to put pressure on tardy debtors, and received taxes and dues in return. In general, Enryakuji retained its rights to tax and protect the guilds (especially from competition), but changes within the commercial sector in the fourteenth century strained the old patron system. "New guilds" began to appear, challenging the monopolies enjoyed by the old *za*. In essence, whereas the older guilds developed in the service of the capital elites, the newer ones were geared to trade and business. Though they still paid their dues, their relationship with traditional patrons was now more contractual.[61]

The movement from below that the new kinds of guilds represented initially provided the temple with more clients and thus more income. In the cotton trade, for example, the older guild, under the protection of the Gion Shrine (a branch shrine of Enryakuji), lodged a complaint with the Northern Court in 1343 against merchants who were trading in the villages around Kyoto. The members of the guild disapproved of the new organization whose members were allowed to trade by the Gion Shrine for only a small annual fee. The court decided in favor of the original guild and prohibited the members of the newer guild to engage in commerce. However, the hierarchy of Gion, which did not mind the extra income, petitioned, and ultimately convinced, the court to reverse its verdict.[62]

Although the Gion Shrine benefited from the addition of such new *za* in the 1340s, the growth of commerce made it more difficult for Enryakuji to maintain itself, in the end, as a successful patron. On the other hand, the role of the Bakufu became increasingly important as the authority of the old elites proved insufficient to control the conflicts between the old and the new guilds. This situation resulted in a diminished status for the former patrons and an enhanced authority for the Bakufu in an area in which the preceding warrior government was not involved. The case of the Kitano sake malt guild provides an illustrative example.

The exclusive right to supply malt to the sake brewers of Kyoto was held by the sake malt guild under the protection of Kitano, another branch shrine of Enryakuji. Starting in 1379, the Bakufu acknowledged the guild's monopoly, but also started to levy taxes of its own. This income became the incentive for the Bakufu to support the monopoly for the next half-century.[63] In 1419, for example, it was challenged by the sake brewers, who started to get cheaper malt elsewhere. In response, the Bakufu, not Enryakuji, issued edicts in support of the za, which was allowed to destroy the "illegal" malt chambers.[64] That policy was continued for another two decades while the sake brewers, for their part, sought to weaken the monopoly. Finally, in 1444, the sake brewers openly refused to buy any malt from the za. The Kitano Shrine tried to pressure the Bakufu once again to support its monopoly, but both the Bakufu and Enryakuji, Kitano's own patron, now found the monopoly increasingly unsustainable and disruptive to commerce. To the dismay and anger of the members of the shrine, the Bakufu now reversed its earlier policies and supported the sake brewers. In the end, the Bakufu had to subdue the shrine with force after which the Kitano malt za was abolished and its surviving members forced out of the capital. A section within Enryakuji became the patron of the new za.[65]

These guild incidents show that the new social forces could no longer be controlled within the old patron-client system. Enryakuji itself now collected taxes from the new guilds, though its control was less strict than it had been over their predecessors. At the same time, it had become clear that the Bakufu was needed to adjudicate disputes involving such non-warrior antagonists. Finally, the Bakufu had also shown that Enryakuji's control was no longer autonomous, since it was now levying its own taxes on guilds protected by the temple.

In the economic sphere, changes in the kenmon status of Enryakuji were also felt in other ways. For instance, beginning in the Kamakura period, the flow of income from the temple's estates was being disrupted. In particular, local warriors, often as land stewards (jitō), sought to increase their share of revenues at the central proprietor's expense. The Bakufu, whose principal role was to keep the peace, often judged against its own vassals, as, for example, in the case of the Sasaki who were shugo of Ōmi. In 1191, 1213, and 1235–36, disputes over rights to income between retainers of the Sasaki and members of the Enryakuji organization resulted in violent conflicts and follow-up lawsuits. The Bakufu ruled in favor of Enryakuji in all those cases.[66]

If the Kamakura Bakufu was disposed to protect the legitimate rights of the *kenmon*, it became increasingly difficult to sustain such equilibrium in the fourteenth century. In other words, with local powers now questioning the authority of the central *kenmon*, divisions of estates (*hanzei*) with original proprietors now began to occur. Like its predecessor, the Ashikaga Bakufu was concerned with the maintenance of stability, and it thereby confirmed *hanzei* in order to avoid friction. But at the same time, the Bakufu was also willing to recognize the proprietary rights of the *kenmon*, as can be seen from its confirmations of temple land on several occasions.[67] Some of its edicts condemned warrior intrusions on temple and shrine estates, others prohibited the *hanzei* alluded to above. In any event, the frequency of such edicts suggests that the Bakufu was something less than successful in the curtailing overall of warrior encroachments. Gradually, most central elites experienced a decline in their income and control, except for estates situated in the capital region.

But what do the Bakufu's confirmations of temple privileges indicate? In spite of its religious policies, was it committed to supporting the system of shared rulership? Why did the Ashikaga Bakufu seek to slow its own warrior allies from taking control of the land? The answer, I believe, is embedded in its desire to maintain the status quo on one level so as to be able to focus on the policies it wished to implement on another level. At the same time, the Bakufu's control of even the capital region could be shaky, as, for instance, during the 1350s. After ousting his brother in the Kannō Disturbance (1350–51), Takauji appointed his son Yoshiakira to handle Bakufu affairs in Kyoto. But Yoshiakira's position soon became precarious, and he was obliged to leave the capital in the intercalary second month of 1352. On that occasion, forces of the Southern Court ousted both the rival court and the Bakufu itself. A month later, Yoshiakira successfully recaptured Kyoto, thereby reestablishing the Ashikaga Bakufu in the country's capital.[68]

With the Bakufu's authority and position so seriously threatened at this time, it was moved to compensate by adopting a favorable stance toward Enryakuji. Both Takauji and Yoshiakira were unusually generous to the temple as a way of assuring its neutrality during this conflict. Accordingly, Takauji granted it three *shōen* in 1351,[69] and Yoshiakira responded in kind. Not only did he confirm Enryakuji's rights on several occasions,[70] but also

he granted it new estates as well as *jitō* perquisites.[71] Realizing the importance of having as many supporters (or as few enemies) as possible, the
Bakufu needed to maintain a precarious balance. The donations and confirmations to Enryakuji were both bribes and rewards for not allying itself
on the side of the Southern Court.

The Bakufu's confirmations of the rights of Enryakuji and of other
central landowners were done, then, either out of political need, as in
Yoshiakira's case, or out of a desire to limit local land intrusions and
thereby to control warriors. Equally important, such acknowledgments of
the proprietary rights of the old elites did not fundamentally compromise the Bakufu's authority. To the contrary, its ability to adjudicate land
issues across the board demonstrated that the Muromachi polity was built
around the rule of the warrior.

The authority of the Bakufu expanded in several other traditional areas
of *kenmon* control. For example, toll gates were an important source of
income that the warrior regime now began to concern itself with. The
seven highways entering the capital all had toll stations, which were controlled by traditional Kyoto aristocrats. In addition, other private barriers
were occasionally erected and tolerated by the Bakufu, if they were not an
obstacle to the flow of goods.[72] As we have seen in the Nanzenji Gate incident, the Bakufu also allowed toll gates to finance specific enterprises.

In the fourteenth century, Enryakuji probably controlled seven toll
gates close to Sakamoto on the shores of Lake Biwa.[73] The Bakufu respected these rights, but made it clear that toll gates did not imply extrater-
ritoriality. Accordingly, in 1363, it required permission from itself to erect
any new gates.[74] An additional indication that its own power was intended
to supersede that of Enryakuji was the licenses it issued to facilitate trans-
port.[75] The right to collect toll dues was thus restricted by the Bakufu's
exemptions, which, to make matters worse for Enryakuji, most frequently
benefited Zen temples.

I have already shown that Enryakuji's authority as a patron of guilds
declined, necessitating Bakufu intervention to control conflicts among
merchants and traders. In addition, the Bakufu imposed a tax of its own,
increasing both its influence and its revenues. At the same time, Enryakuji
lost more of its traditional rights by being restricted in its adjudication of
matters concerning its guilds. In 1370, the Bakufu prohibited members of
the Enryakuji community from harassing debtors in Kyoto in an attempt
to assist the guild of moneylenders (*dōso za*). That prohibition was repeated
in an edict of 1386, when it was also added that disputes regarding late pay-

ments should be handled by the Bakufu.[76] These edicts were designed to enhance the position of the Bakufu in two ways. First, the Bakufu needed to fulfill its policing duties and to maintain peace in the capital if it was to succeed as the country's legitimate government. Second, in seeking to realize this goal, the warrior regime was attempting to expand its authority in areas that had previously been under *kenmon* control. In fact, the Ashikaga Bakufu was much less inclined than its predecessor to respect the judicial immunities of Enryakuji.

During the Kamakura period, neither the court nor the Bakufu could restrict Enryakuji's immunities or control it directly. Government officials had no jurisdiction on Mount Hiei, and they would not even ascend the mountain without the clergy's permission. In fact, the Enryakuji compound was a sanctuary that was occasionally used by criminals to escape punishment. Temples were expected to extradite such villains, but the records reveal that they refused in many cases. To make matters worse for the secular powers, Enryakuji's immunity and military strength also created severe problems in the capital proper. While relying on their religious immunity, the monks often voiced their opinion by demonstrating and fighting government warriors. Occasionally, the Kamakura Bakufu attempted to protect Kyoto by forbidding the monks to carry arms, but such edicts had little effect, as evidenced by the activities of Enryakuji's armed monks.[77]

The head abbot, appointed by the imperial court, was the original means of communicating with and controlling the Enryakuji clergy. By the early thirteenth century, however, this office had become little more than a lucrative source of income for the sons of either nobles or the imperial family, who lacked any substantial support within the temple complex.[78] The abbots of the three largest cloisters—Shōren'in, Nashimoto (Kajii), and Myōhōin—emerged as the leaders through whom the court and the Bakufu attempted to communicate with the clergy. But in the second half of the fourteenth century, changes in Enryakuji's internal power structure undermined the authority of these abbots. Reminding us again of the aforementioned trend of "the lower overturning the higher," new warrior leaders, who performed administrative and managerial duties at the cloisters, now began to challenge their masters. The first references to these commanders, sometimes even referred to as *daimyō*, can be found in documents from the 1360s.[79] In fact, a marked change can be seen between the incidents of 1345 and 1368. In the earlier Tenryūji incident, the Bakufu managed to contain the clergy by threatening to depose all three noble abbots and confiscate Enryakuji property if the portable shrines were brought into the capital.[80] The same method was used in the Nanzenji Gate incident more than two decades later, but this time with no effect. The abbots were repeatedly asked to calm the monks and to stop them from entering Kyoto, but they failed, and two of them who had sided with the Bakufu were even chased off Mount Hiei. The Bakufu responded on that same day by creating a new post designed to oversee the temple. It was called the Enryakuji magistrate (*sanmon bugyō*).[81]

The new office did not accomplish what the Bakufu leaders had in mind. The choice of Sasaki Takanaga, the *shugo* of Ōmi Province, was problematic from the start, since that family was an old enemy of Enryakuji. Disputes over rights to taxes and land had been a recurrent theme in their relationship since the 1190s, and Takanaga proved unable to exercise any real authority over Enryakuji. The magistrate appointment nonetheless reflected the Bakufu's wish to assume direct control over the temple, thereby negating the older concept of cooperative rulership under the *kenmon*.

During the tenure of the third shogun, Ashikaga Yoshimitsu, the problem of authority was resolved when the aforementioned military figures within the temple were appointed as Enryakuji constables (*sanmon shisetsu*). The match was a judicious one for both sides. Though the new commanders were powerful, they were also newcomers who lacked traditional status within the temple. The Bakufu appointment gave them the official status and the additional authority to make them the undisputed powers on Mount Hiei.

For Yoshimitsu's part, the magistrates were instrumental in expanding his authority both within Enryakuji and against competing warriors in Ōmi.[82] Indeed, the timing of the creation of these offices indicates how important they were in the overall political scheme. The magistrates were appointed at the time of a palace coup in 1379 when Yoshimitsu ousted Hosokawa Yoriyuki and now took control of the Bakufu himself.[83]

Owing to Yoshimitsu's ability to identify well-placed allies within Enryakuji, the magistrates now came to serve the Bakufu's purposes variously. They acted as its own deputies, adjudicating internal conflicts, collecting and forwarding rents and taxes, and curtailing unruly monks.[84] The *sanmon shisetsu* were, in short, *shugo*-like officials specific to Enryakuji. For that matter, they even had the right to levy the special taxes (*tanzen*) associated with *shugo* on Enryakuji estates.[85] The success of this policy is evident in the astonishing absence of incidents involving Enryakuji monks for nearly the next half-century.[86]

CONCLUSION

There can be little doubt that Enryakuji experienced drastic changes during the fourteenth century. Its status as a proprietor and patron was challenged first by local warriors and then by a growing number of merchants and entrepreneurs. In addition to these slower-moving developments, there were also sudden political jolts caused by the establishment of the Ashikaga Bakufu in Kyoto. This new warrior regime envisioned a much less restricted authority than that of its predecessor.

The Ashikaga Bakufu expanded its authority at the expense of Enryakuji in two areas and in two stages. First, the Bakufu's religious support was geared toward Zen from the start. As a result, Enryakuji's public role as a provider of doctrine and ceremonies was now diminished. Moreover, the Bakufu threatened to replace the whole multidoctrinal system with a religious hierarchy consisting of a single controllable doctrine. Enryakuji opposed this move but had little success. Its spiritual influence in the early Muromachi polity was kept to a minimum.

Second, during Yoshimitsu's tenure, Enryakuji's judicial privileges came to be severely restricted. While Yoshimitsu acknowledged Enryakuji's economic privileges, he limited it judicially through restrictions of its *kenmon* immunities. He also sought to control it politically by appointing warrior leaders within the temple to function as Bakufu deputies. These policies resulted in an unprecedented expansion of Bakufu authority at the expense of Enryakuji, which was now neutralized for half a century. The temple did not regain control over its own organization until the Bakufu itself started to crumble in the mid-fifteenth century.

To put these conclusions in a slightly different light, we can use Kuroda's *kenmon* terminology. Kuroda claimed that the *kenmon* system prevailed until the Ōnin War, but that conclusion cannot be accepted based on his own definition of *kenmon* cooperative rulership. The Ashikaga Bakufu not only favored but also controlled Zen. There was consequently no mutual dependence between the two. The traditional *kenmitsu* schools such as Enryakuji, on the other hand, were simply excluded from the Ashikaga polity. In addition, old *kenmon* privileges such as immunity and self-rule were limited, expanding the Bakufu's own control of state matters. During its zenith, the Bakufu indeed managed to restrict Enryakuji, but the Ashikaga hegemony did not last long enough to extinguish the power of the old elites. In the long run, the Bakufu policies of the early Muromachi age resulted in an elimination of the fundamental conditions for *kenmon* cooperative rule, leaving Enryakuji as a separate and alienated power. The Ashikaga vision of religious institutions strictly in their own service did not materialize until the late sixteenth century when the new hegemons brought all major temples under their control.

CHAPTER 12

Musō Soseki

MARTIN COLLCUTT

THE FOURTEENTH CENTURY was a critical dividing point in the development of medieval Japanese Rinzai Zen and the relation of the Zen schools to the changing medieval power structure and religious world. In these years Rinzai Zen, especially the officially sponsored monasteries making up what is known as the *gozan*, successfully passed a crossroads at which, like the old garrison center of Kamakura in which it had been nurtured in the thirteenth century, it might have slipped into gentle obscurity. Not only did Rinzai Zen survive and flourish in Kyoto under the new regimes of Kenmu and Muromachi, it also was subtly transformed into a more self-consciously Japanese religion and institution.

This transformation will be explored through the career of the monk Musō Soseki (1275–1351). Musō is a central, ubiquitous, and controversial figure in the religious, cultural, and political history of the fourteenth century. He seems to crop up everywhere and to have a finger in most of the religious and political pies of his age. Quite apart from his crucial role in the development of Rinzai Zen, he had connections with the "old regime" in Kamakura, with Emperor Go-Daigo who engineered its destruction, with the Ashikaga brothers who built a renewed Bakufu in Kyoto, with Go-Daigo's rivals, the emperors of the Northern line in Kyoto, and with many provincial warriors. He traveled widely in the provinces of eastern and northeastern Japan in his early life and was at storm center in the monastic rivalries between Tendai Buddhism and Zen in Kyoto later in his life. After a reclusive early life, he came to be revered and lionized by monks and laymen and frequently honored with the title National Teacher (*kokushi*).

In spite of this prominence, perhaps partly because of it, he remains something of an enigma. And what people do know about him they generally do not like very much. He has earned an unfortunate reputation as a second-rate Zen master, whose enlightenment was questionable and whose Zen was polluted by Tendai and Shingon practices, a monastic administrator and institution builder rather than a truly insightful religious leader, an aristocratic place-keeper who parlayed family ties and a doubtful imperial ancestry into monastic preferments, a politically manipulative monk hungry for connections and titles, and a weathercock, ever ready to swing with the changing winds of politics and power. Musō is usually compared, unfavorably, with another Rinzai master of the mid-fourteenth century, Shūhō Myōchō (Daitō Kokushi), who has an unassailable reputation as an austere, deeply enlightened master.[1]

This rather negative view of Musō existed in his own day, at least among partisans who favored Daitō, and it runs through the modern biographies of Musō by Tamamura Takeji and others.[2] This kind of negative case is easy to make. But I have more than a sneaking respect for him as, on the one hand, a reclusive monk struggling between an inclination to shun the world and concentrate on his own spiritual problems, and on the other, a teacher who came to feel a strong sense of obligation to promote a well-ordered Zen community life, to enforce monastic discipline and Zen training for monks, to advise those who had the power to shape society, and to teach about Zen—even if he could not directly impart Zen itself—to provincial warriors and Kyoto townspeople. Musō may not have been a supreme master of Zen insight. He does come through to us a very human, approachable monk, sincere and struggling to find himself and to help others in a troubled age. So I will try to offer evidence to at least partially rehabilitate him. Musō's life is interesting in itself. By tracing Musō's religious, cultural, and political activities we can also derive a good understanding of the changing character of Rinzai Zen monastic life in the great metropolitan monasteries of Kamakura and Kyoto and the patterns of association of Rinzai Zen with political power-holders and the medieval state.

At the opening of the fourteenth century, in the year 1300–1301, Musō was a twenty-five-year-old monk still seeking a deep enlightenment experience (*satori*). He was practicing Zen in the monastery of Unganji in Shimotsuke Province. His life was little different from that of the thousands of wandering Zen monks (*unsui*) who filled the Zen halls of the officially sponsored Rinzai monasteries of Kyoto, Kamakura, and the provinces. Tracing the fragmentary record of his life we are struck at first by a bewildering sense of movement. Until the age of fifty, he hardly stayed in one spot, or studied with any one master, for more than a few months at a time. As we look more closely, however, we can see patterns in his life as a monk. Some of these patterns were common to monks of his age. But some of them were unique to Musō.

Musō was born in 1275 (Kenji 1) in Ise.[3] The year before had seen a foiled Mongol invasion attempt; and in 1275, a Mongol envoy was killed by order of the regent Hōjō Tokimune who determined to resist any further invasions. The country was tense. Musō's father was a warrior of the Sasaki family, a branch of the Murakami Genji based in the Ise area. His mother was a Taira woman, perhaps a member of a branch of the Hōjō family. It was rumored that Musō had distant imperial ancestry.[4] In 1283, when Musō was eight years old, the family moved to Kai where, at age nine, Musō entered a local monastery and studied with the monk Kūa. He studied not only esoteric Mahayana Buddhism but also Confucianism, Taoism, and secular learning.[5] It is not surprising that he should not have found his way directly to a Zen monastery. Although by this time Zen had taken hold in Hakata, Kyoto, and especially Kamakura, and was beginning to find provincial warrior patrons, it was still very much a minor current in the Japanese religious world. Most Japanese monks and nuns were either committed to the older Shingon and Tendai monastic centers or, rejecting monastic Buddhism, turning to the newer Pure Land or Lotus devotional schools. Musō's early training in Shingon and Tendai was a core of basic Buddhist teaching shared by the vast majority of Buddhist devotees in his age.

At the age of eighteen or so (1292) Musō "took the tonsure" and went to Nara, staying with a relative, Uchiyama Myōchin. The real reason was probably to advance his training as a monk. Like other young monks of his age who wanted to commit themselves to the religious life in one of the older schools of Buddhism, he needed to take the vows of an ordained monk. This he did in Nara at the Kaidan'in precept platform in Tōdaiji. He took the tonsure (*tokudo*) under the Ritsu (Vinaya) master Jikan.[6] He

probably received the Mahayana *gusoku* precepts. Musō was laying esoteric and Vinaya foundations for his religious life.

Around this time (1293/Einin 1) Musō began to develop an interest in
Zen. He described a vivid dream in which he visited two famous Chinese
monasteries. In Japanese their names were Sozan and Sekito. In Sekito a
monk led him into the sickbay of the monastery where he met an ailing
elderly monk. The old monk made room for Musō and urged him to sit
with him. After a while the monk who had led Musō into the chamber approached the elderly monk and said to him: "The reason why this monk
[Musō] has come so far, is to seek a sacred image, *shōzō*. I beg you, venerable abbot, help him." Whereupon the old monk took out a hanging scroll
and gave it to Musō. When he looked at it he found it was a half-torso
portrait, *chinsō*, of Bodhidharma. Musō was delighted. As he was rolling
this up he awoke from his dream. Through this dream Musō came to believe that he had a particular serendipitous connection (*kien*) with Zen.[7]
Later on he took a character from each of the two temple names to make
the name Soseki.

Convinced that he should change the direction of his religious quest,
he set out in search of Zen. He first intended to visit the reclusive monk
Muhon Kakushin in his hermitage at Yura, in the Kii peninsula.[8] On the
way he met an old acquaintance, the monk Tokushō Zennin. Tokushō
told him that before he committed himself to the life of a Zen recluse he
had better first do some basic training in Zen and master the rules of Zen
monastic life in one of the official monasteries (*sōrin*).[9] Although Musō
may not have recognized it, this decision helped to shape his later career. A
reclusive inclination continued to run strong in Musō, and for much of his
life he fostered it. By accepting training in the large and highly regulated
Rinzai monasteries of Kyoto and Kamakura, however, Musō was laying an
essential foundation for his eventual career as founder-abbot of large Rinzai communities, as the leader of a large "school," and as monastic legisla-
tor and *gozan* administrator. Following Tokushō's advice Musō enrolled in
the Kenninji, Kyoto, changed his robes for those of a Zen monk (*unsui*),
and began serious practice of Zen under Muin Enpan.[10] Muin had studied
under Lan-ch'i Tao-lung in Kenchōji in Kamakura, then visited monasteries in Yüan China where Zen (Ch'an) was taught. When he returned to
Japan he was installed in Kenninji as its head monk. Although he had enrolled in a Kyoto Zen monastery, Musō was immediately connected with
the Zen world of Kamakura, with its very Chinese flavor, through Muin
and other disciples of Lan-ch'i.

Young Zen monks were not expected to remain for long in one monastery under a single master. The traditional pattern, in China and in Japan, was for *unsui* to move like "clouds and vapor" from master to master, testing their experience and insight in encounters (*mondō*) or Zen exchanges (*sanzen*) with several different masters. Once they were directly convinced of their enlightenment, and had demonstrated that enlightenment to a master, they would be granted some sign of transmission of the *dharma* and might settle for a while with that master. For Musō, as for many young monks, this time of wandering, self-doubt, and self-searching was to be a long and arduous process.

As a wandering monk, Musō began by moving around from teacher to teacher in the Lan-ch'i (Daigaku) lineage. At age twenty (1295/10) he went to Kamakura and encountered Mukyū Tokusen and Ikō Dōnen, disciples of the Chinese masters Lan-ch'i and Wu-hsüeh. In 1296 he had encounters in Engakuji with Tōkei Tokugo and in Kenchōji with Chidon Kūjō. At the invitation of the latter Musō served as the "guest" in a formal Zen encounter held at the first lecture after the accession of a new abbot at Engakuji. His role was to participate in a formal debate before the community in which he was expected to respond to a Zen *mondō*. The monks applauded him.[11] The installation ceremony of a new abbot was an important ritual moment in the community life of any monastery. For Musō to be chosen for an important ceremonial role suggests that monks in Engakuji recognized some promise in him. After gaining experience and rising in the ranks of the Kamakura monasteries, he returned to Kyoto and, reentering Kenninji, continued his practice under Muin Enpan. All the above five teachers were disciples of Lan-ch'i. They were, at the time, the Zen monks in Japan who had the fullest training in Sung-style Zen and knowledge of the Sung rules of monastic life. It was perhaps natural that Musō should move from one to another to broaden his experience.

By the time of Musō's youth, Rinzai Zen was becoming a force to be reckoned with in the Japanese religious world. In spite of the efforts of the older schools of Japanese Buddhism to restrict its independent sectarian development, Zen had clearly put down deep roots in Japan by the year 1300. These roots were set in the centers of political power, Kyoto as well as Kamakura, and in the provinces. In the case of Rinzai Zen the main centers of growth and dispersion during the thirteenth century were Hakata, Kyoto, and Kamakura. Zen spread from these centers out into the provinces. That diffusion was still limited at the end of the thirteenth century, but it was gaining ground as the Hōjō regents and many provincial warrior families committed themselves to the patronage of Zen monks and the building of family mortuary temples, *bodaiji*. Under Hōjō patronage, the system of official Zen monasteries that we commonly refer to as the *gozan* was beginning to take shape.[12]

Although Kyoto had several large Rinzai temples, among them Kenninji, Tōfukuji, and the newly built Nanzenji, on the whole it was the Kantō, especially Kamakura, that was the vital center of Rinzai Zen diffusion in the late Kamakura period. This was due not only to the enthusiasm of Hōjō Tokiyori and his successors for Zen; it was also attributable to the presence and powerful influence of a succession of Chinese émigré masters who headed the great Kamakura monasteries of Kenchōji, Engakuji, and so on. The leadership shifted from Japanese Zen pioneers in the generation of Eisai (Yōsai) and Ben'en Enni to Chinese émigré masters from around the Mongol invasions until the early fourteenth century. They naturally introduced the kind of Zen practice, codes, *kōan* use, and teachings they had learned in China. Some were invited to Kyoto but most of their time and energy was spent in Kamakura; and it was to Kamakura, to practice with them, or at least with their immediate Japanese disciples, that young Zen monks felt impelled to go in order to test their mettle and insight.

The influx of Chinese émigré monks, brought about largely by the upheavals surrounding the Mongol conquest of China and Korea, was quite a remarkable cultural phenomenon.[13] At least a score of Chinese émigré Ch'an monks found their way to Japan between 1246 and 1330. Some stayed a few months or a few years. Several ended their lives in Japan. Among the most influential were Lan-ch'i Tao-lung (Rankei Dōryu, 1213–78), Wu-hsüeh Tsu-yuan (Mugaku Sogen, 1226–86), and I-shan I-ning (Issan Ichinei, 1247–1317). It was with Issan that Musō's path was, quite painfully, to cross.

Musō went to Kamakura to seek insight under the guidance of I-shan in 1299. Hōjō Sadatoki had continued the policy of inviting Chinese Zen masters to Kamakura and building or rebuilding Zen monastery buildings. During his term in office, new developments can be detected: the Chinese literary and cultural tone of the Kamakura monasteries became very much more pronounced; and Zen monasteries were subjected to greater formal Bakufu regulation and control. Sadatoki's principal Zen mentor was the learned Chinese monk I-shan I-ning who came to Japan as a Mongol emissary in 1299. Suspected of being a Mongol spy by the Bakufu, he was initially confined to the Shuzenji in Izu. Sadatoki quickly recognized I-shan's qualities and installed him as abbot of Kenchōji and later of Engakuji and Nanzenji in Kyoto. Where Lan-ch'i and Wu-hsüeh had largely confined their activities to Zen training, I-shan, who was well read in neo-Confucian philosophy, Chinese literature, and classics, besides being a talented calligrapher and connoisseur of Chinese painting, introduced these more scholarly and literary interests to the young Japanese monks who studied with him and to his secular patrons in Kamakura and Kyoto. He was therefore instrumental in first giving to the metropolitan Zen monasteries that Chinese aesthetic tone that was to find expression in the Literature of the Five Mountains (*gozan bungaku*) in ink painting, and in the other arts associated with medieval *gozan* Zen.

For young Japanese monks, Kamakura was the mecca for Rinzai Zen training and I-shan was the most attractive and challenging master in Japan. They began to flock to his monastery. To select the most promising among them, I-shan set a written examination in Chinese. Musō did well on the literary test, being one of only two monks ranked in the highest of three classes,[14] but unfortunately there was no real spark of Zen (*kien*) between them. Musō seems to have left I-shan in frustration after only a few months of encounters with him. I-shan was critical of Musō's bookishness and his attachment to the scholastic and mystical features derived from his early training in Shingon and Tendai Buddhism. For Musō his encounters with I-shan, unrewarding as they were, provided some of the most critical moments in his religious life. They must have starkly revealed to him his own limitations and the difficulty of the path he had chosen.

In the following year (1300) Musō went to northeastern Japan. While he was in Matsushima he heard a Tendai monk lecture on the *Makashikan*, a text on Tendai-style meditation. He is said to have been moved by this talk.[15] Originally, Musō had been trained in scholastic and esoteric Buddhism. With his change of sectarian interest to Zen, he had suppressed his early interest in Tendai teachings. Because his encounter with I-shan had not been productive and he felt frustrated in his Zen practice he was no doubt receptive to other teachings. Thus for him the lecture probably fell like rain on parched earth. Immediately after the lecture, during *zazen*, Musō thought he had attained an enlightenment experience, in that he felt that he understood for the first time the differences among the various sects of Buddhism. But he later realized it was not a true *satori*.[16] It is possible that he may have wavered briefly in his commitment to Zen, but it is more likely that this eclectic mix of teachings was part and parcel of Zen monastic life, especially outside the most strongly Sung-influenced Kamakura monasteries.

At about this time (1300–1301), thinking about Tendai Buddhism as well as Zen, and frustrated in his efforts with I-shan, Musō seems to have heard of a reclusive Japanese monk, Kōhō Kennichi, who had been trained in Kamakura by Chinese masters but was now living in a small mountain temple in Kai Province. Although Kōhō had practiced Zen under the Chinese monk Wu-hsüeh, he was said to have a Japanese viewpoint. Musō set out to practice with him. Unfortunately, by the time Musō got to his temple, Kōhō had left for Kamakura where he was installed as the head monk of Jōmyōji. Unable to meet Kōhō, Musō did not immediately pursue him to Kamakura. Instead, he spent the following year or so (1301) wandering in the northeast, ending at the Unganji where he suffered a bout of sickness, served as registrar (*inō*) for a few months, and engaged in devotion to Kannon as well as Zen practice.[17] This suggests that his determination to seek Kōhō's guidance was not yet very strong. Musō determined to try again with I-shan, who then headed Kenchōji. When in the following year (1302) I-shan moved to Engakuji, Musō went with him. Although he studied under I-shan for two more years, he could not convince the Chinese master that he had attained deep insight. In the end Musō made a desperate appeal: "I have not been able to clarify myself . . . please show me." I-shan is said to have replied cuttingly: "In our school (*shū*), there are no words to show self, and I have no *dharma* to give you."[18] This was a classic Zen opening gambit but Musō was unable to respond to it. No doubt with a sense of redoubled failure, Musō left I-shan and Engakuji in 1303. It is important to note that this incident is recorded in the *Nenpu*. In other words, Shun'oku Myōha heard from Musō himself about his failure with I-shan. This suggests a considerable integrity on Musō's part that he was willing to expose for his disciples and posterity what can only have been a bitter experience.

If Musō had not succeeded in convincing I-shan of the depth of his Zen experience, he had succeeded in deepening his literary insights, both Chinese and Japanese. Although I-shan was a poet and literatus, and expected the monks who worked under him to be literate, he may have felt that Musō's insights were bookish rather than rooted in direct experience. One of the problems Musō and many other Zen monks had was an inclination toward a literary Zen in which responses in encounters were perceived by the master to be based more on learned phrases from the Zen classics or sutras than on direct experience. This inclination was by no means unique to Japanese Zen, or to the fourteenth century, but it became quite pronounced in Japanese Rinzai monasteries during the fourteenth century.

Musō, in I-shan's eyes, may well have been confined to a "Zen of words and letters" (*moji Zen*).[19]

After quitting Engakuji, Musō went to see Kōhō Kennichi, who was now the abbot of Manjuji in Kamakura. Musō now met him for the first time. Kōhō received him sympathetically. Musō seems to have wanted to take Kōhō as his master but felt he needed to prove himself first. He is said to have promised Kōhō, "Until I realize my *satori* I won't return to your place" and set off again as an itinerant monk.[20] He went north, and in 1304, while he was in Hitachi Province, he attained enlightenment while watching the shadows of bamboos against the paper screens of a window.

Having attained his "great *satori*," he returned to Kamakura in 1305, visited Jōchiji where Kōhō was serving as abbot, and demonstrated his *satori* to Kōhō who granted him a certificate of *inka*. Musō was thirty-one.[21]

Instead of staying in Kamakura, Musō returned to Kai and lived in the Jōkyōji. For the next few years he moved between Kai, where he had lived in childhood, and Kamakura. In 1307, he went from Kai to Kamakura and met Kōhō in Manjuji and received from him a robe and portrait (*chinsō*) with a verse by Kōhō on it.[22] In doing so, Musō, as well as Kōhō, acknowledged that he was Kōhō's *dharma* heir. He served as registrar (*inō*) in Manjuji and heard *dharma* talks (*hōgo*) by Kōhō. In 1308, he returned to Kai. Sometime during this year Musō met his old Shingon teacher Jōtatsu. He may well have gone to tell Jōtatsu about his receipt of *inka* from Kōhō. In return Musō seems to have been asked by Jōtatsu also to accept an esoteric transmission. It is not clear from the *Chronology* whether he did so or not. But it is not unreasonable to assume that Jōtatsu would not have raised the issue if he had not thought Musō would be receptive. This can be taken as an indication of Musō's continued, and well known, attachment to the esoteric traditions in which he had received his early training.[23]

The next decade, from 1309 to 1319 or so, Musō continued to spend in relative obscurity, wandering from one small temple to another, heading some and then moving on, covering much of Japan in his travels. There is no discernible relationship with political figures in the Kantō or with Go-Daigo or members of the imperial court in Kyoto. Nor does Musō seem to have consorted with other monks or gravitated toward major *gozan* monasteries. He seems, rather, to have been driving himself deeper into the wilderness. He devoted some of his energy, insight, and feeling for nature to the design of temple gardens, at which he was to become a master. Musō, in his thirties and forties, was a relatively obscure monk, one of thousands of wandering *unsui*, concerned with his spiritual experience and his relationship with his master, Kōhō, and indifferent to the political and social movements of the age.

His relationship with Kōhō and with other disciples was not always easy. In the spring of 1309, he returned to Unganji at Kōhō's suggestion and was appointed secretary (*shoki*). According to Tamamura Takeji, he seems to have become involved in a dispute with a fellow disciple of Kōhō who complained to Kōhō about him.[24] He soon left, without getting Kōhō's permission. Perhaps because of this dispute some strain seems to have developed between Musō and Kōhō. In the twelfth month, Musō sent Kōhō a letter of apology. A year later (1310 Autumn), Musō still seems to have been concerned about Kōhō's feelings toward him. He added a *chakugo*, turning word, to a verse (*gatha*) that Kōhō had written in a letter, and sent it to him. He also had a *chinsō* of Mugaku Sogen, Kōhō's master, painted, sent it to Kōhō, and asked for an inscription.[25] Thus he seems to have planned to restore his relationship with Kōhō. In the spring of 1311, Musō built a small hermitage, the Ryūzan'an, in Kai and lived there until the following year when it was destroyed by fire. Some commentators have suggested that a rival monk in Kōhō's lineage, jealous of Musō, might have resorted to arson.[26]

In 1313, with the advice and help of Gennō Hongen, a brother disciple, Musō moved to Nagaseyama in Mino where he built the hermitage of Eihōji in a narrow ravine and lived in seclusion for several years. The following year he built a Kannon Hall there, reflecting his lifelong devotional interest in Kannon.[27] Musō obviously liked and trusted Gennō, who himself built a hermitage nearby. The place and the relationship may have provided some solace after the difficulties at Unganji and any misunderstandings with Kōhō. Kōhō died at the Unganji in 1316 (10/20). Musō, although his *dharma* disciple, was not with him when he died.[28] After Kōhō's death, Musō went to Kyoto and moved into a hut in Kitayama. But within a few months he was on his way to distant Tosa (1318). He had heard a rumor that, following Kōhō's death, the nun Gakukai Enjō, widow of Hōjō Sadatoki, following Kōhō's wishes, wanted to have him installed as abbot of Unganji and he fled to avoid the honor.[29] Musō made a habit of avoiding secular connections when they were first offered. He also tended to yield to them if they were repeated.

Musō had settled into a reclusive life in small provincial temples, avoiding both Kamakura and Kyoto. His name, however, was coming to the attention of well-placed patrons in Kamakura, some of whom were eager to draw him out of the mountain valleys he had sought. Between 1319 and 1325, Musō came rather hesitantly under the patronage of the Kamakura regime. In his biography of Musō, Tamamura Takeji argues that Hōjō Takatoki and his mother were eager to patronize Musō but that, disinclined to quit his reclusive mode of life and unimpressed by the Kamakura warrior regime, he rebuffed them. Although there is evidence that Musō was attracting some attention in Kamakura it is not clear that he was yet viewed as one of the great Zen masters or eminent Buddhist priests of his age. He was offered some advancement but not immediate promotion to leadership in the Zen world in Kamakura. This is not particularly surprising. Musō was personally not well known in Kamakura. He had not made his mark in the Chinese Zen circles of Engakuji or Kenchōji. He had not yet written any significant Zen commentaries or verse. His master, Kōhō, was liked and respected but had himself risen in the Kamakura religious establishment only to the headship of the middle-ranking Manjuji.

In 1319, Musō responded to repeated appeals by Gakukai, the widow of Sadatoki and mother of Takatoki, to visit Kamakura as a lecturer. She offered him the headship of the Unganji, the large and influential Zen monastery in Shimotsuke, some way from Kamakura, which he declined. The Unganji had been Kōhō's monastery but it may not have held particularly happy memories for Musō. For the next few years Musō remained on the fringes of the powerful Kamakura *gozan* monasteries, headed by Engakuji and Kenchōji, in which he had trained. If he had sought it, it is quite possible that he might have secured an appointment in one of the Kamakura *gozan*—Gakukai was eager to promote his interests—but he seems to have kept his distance, preferring to remain on the margins of Kamakura warrior society. There is little evidence that the Hōjō had marked Musō for a leadership role in the Kamakura Zen world, or that they felt rebuffed by his hesitancy. Musō was only one of many admirable Zen monks in Kamakura. In the summer of 1319, he moved to a hermitage on the Miura peninsula—the Hakusen'an. For the next five years or so he spent much time in the Kamakura area building small retreats. In 1320, the Chinese émigré monk Rinsan Dōin (Ling-shan Tao-yiu) visited him. Rinsan admired Musō's reclusive way of life and probably felt a kindred feeling for him. In 1321, Musō built a pagoda, the Kaiintō, behind the Hakusen'an. Then, suddenly, he abandoned the hermitage and in 1323 moved across the bay to Kazusa and built the Taiō'an.[30]

All this activity in building small hermitages and retreats raises the question of economic support. How was he able to build huts or hermitages in such profusion? Did he have his own resources? If not, who were Musō's patrons in these wilderness years? Although Musō is rumored to have had courtly connections and came of a substantial local warrior family, it was not a particularly wealthy one, and his branch of it had fallen on hard times. He seems to have had no resources of his own. While he stayed in *gozan* monasteries he was well provided for, but once he moved outside the orbit of the Zen cloisters and began to set up his own small temples he had to provide for himself. In this phase of his life he seems to have relied on the support of monks like Kōhō or the patronage of provincial warrior families. During Musō's travels in the northeast, a provincial warrior devotee of Zen, Hisa Koji, seems to have built a small hermitage for him. Ishii Susumu has suggested that the local warrior Nikaidō Dōun may have built the Jōkyoji in Kai for Musō.[31] Jōkyoji, the first temple that Musō really founded, was built within the Maki estate (*Maki-no-shō*) with which the Nikaidō family is thought to have been associated. Musō was to establish a number of small retreats in the next few years. Although in many cases the patrons are unknown, in a few cases Musō's name is associated with those of Nikaidō Dōun or Miura Sadatsura, a local warrior in Sagami who sponsored the Hakusen'an. This suggests that his principal patrons in these years were, like himself, members of the class of small-scale provincial warrior families. Both Nikaidō Dōun and Miura Sadatsura had ties with Musō's home province of Kai. Dōun had land rights there and Sadatsura had been born into the Takeda family before being adopted by the Miura. Through these fragmentary connections we can get a sense of the way in which Rinzai Zen was spreading into the provinces through the patronage by local families of monks like Musō with whom family leaders felt some personal affinity.

In Kamakura, the patronage of Rinzai Zen had been continued by Hōjō Takatoki, who was still a child when he was appointed *shikken* in 1316. Actual power was held by warrior-advisers, and his regency (1316–26) was plagued by the political upheavals attending Emperor Go-Daigo's initial attempts to overthrow the Bakufu and restore direct imperial rule. In these troubled circumstances, and with dwindling resources, Takatoki's patronage of Zen was necessarily more modest than that of his predecessors. He did, however, try to continue the two-pronged Hōjō policy of patronage and strict regulation. Although he himself did not invite Zen masters from China, Takatoki extended a welcome to those who came to Japan at the invitation of powerful warrior-leaders in northern Kyushu and around the Inland Sea. The Chinese monks Ch'ing-cho Cheng-ch'eng (Seisetsu

Shōchō, 1274–1339), Ming-chi Ch'u-chun (Minki Soshun, 1262–1336), and Chu-hsien Fan-hsien (Jikusen Bonsen, 1292–1348) were invited to Kamakura by Takatoki and appointed to the headships of major Zen monasteries. All three shared the cultural and literary avocations of I-shan. Besides encouraging the practice of meditation, they did much to strengthen the cultural tone of metropolitan Zen and helped spread Sung and Yüan Zen teachings in provincial centers as well as in Kamakura and Kyoto. Ch'ing-cho reemphasized the importance of the Ch'an monastic rule by encouraging in Japan the veneration of Pai-chang Huai-hai, the accepted author of the first Ch'an monastic rule, and by compiling a monastic code, based on prevailing Chinese codes, appropriate to Japanese monasteries with their smaller scale and different social circumstances.

Although Musō's reputation as a dedicated Zen monk was probably growing, his life in small country retreats was quite different from that of the populous, highly regulated, and Chinese-oriented Kamakura *gozan*. Had he remained in the Kantō and responded to the blandishments of Hōjō patronage he might, before long, have been installed as abbot of one of the smaller Kamakura *gozan* monasteries and then advanced up the hierarchy. He was well known to Takatoki and his mother Gakukai, both of whom wanted to advance his interests. By 1325, however, Musō was getting requests from Kyoto that were harder to turn aside. Before much promotion took place in Kamakura he was pressed to turn to Kyoto and offered rapid advancement by the principal antagonist of the Hōjō. He had come to the attention of Emperor Go-Daigo and was being urged to come and head the monastery of Nanzenji.

Why should Go-Daigo have called on Musō, a young and relatively obscure monk from the Kantō? Like several of his predecessors in the Daikakuji line of the imperial house, Go-Daigo was interested in Rinzai Zen. He was a patron of Daiō Kokushi and Daitō Kokushi, the founders of Daitokuji. He also had Nanzenji in his gift. He may have heard of Musō from Kōhō Kennichi, a member of the imperial family, or from one of the courtiers who had visited Kamakura. He certainly knew that Musō was Kōhō's disciple. At the same time, Go-Daigo, like other members of the imperial house, was deeply committed to tantric Buddhism, even indulging in what is known as "left-handed tantra." Rather than the heavily sinified Sung style Zen of the Chinese masters in Kamakura and their closest Japanese disciples, Go-Daigo probably found the Japanese-style Zen of Kōhō and Musō, with its openness to Shingon Buddhism and other Japanese folk beliefs, more attractive. Kōhō would certainly have mentioned

Musō to members of the court, if not directly to Go-Daigo. Musō may also have been brought to the attention of Go-Daigo by Reizei Tame-suke, a noble who spent several years in the Kantō, knew Kōhō, Musō, and Nikaidō Dōun, and engaged in poetry meetings and discussion of Buddhism with them. One or another of these would surely have made it known that Musō claimed a remote imperial connection.

Although the Hōjō and their allies and vassals in Kamakura were the principal patrons of Zen in the late Kamakura period, the new Chinese teachings were not ignored by the imperial house in Kyoto. Rinzai Zen was by no means absent from the Kyoto religious world. In the mid-thirteenth century Ben'en Enni of Tōfukuji was instrumental in introducing some knowledge of Sung Zen teachings to Kujō Michiie and the imperial court. Enni was patronized by Emperor Go-Saga (1220–72), who also invited the Chinese monk Lan-chi Tao-lung to instruct him in Zen. At Go-Saga's death, the imperial house was split by a succession dispute into the rival factions later known as the Jimyōin and Daikakuji lines.

The first three emperors of the Daikakuji line, Kameyama (1249–1305), Go-Uda (1267–1324), and Go-Daigo (1288–1339), all patronized and studied Zen. Kameyama began the construction of Nanzenji, which was to become a major link between metropolitan Zen and the imperial court. Go-Uda installed the Chinese master I-shan I-ning as third abbot of Nanzenji and practiced Zen under his guidance. This was the first close contact between continental Zen and the Japanese imperial family. No doubt I-shan's talents as a calligrapher also impressed Go-Uda. On I-shan's death, Go-Uda arranged for the Chinese monk to be buried near the tomb of Kameyama. He continued his study of Zen with I-shan's disciples. Go-Daigo became a devoted patron of the Chinese monk Ming-chi Ch'u-chun and of Musō Soseki, whom he persuaded to serve three times as abbot of Nanzenji. After Go-Daigo's death, from the mid-fourteenth century, the ties between the Daikakuji line and Musō followers in the emerging Musō school remained close, and a number of imperial princes, sons of Emperors Go-Daigo and Go-Murakami (1328–68), subsequently entered the growing number of Musō-lineage monasteries to train as monks.

The commitment of Kameyama, Go-Uda, and Go-Daigo to Zen, though deep, was only partial. They were attracted by the aristocratic quality of Rinzai Zen, by its novel emphasis on self-reliance, and by the vistas it offered into Chinese culture. Zen did not supplant esoteric Buddhism in their lives, however. Go-Uda, for instance, while supporting Nanzenji, embarked upon the rebuilding of the ancient Shingon temple of Daikakuji. Go-Daigo, who needed all the support he could muster in his struggle for power, was careful to maintain amicable relations with the monasteries of the established Buddhist sects which had powerful monk armies. He installed his sons and relatives as abbots of leading Tendai and Shingon monasteries. Even his patronage of Musō can be seen as a politically motivated compromise with Zen, since Musō's Zen was didactic and esoteric in tone, and Zen was a factor to be reckoned with in the contemporary political arena. Moreover, although these emperors practiced meditation, that too was probably conceived of as as much a source of magical power and a means of exorcising baneful spirits as a means of personal spiritual enlightenment. In the conversion of an imperial residence into the monastery of Nanzenji, Shingon priests were called in to exorcise restless spirits of the dead who were believed to haunt part of the site. When the Shingon priests admitted defeat, a Zen monk was asked to do meditation, *zazen*, at the site. It was believed by his imperial patrons that the power of *zazen* had dispersed the baneful influence of the spirits.

One of the first emperors of the rival Jimyōin line to show a positive interest in Zen was Hanazono (1297–1348). A classical scholar and fine *waka* poet, Hanazono also devoted himself to the practice of Zen under the stern Japanese master Shūhō Myōchō (Daitō Kokushi, 1282–1337), for whom the emperor helped establish the monastery of Daitokuji. For the last decade or so of Daitō's life, Hanazono and Go-Daigo competed in heaping favors on him. Hanazono, however, went much more deeply into Zen practice than Go-Daigo, so much so that Shūhō recognized his enlightenment. Hanazono, therefore, had the deepest understanding of Zen among members of the imperial line in the thirteenth and fourteenth centuries. After Shūhō's death, Hanazono continued his Zen practice under the guidance of Shūhō's disciple Kanzan Egen (1277–1360), the founder (*kaisan*) of Myōshinji. Though eclipsed by monasteries affiliated with the Musō school in the fourteenth century, Daitokuji and Myōshinji and their branches came into their own after the mid-fifteenth century, and it is from these two monasteries that modern Japanese Rinzai Zen derives.[32]

Hanazono did not have a high opinion of Musō. He was among those who criticized Musō's Zen as bookish and derivative. On one occasion he complained that Musō's Zen was "bound by a rope of doctrine." [33] Hanazono's comments on Musō were based on his own intensive practice of Zen, but they were no doubt colored by his admiration for Daitō, whose Zen he believed to be dynamic and direct. It is also possible that in assessing Musō he was affected by a sense of rivalry with Go-Daigo, also a patron of Shūhō Myōchō, who was actively promoting Musō's fortunes in the Kyoto Zen world, to the disadvantage of Daitō and Daitokuji. In his diary Hanazono damned both Go-Daigo and Musō: "Everyone says that his majesty [Go-Daigo] earnestly desires the Buddha-Dharma to flourish. So I do not understand why he tries to make a secret of his reliance [on Musō]. To treat this man as a venerable abbot is to destroy the patriarch succession of the Zen school. One cannot help grieving." [34]

In spite of Hanazono's distaste for Musō, his imperial successors in the Jimyōin line, Kōgon (1313–64), Kōmyō (1321–80), and Sukō (1334–98), had close ties with Ashikaga Takauji and his successors, and through them with Musō and the Musō lineage. They studied Zen with Musō or his disciples, took the vows and tonsure, and for part of their lives lived Zen-style monastic lives in private hermitages. Kōgon was the first emperor to be given a formal Zen funeral. Many of their offspring, too, entered Zen monasteries. This infusion of imperial blood into Zen cloisters naturally affected the character of medieval Japanese metropolitan monasteries, especially those of the Musō line, accentuating the aristocratic tone and also the stress on literary and artistic pursuits of that lineage.

Musō's connections with Go-Daigo date from around the spring of 1325 when Musō was fifty. Like his encounters with I-shan and Kōhō, this was to be one of the critical relationships in Musō's life. In life and, especially, in death, Go-Daigo was to exert a profound impact on Musō. The relationship between them was to have important implications for Ashikaga Takauji and his brother Tadayoshi, as well as for the development of Rinzai Zen in Kyoto. Go-Daigo's deepest religious interests were probably in esoteric Buddhism—he frequently participated in Shingon rituals led by monks from Daigoji and Enryakuji—but he had studied Sung-style Zen with various monks of the Matsubara and Daiō lineages, including Shūhō Myōchō (Daitō Kokushi). He invited Chinese Zen masters to head Nanzenji in Kyoto and had them lecture before him on Zen.

Go-Daigo came to hear of the reclusive Musō and wanted to appoint him abbot of Nanzenji, an imperially sponsored temple in Kyoto. The patrons of Nanzenji were emperors of the Daikakuji branch of the imperial line, so the headship was in Go-Daigo's gift. Even so, it is not clear why he should so suddenly have wanted to bestow such an honor on Musō, who was still a rather obscure figure. No doubt news of Musō had come to the court from Kōhō Kennichi and courtiers who visited him in the Kantō. One of these was Reizei Tamesuke, the son of the nun Abutsu-ni who made her way to Kamakura to appeal to the Bakufu for the protection of his landed inheritance. After Abutsu-ni's death Tamesuke himself went to the Kantō to try to secure his interests. The appeal dragged on and Tamesuke stayed on in Kamakura where he got to know Kōhō and, no doubt, Musō. On at least one occasion Tamesuke visited Nikaidō Dōun's residence in Kamakura where Musō talked about Zen and engaged in a poetry gathering. It is not too great a stretch of the imagination to suggest that Reizei Tamesuke came to know and admire Musō and conveyed this admiration to Kyoto, perhaps directly to Go-Daigo.

Go-Daigo may have liked Musō's claims of aristocratic ancestry and his connections with the courtly Kōhō Kennichi. He may have wanted to draw this potentially influential prelate away from the Hōjō. He may have been looking for information about conditions in Kamakura. He may have detected in Musō's Zen esoteric and Japanese elements that Go-Daigo himself could appreciate. Or he may simply have heard that Musō was a sincere and dedicated monk who shunned politics and kept himself at a distance from the warrior regime in Kamakura.

In the spring of 1325, Go-Daigo sent a messenger to the small temple in Kazusa where Musō was then staying. Musō declined Go-Daigo's invitation on the first request, claiming illness. In the seventh month of the same year, Go-Daigo had Hōjō Takatoki intervene, and the renewed offer was accepted.[35] In the eighth month, Musō set out for Kyoto. He visited his old temple in Mino. Here several monks, including Shunoku Myōha, came to receive the tonsure from him. Picking up Gennō Hongen, who still lived there, Musō made his way to Kyoto. After lecturing on Zen before the emperor at the imperial palace, he was installed as the ninth-generation head of Nanzenji (8/29).[36] Go-Daigo visited Nanzenji several times each month to hear Musō lecture on Zen. Musō had now established patronage connections not only with the Kamakura Bakufu but also with Kyoto courtiers, Go-Daigo, and the Southern line of the imperial court. With appointment as abbot of Nanzenji, he was catapulted from relative obscurity to prominence in Rinzai Zen circles in Kyoto, with reverberations in Kamakura and throughout Japan. Some of these reverberations were less than complimentary. In the twelfth month of 1325, according to Hanazono's diary, the *Shinki*, Musō was severely criticized for his lack of insight in Zen by both Shūhō Myōchō and cloistered emperor Hanazono. He was, no doubt, viewed as something of a pretentious upstart in the aristocratic Zen world of Kyoto.

Musō clearly did not consider this commitment to Go-Daigo, Nanzenji, or Kyoto a long-term one. If a report of Hanazono's criticism reached him, he may have felt unwelcome in Kyoto. In any case, his inclination to re-clusion ran deep. Elevated to the position of abbot of Nanzenji, Musō was now an even more venerated figure in Kamakura. He had hardly settled in Kyoto than he began to get invitations from Hōjō Takatoki to return and head monasteries in Kamakura. In 1326/7/15, Takatoki sent a messenger in-viting Musō to head the Jufukuji in Kamakura.[37] Musō declined but in the same month quit Nanzenji and went via Nachi, Kumano, and the Zenōji, near his birthplace in Ise, to Kamakura where he was appointed founder abbot of a small hermitage, the Nanpō'an, by Nikaidō Dōun (Sadafuji), a high-ranking Bakufu official and longtime patron.[38]

In 1327/2/12 on orders of the Bakufu, i.e., by Takatoki, he was briefly appointed abbot of Jōchiji.[39] In the same year (7/13), he withdrew from Jōchiji and returned to head the Nanpō'an. Nikaidō Sadafuji built the Zuisen'in (later Zuisenji) nearby, and Musō now moved there. He built a hall for worship of Kannon and a retreat, "the hut from which to view the turning world," where he invited friends to poetry gatherings, on the hill-top above the monastery. This mountain temple in Kamakura was also to be the site of one of his most renowned gardens.[40]

In the winter of that year, 1327, he was asked by Takatoki to head En-gakuji, but refused firmly. In 1329, he was asked again and this time ac-cepted.[41] He does not seem to have had any presentiment that the Bakufu was facing disaster or that he should remove himself from Kamakura. Nor does he seem to have had the strong antipathy to the Hōjō as patrons that Tamamura Takeji asserts in his biography of Musō. If anti-Hōjō and pro–Go-Daigo sentiments were motivating factors in his decisions, he would hardly have returned from Kyoto to Kamakura or accepted, however re-luctantly, the headship of Jōchiji and Engakuji. I would prefer to argue that Musō, after years of semiretirement and outright reclusion, was shy of all authority figures and large institutional monasteries. He was, however, being tugged steadily and somewhat reluctantly out of obscurity and into the mainstream of Rinzai Zen by powerful would-be patrons who were unwilling to take no for an answer.

Later, in *Muchū Mondō* (Dialogues in Dreams) Musō wrote apprecia-tively of several of the Hōjō Regents, especially Tokiyori and Tokimune, as patrons of Zen:

The faith of lay practicers was as great as that of monks, as demonstrated by the Zen disciple Hōjō Tokimune. In the Kōan period [1278–87], the world was in an uproar because the Mongols were invading. The lay disciple Tokimune, how-ever, remained composed, and every day he summoned Zen master Wu-hsüeh

Tsu-yüan, then head of Kenchōji, or various experienced Zen monks, and they would speak about matters of *Dharma*. This attitude was so praiseworthy that it was noted in Wu-hsüeh's *Discourses*. Later, Tokimune built Engakuji, continuing to foster the prosperity of the Zen school. The world was kept secure during the two generations of father and son, and both men are reported to have died in an exemplary manner.[42]

These are hardly the words of somebody who disliked the Hōjō family or spurned their patronage of Zen.

After serving as abbot of Engakuji for a year or so, Musō returned (1330/9) to the Zuisen'in. Then he set out for Kai, where, with the backing of the Nikaidō family, he opened the Eirinji. Early in 1331, he returned to the Zuisen'in in Kamakura. He was asked by Takatoki to head Kenchōji but declined. In the spring of 1332 he returned to the Eirinji in Kai. Later in the same year he was asked again to head Kenchōji but declined again on grounds of ill health. In 1332 he was appointed head of the Zuikōji in Harima. In 1333/1, he was once again asked by Takatoki to head Kenchōji but again declined on grounds of ill health. In 1333/3, he returned to Zuisen'in.[43] Two months later (1333/5) the Kamakura Bakufu was overthrown by Nitta Yoshisada and his forces, and the Hōjō family was virtually wiped out. Musō, based in the Zuisen'in, was said to have saved many people's lives.[44]

The overthrow of the Kamakura Bakufu was to have serious implications for Musō as well as for Rinzai Zen. The political balance quickly shifted to Kyoto. Kamakura Rinzai monasteries including Engakuji, Kenchōji, Manjuji, Jufukuji, and Jōchiji, all of which Musō knew well, were deprived overnight of their principal patrons, the Hōjō family. With Go-Daigo and the Ashikaga active in establishing a new political regime in Kyoto, it would not be long before Rinzai monasteries there, Daitokuji, Myōshinji, Nanzenji, Tōfukuji, and Kenninji, attracted new patrons and began to outstrip their Kamakura counterparts in influence, in scale, and in wealth. Had Musō remained in the Kantō he would most likely have settled back into the obscurity that so often pulled him. His reputation was now so great, however, that he could not easily maintain a reclusive life.

Following the fall of the Kamakura Bakufu, Go-Daigo returned to Kyoto in the sixth month. Almost immediately he ordered Ashikaga Takauji to have Musō head Nanzenji for a second time. An official messenger (*kanshi*) representing Go-Daigo was sent by Takauji to the Zuisen'in.[45] Musō went to Kyoto (seventh month), lectured before Go-Daigo, and, after heading the small monastery of Rinsenji to the northwest of the city for a while, moved briefly into Nanzenji. In 1334/9 Go-Daigo invited Musō to the imperial palace and "received the robe" (i.e., became his disciple).[46] He requested Musō to head Nanzenji again. As usual Musō declined at first, then accepted (10/10) and again became abbot of Nanzenji. To help him, Musō called the monk Mukyoku Shigen from Engakuji in Kamakura to serve as leader, known as chief seat (*shuzo*), in the Zen meditation hall.[47] Because the Zen schools were being criticized for laxity by monks of the old Kyoto religious establishment, Musō invited the emperor and his courtiers to visit Nanzenji to see for themselves that monks in Musō's temple observed the rules of monastic life (1334/11/28). It is said that this ended the criticisms. Go-Daigo must have been pleased. Within a few days he awarded more landholdings to Nanzenji (12/3).[48]

On 1335 (Kenmu 2)/5/25, Go-Daigo made a gift of Nikaidō Dōun's (Sadafuji's) holdings in Maki-no-shō in Kai Province to Rinsenji, the Kyoto temple that was to become most closely associated with Musō. Rinsenji had been converted from an imperial residence into a Buddhist temple by Go-Daigo (1330/7/25) in memory of his deceased son, Prince Sera. Musō's fellow monk, Gennō Hongen, with whom Sera had studied Zen, was named founder abbot. In the following year (1331/3/27) estate holdings in the provinces of Sanuki, Hitachi, and Kaga were granted to Rinsenji in memory of Prince Sera. Gennō died in 1331 before the transformation of Rinsenji into a Zen monastery was complete. It was natural for Go-Daigo to think of this new temple as a place in which to install Musō, a fellow disciple of Gennō, who had just arrived from the Kantō. Go-Daigo would have been aware that Nanzenji was regarded as an official, or public, monastery and that its abbacy frequently changed. Even if Musō wished to remain in Kyoto, he would not have been able to stay indefinitely as abbot of Nanzenji. A private temple would have to be made available for him. In the seventh month of 1333 (twenty-third day) Go-Daigo issued an edict addressed to Musō offering him "oversight" (*kanryō*) of Rinsenji and granting more landholdings to the temple. In the tenth month of that year (twenty-eighth day), Rinsenji was awarded lands in the neighboring village of Oi. Having provided for the economic base of Rinsenji, in 1335 (10/11), Go-Daigo issued a directive making Musō founder abbot (*kaizan*) of Rinsenji in place of Gennō. No doubt he intended Musō to treat Rinsenji as a memorial temple for Prince Sera. In the edict of designation he was referred to as "Musō Kokushi." He was thus first awarded the title of Kokushi, or National Teacher, while he was still alive.[49]

Musō was thus provided with a large, well-supported site in the beautiful area of Saga-Arashiyama to the northwest of the city as a base for his activities and for the training of the monks and lay people who would seek him out. Rinsenji was to remain the base for the Musō lineage. Within the grounds of Rinsenji he built a founder's pagoda. Although Rinsenji was becoming the head of a Musō lineage, it had been ranked among the monasteries in the second tier (*jissatsu*) of the *gozan* system; and as such it was nominally a public temple, open to monks of all lineages. In order to maintain greater control over the leadership of Rinsenji, Musō established a subtemple (*tatchū*) within Rinsenji called the San'ein. It was the abbot of this *tatchu*, even more than the head of Rinsenji, who would exercise control over the Musō lineage. After a long, itinerant life marked by periods of reclusion, Musō was now beginning to demonstrate administrative ability and the desire to organize a lineage of his own.

Go-Daigo, of course, was not exclusively committed to Zen or to Musō. His deepest interests probably lay in Shingon Buddhism and *kami* worship.[50] Throughout the period of the Kenmu regime, however, he kept Musō in Kyoto and, obvious to all, became his patron and student in Zen.

Musō was, by 1333, known to Ashikaga Takauji and his younger brother Tadayoshi. Go-Daigo had used Takauji to get Musō to come to Kyoto early in the regime, and the Ashikaga brothers had lived in the Kantō before 1333. They knew Kōhō Kennichi and his disciples, including Musō. They were also becoming familiar with Zen. They had close connections with the Uesugi warrior family which was a patron of Zen monks, including several Chinese masters who were active in Kamakura. Among these was Chu-hsien Fan-hsien (Jikusen Bonsen) whom Takauji and Tadayoshi both got to know. Takauji probably had Chu-hsien installed as abbot of Jōmyōji in 1332. In the ninth month (fifth day) of that year Chu-hsien led the first-year memorial service for deceased Ashikaga Sadauji and gave a *dharma* lecture (*shinzō seppō*). Takauji and Tadayoshi remained patrons of Chu-hsien even after their move to Kyoto and the opening of the Kenmu regime, and later (1341) invited him to Kyoto as abbot of Nanzenji.[51] A few months later both Takauji and Tadayoshi visited Nanzenji to hear the Chinese master expound Zen.[52] Until Chu-hsien's death in 1349, Takauji remained a devoted patron of the Chinese monk. Takauji's patronage was generous but it does not seem to have involved a very deep commitment to Zen practice. Tadayoshi had a much deeper interest in Zen and a better command of Chinese culture. In addition to Chu-hsien, Tadayoshi practiced Zen with the Japanese monk Kosen Ingen.

When the Kenmu Restoration collapsed in early 1336 (Kenmu 3) Musō was sixty-two years of age. On the tenth day of the first month Go-Daigo fled to Enryakuji. The following day Ashikaga Takauji entered Kyoto. Because of the disorder in the city, Musō left Nanzenji for Rinsenji. Takauji gave his support to the Northern line of the imperial family represented by cloistered emperor Kōgon, by whose edict Emperor Kōmyō was installed on the throne. In addition to promoting the Northern line, Takauji and his brother Tadayoshi also courted the religious leadership in Kyoto. They were particularly assiduous in their patronage of Musō, who was both a leading prelate and one who had close ties with the ousted Go-Daigo. While Go-Daigo was active in the Kenmu regime neither Takauji nor Tadayoshi seems to have made much of an effort to patronize Musō; they may have felt that it would be presumptuous to lay much claim on a monk clearly favored by Go-Daigo. With Go-Daigo gone, the Ashikaga quickly realized that Musō was one of those prelates whose support and visible charisma they needed if they were to assert control over the religious as well as the political arena in Kyoto. In that year (1336) Ashikaga Takauji declared himself Musō's disciple, "received the robe" (*jue*), and asked for his guidance in Zen. He also ranked Musō's monastery of Rinsenji among the official monasteries in the third tier of the *gozan* hierarchy (*shozan*).

There is a strong possibility that Takauji's sudden interest in Musō sprang in part from tactical political concerns and in part from a sense of guilt at his treatment of Go-Daigo, as well as from an effort to make amends to Musō who had been deprived of his imperial patron. Takauji's commitment to Zen was by no means exclusive and he did not immediately confine his patronage of Zen monks to Musō. Takauji's attachment to Chu-hsien meant that until the Chinese monk's death in 1349, his patronage of Musō remained divided. Although Takauji formally became Musō's disciple, it is not clear to what degree he actually practiced Zen. His religious belief seems to have been one of rewarding good and punishing evil, of sinfulness and relief through the efficacy of devotion to Jizō. No doubt Takauji found Musō more approachable than any Chinese monk. He could talk to him about political problems and ask him for moral guidance. Musō's openness to esoteric Buddhism and his directness and willingness to teach and explain things at length would also have been appealing to Takauji. But Takauji does not seem to have been interested in, or able to commit himself to a rigorous search for *satori* under the guidance of Musō or any other Zen master.

Tadayoshi was very different. He had more interest in culture and learning than Takauji, and like many of the Hōjō leaders, was attuned to Chinese culture and Chinese Zen. He mixed with many Chinese and Japanese Zen masters in the Kantō and Kyoto, practiced *zazen*, and engaged in *mondō* with them. He was better able than his brother to put Musō in context as a Zen monk, and he may not have been overly impressed with him. He did study Zen with Musō. Musō wrote the *Muchū mondō* for him in 1344. But Tadayoshi did not formally become a disciple of Musō until 1349 (third month) when he "took the robe." When he did so, he told Musō that he had already taken the robe from masters in the lineage of Mugaku Sogen in Kamakura, and he asked Musō if it would be proper to take it again from Musō in view of the emphasis in the Zen school of recognition by a single master (*isshi inshō*). Musō responded that since he himself was a third-generation disciple of Mugaku it was "in the family," so to speak, and therefore quite acceptable. By his question, Tadayoshi revealed both his seriousness of purpose and his considerable understanding of Zen and the Zen transmission. Tamamura Takeji suggests that the *Muchū mondō* shows Tadayoshi deliberately exposing the weaknesses in Musō's Zen by asking questions that called for Musō to reveal his rather didactic, literary, Shingon-oriented Zen, but this seems to be crediting Tadayoshi with more calculation and a much better grasp of Zen than he may have actually had. At the same time, it is true that in spite of receiving careful guidance from Musō in the *Muchū mondō* from 1344, he was not in a hurry to become a formally recognized disciple. It is perhaps significant that when he did become Musō's disciple in 1349, he had just quarreled with Kō no Moronao and Takauji and had been ousted from the Bakufu.[53]

Shūhō Myōchō, Musō's rival, died (age fifty-six) in 1337. Shūhō and his monastery of Daitokuji had enjoyed the patronage of Emperors Hanazono and Go-Daigo. His disciple Kanzan Egen founded Myōshinji in Kyoto. Musō's Zen insight had at times been compared unfavorably with his. His death left Musō as the most venerated and imperially well-connected Zen monk in Kyoto. Had Go-Daigo remained in Kyoto at the head of the Kenmu government it is very likely that Daitokuji and Myōshinji would have continued to flourish, rivaling Musō-related monasteries for leadership of the Kyoto Zen world. The Ashikaga had few ties with Daitokuji or Myōshinji. When they threw Bakufu support in the direction of Musō and his lineage, and the other *gozan* lineages, Daitokuji and Myōshinji fell on hard times.

Musō put Mukyoku Shigen, a monk with imperial blood in his veins, in charge of Rinsenji while he himself became the head of the San'ein and withdrew there. Musō seems to have seen in Mukyoku, with his imperial connections, a future head of the Musō lineage. At the same time, by with-drawing to the San'ein Musō was not relinquishing his leadership role. The San'ein, at least during Musō's lifetime, served as a kind of command post or nerve center for the Rinsenji and the Musō lineage. In 1339 (fifth month), Musō wrote the *Rinsen kakun* and *San'ein ikai* to provide guidance for his disciples. They laid down rules for the leaders of his lineage.[54] Dur-ing this year he also began the restoration of the garden retreat that came to be known as the "Moss Temple," Saihōji.[55] These three temples continued to compel his attention. In 1343 Musō had a sutra repository (a place for storing the blocks for the great tripitika) built at Rinsenji. This suggests that Rinsenji had been provided its own set of the tripitika (1343/8).

From 1339, however, Musō's energies were increasingly taken up with the building of a new temple, one that would link him and the new Bakufu even more closely with Go-Daigo, who had died at Yoshino on the six-teenth day of the eighth month. It is not clear what contacts, if any, Musō had maintained with Go-Daigo after the emperor's ouster from Kyoto in 1336, but Go-Daigo was in Musō's mind. Shortly before Go-Daigo's death Musō had a dream in which he saw the emperor in the robes of a monk riding in a phoenix cart entering the Kameyama detached palace (twenty-fourth day of the sixth month of this year). Musō mentioned this dream to his followers.[56] When, two months later, Go-Daigo died, it was taken as a portent that Go-Daigo's restless spirit (*onryō*) wanted a temple built as a means of pacification. Musō persuaded Tadayoshi and Takauji that it would be spiritually appropriate, and politic, to build a great memorial where the troubled spirit of the emperor could be laid to rest. The Ashi-kaga welcomed the proposal. Takauji, who must have felt some remorse for turning against Go-Daigo, and Tadayoshi, an enthusiastic supporter of Zen, appealed to cloistered emperor Kōgon to have the Kameyama de-tached palace, an imperial villa, converted into a Buddhist temple. Kōgon agreed.[57] Initially, it was not specified to which school of Buddhism it would belong, but it was quickly decided that it should be a Zen temple, and Kōgon appointed Musō to head it.[58] Musō was named founder abbot (*kaizan*).[59] At first Kōgon had the new temple named Ryakuōji after the year period.[60] The name was changed to Tenryūji, Temple of the Heavenly Dragon, in 1341, no doubt to honor Go-Daigo. Musō had the able monk Kosen Ingen appointed chief fund raiser, *daikanjin*.[61]

Tenryūji was built at a time when the foundations of the Ashikaga Bakufu were not yet very firm. There was also considerable resistance from Enryakuji and other old Buddhist monasteries around the capital, which regarded Musō and the network of well-connected temples—Rinsenji, San'ein, Saihōji, and now Tenryūji—he was creating with suspicion and disfavor. The hall-opening *dharma* lecture for Tenryūji was not held until 1345, the seventh-year anniversary of the death of Go-Daigo.

In the meantime, the building and endowment of the new monastery moved ahead. Ashikaga Takauji, Tadayoshi, Emperor Kōmyō, and especially cloistered emperor Kōgon took an active interest in the new temple. Kōgon visited the site on several occasions and he and Takauji granted land rights in estates in Bingo, Hyūga, Awa, Yamashiro, and Tamba provinces. Building work actually began in the spring of 1340.[62] To mark the occasion, Takauji granted Ryakuōji a *jitō shiki* to the Mitani-no-shō in Bingo Province.[63] One of the first buildings to be constructed was a Memorial Treasure Hall (*tahōin*). The Buddhist ceremony for the start of work on this hall was held on 4/27.[64] In the sixth month of 1340 Takauji granted to Ryakuōji income rights from the Kanoyama-no-shō in Hyūga Province.[65] In the following month he arranged a swap of income rights in which land rights in a nearby *shōen* in Yamashiro Province belonging to the Daikō-myōji temple were transferred to Ryakuōji, and in exchange the title to the distant Hyūga *shōen* was given to the Daikōmyōji.[66] No doubt Ryakuōji got the better portion of the exchange. A month later cloistered emperor Kōgon awarded a *jitō shiki* to a *shōen* in Tamba Province to Ryakuōji as a building resource (*zōei ryosho*).[67]

To further provide for the building expenses and economic support of the new monastery, Ashikaga Tadayoshi proposed in the winter of 1341–42 that two vessels go on a trading mission to Yüan China.[68] Musō supported the plan, which seems to have been derived from the earlier example of the Kenchōji vessels. Over the objections of Enryakuji monks and their supporters among the court aristocracy, the Tenryūji vessels set sail the following autumn. A Hakata merchant organized the venture and promised to raise 5,000 *kanmon* for the monastery. In spite of a growing Japanese "tilt" in Rinzai Zen circles, there were still plenty of monks eager to be allowed to study in Chinese monasteries.

The first Buddhist ceremony was held in the memorial pagoda (Tahōin) in 1340 and Ryakuōji began to function minimally as a temple. Because everything was going smoothly Musō reassumed the abbacy in 1341. The name was changed to Tenryūji (1341/7). It is said that Tadayoshi recommended the name to ex-emperor Kōgon after a dream in which he saw a golden dragon rising from the river to the south of the temple. Kōgon also visited Musō in Saihōji, located to the west of the city, where he "took the robe" from Musō and became his disciple (1342/4/8).[69] In this year the ceremony of raising the ridgepole for Tenryūji was held. Musō acted as celebrant (1342/12/2).[70] As a mark of reverence for the new monastery an envoy from Kōgon and the brothers Takauji and Tadayoshi visited Tenryūji. At the request of the Bakufu, Kōgon had fixed the ranking of the *gozan* and *jissatsu* monasteries. Tenryūji was ranked very high from the outset, at *gozan* number two (1342/12/5). Kōgon made several more visits to Tenryūji (1343/1344) to attend various ceremonies connected with the construction.[71]

By 1344, Tenryūji was virtually completed. A proposal was made that Kōgon should attend the seventh-year anniversary services for Go-Daigo to be held at the new monastery in 1345. When Enryakuji monks, who had no desire to see the Zen sect flourishing in Kyoto or usurping Enryakuji claims to court patronage, got wind of this, they descended (8/14) on the city in an armed appeal (*gōso*) demanding that the "evil monk" Musō be banished and Tenryūji razed. In the face of Enryakuji's threats to bring the sacred portable shrine (*shin'yo*) into the city, and to call up the support of soldier-monks from Kōfukuji and Tōdaiji, Kōgon decided not to attend the Tenryūji ceremonies in person and sent an imperial messenger instead. He visited the monastery a day later.[72] In spite of the opposition from Enryakuji, Musō had secured for Tenryūji a deep spiritual bond with Go-Daigo, and with the imperial leaders of the Northern line as well as the Ashikaga.

The Ashikaga, eager for any chance to assert their control over Kyoto and break the grip of Enryakuji on the city, took a hard line. They threatened to confiscate all the resources of Enryakuji monks if they brought the sacred palanquin into Kyoto. The memorial ceremonies and feasts went ahead. The Ashikaga thus used Tenryūji as Yoritomo had used the rebuilding of Tōdaiji—as the occasion for a show of shogunal strength, affluence, and benevolence. In the eighth month of 1345, Takauji and Tadayoshi, with their leading generals Yamana Tokiuji and Kō no Moronao, headed a procession of many hundreds of armed warriors to a great celebration feast at Tenryūji. According to such contemporary chronicles as the *Kōmyōin shinki* and the *Entairyaku*, the streets of the city were thronged from early morning with townspeople hoping to catch a glimpse of the military pageantry. It was impressed upon the city that the Bakufu, not Enryakuji, was the military master of Kyoto and that henceforward Zen was to be the privileged Buddhist school within the capital.

On the occasion of the opening of the Meditation Hall (*zendō*) in 1345 (fourth month, eighth day), Musō performed the ceremony before Takauji and Tadayoshi and delivered a sermon in which he stressed that Tenryūji was the very embodiment of the Buddha's teaching as transmitted through the Zen patriarchs of China and Japan.

The privileged status of Zen and its intimate relation with the Ashikaga were further symbolized by the rebuilding of Tōjiji in 1336, close to the seat of the Bakufu in the center of Kyoto. Until Yoshimitsu built Shōkokuji in 1382, Tōjiji served as the Ashikaga family temple (*bodaiji*) in Kyoto. Its first abbot was Kōsen Ingen (1295–1374), who studied Zen in China from 1318 to 1326 and was patronized especially by Tadayoshi.

After Tadayoshi's fall from power in 1350, Kōsen moved to Kamakura. Tōjiji was made a branch temple (*matsuji*) of Tenryūji. The monastery was then restricted to monks of the Musō lineage. Together with Rinsenji and Tenryūji, Tōjiji became a major center of Musō school influence in Kyoto. In spite of its being a "closed" monastery, it was subsequently ranked as a *jissatsu* in the official *gozan* system. The fact that Tōjiji was permitted to retain its exclusive character while being included as an official monastery set a precedent under which the Zen family temples (*ujidera*) of local magnates could be raised to the status of official monastery.

The building of Tenryūji, with its manifold meanings, and the related promotion of Tōjiji as a Musō-lineage Ashikaga *bodaiji* should be seen in the context of the decision by the Bakufu to promote a major nationwide temple-building effort. At the same time that Takauji and Tadayoshi were using Zen as an instrument in their assertion of control over Kyoto and as a means of strengthening ties with local warrior chieftains, they were also making use of Buddhist monasteries of the Shingon and Tendai schools in their pacification of the rest of the country. This strategy is described in a number of articles by Professor Imaeda Aishin. Tadayoshi played a leading role in developing a Bakufu-connected nationwide network of Zen and Shingon temples known as the Ankokuji and Rishōtō. Some of the inspiration for this policy came from Musō. The whole policy was motivated by a blend of genuine compassion and political calculation.[73]

The policy of building Ankokuji and Rishōtō dates from 1337. By the spring of 1337, resistance by supporters of Go-Daigo was crumbling. Pro-Ashikaga forces were clearly gaining the upper hand. Although the fighting was not over, many felt that a time had come to try to heal some of the wounds opened in the years of civil war. Musō proposed that a pagoda and temple should be built in each of the provinces of Japan where prayers could be offered for the spirits of warriors who had fallen in battle and for lasting peace. This suggestion was taken up by Takauji and executed by Tadayoshi. Although the plan resembles the ancient Japanese network of official temples, the Kokubunji system, the direct inspiration was derived by Musō and Tadayoshi from Sung China.

In 1338 and 1339, Tadayoshi ordered the provision of funds in the form of *jitō shiki* for the construction (in some cases reconstruction) of five-story pagodas in the Kumedadera in Izumi Province, the Jōdoji in Bingo, the Tōmyōji in Hizen, and the Eikōji in Noto. Of these, the Jōdoji actually petitioned the Bakufu to be allowed to build such a pagoda. In the eighth month of 1338, the community of monks at the Gakuonji in Iga Province also requested the Bakufu to be permitted to build a pagoda in their temple. According to their petition, Niki Yoshinao, the local *shugo*, an Ashikaga appointee, had fortified the Gakuonji and used it as a strongpoint in his struggles with warrior supporters of Go-Daigo in Iga. Gakuonji monks, in support of their claim, protested that they had actively supported Yoshinao and amply demonstrated their loyalty to the Ashikaga.[74]

In 1344, the Bakufu declared that the pagodas were to have the title of Rishōtō (Pagodas of the Buddha's Favor) and that the temples would be known as Ankokuji (Temples for Peace in the Realm). Ankokuji and Rishōtō were separate institutions. The pagodas were established not in Zen monasteries but principally in powerful provincial Tendai and Shingon monasteries. Ankokuji were designated from among existing Zen monasteries belonging to the *gozan* lineages, especially the Musō and Shō-ichi (Ben'en Enni) lineages. Both the Ankokuji and the monasteries containing the Rishōtō were patronized by *shugo*. In many cases, the Ankokuji were the clan temples (*ujidera*) of their *shugo* patrons and thus the most influential local Buddhist foundations. As leading provincial Zen monasteries, Ankokuji were also rapidly incorporated into the middle and lower tiers of the expanding *gozan* network of official Zen monasteries. Although very few Ankokuji or Rishōtō buildings survive today, Professor Imaeda, on the basis of careful research of contemporary documents, has concluded that, by 1350, Ankokuji and Rishōtō had been established in every province of Japan, with the possible exception of Yamato, where entrenched Kōfukuji power may have prevented the establishment of a rival Zen Ankokuji.[75]

Inspired initially by religious impulse, the policy of building Ankokuji and Rishōtō rapidly assumed political and military implications in the eyes of the Ashikaga. Tsuji Zennosuke has suggested that the foundation of a temple represented an assertion of territorial control by its patron. If this is so, then the successive creation of Ankokuji and Rishōtō provides an index of the growing authority of the Ashikaga and of their claim to exercise benevolent rule over the whole of Japan. Ankokuji and Rishōtō were strategically sited within the areas of *shugo* jurisdiction. The example of Gakuonji in Iga suggests that *shugo* and Bakufu planned to use these religious centers as military fortifications and centers of surveillance.

Through the Ankokuji and Rishōtō, the Bakufu was able to supervise and support the *shugo* and tie localities more closely to the center of power in Kyoto. Since monasteries and their local patrons petitioned for the grant of Ankokuji or Rishōtō status, there was obviously considerable incentive. This was partly economic, involving the grant of additional land rights to the value of two or three hundred *kanmon* per annum. Their enthusiasm was also spurred by a desire for local prestige and the advantages of a direct tie with the Ashikaga. Through the granting of the Rishōtō title, Tadayoshi skillfully maintained the support of powerful monasteries belonging to the older Buddhist sects. At the same time, through the Ankokuji, he was promoting the nationwide diffusion of the *gozan* Zen lineages, especially the growing lineage of Musō, and encouraging *shugo* to follow the lead of the Ashikaga in patronizing Zen.

With the death of Musō in 1351, the assassination of Tadayoshi in 1352, and the death of Takauji in 1358, the Rishōtō, which no longer served a vital military function, had no self-sustaining central organization, and were a financial burden to the *shugo* responsible for their upkeep, were allowed to fall into neglect. Ashikaga Yoshimitsu devoted his energy to reorganizing, expanding, and centralizing the *gozan* system into which most of the Ankokuji were eventually absorbed.

With Tenryūji completed, Musō devoted the remaining years of his life to the consolidation and regulation of the rapidly growing Musō lineage, to popularizing Zen, and to keeping the peace between the various factions within the Ashikaga regime. He was laden with honors in the form of repeated designations as "National Master" by Kōgon and Kōmyō. In 1344, he compiled the *Muchū mondō* as a guide to Zen for a warrior layman. In it he stressed that he and other Zen masters felt free to use any teaching, Buddhist or not, in the service of Zen:

> Clear-sighted masters of the Zen sect do not have a fixed doctrine which is to be held to at any and all times. They offer whatever teaching occasion demands and preach as the spirit moves them, with no fixed course to guide them. If asked what Zen is, they may answer in the words of Confucius, Mencius, Lao Tzu or Chuang Tzu, or else in terms of the doctrines of the various sects and denomi-

nations, and also by using popular proverbs. Sometimes they draw attention to the immediate situation confronting us, or they swing their mace and shout out "*katsu*" or perhaps they just raise their fists or fingers. All of these are methods used by the Zen master and known as the "vigorous treatment of the Zen Buddhist." They are incomprehensible to those who have not yet ventured into this realm.[76]

Until the end of his life Musō conducted lavish annual memorial services for Go-Daigo in Tenryūji. At one of these in 1351, he reflected on the discord between Go-Daigo and the Ashikaga and the reasons for the building of Tenryūji. Though he eulogizes Go-Daigo, he does not spare him from criticism. He presents Tenryūji both as a place for the pacification of Go-Daigo's troubled spirit and as the vehicle by which the fully enlightened sovereign may extend peace to the realm and legitimacy and continuity to the new regime:

The virtuous rule of Emperor Go-Daigo was in accord with Heaven's will and His wisdom was equal to that of the ancient sage-kings. Therefore the Imperial fortunes rose high and the whole country was brought under His sway. A new calendar was proclaimed and a new era of magnificence and splendor was inaugurated. The barbarian peoples showed themselves submissive and His subjects were well-disposed. This reign, men thought, would be like that of the Sage Emperor Yao [in ancient China]; it would endure and never come to an end. Who would have thought that this Sage-like Sun would soon set and disappear into the shadows? And what are we to make of it—was it a mere trick of fate? No, I surmise that His late Majesty paid off all the debt of karma incurred in the world of defilement and straightway joined the happy assemblage of the Pure Land. It is not so much that His august reign was brought to an untimely end, but that the great mass of the people were caused so much suffering and distress. As a result, from the time of His passing right up to the present there has been no peace, clergy and laity alike have become displaced, and there is no end to the complaints of the people.

I pray therefore that our late Emperor will turn away from his past confusions and free Himself from bondage to illusion, bid farewell to karma-consciousness and prove Himself the master of enlightened knowledge. Thus He may pass safely beyond the dark crossroads of differences between friend and foe, and attain that spiritual region wherein the identity of confusion and clear insight may be seen. Yet may He not forget the request of the Buddha at Vulture Peak, and extend an invisible hand to protect His teaching, so that with His spirit ever-present in this monastery of Kameyama His blessings may extend to all mankind.

This is indeed the wish of the Military Governor [Takauji], and so we have reason to believe that the Imperial wrath will be appeased. Such a worthy intention [on the part of Takauji] is no trifling thing, and the Buddhas in their profound compassion are certain to bestow their unseen favor and protection upon us. Then may warfare come to an end, the whole country enjoy true peace, and all the people rest secure from disturbances and calamities. May the rule of the Military Governor pass on to his heirs generation after generation. Our earnest desire is that all mankind should share in its blessings.[77]

After the thirteenth-anniversary services were held in 1351, Musō, now a sick man, retired from Tenryūji and secluded himself in the San'ein inside Rinsenji. He cut his ties with the world and waited quietly for the end. Monks and lay people sought to visit him in large numbers. In 1351, he heard that Takauji and Tadayoshi were at odds and sent one of his monks to try to make peace between them. In turn, Takauji informed him that he had ordered that all descendants of the Ashikaga should honor Musō and his lineage at Tenryūji and that anyone who broke this pledge would no longer be considered a member of the Ashikaga house.

Musō died at age seventy-seven on the thirtieth day of the ninth month, 1351. He had been a monk for sixty-nine years. According to his tomb inscription, more than twenty disciples inherited his teaching and more than thirteen thousand people could be counted as his disciples. The four foundations of Tenryūji, Rinsenji, San'ein, and Saihōji, the Bakufu *bodaiji* of Tōjiji, and many of the Ankokuji were all firmly established and provided the basis for his rapidly growing lineage. His leading disciples Mukyoku Shigen, Shunoku Myōha, Gidō Shūshin, and Zekkai Chūshin would carry on his work of promoting and popularizing Rinzai Zen, shifting the center of gravity of the *gozan* to Kyoto, and giving it a more Japanese style and leadership.

What, then, does Musō's life tell us about the changing place of Rinzai Zen, especially *gozan* Zen, in the fourteenth century and the place of Zen monks in politics? Ironically, for a monk who fought shy of politics for most of his life, Musō brought Rinzai monks into politics in a much greater way than had ever been the case. He gained the favor of members of the Hōjō regency and then won the patronage of the Ashikaga who helped to destroy them. Respected and revered by the Ashikaga and emperors of the Northern line, he also served as the protégé and keeper of the spirit of Go-Daigo. The growth of Zen in Kamakura and Kyoto had always had political overtones. His activities in Kyoto tightened the political connections between his lineage, and the *gozan* schools in general, with the Ashikaga regime. For better or worse, *gozan* Zen now became a satellite of the Muromachi Bakufu.

Although he had close ties with Kamakura and Kantō monasteries, Musō's manifold connections with Kyoto, especially with the emperors and ex-emperors of the Southern and Northern lines, helped swing the axis of Rinzai *gozan* Zen from Kamakura to Kyoto. Had this not happened, and had a monk like Musō not come forward, Rinzai Zen (at least the *gozan* lineages) might well have made only a modest development in Kyoto, and thus languished. Conversely, if Musō had not been so successful in Kyoto, it is possible that Daitō's lineage, which had enjoyed imperial patronage in the capital, would have remained, or emerged much sooner, as the dominant branch of Rinzai Zen in Kyoto. Daitō's connections were almost exclusively imperial and it is unlikely that Daitokuji and Myōshiji would have become as supportive of the new Ashikaga warrior regime as Musō and his disciples were prepared to be.

Musō won the favor of Go-Daigo in life; and in death he became the keeper of the emperor's restless spirit (*onryō*). This bond was in many ways the key to his contemporary influence on political leaders of all affiliations. The need, and the desire, to honor Go-Daigo in death led to the building of Tenryūji and the associated rise to influence of Rinsenji, San'ein, and Saihōji. The energy provided by the pacification of Go-Daigo and the restless spirits of those who had died in the wars fed into the building of Ankokuji and Rishōtō and helped to promote *gozan* Zen in the face of opposition from Enryakuji. Whatever his personal motivation, Musō was able to harness that energy to win for Rinzai *gozan* Zen the kind of position in the Kyoto religious world that it had earlier enjoyed in Kamakura.

While Musō may not have emanated the personal charisma or powerful Zen spirit of Daitō Kokushi, he seems to have been an approachable and kindly monk who was prepared to make Zen accessible to lay people on terms they might understand. This is evident from his *dharma* lectures (*hōgo*), many of which were written in Japanese, as well as from the *Muchū mondō*. For much of his life he was unapproachable, reclusive, and hesitant or difficult in his human relations. He seems to have mellowed in his fifties, however, as he became more involved in politics, monastic administration, and the promotion of Zen. When he settled down in Kyoto after his early peripatetic life in the Kantō, monks and lay people flocked to him.

Like many other Japanese religious leaders of the fourteenth century, Musō found it within himself to be an institution builder. In this he shares something with Keizan Jōkin, who revived and promoted the fortunes of Sōtō Zen, as well as with the leaders of the Ji school who were also giving sectarian form to the simple teachings of Ippen. On the other hand, Musō's interest in the secular learning of Confucianism and Taoism remained with him, as did his early interest in scholastic and esoteric

Buddhism, the latter of which surfaces from time to time in his writings. He also maintained considerable devotion to Kannon. In his acceptance of a mixed or "diluted" Zen which could embrace esoteric and devotional elements as well as the *zazen*, he may not have been a Sung purist. But he was entirely in the tradition of monks like Eisai and Ben'en Enni and thus in step with the mood of his age. He was willing to employ the teachings of any branch of Buddhism or, indeed, of any secular tradition, but he did so in order to promote Rinzai Zen. In other words, he was tolerant and flexible enough to try to explain Zen in terms that could readily be understood, and to set that teaching in a larger Buddhist context. Without rejecting the Chinese character of Rinzai Zen, Musō may be said to have legitimated a Japanese religious context and content for Kyoto *gozan* Zen.

Musō also pushed the door open further for the practice of Japanese literary arts by *gozan* monks. Although he railed against monks who devoted themselves exclusively to literary or artistic avocations at the expense of Zen, he wrote poetry in Japanese as well as Chinese. He was not the first Japanese Rinzai monk to do so, but he helped to legitimate the practice of Japanese literary expression in the still very Chinese cloisters of the Kyoto *gozan*.

As we look at Musō's life, can we say that it represented the attainment of a "medieval Japanese" Rinzai Zen? The "Japanese" element is easier to elucidate. Without breaking with its Chinese character, Musō helped to shift the leadership, religious and literary focus, and center of gravity of Rinzai Zen back in a Japanese direction. These changes might well have taken place without Musō; contacts with China were tenuous and the supply of Chinese émigré monks would have dried up in time anyway. But Musō gave Rinzai Zen a decisive push toward a fuller recognition of itself as a Japanese institution. Henceforth, it would be capable of organizing, regulating, and training monks under Japanese masters who had fully and confidently imbibed the best of Chinese practices and made them their own. Visits to China or study under Chinese monks were not precluded. But they were no longer essential to full authentication as a Zen monk or to the confirmation of religious insight.

The "medieval" component of Musō's contribution is harder to assess. In many respects he harks back to the eclectic style and interests of Eisai and Ben'en Enni. At the same time, the Kyoto-centered *gozan* that he helped to shape was very much part of the medieval polity that emerged from the overthrow of the Kamakura regime, the Kenmu Restoration, and the war between the courts. This recentered *gozan* was strong enough to resist the pressures of the older Buddhist centers, and it was also vigorous and attractive enough to appeal to the provincial warriors who would be the shapers of the new age. While Musō's Tenryūji and other Kyoto *gozan* monasteries still depended on *shōen* titles, they were now involved in foreign trade, moneylending, and commerce—activities that were more in step with an emerging mercantile economy than with the older land-based order. Musō might well have seen no great change in the Zen institution within which he was working. We, however, can see a much more active participation by organized Zen in a political and social world in which the realities of power would never be the same.

CHAPTER 13

Kokan Shiren and the Sectarian Uses of History

CARL BIELEFELDT

THE PERIOD of Japan's transition from aristocratic to warrior rule was a time when history mattered. The transition was a long and fitful process, stretching from the disturbances in the twelfth century that brought about the establishment of the Kamakura Bakufu through Emperor Go-Daigo's failed imperial restoration in the fourteenth century. Though they did not know where history was taking them, the generations living through this long process were well aware that things were changing. No doubt at some level every age is sensed by the people living through it as a period of transition, but it does seem that the people living in this particular age—especially those living close to power—were more acutely aware than their predecessors of their own time as one of profound, perhaps even unprecedented change. The evidence for this awareness comes not only in the mannered lamentations over the passing of the old order seen in courtiers' diaries and poems but also in the marked interest in various genres of writing that sought to record and interpret the events of history, both current and past: "historical tales" (*rekishi monogatari*), "military tales" (*gunki monogatari*), "tale" literature (*setsuwa bungaku*), and of course more comprehensive, more self-consciously historiographical works like the celebrated *Gukanshō* and *Jinnō shōtōki*.[1]

The Buddhists of this period were no exception to the sensitivity to change and the desire to locate it in history. Indeed, it is often held that the new historical consciousness of late Heian and Kamakura culture is a product not only of real (or felt) sociopolitical changes but of the spread of Buddhist visions of time—especially what we might call its "metahistorical" vision of the decline of time, through a series of spiritual stages, toward the dissolution of Śākyamuni's religion at the period of the final dharma (*mappō*). By this account, Japan's social changes (along with its earthquakes, fires, famines, and the like) were seen through and magnified by the theological lens of *mappō* thought, according to which history was held to have had entered (typically in the year 1052) the final age of the aeon predicted by the sūtras—an age of religious and secular conflict, in which life would be brutish and short, and spiritual enlightenment no longer possible. In an overlay of local and cosmic time, then, the decline of the old sociopolitical order was read as evidence that the forces of evil karma were out of control and salvation from karma out of reach. Given this evidence, the aristocratic mood is said to have gravitated from a high Heian feminine aesthetic sensitivity for the ephemeral (*hakanashi*) toward the more masculine existential angst over impermanence (*mujō*) that would sound in the opening lines of the *Heike monogatari*.[2]

However neatly the Buddhist *mappō* doctrine may fit certain works of literature, both secular and sacred, we should probably avoid exaggerating this characterization of the Kamakura period as a time of general spiritual malaise brought on by a sense of living in the last age. Buddhist ideas may have been important at the time and the notion of *mappō* a common literary trope and cultural cliché, but we need not imagine an entire society of religious fundamentalists reading historical events as "signs of the times" predicted in the sūtras. The Buddhists of this period produced a wide range of literature that we may loosely call "historical"—from chronologies and hagiographies of past masters (*nenpu, denki, gyōjō*), collections of edifying historical tales (*setsuwa, ōjō den*), temple legends (*engi*), esoteric sectarian traditions (*kuden, kirigami*), and the like, to broader surveys of the Buddhist tradition as a whole. Yet surprisingly little of this literature seems particularly invested in the idea that its readers are living in a uniquely dark time at the mercy of the cosmic forces of history. Kamakura Buddhist authors continue, of course, to make the usual Buddhist complaints against the problems of life in saṃsāra, but most also continue to offer the standard Buddhist solutions. Their use of terms like *mappō*, *masse*, or *matsudai* to discuss saṃsāra may—I think probably does—reflect an increased tendency to locate both the problems and their solutions in history, but we need not read into that use an increased sense of despair.

One of the standard solutions to the problems of life in saṃsāra was, of course, faith in the salvific powers of the buddhas and bodhisattvas. It is in theological service especially to such faith that we find the most persistant emphases on the final dharma among Buddhist authors, especially in the new religious doctrines of figures like Hōnen, Shinran, and Nichiren, who required the dogma of historical decline as justification for their dismissals of traditional Buddhist soteriology in favor of sole reliance on the trans-historical powers of Amida or Śākyamuni. The rise of these new doctrines has traditionally dominated our view of the Kamakura as a period of radi-cal Buddhist reformation; but recent scholarship—at least in nonsectarian circles—has tended increasingly to question this view as a product of the founding myths and theological claims of the Buddhist schools that trace their origins to the period, and to emphasize instead the continuity of Heian and Kamakura Buddhism in what is often called, in the late Kuroda Toshio's popular phrase, the "exoteric-esoteric establishment" (*kenmitsu taisei*)—that is, the major Buddhist institutions of Nara and Kyoto.³ Need-less to say, the representatives of these institutions had no vested interest in the revolutionary religious possibilities of the last age. On the contrary, for them, history served less to open up than to close off possibilities: it was not that historical doctrine justified religious change but that the religious changes going on around them necessitated a historical doctrine to con-trol the proliferation of competing Buddhist ideologies and institutions.

In short, then, the increased Buddhist concern for history and histori-cal writing that we see in this period was by no means merely a matter of cosmic cycles of the dharma; it was also a reflex of real sectarian conflicts and institutional interests. If the last age was supposed to be a time of conflict, the doctrine of the last age in this time of conflict was itself only one weapon in a struggle to lay claim to history; ranged against the doc-trine were other powerful historical visions—of lineages and transmissions, precedents and traditions—that linked the present to particular pasts and thus bound it to particular interests.

The power of the past as a weapon of sectarian struggle is already appar-ent in one of the earliest and most famous examples of religious conflict in the Kamakura period: the Kōfukuji petition of 1205 seeking government proscription of Hōnen's Pure Land teachings. There, in his opening argu-ment, the author, Jōkei (1155–1213), objects to the creation of a new Pure Land school by reminding the court that for centuries it had recognized only eight orthodox forms of Buddhism, all of which had been transmit-ted to Japan from the continent in ancient times by Saichō, Kūkai, and the other founders of Japanese Buddhism; there is, Jōkei holds, no such founder of Pure Land and no proper precedent for Hōnen's establishment of a new Japanese Buddhist school.[4]

Here Jōkei is invoking not only the venerable political consensus that the court had authority to regulate the Japanese Buddhist establishment but also the long-standing religious agreement within the establishment that the divisions of its members would be limited to eight. This sacred number had in fact already been fixed in the Buddhist literature of the early Heian period, where it was regularly used by scholars to describe and rank the various theological positions of the religion, in the genre known as "doctrinal classification" (kyōsō hanjaku). The same classical genre, borrowed from medieval Chinese Buddhist scholarship, continues into the Kamakura as one vehicle of scholastic exposition and sectarian debate; eventually it comes to include, and itself be used by, the new movements of the day that did not figure among the ancient eight.[5]

In modern times, we are used to thinking of the various schools of Japanese Buddhism as independent religious bodies, each with its own clergy and lay membership. This way of thinking reflects conditions since the seventeenth century, when the new Tokugawa administration passed a series of laws that defined a fixed set of authorized Buddhist organizations and required all citizens to register with a local temple belonging to one or another such organization. The "eight schools" of Heian and Kamakura times were hardly such religious bodies. The ancient government recognition invoked by Jōkei was little more than the appointment of annual scholarship monks (nenbun dosha) granted by the old ritsuryō government for the specialization in the eight systems of Buddhist thought studied in the Nara and early Heian periods. The major Heian monasteries did, of course, develop networks of branch temples that tended to link them in institutional factions, and the Tendai and Shingon religious systems did involve certain rituals of ordination and initiation that tended to distinguish them as separate ecclesiastical orders; yet throughout the Heian and into the medieval period, many temples (especially at the local level) probably remained, as it were, "nondenominational," and many monks (at least of the scholarly type) seem to have shared the same traditional ordination rituals and moved about among the monasteries, studying various specializations. And of course most of the laymen who worshiped at the temples and watched the rituals of the monks had little concern for their sectarian divisions, let alone a sense that they themselves belonged to a particular Buddhist denomination.

In his petition against the Pure Land teachings, Jōkei is reacting to, and seeking government intervention against, the perceived threat to this Heian religious style posed by Hōnen's new type of "selective Buddhism" (*senchaku bukkyō*) — that is, a type that selects from the wide range of traditional Buddhist alternatives a particular spiritual practice for exclusive cultivation (*senju*). The worship of Amida and the practice of calling his name (*nenbutsu*) were ancient and accepted features of Mahāyāna religion, but Hōnen went further, suggesting that they constituted the sufficient and, especially in the age of the final dharma, perhaps even the necessary conditions for salvation. Jōkei rightly perceives in such a suggestion the threat of a separate Buddhist movement of Amida devotees outside the old establishment. In his *Senchaku shū*, Hōnen in fact creates an orthodox precedent for a separate Pure Land tradition through a "lineage" of Chinese masters of the faith; in his petition, Jōkei counters by creating an orthodox Japanese Buddhism embodied in the convention of the eight schools. The two men may disagree on which schools are orthodox, but to the extent that they both imagine their schools as historical realities, they share a historical fiction. They may be far apart in their religions, but insofar as they are invested in this fiction, they join in a growing consensus that, in matters of religion, history matters.

The growing consensus is reflected in the later Kamakura literature on the Buddhist schools. The older genre of theoretical, largely ahistorical doctrinal classification is supplemented by new treatments that include not only the distinctive doctrinal positions of the schools but material on their particular historical traditions: their lineages in India and China, their transmissions to Japan, and their prominent founding figures and monasteries. This is the style of treatment that turns up, for example, in the brief account of the Buddhist schools appearing in the *Jinnō shōtōki*. It achieves its highest expression in the works of the prolific Tōdaiji scholar Gyōnen (1240–1321), whose use of the style in his famous *Hasshū kōyō* created a model for Buddhist historiography that has continued to influence our understanding of Japanese Buddhism right up to the present.[6]

In modern times, the *Hasshū kōyō* has often been praised for its relatively even-handed, descriptive account of the Buddhist schools, in contrast to the more polemical doctrinal hierarchies of the *kyōsō hanjaku* systems. In a narrow sense, I suppose we can say that Gyōnen is nonsectarian; but there is a broader, more important sense in which his vision of Buddhist history expresses the degree to which sectarian divisions in the late Kamakura were becoming institutionalized and sectarian identities were becoming defined not merely as a matter of specialization in a particular philosophical doctrine or religious practice but as membership in a specific ritual community and lineage tradition. To be sure, we can trace the roots of this development to earlier times, and it would yet be several centuries before the Tokugawa religious policies would fix the Buddhist schools as separate legal bodies; still, I think it fair to say that the close linkage of distinctive theological position with specific historical tradition that we see in Gyōnen's works represents a major intellectual step toward the division of Japanese Buddhism into the sort of exclusive denominations that we now take for granted.

In addition to his most famous book, composed in 1268 when he was still in his twenties, Gyōnen went on to write a shorter piece in the same survey genre, the *Naiten jinro shō*, as well as a more ambitious work, the *Sangoku buppō denzū engi*, covering, as its title indicates, the course of Buddhism in the three kingdoms of India, China, and Japan. In each of these texts, he views the history of his faith through the lens of its sectarian divisions, understanding that history in effect as a set of discrete doctrinal positions handed down through specific lineages of teachers. His interest in the past, then, is not in the individual people, places, and events of Buddhist history, except as they fit into the origin and transmission of the various schools; he is not looking to recover the historical lore of his religion but rather to define the range of its orthodox forms through historical pedigree. Indeed, though his work focuses on the eight forms specific to the Japanese understanding of orthodoxy, he usually loses interest in them and gives little account of their actual histories in Japan once he has established their doctrinal characteristics and the circumstances of their proper transmission from China.

Although Gyōnen's mix of intellectual schools and institutional lineages became a standard model for accounts of the Buddhist tradition, it was not the only style of Buddhist historiography practiced in the late Kamakura. In 1322, the year after Gyōnen's death, there appeared a major work that took a rather different approach to the religious past: the *Genkō shakusho*, "An Account of the Śākya [House] from the Genkō [Era]," by Kokan Shiren (1278–1346). This book, composed in thirty fascicles by the abbot of Tōfukuji, is said to have been the fruit of ten years of research and writing. Immediately upon its completion, the author presented it to the imperial court of Go-Daigo, with the request that it be included in the Buddhist scriptural canon. Although this and a subsequent appeal to the Northern Emperor Kōgon did not bear fruit, the book did ultimately make it into the *daizōkyō* after its author's death and was finally printed in 1377. It became a major source for later histories of Japanese Buddhism and is still regularly consulted for its biographies of many early Japanese Buddhist figures.[7]

The *Genkō shakusho* is widely identified as the first general history of Japanese Buddhism; yet surprisingly it does not seem to have attracted the kind of attention from scholarship that such a groundbreaking work might be expected to receive.[8] Buddhist scholars of course often cite (or sometimes criticize) the text as a source of information on the biographies of individual monks, but they seem less often to take the work itself as an object or ask in detail how the creation of such a work might be related to the Buddhist scene at the time of its production. I myself have tended to treat the book simply as a reference tool, but recently I have come to wonder if there may not be more to it than this. In what follows here, then, I should like to offer some first thoughts on what more there might be, by suggesting that, when viewed against the intellectual and institutional conflicts of its time, the *Genkō shakusho* can be seen in part as a political document. In particular, I want to argue that its new vision of history and style of historiography may represent a reaction against Gyōnen's model of the Buddhist tradition—a reaction not unconnected with the situation of its author as the abbot of Tōfukuji. First, I should say a word or two here about the abbot and his situation; then I shall try to make my argument.

KOKAN SHIREN was one of the leading prelates of the Zen school in the imperial capital during the first half of the fourteenth century. His monastery, Tōfukuji, was one of the great Buddhist institutions of the capital. It had been founded in the preceding century by the powerful minister Kujō Michiie, boasted as its first abbot the prominent early exponent of Zen Shōichi Kokushi (Enni, 1202–80), and, by Shiren's day, was designated one of the "Five Mountains" (*gozan*), the select group of Zen monasteries officially recognized by the Bakufu. Shiren was born in Heian-kyō, the scion of a prominent Fujiwara house. He was sent to Tōfukuji as a boy, to study under its second abbot, Tōzan Tanshō (1231–91). Although Shiren is usually associated with Tanshō's spiritual lineage, in fact the old abbot died within a few years of the boy's arrival; and Shiren went on to study with a number of other Zen masters at various monasteries in Kyoto and Kamakura, including the prominent figure Kian Soen (1261–1313) of Nanzenji and the important Chinese missionary I-shan I-ning (Issan Ichinei, 1247–1317). In addition to his Zen training, he also studied other forms of Buddhism, especially the esoteric (*mikkyō*) forms, as well as Chinese philosophy and letters. He became renowned as a scholar, served as abbot of both Tōfukuji and Nanzenji, founded several temples of his own, and enjoyed the patronage of high officials in both capitals and emperors in both courts, from Go-Fushimi to Go-Murakami and Kōmyō. He had numerous well-placed disciples and left his name to the *gozan* branch of his Shōichi lineage known as the Kaizō-ha (after his residence at Tōfukuji).[9]

Shiren is probably best known today as the author of the *Genkō shaku-sho*, but he left a fair corpus of other works, reflecting both his broad scholarly interests and his role as a Zen master. In the latter vein, for example, we have several short religious tracts on typical Zen themes, such as the *Zenmon ju bosatsu kaiki* (1325), on the Buddhist precepts; *Goke ben* (undated), on the Five Houses of Chinese Zen; and *Shōshū ron* (1343), on the principles of Zen spiritual training. Shiren was responsible for compiling the Zen sayings of the founder of Tōfukuji, Enni (*Shōichi kokushi goroku*), as well as the records of his teacher I-shan (*Issan kokushi gyōki*); his own lectures on Zen are preserved in three fascicles known as the *Jūzenshi roku* and *Zoku jūzenshi roku*.

Although Shiren is historically important as the founder of a sublineage of *gozan* Zen, and some in his lineage did read his Zen teachings in medieval and early modern times, today these teachings rarely attract much attention and typically do not make it into modern collections of the major Japanese Zen texts—which tend to prefer some of Shiren's more illustrious contemporaries, like Musō Soseki (1275–1351) and Shūhō Myōchō (i.e., Daitō Kokushi, 1282–1337). Where Shiren appears more often is in collections of the medieval *gozan bungaku*. Indeed, he is regularly regarded as a founding figure of this tradition of Zen "sinological" literature, an honor he often shares with a fellow student of I-shan, Sesson Yūbai (1290–1346). His representative text in this tradition is the *Saihoku shū* (after the name of his residence in Shirakawa), which collects in twenty fascicles his poetry and several of his short essays. Early in his career, he wrote the first Japanese dictionary of Chinese poetics, the *Shūbun inryaku* (1306), and near the end of his life, added a shorter manual on Chinese verse, the *Zengi gemon shū* (1341), which provides a primer for Zen monks in the art of elegant *kanbun* composition; both these works were much studied in medieval and early modern times.

Beyond such religious and literary efforts, Shiren wrote in a variety of genres on a number of disparate topics. One of his earliest texts, for example, the *Byōgi ron* (1320), is an unusual piece on medicine, an interest reflecting the author's own lifelong struggle with the health problems of a weak constitution. In a quite different vein, Shiren tried his hand as well at Gyōnen's genre of scholastic survey of the Japanese Buddhist schools, in a little—and seemingly little-noticed—work called the *Hakkai ganzō* (undated).[10] Much more ambitious was his *Butsugoshin ron*, in eighteen fascicles (1325), providing the first Japanese commentary on the *Laṅkāvatārasūtra*. This scripture, of course, was particularly important for the Zen tradition because of its legendary association with the school's First Patriarch, Bodhidharma—a figure of special interest to Shiren. The depth and character of that interest is revealed in another of his texts, the controversial *Shūmon jisshō ron* (1338), a short tract providing, as its title indicates, ten reasons why the Zen school is superior to all others. This last work, in a genre we might call Zen "apologetics," is particularly interesting for our purposes here because it provides us some insight into the polemical context of sectarian dispute within which Shiren wrote his history of Japanese Buddhism. Before we come back to the history, we need to make an excursus into this context.

TO SOME it may seem odd that the abbot of a Zen monastery in the fourteenth century should have taken the trouble to write an apologetic piece defending his faith. After all, by the time the abbot wrote the piece, his faith had been practiced in Japan for some 150 years, since the earliest days of the Kamakura period, and had long since become a well-established element of Japanese religious life. Indeed, we are used to thinking of this time as "the age of Zen," the age when Shiren's faith was the dominant form of Buddhism in Japan—the religion of choice among the ruling samurai, the new elite religion, whose government-sponsored institutions in the two capitals were the centers of medieval high culture. Shiren was himself head of one of the foremost of these institutions, himself a major figure in elite society and high culture, with easy access to the halls of both aristocratic and warrior power.

It is true that the rapid advance of Zen from the outskirts to the center of the Japanese Buddhist world represents one of the great success stories of the Kamakura period. It is less true that the advance, as is sometimes imagined, filled a vacuum at the center left by the retreat of the established Buddhist institutions of Nara and Kyoto. As Kuroda and others have emphasized, these institutions endured and often even prospered throughout the Kamakura, continuing to enjoy the loyalty and receive the support of both court and Bakufu. Just as the founding of the Bakufu did not replace but rather supplemented the court administration, so the founding of the Zen monasteries simply added an additional player to the Buddhist world. Like the Bakufu, Zen was a powerful player; but like the Bakufu, it played in a game for which the rules—at least those governing issues of legitimacy—were still largely set by the old establishment. Just as the court continued, throughout the Kamakura and well into the fourteenth century, to use its imperial authority to resist a Bakufu hegemony, the Buddhist establishment, especially the Tendai center of Enryakuji, employed the norms of Buddhist orthodoxy, the prestige of its tradition, and its connections with the court to contain the advance of Zen.

Signs of what would become a persistent (or at least recurrent) tension between the old order and the new Zen movement appear already in the first years of the Kamakura period, when pressure from Enryakuji led to the proscription of the "Bodhidharma" school of Dainichibō Nōnin. Eisai, who had just returned from his study of Zen on the mainland, got caught up in the same proscription. Again, a few decades later, Eisai's follower Dōgen ran afoul of the mountain monks of Enryakuji when he tried to spread Zen in the capital; and the founder of Shiren's own monastery, Shōichi Kokushi, faced Tendai opposition to his early attempts to found Zen institutions in Kyushu. In the 1260s, Tendai monks from Miidera attacked the Zen monastery Shōdenji in Kyoto; and in the 1270s, Tendai leaders again petitioned the court to proscribe the Zen school. Indeed, during Shiren's own lifetime, when Zen was seemingly now well established, Enryakuji protested against plans for the founding of Zen temples in the capital by both Kameyama (1294) and Go-Uda (1305), Kōfukuji attacked a Zen temple in Yamato (1305), and monks from both capitals renewed the long-standing appeal for proscription of the school (in the so-called Shōchū debate of 1325). And of course in the last years of his life, Shiren witnessed the nasty dispute, discussed elsewhere in this volume, over the recognition of Tenryūji as a memorial to Go-Daigo.[11]

Hence, despite—or in large measure because of—their striking institutional success, the Zen masters could hardly remain content to sit on their meditation cushions contemplating the enigmatic sayings of their Chinese predecessors; prodded by continuing questions about their right to a place in the Japanese Buddhist community, they were forced out into the fray of Kamakura sectarian dispute. The Zen documents from the Tenryūji affair represent the latest in a series of apologetic works that reaches back to Eisai's famous *Kōzen gokoku ron* (1198) and includes such tracts as Dōgen's *Bendō wa* (1231), Enni's *Zazen ron* and *Jisshū yōdō ki* (undated), the *Kōzen ki* by Jōshō (1270s?), and Shiren's own *Shūmon jisshō ron*. The styles and

arguments of these texts differ considerably, from scholastic *kanbun* treatises citing scriptural proof texts to vernacular homilies praising the benefits of Zen meditation; but they all reflect a strong sense of sectarian de-
fensiveness and a clear concern to convince the reader that their authors'
religion is a legitimate form of Buddhism.

To be recognized as a legitimate form of Buddhism in the Kamakura
period meant, in effect, to break into the list of schools accepted as orthodox by establishment scholars like Jōkei and Gyōnen. For this, as we have
seen, it was necessary to claim both a distinctive doctrinal position and a
separate historical lineage. In arguing for its doctrinal position, Zen was
at some disadvantage. To be sure, Shiren's predecessor Enni had struggled
to establish Zen's credentials as a theology, through reliance on Chinese
scholarly texts like Yen-shou's *Tsung-ching lu* and the writings of Tsung-mi;
and in fact we do find Zen thought taken seriously by some Kamakura in-
terpreters and set alongside the systems of Hossō and Kegon in thirteenth-
century works like Ryōhen's *Shinjin yōketsu* (1244–46) and Shōjō's *Zenshū
kōmoku* (1255). Still, the antiintellectual thrust of much Zen literature made
it difficult for the movement to compete in theology with the elaborate
technical systems of Kegon, Tendai, Shingon, and the like. Instead it was
forced to make a virtue of its intellectual simplicity, by claiming to represent the "Buddha Mind" school (*busshin shū*), based on a direct experience
of the Buddha's own enlightenment that could not be described in speech,
"did not depend on the written word" (*furyū monji*), and thus transcended all theological teachings. Needless to say, such resort to a higher
silence, however ingenious as a rhetorical move, hardly silenced the doubts
of Buddhist scholars about the resorter's right to a place among them.

Yet, in a world where sectarian lineage was becoming increasingly important, Zen did have a distinct advantage. Contrary to many modern
apologies for the religion, in the Kamakura period the key to Zen's place
among the Buddhist schools lay less in its sublime philosophical insight
than in its unique historical claim to represent "a special transmission
outside scripture" (*kyōge betsuden*) that had been handed down "mind to
mind" (*ishin denshin*) from Śākyamuni himself through the lineage of its
patriarchs in India and China. Of all the forms of Buddhism, then, Zen—
or what was often called the "Bodhidharma school" (*daruma shū*)—was
probably the most heavily invested in a particular historical vision and the
most acutely conscious of its unique historical tradition. By the time it
began entering Japan at the beginning of the Kamakura, the Sung monasteries of the school had already developed a distinctive lineage cult, and

Sung authors of the school had produced a massive corpus of historical writing on the lineages of the "Five Houses and Seven Schools" and the sayings and doings of the masters.

In his *Shūmon jisshō ron*, Shiren invokes this historical vision. The work opens with the argument that, of all the Buddhist schools, only Zen warrants the name *shūmon* ("essential gate") because only Zen derives from the essential teaching of the Buddha Śākyamuni himself—the others having been founded by later figures in India and China. This essential teaching is accessible only to the highest type of practitioner. Shiren then proceeds to the ten points of superiority referred to in his title. (1) Zen is a direct, unbroken transmission of "the treasury of the eye of the true dharma, the mystic mind of nirvāṇa" (*shōbō genzō nehan myōshin*), through the twenty-eight patriarchs of India. (2) Of all the missionaries from the west, only Bodhidharma had the supernatural body of an advanced bodhisattva—an accomplishment revealed by the fact that, immediately upon arriving in China, he was able to converse in the local language with the Emperor Wu of Liang and, upon death, rose from his grave and was observed returning to India across the deserts of Central Asia. (3) Only the patriarchs of Zen have general currency throughout China—a status seen from the fact that mountains associated with their lives are known simply as "Third Patriarch" or "Fourth Patriarch" mountain; the patriarchs of other schools are always identified as such-and-such a patriarch of such-and-such a school. (4) After the Fifth and Sixth Patriarchs, Zen spread widely throughout China, developing into the Five Houses and Seven Schools whose members far exceed those of any other tradition. (5) Other schools flourished and declined in China, whereas Zen has enjoyed the continued prosperity predicted by Bodhidharma's Indian master, Prajñātāra. (6) Zen, being based on a state of enlightenment that is unobstructed by the written word, has been free to develop a huge corpus of texts, the equal of the Buddhist canon itself; other schools may specialize in the written word but cannot match Zen in literary productivity. (7) Zen is based on the monastic rule of the T'ang patriarch Po-chang, which, though imitated by other schools, alone preserves the true form of Śākyamuni's religion. (8) Other schools may attract the faith of kings and ministers, but only Zen records a large number of direct religious interactions of the masters with the emperors and high officials of China. (9) Zen taps the deep wisdom of the sages, as seen from the fact that Bodhidharma's teachings were anticipated by such legendary Chinese sages as Chih-kung and Fu Ta-shih, and expressed by such transcendent types as Han-shan and Shih-te. (10) The Chinese historians, both Buddhist and lay, treat Zen as the foremost school.[12]

This rather odd list of arguments may not reflect well on its author's powers as a Buddhist theoretician, but it does well reflect the degree to which he seeks to ground his religion in its historical tradition. The superiority of Zen lies in the lineage of Śākyamuni, the remarkable gifts of Bodhidharma, and the books, monastic forms, and cultural testimony of Chinese history. There is almost nothing here of the sort of metaphysical and soteriological defense of Zen that we find in other apologetic tracts of the period—no account of the transcendental "buddha mind" that stands behind and runs through Zen history; no offers of a "sudden awakening" to that mind through the power of Zen religious practice. More important for our purposes—and most surprising given that the author of the *Shūmon jisshō ron* had already written the first general history of Japanese Buddhism—there is nothing here of Japan, nothing of the place of Zen in Japanese history or the justification of Zen as a Japanese Buddhist school.

The absence of any reference to Japan in a work dedicated to arguments for the Japanese Zen school may well reflect the somewhat awkward situation into which Japanese history had put apologists for the school. Their strength may have rested in the claim to represent the ancient, unbroken lineage of Bodhidharma, but the historical implication and political value of that claim were complicated by the fact that, by the time Sung-dynasty Zen began to arrive in the early Kamakura period, the Bodhidharma lineage already had a long "prehistory" in Japanese Buddhism. Gyōnen and other contemporaneous commentators on the new Kamakura movement regularly remark on a prior transmission of the Buddha Mind school from the T'ang dynasty by the Tendai founder, Saichō, and note its inclusion in the religion of early Tendai scholars like Enchin and Annen.[13]

In view of this widely recognized evidence for an early Heian Zen presence, exponents of the "mind transmission" in the Kamakura period had to accommodate two views of its history: one that saw the school as an ancient but arrested tradition of Japanese Buddhism and tended to overlook its florescence under the Five Houses in China; the other that focused on the continuity of the lineage on the continent and largely ignored its prehistory on the islands. The former view had the advantage of sheltering the religion under the orthodox Enryakuji tradition but ran the risk of restricting it to a branch of Tendai learning—in a status sometimes called an "attendant school" (*gushū*); the latter view, while capitalizing on the prestige of Chinese tradition, left the Japanese movement exposed as a new religious cult subject to establishment criticism and in need of independent justification. Thus, historical arguments in Kamakura Zen apologetics were faced with something of a dilemma, and in fact we see them tending toward one or the other horn. In general, the more conservative authors, like Eisai, opt for accommodation with Tendai and seek to capitalize on the earlier Japanese transmission; a sectarian purist like Dōgen takes the opposite approach, making much of his own Chinese lineage and explicitly rejecting the notion that authentic Zen had ever previously been transmitted to the islands.[14]

This difference in historical vision is but one aspect of a broader distinction, regularly made in modern accounts of the development of Zen sectarian style in the Kamakura, between what is often called "joint practice" (kenshū) and "pure Zen" (junzen) — that is, between a religious style that sought to combine the study of Zen with the existing forms, especially the mikkyō forms, of Japanese Buddhism; and a style wholly devoted to the new teachings and practices arriving from the continent. The former is usually associated with an earlier phase of the movement, as exemplified by pioneering figures like Eisai, Enni, and Kakushin, who were largely active in and around the imperial capital; the latter is seen as a more mature phase, developing in the second half of the thirteenth century with the arrival in Kamakura of Chinese masters like Lan-ch'i Tao-lung (Rankei Dōryū, 1213–78), Wu-hsüeh Tsu-yüan (Mugaku Sogen, 1226–86), and Shiren's teacher I-shan. Under the tutelage of the Chinese monks and with the support of the Kamakura shoguns, the Zen movement worked its way free from the legacy of Japanese mikkyō and established an independent school, replicating the form of the tradition in China. It is this pure style that we find institutionalized in the gozan system, with its distinctive monasteries, rules, and rituals, and its specialization in the study of Sung philosophy, literature, and the like.

Shiren, of course, is counted as one of the founding figures of this "mature" Zen of the late Kamakura. He was in fact a monk of highly sinified tastes. Born in the last quarter of the thirteenth century, he came of age in a Japan already dotted with Chinese-style Zen monasteries and populated with Zen missionaries from the mainland. Though he dreamed of traveling to the mainland, in the end his weak constitution (and, we are told, the protestations of his mother) prevented him from making the arduous trip to the source. Instead, he immersed himself in the imported culture, not only in the characteristic Zen literature recording the sayings of the Chinese masters but in the broader literary world in which the masters moved. He went on, as we have seen, to produce not only Chinese-style goroku for his Zen predecessors but other works in characteristic Zen genres, as well as a substantial corpus of Chinese poetry, literary theory, and composition manuals.

As the abbot of a *gozan* monastery in the imperial capital, Shiren must have been particularly sensitive to the weight of Tendai authority and the political risks of borrowing on that authority by associating his religion with Saichō and the founding of Enryakuji. While the establishment of independent Zen institutions in the Bakufu town of Kamakura does not seem to have provoked much response from the Nara and Kyoto monasteries, in the capital area, in the shadow of Mount Hiei, things were different. Eisai had succeeded in founding Kenninji in the capital only on the premise that it would represent a branch temple of Enryakuji; and, as we see in the dispute over Tenryūji, even in the fourteenth century the monks of Enryakuji were still resisting the development of independent Zen monasteries in the capital by claiming that, in principle, such institutions should be subject to Tendai authority. Indeed, Shiren's own Tōfukuji had been established by Michiie on the understanding that it would combine Zen with the practice of Tendai *mikkyō*.[15]

Given his situation as abbot of Tōfukuji and his personal devotion to Sung culture, therefore, it is not so surprising that Shiren's advocacy of Zen in the *Shūmon jisshō ron* should ignore the early history of the religion in Japan and focus exclusively on China; rather, the question becomes why such a seemingly "pure" Zen master, so invested in his Chinese heritage, should have decided to write the first general history of Buddhism in Japan. Part of the answer to this question may lie in the kind of history he decided to write.

THE *Genkō shakusho* is not a general history, if we mean by that a work that provides a coherent narrative of past events. The book as a whole has no explicit narrative structure and indeed does not cohere even as a single essay; rather, its thirty fascicles are divided into three distinct sections, each of which represents a different genre and takes a different approach to organizing the past. The first two-thirds of the work, the *den*, or "Biography" section, is devoted to accounts of past Buddhist worthies, arranged in groups according to their particular religious claims to fame; the second part, the *hyō*, or "Annals," provides a running record of events in the history of the Buddhist religion, arranged by year of the imperial reign from 538 to 1221; the final three fascicles, the section called *shi*, or "Records," collects material on miscellaneous aspects of Buddhism—temple legends, major ritual events, traditions of music and chanting, sectarian teachings, religious disputes, and so on. In addition, the author provides throughout his own comments on this material, in passages he identifies as *san*, "appreciations," and *ron*, "discussions."[16]

The *Genkō shakusho* may not be a work of narrative history, but it is clearly a work much more concerned with the actual (or legendary) events of the Japanese past than with Buddhist metahistorical models of cosmic aeons. Shiren shows here little concern here for the implications of the last age and largely avoids gloomy lamentations over the decline of the dharma or dark forebodings about what is to come. The fateful year 1052 passes in his "Annals" with an entry only on several sūtra-reading ceremonies that cured epidemics.[17] Where Shiren dips into the spiritual realm, he does so not to the deeper levels of cosmology (or metaphysics) but to the more familiar world of the supernatural order—the world of miracles, powers, epiphanies, and the like, that have always hovered about Buddhist historical writings. For the rest, he takes a more or less matter-of-fact view of the course of history and, if anything, is rather upbeat in his obvious assumption that the great figures of the past whose hagiographies he records can serve as evidence for the enduring value of the Buddhist religion and as models for emulation in the future. To this extent, Shiren is rather like Gyōnen in his respect for the continuities of tradition.

Shiren's sense of tradition, however, is much more concrete than Gyōnen's. The *Genkō shakusho* shows little taste for the doctrinal matters so prominent in the *Hasshū kōyō* and devotes scant attention to the teachings of the various Buddhist schools—a discussion it relegates to a brief account in the miscellaneous material of its final section. Shiren may conceive of history as more than a mere record of the past and mix into his record edifying legends and stories (as well his own religious judgments), but he is at least interested in the details of specific events. He may not be very good at telling his stories and bringing out the details (his overly wrought *kanbun* having little of the charm and immediacy of the vernacular *setsuwa* literature from which he sometimes draws), but he does provide accounts—often quite extended accounts—of individual figures from the past, including some nuns and lay folk. As a historian, then, Shiren is interested simply in recording the lore of the past; as a Buddhist historian, he has didactic interests in this lore as exemplary for the faith. Yet as a Zen Buddhist historian, he has some additional interests that guide his selection and handling of the past and that also mark him off from Gyōnen.

There is an old rumor, started in the fifteenth century by the author of a diary called the *Hekizan nichiroku*, that the bulk of the *Genkō shakusho*, its twenty fascicles of biography, was originally the work of Gyōnen, to which Shiren then added his last two sections. Yet the gap between the approach of this book and Gyōnen's style of theological history makes this seem pretty unlikely. It becomes very unlikely when we consider the place of Zen here. Gyōnen always considers Zen a marginal religious movement, outside the mainstream of Japanese Buddhism; the *Genkō shakusho* puts it at the very center of its history.[18]

By the time Gyōnen wrote his *Hasshū kōyō* in 1268, the new movements of Pure Land and Zen were difficult to ignore. As the title of his work indicates, Gyōnen sought to limit what he elsewhere calls the "standard" (*kiku*) Buddhism to the eight schools of Nara and Heian tradition; but he did acknowledge the recent popularity of the two new movements and treated them briefly in an appendix to his work, giving an abbreviated summary of their doctrinal positions and historical lineages. Of the two, he seems to have preferred the Pure Land and, toward the end of his life, apparently sought to bring it into the fold of orthodoxy; Zen, on the other hand, is never so favored and remains but a footnote to history.[19]

The *Genkō shakusho* may lack an explicit narrative and may be more interested in the particulars of the Japanese past than in the divisions of its sectarian theologies, but one need not read far in the book to recognize that these particulars tell a certain sectarian story very different from that of the *Hasshū kōyō*. The first of Shiren's ten categories of biography deals with those monks who "transmitted wisdom" (*denchi*) — that is, those responsible for the introduction of Buddhism to Japan. After notices on a number of familiar figures of the Nara and early Heian periods regularly credited with founding the various Buddhist schools, the concluding entry here, and the longest in this category, is devoted to the Kamakura monk Eisai.[20] The message is unmistakable: that Eisai's introduction of the Zen school from the Sung places him in the company of such ancient worthies as Saichō and Kūkai as one of the founding fathers of Japanese Buddhism — or, to put the matter from the other side, that Eisai's company here places his school among the legitimate traditions of Japanese Buddhism. This image of Eisai as a central historical figure is then reinforced in the "Annals" section of the book, where the only event worthy of entry for the year 1194 is the return of Eisai from his Zen studies in China, and where indeed almost nothing happens in the Buddhist world during the years thereafter that does not concern events in the life of this latter-day patriarch.[21]

Once the patriarch's work of transmission is done, his school can take its rightful place among the forms of Japanese Buddhism recognized as orthodox by scholars like Gyōnen. In the "Records" section of the *Genkō shakusho*, where Shiren offers his own brief account of the teachings of the various schools (*shoshū*), we find a new list of seven orthodox traditions, of which Zen is given as the last (the Nara schools of Jōjitsu and Kusha, as well as the Jōdo, being reduced here, for lack of separate lineage, to "attendent schools").[22] As Shiren makes explicit elsewhere in his writings, the distinctive feature of this seventh school is its specialization in the meditation (*zazen*) practice from which it takes its name. The school's specialization becomes obvious in the *Genkō shakusho* when we look for the biographical notices on its members, which are found collected under the category "pure meditation" (*jōzen*)—that is, the section on monks noteworthy as contemplatives. Indeed this entire category is occupied solely by figures belonging to the new Zen movement, almost as though the movement had a monopoly on Buddhist meditation practice. One full fascicle of this section, by far the longest biography in the book, is given over to the founder of Shiren's own Tōfukji lineage, Shōichi Kokushi; the section concludes with a notice on the author's teacher Soen.[23]

Clearly, then, the selection and organization of material in the *Genkō shakusho* serves a particular sectarian agenda, which seeks to provide the Zen movement with the proper founding patriarch and distinctive religious character that would qualify it for a place among the Japanese Buddhist schools. Indeed, Yanagida Seizan has characterized the book as less a general history of Japanese Buddhism than a history of the Japanese Zen school. Similarly, Funaoka Makoto has singled out the book as the one source primarily responsible for establishing the Zen sectarian tradition, with Eisai as its founding figure, that would become the standard model for later historiography of the school.[24] As Funaoka complains, this model, by focusing almost exclusively on the new Zen arriving from China in the Kamakura, conveniently ignores the long prehistory of the religion in Japan. Thus, if Funaoka is right, the *Genkō shakusho* seems squarely in the camp of those late Kamakura "purists" of the mature Zen style who abandoned compromise with the Japanese Buddhist establishment, rejected religious eclecticism, and sought to isolate their religion as a distinctive new denomination. But Funaoka may not be right, or may be only partly right; for the *Genkō shakusho* seems to have a somewhat different, more ambitious agenda, which seeks not just to insinuate Zen into Gyōnen's picture of the legimate schools but to call into question the legitimacy of that picture itself.

Whatever its emphasis on Eisai and the new Kamakura Zen movement, it is hardly fair to say that the *Genkō shakusho* ignores the earlier record of the religion in Japan in favor of a pure sectarian lineage transmitted from the Sung. In its biography of Saichō, for example, it repeats with no apparent discomfort the standard account of his inclusion of the Buddha Mind (i.e., Zen) school in the Tendai order he founded on Hieizan; and among others who "transmitted wisdom," it also reports the long-standing tradition, noted by Gyōnen and other contemporaneous authors, of an earlier introduction of Zen by the Nara monk Dōshō (628–70).[25] The inclusion of such notices obviously tends to diminish the stature of Eisai as founding patriarch, to compromise the claim that Eisai's Zen transmission represents a unique lineage of mind-to-mind transmission in China, and thus to raise again the question of Zen's identity as a separate Japanese school. To this extent, the author of the *Genkō shakusho* seems caught between his fidelity to Chinese Zen and his job as a Japanese historian.

Yanagida is of course exaggerating when he describes the *Genkō shakusho* as a history of the Zen school. Shiren may want to put his own school at the center of Japanese Buddhism, but he is after all writing a global, rather than a sectarian, history and does in fact provide full coverage of representative figures from all the traditions—with perhaps the most conspicuous exception being the recently deceased Gyōnen, who does not merit mention.[26] Most striking perhaps for one of Shiren's obvious sectarian leanings is the ample attention he gives to *mikkyō*, which was the dominant style of establishment Buddhism in both Kyoto and Nara and thus the chief competitor of the new Kamakura movements. In his biographies of those who "transmitted wisdom," Shiren goes out of his way to record the legend that the Indian Tantric master Śubhakarasiṃha (Zenmui, 637–735), a figure central to the Shingon lineage, brought esoteric Buddhism to Japan; and the subsequent Japanese tradition of *mikkyō*, from Saichō and Kūkai on, receives generous treatment throughout the book. In fact, we know from Shiren's biography that, like Eisai, Enni, Kakushin, and many other Kamakura Zen masters, he himself studied and practiced the esoteric rites.[27]

Thus in both its genre and its content, the *Genkō shakusho* hardly reads like a serious sectarian history. Shiren had ample recent precedent for such a history, in works like Shōchō's *Meishō ryakuden*, on biographies of the *mikkyō* masters of India, China, and Japan, or Gyōnen's own *Risshū kōyō*, on the Vinaya school, and *Jōdo hōmon genru shō*, on the Pure Land tradition. Perhaps more to the point, given his fondness for things Chinese, he had the obvious model of the famous Zen sectarian histories from the Sung and Yüan, in the genre of the *Ch'uan teng lu*—material that had already been exploited for apologetic purposes in works like Dōgen's *Shōbō genzō* and Keizan's *Denkō roku*. In contrast to such narrowly sectarian treatments, Shiren opts instead to locate his religion within a broader, more ecumenical account of Japanese Buddhism that draws on other Chinese historiographic models.

According to his biographers, Shiren undertook to write the *Genkō shakusho* at the prompting of his Chinese master, I-shan, who is said to have found it odd that a monk of Shiren's learning should know so much about continental history and so little about his native Buddhist tradition. Whether or not the story is true, it is expressive of the degree to which the book casts the native tradition in the mold of its author's Chinese learning. The Sung literature to which Shiren devoted himself provided an abundance of models, both secular and sacred, for a new historiography. In addition to the sectarian collections of the Zen, Pure Land, and Tendai traditions, Buddhist authors had produced monumental works in several genres—biographies, like Tsan-ning's tenth-century *Sung kao-seng chuan*; chronicles, like Tsu-hsiu's *Lung-hsing t'ung-lung* (1164); and general histories, like Chih-p'an's *Fo-tsu t'ung-chi* (1269), that adapted various traditional forms of secular historiography to Buddhist materials.[28]

As Shiren himself says of his own work, it is intended to provide for Japanese Buddhism a proper history of the sort found on the mainland. Thus, while he draws on such popular indigenous genres as *setsuwa*, *ōjō den*, and *engi* (themselves not without continental antecedents), like some of his continental models, he arranges his material according to a combination of traditional Chinese historiographical styles. The most obvious of these, of course, is provided by the several Buddhist collections known as the *Kao-seng chuan*, from which he borrows both the genre of sacred biography itself and the technique of religious typology through which the biographies are organized. The twenty fascicles devoted to this genre are then supplemented by the "Annals" and "Records," both of which are based on classic historiographical forms dating back to Ssu-ma Ch'ien's *Shih-chi*. The very title of the work, Shiren himself says, derives from analogy with Chinese secular histories like the *Han shou*, *Chin shou*, and *T'ang shou*.[29]

AS A PERSONAL PROJECT, then, the *Genkō shakusho* can be read as the attempt of a monk who never made it to the mainland to bring the mainland to the islands. As a political statement, this revisioning of the insular Buddhism in a continental style had several obvious advantages for its author. The very foreignness of its vision, first of all, could not but remind the reader that its author, though he never himself made it to the mainland, stood in the great tradition of Chinese culture that had always been the proper source of Japanese Buddhism. Just as the glories of T'ang civilization had once been transmitted through the Buddhist institutions of Nara and Heian, so now the new Sung and Yüan culture was being introduced at Tōfukuji and the other monasteries of the Five Mountains. Like other literary products of that culture studied and mimicked in the *gozan* monasteries—the new poetry and philosophy, the novel genres of *goroku* and *kōan*—the new historiography (as well as the florid Chinese literary style) of the *Genkō shakusho* could serve to advertise the Zen movement as the chief representative of the latest continental learning. The prestige of association with and support for the representative of this learning would not, of course, have been unwelcome to the movement's Bakufu patrons in their competition with the Kyoto establishment for social and political legitimacy.

As a Zen master in the imperial capital, however, Shiren could hardly afford simply to appeal to the cultural conceits of Kamakura. In fact the new style of the *Genkō shakusho* could be attractive to the Kyoto court establishment itself, insofar as it envisioned a national Buddhist history on a par with that of the great imperial tradition in China. The work was intended precisely to create such a history and was, we may recall, presented to the Emperor Go-Daigo in 1322, at a time when he was no doubt already giving thought to the possibilities of restoring direct imperial rule. The text is lavish in its praise of the imperial line and of Japan as the land of the gods.[30] Moreover, the organization of the text, by de-emphasizing the separate traditions of the various Buddhist schools, offered a welcome new vision of a single Japanese saṅgha transcending the competing claims of the fractious Buddhist institutions. The "Annals" section of the text in particular, by displaying the role of Buddhism in the history of imperial rule, provided an attractive model of a church in service to the court. It is probably no oversight that the "Annals" comes to a seemly but seemingly premature end in 1221, on the eve of the failed Jōkyū uprising that dealt a heavy blow to aristocratic political fortunes.

Shiren's vision of a national Japanese Buddhism along Chinese lines leads to an interesting tension in his text between its continental model and its native application. In fact, for all his personal and political investments in Chinese learning, Shiren is no slavish imitator of his Chinese tutors. On the contrary, he is explicitly critical of what he sees as shortcomings in the historical scholarship of the *Kao-seng chuan*, which his own work seeks to revise and supplement. In his book on Japanese literary approaches to China, *The Fracture of Meaning*, David Pollack has noted the degree to which Shiren, while deeply immersed in Chinese studies, retains an independent Japanese sensibility and a remarkably critical distance from his Chinese sources.[31] Nowhere are that sensibility and distance more forcefully expressed than in the postface (*josetsu*) of the *Genkō shakusho*, where Shiren provides his argument for departing from his Chinese historiographical model.

Although the biographies of the *Genkō shakusho* are arranged according to a schema based on the *Kao-seng chuan*, Shiren in fact alters somewhat the categories of that schema, in order to organize his own work around the traditional Mahāyāna list of bodhisattva virtues known as the "ten perfections" (*jūdo*, or *jū haramitsu*). In his postface, the latter part of which proceeds by a standard question-and-answer format, he poses the question of his justification for this innovation and especially whether it is meant to imply that the figures appearing in his book are all themselves bodhisattvas of the Mahāyāna persuasion. The answer is yes: Japan may be a small country, but it is unique among the three kingdoms in that it alone is devoted purely to the Mahāyāna, without admixture of the Hīnayāna or competition from non-Buddhist religions like the Indian Brahmanism or the Chinese Confucianism and Taoism. Japan is the place indicated by the *Mahāprajñāpāramitā-sūtra* in its ancient prediction that, following the nirvāṇa of the Buddha, the Mahāyāna "perfection of wisdom" would spread from Jambudvīpa to the northeast. China may also be to the northeast, says Shiren, but China is only "largely pure with minor defects" (*daijun ji shōshi*); Japan is "purity itself" (*junko junsha*).[32]

Here we are clearly in a world of purity quite different from that imagined for the pure, sinified Zen master—a world so different that it seems to have led some in prewar Japan to read the *Genkō shakusho* as a Buddhist work of Japanese nationalism; even today it probably reminds us more of Nichiren's vision of a sacred teleology culminating in the East than any Zen story of Bodhidharma coming from the West.

Yet Bodhidharma did come from the West. If the *Genkō shakusho* section on the biographies of the founders of Japanese Buddhism ends with Eisai, it begins with Bodhidharma. The very first notice of the book is devoted to the First Patriarch and the venerable legend that he manifested himself in Japan and appeared as a starving beggar to Prince Shōtoku. The legend goes back to a story in the *Nihon shoki*; it developed as part of a complex set of traditions that associated Bodhidharma with the early Tendai movement in China and imagined Shōtoku as the incarnation of the Chinese Tendai patriarch Hui-ssu.[33] The symbolic significance of this legend at the opening of the *Genkō shakusho* can hardly be missed: the school of Bodhidharma is no new immigrant applying for a place among the old families of Japanese Buddhism; it is the most ancient Buddhism of the country, predating the transmission of the various schools—the religion of Shōtoku himself, the father of the country and first great patron of the church. The author of the *Genkō shakusho* did not miss this symbolic significance: elsewhere in his writings he repeats the claim that Bodhidharma was the founder of Japanese Zen; indeed, so invested was Shiren in this claim that he created a new annual ritual at Tōfukuji for the celebration of the Patriarch's advent.[34]

Finally, the new national Buddhism founded by Bodhidharma and Shōtoku provides Shiren with an ingenious solution to the dilemma for Zen apologetics posed by Gyōnen's sectarian historiography. By refiguring the tradition as a single saṅgha, the *Genkō shakusho* deftly sidesteps the issue of orthodoxy. By substituting the Chinese genres of biography, annals, and records for Gyōnen's organization by sectarian division, it largely obviates the need to define the sectarian status of Zen in Gyōnen's terms, either as an early branch of Tendai or as a recently arrived addition. With the dismissal of Gyōnen's list of eight schools as measure and limit of legitimacy, Zen need no longer argue its way from the margins of Japanese Buddhism onto that list; in effect, the schools themselves have become marginal to the global vision of a "nonsectarian" tradition with Zen at its center.

Such, for the most part, was the vision of Buddhism on the continent, where the old scholastic traditions had never been strongly institutionalized and the Zen lineages had come to dominate the ecclesiastical world of the Sung and Yüan. In fourteenth-century Japan, charged as it was with strong sectarian consciousness and competition, the turn to such a continental vision can be seen as a new, more aggressive approach to Zen apologetics and as testimony to the confidence of the Zen movement at the end of the Kamakura period. Shiren's model for a Zen "ecumenical hegemony" may never have been fully realized, but his confidence as it turned out was well warranted by the subsequent growth in the power of the *gozan* system under the Ashikaga. To this extent, his history is as much an accounting of the present as a recounting of the past. The *Genkō shakusho* sends a message to the Japanese Buddhist establishment on the eve of the Ashikaga takeover that times have changed, that the Zen school in the Genkō era has come of age, and that the game will no longer be played by the rules of the old order.

PART FOUR

Ashikaga Takauji and the Fourteenth-Century Dynastic Schism in Early Tokugawa Thought

I. J. MCMULLEN

MANY MODERN HISTORIANS of pre-Restoration Japan trace the origins of their discipline back to the Tokugawa period. Just as students of Japanese language and literature see the work of the great Tokugawa philologists such as Motoori Norinaga (1730–1801) or Fujitani Mitsue (1768–1823) as the founders of their subject, so Hayashi Razan (1583–1657) and Hayashi Gahō (1618–80), Arai Hakuseki (1657–1725), and the early Mito historians are viewed as the first practitioners of a recognizably modern historiography in Japan.[1] The grand achievements of these men and their successors in the period, already introduced to readers of English through the work, among others, of Herschel Webb, Kate Nakai, and, most recently, John Brownlee, attest to a flourishing of the muse of history in the Tokugawa period.[2] They, together with those who followed, achieved success in adapting Chinese historiographical models and acquiring a growing and cumulative sophistication in gathering and criticizing material and in rational analysis, periodization, and presentation. Nor were works such as the *Honchō tsugan* (Comprehensive Mirror of This Court, 1670), *Tokushi yoron* (A Reading of History, 1712), and the *Dai Nihon shi* (History of Great Japan, inaugurated 1657) isolated achievements. It is clear that a vast amount of thinking about the meaning of the past, both generally and in relation to particular periods, went on among intellectuals throughout the period. Analysis of history was an important mode whereby Tokugawa Japanese defined the nature of their own polity and society.

It is a truism that no history can be wholly objective. At the same time as the empirical discipline of history took root in Japan, whether consciously or not, Tokugawa thinkers shared a widespread, less disciplined, and logically incongruent tendency to project back into history the immediate concerns of their present. In the Tokugawa period, history was interpreted—often to modern eyes crudely manipulated—to support and legitimate a variety of ideological or political objectives such as the ascendancy of the samurai estate, Tokugawa dynastic rule itself, and the extension of Bakufu powers. Historically the most important legacy of this tendency was the tradition known as *taigi meibun* (great duty and names and status) or *kōkoku shikan* (imperial land view of history), an emperor-centered, nationalist ideology, constructed around the belief that Japan had enjoyed an unbroken line of imperial successions and intended to establish a cohesive polity to resist the national crisis precipitated by foreign threat and domestic decline.

There thus coexisted two readily identifiable contradictory tendencies in historical thought: cumulative breadth of sources and growing sophistication in the critical handling of historical materials on the one hand, and a sensitivity to contemporary issues and a sometimes shrill politicization on the other.[3] Both tendencies were part of the broader legacy of Tokugawa historians to their post-Restoration successors. The working out of the tension between them forms a theme in Japan's modern intellectual history. As is well known, this tension could erupt onto the stage of national affairs. Particular examples concerning fourteenth-century historiographical issues are the textbook controversy of 1911 surrounding the historiographical treatment of the Northern and Southern courts,[4] and the enforced resignation of the Minister of Trade and Industry, Nakajima Kumakichi, in 1934, the six hundredth anniversary of the Kenmu Restoration. Nakajima's offense had been to publish an article praising the qualities of Ashikaga Takauji, a man condemned as an antiimperial traitor in the nationalist historiography of the time.[5]

The fourteenth-century crisis was among the episodes of Japanese history that most challenged the imagination of thinking Japanese of the early Tokugawa period. One reason for this preoccupation may have been cultural. The narrative of the Kenmu Restoration was widely familiar through public recitations of what was, for contemporaries, the major historical source for the period, the warrior prose epic *Taiheiki* (Chronicle of Grand Pacification). Through the activities of *Taiheiki* reciters (*Taiheiki yomi*), this work had enjoyed growing popularity at least since the sixteenth century, and there had developed a cult of its major heroes, particularly Kusunoki Masashige (d. 1336). The *Taiheiki*, furthermore, seems to have been widely read as well as heard, more even than its greatest rival as a warrior epic, the earlier *Heike monogatari* (Tale of the Heike). The *Kokusho sōmokuroku* (National Bibliography) lists no fewer than twenty-five printed editions of the former in the years 1603–1703, as against eighteen for the latter.[6] Nor is this high level of interest surprising. The events themselves were dramatic and many of the actors possessed heroic characteristics. To a militarized society, the deeds of warriors were always interesting. The story also involved men whom the elite of the Tokugawa regime claimed as their own direct ancestors. Furthermore, the decline of Japan's first warrior regime, the dynastic schism, the brief and unsuccessful revival of direct imperial rule, and the reestablishment of warrior administration under the Ashikaga raised insistent questions concerning the nature of the Japanese polity, the legitimacy of governments, and the proper object of loyalty. Essentially, the events of the Kenmu Restoration recapitulated in a single brief episode the historical evolution of the Japanese state and the displacement of courtly by warrior political control. Questions of regional and cultural allegiance may also have been suggested, since the *Taiheiki* narrative often contrasted the Kyoto court with its enemies, the "eastern warriors."

Tokugawa historians and thinkers, therefore, devoted considerable attention to the fourteenth century and the events surrounding its central episode, the Kenmu Restoration. Rather than attempt a general survey of ground that is already familiar, however, this essay will restrict itself to an exploration of the early Tokugawa origins of two contrasting approaches to this episode, as exemplified in the thought of two influential Confucian thinkers, Asami Keisai (1652–1711) and Yamaga Sokō (1622–85). Neither of these men is normally identified primarily as a major historian. Sokō's *Buke jiki* (Encyclopedia of the Warrior Houses, 1673), it is true, is an important work, of which it has been claimed that it was the first historical work in Japan to make use of warlord household documents for historical research.[7] Keisai's major work in this field, his *Seiken igen* (Last Testaments of Calm Self-Sacrifice), was a scissors-and-paste compilation of no great technical originality. Yet both men thought interestingly about the fourteenth-century crisis, and their views illuminate the historical roots and ideologi-

cal background to the two trends in Tokugawa-period historiography identified above. Neither thinker exemplified either approach in a pure form.
In what follows, it is the underlying approach to history that provides the
main focus, rather than the details or forms of historiographical practice.
It is argued that Asami Keisai was the author of a synthesis of the historical
thought of two Chinese neo-Confucian thinkers, Ssu-ma Kuang and Chu
Hsi, which was destined to be a seminal influence in the formation of *taigi
meibun* ideology. Yamaga Sokō, by contrast, achieved a greater detachment
from the neo-Confucian tradition and adopted an approach that owed
more to indigenous sources and might be termed empirical and realist.

Japanese thinkers of the early Tokugawa period, who pondered the significance of the dynastic schism, the Kenmu Restoration, and the activities
of Ashikaga Takauji, evolved their views in response to a complex variety
of influences. First, as Confucian scholars, many of them tended to survey
the period through the lenses of the Chinese Confucian historiographical
tradition, of which they were students. This tradition provided many of
their basic ideas on the function of history. It was not, however, a homogeneous tradition, but accommodated divergent assumptions on political
and moral conduct. Of the two thinkers under review, Asami Keisai was
particularly and directly influenced by Sung neo-Confucian historians,
while Yamaga Sokō's work seems largely to ignore them. But Tokugawa
thinkers also necessarily learned of the incidents themselves through indigenous Japanese accounts. Of these, the most important was the *Taiheiki*
itself, followed by the *Jinnō shōtōki* (A Chronicle of Gods and Sovereigns)
by the Nambokuchō loyalist courtier and general, Kitabatake Chikafusa
(1293–1354). These works, too, are informed by different assumptions concerning the legitimacy and exercise of power. This overall heterogeneity
was one factor that encouraged a corresponding variety in the thinking of
Tokugawa scholars. To understand the thought of Keisai and Sokō, it is
first necessary to glance at the Chinese and Japanese sources on which they
drew. In the case of Keisai, in particular, because the influence of the Sung
dynasty historians Ssu-ma Kuang (1019–86) and Chu Hsi (1130–1200) is
so important, it is from an account of their understanding of history that
exploration of his views on the fourteenth century must begin.[8]

CHINESE INFLUENCES: SSU-MA KUANG AND CHU HSI

Ssu-ma Kuang was the author of the *Tzu chih t'ung chien* (Comprehensive
Mirror for Aid in Government),[9] a massive work of history in 294 *chüan*

covering 1,362 years from 403 B.C. to A.D. 959 that took nineteen years to complete. The main narrative drew on the standard dynastic histories, supplemented by 222 less formal sources. The work was compiled from existing narratives, but Ssu-ma also offered his own analyses in special comments. It is the model of the political order developed in these comments that most influenced Keisai. Chu Hsi initiated an immensely influential redaction of Ssu-ma's work under the title, *T'ung-chien kang-mu* (Outline and Details of the *Comprehensive Mirror*), in fifty-nine *chüan*.[10] His procedure was to create his own headings (*kang*), which, through choice of vocabulary specified in his *fan li* (general principles), reflected his own moral judgments, and to amplify them with material (*mu*) taken from Ssu-ma's text. The resulting clarity of moral judgment particularly aroused the admiration of Keisai.

Ssu-ma and Chu both accepted the traditional Chinese belief that the purpose of history was didactic and "remonstrative": it was the function of the historian to compile history according to Confucian normative assumptions on political and moral behavior, noting departures so as to provide a "mirror" for the guidance of subsequent generations. They also shared an interest in the question of legitimacy in political control, and with that most problematic of all episodes in Chinese history, the replacement of one dynasty by another. The question here was how the Confucian imperative to loyalty to an established dynasty could legitimately be broken and the dynasty overthrown. Normally, in Confucian thinking, political power was legitimately transferred between one dynasty and another when "Heaven," believed by many Confucians to refract the condition of the people,[11] lost confidence in one dynastic lineage and intervened, through the course of events, to select another.[12] The task of the historian was to identify, through the conventions of historiographical practice, which constituted legitimate dynastic successions and which acts of usurpation. Here was a field of inquiry to which Tokugawa Japanese, reviewing the history of dynastic schism in fourteenth-century Japan, were obviously sensitive.

While Ssu-ma and Chu would have agreed on the central purposes of writing history, they differed in certain important basic assumptions and emphasis over the criteria for judging legitimacy. Ssu-ma Kuang, as a recent study by Peter Bol has shown, was an intensely conservative historian.[13] He was a member of an established official family, and himself inherited rank through the *yin* system of hereditary privilege,[14] familiar to students of Japanese history in its Japanese adaptation as the *on'i* system employed to transmit court rank among the ancient court nobility.

By Northern Sung times, however, the old aristocratic order was breaking down. Ssu-ma wrote against the background of "pressure from newer men," but believed "Government was to be the enterprise of an existing national elite. It should not try to create a new elite."[15] His position was the conservative one that order could only be preserved if men adhered to their existing functions within the polity. The role of the emperor was to preserve the established structure.[16] This did not, however, mean absolutist imperial control over administration.[17] Ssu-ma's concern was to emphasize the formal criteria of lineage and the "so-called unconditional preservation of status of ruler-subject relationships with the exception of extremely special cases."[18] The function of the ruler was to legitimate and maintain the status hierarchy of society. As Ssu-ma expressed it in one of the best-known editorial insertions in his work: "In the office of the Son of Heaven, there is nothing as important as enacting ritual. With regard to enacting that ritual, there is nothing as important as preserving status (*fĕn*; Jap. *bun*). With regard to preserving status there is nothing as important as rectifying names (*ming*; Jap. *mei*)."[19] Failure to "preserve status" and "rectify names" — in other words, failure to maintain the hereditary status order of society — precipitated political and social disintegration.

Ssu-ma began his history of China in the Chou dynasty from the fifth century B.C., where the *Tso chuan* (Commentary of Tso), a canonical commentary on the *Ch'un ch'iu* (Spring and Autumn Annals) of Confucius himself, had broken off, with the wrongful division of the feudal state of Chin into three fiefs, each to be ruled by a rear-vassal of the Chin lord. This event held a particularly cautionary significance because it had been delinquently permitted by the Chou sovereign. It was an act that violated the "name and status" of the feudal order that had been maintained in the dynasty up until that time, and its consequences for China were destructive:

Truly the ritual [relationship] between ruler and subject was destroyed at this point. Thereafter, the realm was transformed into an age of struggle based on cleverness and strength. It was made impossible even for feudal princes who were known to inherit the blood of sagely kings or worthy princes to preserve their states. As a further result, the lives of the people were almost completely destroyed.[20]

However weak royal political power, therefore, its function must remain to legitimate and conserve the existing formal, hereditary status order. "The positions of ruler and subject," Ssu-ma wrote, "like the relationship between Heaven and Earth, cannot be exchanged. . . . Even when the power of the royal house declined, [Confucius in writing the *Ch'un ch'iu*] placed it above the feudal princes."[21] Significantly, Ssu-ma criticized the Mencian, contingent view of sovereignty, according to which a delinquent, inhumane sovereign might morally be overthrown by his subjects.[22] This aspect of Ssu-ma's thought, his emphasis on rigid adherence to existing structures of status however depleted of actual power, explains why he is characterized as "conservative." It was this rigidity that was to appeal most to Keisai.

In Chu Hsi, by contrast, the reflexes of the moralist seem to have predominated over those of the historian. Chu condemned the style of scholarship that "hold[s] that . . . [Ssu-ma] Ch'ien and [Pan] Ku are superior to Confucius."[23] The *T'ung-chien kang-mu* placed greater emphasis on the "correctness" of the ruler—that is, on his personal moral qualifications to rule—than on the formal, conservative criteria adopted by Ssu-ma Kuang. This position was consistent with Chu's more general view that the moral cultivation of the individual, particularly that of the ruler, was the basis of social order. Thus Chu Hsi accepted the Mencian argument that though the office of emperor should normally be hereditary, moral delinquency disqualified him for rule and justified his overthrow.[24]

This difference in emphasis between the two men is associated with selection of different lines of dynastic legitimacy in their respective accounts of Chinese history. In the period of disunion following the collapse of the Han dynasty (202 B.C.–A.D. 220), Ssu-ma Kuang had structured his chronicle through the Wei dynasty (220–265), on the grounds that that dynasty had actually controlled most of the territory of China and that it was expedient for the historian to recognize this fact when structuring his work.[25] Chu, however, chose, not the Wei, but the outlying Shu Han (221–264), founded by Liu Pei (162–223), a genealogical descendent of the Han emperor Ching ti (r. 156–140 B.C.). It has been suggested that Chu made this choice on the grounds that he regarded Ts'ao P'i (188–227), the founder of the Wei, as a usurper and thus morally disqualified to succeed the Han.[26] Another consideration was surely that Liu Pei, in contrast to Ts'ao P'i, was genealogically and thus "legitimately" descended from the Han imperial house.[27] To Japanese such as Keisai, schooled in the belief that their own imperial house had enjoyed an unbroken lineage, Chu's position had an obvious appeal.

In addition to his views on the legitimacy of specific dynasties, Chu influenced the historical thought of such neo-Confucians as Keisai, no less importantly, through his more general ideas, particularly on moral cultivation. The great achievement of the neo-Confucian synthesis, of which he was the main author, was to find a new and more cogent metaphysical basis for Confucian moral imperatives, and a new methodology of self-cultivation. In the neo-Confucian revival, the charge to the individual student of the tradition was clear. He must rigorously know and act out, or "exhaust" (Chin. *ch'iung*; Jap. *kyū*), the moral principles believed to inhere in the world of appearances. These principles were accessible also in the record of the past. Thus, since all knowledge was moral knowledge, neo-Confucian history itself tended to become a retrospective branch of morality.

JINNŌ SHŌTŌKI AND TAIHEIKI

Keisai's discussions of history demonstrate familiarity with and influence from the historical writings of both Ssu-ma Kuang and Chu Hsi. Ssu-ma Kuang, however, influenced his view of the fourteenth-century crisis not only directly through the *Tzu-chih t'ung chien*, but indirectly through his influence on the source that seems most to have determined Keisai's perception of the episode, the *Jinnō shōtōki*. There is some evidence to suggest that the ideas of both Ssu-ma Kuang and Chu Hsi were already known to the leading figures in the Kenmu Restoration, chiefly through the activities of the monk Gen'e (d. 1350). According to *Sekiso shōsoku* (Letters and Correspondence), a work attributed to Ichijō Kanera (1402–81), Gen'e is claimed to have taught both Sung neo-Confucianism to Go-Daigo himself and Ssu-ma's *Tzu-chih t'ung-chien* to Kitabatake Chikafusa.[28] If indeed Gen'e transmitted both these approaches, it was that of Ssu-ma Kuang that particularly influenced Kitabatake Chikafusa's *Jinnō shōtōki*.[29] Ssu-ma and Chikafusa, in fact, shared a common orientation. Like Ssu-ma in the eleventh century, Chikafusa in the fourteenth was a member of a privileged hereditary elite confronted with the slow unraveling of an order of inherited status and prestige. In the Northern Sung, however, the new pressures were accommodated within the established framework of bureaucratic government and a primarily civil state structure. In medieval Japan, by contrast, they came much more radically from outside the civil polity, from an ascendant military estate which was perceived by the old aristocracy as usurping the functions of governance.

Like Ssu-ma, Chikafusa expressed his reaction to this situation with a work of history. In formal historiographical terms, *Jinnō shōtōki* bears little resemblance to Ssu-ma's monumental work. It is relatively short, consisting of three parts, and was written under conditions of deprivation, when its author was at Oda Castle, with access only to an imperial genealogy.[30] The work presents a framework of Japanese imperial reigns, but includes also more discursive passages. Here, the author, like Ssu-ma Kuang, developed a highly conservative view of society.[31] His work is in effect a defense of the imperial and oligarchic order of the late Heian period. Its author believed that the legitimate rulers of Japan were determined theocratically and genealogically by the intervention of the Shinto gods in human society. These rulers were the emperors, assisted by the Fujiwara, whose lineage enjoyed a position coeval with the imperial family and the Murakami Genji, from whom Chikafusa himself was descended.[32] The warriors had a legitimate and beneficent role within this scheme as maintainers of order. But problems arose when, as with the Taira, they had intruded into the civil aristocracy, insubordinately exceeding their proper status in life. This had precipitated disorder. "The positions of high and low are fixed," and "it is the greatest of offenses for social inferiors to succeed their superiors." [33] In this context, loyalty, a particularistic submission to the status quo, was an absolute imperative;[34] "name" and "status" must remain inviolable. Following Ssu-ma Kuang, Chikafusa quoted words attributed to Confucius in the *Tso chuan*: "It is only peculiar articles of use, and name, which cannot be granted [to other than those to whom they belong];—to them a ruler has particularly to attend. It is by [the right use of] name that he secures the confidence of [the people]." [35] Chikafusa's thought thus appears a synthesis of the preservation of "name and status" of Ssu-ma Kuang with Shinto theocratic beliefs in the inviolability of the imperial lineage. For him, as for Ssu-ma, it was only through the preservation of traditional status relationships that social disorder and upheaval could be avoided. He, too, may justifiably be called conservative.

The second major source for the period to which Keisai alluded, the *Taiheiki*, belongs to a different genre from that of *Jinnō shōtōki*. Where the latter has been described as a political tract, the former is in the established tradition of *gunki monogatari* (warrior tales), part historical record, part work of epic literature. It is a long work of forty *kan*, possibly by several hands, and is episodic in structure, consisting of successive incidents under descriptive headings. In some respects, it is guided by assumptions similar to those of the *Jinnō shōtōki*. It, too, assumes that the emperors are the theocratically ordained rulers of Japan. But it is less coherent ideologically and implicitly accepts views on the exercise of political power that Ssu-ma Kuang and Kitabatake Chikafusa would have rejected. Its main assumption in that respect seems to be that failures in moral rectitude, delinquency, or indulgence by rulers deprive them of the right to legitimate exercise of power. This is, in effect, a version of the Mencian view of sovereignty that Ssu-ma Kuang had rejected. Thus in Japan, with decline in the quality of imperial rule, the emperors had been replaced as rulers and maintainers of order by the Hōjō, who had flourished and ruled effectively in the interests of the people for some generations. Latterly, however, the fourteenth Hōjō regent, Takatoki (r. 1316–33), had behaved indulgently. His rule was implicitly compared with that of the T'ang emperor Hsuan tsung (r. 712–56),[36] whose final decade as emperor had archetypically exemplified defective imperial rule. A complex of forces, the operation of the principles of the *I ching* (Book of Changes), Buddhist karma, the Confucian mandate of Heaven, had combined to destroy the Hōjō administration. There is little sense, however, that in assuming power originally the Hōjō had acted with insubordination. Their only act of hubris seems to have been banishing an emperor, and their earlier rule was looked back to with nostalgia in the *Taiheiki* itself. Warriors thus had a rightful place in the polity, though it was contingent upon responsible exercise of power. This essentially functional, realist approach applied also to the imperial lineage. In the Kenmu Restoration, Go-Daigo (r. 1318–39) attracted support because at first he seemed the more virtuous political authority, not simply because he was the emperor; conversely, it was his ineffectual administration that led eventually to the restoration of warrior rule. The concept here that legitimacy in the exercise of power derives from moral and administrative competence may be identified as a kind of incipient realism. It was clearly a way of explaining, and therefore implicitly justifying, the expanding role of the warriors in the Japanese polity.

The authors of the *Taiheiki* seem, however, less interested in questions of political legitimacy than in the professional ethos of the warrior and his conduct in battle. Loyalty is an important concern, but it is primarily a parochial, professional military loyalty on the battlefield, rather than political loyalty. Loyalty may be the highest value for warriors, but the ultimate political ends to which it is extended are not necessarily subject to searching scrutiny or constraint. There could be exemplary men on both court and warrior sides. Status, as in the *Jinnō shōtōki*, is certainly a matter of concern, but it seems less assymetrically distributed between court and warriors than in Chikafusa's work, and more to reflect the realities of power. The main concern in the *Taiheiki* is that high-status warriors should not demean themselves by fighting with unworthy opponents or allow themselves to be killed by those of inferior status.

The *Jinnō shōtōki* and *Taiheiki* thus represent divergent ideological positions, particularly on the criteria for the legitimate exercise of political power. Despite its gestures in the direction of the view that the achievement of virtue was necessary for effective rule,[37] the *Jinnō shōtōki* remains a text dedicated to deeply particularistic and ascriptive norms of social and political order, like those upheld in Ssu-ma Kuang's *Tzu-chih t'ung-chien*. It promotes a thoroughly conservative view of society, a true preservation or restoration of Japan's ancient order of status and privilege. The *Taiheiki*, by contrast, has moved further in the direction of adapting ideologically to the warrior political ascendancy. It sees achievement as a legitimate basis for the exercise of political power. In its view, achievement transcended inherited status, and it may thus be claimed as more universalistic. Though the view of political legitimacy implicit in the *Taiheiki* is closer to Chu's "moralism" than to the "conservative" thought of Ssu-ma Kuang, its acceptance of the fact of warrior ascendancy may perhaps be described as incipiently "realist."

THE HISTORICAL THOUGHT OF ASAMI KEISAI

The foregoing summary suggests that a seventeenth-century Japanese neo-Confucian scholar seeking to inform himself of the fourteenth-century crisis would be confronted with a variety of approaches implicit in the work of his Chinese mentors and the indigenous material relating to the period. It is argued here that Keisai, although he professed adherence to Chu Hsi's moralistic understanding of history, was deeply influenced also by the conservative approach of both Ssu-ma Kuang, whose work he criticized, and Kitabatake Chikafusa, of whom he expressed approval. Keisai's view of the fourteenth-century crisis may, in fact, be characterized as a synthesis of Chu Hsi moral rigorism with the conservative understanding of history of Ssu-ma and Chikafusa. Yamaga Sokō, on the other hand, was to be closer to the *Taiheiki*.

Asami Keisai was a first-generation disciple of the Chu Hsi neo-Confucian scholar Yamazaki Ansai (1618–82) and a member of Ansai's influential Kimon school. A commoner and a native of the Kansai, Keisai brought to the study and practice of neo-Confucianism a peculiar intensity. The Confucian Way was universal, changeless across time and space.[38] It was not, however, the aspect of the Way as a substantial unity or any mystical satisfaction to be derived from it that attracted Keisai. Rather, it was the exigencies that arose in observing discrete moral imperatives that commanded his attention. For him, as for his teacher, Yamazaki Ansai, these imperatives were ordered in a hierarchy, with the duty owed by a subject or vassal to his ruler or lord occupying first place, before the filial duty owed by a son to his father. Here was an ordering that, in the contemporary perception, reversed the priority accorded to the father-son relationship by Chu Hsi himself.[39] Keisai particularly stressed *taigi* (the greater righteousness), the duty owed by a subject to the ruler of his country, together with the preservation of "name and status," much in the manner of Ssu-ma Kuang himself. This duty transcended other moral claims. Keisai infused the ruler-subject relationship with the absolute value and emotional intensity more usually reserved in traditional Confucian thought for that between father and son. The loyalty required by *taigi* was not abject or uncritical, though Keisai, a man much interested in military matters, admired such loyalty on the battlefield.[40] It was, rather, a reasoned grasp of moral duty achieved only after intense and sustained study and thought, uninfluenced by prejudice, temperament, or jumping to conclusions.[41] Such study was based on the Chu Hsi neo-Confucian technique of "exhaustion of principle" (*ch'iung li*, Jap. *kyūri*), whereby, through reading and thought, the student identified and acted out the unchanging moral principles believed to inhere in the world of appearances.[42] This loyalty, Keisai insisted, was properly directed to the legitimate ruler of a man's country; and legitimacy, in its turn, for Keisai as for Ssu-ma Kuang, was based on genealogical descent rather than on any other criterion such as virtue.[43] In this way, Keisai substituted his own brand of ethical particularism for the universalism that was an aspect of mainstream Confucian moral and political thought.

Keisai was a voracious student of history. His public predelection among historians was for Chu Hsi. He is said to have read Chu's *T'ung-chien kang-mu* forty-two times.[44] His belief in unchanging and inflexible loyalty combined with his faith in the Chu Hsi view of individual morality as the key to social order led him inexorably to a reductionist theory of history. According to this view, the past actions of men were judged with reference to their conformity or departure from the single, unchanging principle of *taigi*. Inevitably, this meant a history that was rigid and essentially ahistorical, a branch of morality. Keisai's own major historical work, *Seiken igen*, completed in 1687, was little more than an anthology of Chinese exemplars of loyalty compiled from Chinese sources. Keisai, however, believed explicitly that works of history, such as Confucius's *Ch'un ch'iu* and Chu Hsi's *T'ung-chien kang-mu*, were "dedicated to the same purpose" as moral treatises. He intended *Seiken igen* to be not so much a work of history as a supplement to the *Hsiao hsueh* (Lesser Learning) of Chu

Hsi, a moral primer for children.⁴⁵ In Keisai, the moralist vanquished the historian; little or no difference was admitted between past and present, China and Japan, no concession made to variations in human experience, historical evolution, or differences in societies across time or space.

This fiercely reductionist view of history is present in Keisai's discussions of the principles of historiography, of particular historical episodes, and the actions of historical individuals. In his *Satsuroku* (Collected Notes, preface, 1706), Keisai adopted a well-worn distinction between three methods of writing history: *hennen* (chronological annals), which was structured on "continuity through years, months, and the sexagenary cycle," like Confucius's *Ch'un ch'iu* or Chu Hsi's *T'ung-chien kang-mu*; *kiden* (biographies), individualized biographical accounts, such as included in the *Shih chi* (Records of the Historian) or the *Han shu* (History of the [Former] Han); and *kiroku* or *jiki* (monographs), discrete accounts of particular subjects, such as the *Shu ching* (Book of documents), *Kuo yü* (Narratives of the states), or *Chan kuo tsê* (Intrigues of the Warring States).⁴⁶ Of these methods, Keisai was in no doubt that it was the *hennen* that best illumined the course of history. Confucius's use of this method in his coverage of 242 years of Chinese history in the *Ch'un ch'iu* had revealed "the three bonds (*sangō*—the relationships between ruler and subject, father and son, and husband and wife) resounding clearly through the realm to later ages, like the sun and the moon, thunder and lightning."⁴⁷ This preference was determined, presumably, because the *hennen* format was transdynastic, and therefore exposed the critical transitions between dynasties or regimes to the moral scrutiny of the chronicler. Keisai quoted Chu Hsi: "After the method of annual compilation [was abandoned], it [became] difficult to discern the sequence of order and disorder or flourishing and decline."⁴⁸ Between Ssu-ma Kuang and Chu Hsi, Keisai preferred the latter, the moralist over the conservative historian. Ssu-ma had been provided with access to imperial libraries, "but because [he] had not been previously enlightened in the discipline of order and disorder and name and status, [Ssu-ma] made a great many mistakes over the correct successions." Chu Hsi had, therefore, made a recension of the work, and "the sequence of annual compilation was clarified, the facts were detailed, right and wrong, success and failure, the name and status of the three bonds and five norms were none omitted. [The *T'ung-chien kang-mu*] deserves the description of the [most] valuable book in the realm, past or present."⁴⁹

Turning to his own country, Keisai found that the *Nihon shoki* (Chronicles of Japan, 720), *Shoku-Nihongi* (Chronicle of Japan Continued, 797), and *Nihon kōki* (Later Chronicle of Japan, 840) were in the *hennen* style, so that "the historical sequence of successive ages in our country is clear, and later generations admire them." Thereafter, historiography had declined:

Coming down to the *Hōgen* and *Heiji* [*monogatari*] (Tales of the Hōgen and Heiji, year periods), *Genpei seisuiki* (Rise and Fall of the Minamoto and Taira), *Taiheiki*, and the like, they are basically written in the monograph style, and thus though the chronological framework seems apparent, because they are not based on the annual compilation (*hennen*) style, sequences are difficult to see and linkages between events, unless the reader devotes much care to mental connections and linkages, are difficult to perceive. . . . It is because [the above-mentioned works] are all unillumined over the discipline of name and status, that they therefore all concentrate on material for reading for amusement, rather than on the sequence of a true record.[50]

Thus, for Keisai, the major historical source for the fourteenth century, the *Taiheiki*, was deficient, because its structure was thematic rather than chronological. The *Jinnō shōtōki*, by contrast, followed a chronological framework of imperial reigns, and was omitted from Keisai's list of inadequate works. More recently written *hennen*-style histories, such as the *Ōdai ichiran* (Conspectus of Royal Reigns, 1652) of Hayashi Gahō, and the *Nihon tsūki* (Comprehensive Record of Japan) of Nagai Teishū (1698), were an improvement over such works as the *Taiheiki*, but they all contained errors. Ultimately, their authors had not mastered the "discipline of name and status."[51]

THE DEMONIZATION OF TAKAUJI

Keisai found the *Taiheiki* narrative of the dynastic schism and the Kenmu Restoration particularly deficient in respect of "names and status." Its section headings (*mokuroku*), he maintained, seriously violated the "name and status of the three bonds and five relationships." If the headings were revised, the work could be made to achieve the same purpose as Chu Hsi's *T'ung chien kang-mu*. Keisai, no doubt inspired by Chu's own redaction activity, had hoped to undertake this task himself, but "I still have not yet had the leisure to take up my brush."[52] An example of the *Taiheiki*'s failings was its treatment of the fourteenth-century dynastic schism. Here, Keisai declared his preference for the legitimacy of the Southern Court: "[The *Taiheiki* and other such works] are not clearly based on the legitimate succession of the Southern Court, nor are circumstances in Kyoto written basically from the point of view of the Southern Court."[53] Keisai does not state the reasons for this choice. It may, however, be surmised, as has been suggested of his teacher Yamazaki Ansai, that he was influenced by Chu Hsi's preference for the Shu Han court. Indeed, the circumstances of the Shu Han, a genealogically legitimate dynasty on the periphery of the Chinese world, could be regarded as similar to those of Go-Daigo's Southern Court in the mountains of Yoshino.[54]

By contrast to his critical attitude to the *Taiheiki*, Keisai strongly approved of the *Jinnō shōtōki*'s view of the Southern Court as perpetuating the correct succession and its identification of Takauji as a rebel.[55] This, as Keisai put it, was "an outstanding opinion and the pattern for ten thousand generations."[56] But this judgment did not necessitate ruthlessly reordering history from a retrospective vantage point. Chu Hsi himself, Keisai argued, had still referred even to such a regicide and parricide as Sui Yang ti (r. 605–18) as "emperor," implicitly accepting his *de facto* rulership over China, but had nonetheless clarified his guilt and made him "a mirror for ten thousand generations."[57] In the same way, it had been correct for Chikafusa to identify the Southern Court as legitimate and Takauji as a traitorous rebel, even though implicitly it had to be accepted that sovereignty had subsequently reverted to the Northern line.[58] In this way, Keisai was relieved of the uncomfortable necessity of declaring the emperors of his own time, who were descended from the Northern Court and had appointed the Tokugawa as shoguns, to be illegitimate.

Takauji's treacherous treatment of Go-Daigo may have put Keisai in mind of the conduct of Ts'ao Ts'ao (155–220), traditionally one of the miscreants of Chinese history, in forcing the last emperor of the Eastern Han, Hsien ti (r. 190–220), off the throne.[59] Furthermore, Takauji had been a long-term disruptive influence in Japanese history, and Keisai seems to have been in the forefront of the movement to demonize him in the early Tokugawa:

Takauji despised the emperor and, for private purposes, attacked and destroyed [Nitta] Yoshisada, who was of the same [Genji] clan. For a while, he was strong and stole the title of shogun. However, during the fifteen [Ashikaga] reigns, not one reign achieved a proper governance. They were all defied and killed by rebellious vassals and patricidal sons. With the disturbances of the Ōnin (1467–69) and Meitoku (1390–94) [year periods], they became like the last lingering fruits on a [dying] tree. That they were in the end destroyed by Nobunaga of the Heishi should be described as no accident in the response of the Mandate of Heaven. During this time, they amused themselves mainly with the tea ceremony and with *sarugaku* [monkey dances]. A state of affairs prevailed in which there was a dearth of actions, edicts, or morals bearing any resemblance to loyalty or filial piety. The Akamatsu and others, too, turned their backs on the Son of Heaven, and, after they joined Takauji, their descendants emulated his morals, and perpetuated internecine murders. As a result of the calamities of murders and revolts by rulers and subjects, they are now without issue. In the whole family, there was not one who lived and died by loyalty.[60]

Keisai insisted that the historical record must not underplay Takauji's guilt. He expressed his indignation against the wording used in such works nearer his own time as the *Shinchō ki* (Record of Nobunaga, c. 1600) of Ōta Gyūichi (1527–1610?) to describe Takauji's actions:

It . . . says [in the *Shinchō ki*] that "when Takauji grew in power and his minor acts of unrighteousness became manifest, [the emperor] issued orders to [Nitta] Yoshisada and attacked him." What does it mean by "minor acts of unrighteousness"? This sort of thing consistently violates the great rule. If Takauji's unrighteousness is called "minor," then there would be no one who is [truly] unrighteous. The countless records compiled since the *Genpei seisuiki* and *Taiheiki* differ little among themselves. Because they are all compiled by men ignorant of anything beyond conventional discussions of righteousness and prestigious martial deeds, they never make clear judgments.[61]

Another offender was the *Hōjō kudaiki* (Record of the Nine reigns [under] the Hōjō, date and authorship unknown): "In the headings of the recent book, the *Hōjō kudaiki*, we have 'The emperor Go-Daigo's rebellion.' No one reading this has censured or refuted this [wording]. This proves the frequent obfuscation of the discipline of the three bonds and five constants."[62] Keisai's opprobrium extended beyond Takauji himself to Ashikaga rear-vassals who had been so purblind as to follow him in his immoral cause. In his *Chūkō ruisetsu* (Classified Views on Loyalty and Filial Piety), a work devoted to analysis of the casuistical problem posed by the conflict between loyalty and filial piety, Keisai commended the Ashikaga vassal Ishidō Uma no Kami for reporting the defection of his father from the Ashikaga side, but condemned him for "the extremity of delusion over the greater righteousness," for serving Takauji, a betrayer of the imperial cause.[63]

The demonization of Takauji opened the way to approval of the moral conduct of their opponents, the Nitta, claimed to be the progenitors of the Tokugawa line, for in spite of the vehemence of his pro-emperor rhetoric, Keisai was not inclined to challenge the Tokugawa status quo:

In the *Taiheiki*, there isn't the slightest cause for anxiety over the conduct of any of the gentlemen who bear the name of Nitta. Those designated as the Prince's allies or the government army were all like this. Even though Takauji turned his back on the administration [of the emperor], and, exploiting a power vacuum, perpetrated the evil of his own brigandage and the whole Nitta kindred almost perished, ultimately the perfection of their loyalty was not rejected by the Mandate of Heaven nor did it disappear from men's minds. So, in the end, Lord Ieyasu arose, honored the Son of Heaven, pacified all sides, established the lineages of the various houses, heard lectures from [Fujiwara] Seika, even while busy with military duties, exhaustively studied and mastered books on administration, appointed the Hayashi as his Confucian officials, and, furthermore, established and observed the *sekiten* [sacrificial] ritual to Confucius.[64]

Thus while the founders of earlier military regimes had been scheming usurpers,[65] the Tokugawa bore an unexceptionable moral inheritance. Nor could the foremost exemplars of loyalty in the *Taiheiki*, the Kusunoki, be omitted from the roll of honor. "There was not one of them," Keisai wrote, "who was not sound in his aspiration to loyalty."[66]

What lies behind Keisai's enthusiasm for Chu Hsi's *T'ung-chien kang-mu* and the intense commitment to imperial loyalism so evident in his review of fourteenth-century history? It is clear, first, that it is a synthesis of different elements. In spite of Keisai's claim to loyalty to the teachings of Chu Hsi and his explicit preference for the *T'ung-chien kang-mu* over Ssu-ma's *Tzu-chih t'ung-chien*, his conservative view of history owes quite as much, or more, to Ssu-ma Kuang and his views on "name and status." It was Ssu-ma, rather than Chu, who supplied Keisai with his main rhetorical concepts. As Professor Bitō Masahide has pointed out, the concept of "name and status," ubiquitous in Keisai's thought, is characteristic of Ssu-ma rather than of Chu, who "mentions it only extremely rarely."[67] The contribution of Chu Hsi neo-Confucianism to Keisai's synthesis was that its techniques of moral cultivation, especially the "exhaustion of principle," added an important authority and metaphysical depth to the imperative to loyalty, particularly when interpreted with Keisai's relentless rigorism. Keisai's loyalism also seems clearly formed by his reading of the *Jinnō shōtōki*, and, though he himself did not belong to the Shintoist branch of the Kimon school, by the indigenous views on the divine descent of the imperial lineage prominent in that text. This combination of moral rigorism and conservative political reflexes resulted in an ideology that was undeniably both potent and inflexible.

It is possible to suggest other influences in Keisai's thinking. The fact that he was a commoner and a longtime resident of Kyoto may have played a part. That city was still the seat of the imperial lineage, but had declined in political importance under the Tokugawa regime, while eastern Japan, referred to sometimes pejoratively in the *Taiheiki*, had grown in power and importance. It is possible also to cite structural features of Japanese society, such as the relative weakness of familial values, which facilitated the elevation of loyalty to the head of the hierarchy of moral imperatives in Keisai's mind.[68] Perhaps most important, he must have shared the fear of disorder adduced by H. Paul Varley as a cause of the disfavor in which Takauji was held in the Tokugawa period. Varley argues that Takauji's "new historical unpopularity" derived from the perception that he was responsible for the disorder of the Sengoku period.[69] Keisai's extended indictment of Ashikaga misrule quoted above suggests that, for him, too, fear of civil disorder lay behind his opprobium of the Ashikaga.

Unlike Chikafusa, with whom at the formal level his ideas on the focus of loyalty shared much, Keisai was not interested in preserving an oligarchy, nor did he seek to restore a vanishing political and social order. He lived in a different historical milieu from the fourteenth century, and his ideas were directed to a different end. He saw himself as encouraging samurai spirit,[70] and one of his objectives was to inculcate a sense of moral responsibility far more widely than Chikafusa could ever have entertained, morally to enfranchise, metaphorically speaking, a whole new stratum of society. It is possible that as a resident and teacher in Kyoto, he sought to impose a moral discipline also on the lives of city dwellers. His debt to Ssu-ma Kuang and Kitabatake Chikafusa demonstrates how ideas from one historical context can reemerge and regain purchase in another quite different historical setting. In some measure, this was facilitated precisely by the conservative, ahistorical nature of the ideas themselves.

AN ALTERNATIVE VIEW: YAMAGA SOKŌ

Keisai's moral and historical thought owed much of its intensity to his belief in the Chu Hsi system of self-cultivation, whose methodological assumption was that the moral regeneration of the individual held the key to social and political order. Chu's system led, logically, to views that were basically ahistorical; all that was necessary for the achievement of the ideal society was for all individuals to act out unchanging moral principles in their lives. The chief function of history was merely to chronicle their successes or failures in this respect. Alternatives to Chu Hsi's ideas had, however, already been explored in several quarters in Japan when Keisai formed his ideas in the 1680s. As might be expected, the challenge to the belief in the centrality of an objective morality facilitated the development of different approaches to history.

One of the first to express doubts about the Chu Hsi world view in Tokugawa Japan had been the samurai thinker Yamaga Sokō. Sokō had studied the writings of the Sung philosophers during his youth, but felt that their "techniques of preserving respect and quiet sitting" inclined him to become "depressed" and therefore sought to return to a more direct relationship with the early founders of the Confucian tradition.[71] Like his contemporaries, the Bakufu official historians Hayashi Razan and Hayashi Gahō or later samurai historians such as Arai Hakuseki, Sokō was, of course, concerned to justify the permanent political ascendancy of his own samurai estate. Sokō's view of warrior rule, the fourteenth-century schism, and the Kenmu Restoration is to be found in the survey of Japanese history that makes up the first three chapters of his encyclopedic compilation of warrior history, genealogy, and institutions, the fifty-eight–chapter *Buke jiki* (1673).[72] In this survey, he placed an emphasis, inconceivable in a thinker like Keisai, on the effective exercise of political power, military force, institutions, and law. Sokō accepted the Shinto belief in Japan as the "divine country," a land sacralized and protected by Shinto deities, with an inviolable imperial lineage. But, as a samurai himself, he did not subscribe to the conservative view that divine descent necessarily entitled the imperial lineage to remain politically powerful indefinitely. Rather than hereditary status, the ultimate criterion for the exercise of political power was administrative and military competence. His survey pays attention, therefore, to institutional and military matters. The high points of pre-Kamakura history for him were the ancient invasions of Korea, which demonstrated Japan's abiding martial character, the "constitution" of Prince Shōtoku (604), Fujiwara no Fubito's *Ritsuryō* (Penal and Administrative Codes, 701), and the supplementary legal codes of the ninth and tenth centuries. At its most successful, he pointed out, court government had been based on a process of administration by legal precedent: "Were there to be irregularities in the way of administration, scholars in law would invariably be consulted and offer judgments. The identification of the right course based on these judgments formed the precedents for court administration."[73]

However, in Sokō's perspective, the effectiveness of court government had eventually waned. Owing to the "daily decline of imperial authority and its transforming influence not reaching distant provinces,"[74] the Masakado (935–40) and Sumitomo (939) rebellions had taken place. Sokō was at pains to identify the cause of the failure of imperial governance not in warrior insubordination or usurpation, as Chikafusa or Keisai did, but squarely in delinquency on the part of the court, its indulgence in specious pleasures, and lack of familiarity with conditions in the country. Warrior government, when it came, did so essentially by default; the warriors had been in no way culpable:

It is not the case that warrior subjects administered the world out of contempt for their superiors. Because those above them were not illumined as to the way of the ruler, their military subjects inherited [administration] and brought peace to the realm. From the Hōgen to the Kenmu Disturbances, it is not that, despite the correctness of the court's rites, music, and administration, the warrior subjects acted self-indulgently. Rather, because the realm was at an utter impasse, the warrior subjects became daily more powerful and brought peace to it.[75]

Yoritomo's institutional innovations were evaluated in terms of their success in bringing order to the country:

Because there were many remaining bands [of Taira supporters] in the provinces, order could not be restored by entrusting the judicial decisions to the deliberations of the court. So Yoritomo, through Taira no Tokimasa, requested of Go-Shirakawa to be the Sōtsuibushi [General sheriff] of the provinces, and the retired emperor gave his consent without qualification. Thereby, constables (shugo) were placed in the provinces, the authority of the provincial governors was suppressed, and they scarcely preserved the name of officials. Stewards (jitō) were attached to shōen, and controlled the activities of the administrative headquarters (honjo). On this basis, the sixty and more provinces became tranquil, and no group in them devised selfish intents. However, the outcome was that the whole realm had passed into the control of the warrior houses, and the court became unable to exercise administration or the provincial officials to prosecute their business.[76]

Sokō evaluated Hōjō administration and legislative achievements highly. He was at pains to point out that the Hōjō ascendancy had not been due to a selfish act, but, in its turn, had been precipitated by the decline in Minamoto virtue. From this period on, the emperors ceased to be politically important, and imperial reigns no longer provided the framework for surveying the past. But Hōjō rule, too, had declined and run to extravagance. During the regency of Tokiyori (1246–56), Buddhism, to which Sokō, like most Tokugawa Confucians, was hostile, had gained as ascendancy.[77] The new legislative formulary of 1284, the *Shin go shiki-moku* (New Formulary for the Palace), had been ineffective.[78] The ninth Hōjō regent, Sadatoki (r. 1284–1301), had been a good ruler, but thereafter, further decline had taken place. Of Takatoki, the fourteenth regent, Sokō remarked that "his natural disposition did not correspond to that of a regent."[79] Wholly addicted to wine and venery, he was ignorant of the insubordination of his deputies.

Of the dynastic schism itself, Sokō wrote that it had been devised by Hōjō Tokimune (r. 1268–84) "in order to split the power of the court."[80] Beyond that, he paid it little attention. The Kenmu Restoration was treated not radically differently from the rise of the Minamoto or the Hōjō. All had been preceded by moral and administrative decline. Nor did the possession of the regalia or the question of dynastic legitimacy greatly concern him. The restoration was simply the consequence of the decline of Hōjō power. It derived no very special luster in Sokō's eyes from imperial participation: "Because Kamakura administration had declined year by year and the virtuous rule of the court had increased daily, groups that rejected the warrior houses emerged in the provinces as day succeeded day."[81] But the restoration was, in its turn, undermined by the inefficiency, indulgence, and corruption of its leaders and the failure of its administration. The situation had only been retrieved with the military ascendancy of Ashikaga Takauji and the reversion to rule by the military houses. Far from participating, like Keisai, in the demonization of Takauji, Sokō praised him for his legislative achievements in having a new set of legal institutions, the *Kenmu shikimoku* (Kenmu Formulary), drawn up,[82] and for his soldierly virtues. He summed up the "thirty-three years" of Takauji's rule in evident satisfaction that contrasts sharply with Keisai's condemnation: "During the time of Lord Takauji, there took place a restoration of the warrior houses, and the realm once more reverted to military virtue."[83] When, in due course of time, the Southern emperor, Go-Kameyama, had returned the regalia to the Northern Court, the fifty-six-year schism had come to an end. But Sokō was in no doubt as to the agency behind this resolution: "This . . . stemmed from the authority and virtue (*itoku*) of the military houses."[84]

Sokō's use of terms such as "military virtue" and "the authority and virtue of the military houses" constitutes a positive recognition of the role of force in the polity. Combined with his strong interest in law and institutions, it suggests an understanding of history very different from the moralism of Chu Hsi or, for that matter, the conservatism of Ssu-ma Kuang, Kitabatake Chikafusa, or Keisai. Here was an approach that developed further the realism of the *Taiheiki*.[85] Sokō's understanding of history is, in effect, largely indigenous, shaped by a specifically Japanese historical experience, and inspired by the need to rationalize a polity based on warrior, rather than civil, power. In contrast to Keisai, there is little suggestion here of influence from Chinese neo-Confucian historians.

CONCLUSION

The two Japanese Confucian thinkers whose views of the fourteenth century are summarized above have much in common. Both were nationalistic, advanced the claims of Japan, rather than China, to be regarded as the "central" land, and placed loyalty at the head of the hierarchy of values to which men should conform. Both accepted that their country was sacralized by Shinto deities and venerated an unbroken imperial lineage. Both would have claimed to respect the facts of history. In the historical thought of both, an ideological element is easily recognized. That said, they subscribed to different world views, and responded differently in interpreting the fourteenth-century crisis.

For Keisai, history was an application of a changeless moral teaching, of which the most important element reduced to a particularistic, uncompromising loyalty to the imperial lineage. His main vocation was that of a fundamentalist Chu Hsi neo-Confucian moralist, as he would have been the first to recognize. He undertook no systematic study of the past himself. His ideas on history, a strident synthesis of the conservative thought of Ssu-ma Kuang, Kitabatake Chikafusa, and the moral rigorism of Chu Hsi neo-Confucianism, were reductive and ahistorical. These basic assumptions led him to reject the transition to warrior rule as an act of usurpation and to condemn Ashikaga Takauji, its restorer, as, in his turn, a disloyal usurper.

But the obvious inflexibilities and limitations of Keisai's thinking on the past in no way diminished its influence. His ideas and those of the Kimon school passed into the Mito school of history writing, for both Miyake Kanran (1674–1718) and Kuriyama Sempō (1671–1706), two of the three scholars dominant in early Mito historiography, were Kimon disciples. The legitimacy of the Southern Court was, as is well known, one of the *sandai toppitsu* (three major special arguments) of the *Dai Nihonshi*. Eventually, with the suppression from that work of the intellectually richer *ronsan* (appraisals) contributed by Asaka Tanpaku (1656–1737),[86] elements of Keisai's thought, particularly *taigi meibun*, came to dominate the thought of the Mito school.[87] Emphasis on "name and status" was revived yet again in the late eighteenth and the nineteenth centuries, in an increasingly politicized tone and for a fresh ideological purpose, the preservation of national cohesion against both external and internal threats. Through late Mito thought, the rhetoric of *taigi meibun*, first extensively employed by Keisai three centuries earlier, became an element in Meiji and twentieth-century statist ideology. It was exploited, perhaps without Keisai's moral conviction and ardor, in politically motivated attempts to inhibit more objective inquiry into the past.

Sokō's history was scarcely less ideologically motivated than Keisai's, for he obliquely pleaded the legitimacy of the warrior regime under which he lived. It was, however, his task as a samurai historian to account rationally and analytically for, and thus to justify rather than deplore, a fundamental change in the Japanese polity. Insofar as it sought rationally to explain this change, his history has a more secular and persuasive ring to modern ears than Keisai's. His recognition of the warrior right to exercise administration, his premise that court and warrior governance were subject to the same laws, and his recognition of the role of force place his thought closer to the incipient realism of the *Taiheiki* than to the conservatism of the *Jinnō shōtōki* that inspired Keisai. It is also clear that Sokō's rejection of the Chu Hsi system created intellectual space for him to adopt a remarkably realist understanding of the past. Unpreoccupied with the rigorous evaluation of discrete moral actions by particular historical figures or by a constricting emperor-centered view of loyalty, he was free to expand inquiry into other fields, such as those in institutions and administrative control. Here were the beginnings of an approach to history that seems recognizably empirical. Though it would be exaggerated to claim that Sokō himself lies behind the development of an empirical school of historiography, it can be accepted that he is an early, perhaps precocious, exemplar of a trend in Tokugawa Japan toward intellectual modernity. By freeing historical thought from the constraints of a medieval world view, he broadened historical discourse beyond fundamentalist inquiry into observance of an ahistorical morality. Nor was Sokō without heirs in his approach to history in the Tokugawa period. In the next generation, Ogyū Sorai (1666–1728), in recent years the most admired thinker of the Tokugawa period, believed profoundly in the importance of disciplined historical study. Sorai was only incidentally a historian, but he could still claim that "because learning refers to broad observation and comprehensive familiarity with facts, it is ultimately historical."[88] Sorai's positivist, empirical understanding of the study of the past led him to an emphatic rejection of the moralistic Chu Hsi approach and a preference for what he perceived to be the more objective approach of Ssu-ma Kuang:

The arguments in the *Kang-mu*, like the impressions of a seal, are no more than the stamping of fixed forms and predetermined principles. Both Heaven and Earth and man are living things; to regard them as though they were trussed up with rope is a truly unacceptable [form of] learning and only serves to bolster people's speciousness. Therefore, the *Tzu-chih t'ung-chien*, which is just facts, is far better.[89]

Sorai's contemporary, the rational, euhemerist Arai Hakuseki, though formally, unlike Sorai himself, a Chu Hsi neo-Confucian, applied something of his approach in writing history. Hakuseki set standards of rational historiographical practice that were to influence later Tokugawa historians and to impress their post-Restoration successors. In his review of the fourteenth-century crisis, Hakuseki argued that the emperors of the Northern Court were pretenders, and, like Keisai, accepted that those of the Southern Court were legitimate. This position, however, was associated with a realist argument that would have outraged Keisai, believing as he did in an unbroken imperial lineage, but might well have elicited a certain sympathy from the more realist Sokō. For Hakuseki argued that, with the eventual failure of the Southern Court to rule competently and to perpetuate its succession, the rulership of the Japanese imperial lineage had effectively come to an end.[90]

CHAPTER 15

The Fourteenth Century in Twentieth-Century Perspective

ŌYAMA KYŌHEI

T HERE HAVE been four main currents in historical studies of the fourteenth century. The first approach has been "political," beginning with Kume Kunitake, and continuing with Tanaka Yoshinari, Hiraizumi Kiyoshi, and Satō Shin'ichi, all of whom were professors at Tokyo University. The second approach has been "cultural," beginning with Hara Katsurō, and followed by Nishida Naojirō, Nakamura Naokatsu, Shimizu Mitsuo, and Hayashiya Tatsusaburō. The members of this group were all associated with Kyoto University. Except for Satō and Hayashiya, all these scholars completed their major research activities before 1945.

The end of World War II marked a major turning point in Japan's historiography, with the appearance of a number of studies strongly influenced by Marxism, representing the third approach. Scholars like Nagahara Keiji continued the work begun by Ishimoda Shō and Matsumoto Shinpachirō, who were already active before 1945. At the same time, political and cultural history had to respond to the new Marxist influences, with Satō and Hayashiya leading the way.

By the 1960s, historians were broadening their horizons everywhere, leading to the fourth approach, which is diverse and eclectic. Thus whereas Kuroda Toshio derived his *kenmon* theory from his study of religious institutions, Amino Yoshihiko's work, *Muen kugai raku*, pioneered an ethnological approach. In addition, the works of Murai Shōsuke, Kawazoe Shōji, and Itō Kiyoshi have placed the fourteenth century in the context of the history of East Asia. We may say that the field is developing as these trends intertwine.

THE CURRENT OF POLITICAL HISTORY

Kume Kunitake (1839–1931)

The pioneering political historian of the fourteenth century was Kume Kunitake. Kume published an article in 1891 entitled "*Taiheiki* wa shigaku ni eki nashi" (*Taiheiki* Offers No Benefit for the Study of History, *Shigakukai zasshi*, vol. 2, nos. 17, 18, 20, 21, 22), which claimed to establish a modern historiography based on accurate historical sources, quite unlike the storytelling history of the *monogatari* type. A year later, however, Kume was involved in an unfortunate incident, which led to his resignation from the professorship at the Humanities College of the Imperial University (the present-day University of Tokyo, Faculty of Literature). Transferring to Waseda, he later published a collection of his lectures there as *Nanbokuchō jidai-shi* (The History of the Nanbokuchō Period; Waseda University Press, 1907).

In fact, Kume's academic position derived from an earlier government-sponsored project of compiling a national history of Japan. Following the model of China and Korea, and its own ancient experience with histories of the chronicle type, the new Meiji government was determined to revive this time-honored tradition. In 1869, plans were laid for a one-thousand-year history beginning with the coronation of Emperor Uda in 887, where the *Nihon sandai jitsuroku*, the last of the old chronicles, left off. In connection with that project, the Shiryō Henshū Kokushi Kōsei-kyoku, an institute for historiographical research, was established. This governmental institution, changing its name several times to Shūshikyoku and Shūshikan, was initially administered by the Dajōkan (Council of State), but later by the newly established modern cabinet (Naikaku). It underwent several institutional changes, and in 1888, when the Department of National History was established at the Humanities College of the Imperial University, it was placed within its organizational framework, and was the predecessor of what is now the Tōkyō Daigaku Shiryō Hensanjo. Kume, who accompanied the Iwakura Mission as a secretary and traveled to Europe and the United States, entered the Institute in 1879 and became involved with the compilation project, which was initially called the *Dai Nihon hennen-shi* (The Chronological History of Japan).

The *Dai Nihon hennen-shi* was planned as a successor to the *Dai Nihon-shi*, which had been prepared, in the late Tokugawa, by the Mito domain. The latter, which was to be built around a massive collection of primary sources, may be said to have served as the springboard for Japan's modern historiography. However, in its description of the Nanbokuchō period, it had taken the accounts in the *Taiheiki* as historically accurate. Thus, once Kume and other scholars started to gather more objective historical sources, they began to question the details of the account in the *Taiheiki*. As previously noted, the 1891 article by Kume proclaimed the independence of Japanese history from the *monogatari*-type storytelling, but a second article, published in 1892, drew strong criticism from nationalists and the public. This second article, entitled "Shintō wa shiten no kozoku" (Shinto Is an Old Religious Custom), evoked a storm of controversy that in 1893 resulted in the suspension by the government of the chronological history project, and in Kume's resignation.

It was at this juncture, and upon the invitation of Okuma Shigenobu, that Kume transferred to Waseda University. The collection of his Waseda lectures, *Nanbokuchō jidai-shi*, published in 1907, is divided into four parts: Causes, Early Stages, The Separation into Northern and Southern Courts, and The Flourishing of the Southern Court and the Decay of the Northern Court. Kume began his treatise with the origins of the *insei* (retired emperor rule) in a search for the backdrop to both the division of the imperial line and the support the Ashikaga gave to its northern branch. He describes in detail the chronological history of the Nanbokuchō period, and his reliance on original sources reflects his belief that in them lay the basis for historical narrative. Kume's lectures are full of moralizing, but they constitute the representative work of a Meiji intellectual.

Tanaka Yoshinari (1860–1919)

Tanaka Yoshinari succeeded Kume as professor of medieval Japanese history at the Imperial University. Though Tanaka was twenty-one years younger than Kume, he was originally hired at the Institute in 1876 — three years before Kume — when he was only seventeen, and after Kume left, he became the dominant figure. Two events of major importance occurred during the 1890s. The first was the reestablishment of the Historiographical Institute (Shiryō Hensan Gakari) in 1895, and the second was the initiation of the *Dai Nihon shiryō* project. Quite dramatically, the state-sponsored historical narrative, the *Dai Nihon hennen-shi*, had been converted into a more objective, chronological collection of historical sources. In the process, the nature of modern Japanese historiography also changed. On the positive side, the main agenda of historical studies were now shielded from political issues, with the result that an objective academic tradition would not be affected by political movements. On the negative side, a methodology built around documents precluded, at least potentially, judgment and interpretation.

The first volume of the *Dai Nihon shiryō* appeared in 1901; Tanaka was the person most responsible for its preparation. This initial volume (in the sixth series) dealt with the Nanbokuchō period, beginning with the founding of the Kenmu regime by Emperor Go-Daigo. Tanaka had the reputation of devoting his life to the "compilation of historical sources," but also to the periodic revision of his lectures as he discovered previously unstudied primary materials. It is said that Tanaka would offer a clear conclusion every time he encountered a new document.

In 1919, Tanaka gave up his academic post on grounds of ill health. The manuscripts for his lectures were edited by his students, Hiraizumi Kiyoshi, Fujimoto Ryōtai, and Nishioka Toranosuke, and were published as the *Nanbokuchō jidai-shi* (The History of the Nanbokuchō Period; Meiji shoin, 1922). The book, a political history in seventy-five chapters, is considered a masterpiece. Six chapters in particular contain especially detailed treatments, suggesting that Tanaka believed their subjects to embrace central themes: chapter 25, "The Assault on Kamakura"; chapter 29, "The New Government Under the Kenmu Restoration"; chapter 31, "The Rebellion of Takauji"; chapter 47, "The Plans of the Southern Court"; chapter 62, "Theories on Ashikaga Takauji"; and chapter 70, "The Kyushu Strategy of Ashikaga Yoshimitsu."

Kume's and Tanaka's *Nanbokuchō jidai-shi* are opposite in many ways. Kume was determined until the end to write a chronological history, believing that a compilation of sources would be too massive for anyone to read, and indeed, he did not find much meaning in the publication of primary sources by themselves. Stylistically he favored ornate literary prose, with primary sources cited extensively. By contrast, Tanaka's narrative is written in a graceful and lucid contemporary style, with each statement accompanied by a concise citation. Though his use of sources is straightforward and much less complicated than Kume's, it is inseparable in practice from the *Dai Nihon shiryō*, that is, history as a sequence of people, places, and events.

Ignoring government pressure to the contrary, Tanaka insisted on using "Nanbokuchō" rather than the more politically acceptable "Yoshino-chō." At the same time, he adopted a less dismissive attitude toward the *Taiheiki*, and used some of the accounts in it that Kume had refused to accept. His convictions defined for many what academics should be, and his views on scholarship have greatly influenced later historians.

Hiraizumi Kiyoshi (1895–1984)

A few years after Tanaka's death, Hiraizumi Kiyoshi succeeded him as the leading professor of medieval Japanese history at Tokyo Imperial University. He was a new type of historian, who had from the very beginning received his education under the modern school system. He graduated from Tokyo Imperial University in 1918, became a lecturer in 1923, an assistant professor in 1926, and in the same year published *Chūsei ni okeru seishin seikatsu* (The Spiritual Life in Medieval Japan) and *Chūsei ni okeru shaji to shakai to no kankei* (The Relationships Between Shrines and Temples and the Society of Medieval Japan). These books helped to open up a new field, incorporating the movements in European medieval history. In 1930–31 Hiraizumi traveled in various countries of Europe and had an opportunity to associate directly with academics there.

Upon his return, Hiraizumi rapidly turned to the right. Among his publications were *Kokushigaku no kotsuzui* (The Heart of National History) and *Kenmu chūkō no hongi* (The True Meaning of the Kenmu Restoration; Shibundō, 1934). The latter work in particular reveals the extent to which the emperor was now situated at the heart of an extreme ethnocentrism. Among various topics, Hiraizumi discussed "The Aspiration [of the Emperor] for the Restoration of Japan," and "The Administration [of the Emperor] on Behalf of the Kenmu Restoration." Overall, Hiraizumi was concerned with the noble ideas of Emperor Go-Daigo, the failure of whose movement he attributes to the people whose hearts had forgotten "justice." Such persons were blinded by "profit" and tempted by the pragmatic traitor Ashikaga Takauji.

Interpretations of this kind did not grow out of scholarly research. However, embedded in Hiraizumi's extremism were some outstanding arguments, which suggest that he was indeed a student of Tanaka. The examination of Go-Daigo's authorship of the *Nenjū gyōgi* is one such example.

Hiraizumi rejected the older view that it was written by Kitabatake Chikafusa, and asserted that it was the emperor himself who wrote it in 1335. Hiraizumi's method of pointing to nine narrative sections in the original document in order to support his theory is outstanding.

Satō Shin'ichi (1916–)

Hiraizumi left the University of Tokyo after Japan's defeat in World War II. With the rise in interest on such subjects as the *shōen*, serious research on political history was no longer a leading topic. The professor of medieval political history at Tōdai at this time was Satō Shin'ichi, who published a celebrated volume, *Nanbokuchō no dōran* (The Nanbokuchō Disturbance), in 1965. In this book he severely criticized Hiraizumi as a historian, who had also, he claimed, collaborated with the rising military authority of the 1930s. Satō further stated that it was important for scholars of the Nanbokuchō to restart their research in a simple but liberal way in the pre-Tanaka mode. With this book, Satō succeeded in writing a work that set a new standard for scholarship, creating a framework for the study of the fourteenth century that continues to the present day.

After Hiraizumi, and by Satō's time, the political history of the Nanbokuchō centered less on chronology and more on government organization and institutions, in particular the political power framework of the Kenmu government and the Muromachi Bakufu, and the nation-state under Go-Daigo and Ashikaga Takauji. According to Satō, Go-Daigo's Kenmu government was modeled on the absolute monarchy of the Sung with its massive bureaucratic foundation. He identified as the mainstay of politics over many centuries such central organizations as the *Daijōkan* and the eight ministries, supported by local administrative agencies. He suggested that the ideal political system was one in which all authority was concentrated in the emperor, and that a model of this kind was understood to be the true form of Japanese politics from the tenth century onward.

More specifically, according to Satō, Go-Daigo's political plans were aimed initially at abolishing such institutions as the Bakufu, *insei*, and *sesshō kanpaku* (Fujiwara regency), all of which were seen to compromise the authority of the emperor himself. Thus in 1321, three years after ascending to the throne, Go-Daigo expelled the ex-emperor Go-Uda and abolished the *insei* system. In 1333, following the earlier failures of 1324 and 1331, he overthrew, by force, the Kamakura Bakufu. He then dismissed Takatsukasa Fuyunori from the office of *kanpaku*, and attempted to abolish the almost 500-year-old regency.

Beyond that, Go-Daigo sought to reduce the *Daijōkan kaigi* (The Assembly of the Great Council) to a mere formality. This assembly had always compromised the expression of the emperor's free will. Go-Daigo therefore appointed *Daijōkan*-level aristocrats of the highest ranks to head the eight ministries, which had until then been positions held by low-ranking nobles. At the same time, Go-Daigo sought to bring the wealthy city of Kyoto under his direct control. He appointed his close retainer Nawa Nagatoshi as the administrator (*shō/chōkan*) of the eastern market, and through him attempted to regulate the developing industrial base of Kyoto as the economic foundation of his regal power. Finally, as described by Satō, Go-Daigo placed both a civil governor and a *shugo* in each province, and had them serve as checks on each other. The policy was an imitation of one in Sung China, which also had a system of mutual supervision between the prefectural governor and controller general.

The political system designed by Go-Daigo would not have been possible without the foundation of a mature bureaucratic system. However, a system of hereditary officials had been rooted deeply in Japan since the Heian period, and was now made subject to more arbitrary management by the emperor. Satō describes the dictatorial nature of Go-Daigo's rule by examining the personal edicts (*rinji*) issued by him as emperor. Expressing the emperor's will under the signature of an imperial secretary, these edicts now came to supersede those of the *Daijōkan*, and also those of the *kirokujo*, the highest judicial agency in Kyoto. Both had been the basis of imperial governance for centuries.

Satō's analysis is indeed a splendid one, borrowing from the archival method passed on to him by his teacher, Aida Nirō. This approach, highlighting the different types of documents, has exerted great influence on later historians.

THE CURRENT OF CULTURAL HISTORY

Hara Katsurō (1871–1924)

Concurrently with the trend of political history that was developing in Tokyo, a clearly distinct cultural history was emerging in Kyoto. After the establishment of the history department at Kyoto Imperial University in 1907, Hara Katsurō returned from his studies in England and the United States and immediately became a professor of Western history. Hara had in 1909 already published a book, *Nihon chūsei-shi* (The History of Medieval Japan)—in fact, he was the first to use the term "*chūsei*" to signify a particular periodization—in which he defined the warrior class as the bearers of the new period and culture. Hara is thus considered by many to be the founder of modern historiography in Japan. His articles include "Ashikaga jidai wo ronzu" (A Theory on the Ashikaga Period) and "Higashiyama jidai ni okeru ichi shishin no seikatsu" (The Life of a High-Ranking Official in the Higashiyama Period).

Nishida Naojirō (1886–1964)

Nishida Naojirō, one of the first of the Hara graduates of the Humanities College of Kyoto Imperial University, set the study of cultural history on its way. Nishida had studied in England and Germany, returning in 1922, and he received his degree in 1924 with a thesis, "Ōchō jidai no shōmin kaikyū" (The Commoner Class in the Imperial Age). From that juncture he began to teach medieval history at Kyoto. His major work is *Nihon bunka-shi josetsu* (A Prelude to the Cultural History of Japan), which is an edited version of the eleven lectures he gave in 1924.

The chief characteristic of Nishida's studies of cultural history is his discovery of "the people." According to Nishida, Japan experienced two major changes between the late Heian and late Kamakura periods. The first was the establishment of warrior politics and the development of social ethics by the *bushi* class, the second the rise and spread of the Pure Land and the other new religions. These points in themselves are not especially noteworthy, but Nishida saw in them the emergence of "the mass" in the late Heian period, and with it, the cultural transformation of the commoner class.

Taking a general view of the history of Japan, Nishida referred to the *jōdai* (the early period) as the age of the aristocrats, to the *chūsei* as the period of the warriors, and to the early modern as the epoch of the rise of the commoners. At the same time, however, he paid particular attention to the changing condition of the people in the late Heian period. His "Ōchō jidai no shōmin kaikyū" was written to explain this phenomenon, as opposed to the view of seeing the beginning of the early modern around 1600, and thereby positioning the rise of a middle class similar to that in Europe. Nishida emphasized the need to look far back in history, indeed, to the final phase of the Heian period.

Nishida had been strongly influenced by the methodology advocated by Gothein (*Die Aufgaben der Kulturgeschichte*, 1889) and also by Karl Lamprecht, whose *Was ist Kulturgeschichte?* stated that the purest form of cultural history is "the history of ideas." Nishida, taking up Lamprecht's view that "history is social psychology," argued against traditional historiography (political history) with its focus on individual facts, and in favor of cultural history with its stress on the collective sense, and on the thoughts and emotions that drive the mass. Although Nishida did not write anything specifically on the fourteenth century, in his *Prelude to the Cultural History of Japan* he discussed the history of the Ashikaga epoch in three sections: a conviction toward power, the world of ego, and the economic people. As part of this effort, he defined the Kenmu Restoration as the beginning of a realization of the true nature of Japanese politics in which the illegitimate Bakufu government was overthrown and a direct rule by the emperor was attempted.

At the same time, Nishida focused on mass movements reflected in the social phenomena of the period, and explained them as a product of various economic situations, collective organizations (guilds, etc.), and popular movements (e.g., of the Ikkō and *hokke* deriving from religious beliefs). He saw in such movements the rise of a more practical spirit that pursued specific goals. Nishida also compared the *wakō* (pirate bands) to medieval Italian *commenda* (overseas merchants), and discussed the significance of foreign trade in the Ashikaga period in terms of the development of a "spirit of the Nation." He saw this trade as having motivated a fundamental entrepreneurial spirit in medieval commerce and industry.

Nakamura Naokatsu (1890–1976)

Nakamura Naokatsu was almost contemporary to Nishida and taught medieval history a little after him. His study of the *shōen* and *za*, in *Nihon bunka-shi—Nanbokuchō jidai* (The Cultural History of Japan—The Nanbokuchō Period), published in 1922, presented the academic world with a new image of the fourteenth century. This was the year of Tanaka Yoshinari's *Nanbokuchō jidai-shi*, published in Tokyo, and the difference between scholarly trends of political and cultural history became apparent with these two works.

Nakamura's book consists of nine chapters: (1) Introduction, (2) The Trends of the Period, (3) Aspects of the Society, (4) Economic Problems, (5) Participation of Priests in Politics, (6) The Unification of the Two Imperial Houses, (7) Thoughts and Beliefs, (8) Art and Literature, and (9) Conclusion. Chapter 3, besides discussing the origins of daimyo, deals with the development of the new professional groups (the *za*, *kugonin*, and *jinin*), and gives details of the various new professions that characterize the period: the cotton *za* of Gion Shrine, the wine and malt *za* of Kitano Shrine, and the *za* of Ōmi Tokuchin *ho*; the *kugonin* of Awazu, Abiki *mikuriya*, and Sugaura, as well as the *tōrō* (lantern) *kugonin*; and the Iwashimizu Hachiman *jinin*, the Gion *inu-jinin*, and the Settsu Imamiya *jinin*. Society's mainstream at this time consisted of merchants and craftsmen. Nakamura emphasizes the early-modern aspects of the period by noting its active mercantile trade and the flowering of cities, along with the rise of financial organizations, transportation systems, and markets.

Nakamura took up a similar theme in *Yoshino chō-shi* (The History of Yoshino-chō), published in 1935. This work characterizes the fourteenth century as marking the end of Japan's medieval period and the beginning of its early modern age (*kinsei*) — the differences between these ages being (1) the transition from a rice to a monetary economy, (2) the change from the world of buddhas and gods to the world of people, and (3) the development of and awareness of a nation-state. Nakamura cites Go-Daigo's policy of terminating the *honke* and *ryōke shiki* (patron and proprietor titles) of the *ichinomiya* and *ninomiya* (first and second shrines) in each province, explaining it as a means to avoid the encroachment of moneylenders as well as an effort by the state to regulate the administration of land. Go-Daigo's plans to issue paper money were another indication of his seeking to place the economy on a monetary basis.

Discussing the transition from buddhas and gods to the people, Nakamura focused on the development of the *Shinkoku* (Japan as a divine country) theory, which took root at the time of the Mongol invasions. This theory argued that since the "Age of the *Kami*," the gods of Japan had been extensions of the people with the same feelings and weaknesses. Concepts of nationhood, Nakamura's third defining point, were accordingly promoted.

Nakamura's analyses, though they have a sense of spontaneity, are supported by a rich tapestry of evidence, and his contribution to the study of the common people in medieval Japan will always be acknowledged.

Shimizu Mitsuo (1909–1947)

Nishida's cultural history captured the people as the main body of history, and concentrated on the analysis of the development of the spirit carried on by a diverse populace. This was a methodology that expanded the vision of society far beyond anything seen in the work of contemporary scholars at Tokyo University (e.g., Tanaka).

Shimizu Mitsuo discussed fourteenth-century society in a chapter in his *Nihon chūsei no sonraku* (The Villages of Medieval Japan), published in 1942. In this chapter, entitled "Kenmu chūkō to sonraku" (The Kenmu Restoration and the Villages), Shimizu, writing from a pro-Marxist point of view, identified the significance of the Kenmu Restoration in its integration of the reconstructed *kokushi-shugo* (civil and military governor) system with the villagers who were now brought into a nation-state structure. Sentiments on the part of locals were now turned back toward their villages, leading to the establishment of a new autonomy. In other words, Shimizu posited the "autonomous village" as having been realized by the regional organizations of the "*kokushi-shugo*" era, assisted by what he called the "patriotism of the villagers." The establishment of a nation-state, as so defined, was an objective of the Kenmu Restoration.

Shimizu also saw the Restoration as having "opened the way to the emergence of early modern "nation-people." They achieved their "liberation" by their new "awareness of their way of life." Thus, villagers could break away from the "narrow sphere of living within the *shōen*" on the occasion of the establishment of a "larger territorial life centered around the *kokushi* and *shugo*." One can clearly identify the influence of Nishida's cultural history on Shimizu's theoretical framework.

Shimizu's main emphasis was on the transformation of the village in medieval Japan. For him, the defeat of the Hōjō meant the decline of the *jitō* in village history. In the Kamakura period, much of the mental and political energy of villagers was organized against the illegal activities of the *jitō*. The schemes to overthrow the Bakufu therefore grew out of the villagers' eagerness to defeat the *jitō*, and the similar expectations on the side of *shōen* proprietors. Shimizu saw this alignment of interests as the reason for the new government's use of *shugo* and *kokushi* as the basis for local administration, at the expense of any emphasis on *jitō*.

Shimizu was clearly under the influence of Marxism, then at its height (he was arrested in 1938 under the Maintenance of Public Order Act), and his emphasis on the transition in landlord-like administration by the *jitō* may reflect Marxist theory on land rents. Specifically, he identified the decline of *jitō* as deriving from the shift of cultivation by their privately owned *genin* (subordinates) to a condition in which landlords collected only taxes. That is, free tenant-landlord relationships now developed, as villagers with shared interests came together. At the top of this system were *kokushi* and *shugo*, with their administrative base resting on unified villages.

If Nakamura enthusiastically explored and opened up the field of *shōen* studies, Shimizu, using Nishida's historical and theoretical background, succeeded in bringing Nakamura's research into the context of cultural history. But with regard to aspects of commerce and distribution, Shimizu did not advance Nakamura's work very far. It would be left to Amino Yoshihiko to take Nakamura's pioneering efforts to a new stage.

SOCIAL STRUCTURAL HISTORY

Ishimoda Shō (1912–1986)

The Marxist-influenced school of history came into its own at the end of the war. In rebellion against ultranationalist historians like Hiraizumi, this new school of historians pursued topics such as the ancient slavery system, medieval feudalism, and modern capitalism, which focused on transitions in social structure. Dramatic changes in the academic world discredited not only Hiraizumi but also scholars of cultural history like Nishida and Nakamura, who were now expelled from Japanese universities and disappeared from the front ranks of historians. Even Shimizu, for all his former Marxist stance, ended his days in a concentration camp in Siberia.

There were good reasons for Marxist historical analysis to become the major trend in postwar Japan. For one thing, an emphasis on changes in the social structure contrasted sharply with the one-sided nationalistic historiography based on *kokutai* and the emperor. For another, Japanese Marxist historiography, which began in the 1920s, had now matured to a point of sophistication. It was in this context that Ishimoda Shō's *Chūseiteki sekai no keisei* (The Formation of the Medieval World) made its appearance in 1946. Written in 1944 during the American bombing, its publication after Japan's defeat seemed to herald a new age.

The subject of Ishimoda's book was the residents of a Tōdaiji *shōen* called Kuroda, located in the Nabari district of Iga Province. This site had previously been studied by Nakamura, Shimizu, and their contemporary Takeuchi Rizō, but Ishimoda gave it a rich new interpretation. In a chapter dealing with the fourteenth century, "Kuroda no akutō," Kuroda discusses the lawless activities of local warriors (*akutō*), which show the era to have been one of historical decadence leading to the formation of a medieval world. Following Ishimoda, *akutō* have since become a central theme of studies of the fourteenth century.

Though the book deals with a small *shōen*, the history of its people is made to embody a larger medieval world. Such was the level of analysis and narration that Ishimoda's work has become a classic, a proper beginning for postwar medieval studies in Japan.

Matsumoto Shinpachirō (1913–)

Even more influential than Ishimoda was Matsumoto Shinpachirō, who published a series of articles during the 1940s that were later brought together in his *Chūsei shakai no kenkyū* (Studies on Medieval Society, 1956). In this book, Matsumoto describes the Kenmu Restoration and the civil wars of the fourteenth century as constituting an age of feudal revolution in which the society based on ancient slavery disintegrated, to be replaced by a medieval and feudal Japan. Matsumoto emphasizes the thoroughness of the social transformation in that century, and argues that "in terms of its scale and the results it brought for the development of the people, it was comparable to any feudal revolution in the world." Matsumoto further suggests that it brought an end to the power structure of the ancient emperor system, as well as to the "dual polity" of the Kamakura era, which was parasitic to this system. Matsumoto's theory is based on the concept of the "*sōryō* system," in which the Kamakura Bakufu, resting on a feudal organization, was maintained by an apparatus of domestic slavery. The power structure that had been formed represented the interests of the warrior heads, known as *sōryō*, which meant that one of the tasks of the revolution was to overthrow this exploitative system.

The second and third consequences of the civil war had economic implications, according to Matsumoto. The first was the termination of the double collection of taxes, which had resulted from the dual nature of the Kamakura system of government. In other words, the people were now seeking the realization of a new, unified system of taxation under a single authority (the second consequence), which would give them a lighter tax burden and would also replace the disorderly collection of goods and services. Thus the courtier and warrior tax systems would be collapsed into one, in part by the breakdown of the *sōryō* system, and in part by the development of land rent based on peasant economy. In the end, Matsumoto viewed the feudal peasants and lower-level warriors who organized them into bands as the dominant forces behind the fourteenth-century revolution. In spite of certain differences in approach and emphasis, Matsumoto's work bears an obvious similarity to that of Shimizu.

TRENDS TO THE PRESENT

If Matsumoto's theories can be seen today as lacking concrete evidence, in the immediate postwar period his work had a strong impact. Shimizu had returned to emperor-centered history by the time he died, and the field of fourteenth-century studies was without leadership when Hiraizumi, Nishida, and Nakamura retired. It was at this juncture that Matsumoto's theories were seen to fill the gap, and the work of Satō Shin'ichi in political history may be viewed as a reaction and reply.

Satō was born in 1916, and Kuroda Toshio and Amino Yoshihiko in the late 1920s. The latter two began their academic careers much influenced by Matsumoto before they then went on to develop their individual approaches. Curiously, however, few scholars who followed soon after them were much concerned with the fourteenth century. Evidently, historians born in the 1930s were too young to feel the need to confront the emperor-centered assumptions of their forebears.

Kuroda Toshio (1926–1993)

Kuroda's theories on the Nanbokuchō were first enunciated in his 1953 essay, "*Taiheiki* to Nanbokuchō nairan" (The *Taiheiki* and the Nanbokuchō Disturbance), first presented at a 1952 conference on the theme, "images of people in times of transition." In this essay, Kuroda argued that the civil war witnessed the destruction of the ancient emperor, court, and *shōen* systems, not to mention the Kamakura Bakufu, which had been unable to overthrow these systems on its own. Kuroda also posited for the working peasants of that era an enhanced right to cultivate their own fields and control their own villages, and he saw a more decentralized and advanced feudal system in the form of the newly emerging provincial magnates (*shugo ryōgoku*). This is, of course, the essence of Matsumoto's core theory. At the same time, Kuroda divided the revolution into four stages and analyzed the roles played by each of four groups: the emperor and the aristocracy, temples and shrines, great warrior houses in the east, and mid- and small-sized warriors and peasants in the center and west.

The historiographical significance of Kuroda's paper lay in his revived use of the same *Taiheiki* once dismissed by Kume Kunitake. His focus was not on the specific facts mentioned in that work, however, but rather on its images of people through depictions of heroes and commoners. Kuroda discerned new categories of persons: the antiauthoritarian warriors of high rank, more locally based warriors associated with *akutō*, and men of influence (*jizamurai*) and peasants who were close to the soil.

Later, in his "Akutō to sono jidai" (*Akutō* and Its Period, 1957), Kuroda redefined the *Taiheiki* as a literary piece, whose dominant characters were rebellious *akutō* types, along with demonic *tengu* who disturbed the world in that unsettled epoch. Continuing the debate on *akutō* initiated by Ishimoda, Kuroda defined the century as one best represented by *akutō*-like phenomena in the social, religious, and literary spheres. Still relying on the *Taiheiki*, Kuroda eventually came to see in it "the thoughts of people who could hardly conceive of the future" — "Henkaku no ishiki to shisō" (Thought and Consciousness During the Period of Transformation), in *Rekishi kōron*, 1979. In assessing these various studies, we should keep in mind the Cold War mentality of the era in which he was writing.

In 1963 and 1967, Kuroda published his "Chūsei no kokka to tennō" (The State and Emperor in Medieval Japan; Iwanami kōza, *Nihon rekishi*, vol. 6), and his *Shōen-sei shakai* (*Society Under the Shōen System*, Nihon Hyōron-sha). In these works, he posed his classic theory of the *kenmon taisei*, which has had a remarkable impact on medieval studies in Japan. In it he challenged the traditional emphasis on the role of the warrior in our efforts to understand medieval Japan. Dismissing the theoretical framework that saw the *shōen* system as ancient and the warriors as feudal landlords, he in effect rejected the victory of the latter over the former as marking the transition to the medieval.

Since as far back as Hara Katsurō, the rise of the warrior class, as in Europe, has been understood in terms of the origins of medieval society in Japan. However, Kuroda believed that the political framework embraced a structure in which the courtiers, warriors, and religious institutions — the three *kenmon* powers — stood in a mutually supportive relationship with each other, and divided the functions of state while controlling the peasantry. He thus criticized the warrior-centered view of medieval Japan, casting its birth and development instead within a *kōbu* (court-warrior) framework. He condemned modern Japanese intellectuals for allowing themselves to be trapped by nationalist ideology, authoritarianism, and the lure of military power.

Kuroda emphasized especially the role of the religious institutions, which were in reality themselves major *shōen* proprietors. He thus sought to identify the religious power bloc as one of the dominant moving forces in medieval Japan. Though the point is an obvious one so far as it relates to political influence, commercial activity, and cultural supremacy, the religious institutions, in Kuroda's explanation, became integral to Japan's medieval system. He called the brand of establishment Buddhism esoteric (*kenmitsu*) and posited its national authority as exemplifying a *kenmitsu taisei*.

In the 1970s, Kuroda began examining the Kenmu regime from this new perspective. In 1972, he published "Kenmu seiken no shoryō ando seisaku" (The Land Rights Confirmation Policy of the Kenmu Regime), in which he criticized Satō Shin'ichi's understanding of Go-Daigo's political policies. The debate hinged on a personal edict (*rinji*) of 1333/6/15, and on a government edict (*kansenji*) of 7/23. Satō saw the earlier decree as an order designed to confirm private land rights under the emperor's imprimatur, deriving from Go-Daigo's misplaced belief in the efficacy of his personal edicts; the edict of a month later represented a concession to reality. Kuroda, by contrast, claimed that both edicts were based on Go-Daigo's unfolding policy of land-rights protection. The debate was subsequently carried on by other scholars (e.g., Ogawa Makoto, Iikura Harutake, and Mori Shigeaki).

In 1975, Kuroda published "Kenmu seiken no shūkyō seisaku (The Religious Policies of the Kenmu Regime), in which he dealt with the emperor's policy of abolishing the administrative headquarters (*honjo*) of the official "first" and "second" shrines (*ichinomiya* and *ninomiya*) of each province. Above all, he argued, Go-Daigo's religious policies were designed to place the *kenmitsu taisei* under the emperor's personal control. In this context, old Buddhism and new Buddhism, including Zen and all other systems of thought, were to be made adjuncts to the nation-state. For the same reason, Go-Daigo excluded the Atsuta Shrine when he gave back former holdings to the rival imperial line (the Jimyōin) upon his return to the capital from exile in Oki. Kuroda interprets this decision as showing the emperor's determination to establish the imperial regalia (the sword at Atsuta, the jewel at the palace, and the mirror at Ise) as the religious foundation for his control of the nation. At the same time, Go-Daigo's policy toward the *ichinomiya* and *ninomiya* was simply part of his larger effort to place shrines and temples under his own authority. Seeking thereby to enhance his regional control, he sought to convert these shrines into religious vessels for the state. In this way, then, Kuroda defined the Kenmu regime as a political structure, religiously based (his term was *kenmitsu shugi*), which aimed for a religious-feudal monarchy. Go-Daigo and the imperial institution would dominate all organized religion.

Kuroda's theory of the *kenmon taisei* led to the discovery of the power of religious institutions in medieval Japan, and also exposed the earlier warrior-centered view as flowing from modern ideology. Where Kuroda did not succeed, however, was in grasping the totality of the world of Japan's medieval people, which the pioneering scholars of cultural history had introduced. Merchants and craftsmen were not within Kuroda's visual orbit.

Amino Yoshihiko (1928–)

It was left to Amino Yoshihiko to rediscover the significance of the next rung of society in such works as *Muen kugai raku* (Heibonsha, 1979), *Nihon chūsei no minshū-zō* (Images of the Common People in Medieval Japan; Iwanami shinsho, 1980), "Nanbokuchō nairan no shakaiteki igi" (The Social Significance of the Nanbokuchō Disturbance), and *Igyō no ōken* (Heibonsha, 1986). In these studies, Amino has argued that the fourteenth century marked a transition in Japanese ethnographic history. The late Heian to Sengoku periods were based on the system of landed estates, and the hierarchy of classes and forms of written documents express what may be considered a unified structure. Beginning in the fourteenth century, however, a notable series of changes took place in the nature of the people as perceived in their folk customs. Hitherto, Japanese society was a society of the senses, rich in primitive sorcery and the arts of magic. In such a society, foreigners, outcasts (*hinin*), and prostitutes were not yet confined to a world of exclusion, and there was an openness in which they could still be active as independent groups. Moreover, Japan was not yet unified into a homogeneous whole; thus the Tōhoku, Tōgoku, Saigoku, and Kyushu regions still had the potential to evolve separately.

Amino has sought to refute two basic arguments: that the Japanese people consist of one ethnic group speaking one language, and that, since Yayoi times, Japanese society has developed on the basis of rice culture. Instead, he has established a category of nonagricultural people—*jinin*, *kugonin*, hunting and fishing people, and various craftsmen—as the key to understanding medieval society.

Concerning the fourteenth century in particular, Amino has cited three developments, especially in the western provinces: the decline of imperial power, the diminution in dignity of the emperor and the gods, and the formation of the structure of discrimination. In this conception, Go-Daigo emerges as an *igyō no ōken*, an "eccentric symbol of sovereign power." Amino discovered from signatures in the interior of a statue of Manjushiri seated on a lion (*Hakkei monju bosatsu kishizō*) at Hannya-ji that the major donors of the statue (1324) were Monkan of the Tachikawa sect and Fujiwara Kanemitsu, the head of the *hikitsukeshū* (board of coadjutors) at the Bakufu's Rokuhara headquarters, and at the same time a member of the *hyōjōshū* (board of councillors). From this evidence, Amino explains how the two men, as Go-Daigo's "brain trust," came to constitute the backbone of the Kenmu regime: "Go-Daigo mobilized the non-persons (*hinin*), and through the use of the power of sexual intercourse in order to strengthen kingship, projected the emperor into the heart of Japanese society." By way of explanation, the Tachikawa sect placed sexual intercourse at the center of its worship, and Yamato Hannya-ji was a temple mainly for the *hinin*. The new government of the emperor was replete with such men.

Deriving his initial inspiration from Matsumoto, Amino condemned previous studies for their one-dimensional emphasis on rice fields and their neglect of nonagricultural people. How then would Amino assess the work of a scholar like Nakamura Naokatsu? In fact, Amino is in his debt even as his own writings have much advanced that perspective. Shimizu Mitsuo, though he profited from Nakamura's achievements in *shōen* history, did not continue the earlier historian's work on *kugonin* and *za*. Moreover, the postwar emphasis on social structure inevitably tied change to transformations in agriculture. Since these studies did not pay much attention to the significance of the formation of the new and diverse professional groups, there was ample space for Amino to develop his criticisms.

The greatest shortcoming of the scholarship of Nishida and Shimizu and other pre-1945 cultural historians was its failure to comprehend the complexities of the people of the Japanese archipelago. Amino's "Chiiki-shi kenkyū no ichishiten" (One Perspective on the Study of Regional History, in *Shinpen Nihon-shi kenkyū nyūmon*; Tokyo University Press, 1982) describes eastern and western Japan as ethnically different regions, thus breaking down the theory of homogeneity in Japanese society. Amino also notes that the areas along the Inland Sea were linked by means of water transportation, and he further emphasizes the existence of "Pan-China Sea" or "Pan-Japan Sea" regions. In addition, he has sought to elucidate and place in context those people who were not part of the framework of the nation-people and nation-state. Two works dealing with these respective subjects are *Higashi to nishi no kataru Nihon no rekishi* (Japanese History as Told by East and West; Soshiete, 1982), and *Nihon shakai saikō— kaimin to rettō bunka* (Rethinking Japanese Society: The Sea People and the Culture of the Archipelago; Shōgakukan, 1994).

Murai Shōsuke (1949–)

Though Amino's arguments are clear and straightforward, he has at times tended to oversimplify. A methodological successor to Amino is Murai Shōsuke of Tokyo University, who has published such articles as "Kenmu/Muromachi seiken to higashi Ajia" (The Kenmu-Muromachi Regimes and East Asia), later incorporated into his book *Ajia no naka no chūsei Nihon* (Medieval Japan Within East Asia; Kōsō shobo, 1988). A striking characteristic of this work is its vision of the people of Ryūkyū, Ainu, and Wa (Murai describes them as "Nihon" in quotation marks) as representing different ethnic groups existing in the fourteenth century. He describes a movement in the direction of a more uniform identity and examines the progress of medieval Japan in relation to such changes during the course of that and the next century. As part of his analysis he posits a pan–China Sea region in the south and a pan–Japan Sea region in the north—each with distinctive cultural and economic spheres.

Beyond that, Murai has studied with great enthusiasm the Zen priests and pirate-like sea merchants who engaged in international cultural exchanges and trade at the time. In particular, the *wakō* (pirates) constituted a vanguard for the formation of a cross-boundary region not subject to the authority of the state. But Murai has also seen negative aspects of these same developments, including the expulsion by force of the Ryūkyū merchants from the trade market of Korea, and the plundering of the coastal regions of Korea and China. Murai discerns in these a friction between the state and the people, thereby injecting a bit of realism in contradistinction to Amino's one-sided optimism.

Murai has succeeded in redefining Japanese politics within the framework of an East Asian international order, and in so doing he has offered a new interpretation of the individual careers of figures such as Prince Kanenaga, Shōni Motofuyu, Shimazu Ujihisa, Imagawa Ryōshun, and Ōuchi Yoshihiro. By defining the roles of these men who may have considered themselves as centers of their own diplomacy, Murai has brought out the unique structure of the fourteenth-century East Asian international order.

A recent book by Itō Kiyoshi, *Nanbokuchō no dōran* (The Nanbokuchō Disturbance; Shūei-sha, 1992), is a successful narrative of the century along the outlines of Murai's views. Itō examines Japan within the context of East Asia, calling the period that of the *Taiheiki*. But Ito's *Taiheiki* world is far different from that of Kume or Tanaka. He emphasizes Tosa and Hakata as windows to the North and West, and studies various sea routes as well as the international and domestic exchange of both people and goods. He also examines the *Taiheiki*, especially Part Three (vols. 23–40), from a much more sophisticated perspective that takes account of recent archaeological discoveries such as the great "Chinatown" in Hakata and the implications of Satsumon earthenware. Itō's book has taken historiography up to "the present."

CONCLUSION

Amino and Murai have argued for the independence of the eastern provinces from the western provinces, thereby taking a position that there were two separate states in medieval Japan. Such a view, which is representative of present studies, attempts to transcend the framework of the "nation-state."

I should like to raise a couple of questions about this perspective. As Murai himself is fully aware, there is a problem of the degree to which these regional cultures could actually invalidate the framework of a medieval Japanese nation-state and its links to the emperor. Can Amino's notion of the eastern provinces truly transcend the concept of the state that existed in medieval Japan?

Amino has depicted the people of the fourteenth century as figures who were part of the historical evolution of the sacred to the secular and the uncivilized to the civilized. He has also described a process by which certain persons became objects of discrimination as outcasts. Claiming, as he does, to have acquired a unique interpretation of Marx, and especially of Engels, his image of the people has become very nearly ahistorical. In other words, his methodology is quite different from that of earlier cultural historians who tried, from the vantage point of their own discipline, to analyze the collective psychology and behavior of the diverse people of medieval Japan. Put differently, much work remains to be done by historians of the fourteenth century.

Though research on medieval subjects has obviously continued apace, a good deal of the work of recent decades uses the framework of political history established by Satō, making detailed examination, for instance, of the organs of the Kenmu and Muromachi governments. Others, such as Ogawa Makoto's *Ashikaga ichimon shugo hatten-shi no kenkyū* (The Study of Shugo Development Among the Ashikaga Kinsmen; Yoshikawa Kōbunkan, 1980) and Mori Shiegaki's *Nanbokuchō kōbu kankei-shi no kenkyū* (The Study of Court-Warrior Relationships in the Nanbokuchō

Period; Bunken shuppan, 1984), reveal that positivist history is alive and well. Still, this approach, for all its virtues, has not succeeded in understanding the mentality of the people. I might even say that this subject, from beginning to end, was not deemed significant, making it incumbent on positivist scholars of political history to address this major shortcoming.

Reference Matter

Notes

Introduction

1. See, e.g., Hirata Toshiharu, *Yoshino jidai no kenkyū*, published in 1943.

2. Andrew Goble has recently reopened some of this controversy by changing Go-Daigo's "restoration" to a "revolution." See his *Kenmu: Go-Daigo's Revolution*.

3. Nagahara Keiji, review of John W. Hall and Jeffrey P. Mass, eds., *Medieval Japan: Essays in Institutional History*, in *Journal of Japanese Studies* 1, no. 2 (spring 1975): 445.

4. There is of course much more to be said on this subject, and we are only now in the opening stage of a comprehensive reappraisal. Needless to add, for scholars in Japan the subject has had a long history, with opinions expressed that posit medieval beginnings across eight centuries. See, e.g., Yasuda Motohisa, "History of the Studies of the Formation of Japanese Hōken System."

5. The original phrase, one of the best known in our field, was penned by James Murdoch; see his *A History of Japan*, 1: 580. John Whitney Hall quoted it in full in his "Foundations of the Modern Japanese Daimyo" (p. 65), which now 35 years later bears repeating: "Takauji may indeed have been the greatest man of his time, but that is not saying very much, for the middle of the fourteenth century was the golden age, not merely of turncoats, but of mediocrities."

6. See Tonomura, *Community and Commerce in Late Medieval Japan*; and Keirstead, *The Geography of Power in Medieval Japan*.

7. As Hurst notes, actual authorship of the Takauji testament has been frequently questioned. Yet the ideas expressed in this document seem to be those that reflect the great man's own thinking.

8. The periodization of George Sansom (pre-Kuroda) makes the point most forcefully. Sansom's history of Japan posited a progression of mutually exclusive ages, each represented by a usurpation and a further deformation of the imperial model; see, e.g., *A Short Cultural History*, 300. For my own critique of the pre-Kuroda approach, see chaps. 1, 2, 6, and 7 in my *Antiquity and Anachronism in Japanese History*.

9. Suzanne Gay remains a forceful spokesman for the applicability of the Kuroda thesis to the Nanbokuchō; see her "Muromachi Bakufu Rule in Kyoto: Administrative and Judicial Aspects"; and her unpublished Ph.D. thesis.

10. Among the scholars considered for inclusion here were Nagahara Keiji, Kawazoe Shōji, Sugiyama Hiroshi, and Toyoda Takeshi—not to mention Seno Seiichirō and Ōyama himself. The Japanese-language bibliography on the fourteenth century is vast.

Chapter 1

I am grateful to Andrew Goble for reading and commenting on a late draft of this paper.

1. For an elaboration of this view, see Mass, "The Missing Minamoto in the Twelfth-Century Kantō." Also, Friday, *Hired Swords: The Rise of Private Warrior Power in Early Japan.*

2. The literature is now quite substantial on what has come to be referred to as the "dual polity," or dyarchy, of Kamakura times. A collection of essays has sought to elaborate some of its major themes; see Mass, ed., *Court and Bakufu in Japan: Essays in Kamakura History.*

3. See, e.g., *Kamakura ibun* (hereafter *KI*), 31, doc. 23722 (1309/6), with its reference to hundreds of outsiders pouring into a troubled estate and wreaking havoc. Unlike earlier documentation, vividness of detail had now become standard. Moreover, petitions now tended to be accompanied by huge complements of supporting documents, for example, 25 and 45, respectively; see *KI* 36, doc. 27819 (1321/7), and 41, doc. 31669 (1332/1). In both cases, the issuing authorities were extremely diverse.

4. The orderliness of that predecessor is a theme of my work on the Bakufu-directed governance of the thirteenth century; see, esp. Mass, *Warrior Government in Early Medieval Japan* (hereafter *WG*), chap. 5 (on the *jitō/gesu* division); and Mass, *The Development of Kamakura Rule, 1180–1250* (hereafter *DKR*), chap. 5 (on the judicial ladder).

5. *KI* 41, doc. 31907 (1332/12/1); and 41, doc. 31979 (1333/2/3). The recipient was Shimazu Sadahisa.

6. *KI* 41, doc. 31669 (1332/1); and 41, doc. 32452 (1333/8/6).

7. For the first, *KI* 40, doc. 31165 (1330/7), and 41, doc. 31741; for the second, 36, doc. 28284 (1322/12/17).

8. *KI* 41, doc. 31829 (1332/8/27).

9. For the "fractional" *jitō* phenomenon, see Mass, *Lordship and Inheritance in Early Medieval Japan*, docs. 18, 121, 135, 141, etc. (hereafter *LAI*). At the same time, siblings who were neighboring *jitō* were often rivals, as in the case of an accused *jitō* who asserted that it was his *jitō* brother, not himself, who was guilty; *KI* 26, doc. 19960 (1299/2).

10. What, e.g., are we to make of someone who identified himself as a "deputy *shugo* plus a two-thirds deputy *jitō*" (*shugodai ken tōgō sanbun no ni sōjitōdai*)? *KI* 31, doc. 23815 (1309/11/19).

11. See, e.g., the Bakufu's confirmations of a sequence of transfers by sale across several decades; *LAI*, docs. 124–31. By the fourteenth century, there was little to distinguish suits over properties that had been purchased from suits that derived from the purchases themselves. See, e.g., *KI* 41, doc. 31913 (1332/12/5), for a Bakufu (Chinzei) verdict in a money and purchase suit.

12. Asakawa was the originator of this notion, followed by Sansom and virtually all others. For the significance of the misrepresentation, see my critique in Mass, *Antiquity and Anachronism in Japanese History*, 17 (hereafter *AA*).

13. In English, see Brown, "The Japanese Tokusei of 1297," and Kyotsu Hori, "The Mongol Invasions and the Kamakura Bakufu," chap. 7.

14. In 1323, e.g., the possession rights (*chigyō*) of a local purchaser were invalidated, with the rights of the earlier holder restored as a result; *KI* 36, doc. 28313 (1323/1/28). In 1330, a seller was summoned to stand trial; 40, doc. 31194 (1330/8/29).

15. There are almost countless examples of these preemptive invalidations of *tokusei*-style invalidations, e.g., *KI* 36, doc. 27664 (1320/12/20); 36, doc. 27709 (1321/2/6); and 38, doc. 29222 (1325/10/10).

16. See, e.g., *KI* 31, doc. 23947 (1310/3/22). A variety of different repayment mechanisms came to be used.

17. For example, *KI* 31, doc. 23761 (1309/9/6); and 38, doc. 29485 (1326/7/22). Persons who claimed falsely to be relatives were likewise enjoined; 38, doc. 29222 (1325/10/10).

18. For the sale, e.g., of a *myōshu shiki*, *KI* 31, doc. 23968 (1310/4/18).

19. See, e.g., the Bakufu's invalidation of the sale of a *jitō shiki* in Kyushu to another *gokenin* from the same province (Buzen); *KI* 31, doc. 23700 (1309/6/12). On the other hand, the sale of managerial *shiki* was not unknown; see, e.g., 20, doc. 15176 (1284/int. 4/13), for the sale of a *gesu shiki*.

20. See, e.g., the admonition of a proprietor against selling or bequeathing to "just anybody" (*kō-otsu no tomogara*); *KI* 38, doc. 29372 (1326/3/6).

21. See Arnesen, "The Struggle for Lordship in Late Heian Japan," and Mass, "The Missing Minamoto in the Twelfth Century Kantō."

22. For example, *KI* 36, doc. 27875 (1321/10/19), by the ex-emperor Go-Uda to the Tōji.

23. For the shogun, e.g., *KI* 36, doc. 27808 (1321/6/22); for the Hōjō (e.g., by the Chinzei *tandai*), 36, doc. 27742 (1321/2/2); and for the Bakufu (e.g., a "Kantō kishinjō" to Kōyasan), 38, doc. 29783 (1327/3/22).

24. See, e.g., the commendation document signed by a "*ryōke* Fujiwara"; *KI* 36, doc. 27643 (1320/11). A local shrine had been ravaged by invaders, leading to the endowment of timber land by a proprietor.

25. See, e.g., *KI* 41, doc. 31730 (1332/4/7), for a commendation of one *tan* of paddy to a local temple in Kii. Or, 36, doc. 27865 (1321/9/20), in which ex-emperor Go-Uda confirms a commendation by a priest to a local temple.

26. *KI* 36, doc. 27698 (1321/1/21); and (another example), 36, doc. 27767 (1321/4/21).

27. For example, *KI* 36, doc. 27897 (1321/11/7).

28. See, e.g., a commendation to the Katsuodera of three *chō* from among the holdings of a *jitō* in Settsu Province; *KI* 36, doc. 27780 (1321/5/4). Or, e.g., a commendation of the proceeds (*jobun*) from an estate in Yamashiro, even as the commender, a woman, retained ultimate property rights (*shitaji*); 31, doc. 23929 (1310/3/5).

29. *KI* 38, doc. 29235 (1325/10/22).

30. See, e.g., a commendation of a *jitō shiki* in Shinano Province to the much patronized Shōmyōji of Musashi Province; *KI* 23, doc. 23877 (1310/1/22). See also note 23.

31. *KI* 40, doc. 31234 (1330/10/13).

32. For example, *KI* 38, doc. 29246 (1325/11/7); and 41, doc. 31730 (1332/4/7).

33. *KI* 38, doc. 29364 (1326/2/27).

34. An excellent introduction to the subject is Harrington, "Social Control and the Significance of *Akutō*." The literature in Japanese is appropriately vast.

35. As one complainant put it, accusing the *shugo* of great evil (*dai akugyō*): "*Shugo* are placed in the provinces to protect against despoilments (*rōzeki*); but this *shugo* [of Bingo Province] is behind [the current] banditry." *KI* 36, doc. 27558 (1320/8).

36. See, e.g., the accusation against hundreds of a local temple's "farmer-residents" *jūnin hyakushō*; *KI* 31, doc. 23722 (1309/6). Or, again, against the "locals" (*domin*) on another temple's holdings; 31, doc. 13979 (1310/4). A survey of the leadership of ten *akutō* between 1275 and 1335 identifies different status levels in each case—from true locals, to former or current *shōen* officers, to *gokenin*, to deputy governors; see *Shiryō Nihonshi*, 54–55.

37. *KI* 38, doc. 29654 (1326/11/16); and *KI* 31, doc. 23722 (1309/6).

38. See, e.g., an inventory (*kyōmyō*) of murderers (*setsugainin*) in an area of Ōmi Province; the accused were a local constable (*sōtsuibushi*) and five of his sons (a certain younger brother was specifically excluded); *KI* 36, doc. 27723 (no date). Or see an "inventory of gang members" (*akutōnin kyōmyō*), consisting of seven persons, two of whose names (*jitsumyō*) are "unknown"; 38, doc. 29618 (1326/9).

39. See p. 29 below; and the essay by Thomas Conlan in this volume (Chap. 2).

40. See, e.g., the mustering of the *jitō gokenin* of Hyūga Province; *KI* 38, doc. 29377 (1326/3/8); or the mustering of *jitō gokenin* from "this [Iga] and nearby provinces" (*tōgoku kinkoku*); 38, doc. 29755 (1327/2).

41. *KI* 41, doc. 31777 (1332/7/12).

42. See Mass, "*Jitō* Land Possession in the Thirteenth Century"; and Mass, *WG*, chap. 7.

43. In an interesting usage, see Hanazono's association of a low-status, would-be troublemaker like Kusunoki Masashige with "the rise of *akutō* in the western provinces"; *KI* 41, doc. 32021 (1333/int. 2/24). Or, more mundanely, Go-Uda's

conveyance of depositions to be sent to the Bakufu in the matter of an *akutō*'s ravagings in Bingo Province; 36, doc. 27584 (1320/10/6).

44. *Akutō* (referred to as such) were a phenomenon of central and western Japan.

45. For example, *KI* 36, doc. 27558 (1320/8), describing conditions in Kōyasan's Ōta Estate; and 38, doc. 29617 (1326/9), describing the mayhem in Tōdaiji's Kuroda Estate.

46. *KI* 36, doc. 27558 (1320/8).

47. For example, *KI* 36, doc. 27602 (no date); and 38, 29225 (1325/10/13).

48. See the two documents in *KI* 36 and 38 for the charge in both directions (the first a defense statement, the second an accusation).

49. See, e.g., *KI* 38, doc. 29629 (1326/10/11); and 41, doc. 31838 (1332/8). For the subject of forgeries and the judicial process, *DKR*, chap. 3.

50. For the first, e.g., *KI* 23, doc. 23952 (1310/3); for the second, 40, doc. 31166 (1330/7).

51. *KI* 31, doc. 23924 (1310/2).

52. For example, the Tōdaiji complained of someone claiming to be a descendant of Ōe Hiromoto (adviser to Yoritomo), and therefore, accordingly, the *jitō* of record. For its part, Tōdaiji proclaimed the estate to have had no *jitō* in the beginning, but it also cited an imperial edict (*rinji*) requesting a *jitō* cancellation. To bolster his own argument, the would-be *jitō* averred the existence of a *"jitō* receivership" (*jitō ukesho*) since the 1220s; *KI* 38, doc. 29538 (1326/7).

53. See next note.

54. For example, *KI* 31, doc. 23761 (1309/6); 36, doc. 27819 (1321/7); 38, doc. 29360 (1326/2/19); and 38, doc. 29765 (1327/3/7).

55. For a petition for a judgment against a *jitōdai*, see, e.g., *KI* 40, doc. 31195 (1330/8). For a defense brief by a *jitōdai*, 40, doc. 31259 (1330/10/27). For the Bakufu's summoning of a *jitōdai* to trial, 41, 31741 (1332/4/16).

56. For example, see the Bakufu's call for particulars in response to a *jitōdai*'s complaint against a man and his followers accused of murder and of building a fortress; *KI* 40, doc. 31248 (1330/10/25). For a trio of accords (*wayojō*) between a proprietor's deputy (*azukari dokoro*) and three deputy *jitō*, see 36, docs. 28321–23 (1323/2/5).

57. Indeed, the same person might now be both a *jitō* and a *jitōdai* in different estates, e.g., *KI* 36, doc. 28249 (1322/11/26). No longer a matter of status and therefore relative influence, *jitō* would not necessarily have eschewed the deputy title.

58. Of course the opposite could also happen—the exclusion of a *jitōdai* by a conspiracy of rivals, e.g., in Ōta Estate in Bingo Province, involving the policing authority (*kendan*). Thus a proprietor's deputy (*azukari dokoro*), his deputy (*azukari dokorodai*), a fractional *jitō* (*ichibu jitō*), and a local constable (*sōtsuibushi*) divided that authority among themselves; the *jitōdai* was pointedly left out. See *KI* 40, doc. 31230 (1330/10/3).

59. *KI* 38, doc. 29633 (1326/10/14).

60. The classic statement came in a will of 1301: "For now and ever more, let no release take place—for as much as a *tan* or *bu*—to a youngest son, a daughter, a widow, or to any different clan-named outsider." See *LAI*, doc. 132.

61. For details, see Kyotsu Hori, "The Mongol Invasions and the Kamakura Bakufu," chap. 6.

62. These documents, known as *fukkanjō*, were issued by *shugo* between 1272 and 1310; see Kawazoe Shōji, *Mōko shūrai kenkyū shiron*, 33–35. However, the phenomenon clearly continued, as we see from a Bakufu edict of 1332, which railed against would-be *gokenin* on the basis now of documents purportedly by *deputy shugo*; *KI* 41, doc. 31850 (1332/9/23).

63. See, e.g., *KI* 7, doc. 4662 (1234/5/20).

64. See, e.g., the complaint by an estate's residents of vandalism by *jitō gokenin* in their capacity as "Bakufu (*buke*) agents"; *KI* 38, doc. 29806 (1327/4/10). Also, an estate deputy's petition against someone who was calling himself a *gokenin* in order to justify his use of force; 40, doc. 31166 (1330/7).

65. In one instance, a proprietor, plagued by local trouble, took the unusual step of requesting that a series of *jitō* be appointed. The Bakufu, unsurprisingly, obliged; *KI* 36, doc. 27652 (1320/12/7).

66. Andrew Goble has made this same point in a somewhat different context in his *Kenmu: Go-Daigo's Revolution*, chap 5.

67. An awareness of the manipulative potential of personal names came earlier (the era after Yoritomo's death); see *AA*, chap. 4. But *keizu*, in large numbers, appear only now. Among numerous examples, see, e.g., the references to the appending of a *keizu* in legal briefs; *KI* 31, doc. 23853 (1310/2); and 36, doc. 28298 (1322/12/6). In the first, the *keizu* was the only supporting document submitted; in the second, it was the final supporting document listed.

68. This constitutes my major argument in *LAI* in which I translate a number of verdicts that underline the point.

69. Most collections of warrior documents indeed begin in the 1180s, with even the exceptions rarely starting more than a generation or two earlier; see the annotated bibliography in Mass, *The Kamakura Bakufu: A Study in Documents* (hereafter *KB*). An oldest document from, e.g., 1183/6 might be considered typical, as in a group appended to an appeal of 1322; *KI* 36, doc. 28298 (1322/12/6).

70. *KI* 38, doc. 29645 (1326/10).

71. *KI* 38, doc. 29538 (1326/7).

72. *KI* 33, doc. 25757 (1316/2).

73. For a discussion of these concessions, see Mass, "Jitō Land Possession in the Thirteenth Century"; for actual examples, *KB* docs. 117–30. The standard work on the subject is Hirayama Kōzō, *Wayo no kenkyū*.

74. For the background to the temple and its association with Go-Daigo and Musō Soseki, see the paper below by Martin Collcutt.

75. *KI* 41, doc. 31771 (1332/6). The document had a complicated political con-

text, i.e., the divisions within the imperial house as they affected the security of the temple's assets. In 1332, Go-Daigo was in exile, meaning that Rinsenji would have been seeking a confirmation of its holdings from the imperial branch that was not the source of its original legacy.

76. The "disturbance" referred to related to the rumblings associated with the exile of Go-Daigo in 1331.

77. A case in point is the accusation of rent theft from Yamato Province's Hata Estate by an imperial prince (a prince, incidentally, from the non–Go-Daigo branch of the imperial house; see note 75). A year later, after the Bakufu's destruction, Go-Daigo confirmed, without comment, a selection (but only a selection) of Rinsenji's holdings; *KI* 41, doc. 32387 (1333/7/23).

78. *KI* 41, doc. 31837 (no date).

79. See the papers below by Mikael Adolphson and Martin Collcutt.

80. For this monumental tale in all its richness, see Goble, *Kenmu: Go-Daigo's Revolution*.

81. See ibid., chap 4, for an expert analysis of the prince's recruiting efforts. Morinaga's name is sometimes read Moriyoshi.

82. See, e.g., *KI* 41, doc. 31937 (1332/12/26); and 41, doc. 31933 (1332/12/25).

83. See, e.g., the Bakufu's call to the Kumagai to suppress both the prince and Kusunoki Masashige; the Kumagai's positive reception to that overture; and the prince's response to that response; *KI* 41, docs. 31915, 32011, and 32074 (1332/12/9, 1333/int. 2/8, and 1333/4/1). Or see the prince's overture to the head of the Miura-Wada—one of the original ranking vassal houses of the Kamakura Bakufu; 41, doc. 31971 (1333/1/20).

84. *KI* 41, doc. 31937 (1332/12/26).

85. *KI* 41, doc. 31983 (1333/2/6).

86. *KI* 41, doc. 31996 (1333/2/21).

87. For example, *KI* 41, doc. 32003 (1333/2/30).

88. For example, *KI* 41, doc. 31988 (1333/2/15); and 41, docs. 32132–33 (1333/5/5).

89. *KI* 41, doc. 32073 (1333/4/1).

90. *KI* 41, docs. 32075 (1333/4/1), from the prince to the Kutsuna house of Iyo.

91. *KI* 41, doc. 32084 (1333/4/10).

92. *KI* 41, doc. 32107 (1333/4/26).

93. For example, *KI* 41, doc. 32171 (1333/5/18).

94. For example, *KI* 41, doc. 32145 (1333/5/9).

95. There are large numbers of these documents, e.g., by a warrior who referred to himself as a "Harima *gokenin*" and a "*gesu-kumon*; *KI* 41, doc. 32150 (1333/5/10). Or by a warrior from Echigo who, though failing to cite his status and his titles, noted the current "treachery" (whose?) as the rationale for his appearance; 41, doc. 32179 (1333/5/21). Both documents were countersigned by Ashikaga Takauji. For an elaboration of this subject, see the paper below by Thomas Conlan.

96. In Kyushu, for example, warriors who attacked Hōjō Hidetoki were re-

ceived by Ōtomo Sadamune. See, e.g., *KI* 41, doc. 32229 (1333/6/2), for an arrival document by the Munakata, to which was affixed Sadamune's countersignature. In the east, Nitta Yoshisada performed a similar role, e.g., 41, doc. 32247 (1333/6/7).

97. *KI* 41, doc. 32148 (1333/5/10).

98. A common request was for immunity from trespass by armies on the move, a desire that Takauji must have found easy to grant. On a single day, he issued protection orders for the Tofukuji, and for temples in Tango and Hizen; see *KI* 41, docs. 32171–73 (1333/5/18).

99. *KI* 41, doc. 32230 (1333/6/2).

100. For example, *KI* 41, doc. 32264 (1333/6/13), on behalf of the Kujō; and 41, doc. 32280 (1333/6/16), on behalf of the Saidaiji.

101. *KI* 41, doc. 32272 (1333/6/14).

102. *KI* 41, docs. 32370–71 (1333/7/17, 7/19).

103. For example, *KI* 41, doc. 32304–5 (1333/6/29); and 42, doc. 32562 (1333/9/14).

104. For the admonitions, *KI* 41, docs. 32320 and 32336 (1333/7/2, 7/7); for the reassignments to the Tōji, 42, doc. 32540 (1333/9/1). For an imperial censure now of the *former jitō* of Ōyama, 42, doc. 32574.

105. For Tara Estate in Wakasa Province, see Yamamura, "Tara in Transition: A Study of Kamakura Shōen," 349–91; *WG*, 177–78; *KB*, doc. 89; *DKR*, docs. 124, 133. For Ōyama Estate in Tanba, see Mass, "Jitō Land Possession in the Thirteenth Century," 173–77, 181; and *KB*, doc. 127. The two *shōen*, for which voluminous sources survive, are among the most exhaustively studied of medieval estates.

106. *KI* 41, doc. 32452 (1333/8/6).

107. *KI* 41, doc. 32372 (1333/7/19).

108. For the *jitō* holdings of the Kamakura-era Kobayakawa, see *LAI*, docs. 84–85, 120; and *DKR*, docs. 41, 78. There is a substantial literature in Japanese on this prominent family.

109. *KI* 41, docs. 32505–10 (1333/8/29).

110. *KI* 41, doc. 32389 (1333/7/24); and 41, doc. 32415 (1333/7/26). Both estates were located in Harima Province. For the political significance of the Kujō's dispute here with the Akamatsu of Harima, see Goble, *Kenmu: Go-Daigo's Revolution*, chap. 5.

111. *KI* 41, doc. 32489 (1333/8/20). The original grant, dating from the Shōō era (1288–93), had been an award for loyal service against the Mongols ("Mōkonin").

112. See, e.g., the emperor's confirmation of Sasaki Tokitsune in the *jitō shiki* of Kuchiki Estate in Ōmi Province; *KI* 41, doc. 32466 (1333/8/10).

113. *KI* 41, doc. 32567 (1333/9/?), on behalf of a holding of the Tōji. Or 41, doc. 32326 (1333/7/3), in which the object of the censure was the "violations of an *akutō*" (*akutō no ranbō*) in Wakasa's Kunitomi Estate.

114. For example, the condemnation of a *jitō* in Bizen (*KI* 41, doc. 32467

[1333/8/12]), or of a *kumon* et al. in Owari (42, doc. 32618 [1333/10/9]). In another case, the censure was of the "provincial headquarters" (*kokuga*) in Satsuma; 42, doc. 32558 (1333/9/12).

115. Thus he might be shorn of all his titles, as in "Kamakura Takatoki" (e.g., *KI* 41, doc. 32309 [1333/6]); or he might be referred to by a nominal Buddhist title, as in "Takatoki *hosshi*" (in a Go-Daigo edict; 41, doc. 32219 [1333/5/29]). Most damning of all was to highlight the undistinguished origins of his family, as in "Izu Province local official (*zaichō*) Takatoki" (41, doc. 32145 [1333/5/9]). His clan of origin might also be recalled, as in "the former Sagami governor Taira Takatoki" (41, doc. 32256 [1333/6/9]).

116. See, e.g., the arrival statements of *gokenin* from Harima, Kii, and Kaga provinces, respectively; *KI* 41, doc. 32150 (1333/5/10); 41, doc. 32261 (1333/6/10); and 41, 32310 (1333/6). In all three cases, the word *gokenin* preceded any *shiki* that might have been held (*gesu-kumon* in Harima, none in Kii, "partial" *jitō* in Kaga). A disproportionately large number of the arrivals listed no *shiki* at all (e.g., *gokenin* from Izumi and Harima; 41, docs. 32154, 32157 [1333/5/11, 1333/5/12]), though there were also others who cited neither *shiki* nor *gokenin* status; these last included their names and provinces only (e.g., 41, doc. 32174 and 32212 [1333/5/18, 1333/5/27]).

117. *KI* 41, doc. 32350 (1333/7/10).

118. *KI* 42, doc. 32578 (1333/9/28).

Chapter 2

1. These incentives for the Ōtomo were *jitō shiki* grants. For a summary of the events of 1375, see Tanaka Yoshinari, *Nanbokuchō jidaishi*. For the offers to the Ōtomo and Shimazu, see *Nanbokuchō ibun, Kyūshū hen* (hereafter *NBIK*), 5, docs. 5229, 5232. For one of the few nearly contemporary documentary references to Fuyusuke's "chastisement," see *NBIK* 5, doc. 5392.

2. Craig, *Chōshū in the Meiji Restoration, 1853–1868*, 145.

3. Murdoch, *A History of Japan*, 1: 580. George Sansom echoes Murdoch: "The disintegration of the old warrior society . . . was hastened by the war between the Courts, when . . . a warrior's loyalty to his overlord was weakened to such a degree that the turncoat became a common phenomenon." See Sansom, *A History of Japan, 1334–1615*, 205.

4. Arnesen, "The Provincial Vassals of the Muromachi Shoguns," in Mass and Hauser, eds., *The Bakufu in Japanese History*, 115.

5. For *kitō chūsetsu*, see *NBIK* 1, doc. 831 (*kitō chūkin*); 2, doc. 1473 (*kitō chūsetsu*); doc. 2090 (*kitō chū*); *Nanbokuchō ibun, Chūgoku shikoku hen* (*NBIC*), 5, doc. 4518 (*kitō chūsetsu*); for the *chūsetsu* of festivities, *NBIK* 4, doc. 4159; for *jimu kōkō chūsetsu*, *NBIC* 5, doc. 4489.

6. For *kassen chūsetsu*, see *NBIK* 1, doc. 945; and *NBIC* 3, docs. 1976–77; for wound *chūsetsu*, *NBIK* 3, doc. 3724; for the *chūsetsu* of the capture of an enemy's head see *NBIK* 3, doc. 3723; and *NBIC* 1, docs. 400–401 for the *chūsetsu* of one

prisoner and two heads taken; for the use of *chūsetsu* for those who had arrived at an encampment, *NBIC* 5, doc. 4130; for those praised for persuading other warriors to become allies, *NBIK* 3, doc. 2633; for those who recently switched sides, *NBIK* 3, doc. 2633; for the *chūsetsu* of building an arrow storehouse (*yagura*), see *Kanagawa kenshi* 3.1, doc. 3481.

7. For the service of being cut down in battle (*uchishi chūkin*), see *NBIK* 6, docs. 6294–95; for a father's receipt of a *jitō shiki* for his *chūsetsu* and the death of two sons, *NBIK* 5, docs. 5776–77; and finally, *NBIK* 2, docs. 2289–90, 2309, 2313, and 2315 for documents issued to Aso Koretoki. In a period of eight days during the third month of 1347, Koretoki was praised by Ashikaga Tadayoshi and by Emperor Go-Murakami for his military service (*chūsetsu* and *gunchū*, respectively).

8. See *DNK, iewake 14, Kumagai-ke monjo*, doc. 225 (1337 [Kenmu 4]/8th month Nomoto Tomoyuki Shisoku Tsurujūmaru gunchūjō); and *Baishōron* (1975 ed.), 99.

9. H. C. McCullough, trans., *The Taiheiki*, 245. See *Taiheiki* (1980 ed.), maki 9, "Ashikaga dono Ōeizan uchikoetamau koto," 28.

10. For one such reference to being born in a *yumiya no ie*, see *NBIK* 1, doc. 1232 (1338/8/15 Kino Takeshige kishōmon); for warrior honor (*yumiya no menmoku*) see *NBIK* 5, doc. 5592 (1380/4/16 Tachibana Kinshige kishinjō).

11. Steenstrup, "*Sata Mirensho*: A Fourteenth-Century Law Primer," 418. Steenstrup translates *jitō gokenin* as *jitō* and *gokenin*. I believe these two were a compound term in the *Sata Mirensho*. See "Sata Mirensho" in *Zoku gunsho ruijū* 25.1, 1–14. Although *jitō* and *gokenin* were distinct during the early Kamakura period—the former being a tangible office and the latter being a more nebulous status—the terms came to coalesce into *jitō gokenin* in the late Kamakura period. The reason for this amalgamation remains unknown.

12. *Miuchi*, in particular, were not limited to followers of the Hōjō *tokusō*. See Ogawa Makoto, *Ashikaga ichimon shugo hattenshi no kenkyū*, 355.

13. *Taiheiki*, maki 38, "Shokoku Miyakata hōki no koto tsuketari Etchū ikusa no koto," 353–54. Ashikaga Tadafuyu was an estranged son of Ashikaga Takauji.

14. Significantly, instead of "service" (*chūsetsu*), the term *gi*, best translated as "duty," often described the obligations of *miuchi*. For this insight I am indebted to Thomas Nelson.

15. *Taiheiki*, maki 17, "Kankō kyōhō no hitobito kinsatsuseraruru koto," 165.

16. The *Baishōron* does not mention this at all, so I am inclined to think the *Taiheiki* account a fabrication. Regardless of its veracity, the *Taiheiki* had to "ring true" to fourteenth-century audiences. In other words, a rebellion by *miuchi* could drive a *tozama* to suicide. See *Taiheiki*, maki 16, "Shōni, Kikuchi to kassen no koto," 18–19.

17. McCullough, trans., *The Taiheiki*, 297–98. See also *Taiheiki*, maki 10, "Shioda oyako jigai no koto," 117.

18. *Taiheiki*, maki 15, "Ōshū sei sakamoto ni tsuku koto," 396.

19. Ibid., "Miidera kassen narabi ni tōji tsukigane no koto tsuketari Tawara Tōda ga koto," 398.

20. Ibid., "Shōgatsu nijū shichi nichi kassen no koto," 421.

21. *Taiheiki*, maki 21, "Tenka jisei shō no koto," 377.

22. Ogawa, *Ashikaga ichimon shugo hattenshi no kenkyū*, 339.

23. Ibid., 338.

24. *Taiheiki*, maki 36, "Hayami kokoro kawari no koto tsuketari Hatakeyama dōsei ga koto," 292.

25. *NBIK* 6, doc. 6848, *Hennen Ōtomo shiryō*, Takita Manabu, comp., 2, doc. 748.

26. Ibid.

27. Ibid.

28. *NBIK* 2, doc. 2197 (of 1346/5/17); *NBIK* 5, doc. 5233 (of 1375/9/2). One of these *jitō shiki* was granted to Aso Koresumi in 1347 by the Southern Court's Prince Kaneyoshi. See *NBIK* 2, doc. 2391.

29. According to the Suwa Daimyōjin e-kotoba (in *Zoku gunsho ruijū, jingi bu 3*, maki 73, p. 512), the Ki and Sei bands of "Utsunomiya housemen" (*kenin*) suffered heavy casualties while fighting in northern Honshū (Tsugaru).

30. Satō Shin'ichi used the phrase "freedom of movement" to describe *jitō gokenin* in his *Nanbokuchō no dōran*, 175–78.

31. Steenstrup, "*Sata Mirensho*," 418, and *Zoku gunsho ruijū*, 25.1.

32. For one example, see *Hizen Matsura tō Ariurake monjo*, Fukuda Ikuo and Murai Shōsuke, eds., doc. 17 (Chinzei gechijō an), 42–43. Seno Seiichirō addresses this question in *Chinzei gokenin no kenkyū*, 159–60. Confirmations of *gokenin* status were rare, particularly in western Japan.

33. An analysis of Go-Daigo's abolishment of *gokenin* appears in Goble, "Go-Daigo and the Kemmu Restoration," 369.

34. *Taiheiki*, maki 13, "Ryūme Shinsō no koto," 262–63; and maki 14, "Setsudoshi gekō no koto," 325.

35. See, e.g., 1333/10/18 Migita Sukeie chakutōjō, and 1333/11 Migita Sukeyasu gonjōjō, *Dai Nihon Shiryō* (DNS), 6.1: 265, 298; 1334/7/18 Ōe Michihide chakutōjō, *NBIK* 1, doc. 85; 1336/1/4 Ogawa Shigeharu hirōjō, *DNS* 6.2: 687, 1333/7/20 Kenbu (Nejime) Kiyotake chakutōjō, *Kamakura ibun* (KI), 41, doc. 32383; and 1333/11 Hizen Aokata Takanao mōshijōan, *KI* 42, doc. 32728. Warriors referred to themselves as *gokenin* into the 1350s. See *DNS* 6.14: 703, 719 (1351/1[?] Yokomine Nagatane mōshijō and 1351/6 Migita Sukeuji gunchūjō).

36. *NBIK* 1, doc. 519 (of 1336/3/26); doc. 937 (of 1337/5/16); and *NBIK* 2, doc. 1391 (of 1339/8/28).

37. *NBIK* 2, doc. 1391 (of 1339/8/28); doc. 1684 (of 1341/7/23); doc. 1883 (1342/12/11 Shimazu Dōkan kyōjō); *NBIK* 3, doc. 3166 (1351/8/21 Hatakeyama Tadaaki kyōjō); docs. 3174–75 (1351, 8th month Nejime Kiyonari gunchūjō).

38. *NBIK* 1, doc. 823; *NBIK* 2, doc. 1394; *NBIK* 3, doc. 3177. Kiyotane does

not appear at all on Kiyonari's petition (*gunchūjō*); see *NBIK* 2, doc. 1684, and *NBIK* 3, doc. 3175.

39. *NBIK* 1, doc. 383 (1336/1/11 Toriihama Kiyoyoshi tō rensho keijōan). Kiyonari and Kiyotane signed this document, as did the Nejime *gokenin* named Kiyotake, Dōkei, and Kiyoyoshi. One Nejime signer, Raijun, remains otherwise obscure. Kiyotake was a *gokenin* summoned to fight in 1333 and 1336. *KI* 41, doc. 32383 (1333/7/20, Kenbu Kiyotake chakutōjō). See also *NBIK* 1, docs. 787–88 (1336/11/21 chakutōjō, for Kiyotake and Kiyotane). For Kiyoyoshi's *gunchūjō*, see *NBIK* 1, doc. 634 (1336/6/17 Kenbu Kiyoyoshi gunchūjōan). Dōkei controlled large holdings of land: see 1323/10/20 Kenbu Takakiyo [Dōkei] yuzurijō, *Kagoshima ken shiryō kyūki zatsuroku jūi, iewake* 1: 465, doc. 718.

40. An analogous situation where aristocratic leaders could lead their peers with great difficulty is admirably elucidated in Leyser, *Rule and Conflict in an Early Medieval Society.*

41. *NBIC* 1, doc. 376 (1336/6/14 Ashikaga Tadayoshi gunzei saisokujō an).

42. Ibid., doc. 440 (1336/8/4 Ashikaga Tadayoshi gunzei saisokujō an).

43. Ibid., doc. 530 (1336/10 Ashikaga Tadayoshi gunzei saisokujō an); also doc. 531. This order was duly repeated two months later; ibid., docs. 562–63 (1336/12 Ashikaga Tadayoshi gunzei saisokujō an).

44. The Tokuno, for example, fought fervently for the opposing Southern Court.

45. For the actions of the Kutsuna, see *NBIC* 2, doc. 1190 (Kutsuna ichizoku gunchū shidai). The Ōtachi led the forces that captured Setanojō, the main Kōno castle; *Taiheiki*, maki 22, "Yoshisuke Ason byōshi no koto tsuketari Tomo ikusa no koto," 459.

46. *NBIC* 2, doc. 1167.

47. Ibid., doc. 1203 (1342/10/20 Kobayakawa Ujihira gunchūjō an). See also ibid., docs. 1205, 1280–81. From this point onward, tensions between the Kōno and the Hosokawa increased, culminating in the Kōno's allegiance with the Southern Court. With the fall of Hosokawa Yoriyuki the Kōno again allied with the Northern Court.

48. *NBIC* 2, doc. 1789.

49. *NBIC* 5, doc. 4627 (1380/8/6 Ashikaga Yoshimitsu migyōsho an).

50. For outright grants of lands as rewards by the Hosokawa in Tosa Province, for example, see *NBIC* 1, docs. 933, 966. Most surviving Kōno documents are mere commendations. For six commendations (*kishin*) to Zennōji temple, see *NBIC* 4, docs. 3194–95, 3228–29, 3277, 3281.

51. See Ogawa, *Ashikaga ichimon shugo hattenshi no kenkyū*, 29ff. and 333ff.

52. For further evidence of the refusal of *tozama* to obey the Shimazu in Ōsumi and Satsuma provinces, see *NBIK* 4, docs. 3831, 3845, and 3883. See also, *Taiheiki*, maki 38, "Shokoku Miyakata hōki no koto tsuketari Etchū ikusa no koto," 352, 358–60.

53. Urushihara Toru. "Nanbokuchō shingi ni okeru shugo kengen no ichi kō satsu," 57–72, particularly p. 69.

54. *Kutsuki monjo*, Okuno Takahiro, ed., 1: 5–7, docs. 7–9, 11. For Yoriuji's service under Hosokawa Akiuji, see ibid., 1: 8, doc. 14 (1347/8/9 Ashikaga Tadayoshi migyōsho). For Yoriuji's reluctance to serve under the Sasaki, see ibid., docs. 56–58 (1338/8/16, 8/27, 9/3 Kyōgoku Dōyo kakikudashi); and ibid., doc. 10 (1338/10/2 Ashikaga Tadayoshi migyōsho).

55. For examples of *tozama* abandoning forces, see *Taiheiki*, maki 19 "Nitta Yoshisada Echizen no fu no shiro o otosukoto," 275; and maki 38, "Shokoku Miyakata hōki no koto tsuketari Etchū ikusa no koto," 359–60.

56. These included the Momonoi, Kira, and Ishibashi. See Ogawa, *Ashikaga ichimon shugo hattenshi no kenkyū*, 5.

57. *NBIC* 5, doc. 4572.

58. *NBIC* 3, doc. 2324.

59. For a sampling of the Ōuchi documents, see *NBIC* 5, docs. 4054, 4266, 4370, 4581, 4601–2, 4607–9, 4621, 4641, 4647–48, 4726, 4736, and for confirmation of some Kumagai holdings, 4731.

60. For the prohibitions, see *NBIC* 5, doc. 4734. Documentation for the rebuilding of shrines appears in *NBIC* 4, docs. 3543, 3785.

61. Perhaps the Ōuchi usurpation of hegemonic prerogatives contributed to the Bakufu's campaign against them in 1399 which ended in Ōuchi defeat.

62. *NBIC* 5, doc. 4252. The term *ichizoku kenin*, or family members and housemen, is used in this document.

63. For this estimate, see Satō Shin'ichi, *Nanbokuchō no dōran*, 450.

64. *NBIC* 5, docs. 4065, 4665. For a later confirmation by Hosokawa Yoriyuki, see ibid., doc. 4112.

65. *NBIK* 5, doc. 5332.

66. Varley, trans., *A Chronicle of Gods and Sovereigns: Jinnō Shōtōki of Kitabatake Chikafusa*, 260–61.

67. Ibid., 263.

68. For more on the nature of symbolic capital, see Bourdieu, *Outline of a Theory of Practice*.

69. For an important article on the personal nature of lordship, see Schlesinger, "Lord and Follower in Germanic Institutional History," from F. Cheyette, *Lordship and Community in Medieval Europe*, 65–99. See in particular p. 75: "The man who sought to erect a royal lordship depended on his followers; these were the chief props of his future power."

70. *"Mukashi wa mukashi ima wa ima on koso shu yo."* Passage from *Genpei Jōsuiki*, maki 20, "Ishibashi kassen no koto." Quoted by Tsuda Sōkichi, *Bungaku ni arawaretaru kokumin shisō no kenkyū 2*, in *Tsuda Sōkichi Zenshū 5*, 135.

71. In a particularly well known case, Go-Daigo bestowed the "taka" of Takaharu (his name as imperial prince) to Ashikaga Takauji in recognition of his ser-

vice. For a more general reward of names, see *NBIK* 3, doc. 3723 (1354/9/3 Ashikaga Takauji kanjō an). The 1351/3/29 entry of the *Jizōin nikki* (most readily accessible as the *Kannō ninnen hinami ki*, in *Zoku gunsho ruijū*, 29.2: 364–65) tells of the grant of a battle flag (*mihata*) from Ashikaga Takauji to a deserving warrior. According to p. 79 of the *Baishōron*, two *kenin* of the Yūki fought so valiantly at Tenryūgawa in 1335 that Ashikaga Takauji gave each a sword in appreciation. Confirmations (*ando*) are also numerous. For one instance of lands entrusted to the Tsuchimochi by the Imagawa for military provisions, see *NBIK* 5, docs. 5001, 5008. For confirmations of hereditary homelands (*honryō*), see *NBIK* 5, docs. 5003, 5309. For an offer of new lands, see *NBIK* 5, doc. 5426; for the offer of a *shugo shiki* and lands, see *NBIK* 4, docs. 4339–41, 4416. Perhaps some will object to my use of the admittedly vague term "lands" to describe the variety of *shiki* that were bestowed to warriors. Although rewards for *jitō shiki* were perhaps most common, warriors were also rewarded *ryōke shiki* for their efforts. See *NBIC* 3, docs. 2118, 2123, and 1354 (1344/8/7 Ashikaga Tadayoshi saikyojō). Although some later documents offer *jitō shiki*—*NBIK* 5, doc. 5008, and *NBIC* 3, docs. 2119, 2128—others simply offer lands to be entrusted and make no distinction between *jitō*, *ryōke*, or any *shiki* at all, for that matter. See *NBIK* 5, doc. 5001. I have lumped these various grants under the term "land" because I believe no significant division existed among these categories, although I may be forced to revise this in light of more systematic research on this subject.

72. *Baishōron*, 140. The *Yoshisadaki*, attributed to Nitta Yoshisada but probably apocryphal, also stresses the importance of rewarding warriors commensurate to the degree of service they performed. See Hurst, "The Warrior as Ideal for a New Age" 221–22.

73. *Taiheiki*, maki 13, "Ryūme shinsō no koto," 262.

74. *DNS* 6.1: 90–91 (1333/6/7 Go-Daigo tennō rinji). See also, Tanaka Yoshinari, *Nanbokuchō jidaishi*, 108–9.

75. The pioneering study on "gift giving" and authority is Marcel Mauss, *The Gift*.

76. Goble, "Go-Daigo and the Kemmu Restoration," 352–53. For the *Taiheiki*'s appraisal of Akamatsu Enshin's rewards, see McCullough trans., 365.

77. Goble, "Go-Daigo and the Kemmu Restoration," 379. For documents relating to Kyushu, see *NBIK* 1, docs. 93–94, 199–200, 330.

78. A Ryūzōji Ieyasu document contains references to his military service (*gunchū*), yet the only tangible service Ieyasu seems to have accomplished is to arrive at an encampment; *NBIK* 1, doc. 435. For another document that equates encampment with military service, see ibid., docs. 421–22.

79. Goble, "Go-Daigo and the Kemmu Restoration," 386–87. For Ashikaga grants of Izu lands to the Uesugi and the Kō on 1333/12/19, see *KI* 42, docs. 32807–9. For the Ashikaga confiscation of Nitta lands, see Satō Shin'ichi, *Nanbokuchō no dōran*, 119. For a sampling of grants by Ashikaga Takauji in 1335, see *NBIC* 1, docs.

167–68 (1335/9/27 Ashikaga Takauji kudashibumi); for a grant by Ashikaga Tada-yoshi to the Nagai in Harima (which was a proprietary province—*bunkoku*—of the Nitta) see *NBIC* 1, doc. 210 (1335/12/26 Ashikaga Tadayoshi kudashibumi). A 1335/9/27 Ashikaga Takauji kudashibumi, granting Mutsu, Kawachi, Sagami, Settsu, Shinano, Bungo, and Kōzuke lands to the Miura can be found in *NBIK* 1, doc. 304. See also *NBIK* 1, doc. 353 (of 1335/12/21).

80. *NBIC* 2, doc. 1354 (1344/8/7 Ashikaga Tadayoshi saikyojō). See also, *Kagawa kenshi* 8, Zentsūji monjo, doc. 42, pp. 44–45. The *onshōgata* was the ad-ministrative organ of the Muromachi Bakufu responsible for rewards. *Bettō shiki* had been previously granted to Daisō Shōbō of Zuishin'in on 1341/5/14, imply-ing a right of management (*kanri*). See *NBIC* 2, docs. 1078, 1082. Daisō Shōbō was able to maintain his *bettō shiki* rights, which were later transferred to another temple. See *Kadokawa chimei daijiten* 37: 466. The ultimate fate of Takatsuna and his companions is unknown.

81. See, e.g., *NBIC* 5, doc. 4521.　　82. Ibid., doc. 4260.

83. *NBIK* 3, docs. 3304–5.　　84. *NBIK* 1, docs. 1128, 1231, and 1284.

85. *Baishōron*, 140.

86. The best account of this incident appears in the "Kannō ninnen hinami ki," 361–62.

87. See Tōin Kinkata's *Entairyaku*, 1351/3/3. Supporting documentary evidence can be found in *NBIK* 3, docs. 3021–22 (1351/3/1 Ashikaga Takauji kanjō). The only reference to Tadayoshi's oath appears in the latter documents. See also, Satō, *Nanbokuchō no dōran*, 248–49. Some discrepancy exists: according to the Zoku gunsho ruijū kanseikai edition of *Entairyaku* (v. 7), Takauji secured rewards for 43 warriors, while the version found in *DNS* 6.14: 858–59 has it as only 42.

88. Satō, *Nanbokuchō no dōran*, 248–49.

89. *Entairyaku*, 1351/3/3 in *DNS* 6.14: p. 859. Tōin Kinkata wryly commented that Akiuji showed fear for the first time since coming to the capital.

90. Tadayoshi was defeated, imprisoned in a Kamakura temple, and poisoned exactly one year after his triumph over the Kō brothers.

91. *NBIK* 3, docs. 3095, 3220. Yasutomi suggested that it was distance that had led to Tadafuyu's mistaking Buzen for Chikuzen province. Tadafuyu duly cor-rected his error.

92. For more on Tadafuyu's *uragaki ando*, see Kawazoe Shōji. " 'Chinzei tandai' Ashikaga Tadafuyu: Kyūshū ni okeru Kannō seihen," 187–242.

93. *NBIK* 3, docs. 2802, 2829. See also, Yamaguchi Takamasa, *Nanbokuchōki Kyūshū chūseishi kenkyū*, 2, 21.

94. *NBIK* 3, doc. 3095 (Yasutomi Yasushige mōshijō).

95. Isshiki Dōyū suffered from confused jurisdiction, few lands, and little sup-port. See *NBIK* 2, docs. 1475, 1481.

96. See ibid., doc. 1469 for *jitō shiki* granted to the Fukabori.

97. *NBIK* 1, doc. 840. The Ryūzōji were *gokenin*. See *KI* 42, doc. 32633.

98. *NBIK* 3, docs. 3304–5.

99. Ibid., doc. 2903. By the first month of 1351 Ryūzōji Iehira received the same. See ibid., docs. 2982, 3292.

100. *Fukushima kenshi*, 1, tsūshihen, 668 and v. 7, shiryō hen kodai chūsei 2, p. 371, Ise Yūki monjo, doc. 17 (1334/4/6 Mutsu kokushi kudashibumi an). Three subdistricts (*gō*) of Ishikawa-no-shō were granted to Yūki Munehiro.

101. *Fukushima kenshi*, 7: 456–57, Endō Ishikawa monjo, doc. 1 (1335/eighth month Ashikaga Takauji kudashibumi).

102. Ibid., 532, Kakuda Ishikawa monjo, doc. 2 (1336/seventh month Ishikawa Yoshimitsu wakatō Yabukigawa Yorimichi gunchūjō). Ishikawa Yoshimitsu was cut down in front of the Jizō-dō on the western slopes of Hiei.

103. Ibid., 503, Matsudaira Yūki monjo, doc. 5 (1338/12/3 Kitabatake Chikafusa migyōsho). The passage cited was a quote from a document of the previous month. See ibid., 501, Matsudaira Yūki monjo, doc. 3 (1338/11/11 Kitabatake Chikafusa sodehan sōshin shojū).

104. Ibid., 501–3, Matsudaira Yūki Monjo, doc. 4 (1340/11/26 Kitabatake Chikafusa sodehan sōshin hōsho).

105. *DNS* 6.7: 573 (of 1343/2/25). This was reconfirmed on 1351/2/27. See *DNS* 6.14: 850.

106. A will (*yuzurijō*) dating from 1369/6/19 lists villages and subdistricts (*gō*) of Ishikawa-no-shō. See *Fukushima kenshi*, 7: 522–23, Shirakawa koji kōshoshū-monjo 1, doc. 3 (Yūki Akitomo yuzurijō an). The members of the Ishikawa who had received rewards from Ashikaga Takauji fought with Yūki Chikatomo. See *DNS* 6.7: 705–8 (1343/8/19, Ishidō Nyūdō migyōsho an, and 1343/ninth month chūshinjō).

107. The Kabata Ishikawa fought against their brethren who joined the Southern Court. See *Fukushima kenshi*, 7: 458, Endō Ishikawa monjo, doc. 7 (1343/11/17 Ishidō Yoshimoto kanjō). Between 1346 and 1353 some members of the main-line Ishikawa apparently supported, once again, the Northern Court. Because documents of this Ishikawa lineage do not survive it remains difficult to chronicle their actions during the fourteenth century. See also, *Fukushima kenshi*, 1: 672–73.

108. Satō Shin'ichi, *Nanbokuchō no dōran*, 181. An instance where a defeated warrior surrendered half his holdings can be found in *Fukushima kenshi*, 7: 211–12, Kunitama monjō, docs. 7–8 (1339/3/23 Satake Katsuyoshi Hōgan Gyōkei rensho uchiwatsejō).

109. *NBIK* 4, doc. 4437; *NBIK* 5, doc. 5426.

110. *NBIK* 4, doc. 3880. The Southern Court promised to confirm only one half of Aso Koretoki's holdings upon his death in 1356, which helps explain why the Aso sided with the Ashikaga in the 1360s. See ibid., doc. 4437. In addition, see ibid., doc. 4281, in which Koresumi goes so far as to complain about "the set rule whereas, irrespective of merit (*rihi o ronsezaru*), all those who ally themselves will receive a full confirmation of their current lands."

111. *NBIK* 3, doc. 2651.

112. *Taiheiki*, maki 16, "Bitchū no Fukuyama kassen no koto," 53.

113. For more on the *kōsan no hō*, see *Taiheiki*, maki 14, "Shōgun juraku no koto tsuketari Chikamitsu uchishi no koto," 380–81; and maki 16, "Bitchū no Fukuyama kassen no koto," 52. An example of a warrior enticed into surrendering with a promise of further rewards can be found in *Iwate ken chūsei monjo*, 1: 65–66, docs. 182, 185 (1340/6/25 and 1341/2/7 Ashikaga Tadayoshi kankōjō). Tadayoshi promised Nanbu Masanaga, a Southern Court stalwart, that if he allied with the Ashikaga he would be amply rewarded.

114. *Sōma Monjo*, 49–50, doc. 61 (1348/ninth month, Sōma Tanehira mōshijōan).

115. Ibid., 35–37, doc. 42 (1336[8?]/8/26 Sōma Tanehira gunchūjō 1336(8?)/8/26).

116. The same seems to have been true for the Nitta, but this assertion needs more research.

117. *NBIK* 6, doc. 6251.

Chapter 3

This paper was translated by Thomas Nelson.

1. Shikata Masakazu, "Kikuchi-shi no kigen ni tsuite"; Morimoto Yoshinobu, "Kikuchi-shi no genryū ni tsuite"; Asoshina Yasuo, *Kikuchi ichizoku*.

2. *Azuma kagami* (hereafter *AK*), 1181/2/29.

3. *AK*, 1185/7/12.

4. While resident in Hakata, a Tōfukuji monk named Ryōkaku described developments in Kyushu, Shikoku, and western Honshu in a diary known to later generations as the *Hakata Nikki*. It was written on the unused, reverse side of a list of documents relating to the Sonogi-no-shō in Hizen (a Tōfukuji property) dated 1329/7/3. It describes events from 1333/3/11 until 1333/4/7. This important source is kept at the Sonkeikaku Bunko.

5. *Ōtomo monjo*, 1333/8/28 Go-Daigo Tennō rinji. All the documents cited in this article may be found in vol. 1 of *Nanbokuchō ibun, Kyūshū hen*, edited by Seno Seiichirō.

6. *Shimazu-ke monjo*, 1334/9/10; 1334/9/12.

7. *Madarajima monjo*, 1334/7/15 Madarajima Todomu chakutōjō; *Ariura monjo*, 1334/7/17 Madarajima Todomu chakutōjō; *Kurushima monjo*, 1334/8/18 Oe Michihide chakutōjō; *Fukabori monjo*, 1334/7/21 Fukabori Myōi chakutōjō; 1334/7/23 Fukabori Tokihiro chakutōjō; 1334/7/28 Fukabori Tokitsugu chakutōjō; *Kōzuma monjo*, 1334/7/22 Miyano Jakue chakutōjō; *Ryūzōji monjo*, 1334/7/24 Ryūzōji Zenchi chakutōjō; *Kondō monjo*, 1334/7/26 Araki Ieari chakutōjō; *Sagara-ke monjo*, 1334/7/28 Sagara Iehiro chakutōjō; 1334/7/28 Sagara Sukenaga chakutōjō.

8. *Munakata Jinja monjo*, 1335/1/21 Go-Daigo Tennō rinji; *Ryūzōji monjo*,

1335/1/23 Ryūzōji Zenchi chakutōjō; *Kōzuma monjo*, 1335/1/24 Miyano Jakue chakutōjō; *Tachibana Nakamura monjo*, 1335/1/–Tachibana Satsuma Shōkū chakutōjō; *Taguchi monjo*, 1335/2/21 Shōni Yorihisa kakikudashi; *Tada Jinja monjo*, 1335/int. 10/–Mutō Sochi mōshijō.

9. *Ōtomo monjo*, 1335/12/12 Hazama Shōku chakutōjō; *Hazama monjo*, 1336/9/– Hazama Shōku gunchūjō; *Nogami-ke monjo*, 1336/9/–Nogami Sukeuji gunchūjō.

10. See, e.g., *Matsura monjo*, 1335/11/22 Go-Daigo Tennō rinji (Hizen); *Aso-ke monjo*, 1335/11/22 Horikawa Mitsutsugu hōreishi (Higo); *Ueda monjo*, 1335/11/23 Go-Daigo Tennō rinji (Buzen); *Iriki Honda monjo*, 1335/12/25 (Satsuma); *Shiga monjo*, 1335/12/15 Go-Daigo Tennō rinji (Bungo).

11. *Fukabori monjo*, 1335/12/14 Ōtomo Sadanori shigyōjō-an; 1335/12/13 Ashikaga Takauji gunzei saisokujō-an; 1335/12/23 Shōni Yorihisa shigyōjō; *Ōtomo monjo*, 1335/12/13 Ashikaga Takauji gunzei saisokujō; *Aokata monjo*, 1335/12/13 Ashikaga Takauji gunzei saisokujō-an.

12. *Yanase monjo*, 1336/1/13 Shōni Yorihisa kakikudashi; *Tsuchimochi monjo* 1336/1/16 Ryōson shojō; 1336/1/18 Hōon Enkan'in shojō; 1336/2/7 Tsuchimochi Nobuhide gunchūjō-an; *Shinohara monjo*, 1336/1/25 Shōni Yorihisa gunzei saisokujō; *Sagara monjo*, 1336/2/4 Ashikaga Takauji gunzei saisokujō; Ashikaga Takauji gunzei saisokujō dated 1336/2/4, quoted in the Sekidō komonjo eihyakushu; *Tomimitsu monjo*, 1336/2/4 Omae Dōtei shojō.

13. *Takuma monjo*, 1338/4/18 Takuma Sadamasa gunchūjō.

14. *Taguchi monjo*, 1336/2/14 Shōni Yorihisa gunzei saisokujō.

15. *Ōtomo monjo*, 1336/2/15 Ashikaga Takauji shojō-an.

16. *Takuma monjo*, 1337/2/–Takuma Yukichika gunchūjō-an; 1338/4/18 Takuma Sadamasa gunchūjō; *Hirose monjo*, 1336/3/20 Shōni Yorihisa kakikudashi; *Aso-ke monjo*, 1348/9/–Aso Korezumi gunchūjō.

17. Before taking his own life, Sadatsune commented: "I give up my life for my commander. This alone should be my funeral rite and memorial. Yorihisa and all those of our clan (*ichizoku*) and of our retainers who are left should demonstrate the utmost loyalty, each man as completely as the next."

18. Six gunzei saisokujō believed to have been issued by Ashikaga Takauji at Dazaifu in 1336/3/3 are to be found in the *Karashima*, *Sata*, *Isshi*, and *Ayabe monjo*, as well as in the Aso genealogy and the *Komonjo-shū* collection.

19. An analysis of surviving chakutōjō, gunchūjō, and kanjō reveals that the following Kyushu warriors joined Takauji: from Hizen: Ryūzōji Zenchi (Ieyasu), Gotō Sadaaki, Fukabori Myōi (Tokimichi), Fukabori Tokihiro, Aokata Takanao, Ryūzōji Jitsuzen (Iefusa), Ōshima Michinobu, Fujiwara Kazukado, Fukabori Tokitsugu, Fukabori Masatsuna, Fukabori Eijō, Madarajima Todomu, Isshi Ryōkaku; from Higo: Shōdai Shigemune; from Chikuzen: Nakamura Hidenaga, Asamachi Mitsuyo, Asamachi Mitsutane; from Chikugo: Miike Sadamoto, Fujiyoshi Mitsudō-maru; from Buzen: Taguchi Nobutsura, Okuma Norizane, Urushijima Kiyomoto; from Bungo: Oga Koreyo, Oga (Tokō) Koremoto, Hirabayashi

Chikazumi, Hirabayashi Ujichika, Hirabayashi Gyōbon (Yorizumi), Betsugi Yoritaka, Tomiki Tadashige, Tomiki Tadataka; from Satsuma: Yamada Tadayoshi, Kawata Keiki, Ohira Narisuke, Kanzaki Shigeyoshi, Shimazu Dōkan (Sadahisa), Yamada Dōkei (Munehisa); from Aki: Hiraga Tomokane.

20. *Hirose monjo*, 1336/3/16 Nakamura Hidenaga chakutōjō; *Madarajima monjo*, 1336/3/26 Madarajima Todomu gunchūjō; *Isshi monjo*, 1336/3/–Isshi Ryōkaku gunchūjō; *Aokata monjo*, 1337/7/–Aokata Takanao meyasu-jō.

21. Isshiki Yoriyuki was sent to attack Kusu Castle in Bungo where Ōtomo Sadamune's eldest son, Sadayori, and his brother Nyūta Shijaku (Yasuchika) had taken shelter together with Dewa Suesada, Betsugi Furen, Kaku Ben'a Jari Kaku Magogorō, Shami Dōen, Oda Akinari, and Uogaeri Saishōbō. Meanwhile Ueno Norihisa was sent to attack Kuroki Castle in Chikugo, and Isshiki Dōyū was sent to attack Yasshiro Kurotori Castle, also in Chikugo. Hatakeyama Yoshiaki and Shimazu Dōkan were ordered to attack Kimotsuki Kaneshiga in Hyūga.

22. *Ōtomo monjo*, 1336/3/17 Ashikaga Takauji kudashibumi.

23. *Shimazu-ke monjo*, 1336/3/17 Ashikaga Takauji kudashibumi.

24. *Arima monjo*, 1336/3/17 Ashikaga Takauji bugyōnin rensho hōsho; *Tsuruta monjo*, 1336/3/27 Ashikaga Takauji kudashibumi-an; *Yamada monjo*, 1336/3/28 Ashikaga Takauji bugyōnin rensho hōsho; *Okamoto monjo*, 1336/4/2 Ashikaga Takauji kudashibumi-an; *Tsugawa monjo*, 1336/4/5 Ashikaga Takauji kudashibumi.

25. *Saidaiji monjo*, 1336/3/24 Ashikaga Takauji kishinjō; *Hinomisaki Jinja monjo*, 1336/3/25 Ashikaga Takauji ando kudashibumi; *Kōsō Hachiman-gū monjo*, 1336/4/11 Ashikaga Takauji kishinjō; Ashikaga Takauji kakikudashi, quoted in the Hokuhi Senshi, dated 1336/3/13; *Shōhōji monjo*, 1336/3/29 Ashikaga Takauji kakikudashi; 1336/3/29 Tomo Shōzen shigyōjō-an.

26. Ashikaga Tadayoshi gunzei saisokujō, in the Hagihan batsu etsuroku, dated 1336/3/23; *Kikkawa-ke monjo*, 1336/3/30 Ashikaga Tadayoshi gunzei saisokujō.

27. *Nejime monjo*, 1336/3/12 Kō Moronao hōsho.

28. *Takeo jinja monjo*, 1336/3/20 Saitō Hen'yū shigyōjō.

29. *Kikuōji-ke monjo*, 1336/3/20 Ashikaga Takauji kakikudashi.

30. *Kikkawa-ke monjo*, 1336/3/30 Ashikaga Tadayoshi gunzei saisokujō.

31. *Takuma monjo*, 1336/4/9 Ashikaga Tadayoshi gunzei saisokujō.

32. *Tomimitsu monjo*, 1336/2/4 Omae Dōtei kenchijō; *Tsuchimochi monjo*, 1336/2/7 Tsuchimochi Nobuhide gunchūjō-an.

Chapter 4

1. Satō Shin'ichi, "Kamakura bakufu no senseika ni tsuite."

2. Matsumoto Shinpachirō, "Nanbokuchō nairan no shozentei."

3. Satō Shin'ichi, "Muromachi bakufu-ron"; idem, *Nanbokuchō no dōran*, 125, 224.

4. There are several variant names for this document. The one given here is

used by Satō Shin'ichi in *Nanbokuchō no dōran*, 125. The document comes from the *Baishōron*, vol. 2, "Ashikaga-zei shokoku tewake narabi ni inzen juryō no koto," 97–98, and is translated here:

"They stayed at the harbor for one or two days and held various discussions about the fighting. [Some people said that] the forces of the court were certain to attack. They suggested that, before Takauji arrived in Kyushu, he should place *taishō* in the provinces to protect his rear. To Shikoku were sent the brothers Hosokwa Kazuuji, Yoriharu, and Morouji. Six of their cousins also went to make a total of nine, Akiuji, Jōzen, Kōkai, Naotoshi, Masauji, and Shigeuji. Kazuuji and Akiuji were ordered to assess the valor of warriors and to reward them accordingly. The Akamatsu were stationed in Harima, Ishibashi Kazutoshi in Bizen, and the Matsuda with their clansmen (*ichizoku*) at Mitsuishi Castle. Bingo received the brothers Imagawa Akiuji and Sadakuni, who set up their encampments at Tomo and Onomichi. Momonoi Yoshimori and the Kobayakawa *ichizoku* went to Aki. Ōshima Yoshimasa, a Nitta *ichizoku*, was made *taishō*, and Ōuchi Nagahiro *shugo* in Suō. Shiba Takatsune was made *taisho* of Nagato, and Kōtō Takatsune its *shugo*. A Sanbōin monk, Kenshun, came as an imperial messenger with a directive (*inzen*) from the Jimyōin [line], and this gave everyone courage, for now the *taishō* could be ordered to hoist the brocade banner without being called enemies of the court."

5. See Chap. 3, by Seno Seiichirō, for details.

6. Imatani Akira, "Jūyon-jūgo seiki no Nihon," 17–18; idem, *Muromachi bakufu kaitai katei no kenkyū*, 228–35. Half-shugoships (*hanshugoshiki*) are explicitly mentioned in the sources, but "*bungun shugo*" is not a contemporary expression and, indeed, the phenomenon was not identified until Satō Shin'ichi noticed that some provinces appeared to have multiple *shugo*; see his *Muromachi bakufu shugo seido no kenkyū*. Warriors who acted as *shugo* only in individual districts (*gun*) are identified in the sources simply as *kunshu*, or lords.

7. Satō Shin'ichi, *Nanbokuchō no dōran*, 224.

8. *Taiheiki*, ed. Gotō Tanji and Kamada Kisaburō, vol. 3, maki 37, "Owari saemon no suke tonsei no koto," 380–81.

9. Okutomi Takayuki, *Kamakura Hōjō-shi no kisoteki kenkyū*, 131–39.

10. Kuroda Toshio, *Mōko Shūrai*, 76–79.

11. Ogawa Makoto, *Ashikaga ichimon shugo hattenshi no kenkyū*; Koyō Hiroshi, "Monjo yori mitaru Ashikaga Yoshiakira no chii to kengen." The propensity for high-ranking *ichizoku* to join Tadayoshi and lower-ranking ones Takauji is clear from the composition of the two camps during the Kannō Disturbance. When Kō Moronao chased Tadayoshi into Takauji's own residence and besieged him there, he was sharply criticized by Takauji for behavior unbecoming a hereditary servant (*Taiheiki*, vol. 3, maki 27, 70–72). Still, victory went to the Kō brothers and Moronao was again appointed *shitsuji*. The Kō were overthrown by a resurgent Tadayoshi and were put to death by the Uesugi, who, though hereditary servants themselves, had broken ranks with Takauji (*Taiheiki*, vol. 3, maki 29, 141).

The shake-up in *shugo* posts gave many to high-ranking Tadayoshi partisans. For example, Ise was passed from Ise Yoshinaga to Ishitō Yorifusa, and Izumo from Sasaki Dōyo to Yamana Tokiuji (Satō Shin'ichi, *Nanbokuchō no dōran*, 251). Again, when Takauji and Tadayoshi came to blows, the lower-ranking Niki, Hosokawa, and Toki joined Takauji, whereas the higher-ranking Momonoi, Hatakeyama, and Shiba joined Tadayoshi (*Taiheiki*, vol. 3, maki 30, 149–51; Satō Shin'ichi, *Nanbokuchō no dōran*, 258).

12. The internal dynamics of the Ashikaga family during the Kamakura period are poorly documented and the most complete description of them in the secondary literature is Kotani Toshihiko, "Kamakura-ki Ashikaga-shi no zokuteki kankei ni tsuite." The more independent collaterals had usually split from the main line earlier and had more integrated landholdings, often separate from those of the main branch. The Niki were closely associated with Takauji, and their lack of status is reflected in their short history as a separate branch and the fact that their holdings consisted of a mere four *gō* on the main Ashikaga estate. The Imagawa were not even descendants of the main line, but merely an offshoot of the Kira.

13. The Shiba and Hatakeyama were both usually in the Tadayoshi camp. The Shiba, with the Kira, were the highest-ranking *ichizoku* and were descended from Ieuji, grandson to Yoshiuji (1199–1254). The premature death of Ieuji's younger brother and progenitor of the Ashikaga main line (Yoriuji) meant that, for a time, it was he who represented the whole of the Ashikaga clan. The Shiba were based away from the Ashikaga main branch and had extensive holdings in Shiba-gun in Mutsu Province. The Hatakeyama are slightly anomalous in being descended from a union in 1205 between an earlier scion of the Ashikaga house and the Hōjō widow of Hatakeyama Shigetada. Shigetada's lands thus passed to an Ashikaga clansman, but the family was treated, from the start, almost as a separate line, joining the other *ichizoku* in giving gifts to the shogun but paying their dues to the Bakufu separately.

14. The Kō and Uesugi had both been Ashikaga *hikan* during the Kamakura period. Fukuda Toyohiko has shown (in "Kamakura jidai ni okeru Ashikaga-shi no kanri kikō") that the Kō served in the administrator's office (*bugyōsho*) from which the Ashikaga administered their lands. Indeed, three of the other bureaucratic (*bugyōnin*) families, the Minami, Mito, and Hikobe, appear to have been Kō *ichizoku*. Families who served as *bugyōnin* were often impoverished *gokenin* or were from clans that had been destroyed in the Wada, Miura, and other revolts.

15. *Entairyaku*, Bunna 4/23/4, cited in *Taiheiki*, 3: 511 n. 1. The event is also described in Satō Shin'ichi, *Nanbokuchō no dōran*, 322.

16. Ogawa Makoto, "Hosokawa Kiyouji no taitō"; idem, "Hosokawa Kiyouji no botsuraku." (Both these articles have been incorporated into Ogawa's *Ashikaga ichimon shugo hattenshi no kenkyū*.)

17. Ogawa Makoto, *Hosokawa Yoriyuki*.

18. Nitta Ichirō, "Taibon sankajō isetsu-jōshiki no saikentō."

19. Imatani Akira, "Jūyon-jūgo seiki no Nihon," 19.

20. Satō Kazuhiko, *Nanbokuchō nairan*, 181–83.

21. Imatani Akira, "Kamakura, Muromachi bakufu to kokugun no kikō," 288. In "Muromachi bakufu kaitai katei no kenkyū," Imatani Akira gives a complete list of the over twenty known divided shugoships. In addition, Kaga, Kawachi, Ōmi, Settsu, Tōtōmi, Suruga, Bingo, Ise, and Hitachi provinces were, at some point, all divided into *hanshugoshiki*.

22. Imatani, "Kamakura, Muromachi bakufu to kokugun no kikō," 290.

23. Ibid., 291–92.

24. In 1351/2/11, Takauji was forced temporarily to side with the Southern Court. He promptly declared the Shōni lands forfeit and gave a number to the Ōtomo, among them Toga Estate and Munakata Nishi-no-gō in Chikuzen, and Kuroda Estate in Bizen (*Nanbokuchō ibun* [hereafter *NI*], Kyūshū-hen, 3: 3242). In 1375/8, Imagawa Ryōshun, the *Kyūshū Tandai*, actually had the Shōni chieftain killed. The complex interrelationship between the Shōni, the Bakufu, the *tandai*, and an important local family called the Munakata is discussed in detail by Kuwata Kazuaki in "Muromachi-jidai ni okeru Munakata-shi no dōkō." In particular, Imagawa Ryōshun sought to turn the Munakata away from the Shōni and into agents of the *tandai*. Repeated injunctions were handed down forbidding Shōni interference in shrine affairs.

25. Urushihara Tōru, "Nanbokuchō jidai ni okeru shugo kengen no ichikōsatsu."

26. Urushihara Tōru, "Nanbokuchō jidai ni okeru shugo hakkyū kanjō no ichikōsatsu." The only real exception was in Kyushu, where Ashikaga clansmen did not benefit from the special advantages they enjoyed elsewhere. Thus, leading *tozama shugo* issued *kanjō* of the type that in central Japan was restricted to senior Ashikaga.

27. See Wintersteen, "The Muromachi *Shugo* and *Hanzei*," for details. Estates belonging to the imperial family, Fujiwara regents, and major religious institutions were made exempt.

28. Murai Shōsuke, "Tokusei to shite no Ōan Hanzeirei."

29. Takahashi Osamu, "Kamakura goki ni okeru chiiki kenryoku to bakufu taisei."

30. *Shimazu-ke monjo*, 1300/26/11 (*Kamakura ibun*, 27: 20653). This document lists every item of the *shugo's* competence and calls on the *on-tsukai* to cooperate with the *shugo* in each. See also, 1284/27/5 (*KI* 20: 15202): "You are to exercise the policing authority (*kendanken*) in the province of Bungo strictly and in partnership with the *shugo*, in accordance with a *Kanto* directive of the 24th day of last month."

31. Goble, "Go-Daigo and the Kemmu Restoration"; and Yamaguchi Takamasa, "Kunijoshi ni tsuite."

32. *Jōdoji monjo*, 1341/23/10 (*NI*, Chūgoku, Shikoku-hen, 2: 1118). Ten years

later, in 1351/29/6, Sugihara Mitsufusa sent orders to local *shisetsu* to suppress outrages on Jōdoji lands (*NI*, Chūgoku, Shikoku-hen, 3: 1057–60). In a separate example, between 1368 and 1371, Ōuchi Hiroyo served the *shugo* Imagawa Ryō-shun in Aki Province. In another document (*Tōji Hyakugō monjo*, 1373/9, *NI*, Chugoku, Shikoku-hen, 4: 3998), Hiroyo is referred to as the "*on-tsukai* Ōuchi-no-suke nyūdō." At the time, Imagawa Ryōshun was in Kyushu as the Bakufu's commander there and had no deputy (*shugodai*). In consequence, Hiroyo effectively discharged many of the functions of a *shugo*. Another example comes from Harima Province, where an undated document from the Yano Estate, believed to be from the early Nanbokuchō era, states that the *shugo* and the *kunishisetsu* had been ordered to put down the *akutō* (cited by Matsuoka Hisato, "Ōuchi-shi no Aki-no-kuni shihai").

33. Matsui Teruaki, "Kunijōshi, kunishisetsu no oboegaki," 20–21. The subject has also been discussed in detail by Tonooka Shin'ichirō in "Kamakura-matsu, Nanbokuchō-ki no shugo to kokujin." He argues that the old *ryōshi* system as inherited by the Ashikaga was continued almost unchanged in some provinces such as Aki, but that it gradually came to be used less frequently and in fewer provinces as the *shugo*'s jurisdiction grew. The destruction of the "bureaucratic *gokenin*" (*rimu-kei gokenin*), most of whom fought for Tadayoshi, signaled the end of the old system. These men had often held little or no land in the areas where they served. Henceforward, the Bakufu would rely more and more on a new type of *shisetsu* recruited from locally powerful *kokujin*, who also served in the *hōkōshū*.

Chapter 5

This chapter draws heavily from my dissertation, "Common Property and Community Formation: Self-Governing Villages in Late Medieval Japan, 1300–1600." My debts to various scholars who have read and commented on my work are too numerous to mention, but I should like to thank Shigehiro Kuramochi, Margaret McKean, Orest Pelech, Conrad Totman, and Kay M. Troost in particular.

1. Not all Japanese scholars see the fourteenth century, or Nanbokuchō as it is often referred to, as the primary turning point in the period 900–1600. Indeed this paper assumes an earlier turning point around 1050, as well as one in the fourteenth century. Some scholars have asserted that either the Genpei wars or the Ōnin War mark the distinctive turn either away from or into medieval society. These debates reflect different analyses of rural organization and are conducted in an explicitly Marxist framework, of a turning from slave to serf society. The issues include family structure, the organization of the agricultural labor force, the nature of "community" (*kyōdōtai*), and relationships between peasants and elites. Thomas Keirstead provides an excellent summary of the debates, especially as they pertain to the *shōen* system and the administrative and fiscal systems governing the countryside, in *The Geography of Power in Medieval Japan*, chap. 5, esp. 99–104.

2. In the eleventh century, between one-third and one-half of all fields listed on the tax rolls were not cultivated in any given year because of drought, floods, or lack of fertilizer. In the fourteenth century, the proportion of fields cultivated increased annually, and abandoned fields ("this year's waste") decreased. See discussion in Troost, "Common Property," chap. 1, esp. 36–44.

3. Influenced by the new trends in social history, research on medieval villages is prolific. For recent scholarship, in addition to the annual May issues of *Shigaku zasshi* and the report of the annual meeting published in *Rekishigaku kenkyū*, the reader may wish to consult *Shinshiten Nihon no rekishi 4, Chūsei hen*, Minegishi Sumio and Ikegami Hiroko, eds., esp., "Shōen koryosei shita no toshi to nōson"; *Sōten Nihon no rekishi, Chūsei hen*, Minegishi Sumio, ed., esp. Kuramochi Shigehiro, "Chūsei sonraku o ika ni ha'aku suru ka?" *Nihon sonraku kōza*, Nihon Sonrakushi Kōza Henshu Iinkai, eds., esp. vols. 2, Keikan I; 4, Seiji I and 6, Seikatsu I, and *Iwanami kōza Nihon Tsūshi, Chūsei hen*, vols. 7–10.

4. For greater detail, see Troost, "Common Property," chap. 1, esp. 85–114.

5. The famine of 1360–61 may have killed a quarter or more of the population, but it seems not to have had a lasting effect. E. A. Wrigley argues in *Population and World History* that once normal harvests resume after a famine, mortality drops to a level well below average, because the most vulnerable members of the population died during the food crisis, and the number of births rises sharply. "As a result populations often recovered their former size in a further decade" (113). It seems likely that this occurred in fourteenth century. Records of famines are drawn from Okajima Hatatsu, ed., *Nihon saiishi*; Fujikawa Yū, *Nihon shippei shi*, is the authoritative work on premodern epidemics. For a table comparing famines, epidemics, and peasant revolts from 900 to 1600, see Troost, "Common Property," 95.

6. Troost, "Common Property," 42–43.

7. This argument is made by a variety of scholars, notably Inagaki Yasuhiko, "Chūsei no nōgyō keiei to shūshu keitai," and Kimura Shigemitsu, "Daikaikon jidai no kaihatsu; Sono gijutsu to seikaku," 149ff.

8. Hotate Mishihisa, "Chūsei minshū keizai no hatten," 178–82.

9. See Nakamura Ken, "Chūsei kōki ni okeru Ōmi no kuni Tokuchinho Imabori gō no nōgyō," 149.

10. Amino Yoshihiko, in *Nihon chūsei no hinōgyōmin to tennō*, argues that population changed from mobile in early medieval Japan to settled in late medieval times, with the fourteenth century as the turning point.

11. Mizuno Shoji, "Chūsei no kaihatsu to sonraku," 8.

12. Okamoto Takenori, "Ōmi ni okeru chūsei sonraku no seiritsu to tenkai," 199–255, esp. 203.

13. Amino dates stable, nucleated settlements from the fifteenth century. Amino Yoshihiko, *Nihon rekishi o yominaosu*, 8–12.

14. *Imabori Hiyoshi jinja monjo shūsei* (hereafter *IM*), Nakamura Ken, ed., 33, 1403/10/2. *Mōto* were newcomers to a village community who had not yet been

given full-fledged status as community members and did not own land. See Naga-hara Keiji, "Village Communities and Daimyo Power," 111. Yasuda Motohisa de-fines *mōto* as lower in status than *myōshu*, and generally without land, unlike the regular cultivator-peasants (*sakunin hyakushō*), but not dependent either, unlike *genin*; *Shōen*, 248.

15. Membership was limited to those born in Imabori or adopted by age seven. The 1460 restriction of travelers from staying over was presumably specific to fes-tival times, since the other regulations in the same law pertained to festivals; by 1489, however, strangers (*tasho no hito*) were forbidden from entering Imabori without a guarantor. *IM* 371, 1460/11/1, and *IM* 365, 1489/11/4; see also *IM* 5, 1556, for another regulation of travelers.

16. Yoshida Toshihiro, "Chūsei sonraku no kōzō to sono henyō katei—shōson-'sankyōgata sonraku' ron no rekishi shirigakuteki sankentō."

17. Koizumi Yoshiaki, "Nairanki no shakai hendō," 128.

18. Sasaki Ginya, *Nihon no rekishi: Muromachi Bakufu*, 120.

19. *IM* 417, 1372/11/21, is the earliest record of new paddy. Other early records include *IM* 23, 1378/10/1, and *IM* 30, 1442/10/5. Development continued to 1600; see *IM* 616, 515, 477, 560, 557, 414, 561, 512, 538, 504, 443, 487, 447, 496 for ex-amples of new land sold or commended, and *IM* 25, 26, 36, 43, 44, 45 for admin-istrative decisions about developing new fields. On ponds and irrigation ditches, see *IM* 26, 1460/2/15, 43 and 44, 1551/4/18, and 265, 1555/12/3. Imabori's fields were predominantly dry in the thirteenth century, but they were almost equally di-vided between paddy and dry fields in 1600.

20. The first documented case was in Owari in 1399. Kinda Akihiro argues for origins after the twelfth century and before the late fourteenth, "Shōen sonraku no keikan," 146–47. See also, *Bishikei to chūsei sonraku*, 161–76.

21. Kinda Akihiro, "Shōen sonraku," 138–41.

22. Minegishi Sumio, "Jūgo seiki kōhan," 399–400. This contrasts with no records of double-cropping for ancient Japan and rates of 50 to 70 percent in 1947, when all feasible land in central and western Japan was double-cropped.

23. Quoted in Inagaki Yasuhiko and Toda Yoshimi, *Nihon minshū no rekishi 2, Doikki to nairan*, 222.

24. Examples can be found in Ichii-no-shō in Yamato in 1135, Yuge-no-shō in a certain province (probably Tamba) in 1160, and Kamo beppu-no-shō in Yama-shiro in 1181. See Kimura Shigemitsu, "Chūsei seiritsuki ni okeru batasaku no seikaku to ryōyū kankei," 9–16. (Kimura's works cited in this paper have been re-printed in Kimura, *Nihon kodai chūsei batasaku no seikaku no kenkyū*.) See also examples from outside the central provinces: Shiga daigaku keizai gakubu shiryō-kan, ed., *Suganoura monjo* (hereafter *SM*), 632, 1472/9/14, indicates that this rate dated from the late fourteenth century; and Wakayama kenshi hensan iinkai, *Oji jinja monjo* (hereafter *OJM*), 142, 1478/3/5; *OJM* 143 (no date, approx. 1478); and *OJM* 148 (no date).

25. Cotton was introduced to Japan in the fifteenth century, and was well suited to intensive cultivation on a small scale. Cultivation spread rapidly after the Ōnin War, except for areas that were too cold. Nagahara Keiji, *Shin-momen izen no koto, Choma kara momen e*, 56ff. Vegetables were grown near large cities on both dry fields and as a second crop on paddy, and oil-producing plants such as sesame became important as well. Miura Keiichi, *Chūsei minshū seikatsushi no kenkyū*, 162.

26. Toda Yoshimi, "Chūsei shoki nōgyō no ichi tokushitsu," 182–83.

27. Kawane Yoshiyasu, *Chūsei hōkensei seiritsushi ron*, 388–89.

28. See Yoshie Akio, "Shoki chūsei sonraku no keisei," 108–10, and Nagahara Keiji, *Nihon chūsei shakai kōzō no kenkyū*, esp. chaps. 6 and 7. Ota-no-shō in Bingo and Iriki-in in Satsuma are two frequently cited examples.

29. This roughly corresponds to the period from late March to late July in the Western calendar.

30. He found only one saucer pond dating from before 1300 in Yamato, the most developed region in medieval times. Kinda Akihiro, "Shōen sonraku," 152–55, and "Heianki no Yamato bonchi ni okeru jōri jiwari naibu no tochi riyō," 96–112.

31. Inagaki Yasuhiko, "Chūsei no nōgyō keiei to shūshu keitai," 171. For further evidence and more detailed discussion, see Kuroda Hideo, *Nihon chūsei kaihatsushi*, and Kimura Shigemitsu, "Daikaikon jidai."

32. *Population and Technological Change: A Study of Long-term Trends*, 96.

33. The government imported a waterwheel to combat drought in 829, but there is no further record of its use in the ninth century; see Farris, *Population, Disease, and Land in Early Japan, 645–900*, 97–100. Kimura, "Daikaikon jidai," 190–92.

34. Man- or animal-powered waterwheels were introduced from China, but water-powered ones were developed in Japan. Rotated by river currents, they worked with fast-flowing rivers, not with the slow currents common in areas with large rivers. Waterwheels continued to be used with little change in form into the twentieth century, though larger ones were developed in the Tokugawa period. Hogetsu Keigo, *Chūsei kangaishi no kenkyū*, 82–86, and Imatani Akira, "Wagakuni chūsei shiyō yōsuisha no fukugen," 17–56.

35. Kuroda, *Nihon chūsei kaihatsushi*, 52–64.

36. This distinction between open-access land and common property follows Margaret McKean, "Success on the Commons: A Comparative Examination of the Institutions for Common Property Resource Management," 250–52. McKean differentiates between unowned non–property, public property, state property, jointly owned private property, common property, and individually owned private property. Laws or customs governing the sale of common property are different from those of jointly owned and individually owned private property: "all co-owners of common property may simultaneously agree to sell by an agreed-upon voting rule but individual co-owners can sell, trade or lease their shares to others only in accordance with very stringent rules laid down by the group."

37. This discussion of ancient and early medieval use of mountain and open land is based on Toda, "Sanya no kizokuteki ryōyū," 280–322.

38. Ibid., 313–15.

39. Sekiguchi argues that the majority of Kamakura boundary disputes were caused by invasions of communal land and attempts to control its customary use by *shōen* lords and local warriors; Sekiguchi Tsuneo, "Chūsei zenki no minshū to sonraku," 149–52. Examples of intervillage disputes abound; the most famous include the ones between Ikatatsu and Katsuragawa (see Yamamoto Takashi, "Rōnin to chūsei sonraku," and Inagaki and Toda, *Doikki to nairan*, 227–33) and between Suganoura and Ōura (see Troost, 239ff).

40. Amino Yoshihiko, "Nōson no hattatsu to ryōshu keizai no tenkan," 120–24. Sekiguchi argues that the Kinai had shifted to *atesaku* by the Kamakura period and that western Japan and Kyushu shifted by mid-Kamakura; Sekiguchi Tsuneo, "Chūsei zenki no minshū to sonraku," 131–35. Yugenoshima illustrates peasant resistance to a *jitō*'s attempts to farm land with labor levies around 1300. See "Iyo no kuni Yugenoshima-no-shō kankei shiryō" (hereafter *YM*), 132, 1296/5/18.

41. Uejima Tamotsu maintains that productivity on Kamikuze-no-shō in Yamashiro more than doubled between mid-to-late Kamakura and late Nanbokuchō. His argument is based on a comparison of documents from 1324 and 1376. *Kyōkō shōen sonraku no kenkyū*, 210, 216–17.

42. Higher yields from improved cultivation practices and double-cropping reduced the amount of land needed to sustain a family. Regular cultivation and the improvement of the soil may have diminished the need for plowing. Plowing was associated with the reliance of small farmers on *myōshu* for access to plows and cows.

43. The full name was *kajishi myōshu shiki*. Suma in his study of Kii-gun in Yamashiro finds examples that suggest mid-Kamakura origin; Suma Chikai, "Yamashiro no kuni Kii-gun ni okeru shōensei to nōmin," 109–12. The selling of *kajishi* was well established in Kamikuze-no-shō by the late fourteenth century. See Kurokawa Naonori, "Jūgo, jūroku seiki no nōmin mondai."

44. For example, a 1297 land sale document listed 1 *koku* 4 *to* to be paid to the *honjo* and 1 *koku* 6 *to* to be paid as *kajishi*; *Tōji hyakugō monjo re*, 13–19, cited in Suma, "Yamashiro no kuni Kii-gun," 110. Sasaki Ginya also cites several examples, such as one from Yamashiro in 1407, with 3 *to* of dues and 8 *to* of *kajishi*; "Shōen sonraku to myōshu hyakushō," 104. See also, Uejima, *Kyōkō shōen sonraku*, 206–16.

45. See Kurokawa Naonori, "Jūgo, jūroku seiki no nōmin mondai," 34.

46. Nagahara Keiji argues that iron tools became widely affordable in the early fifteenth century; see "Chūsei no shakai kōsei to hōkensei," 341–42. The earliest records that allow for a comparison of prices for iron tools and rice or soybeans date from the mid-sixteenth century. In 1548, for example, a sickle was 25 *mon* and a *koku* of rice ranged from 1,149 to 1,515 *mon*; in 1549 a spade was 93 *mon* and a *koku* of rice ranged from 1,000 to 1,053 *mon*. Kadokawa, *Nihonshi jiten*, 1138.

47. A broad ax, two hoes, and a hand ax were listed as confiscated in 1347 from

a peasant who had only a few household goods and no horse or cow. Wealthier landholders had cows and plows; see Kuroda Hideo, *Nihon chūsei kaihatsushi*, 47–49.

48. Ibid., 171–74.

49. Although this example is drawn from eastern Japan where small fields continued to be opened later than in central Japan, a similar process occurred earlier in western Japan; for example, in Yano-no-shō in Harima, 16.4 percent of the land on the registers in 1298–99 were small, new fields. Koizumi Yoshiaki, "Nairanki no shakai hendō," 128.

50. *Isshikiden* were fields within an estate that paid only one form of dues, the rice levy (*nengu*), and were leased, usually on an annual basis, to cultivators, with the dues collected directly by the estate manager. By contrast, the holders of *myō* fields enjoyed a more stable tenure, and the levies, collected by the *myōshu*, were assessed at a lower rate because miscellaneous dues (*kuji*) were also paid. Cultivators of *isshikiden* relied on *myōshu* or local *shōen* officials for tools and seed. Before the growth of the village community in the late medieval period, these cultivators were not full members of the village community but rather had access to communal property through their ties to *myōshu*.

51. Hirose Kazuo argues that the growth of nucleated villages was premised on full cultivation of arable land. "Chūsei e no taidō," 349.

52. Ikeda-no-shō, Ichii-no-shō, and Kohigashi-no-shō are some examples in Yamato. See Kinda, "Shōen sonraku," for a brief summary; for greater detail see idem, "Nara–Heianki no sonraku keitai ni tsuite," 49–117. See also, Inagaki Yasuhiko, "Shōen kaihatsu no ato o saguru — Yamato no kuni Ikeda-no-shō," 1–32, and the work of Hirose Kazuo. Mizuno Shoji traces this transformation in thirteenth- and fourteenth-century Ōmi villages; "Chūsei no kaihatsu."

53. Okamoto Takenori, "Ōmi ni okeru chūsei sonraku no seiritsu to tenkai," 216. Houses of four to twelve *tsubo* were rebuilt twice on average.

54. Yoshida Toshihiro argues that the size of house lots in Imabori decreased because the village required that houses be built within specified boundaries, "Sōson no tenkai to tochi riyō," 137. He also demonstrates that land that had been previously houseland but was not within the village boundaries ceased to be houseland in the fifteenth century, 136–37.

55. "Nara-Heianki no sonraku keitai," 92–93.

56. Kinda, "Shōen sonraku," 128–30. Kohigashi-no-shō had eighteen residences in 1144, eight of which were in two groups near the present-day village while ten were on the high land in between. Kinda, "Nara-Heianki," 87–90.

57. They were grouped together at the site of the present-day village in the mid-fifteenth century. Kinda, "Nara-Heianki," 87.

58. Examples include Wakatsuki-no-shō and Kashiwade-no-shō; Fujioka Kenjirō, *Nihon rekishi chiri sosetsu, Chūsei hen*.

59. Fukuda Ajio, *Ajia no naka no Nihonshi*.

60. "Hori yori higashi o wa yashiki ni subekarazu mono nari," *IM* 363, 1489/11/4.

61. Hitomi Tonomura also argues for a collaborative relationship between village and proprietary lord, *Community and Commerce in Late Medieval Japan*, esp. 94. Shiga Setsuko, in "Chūsei kōki shōen sonraku to kendan," argues that the establishment of village self-government did not rest on a denial of proprietary rights but was a fusion of local customs and proprietary rights.

62. Ōyama Kyōhei argues that the peasants from Ichiidani went to Kyoto to protest the behavior of Tōji's agent and that Tōji took the opportunity to negotiate over the tax rate and to establish the peasants as responsible for the collection of taxes; "Kamakura jidai no sonraku ketsugō—Tamba no kuni Ōyama-no-shō Ichiidani," in Ōyama, *Nihon chūsei nōson no kenkyū*.

63. Thomas Smith defines *miyaza* as a group of families who exercised exclusive ceremonial rights with respect to the village deity and enjoyed a privileged position in the village; *Agrarian Origins of Modern Japan*, 59, 188. For research, see, in particular, Hagihara Tatsuo, *Chūsei saishi soshiki no kenkyū*, and Higo Kazuo, who is known for his study of shrine associations in Ōmi in the early twentieth century, *Ōmi ni okeru miyaza no kenkyū*. A short survey of shrine associations can be found in Takamaki Minoru, *Miyaza to matsuri*. Some villages had temple organizations (*tera no za*) which operated in a similar manner. The earliest example was the Shimoda Kagoshima shrine's Kechin-za in Yamato Prefecture which dates from 1196; see Nagashima Fukutarō, "Yamato Shimoda Kagoshima-shō Kechinza monjo to Chūsei sonraku," 67–82. Relatively few villages in the Kantō and eastern Japan had *miyaza*.

64. Smith, *Agrarian Origins*, 188.

65. *Ōshima jinja, Okutsushima jinja monjo* (hereafter *OJOJM*) 3, 1263/5/8, specified festival obligations for Shima and Tsuda.

66. For example, a local official exempted five *tan* of paddy and some forested land from dues and gave the land to Suganoura's three shrines and a Buddhist chapel, the Kannondō, in 1298 at the beginning of its struggle with the nearby estate of Ōura.

67. Listed as cultivators of the large *geshi myō*, their status is unclear. *YM* 176, 1314/9, and 178, 1314/11.

68. As in Yugenoshima, small peasants and *myōshu* in Kamikuze-no-shō protested together in the late fourteenth and early fifteenth centuries. Between 1339 and 1462, 29 oaths and petitions were sent to Tōji by the residents of Kamikuze-no-shō.

69. Compare *OJOJM* 15, 1298/6/4, *OJOJM* 16, 1298/6, and *OJOJM* 17, 1298, with *OJOJM* 2, 1262/10/11. For more detailed discussion, see Troost, "The Evolution of Self-Governing Villages: From Festivals to Common Land."

70. Okujima residents proclaimed a decision of the group (*shūgi no jo*) in 1342; three years later is the first reference to the *sō*, and eight pieces of land were com-

mended between 1345 and 1348; *OJOJM* 29, 1342/2, and *OJOJM* 30, 1345/12/9. See discussion in Troost, "The Evolution of Self-Governing Villages," 4–6.

71. Although no land had been commended before 1343, four pieces were commended between 1343 and 1347. Thirty were commended before 1420 (out of a total of 40). This coincidence strongly suggests an identification with village interests arising out of pond building. A sense of a nascent community was also seen in the banning of village daughters from serving in festivals in other villages in 1365 (*OJM* 81, 1365/10/14), the commendation of land for a village temple in 1368, and the contribution of 74 *kan* 200 *mon* by 77 people to build it in 1375 (*OJM* 84, 1368/3/14, and *OJM* 86, 1375/1/17).

72. *OJM* 24, 1296/12/27; four and a half *koku* was paid for 35 *bu*; see Kuroda Hiroko, *Chūsei sōsonshi no kōzō*, 119–23.

73. *SM* 830, 1467/2, and *SM* 348, 1516/6/22.

74. See *IM* 392 and *IM* 409, both 1477/11/16; *IM* 562, 1482/11/3; *IM* 439, 1376/2/16; and *IM* 402, 1449/7/10. Imabori also bought vegetable fields, *IM* 493, 1482/12/29.

75. See Maruyama Yoshihiko, "Shōen sonraku ni okeru sōyūchi ni tsuite— Ōmi no kuni Tokuchinho o chūshin ni," 297–323. Maruyama has analyzed two surveys from 1583 and 1584; the first did not record land held by the village. Maruyama gives two figures: 15.8 percent and 18.4 percent; the second includes woods directly held by the shrine. He also says about 20 percent. Imazaike had no paddy fields, hence vegetable fields were the best fields. The village held 51.9 percent of the vegetable fields, 9.8 percent of the best dry fields, and 85 percent of forest land; Maruyama, 301.

76. Since we lack the late-sixteenth-century land registers, it is difficult to be as precise as in the case of Imazaike, but Imabori held about 9 *chō* plus 72.5 *semachi* (unit of measure for vegetable fields, area unknown) of vegetable fields and 23 places (including houses) of shrine land in 1566; total fields not including forest at the time of Taikō kenchi were about 50 chō; Maruyama, "Shōen sonraku," 305.

77. Imabori, Higashimura, Suganoura, and Okujima have left records of dues collected, though Imabori's are by far the most extensive. Imabori has left many dues records (*osamechō*) as well as four registers with cultivator, area, place, and amount of dues (1384, 1463, 1510, 1566). There is one remaining for Okujima, three for Higashimura, and six for Suganoura.

78. *IM* 363, 1489/11/4.

79. *OJOJM* 73, 1372/12/27. *OJOJM* 125, 1436/1/16, said that "the *murando* shall survey the land every year to assess dues (*mainen kenmi*)." Suganoura wrote that "when the fields are bare from drought or water damage, there will be no 7 *to* of dues (*naitoku*). However, in mature years, there will be no deviation," *SM* 351, 1470/6. *OJOJM* 121, 1416/4, shows the right to cultivate (*gesaku shiki*) being reclaimed by the *murando* because of nonpayment of dues. *OJOJM* 106, 1409/10/25, said that if there was any nonpayment of dues, the *sō* could take the sakushiki

("*moshi mishin o mōsaresōrawaba, sakushiki o sō e tori ageraru beki mono nari*"). *IM* 371, 1460/11/1, implies that nonpayment of dues was grounds for loss of cultivation rights. *IM* 448, ?/11/8, said that the *sakushiki* could be taken for nonpayment of dues. *SM* 1260 (undated, about 1346) said that land would be taken if dues and rent were not paid before 10/10.

80. *OJOJM* 72, 1372/8/6.

81. *IM* 371, 1460/11/4. There was, however, considerable continuity; fifteen out of seventeen people cultivating shrine land in 1381 were still cultivating it in 1384; compare *IM* 342 and 318.

82. See Troost, "Common Property," 147–8; and Uejima, 89, 106–7, and 470–71.

83. The first reference to the *sō* by Suganoura was in 1346, *SM* 180, and the first survey of Hisashi and Morokawa was in 1342, *SM* 326.

84. *SM* 576, 1423/3/26; *SM* 575, 1434/11/30; *SM* 572, 1449/12/11.

85. Suganoura assumed responsibility for the collection and payment of taxes (*jigeuke*) in 1412 and thereafter received many pieces of land (*sōyūchi*).

86. This is particularly well illustrated by the case of Kujō Masamoto, the proprietary lord for Hine-no-shō in Izumi. When violence in the capital became excessive in the sixteenth century, he retired to Hine-no-shō and sought to become actively involved in its administration. The villagers, however, sought to resolve matters as much as possible on their own, often leaving him with little alternative other than to agree with the villagers' course of action; see Ryavec, "Political Jurisdiction in the Sengoku Daimyō Domain: Japan, 1477–1573," chap. 3.

87. For the Kawashima, see Gay, "The Kawashima: Warrior-Peasants of Medieval Japan."

88. *SM* 335, 1454/6/2; *SM* 830, 1467/2; *Suganoura ke monjo*, compiled by Shiga daigaku keizaigakubu fuzoku shiryōkan, 12, 1496/12/2; *SM* 224, 1497/12/5; *SM* 342, 1503/6/24.

89. See *OJOJM* 43, 1355/1/13, *OJOJM* 49, 1359/12/26, and Tabata Yasuko, "Chūsei koki ni okeru ryōshu shihai to sonraku kōzō—sōshō sōgō no kinō to yakuwari," 71–72.

90. *OJOJM* 140, 1454/12/3.

91. Uejima, *Kyōkō shōen sonraku*, 322–23.

92. Ryavec, "Political Jurisdiction," 94. Chap. 3 discusses three types of cases where proprietary and villager notions of justice differed: one where the proprietor enforced his notion, several where the villagers enforced their notions, and two where the villagers enforced compromises from higher authorities.

93. *OJOJM* 1, 1241/9, and *OJOJM* 35, 1350/10/9, *OJOJM* 36, 10/10, *OJOJM* 37, 1350/10, *OJOJM* 38, 1350/11/27, and *OJOJM* 67, 1370/8/21.

94. Suganoura had the support of Kaizu Nishihama and Yagi while Ōura had that of Kaizu, Higashihama, and Yagihama. Warriors from Imanishi, Yamamoto, and Asami on the northeastern shore of Lake Biwa supported Ōura, while war-

riors based in the neighboring villages of Anyōji, Kawamichi, and Yagi supported Suganoura. See Troost, "Common Property," chap. 4, esp. 256–62.

95. *IM* 594, 1558/5/28, listed warriors and their retainers (*hikan*).

96. *YM* 176, 1314/9; *YM* 178, 1314/11; and *YM* 179, undated, probably 1314/12/3.

97. Miura Keiichi, "Chūsei ni okeru nōgyō gijutsu no kaikyūteki seikaku — 'kadota naeshiro' o sozai ni tsuite," in Miura, *Chūsei minshū seikatstushi*, 35–54.

98. Tonomura, *Community and Commerce in Late Medieval Japan*, 150; the argument is developed in chaps. 4 and 5.

99. *SM* 126, 1470/4/20; see also *SM* 48 and 840; *SM* 632, 1472/9/14.

100. See Mass, *Warrior Government in Early Medieval Japan*, 176.

101. Ryavec, "Political Jurisdiction," 72.

102. *YM* 30, 1259/2/22.

103. Suganoura required residents to write wills that would be witnessed by the village; *SM* 229, 1491/9/8. *IM* 363, 1489/11/4, banned the keeping of dogs, and set rules concerning fees paid for building and selling houses. *IM* 5, 1556, banned fighting and gambling.

104. 106 *IM* 254, 1599/5/10, addressed cattle eating farm crops. *Chūsei Hōsei Shiryōshū* 63, 1585/6/28, from Kami Omori in Ōmi, also said that villagers needed to receive recompense for crops eaten by others' cows, and specified different punishments depending on whether it was the first time this had occurred.

105. For instance, Popkin in *The Rational Peasant* discusses at length the problem of free-riders—people who abuse the system because it is difficult to prosecute.

106. *IM* 363, 1489/11/4; see also, *IM* 375, 1502/3/9; *IM* 369, 1448/11/14; *IM* 372, 1520/12/26; *IM* 254, 1599/5/10; and *IM* 255, 1626/6/3. Ridges between fields were considered common property, and so Imabori set fines for the enlargement of fields by removing dirt from these embankments. *IM* 375, 1502/3/9; Nakamura Ken, *Chūsei sōsonshi no kenkyū*, chap. 6.

107. Wade, *Village Republics*, 13.   108. *OJOJM* 177, 1502/8/27.

109. *IM* 254, 1599/5/10.   110. *SM* 180, 1346/9.

111. *OJOJM* 165, 1492/12/4. Access to mountain land was contingent upon membership in the community and payment of dues. If someone did not pay his dues, he was required to leave his house, and his household goods and mountain fields became the property of the village community. Villagers could sell mountain fields to each other but not to outsiders.

112. If one *koku* of rice cost one *kanmon*, as it did except in times of famine, then three *mon* would buy 0.3 percent of one *koku*, or about half a liter of rice.

113. "Shugo funyū, jikendan no tokoro nari," *SM* 925, 1568/12/14.

114. *SM* 227, Kanshō 2 [1461]/7/13.

115. Masamotokō Tabihikitsuke, 1504/1/11, translated by Ryavec, 81.

116. Ibid., 82.

117. *SM* 226.

118. The spread of new rice strains was one change that was remarked upon; see Troost, "Common Property," chap. 1.

119. Suzanne Gay in her study of the Kawashima reads the documents closely, but finds little information about peasant life; see "The Kawashima: Warrior-Peasants of Medieval Japan." While both village and warrior documents survive for Suganoura, there is little connection between them, except in the sale and purchase of land; see *Suganoura ke monjo*.

Chapter 6

1. Goble, *Kenmu: Go-Daigo's Revolution*.

2. Imatani Akira, *Muromachi no ōken*; Imatani Akira with Kozo Yamamura, "Not for Lack of Will or Wile: Yoshimitsu's Failure to Supplant the Imperial Lineage"; Itō Kiyoshi, *Nihon chūsei no ōken to ken'i*.

3. *Taiheiki*, Nihon koten bungaku taikei edition (*NKBT*). The passage, in one of the variant editions of the *Taiheiki* (see *NKBT* supplementary note 5, 2: 484–85), is cited in Yagi Seiya, "Muromachi shoki no onryō shisō — Tenryūji sōken wo megutte," 2. The "standard" version reads somewhat less dramatically, but obviously addresses the same story. For a study of the cultural significance of *onryō*, and also of *tengu*, see Haruko Wakabayashi's recent dissertation from Princeton University. For a translation of the first twelve chapters of the work, see H. C. McCullough, *The Taiheiki*. See also, Varley, *Warriors of Japan as Portrayed in the War Tales*, 159–213.

4. For Shigemori's portrait, see *Nihon no shōzō*, ed. Kyoto kokuritsu hakubutsukan, plate 62 (a section in color is reproduced on p. 22).

5. *Gyokueiki shō*, entry for 1340/3/18, cited in Yagi, "Muromachi shoki," 11. Sutoku (reigned 1123–41) died in Sanuki after being exiled there following his defeat in the Hōgen disturbance of 1156. His spirit, which had been deemed to require amelioration for this treatment, also appears in the *Taiheiki*. For Sutoku's portrait, see *Nihon no shōzō*, plate 53.

6. Yagi, "Muromachi Shoki," 4–5. Yagi notes that it would thus be natural for references to Go-Daigo as a vengeful spirit (*onryō*) to be limited in the work, as is in fact the case. Questions of date of compilation and authorship for the *Taiheiki*, apart from the possibility of multiple authorship, are unresolved ones, but there is some consensus that the so-called Tōjiji text was influenced by Tadayoshi.

7. See the essay in this volume by Martin Collcutt. Also, Tomita Masahiro, "Muromachi jidai ni okeru kitō to kōbu tōitsu seiken"; Katayama Shin, "Muromachi bakufu no kitō to Daigoji Sanbō-in."

8. For further discussion of Musō Soseki's ideas on the nation and on sovereignty and religion, and how they were intertwined in the founding ethos of Tenryūji, see Suga Kikuko, "Gokoku to seijō — Tenryūji sōken to Musō Sōseki"; Tamakake Hiroyuki, "Musō Sōseki to shoki Muromachi seiken."

9. See 1333/6/10 Go-Daigo tennō shojō an, *Kamakura ibun* (hereafter *KI*), 41, doc. 32061.

10. See Kraft, "Musō Kokushi's Dialogues in a Dream: Selections"; also Ryusaku Tsunoda et al., eds., *Sources of Japanese Tradition*, 1: 250–55.

11. Yagi, "Muromachi shoki," 13–17.

12. Ibid., 14–15.

13. Ibid., 15–17.

14. Such as Barbara Ruch's use of the portrait of the female Zen teacher Mugai Nyōdai in "The Other Side of Culture."

15. *Hōnen shōnin eden*, ed. Komatsu Shigemi, *Zoku Nihon emaki taisei*, vols. 1–3.

16. *Ippen shōnin eden*, ed. Komatsu Shigemi, *Nihon emaki taisei, bekkan*. See also, Kauffmann, "Ippen hijiri e," and "Nature, Courtly Imagery, and Sacred Meaning in the *Ippen Hijiri-e*"; and Foard, "Prefiguration and Narrative in Medieval Hagiography."

17. See Mori Tōru, "Myōe shōnin no gazō ni tsuite," in *Kamakura jidai no shōzōga*, 49–84.

18. Matsubara Shigeru, "Shōwa sannen hon Shingon hassō zō."

19. Fujikake Shizuya, "Kenmu gan no nenki aru gokei monjū e ni tsuite," and idem, "Monkan sōjō to Hachiji Monjūshiri bosatsu zu." On Monkan more generally, see Moriyama Seishin, *Tachikawa jakyō to sono shakaiteki haikei no kenkyū*, 257 ff.

20. Noted in Amino Yoshihiko, *Igyō no ōken*, 162–71; also Sugiyama Jirō, "Hannyadera Monjū bosatsu zō ni tsuite." For Monjusri worship, see Uchida Keiichi, "Hachiji Monjū gazō no zuzōgaku teki kōsatsu," and "Saidaiji Eizon oyobi Saidaiji ryū no Monjū shinkō to sono zōzō."

21. At least fourteen portraits of Musō are known to exist, eight of which enjoy status as important cultural properties. See Takeuchi Naoji, "Zenrin bijutsushi kō—Musō ha kyōdan no bijutsu ni tsuite," on the painting tradition in Musō's school. The eight major portraits are also reproduced in Mainichi shinbun sha, *Jūyō bunkazai*, 10, *ega IV*, plates 344–51. For a color reproduction of the portrait held in Myōchi'in, see *Nihon no shōzō*, p. 30 (plate 88 has a full monochrome reproduction).

22. *Nihon no shōzō*, plate 89 monochrome, color section, p. 31, produced in 1334 and housed in Daitokuji. A portrait from 1330, which is housed in Myōshinji, with inscription in Myōchō's own hand, is reproduced in color in *Nihon koji bijutsu zenshū, 24, Myōshinji*, plate 20 (monochrome reproductions in Mainichi shinbun sha, *Jūyō bunkazai, 10, ega IV*, plate 341; and in *Nihon no shōzō*, reference plate 40, p. 324). For an undated portrait (housed in Daitokuji), whose inscription is attributed to Go-Daigo, see *Jūyō bunkazai, 10, ega IV*, plate 343. For a study of Daitō, see Kraft, *Eloquent Zen*.

23. *Nihon no shōzō*, reference plate 39, p. 324, monochrome, a 1343 portrait housed in Kaizōin. See also the essay by Carl Bielefeldt in this volume.

24. *Nihon no shōzō*, plate 97 for Tokimune (1251–84), color detail p. 33. See also, Mainichi shinbun sha, *Jūyō bunkazai, 9, ega III*, plate 272.

25. *Nihon no shōzō*, plate 22, plate 23 detail, for Tokiyori (1227–63).

26. See *Kanazawa bunko no meihō*, ed. Kanagawa kenritsu Kanazawa bunko, for color reproductions of portraits of Sanetoki (priestly garb, plate 1), Akitoki (priestly garb, plate 2), Sadaaki (lay garb, plate 3), Sadamasa (lay garb, plate 4), Saneyasu (priestly garb, plate 6; identification as Saneyasu is tentative). For monochrome reproductions, see *Nihon no shōzō*, plates 67, 68, 69 (color detail, p. 25), and 70; also Mainichi shinbun sha, *Jūyō bunkazai, 9, ega III*, plate 271, p. 130.

27. *Nihon no shōzō*, plates 24 and 25 (p. 9 for color photo of plate 25).

28. Portraits of Andō Rensei and his son Enkei, painted in 1330, can be found in *Jūyō bunkazai, 9, ega III*, plates 273, 274; for Rensei, see also *Nihon no shōzō*, plate 98. Mingji (1262–1336) was highly regarded, and had been received in audience by Go-Daigo shortly after his arrival in Japan that year prior to traveling to Kamakura (much to the chagrin of the Bakufu). He played a major role in establishing regulations for Zen temples in Japan (see Collcutt, *Five Mountains*, 79) and was also a noted painter active in landscape painting (see Rosenfield, "The Unity of the Three Creeds," 223–24).

29. See *Nihon no shōzō*, plate 63, color detail p. 23, for the portrait traditionally identified as Yoritomo; for a statue of Yoritomo, see plates 21 and 20 (detail). For a good discussion of the "Yoritomo portrait," see Mori Tōru, "Minamoto Yoritomo zō ni tsuite," in *Kamakura jidai no shōzōga*, 1–24. However, a recent study by Yonekura Michio (*Minamoto no Yoritomo zō—chinmoku no shōzōga*) has questioned this attribution, arguing quite strongly that the portrait is of either Ashikaga Takauji or Ashikaga Tadayoshi. For the purposes of the present paper, however, the accuracy of the identity, provided it is not of someone born after Go-Daigo's period, does not affect the point made in the text. Indeed, if it is a picture of either Ashikaga brother, this would fit very well with my overall portrait of the Ashikaga and their world view.

30. My point here is not that we do not have any pictures of warriors earlier than this time (ready examples being the Mongol invasion scroll *Takezaki Suenaga ekotoba*, or the scrolls of the Heiji and Hōgen incidents), but that portraits of warriors seem not to have been produced even if some—Minamoto Yoshiie, Minamoto Yoshitsune—were accorded great stature in tale literature. As far as I am aware, the first "warrior portrait" is the famous mounted figure that for some time was thought to be that of Ashikaga Takauji.

31. I have been unable to examine the two portraits housed at Rozanji in Kyoto and at Yoshino jingū in Yoshino. As far as I know, they have not been reproduced and are rarely exhibited; the last time they appeared, at least together,

may have been at a 1938 exhibition of Go-Daigo–related writings and paintings (Kyoto hakubutsukan comp., *Go-Daigo tennō shinkan haiten mokuroku*). Accordingly I shall not be referring to them.

32. See the *Tenshi sekkan miei* (along with Zuishin teiki emaki, Nakadono miei zu, and Kuge retsuei zu) in *Zoku Nihon emaki taisei*, ed. Komatsu Shigemi, vol. 18, and *Shinshū Nihon emakimono zenshū*, ed. Miya Tsuguo, vol. 26. The commentaries in both are very useful, though the reproductions in the Komatsu volume are superior. For a discussion of other aspects of this scroll and the similar *Tennō sekkan miei*, see Kuroda Hideo, *Ō no shintai, ō no shōzō*, 223–47.

33. Not depicted are Konoe, Rokujō, Antoku, and Chūkyō, the latter two having died in infancy.

34. Go-Kōgon was still reigning; Shijō, Go-Nijō, and Go-Daigo died in rank; Nijō and Takakura died the year after abdication.

35. Go-Daigo's successor Go-Murakami (r. 1339–68); and Go-Kōgon's predecesors Kōgon (r. 1332–33), Kōmyō (r. 1337–48), and Sukō (r. 1349–51).

36. Translated by H. Paul Varley, *A Chronicle of Gods and Sovereigns*.

37. See Shiroyama Hōtarō, *Shokugenshō no kiso teki kenkyū*; Kaji Hiroe, "*Shokugenshō* no shisō teki kiban wo megutte."

38. *Sonpi bunmyaku*, Kokushi taikei edition.

39. For information on the mechanics of this, see Mori Shigeaki, *Nanbokuchō ki kōbu kankei shi no kenkyū*.

40. For a well-written study of how aristocrats tried to deal with their new environment, based around the *Entairyaku* of Kinsada's father Tōin Kinkata (1291–1360), see Hayashiya Tatsusaburō, *Nairan no naka no kizoku*.

41. Only two other beards examined come close, those of Fujiwara Saneyoshi and Fujiwara Kanemasa. See *Tenshi sekkan miei*.

42. Kuroda Hideo, "Go-Daigo tennō to Shōtoku taishi," plate 3; I should like to thank Professor Kuroda for some stimulating discussions on the general topic of Go-Daigo, as well as for sharing an early version of this essay with me. For some other reproductions, see Itō Kiyoshi, *Nambokuchō no dōran*, 162; Toyoda Takeshi, ed., *Zusetsu Nihon no rekishi, 7, Buke no shōri*, picture no. 1. See also, *Nihon no shōzō*, plate 60, and pp. 259–60; and frontispiece in H. C. McCullough, *The Taiheiki*.

43. See, for example, the frontispiece in Kuroda, *Ō no shintai, ō no shōzō*; see "Shōzōga toshite no Go-Daigo tennō," 248–75, for an analysis of the painting. See also the excellent reproduction in Boston Art Museum, *Courtly Splendor: Twelve Centuries of Treasures From Japan*, no. 22, pp. 70, 71 (detail). The commentary in the latter notes that the Ashikaga "commissioned portraits in which Go-Daigo is essentially apotheosized"; while not elaborating further, the comment suggests that this portrait was one such; the Daitokuji portrait would be another logical candidate.

44. The portrait in the *Tenshi sekkan miei* scroll was painted by the noted

court painter Gōshin, as indicated by an internal notation on the scroll (Komatsu Shigemi, ed., *Zuishin teiki emaki, Nakadono mie zu, Kuge retsuei zu, Tenshi sekkan miei* [Zoku Nihon emaki taisei, 18]). The Daitokuji portrait was possibly painted by a member of the Tosa family: see Miya Tsuguo, picture no. 1, *Zusetsu Nihon no rekishi, 7, Buke no shōri,* ed. Toyoda Takeshi, and, *Nihon no shōzō,* 269–70. For the Shōjōkōji portrait, Kuroda (*Ō no shōzō, ō no shintai,* 260–62) has argued fairly strongly that the artist would have had to enjoy a close relationship with Go-Daigo, be very well versed in Shingon esotericism, and able to conceive of the portrait as *igyō,* factors that eliminate all but Monkan (himself a noted painter) as a reasonable choice. Kuroda thus dates the portrait between 1339 and 1357, respectively the year of death of Go-Daigo and Monkan.

45. Four portraits, including one in *Tenshi sekkan miei.* The three others are all housed in Daikakuji: *Nihon koji bijutsu zenshū, 14, Daigoji to Ninnaji, Daikakuji,* plate 86 color, in brownish cloak over which is a richly designed *kesa,* seated on a dais, holding a three-point *vajra* in right hand and beads in the left; *Nihon no shōzō,* plates 57 (in informal court garb, painted presumably before taking tonsure in 1308, the face resembles that in the *Tenshi sekkan mie* scroll) and 58 (in priestly garb, late in life). These three are also in Mainichi shinbun sha, *Jūyō bunkazai, 9, ega* III), plates 260, 262, 261.

46. Total of four portraits, including one in *Tenshi sekkan miei.* For the 1338 portrait housed in Chōfukuji of Hanazono in simple priestly garb and in his middle years, see *Nihon no shōzō,* plate 59, also in color, section p. 21. A portrait housed in Myōshinji, of Hanazono in his last years (likewise in priestly garb and revealing an intelligence and strength not evident in the earlier works), was painted shortly after his death in 1348: see *Nihon koji bijutsu zenshū, 24, Myōshinji,* plate 18, full size, color. The third portrait, a Muromachi-period work apparently modeled on the previous portrait, is also housed in Myōshinji: see *Myōshinji* reference plate 33. For a discussion of the portraits of Hanazono, see Mori Tōru, "Hanazono tennō ei ni tsuite," in *Kamakura jidai no shōzō,* 143–59.

47. 1333/3/17 Go-Daigo tennō rinji (*KI* 41, doc. 32061): "In order to make use of a substitute treasured sword, if there be a sword among your old sacred treasures then this must be conveyed."

48. For elucidation of some points made here, see Kuroda, "Shōtoku taishi to Go-Daigo tennō"; and Takeda Sachiko, "Igyō no Shōtoku taishi." For reproductions of this painting, the "Shōtoku taishi shōmangyō kōsan zu," see (for multiple advisers) *Hōryūji Shōwa shizaichō chōsa kansei kinen, Kokuhō Hōryūji ten,* plate 141, p. 200; Kuroda, "Shōtoku taishi," plate 1; and (for a single adviser, Soga no Umako) see *Nihon koji bijutsu zenshū, 7, Shitennōji to Kawachi no koji,* color plate 11.

49. A number of versions of this exist. One type, held in such places as the Seattle Art Museum (see Fuller, *Japanese Art in the Seattle Art Museum,* plate 87; I wish to thank Professor Cynthea Bogel of the University of Oregon for this

reference), Hōryūji (*Hōryūji Shōwa shizaichō chōsa kansei kinen, Kokuhō Hōryūji ten*, plate 140, p. 199), or Shitennōji, focuses on Shōtoku taishi himself. Another type, such as the magnificent painting at Hōryūji of Shōtoku taishi with the Four Heavenly Kings ("Shōtoku taishi shitennō zu," *Horyūji Shōwa*, plate 143, p. 201), provides images of Shōtoku taishi amid slightly smaller divine beings and above a much smaller partial figure of an ordinary (and elderly and bearded) human being. In all, however, the center point is Shōtoku taishi, ruler with baton and sword (black scabbard, sometimes gold-inlay decoration, golden jewel-shaped pommel), with mustache, the elongated ears of a Buddha, a lacquer-gauze black hat, a red (*hanezu*) robe with rounded collar, a green belt with some decoration, and seated on mat or dais.

50. See Higo Kazuo, *Rekidai tennō zukan*, 124. This portrait of Daigo is held in Daigoji. Unfortunately, Higo does not provide information on when the portrait was executed, so I am hesitant to associate it with the portraits of Shōtoku taishi and Go-Daigo at this point. It might, for example, be a much later work, as is the case of the Muromachi-period portrait of Saga (786–842) held in the Kunaichō.

51. See translation in Grossberg and Kanamoto Nobuhisa, *The Law Codes of the Muromachi Bakufu*.

52. See Kuroda *Ō no shintai, ō no shōzō*, "Shōzōga toshite no Go-Daigo tennō," 248–75. See 248–52 for Kuroda's comments on earlier efforts, including that of Amino Yoshihiko in his provocative *Igyō no ōken*.

53. See Grapard, *Protocols of the Gods*; Tyler, *Miracles of the Kasuga Deity*.

54. For a description, see Kuroda, "Shōzōga toshite no Go-Daigo tennō," 254–55.

55. For the statue, see, e.g., *Hōryūji Shōwa shizaichō chōsa kansei kinen, Kokuhō Hōryūji ten*, plate 40, p. 86; or the excellent close-up photographs in *Nara roku-daiji taikan, Hōryūji* 4, color plate 33, and *Nihon koji bijutsu zenshū, 2 Hōryūji to Ikaruga no koji*, color plate 23. Kuroda, "Shōzōga toshite no Go-Daigo," 253–54, notes that, *pace* the suggestions of other commentators (including that in *Courtly Splendor*), this is not a jeweled crown, *hōkan*, used for ordination; Go-Daigo did receive ordinations, such as receiving the dharma and accession to the throne, but these are not symbolized here. For another Shōtoku painting with the crown, see *Nihon koji bijutsu zenshū, 7, Shitennōji to Kawachi no koji*, color plate 11.

56. See Takeda, "Igyō no Shōtoku taishi," 27–29.

57. For a discussion of late Sengoku and Tokugawa portraiture, which includes Hideyoshi and Ieyasu, see Kuroda, *Ō no shintai, ō no shōzō*, 276–302.

58. Professor Kuroda notes that the Kongō satta image still needs some analysis, notably with respect to the significance of holding these two implements as a set: similar portraits of Kujō Michiie (1193–1252) and Kōbō daishi ordination, by contrast, have them holding pearl rosaries in their left hand. Kongō satta is the locus of the bodhisattva heart (*bodai shin*, aspiration or mind of enlightenment), which causes it to arise and gives human beings the strength to attain it.

59. An inscription on a painting of Aizen myōō seeking success in an enterprise is traditionally ascribed to Go-Daigo (see Nagai Michiko, "Go-Daigo tennō," 40; for a partial color reproduction, see Anonymous, "Go-Daigo tennō no itsuhin," 131). Although it has been suggested that the painting may be from earlier in the Kamakura period (*Nezu bijutsukan meihin shūsei*, vol. 1, plate 57 black-and-white reproduction; vol. 3, p. 26 commentary), it is not impossible that date of painting and date of inscription are different; we know, after all, that Go-Daigo readily inscribed many treasured objects of which he had knowledge, and on at least one occasion ordered Mount Kōya to conduct Aizen *homa* rites and furnish a statue in order to do so: see 1334/4/14 Go-Daigo tennō rinji, *Dai Nihon Shiryō*, 6.1: 524, 525–26. For Aizen, and also Fuken bodai (Samantabhadra), with their hand postures and holding of pestles, see illustrations and explanations in Sawa Ryūken, *Butsuzō zuten*, 119 (Aizen), and 83–85, Fuken bodai and Fuken enmei bodai (vajramoghasamaya sattva), 51 for Kongō satta.

60. See, e.g., *Hōryūji Shōwa shizaichō chōsa kansei kinen, Kokuhō Hōryūji ten*, plate 144, p. 202 and the commentary.

61. For example, Uda's *Kampyō on ikai* of the ninth century: Yamagishi Tokuhei et al., eds., *Kodai seiji shakai shisō*; Fushimi no miya Sadafusa's *Chin'yōki* of 1432, discoursing on the sorry state of the imperial family: Murata Masashi, *Murata Masashi chōsaku shū, 4, Chūshō Chin'yōki*.

62. 1324/9/21 Go-Daigo tennō rinji, in Murata Masashi and Matsumoto Shūji, *Yoshida Sadafusa jiseki*, 69–71. The document has been missed in *KI*. For a full translation, see Goble, *Kenmu: Go-Daigo's Revolution*, chap. 2.

63. Go-Daigo here refers none too subtly to a passage in the *Shiji* in which an emperor warns against the dangers faced by underlings who presume to raise doubts about an emperor's right to rule. See Watson, trans., *Records of the Grand Historian of China*, 2: 404.

64. For greater detail, see Goble, *Kenmu: Go-Daigo's Revolution*, chap. 6. Go-Daigo's eight era names were Gen'ō (Responding to Fundaments), Genkō (Inheriting the Fundaments), Shōchū (Rectifying the Mean), Karyaku (Auspicious Almanac), Gentoku (Making Virtue Fundamental), Genkō (Broadening the Fundaments), Kenmu (Building the Military), and Engen (Extending the Fundaments).

65. For Tōdaiji's claims (and complaints), see 1333/8 Tōdaiji soshō toshiro (*KI* 41, doc. 32516). On the Shōmu cult, see Hisano Nobuyoshi, "Chūsei Tōdaiji to Shōmu tennō."

66. This translation differs slightly from that in Uyenaka Shuzo, "A Study of *Baishoron*: A Source for the Ideology of Imperial Loyalty in Medieval Japan," 110.

67. See Takemitsu Makoto, "Kenmu nenchū gyōji ni kisareta chōgi no tokushitsu"; also Goble, *Kenmu: Go-Daigo's Revolution*, chap. 6.

68. See 1339/6/16 Go-Daigo tennō shinkan Tenchō inshin, in *Genshoku han, Kokuhō, 11, Nambokuchō Muromachi*, ed. Sawada Iwao, plate 15, reproducing final

15 lines, photo including first 11 (thus 3 overlap) on p. 122 above the commentary (pp. 122–23). See also, Tsuji Zennosuke, *Nihon bukkyō shi, chūsei 3*, 60–61. This privilege was granted by Go-Daigo to Monkan, who on a separate and accompanying sheet noted the circumstances and significance of the act. The original and another copy were subsequently lost, with the result that Go-Daigo's copy became of crucial importance in Daigoji, and by tradition was seen only by the chief priest. The document (written on quality waxen paper imported from China) is 32 cm. in breadth, 93 cm. in length.

69. Kuroda, "Go-Daigo tennō to Shōtoku taishi," 12, citing Abe Yasurō. The source for the information is a citation from 1338, the year before Go-Daigo's death.

70. For Kōyasan (black-and-white reproduction), see Tsuji Zennosuke, *Nihon bukkyō shi, chūsei 3*, 10. For Shitennōji (color), see Anonymous, "Go-Daigo tennō no itsuhin," 134–35; or Itō Kiyoshi, *Nambokuchō no dōran*, 164.

71. For a more detailed discussion, see Goble, *Kenmu: Go-Daigo's Revolution*, chap. 5.

72. As Kuroda, *Ō no shintai, ō no shōzō*, 258, notes, the portrait of Michiie held in Tōfukuji (see *Nihon no shōzō*, plate 65) of him in priestly garb and holding a *gokosho* in his right hand is one that signifies that he had achieved Buddhahood in this very existence.

73. For the development of Hanazono's understanding of Buddhism and achievement of *satori*, see Goble, "Truth, Contradiction, and Harmony in Medieval Japan: Emperor Hanazono (1297–1348) and Buddhism."

74. See Nihonyanagi Kenji, *Bukkyō igaku gaiyō*, 13; Amino Yoshihiko, *Igyō no ōken*, 168–86. For a recent study on Tachikawa, see Sanford, "The Abominable Tachikawa Skull Ritual."

75. The crucial evidence on this point is supplied by the inscription on a copper bowl that was written by Go-Daigo on 1336/6/30, almost three years before his death: he refers to himself as Go-Daigo. See photograph in Anonymous, "Go-Daigo tennō no itsuhin," 133. An intriguing question here, which has yet to be fully pursued, is who determined the posthumous name for Go-Uda. See also note 77 below.

76. *Genkō shakusho* can be mined from several perspectives. See Ōsumi Kazuo, "Genkō shakusho no buppō kan," and "*Genkō Shakusho* to jingi." See also the essay in this volume by Carl Bielefeldt.

77. See the "Memorial Offering Up *Genkō Shakusho*," translated in Marian Ury, "*Genkō Shakusho*, Japan's First Comprehensive History of Buddhism," 185–88. This is the first reference to Go-Daigo's association with the lauded era of emperors Daigo and Murakami, and can be seen as lending evidence to the oft-repeated notion that Go-Daigo's Kenmu slogan, and focus, was something like "back to Engi." However, while it is clear that Go-Daigo thought highly of Daigo's era (see note 75 above), there is no real evidence that Go-Daigo ever had such a

simple-minded approach to his Kenmu programs. For a discussion of the point, see Kawauchi Yōsuke, "Nihon chūsei no chōtei, bakufu taisei," esp. 30ff.

78. Varley, *A Chronicle of Gods and Sovereigns*, 218. For a discussion of the evolution of the significance of the three divine objects (*jingi*) as related to legitimacy of succession—an issue that leaped to the fore in Go-Daigo's wake—see Satō Tokiko, "[Masu kagami] no kōi keishō kan—sanshū no jingi wo megutte."

79. *Genkō Shakusho, kan* 17 (*Kokushi taikei*, 31: 251–53), Shiren's Discourse after the vitagraph about Hōjō Tokiyori.

80. For the *Ruijū jingi hongen*, see Ōsumi Kazuo, ed., *Chūsei shinto ron*, 80–134 and 281–301. For a discussion of some of the issues involving the Watarai stream, see Teeuwen, "Attaining Union with the Gods: The Secret Books of Watarai Shinto." Varley, *A Chronicle of Gods and Sovereigns*, 12–14, suggests that the work was presented to both Go-Uda and Go-Daigo in 1332, but this seems unlikely since Go-Uda had died in 1324 and in 1332 Go-Daigo was either imprisoned in Kyoto or in exile on Oki Island. An internal notation (which could have been written any time up to 1356) in the *Ruijū jingi hongen* itself notes that it had been requested by Go-Uda, and by Go-Daigo "during his reign."

81. For a statue of Chūgan Engetsu, see *Nihon no shōzō*, plates 16 and 17.

82. The ideology was not an academic one, for the same point had been stressed in some of the anti-Hōjō edicts of both Go-Daigo and his son Prince Moriyoshi: see 1333/4/10 Go-Daigo tennō rinji (*KI* 41, doc. 32088).

83. For Engetsu's "Jō Kenmu Tenshi" with its introduction and two sections on Making the People Fundamental (*Genmin*) and Making Priests Fundamental (*Gensō*), see *DNS* 6.1: 303–6.

84. *Chūshōshi* in Ichikawa Hakugen et al., *Chūsei Zenke no shisō*, 124–85.

85. *Hanazono tennō shinki*, entry for 1324/1/5.

86. For a discussion of how Hanazono came to these views, see Goble, "Social Change, Knowledge, and History: Hanazono's *Admonitions to the Crown Prince*"; the *Admonitions* are translated on 121–28. In this article I read the Crown Prince's name as "Tokihito"; this should be amended to "Kazuhito."

87. See Goble, *Kenmu: Go-Daigo's Revolution*, chap. 5.

88. See ibid., chaps. 5 and 7.

89. For an informative overview of Go-Daigo's princes, see Mori Shigeaki, *Ōjitachi no Nambokuchō*. See also, Marra, *Representations of Power: The Literary Politics of Medieval Japan*, 41–54.

Chapter 7

1. Writings of Paul de Man, Dominick La Capra, and Michel Foucault in their works, *Blindness and Insight, Soundings in Critical Theory*, and *The Order of Things: An Archaeology of the Human Sciences*, have inspired my thinking on the question of periodization.

2. "Accounts in Japanese or Western languages seldom do justice to the remarkable creativity of this [Heian] age," states *The Princeton Companion to Classical Japanese Literature*, by Earl Miner, Hiroko Odagiri, and Robert E. Morrell, 27. *Taikō gyoki*, written by Fujiwara Onshi (wife of Emperor Daigo) in the 920s and 930s, apparently is the earliest example; Saiki Kazuma, *Kokiroku no kenkyū*, 2–6. This diary is a daily kept record, unlike later composed memoirs. In the Tokugawa period, diaries and memoirs came to be written by well-educated women in the samurai and merchant classes and daughters of Shinto officials in large numbers. *Shōin nikki* by Ōgimachi Machiko, wife of Yanagisawa Yoshiyasu (Tokugawa Tsunayoshi's favorite adviser), *Sakume nikki* by Nishitani Saku (daughter of a merchant in Kawachi Province), and Enjo's diary serve as examples; see Sōgō joseishi kenkyūkai, ed., *Nihon josei no rekishi*, 156–58.

3. Fukuda Hideichi, "Kaisetsu," in *Chūsei nikki kikōshū*, 511–13.

4. It is not entirely clear to what "Takemuki" refers. Nakada Norio and Mizukawa Yoshio, after considering various possible meanings, have argued that "Takemuki" was probably the name of Meishi's living quarters that faced a garden with a bamboo thicket. This was in the Kitayama Mansion (the residence of her husband's family, the Saioinjis) and adjoined the room assigned to her son, Sanetoshi. Following the convention, she may have been known by her place of occupancy, "Takemuki," and thus the name of her memoir. See *Takemukigaki zenshaku*, Nakada Norio and Mizukawa Yoshio, eds., 24–25.

5. According to Steven D. Carter, the Hino family, "one of the so-called *seigake*, whose heirs could rise no higher than Major Counselor in government administration—had been one of the lesser court clans, distinguished only by its status as a provider of wives for the Ashikaga shoguns." See his "Ichijō Kaneyoshi and the Literary Arts," 39.

6. In English, see the translation by Karen Brazell. The diary covers the period 1271–1306.

7. When Sanetoshi died in 1389 at age 55, he had moved up to the position of Minister of the Right; Nakada and Mizukawa, *Takemukigaki zenshaku*, 335, 338. I used "Takemukigaki," edited by Iwasa Miyoko, in *Chūsei nikki kikōshū*, 271–344, and have followed, for the most part, her notes and interpretations, which seem to be based on a sound understanding of social and political context and differ significantly from those of Nakada and Mizukawa in *Takemukigaki zenshaku*. Meishi's diary was structured into two volumes from the outset. Scholars agree that there is no "missing chapter"; Fukuda, "Kaisetsu," 512.

8. One notable exception is the poetic memoir of Ukyō no daibu who served Kenreimon'in (Tokushi, Taira Kiyomori's daughter and mother of the child Emperor Antoku) and lived through the Genpei War and the early years of Kamakura rule in the late twelfth century. Her memoir focuses on her longing for one of her lovers, Taira Sukemori, who drowned with many other Taira family members

upon the Taira's defeat in the Genpei War. Ukyō no daibu, *Kenreimon'in Ukyō no daibushū*. I thank Aileen Gatten for bringing this work to my attention.

9. Saionji Kintsune (1171–1244) first built a home in Kitayama, a location where now stands Rokuonji, popularly called Kinkakuji, or the Golden Pavilion, built by Ashikaga Yoshimitsu in 1397. *Taiheiki*, ed. Gotō Tanji and Kamada Kisaburō, 2: 21–30.

10. With the tone thus established, Kinmune's treachery (against Go-Daigo) is made genealogically likely. Saionji Kinmune indeed sided with the Hōjō and against Go-Daigo during the Kenmu Restoration. The Saionji was a branch of the Northern line of the Fujiwara; some members held important mediating posts in the Kamakura Bakufu that bridged the warrior government and the imperial court.

11. Aware nari /hikage matsu ma no /tsuyu no mi ni /omoi'okaruru /nadeshiko no hana [Tis too pitiful— /with this dewdrop-body awaiting /only the wilting sun /longing ever draws my mind /to the cherished carnation]. *Nadeshiko*, the wild pink or carnation flower, is a classic conventional metaphor for a cherished child, owing to the semantic value of *nade*—to stroke—and *ko*—child. I thank Esperanza Ramirez-Christensen for rendering this poem into elegant English.

12. Kinmune's arrest and execution differed in reality from the *Taiheiki*'s condensed "pulp" version. Kinmune was arrested on 1335/6/22 and was not executed until 1335/8/2, a month and a half later. Meishi's older brother, Hino Ujimitsu, was also executed then.

13. Changes in pictorial representations of hells from the Kamakura to the Muromachi periods suggest greater social and artistic familiarity with bloody incidents. "Kitano tenjin engi" and "Rokudō-e" of Shōju Raigōji from Kamakura times show gods (Asura) fighting each other. The Muromachi-period representations of the same hells in such works as "Kumano Kanshin Jikkai Mandara" and "Yada jizō maigetsu nikki-e" show that human warriors have displaced Asura. It suggests that violence had come within an easier reach of mortals. In Kuroda Hideo, "Kumano kanshin jikkai mandara no uchū," 243. It seems entirely possible for Hino Meishi to have read or heard about this *Taiheiki* chapter before she wrote her own work. *Taiheiki* covers events from 1318 to 1367 and was completed and circulated among certain aristocrats within a few years after the last event mentioned. As early as 1374, it received notice in a diary written by one of Meishi's husband's relatives, Tōin (Saionji) Kinsada. Scholars debate whether the text was written over the decades as events occurred or all at once. If the former, Meishi could have known about it. Kami Hiroshi discusses the issue of its reception in his *Taiheiki kyōjushi ronkō*, p. 9. For various theories on the identity of author(s) and authorship, see Gotō and Kamada, eds., *Taiheiki*, 1: 5–14.

14. *Oyudono no ue no nikki*, in Hanawa Hokiichi and Ōta Toshirō, eds., *Zoku gunsho ruijū, bui*, 11 vols.

15. Saiki, *Kokiroku no kenkyū*, 9–11. Go-Daigo in 1334 began compilation of *Kenmu nenchū gyōji* (Annual Ceremonial Events in Kenmu) in Japanese. This suggests to Saiki that Go-Daigo may have planned to revive *Denjō nikki*. This soon ended, as did Go-Daigo's restored imperial rule.

16. Saiki, 9–12; Wakita Haruko, *Nihon chūsei joseishi no kenkyū: seiteki yakuwari buntan to bosei, kasei, seiai*, 234.

17. This secretarial role of female officials continued into the early Meiji period. Satō Shin'ichi, *Komonjogaku nyūmon*, 77, 116–19; Tsuchida Naoshige, "Naishi sen ni tsuite."

18. For Emperor Go-Fukakusa, Lady Nijō is a replacement figure for her dead mother for whom he had great fondness. (Lady Nijō's father was not the only sexual partner her mother had. Nijō has a sister by a different father.) In addition to having sex with Lady Nijō, Go-Fukakusa pushes her to have other affairs.

19. Iwasa, "Takemukigaki," 274.

20. Meishi states that Go-Daigo was in fact hiding in Mount Kasagi though it was reported that he was at Mount Hiei.

21. Iwasa, "Takemukigaki," 275–77.

22. Ibid., 282–85.

23. Ibid., 301.

24. Wakita Haruko, "Chūsei kōki, machi ni okeru 'onna no isshō,'" 157.

25. In the sixteenth century, the distinction between *rinji* (imperial edict) and *nyōbō hōsho* (ladies' dispatch) ceased to hold public and private meanings, respectively. The same merging of meanings characterized the warrior government's public documents that took the form of shogun *hōsho*; Wakita Haruko, *seiteki yakuwari*, 234. Wakita views this as but one manifestation of a major trend that privileged the private. To Wakita, the very meaning of "medieval" is founded upon the structure of *ie*, or patriarchal household.

26. Yanagisako and Collier, "The Mode of Reproduction in Anthropology," 138.

27. Located to the northeast side of the Seiryōden's Night Palace; Iwasa, "Takemukigaki," 277 n. 54, 278.

28. Kinmune was then Major Counselor, Senior Second Rank.

29. A neutral place would be, for example, Kinmune's nurse's residence. Iwasa Miyoko, in "Takemukigaki," follows the natural progression in Meishi's narrative and dates this incident in 1332/2, while Nakada and Mizukawa place it after Kinmune's declaration of "eternal spring" in 1333; their logic must be that sex comes after marriage. Iwasa's interpretation is far more convincing. Iwasa, "Takemukigaki," 293 nn. 43, 44; Nakada and Mizukawa, 102, 105.

30. Iwasa, "Takemukigaki," 294.

31. On the thirteenth day of the first month. Ibid.

32. Ibid., 295–96.

33. Ibid., 299–303.

34. McNamara, "Chaste Marriage and Clerical Celibacy," 22.

35. Here we discuss heterosexual relationships. Sexual relations among men were prevalent throughout Japanese history but they never constituted "marriage." Fujiwara Yorinaga records in his diary, *Taiki*, for example, that on 1152/8/24, "Fujiwara Narichika visited [him] at around ten at night. . . . We spilled semen together. How sublime. With this man, it always happens this way. I feel most deeply moved." Yorinaga was thirty-three years old then and had an official wife and concubines. His diary shows at least seven other male lovers who also had wives themselves. See Sōgō joseishi kenkyūkai, ed., *Nihon josei no rekishi: sei, ai kazoku*, 86–87. Although same-sex sexual relations pervaded the lives of aristocrats, monks and priests, and warriors, historians rarely consider seriously their impact on political developments or other social institutions, such as marriage. This is a methodological problem that demands attention.

36. Takamure divides Japan's marriage history in the following way: the Asuka through early Heian periods, early *mukotori*; the mid-Heian period, pure *mukotori*; the late Heian period, "agency" *mukotori* in which the woman's parents establish a structure to receive the man; the Kamakura through Nanbokuchō periods (1221–1336), "fictional" *mukotori*. The century from Nanbokuchō (1336 on) to about the Ōnin War (1467–77) saw the gradual conclusion of *mukotori* marriage and the beginning of *yometori* marriage, or patrilocal marriage, that lasted until 1947, the date of the post–World War II Constitution. She divides this long "patriarchal" period into three segments. The first period, stretching from 1336 through the Ōnin War, saw what Takamure calls the "secret ceremony take-the-bride" marriage (*mitsugi yometorikon*). In this phase, although it is the groom's household head (*kafuchō*) who in fact holds the authority over marriage decision making, the two families maintain the appearance of the earlier social convention in which the husband freely chooses the bride. Takamure's next segment is approximately one century from the Ōnin War through the late-sixteenth-century period under the unifiers. She calls the pattern in this period a "new construction take-the-bride (*shinzō yometorikon*) marriage." In this stage, there is no more need to hide the act of taking the bride. Instead, the head of the groom's household (*ie*) openly demonstrates his role as the primary authority in arranging the marriage. He builds a new structure for the newlyweds in his own residential compound. The woman's physical separation from her natal family becomes definitive but she is not integrated into the established space of the man's family right away. Finally, Takamure calls the four centuries from the unification era to the issuance of the post–World War II Constitution the "pure take-the-bride marriage (*jun yometorikon*)." By this time, the household head (*kafuchō*) of the groom's family makes no pretense of asserting his authority to take the bride for his son into his own residence. The end of take-the-bride marriage brings us to a "mutual (sōgo)

marriage" that once again ensures marriage based on the couple's mutual love and respect. See Takamure Itsue, *Shōseikon no kenkyū*, 1 and 2. This work was first published in 1952, after fourteen years of solitary research and writing.

37. Practically every piece of Japanese scholarship on marriage and women from the last two to three decades makes reference to Takamure's paradigm. *Rekishi hyōron*, for instance, ran a special on "Takamure Itsue o ima . . . ([Re-examining] Takamure Itsue today . . .)" in March 1988, which contains, for example, Fukutō Sanae's "Jun mukotorikon o megutte," and Suzuki Kunihiro's "Chūseishi kenkyū to Takamure Itsue: 'Kafuchōsei kazoku'ron no saikentō kara," no. 455: 2–11 and 12–24. More recently, Takamure's work has met even greater criticism. " 'Nationhood' and 'Motherhood': Reconsidering the Legacy of Takamure's Women's History" was the theme of the 28th conference of the Comparative Family History Association (*Hikaku kazokushi gakkai*) that took place in October 1995. Calling Takamure a nationalistic apologist for "womanhood" and "Japan," the participants seriously questioned the scholarly merit of Takamure's work. See a report by Ueno Chizuko, " 'Takamure joseishi' dō uketsuguka: nashonarizumu to fueminizumu no aidade," *Asahi shinbun*, Dec. 5, 1995, p. 13.

38. For Takamure, *tsumadoi* and *mukotori* are grouped under one category of *shōseikon*, or "invite the *muko* marriage." In both, the man either visits the woman or lives at her house, and he participates in the reproduction of the members of the woman's line. Both models assume a matrilineal descent system. The ceremony, *tokoro arawashi*, had the function of incorporating the man into the woman's line. Based on her own extensive and thorough analyses of historical data, Sekiguchi Hiroko points out the unlikelihood of a man's being taken into the wife's family, "considering the growth of patriarchy." But she firmly agrees with Takamure that the coresidence marriage pattern that historically followed the visiting marriage pattern took place at the woman's residence. Sekiguchi praises Takamure's meticulous research that empirically proved this point and overturned all previous research, calling it "nothing less than splendid." She also has found many other areas for revision. *Nihon kodai kon'inshi no kenkyū*, 2: 348–51.

39. McCullough differs from Takamure, among other things, in locating neo-local marriage at the end of the twelfth century instead of the fourteenth century or later, the time period suggested by Takamure. He also emphasizes that Heian marriages were polygamous for men and monogamous for women. See W. H. McCullough, "Japanese Marriage Institutions in the Heian Period." Nickerson, "The Meaning of Matrilocality: Kinship, Property, and Politics in Mid-Heian," anthropologically expands the discussion of Heian marriage institutions.

40. For example, Suzuki Kunihiro, "Chūseishi kenkyū to Takamure Itsue," 16–17.

41. Along with an expectation that their children would have an appropriately noble position in the "bureaucracy" imbued with familial interests. The Saionji family's genealogy shows that Kinmune was indeed sleeping with at least one

other woman, denoted simply "a lady in the house (*ie nyōbō*)," who produced a daughter. Photo reproduction of a hand-copied text of *Takemukigaki*, kept in the National Diet Library, estimated to date from the eighteenth century, with an introduction by Mizukawa Yoshio, 106.

42. *Kagerō nikki.* In English, Edward Seidensticker, trans., *The Gossamer Years: The Diary of a Noblewoman of Heian Japan.*

43. Takamure would call Meishi's marriage a "fictional" *mukotori* marriage, even if the *yometori* portion was the longer and more dominant.

44. Called "*tokoro arawashi*," the ceremony took place following the proposal from the woman's family to the man's family. Takamure claims that sharing of the food (rice cake) at the woman's house evolved out of a need to distinguish the main wife from the secondary wives in the late tenth century. The taboo against the sharing of the hearth is based on the concept of matriliny, not patriliny. Takamure, *Shōseikon*, 1: 439–54.

45. The Tōin was a branch of the Saionji into which Meishi married.

46. Tōin Kinkata, *Entairyaku*, entry for 1346/8/29, ed. Iwasaki Koyata and Saiki Kazuma, 2: 32–33; Takamure, *Shōseikon*, 2: 1141–42.

47. *Chikanaga kyōki*, 2: 102. Also in *Nobutane kyōki*, entry for 1481/2/11 (Shiryō taisei 41: Naigai Shoseki, 1943), 1: 176. Takamure, *Shōseikon*, 2: 1156. The mother of the groom lived in the main section and was called "Facing the South (*minami mukai*)" while the daughter-in-law was called "Facing the North (*kita mukai*)." As noted earlier, McCullough has found neolocal arrangements as early as the twelfth century. This suggests more variations in marriage modes than the uni-lineally constructed model of Takamure.

48. Much of the information in the following paragraphs comes from Nomura Ikuyo, "Chūsei ni okeru tennōke," 311–13.

49. Emperor Sanjō's daughter married Go-Suzaku; the two daughters of Go-Suzaku's brother (Go-Ichijō) married Go-Reizei and Go-Sanjō.

50. For example, an unmarried daughter of Emperor Shirakawa became *junbo* to her younger brother, Emperor Horikawa (r. 1086–1107). A daughter of Emperor Toba was a *junbo* to her brother, Emperor Go-Shirakawa (r. 1155–58).

51. Although the imperial family began to make lifetime bequests one century after the regents' family did, the two share the context that gave rise to lifetime bequests: insecurity within the family, which called for strong organizational control from the top. There is a scarcity of studies on the female members of the imperial family. For a useful survey, see Nomura Ikuyo, "Nyoin kenkyū no genjō."

52. Kinkazu earned some one thousand *hiki* (10 *kanmon*) for it. He did this thirteen years after taking tonsure. He ended the Tōin line. Kinkata had sixteen sons and eleven daughters. We do not know the financial status of one of Kinkata's daughters who apparently married Meishi's son. *Entairyaku*, vol. 1, intro.: 4–5; genealogy: 1–16.

53. Takamure, *Shōseikon*, 2: 974.

54. The description of this marriage appears in *Gyokuyō* 61 in vol. 3: 707, entry dated 1191/6/2, 6/4, 6/7, 6/25, 6/27. Cited in Takamure, *Shōseikon*, 2: 815–18, 974–75.

55. Kujō Yoritsune was thirteen and Takegosho twenty-eight years old when *yometori* took place; Takamure, *Shōseikon*, 2: 978, 980–82; *Zenyaku Azuma kagami*, 4: 50, 83, 99.

56. The prince was nineteen, considerably older than the fourth shogun at his marriage. 1260/2/5, 2/14, 3/27 in *Zenyaku Azuma Kagami*, 5: 382, 387–88.

57. According to Takamure, the first sign of *yometorikon* was the "abduction-marriage (*ryakudatsu-kon*)" in which men abducted women from the enemy and distributed them among the soldiers. But this was a case of an "exceptional sexual life," not a real marriage. She states that this already demonstrates the perception of the female sex as a "thing (*buppin*)," and the later, Muromachi period *yometorikon* formalized and normalized the notion. Takamure, *Shōseikon*, 2: 809, 1129–30.

58. *Myōhōjiki*, two vols., covering 1466–1561. In *Zoku shiseki shūran* (no date), 7: 17. Cited in Takamure, *Shōseikon*, 1: 346.

59. The more modest Mōri, for example, did not practice ostentatious woman-giving ceremonies. Tabata Yasuko, who has worked extensively on the Mōri family, verbally provided me this information. On other aspects of the Mōri family's marriage in the sixteenth century, see Tabata Yasuko, *Nihon chūsei no josei*, 153–63.

60. See my "Women and Inheritance in Japan's Early Warrior Society"; Takamure, *Shōseikon*, 2: 1065–67. See also, Mass, "Patterns of Provincial Inheritance in Late Heian Japan" on Heian inheritance and his *Lordship and Inheritance in Early Medieval Japan* for Kamakura patterns.

61. "Kobayakawa Shigekage jihitsu yuzurijō," dated 1363/6/29; "Kobayakawa Saneyoshi jihitsu yuzurijō," dated 1363/3/18. *Kobayakawake monjo* 68 and 67: 47–48. Mentioned in Gotō Michiko, "Nanbokuchō, Muromachiki no josei no shoryō sōzoku," 346–67.

62. Although I am uncertain as to the method Fukuo used to calculate this ratio, I would assume it was based on the instances of holding rather than its content. It is extremely difficult to quantify various types of land rights. Fukuo Takeichirō, 90. Ishii Susumu refers to this work in his *Chūseishi o kangaeru*, 91.

63. Tabata Yasuko, *Nihon chūsei joseishiron*, 37.

64. *Takeo jinja monjo* mentioned in ibid., 32–33. Kusome received a certificate of her participation from Shōni Sadatsune in the seventh month of 1333, and another from Ōtomo Sadamune in the eighth month.

65. *Satake monjo*, cited in Tabata, *Nihon chūsei joseishiron*, 39.

66. This point is elaborated in Tonomura, "Women and Inheritance," 594, 617–23.

67. See note 61.

68. For discussion of the gender-differentiated bounds within which sexuality may operate, see my "Black Hair and Red Trousers."

69. Though scholars have insisted that Heian marriage was monogamous for women and polygamous for men, evidence indicates that this was not always so, especially for women who worked in the palace. Lady Nijō—author of *Towazu-gatari*—who, strictly speaking, was not "married" in late Kamakura times surely had multiple relationships simultaneously, even if she did not necessarily want them. Documents from Kamakura times indicate an abundance of instances in which women were sequentially monogamous. For references, see my "Women and Inheritance."

70. Legal treatment of rape and adultery is elaborated in my "Sexual Violence Against Women: Legal and Extralegal Treatment in Premodern Japan."

71. In case either had no fief, both were subject to banishment. *Goseibai shiki-moku* no. 34 in Ishii Susumu et al., eds., *Nihon chūsei seiji shakai shisō*, 1: 27.

72. The samurai was a vassal of the Akamatsu and the sake brewer's son served the Itakura, related to the Yamana.

73. *Nagaoki Sukune nikki*, entry dated 1479/5/23. In Satō Shin'ichi and Ikeuchi Yoshisuke, eds., *Chūsei hōsei shiryōshū*, 2: 237–38; mentioned in Sōgō joseishi kenkyūkai, ed., *Nihon josei no rekishi*, 107.

74. Muromachi Japanese society is distinguished from other societies in which control over female sexuality was also important. For instance, in small, face-to-face societies such as Naples and Cuba, as in Japan, male honor was frequently at stake. Premodern Japan's warrior society contrasts with Naples and Cuba in its lack of communally wide concern for and control over virginity of its female members. Japanese society ignored the concept and the physical state of virginity. It was apparently a non-issue in consideration of honor, marriage, or pollution; it is absent from any noticeable discourse. For reference to Naples and Cuba, see Goddard, "Honour and Shame: The Control of Women's Sexuality and Group Identity in Naples."

75. The ecclesiastical courts imposed less physical sentences such as excommunication, public penance, imprisonment, whipping, money fines, and enslavement; Brundage, "Rape and Seduction in the Medieval Canon Law," 141, 145.

76. See my *Community and Commerce in Late Medieval Japan*, 4–6, 57–61.

77. *Ōji jinja monjo* 81, cited in Kuroda Hiroko, "Chūsei kōki no mura no onna tachi," 193.

78. Tabata Yasuko, "Daimyō ryōgoku kihan to sonraku nyōbō za," 234–35.

79. *Imabori Hiyoshi jinja monjo shūsei*, comp. Nakamura Ken, docs. 541, 496, 237, cited in Tonomura, *Community and Commerce*, 59.

80. Nagahara Keiji, "Joseishi ni okeru Nanbokuchō, Muromachiki," 158–60.

81. See a series of *Shokunin uta awase*, the earliest of which, *Tōhokuin shokunin uta awase emaki*, dates from 1214. The poems it contains may have been composed by Emperor Go-Toba. A hundred years later, Emperor Hanazono made a copy of it as a way of appeasing Go-Toba's spirit. Excellent description and analyses of this genre can be found in Iwasaki Kae, ed., *Shokunin uta awase: chūsei no shoku-nin gunzō*. *Shichijū-ichi-ban shokunin uta awase*, ed. Iwasaki Kae et al., also has

excellent and thorough commentaries on each of the 71 types of artisans. This *uta awase* dates from sometime before 1500. Hanawa Hokiichi, comp., *Gunsho ruijū* 28: 441–606, contains *Tōhokuin shokunin uta awase, Tsuruoka Hōjōe shokunin uta awase, Sanjū-niban shokunin uta awase, Shichijū-ichiban uta awase*, dating from Kamakura through Sengoku times. The *uta awase*, along with picture scrolls (such as *Ippen hijiri e*), are used extensively by historians, such as Amino Yoshihiko and Kuroda Hideo, as valuable sources for understanding the lives of commoners in nonagricultural professions.

82. Fukutō Sanae, "Yūkō jofu kara yūjo e," 245.

83. Iwasa, "Takemukigaki," 290–93.

84. H. C. McCullough, trans., *The Tale of the Heike*, chap. 1.6, pp. 30–37.

85. Geinōshi kenkyūkai, ed., *Nihon geinōshi 2*, 165.

86. Nakada Norio, ed., *Towazugatari zenshaku*, 310, 315; Brazell, *The Confessions*, narrative dated 1288/8, 114–17.

87. Because of their artistic accomplishment, they are believed to have served in the Naikyōbō, the Female Dancers' and Musicians' Office in the imperial palace.

88. Amino Yoshihiko, in many of his works, for example: *Chūsei no hinin to yūjo*, and *Nihonron no shiza: rettō no shakai to kokka*. He gives a concise summary history of female entertainer–prostitutes in "Sanjū ban: tachigimi, zushigimi." Hosokawa Ryōichi lists examples of *yūjo* and *shirabyōshi*'s children rising in the court in his "Kazoku o kōsei shinai josei," 229–30. Tōin Kintada is a brother of the grandfather of Tōin Kinkata, mentioned earlier in reference to marriage.

89. My understanding of these terms comes from Iwasaki Kae, *Shokunin uta awase*, 193–94, 209.

90. Hosokawa, "Kazoku o kōsei shinai josei," 229–30.

91. Takamure finds the situation in Muromachi Japan comparable to one found in ancient Greece. The female chief was called *chōja*. Takamure Itsue, *Josei no rekishi* 1, 284–94, 345–49.

92. Amino, "Sanjū ban: tachigimi, zushigmi"; Amino, *Nihonron no shiza*, 165–77. If Takamure's analysis is based on feminist ideas, Amino Yoshihiko's examination is based on a status-based perspective, although they share the conclusion that "sex for sale" began in the fourteenth century. Amino considers the emergence of a new category of prostitutes within the broader history of nonagricultural people, arguing that discrimination against nonagricultural commoners of various skills (*shokunin*), including women and entertainers, only began with the intensified valuation of rice and rootedness in the fourteenth century. Earlier, artistic and artisanal skills often brought tax-exempt land to these commoners, who could even bring a winning suit, for example in 1249, against officials for levying unjust taxes. Like Takamure Itsue's romanticized perspective on the *mukotori* age of free love, Amino's downplaying of discrimination seems a bit idealistic.

93. Kujō Kanezane, *Gyokuyō* 37-2, p. 584; Jien, *Gukanshō* 3: 148–49. Citations

appear in Wakita Haruko, "Chūsei ni okeru seibetsu yakuwari," 103–6, in which she reads the writing of Kanezane and Jien as a way of stressing the value of maternal function and, by implication, the notion of female chastity for continuing the male-centered descent system. *Jinnō shōtōki* by Kitabatake Chikafusa, completed in 1343, and *Taiheiki* also suggest the link between motherhood and a medieval version of nationalism. See Sasaki Kaoru's analysis in *Chūsei kokka no shūkyō kōzō*, 247–49.

94. For instance, items 18, 22, 26 in *Goseibai shikimoku*, Satō and Ikeuchi, eds., *Chūsei hōsei*, 1: 13, 15, 26.

95. *Goseibai shikimoku*, item 23 in *ibid.*, 15.

96. "Kitano Tenjin engi" (the thirteenth century), "Yūzū nenbutsu engi" (the early fourteenth century), and "Hōnen shōnin eden" (the early fourteenth century) in Hotate Michihisa, *Chūsei no ai to jūzoku*, 189, 183, 200.

97. Tokieda Tsutomu, "Chūsei Tōgoku ni okeru ketsubonkyō shinkō no yōsō," 599.

98. This is a version that comes from Sōkenji in Niigata Prefecture. Kōdate Naomi has identified 23 different versions, mostly from the Tokugawa period. See her "Shiryō shōkai 'Ketsubonkyō wakai': kinseiki Jōdoshū ni okeru ketsubonkyō shinkō"; also Takemi Momoko, " 'Ketsubonkyō' no keifu to sono shinkō"; and Tokieda, "Chūsei Tōgoku," 588. The popularized Japanese version was quite different from the original Chinese version that deals with the sin of approaching the well or the hearth, or of hanging up the laundered polluted clothes in public view within twenty days of childbirth. This sin was borne 70 percent by the woman and 30 percent by the man. In addition, the husband and wife would both descend into the Blood pond after death if they had sexual intercourse on a holy day, served blood to gods and buddhas by mistake, or got involved in other sexually offensive acts. Notably, the Chinese version was applicable to both women and men, though not equally. Tokieda, "Chūsei Tōgoku," 601.

99. Tokieda, "Chūsei Tōgoku," 593.

100. For example, "Yada jizō maigatsu nikki e": illustrations 29 and 35 in Kuroda Hideo, "Kumano Kanshin," 247, 251.

101. Ibid., 258. Kuroda explains that representation of women's hells was promoted by "picture narrators (*etoki*)" who anticipated a female-dominant audience with an interest in tales of salvation tailored to women's taste. For an interesting analysis of pictorial representations of various hells and heavens, see Ruch, "Coping with Death: Paradigms of Heaven and Hell and the Six Realms in Early Literature and Painting," esp. 117–30. She sees a significant thematic change in the works from the twelfth through fourteenth centuries.

102. Takemi Momoko, "Nyonin kyūsai," 68; in English, see her " 'Menstruation Sutra' Belief in Japan." Kōdate Naomi introduces various sources that contain variant versions of the Blood Bowl Sutra and discusses Takemi's position in her "Shiryō shōkai," esp. p. 77.

103. Smyers, "Women and Shinto: The Relation Between Purity and Pollution," 9–10; see a poetic exchange between Yamato Takeru no mikoto and Miyazu-hime during her menstrual period that demonstrates no sense of pollution or embarrassment in *Kojiki*, second volume, 217–19. Donald L. Philippi explains in his note that this song may be "a light and roundabout expression of disappointment that ritual considerations prevent immediate sexual union" because women could be considered "sacred to the gods and therefore unapproachable" during menstruation. He also notes, however, that "women may have been considered polluted during the menstrual period, as in later centuries in Japan." The poem tends to support the first interpretation. Philippi, trans., *Kojiki*, 244–45.

104. Tokieda, "Chūsei Tōgoku," 600.

105. Ibid., 591. Wooden sticks were less than 13.5 centimeters long. Sulfur in the site helped to preserve the wood.

106. Foucault in Rabinow, 11. Foucault is discussing the path to the development of "scientific" understanding of self, especially sexuality in the nineteenth-century West. But a comparable process of self-formation can be found in other societies at other times.

107. Hosokawa Ryōichi, "Kazoku o kōsei shinai josei," 221–22. Hokkeji officially became the nunnery of the Saidaiji-line Ritsu sect when Eison ordained the Bikuni Precept that allowed nuns to become full-fledged members of the sangha. Eison also organized or revived Chūgūji, Shōhōji, and Dōmyōji for women. In English, see Hosokawa's "Medieval Nuns and Nunneries: The Case of Hokkeji."

108. Taira Masayuki, "Chūsei bukkyō to josei," *Nihon josei seikatsushi 2: chūsei*, 105.

109. This idea was suggested to me by Aileen Gatten.

110. Katsuura Noriko, "Josei no hosshin, shukke to kazoku," 253.

111. Hosokawa, "Kazoku to josei," 222. Women often did not necessarily become a "complete" nun (to "shukke," i.e., "leave house") after the husband's death. Instead, as did the mother of Nakahara Moromori, a woman might just receive "Gokai" or Five Precepts. In another case, Madenokōji Tsugufusa's concubine, who gave birth to Tokufusa and a daughter, continued to stay at the house after his death on 1398/8/6 and served his official wife who had adopted Tokifusa to properly incorporate him into the lineage. When Tokifusa turned fifteen, the concubine, as his biological mother, received the authority to manage the household. *Moromoroki* (1339–74), entry for 1345/2/19, and *Kennaiki* (1414–55), entry for 1443/2/26. Cited in Katsuura Noriko, "Josei no hosshin," 257–58.

112. Taira Masayuki, 105–6.

113. Turner, *Dramas, Fields, and Metaphors*, 34–41. Reference and elaboration of this in Raybin, "Aesthetics, Romance, and Turner," 24–26.

114. The deep-level social structure that Pierre Bourdieu calls *doxa*. *Doxa* is different from any discourse that is articulated—heterodoxy or orthodoxy—in that it is simply taken for granted and does not demand acknowledgment beyond

acting in the accepted social convention. See his *Outline of a Theory of Practice*, esp. 164–69.

115. Iwasa Miyoko, "Takemukigaki," 344. My deep gratitude goes to Professor Robert Huey for translating this poem, full of *kakekotoba* and *engo*.

Chapter 8

1. See Huey, *Kyōgoku Tamekane: Poetry and Politics in Late Kamakura Japan*, 77–79.

2. See Huey, "The Kingyoku Poetry Contest," 302.

3. I see Shirakawa's time as pivotal because his *Goshūishū* (1086) was the first imperial anthology to elicit a public critique, and it was during his era that poetry contests became literary battlefields for contending poetic factions (Huey, "The Medievalization of Poetic Practice," 653, 666–67). These were early indications of discontinuity in the world of waka, though imperial control of that world was still firm.

4. The Go-Toba depicted in *Minamoto Ienaga nikki*—the memoirs of a courtier who was, in effect, Go-Toba's personal secretary—is fanatically devoted to waka, and to other arts and pleasures as well. See Ishida Yoshisada and Satsukawa Shūji, *Minamoto Ienaga no nikki zenchūkai*, 34–37, among many passages.

5. For example, Minamoto Michichika had been the initial driving force behind the first 100-poem sequence commission of Shōji 2 (1200), evidently in hopes that Go-Toba would use it as an occasion to start planning an imperial anthology that Michichika and the Rokujō poets could control. In fact, Go-Toba did seize the opportunity, but he quickly took command of the situation himself and left Michichika a bystander.

6. *Meigetsuki*, Kanki 2 (1230)/7/6. Hereafter, page number citations are from Kokusho Hakkōkai, *Meigetsuki*, 3: 224.

7. *Meigetsuki*, Jōei 1 (1232)/6/13; 3: 322.

8. *Meigetsuki*, Bunryaku 1 (1234)/8/7; 3: 424.

9. Kuroita Katsumi, ed., *Kokushi taikei*, vol. 11, sec. 2, *Hyakurenshō*, 177. For leads to this and other documentary materials on *Shinchokusenshū* I am indebted to Kubota Jun et al., *Kenkyū shiryō nihon koten bungaku*, 6 [Waka]: 269–72.

10. Imagawa Fumio, ed., *Gyokusui*, entries for Bunryaku 2 (1235)/1/13 (p. 400) and 2/14 (p. 401).

11. The letter is now known as *Koshibe no zenni shōsoku*, and appears in Sasaki Nobutsuna, ed., *Nihon kagaku taikei*, 3: 385–87. Shunzei no Musume's remarks on *Shinchokusenshū* appear on p. 385.

12. Ibid., 5: 108. The most prominent "warrior poet" in the anthology was the shogun Sanetomo, who ranked sixth among all the poets in the collection with 25 poems. Teika had been his poetry teacher, and was awarded the stewardship (*jitō shiki*) to Hosokawa Estate as a result. (This was the *shiki* much fought over among Teika's descendants, the Reizei, Kyōgoku, and Nijō branches.) Of course

the term "warrior" was relative. In many cases, if the person in question had lived in Kyoto instead of Kamakura his lineage would not have been questioned.

13. From *Koshibe no zenni shōsoku*, in ibid., 3: 385.

14. Shinkan (1203–76) was born Hamuro Mitsutoshi. Because of his family's close ties to Juntoku, he was exiled for a year as a result of the Jōkyū War. He was originally a disciple of Teika's and a friend of Tameie's until he broke with the latter over poetic matters. In particular, he was fond of the Man'yō style, while Tameie became increasingly attached to the first three imperial anthologies (*sandaishū*, that is, *Kokinshū*, *Gosenshū*, and *Shūishū*).

15. Depending on the source, Ieyoshi is identified as being of the Kinugasa or Kujō branches of the Fujiwara clan, though his father was Tadayoshi, of the Rokujō branch of the *sekkanke*.

16. Tokieda et al., eds., *Jinnō shōtōki, Masukagami* (*Nihon koten bungaku taikei 87*), 325; Kokusho Kankōkai, *Honchō Tsugan*, 10: 3212–14. Neither does any of the accounts compiled *Shiryō Sōran* mention this. See Tokyo Daigaku Shiryō Hensanjo, *Shiryō Sōran*, 5: 115, 119.

17. *Nihon kagaku taikei*, 4: 2. For this and other reactions to *Shokukokinshū*, see Fukuda Hideichi, *Chūsei wakashi no kenkyū*, 99–103. Genshō's remark about Shinkan that "he taught as he pleased" is to be taken as derogatory.

18. Such *Man'yōshū* poems as appear in imperial anthologies at least through *Shinkokinshū* are almost inevitably from the *Kokin waka rokujō* rather than directly from *Man'yōshū* itself. This is partly because the *Man'yōgana* code took many centuries to crack, and partly because compilers felt safe using poems from *Kokin waka rokujō*.

19. Sengaku's most important extant writing is his *Man'yōshū chūshaku*, 1269, considered the first comprehensive annotative work on *Man'yōshū*. As early as 1246, however, he had gained a reputation in Kamakura for his textual work on the collection. For a text of Sengaku's study, see Nihon tosho sentaa, ed., *Man'yōshū sengakushō Man'yōshū meibutsukō*, Man'yōshū kochūshaku taisei (Nihon tosho sentaa, 1978), 1–234.

20. Go-Saga was first son of Tsuchimikado, who in turn had been Go-Toba's first son, but owing partly to Go-Toba's desire to keep his own hand strong, and partly to the Jōkyū War, Go-Saga had not ascended directly to the throne. Four emperors intervened between him and his father. His taking the throne at all suggests that for the Bakufu, too, memories of Jōkyū were fading.

21. Go-Fukakusa's account, known as *Shokukokinshū kyōen gyoki*, can be found in Ressei Zenshū Hensankai, ed., *Ressei zenshū*, vol. 19, *Shinkishū I*, 263–66. The *Masukagami* comments are in Tokieda et al., eds., *Jinnō shōtōki Masukagami*, 325.

22. *Nihon kagaku taikei*, 5: 92–93. Ton'a is in turn citing Nijō Tameyo.

23. For more details about this rupture, see Huey, *Kyōgoku Tamekane*, 12–15.

24. *Masukagami*'s assessment is pithy: "Contemporaries said of it, 'There isn't much soul to it, but one can find charm there.'" *Jinnō shōtōki* (1965 ed.), 365.

25. Ton'a says that *Shokushūishū*'s nickname was "The Cormorant Boat Collection" (*Ubuneshū*). This involves a pun on the word *kagari*, which can describe the torches (*kagaribi*) cormorant fisherman used to attract fish to the surface at night, as well as the torches used at the 48 guardhouses (*kagariya*) throughout Kyoto. It can also simply mean the guards themselves. By saying *Shokushūishū* "includes a lot of *kagari*" (*kagari no ooku iritaru*), Ton'a is suggesting that there were many warrior poets cited in it. *Nihon kagaku taikei*, 5: 108. Neither in this instance nor in the case of *Shinchokusenshū*, where he actually uses the term *bushi* (see note 12 above), does Ton'a name names, though it does seem (since *kagari* guards were associated with Kyoto) that one need not live in Kamakura to be in this warrior category. An example of the type of family that literary historians now dub "bushi" would be the Utsunomiya house. They were descended from Fujiwara Michitaka (953–95), younger brother of Michinaga and himself regent and chancellor. By the Kamakura period they had become Bakufu *gokenin*, but maintained a residence in Kyoto and were especially close to Teika, whose son Tameie married an Utsunomiya daughter. They also had ties with Ietaka, and were very active in Kyoto poetry circles into the fourteenth century. (See Ariyoshi Tamotsu, *Waka bungaku jiten*, 52–53; and Inoue Muneo, *Chūsei kadanshi no kenkyū: Nanboku-chōki*, 68–70.) This is a far cry from someone like the *Heike Monogatari* character Tsutsui no Jōmyō Meishū, "the pride of Miidera," who stands, halberd in hand, ready to challenge all comers at the Uji Bridge. Similarly, among the poets in the Miscellaneous section of *Shokushūishū* we find one Norisada, member of the Sahyōe guards. In fact, Norisada did serve three shoguns in Kamakura, and his mother was from the prominent Ōe warrior house. But his father was Asukai Masatsune, who as noted earlier had been called to Kyoto by Go-Toba and had founded one of the capital's most important poetry houses.

26. *Hanazono tennō shinki*, Genkō 2 (1332)/3/24, part 3, 264. (All citations of Hanazono's diary are from Murata Masashi, ed., *Shiryō sanshū*, vol. 80, parts 1–3, *Hanazono Tennō shinki*.) As head of a recognized poetry family, Tameyo could take on and certify disciples as having mastered the art. Hanazono complains that Tameyo is too quick to grant formal approval to many of these pupils, "aristocrats, warriors (*buke*), and commoners" alike. See Huey, *Kyōgoku Tamekane*, 158, for a translation of the passage in question.

27. Familial splits like the ones seen in the imperial family and the Miko-hidari house had become virtually endemic at all levels of society in the Kamakura period. As Jeffrey Mass notes, "Clearly, competition among kin was scarcely an affliction known only to warriors." See Mass, *Lordship and Inheritance in Early Medieval Japan*, 111.

28. See Huey, *Kyōgoku Tamekane*, esp. chap. 1.

29. See ibid., 31–33, for details.

30. *Chisei no kimi*, or *chiten no kimi*, literally "ruler of the land," was the designation for the head of the imperial household, which from late Heian usually

meant the senior retired emperor. Because of the imperial family split at this time, however, the term effectively refers to the oldest active male member of whichever imperial line occupied the throne.

31. Inoue Muneo, *Chūsei kadanshi no kenkyū: Nanbokuchōki*, 122–23.

32. *Tamekanekyōki*, 12/18 and 12/20; Hamaguchi Hiroaki and Ogawa Michiko, eds., "*Tamekanekyōki* Ryakuchū," 65, 67. See also, Huey, *Kyōgoku Tamekane*, 45.

33. The *Sentō gojūban uta-awase* of 1303/4/29.

34. The Tsumori family were hereditary administrators of the Sumiyoshi Shrine in Settsu Province. The god Sumiyoshi had become associated with waka over the centuries, so the Tsumori family, too, practiced the art. Still, they were not one of the old poetic houses in the capital, and their rise to prominence was clearly due to their connections with the Nijō house. They were thus seen as upstarts by many in Kyoto, hence the derogatory mock title. Sasaki, ed., *Nihon kagaku taikei*, 5: 108–9.

35. There is disagreement among waka scholars as to whether this Rensho is modeled on the Bakufu office known as vice-regent. (For example, Ariyoshi Tamotsu states flatly that it is, but does not elaborate, while Inukai Kiyoshi thinks it is not. See Ariyoshi Tamotsu, *Waka bungaku jiten*, 698; and Inukai Kiyoshi et al., eds., *Waka daijiten*, 524, 1075–76.) I do not see a clear connection, since the Bakufu office was held by one person, whereas the Rensho established by Go-Uda (and used for later anthologies as well) involved a group. More likely, the term is a reference to the other meaning of *rensho*, that is, a document (often a critique) that bears multiple signatories. A well-known example in waka circles would be *Kaen rensho no kotogaki* (Poetic Garden Particulars Jointly Signed), 1315, an anonymous attack on Tamekane's *Gyokuyōshū* "signed" by a group of famous, but deceased, poet-priests like Kisen and Saigyō.

36. More than any group, literary scholars both in Japan and, inexplicably, in the West, have consistently taken the side of the imperial family in matters political and historical. According to this view, in the Heian period it was the Fujiwara who usurped the imperial prerogative. Subsequently, it was the warriors from the East. It is a testament to the success of the nationalist scholars (*kokugakusha*) and later the Meiji propaganda machine that scholars accepted without question the notion that culture ought to rest in the hands of the imperial family like some cosmological privilege. Patrons they undoubtedly were, and serious types like Hanazono made honest attempts to put the imperial cultural responsibility in a larger philosophical, cosmological context. But that does not absolve us from our own critical responsibilities.

37. The extant portion of the suits between Tameyo and Tamekane is known collectively as *Enkyō ryōkyō sochinjō*. A text appears in *Nihon kagaku taikei*, 4: 127–37. An English discussion and partial translation can be found in Huey, *Kyōgoku Tamekane*, 53–56 and 164–67. In what still stands as one of the most impressive examples of scholarship I know of, Fukuda Hideichi gives a detailed discussion of

the circumstances surrounding these suits in *"Enkyō ryōkyō sochinjō* no seiritsu," and *"Enkyō ryōkyō sochinjō* no seiritsu ni kansuru shiryō." A shorter version of his findings appears in his *Chūsei wakashi no kenkyū,* 685–710.

38. Fukuda, *"Enkyō ryōkyō sochinjō* no seiritsu," 40; and *"Enkyō ryōkyō sochinjō* no seiritsu ni kansuru shiryō," 39–40.

39. Tokieda et al., *Jinnō shōtōki Masukagami,* 416.

40. The last collection ordered by an emperor and completed was the fourth one, *Goshūishū,* under the direction of Shirakawa (commissioned in 1075, and submitted in 1086). The title of Go-Daigo's anthology—*"Goshūishū, Continued"*—signaled his wish to be associated with Shirakawa's undertaking. After retiring, Shirakawa sponsored *Kin'yōshū* (ordered in 1124 and presented in 1127). Thereafter, all completed anthologies were under the direction of retired emperors until Go-Daigo.

41. In the first year of the Bunpō era, 1317, the Bakufu engineered a compromise among the various contending imperial factions whereby succession to the throne would be alternated between two of the lines, Go-Nijō's and Go-Fushimi's. The other lines, including the descendants of Go-Daigo and Hanazono, were to be left out.

42. For Hanazono's obituary of Tamefuji, see *Hanazono Tennō Shinki,* Genkō 4 (1324)/7/26, part 3, 64–66 (translated in Huey, *Kyōgoku Tamekane,* 155–57).

43. For excellent discussions of Hanazono's thought, see Goble, "Truth, Contradiction, and Harmony in Medieval Japan: Emperor Hanazono (1297–1348) and Buddhism," 21–63; and Iwasa Miyoko, *Kyōgokuha waka no kenkyū,* 99–143.

44. The issue of who actually compiled *Fūgashū* and of the relative roles played by Hanazono and his nephew Kōgon has not been settled. The major arguments are reviewed, with bibliographical references, in Inoue Muneo, *Chūsei kadanshi no kenkyū: Nanbokuchōki,* 441–51; and *Fūga wakashū,* ed. Tsugita Kasumi and Iwasa Miyoko, 20–25. I am following the bulk of current scholarly opinion, which sees Hanazono as the initiator of the idea, and an active supporter behind the scenes (it is certain that he composed the Chinese and Japanese prefaces) while Kōgon was the official "front man" and compiler.

45. *Hanazono tennō shinki,* Genkō 4 (1324)/1/25, part 3, 40–41.

46. A citation of the relevant passage from *Entairyaku* appears in Inoue Muneo, *Chūsei kadanshi no kenkyū: Nanbokuchōki,* 442.

47. Inoue reviews these opinions in ibid., 442–43, and favors the latter.

48. *Fūga wakashū,* 50.

49. Ibid., 52.

50. The following discussion and examples are indebted to Tsugita and Iwasa, *Fūga wakashū,* 4–13.

51. The first example is FGS 2006 (Book XVII, Misc. 2), by Kenreimon'in Ukyō no Daibu ("Lady Daibu" in Harries, *The Poetic Memoirs of Lady Daibu*), and the second is FGS 2008 (Book XVII, Misc. 2) by Zensei Hōshi. Both head-

notes refer to events connected with the Genpei War, suggesting that Hanazono and Kōgon are interested in the *theme* of war, not just in their immediate social circumstances, though other poems address contemporary upheavals (e.g., FGS 1871 and 1872, an exchange between Kinkage and Hanazono about their having to relocate to Sakamoto when Southern forces enter the capital in early 1336). Poem numbers are from the *Shinpen kokka taikan*, and differ somewhat from those in Tsugita and Iwasa.

52. Tsugita and Iwasa, *Fūga wakashū*, 9–11. The two scholars do not provide an especially precise analysis of this point, at times, for example, treating "flowers" as a single image, at other times distinguishing types of flowers, so that their statistics ultimately compare different things. And much of what the two scholars have to say appears to be anecdotal. Still, assuming they are correct in their count, the prominence of the "mountain hut" image is striking and worth comment.

53. Michele Marra interprets the first poems of *Fūgashū* differently, by focusing on the "who" rather than the "what." In spite of a factual error that could have been avoided had he read his own cited text more carefully (FGS 3 is by Kanezane, not Tadamichi), he rightly notes that part of Kōgon's agenda here is to honor the Kyōgoku school and legitimize it as the proper heir to the Mikohidari tradition. (The first nine poems are by Tamekane, Shunzei, Kujō Kanezane, Go-Toba, Saionji Sanekane, Fushimi, Hanazono, Fushimi's daughter Princess Shinshi, and Teika, respectively—all either Mikohidari poets [pre-Nijō] and their patrons or Kyōgoku poets and their patrons.) See Marra, *Representations of Power*, 36. In terms of overall representation, the anthology is similarly one-sided. Fushimi, Eifukumon'in, Hanazono, Tamekane, Tameko, Teika, Go-Fushimi, and Kōgon—the core and essence of the Jimyōin line and the Kyōgoku school—make up the top eight poets. In this sense Hanazono and Kōgon are if anything even more partisan than their Nijō rivals had been in the previous two anthologies.

54. During the decades of their dispute with the Kyōgoku and Reizei branches of the family, Nijō compilers of imperial anthologies had continued to designate their collections "new" (*shin*), "later" (*go*), or "continued" (*shoku*) versions of earlier classics and they had looked askance at Tamekane's choice of *Gyokuyōshū*, with its deliberate reference to *Man'yōshū* and *Kin'yōshū*.

55. See Marra, *Representations of Power*, 37–54, for examples.

56. Though Marra correctly notes the growing Ashikaga impact on imperial anthologies (pp. 11–12), I believe he fails to see how much even the Ashikaga shoguns still chose to work within the old imperial parameters. His chapter on the waka of this period, though the most complete discussion of its kind in English, is unfortunately marred by several basic factual errors. See Marra, *Representations of Power*, 6–54.

57. Entry for Enbun 1 (1356)/6/10 in *Dainihon shiryō*, part 6, vol. 20: 609–12.

58. Entry for Jōji 2 (1363)/2/29 in *ibid.*, part 6, vol. 24: 1014–16.

59. Takauji is in eleventh place with seventeen poems. In fact, the collection

in general includes more deceased poets than living ones, probably because it was made within fifteen years of *Fūgashū* and *Shinsenzaishū*, which had already anthologized much of the best contemporary work. So the lack of powerful Ashikaga patrons among the top ten is probably not significant politically.

60. There is an overlap between the decline of waka and the rise of *renga*. The first imperial *renga* anthology, *Tsukubashū*, was ordered in 1357. However, we must bear in mind that waka never really dies out, and that the most important practitioners of the other literary arts received their initial training in waka, and still held it to be the primary art. See, for example, Steven Carter, "Ichijō Kaneyoshi and the Literary Arts," in Carter, ed., *Literary Patronage in Late Medieval Japan*, 19–44. Other essays in the collection reiterate this point.

Chapter 9

1. See Kawazoe Shōji, *Kamakura bakufu*, 70–71.

2. Ibid., 133.

3. *Nijō-Kawara rakusho* in Satō Kazuhiko, *Nanbokuchō nairan*, 50. The fast horses were for carrying messages to and from the Kantō.

4. *Taiheiki*, ed. Gotō Tanji and Kamada Kisaburō, 3: 252.

5. *Kenmu shikimoku* in Hanawa Hokiichi, ed., *Gunsho ruijū*, 33.

6. Ibid., 34.

7. *Nijō-Kawara rakusho*, 52.

8. Donald Keene, trans., *Essays in Idleness: The Tsurezuregusa of Kenkō*, 118.

9. Gotō and Kamada, eds., *Taiheiki*, 2: 355–56.

10. Wintersteen, "The Early Muromachi Bakufu in Kyoto," and Gay, "Muromachi Bakufu Rule in Kyoto: Administrative and Judicial Aspects."

11. Gotō and Kamada, eds., *Taiheiki*, vol. 1. Takatoki (1303–33), the last of the Hōjō regents, is said to have attended *dengaku* performances "day and night."

12. Hara Tsunehira, "Sasaki Dōyo," 116.

13. Satō Kazuhiko, *Taiheiki no sekai*, 124.

14. Imai Masaharu, *Chūsei o ikita Nihonjin*, 273.

15. See the discussion of the textual development of *Taiheiki* in Varley, *Warriors of Japan, As Portrayed in the War Tales*.

16. Gotō and Kamada, eds., *Taiheiki*, 2: 337–38.

17. Ibid., 338.

18. Satō Kazuhiko, *Taiheiki o yomu*, 118.

19. Gotō and Kamada, eds., *Taiheiki*, 2: 339.

20. Ibid., 403. Shooting a dog refers to the warrior sport of *inuou mono*, which Yoritō and his party had probably engaged in during their outing.

21. Ibid., 405. Kō no Moronao, whom we have identified, along with Sasaki Dōyo and Toki Yoritō, as a prominent *basara* warrior in *Taiheiki*, is also charged in that work with expressing gross disrespect for the imperial family. According to *Taiheiki*, Moronao took advantage of his position as a high-ranking member

of the Bakufu (he held the office of *shitsuji*) to illegally confiscate the mansions and landholdings of others in Kyoto. Angered that the extensive land occupied by the palaces of the emperor and retired emperor were not available to him, he suggested that their majesties be banished. If it was necessary to have an emperor and a retired emperor, he contended, "Why not make them out of wood or cast them in metal?" Gotō and Kamada, eds., *Taiheiki*, 3: 49.

22. Satō, *Nanbokuchō nairan*, 302–3.

23. Gotō and Kamada, eds., *Taiheiki*, 3: 357–58.

24. Satō, *Nanbokuchō nairan*, 303.

25. Gotō and Kamada, eds., *Taiheiki*, 3: 373–74.

26. Ibid., 374.

27. Atsuta Kō, ed., "Nanbokuchō, Muromachi," 153.

28. For example, Varley, "Ashikaga Yoshimitsu and the World of Kitayama," 191–92.

29. Ibid., 188–92.

30. Hara, "Sasaki Dōyo," 128.

31. Gotō and Kamada, eds., *Taiheiki*, 3: 443–44.

32. Ibid.

33. Murai Yasuhiko, "The Development of *Chanoyu*: Before Rikyū," 14–15.

34. Satō, *Taiheiki no sekai*, 130.   35. Ibid., 131.

36. Hare, *Zeami's Style*, 17.   37. See, e.g., ibid.

38. Thomas Hare states that *mugen* plays are those in which the *shite* (main character) is "a being from another dimension of existence, either a god, demon, faerie, or plant spirit or the ghost of a human being."

39. Ryusaku Tsunoda et al., eds., *Sources of Japanese Tradition*, 289.

40. Ibid., 290.

41. Hare, *Zeami's Style*, 185.

42. "*Sandō*" in Rimer and Yamazaki Masakazu, *On the Art of the Nō Drama*, 155.

43. For a discussion of loser-heroes in the war tales, see Varley, *Warriors of Japan*, 56–58.

44. See the discussion in Hare, *Zeami's Style*, 186.

45. Kuwata Tadachika, *Shinchō kōki*, 53–54.

Chapter 10

1. Sansom, *A History of Japan, 1334–1615*, 115.

2. *Buke shohatto*, in *Kinsei buke shisō*, 27: 454. Translation from Tsunoda Ryusaku et al., *Sources of Japanese Tradition*, 335–36.

3. As Japan became more peaceful under Tokugawa rule, subsequent editions of the *Buke shohatto* diluted references to the *bu* element and moved it further down in the list of articles. Edwin Reischauer's claim that Tokugawa Japan represented "the longest period of complete peace and political stability that any size-

able body of people has ever enjoyed" is substantially accurate. Reischauer and Craig, *Japan: Tradition and Transformation*, 91.

4. Hayashi Razan, "On Mastery of the Arts of Peace and War," in *Sources of Japanese Tradition*, 347.

5. Eight signatures appear on the document, but the Nakahara brothers were apparently the primary authors. Scholars still debate the form and force of the document, and Kasamatsu Hiroshi has argued that Takauji's younger brother Tadayoshi was really behind its drafting. See Satō Kazuhiko, *Nanbokuchō nairan*, 124–29.

6. *Kenmu shikimoku*, in Satō Shin'ichi and Ikeuchi Yoshisuke, eds., *Chūsei hōsei shiryōshū*, 2, 3 (hereafter *KS*). See also, Grossberg and Kanamoto Nobuhisa, trans., *Laws of the Muromachi Bakufu*, 15–23.

7. *KS* 3.

8. See Hurst, "The Kōbu Polity: Court-Bakufu Relations in the Kamakura Era."

9. Grossberg and Kanamoto, *Laws of the Muromachi Bakufu*, 16. Of course, the elite included Bakufu vassals like Sasaki Dōyo, whom the derogatory term *basara*, or ostentatious display and excess, aptly described. In his criticism of how warriors have enriched themselves while the courtiers have become impoverished, the author of *Taiheiki* singles out Dōyo as especially venal. *Taiheiki*, Gotō Tanji and Kamada Kisaburo, eds., 3: 252–53 (hereafter *THK*). See also the essay by Varley in this volume.

10. Not content simply to list seventeen articles (they are not numerically ordered) the compilers state in their conclusion, "The above seventeen articles are as stated herein." *KS* 7.

11. Ibid.

12. Ibid.

13. Ibid., 6.

14. Mass, "The Kamakura Bakufu," 79.

15. Kakei Yoshihiko, *Chūsei buke kakun no kenkyū*, 142–43, also makes this point.

16. For a discussion of Nitobe and the development of the idea of *bushidō*, see Hurst, "Death, Honor, and Loyalty: The Bushidō Ideal," 514–16.

17. For an excellent study of Shigetoki's writings, see Steenstrup, *Hōjō Shigetoki (1198–1261) and His Role in the History of Political and Ethical Ideas in Japan*.

18. Kakei, *Chūsei buke kakun no kenkyū*, is the most readily accessible source for the first three texts; see appendix (*sankōhen*) 7–17 (Imagawa), 30–32 (Ashikaga), and 35–42 (Shiba). For the text of *Yoshisadaki*, see Hanawa Hōkiichi, ed., *Gunsho ruijū*, 23: 477–92 (hereafter *GR*).

19. See Kakei, 29 (*Sankōhen*), and Steenstrup, following Kakei, 205. The document is also known as *Saki no Sadaijin Takauji-kyō goisho* and simply *Takauji-kyō goisho*.

20. Although Varley (*The Onin War*, 97) observes that "the history of the Bakufu during the rest of the 14th century . . . can be reduced to the careers

of Shiba Yoshimasa and Hosokawa Yoriyuki," Western sources seldom mention Yoshimasa. *Chikubashō* is translated by William S. Wilson, *The Ideals of the Samurai: Writings of Japanese Warriors*, 46–56.

21. Sansom, *A History of Japan*, 178–79.

22. *Kyūzen* could be used more broadly to refer to "martial arts" in general, but it reflects the continued dominance of mounted archery as the primary warrior fighting skill.

23. The three are forms of mounted archery. *Mato* refers to mounted archery shooting at regular, fixed targets; *kasagake* involved shooting at targets that were originally sedge hats, then sedge targets especially constructed for competition; *inuoumono*, the major archery competition for Muromachi warriors, involved shooting at dogs with specially blunted arrows.

24. Quoted by Nakabayashi Shinji, "Nihon kobudō ni okeru shintairon," 109.

25. Takahashi Tomio, *Bushidō no rekishi*, 1: 287–88. Takahashi equates the compilation of *kakun* and *buke kojitsu*.

26. Kakei, 5 (*sankōhen*).

27. There is considerable literature on Ryōshun in English. For information on Ryōshun's political career, see Harrington, "Regional Administration Under the Ashikaga Bakufu: Power and Politics Outside the Central Provinces," 163–83. Steenstrup, *Hōjō Shigetoki*, 207–8, assesses Ryōshun's text. See also Steenstrup, "The Imagawa Letter: A Muromachi Warrior's Code of Conduct Which Became a Tokugawa Textbook," 295–316, for an annotated translation of Imagawajō. Wilson, *Ideals of the Samurai*, provides a translation on pp. 57–63.

28. For details, see Steenstrup, "Imagawa Letter," 297–98.

29. Steenstrup, e.g., *Hōjō Shigetoki*, 207.

30. The eighteenth-century ceremonial expert Ise Sadataka considered Yoshisada the author, but the work may have been fabricated, possibly around the same time as *Chikubashō*. See Takahashi, *Bushidō no rekishi*, 280.

31. Yoshisada argues that one should not always reward hereditary vassals most highly; a new vassal who displays ingenuity (*kiyō*) should be well rewarded. He warns against "remembering old faults while neglecting new deeds," and says that past misdeeds can be forgiven. Only when the contributions of a new and old vassal are equal should the old vassal be more highly rewarded; normally, rewards should be equal for similar service.

32. Takahashi, 281–82.

33. Morohashi Tetsuji, comp., *Dai kanwa jiten*, 4: 593, provides a number of examples of classical loci for these terms.

34. Wechsler, "T'ai-tsung the Consolidator," 241.

35. Ibid., 200.

36. Rogers, "The Chinese World Order in Its Transmural Extension: The Case of Chin and Koryŏ," 12. See also, Liu, "Yueh Fei (1103–41) and China's Heritage of Loyalty," 297, as also noted by Rogers.

37. Fairbank, *China: A New History*, 11.

38. Hurst, "The Good, the Bad, and the Ugly: Personalities in the Founding of the Koryŏ Dynasty," 1–27 passim.

39. *Heiji monogatari*, in *Nihon koten bungaku taikei*, 2: 189.

40. *Heike monogatari*, in *Nihon Koten bungalev taikei*, 2: 70. Translation from H. C. McCullough, *The Tale of the Heike*, 229.

41. *Yoritomo, Sasaki ni kudsaruru jō*, in *Shibugaki*, GR 27: 157. Kenkyū 2 (1192)/int. 12/28. See also note 54.

42. Steenstrup, *Hōjō Shigetoki*, 123, 213–4.

43. Varley, *Warriors of Japan, As Portrayed in the War Tales*, 178–79.

44. *THK* 3: 392–94.

45. Wajima Yoshio discusses the state of Confucian studies during the long period when Sino-Japanese official relations were curtailed, emphasizing the decline of Confucian knowledge. He concludes that even the rise of the warriors and new support from Kamakura did not lead to an opening of new studies. Wajima Yoshio, *Chūsei no jugaku*, 62.

46. Ibid., 66–91, discusses this phenomenon. Wajima notes that Confucian references in various writings and lectures do not necessarily show individual preference on the part of priests; rather, they indicate the extent of the T'ang-Sung amalgamation of the three teachings—Buddhism, Confucianism, and Taoism.

47. From Tokugawa times, Chikafusa was revered as a great master of the new Sung studies who based much of his own work on Ssu-ma Kwang's *Tzu-chih t'ung-chien*. Wajima has concluded that this view is without merit, and that Chikafusa's Confucian knowledge was of a type that could easily be obtained from familiarity with current Shinto writings and traditional Confucian learning and was not based on any advanced Sung studies. Wajima, 154–55.

48. Translation from Varley, *A Chronicle of Gods and Sovereigns: Jinnō Shōtōki of Kitabatake Chikafusa*, 32–33, 248.

49. Fuji Naomoto, *Buke jidai no shakai to seishin*, 122.

50. Extant Heian *yūsoku kojitsu* texts include *Saigūki* (compiled by Minamoto no Takaakira), *Gōke shidai* (Ōe no Masafusa), and *Hokuzanshō* (Fujiwara no Kintō). As Murai Yasuhiko notes, *Gōke shidai* is the most refined of these, moving beyond a mere listing of details to an analysis of the procedures. *Bungei no sōsei to tenkai*, 201–2.

51. See Niki Ken'ichi, *Chūsei buke girei no kenkyū*, 179. As noted by Ishioka Hisao, archery was one of the "six accomplishments" (*rikugei*) of the gentleman mentioned by both Confucius and Mencius and was so understood in ancient Japan ("*Kyūdō*," in *Nihon budō taikei*, 9: 125–66). Chapter 43 of the *Li Chi* (Book of Rites) on "The Meaning of the Ceremony of Archery" states: "Archers were required to observe the rules. With minds correct, and straight carriage of the body, they were able to hold their bows skillfully and firmly; and when they did so, they might be expected to hit the mark. In this way (from their archery) their char-

acters could be seen" (James Legge, trans., *Li Chi: Book of Rites*, 446). Archery never lost that ceremonial quality in Japan. In fact, archery was intimately related to character development and etiquette long before the introduction of Zen, which has so transfixed Western authors that they refer to Japanese archery as "Zen archery." For further comment, see Hurst, "The Quest for Records: Japanese Archery as Competition," unpublished paper, 1994.

52. The husband of Naka no kimi, for example, is referred to as the "premier warrior in the land" (*"kokka daiichi no musha nari"*) in *Shin sarugakki*, in *GR* 8: 342. The text, compiled by Fujiwara Akisue in the early eleventh century, recounts the various forms of archery and other martial techniques in which he was skilled.

53. *Azuma kagami*, 1194/10/9 (hereafter *AK*).

54. In a document addressed to Sasaki Sadatsuna, for example, Yoritomo claimed that *kojitsu* were even more important to warriors (*yumitori*) than to courtiers (*fumitori*). See *Yoritomo, Sasaki kudasaruru jō*, in *Shibugaki*, in *GR* 27: 158.

55. *AK* 1203/10/26.

56. Fuji, *Buke jidai no shakai to seishin*, 124–25.

57. In English, see, e.g., Varley, "Ashikaga Yoshimitsu and the World of Kitayama," and Grossberg, "From Feudal Chieftain to Secular Monarch: The Development of Shogunal Power in Early Muromachi Japan."

58. Fuji, 125–26. Once, for example, when Yoshimitsu was preparing for an audience at court, he borrowed a sword from Michitsugu and had one made exactly like it. (Court ceremonial dress required straight, double-edged swords patterned on ancient Chinese prototypes and thus different from the curved *tachi* worn and used by medieval warriors.)

59. Ibid.

60. Both texts are reproduced in *GR* 22: 133–36 (*gempukuki*) and 179–81 (*naoihajimeki*).

61. Fuji, 126. Quoting a passage from *Gogumaiki*, Fuji notes that Yoshimitsu once lamented that there were no precedents for warrior authorities.

62. See *Canterbury Tales, General Prologue*, ll. 43–78.

63. See Weir's discussion of Anthony Wydville, Earl Rivers, in *The Princes in the Tower*, 41.

64. *Hōjō Shigetoki*, 229.

65. The first quotation is from *Ōtomo kojitsu* in *GR* 22: 409–24, the second, from *Kyūba no gi ni tsuki taigai kikigaki*, in *GR* 23: 127–98. See Fuji, 131.

66. See, e.g., Imagawa Ryōshun, *Imagawa ōsōji*, in *GR* 22: 478, where Ryōshun details how to offer or receive a bow from a person of status (*kijin*) as opposed to an equal (*dōryō*).

67. *Yoshisadaki*, in *GR* 23: 480.

68. Wechsler, *Offerings of Jade and Silk: Ritual and Symbol in the Legitimation of the T'ang Dynasty*, 21. Chap. 1, 9–36, reviews major works on legitimacy, ritual, and symbolism.

69. Cohen, *Two-Dimensional Man: An Essay on the Anthropology of Power and Symbolism in Complex Society*, 77.

70. See Fuji, 135 on this point, and the general comparison of law with *kojitsu*.

71. Wechsler, *Offerings of Jade and Silk*, 29.

72. Although the Ogasawara were intimately involved in mounted archery competitions in the fourteenth century, their designation as official *kojitsu* specialists and archery instructors to the shogun came in fact in the era of Yoshimasa in the next century. Similarly, the Ise really established their leadership in the mid-Muromachi. For a discussion of these two families, see Niki, 175–210 (Ogasawara) and 211–56 (Ise).

73. See Sadamune's *Meyasu*, in *GR* 23: 95–96. This document, presented in the form of a petition to Takauji, is dated 1343. *Inuoumonoki*, in *Nihon budō taikei*, 4: 467, presents another, later version of the story. In any case, it seems obvious that the story was a later attempt by the family to enhance its reputation, based upon the knowledge that Sadamune was a distinguished early Muromachi Ogasawara archer. See Niki, *Chūsei buke girei no kenkyū*, 189–91.

74. Textual references to numbers of warriors are vexing. Farris deals with the problem of "counting warriors" for the Kamakura period, concluding that *Azuma kagami* and other sources often exaggerate the numbers of vassals in a warrior band. *Heavenly Warriors: The Evolution of Japan's Military, 500 to 1300*, 318, 335–43.

75. Shimokawa Ushio, *Kendō no hattatsu*, 96.

76. *Heike monogatari*, 1: 310–11, describes "The Battle of the Uji Bridge" in which Tsutsui Jōmyō Meishū slashes in all directions, "using the zigzag, interlacing, crosswise, dragonfly reverse, and waterwheel maneuvers." Shimokawa, *Kendō no hattatsu*, 92–94 tries to explain some of these moves; translation from McCullough, 153.

77. *THK* 3: 233.

78. Quoted in Nakabayashi Shinji, "Kendōshi," in *Nihon budō taikei*, 9: 36–37.

79. Steenstrup, *Hōjō Shigetoki*, 227.

80. *Bajutsu* is usually considered a martial art distinct from mounted archery, and there are many schools (*ryūha*) established by families of specialists — often Ogasawara branch families. See Hyūga Hiroyuki's section on *bajutsu* in *Nihon budō taikei*, 6: 539–640, which contains several important works of equestrian etiquette.

Chapter 11

1. Temples are treated as personalized sociopolitical units throughout this study. This will eliminate repeating such phrases as "the monks of Enryakuji" and "the temple community." Although internal disputes between Enryakuji's several subunits and socially diverse groups were not unusual, the clergy tended to act in unison in conflicts with the Bakufu and the imperial court. Accordingly, sources

in the capital describing such incidents frequently refer to the Enryakuji monks as a coherent unit.

2. The use of the term Zen in this study is limited to the monks and institutions of the Ashikaga-favored Rinzai.

3. Goble, "Go-Daigo and the Kemmu Restoration."

4. See Collcutt, *Five Mountains: The Rinzai Zen Monastic Institution in Medieval Japan*; McMullin, *Buddhism and the State in Sixteenth-Century Japan*; Piggott, "Tōdaiji and the Nara Imperium"; Goodwin, *Alms and Vagabonds: Buddhist Temples and Popular Patronage in Medieval Japan*.

5. Kuroda presented the *kenmon* theory in the following works: *Jisha seiryoku* (hereafter *JSR*); *Nihon chūsei no kokka to shūkyō* (hereafter *NCKS*); "Chūsei jisha seiryoku ron," in *Iwanami kōza, Nihon rekishi 6: Chūsei 2*, Asao Naohiro et al., eds., 245–95; and "Chūsei kokka to tennō," in *Iwanami kōza, Nihon rekishi 6: Chūsei 2*, Ienaga Saburō et al., eds., 261–301 (hereafter *CKT*).

6. Kuroda used *kenmon*—a historical term—mainly as an analytical term in his works. The warrior government (Bakufu) and religious institutions are not referred to as *kenmon* in historical sources. Yet there is evidence to support Kuroda's analytical usage. There are frequent references to the prerogatives of the *kenmon* and temples and shrines (*kenmon narabi ni jisha*) in documents and other contemporary sources. Moreover, a document of 1271/7 explicitly juxtaposes the *kuge*, the *buke*, and the *shūke* (the religious establishment). *Kamakura ibun* 14: 290, doc. 10856; see also, Mass, *Antiquity and Anachronism*, 50.

7. *NCKS* 78. Kuroda has been criticized for not explaining exactly how this interdependence worked. See Nagahara Keiji, "Nihon kokka shi no ichi mondai," 45.

8. *NCKS* 17–18, 31, 78; *CKT* 265–79. The court-Bakufu relationship has been explained in English by Hurst, "The Kōbu Polity: Court Bakufu Relations in Kamakura Japan," and by Kiley, "The Imperial Court as a Legal Authority in the Kamakura Age."

9. The most comprehensive treatment so far can be found in Gay's "Muromachi Bakufu Rule in Kyoto: Administrative and Judicial Aspects," 50–52.

10. *NCKS* 7–11, 367; *CKT* 269–70.

11. *CKT* 268.

12. *NCKS* 20–21, 453; *CKT* 279–80.

13. *NCKS* 19; *CKT* 277–80.

14. *CKT* 270.

15. *CKT* 275–76; *NCKS* 455–58.

16. *NCKS* 17–18, 21; *CKT* 275–79. One interesting example supporting this notion can be found in 1221/10/24 when the retired emperor issued an imperial directive (*inzen*) in accordance with an order from the Bakufu in Kamakura confirming an estate's immunity (*DaiNihon komonjo iewake 1: Kōyasan monjo*, vol. 1, doc. 267).

17. Our understanding of the Kamakura period and the Bakufu has progressed greatly during the last two decades in particular thanks to the works of Jeffrey Mass. See, for example, Mass, *Warrior Government in Early Medieval Japan: A Study of the Kamakura Bakufu, Shugo, and Jitō*; *Antiquity and Anachronism in Japanese History*; "The Kamakura Bakufu"; and Mass, ed., *Court and Bakufu in Japan*.

18. *Kenmitsu* was the combined term for the six Nara schools and the two Heian schools (Tendai and Shingon). Tendai and Shingon in particular dominated in the late Heian and Kamakura periods. They used both exoteric (*ken*) scriptures and esoteric (*mitsu*), orally transmitted rituals in their teachings.

19. *JSR* 255–56; *NCKS* 454–55.

20. *JSR* 257.

21. Taira Masayuki, *Nihon chūsei no shakkai to bukkyō*, 94–96.

22. *NCKS* 306, 456.

23. *NCKS* 5–6, 31–32.

24. *NCKS* 306, 457, 460. For more information on the study of religious institutions and religion in premodern Japan, see McMullin, "Historical and Historiographical Issues in the Study of Pre-Modern Japanese Religions."

25. *NCKS* 533, 539–43; *CKT* 291–94.

26. *NCKS* 537. This statement needs to be qualified. My research on Enryakuji actually indicates the opposite. It is possible that Kuroda was referring to the conflicts that involved the relatively new Nichiren and Jōdo Shinshū sects. Conflicts between them and the old Buddhist schools were larger in scope in the fourteenth century than during the Heian and Kamakura periods.

27. *NCKS* 537–41; *CKT* 296–97.

28. *CKT* 291, 296–300.

29. Gay, "The Muromachi Bakufu in Medieval Kyoto," 195.

30. Nagahara Keiji, "Nihon kokka shi no ichi mondai," 48.

31. For a more comprehensive treatment of the development of Enryakuji's organization and leadership during the Heian and Kamakura periods, see chap. 2 in my Ph.D. dissertation.

32. Monks from Enryakuji and Onjōji (also known as Miidera). The two Tendai temples often fought over Onjōji's rights to complete independence during the Heian and Kamakura periods. With this in mind, the joint action becomes a good indicator of the seriousness of the incident.

33. *Chūyūki*, in *Zōho shiryō taisei*, vols. 9–14, entry for Tennin 1/3/21; *DaiNihon shiryō* (hereafter *DNS*), 3:10, 112.

34. *Chūyūki*, entry for Tennin 1/3/23; *DNS* 3:10, 114.

35. *Chūyūki*, entry for Tennin 1/3/30, 4/1, 4/2; *DNS* 3:10, 123–24.

36. Entry for Ennō 1/9/20, in *DNS* 5:12, 538–39, and *Kōtei zōho Tendai zasuki*, compiled by Shibuya Gaiji, 207; *Geki nikki*, in *Zoku shiseki shūran*, vol. 1, entries for Bun'ei 1/3/27, 5/24, 27; *Sanemi kyōki*, (unpublished) entries for Shōō 4/3/8, 16.

37. The four Grand Masters were Dengyō Daishi (Saichō), Kōbō Daishi (Kūkai), Jikaku Daishi (Ennin), and Chishō Daishi (Enchin).

38. *Tendai zasuki*, 312–17; Tsuji Zennosuke, *Nihon bukkyō shi: chūsei 1*, 60–73.

39. Collcutt, *Five Mountains*, 57–61.

40. I have found only a single conflict between Enryakuji and other *kenmitsu* temples during the whole of the period from the establishment of the Ashikaga Bakufu to the end of the fourteenth century: a brawl between Tōji and Enryakuji monks during a religious ceremony at the imperial palace on 1367/8/18. Though there were some fatalities, the fighting did not continue beyond the first day. *Moromoriki*, in *Shiryō sanshū*, 11 vols., entries for 1367/8/18, 19, 20: *DNS* 6:22, 247–72.

41. Collcutt, *Five Mountains*, 103–5.

42. *Sanzen'in monjo*, Kōei 3/12; *Sanmon uttaemōsu*, Kōei 4/6/29; *Kōei yonnen sanmon uttaemōsu*, Kōei 4/7/3, all printed in *DNS* 6:9, 121–24.

43. *Kōei yonnen sanmon uttaemōsu*, Kōei 4/7/20, in *DNS* 6:9, 130–32.

44. *Sanmon uttaemōsu*, Kōei 4/8, in *DNS* 6:9, 201–2.

45. *Moromoriki*, entry for Kōei 4/8/15; *DNS* 6:9, 204–5.

46. *Entairyaku*, entry for Kōei 4/8/8; *DNS* 6:9, 198–99.

47. *Moromoriki*, entry for Kōei 4/8/29. The retired emperor did, however, visit the temple on the next day. Ibid., 8/30; Tsuji, *Nihon bukkyō shi: chūsei 3*, 149.

48. *Moromoriki*, entry for Jōji 6/6/18; Tsuji, *Nihon bukkyō shi: chūsei 3*, 295.

49. *Moromoriki*, entry for Jōji 6/6/26, 7/2; *DNS* 6:27, 127–28.

50. *Gukanki*, in *Zoku shiryō taisei 1–4*, entry for Jōji 6 (1367)/8/8; Tsuji, *Nihon bukkyō shi: chūsei 3*, 295.

51. "The Enryakuji monks are merely the monkeys of the seven [Hie] shrines. They look like humans but they are not" (*Zoku shōbōron* in *DNS* 6:29, 477). Jōzan is undoubtedly making a pun here referring to the numerous monkeys that inhabited the area around the Hie shrines on the eastern slopes of Mount Hiei.

52. *Nanzenji taiji soshō*, Ōan 1/uru 6 in *DNS* 6:29, 483–86. Among other things, the Enryakuji monks claimed that the Shinto deities disliked Zen, that the state was protected by the eight (*kenmitsu*) sects, and that Enryakuji alone was the original temple of the sons of heaven.

53. *Sanmon gōsoki*, Ōan 1/7/10, in *DNS* 6:29, 489–92; Tsuji, *Nihon bukkyō shi: chūsei 3*, 306–7. It is not fully clear what these four incidents of disloyalty were, but Enryakuji's support of Go-Daigo against Ashikaga Takauji is clearly referred to. A second incident may have been one of 1351 when some Enryakuji monks attacked Momoi Naotsune, a retainer of Takauji and the *shugo* of Etchū Province, on his way to the capital (Hioki Shōichi, *Nihon sōhei no kenkyū*, 239). The Tenryūji incident was most likely another sin on the Bakufu's list.

54. *Nanzenji taiji soshō*, Ōan 1 (1368)/8/4, in *DNS* 6:30, 21. The Enryakuji monks were not alone in noting that the Bakufu's policies disrupted the accustomed balance among the sects. For example, Konoe Michitsugu, a high-ranking courtier, was much concerned that these policies broke with the customs of old (*Gukanki*, entry for Ōan 1/7/5; *DNS* 6:29, 494–95).

55. In 1350, for example, Enryakuji monks complained that taxes had not been forwarded from Sasaki-no-shō even though the Northern Court and the Bakufu both had decreed that they be sent. Enryakuji even had a pledge from the Sasaki family acknowledging the temple's right to the taxes. In the end the Bakufu not only denied Enryakuji's rights but even assessed the expenses of the Kamo festival on members of the Hie Shrine (Hioki, 200). Another example, also involving the Sasaki family, occurred in 1357–58 (Hioki, 202; *Sugaura monjo*, in *DNS* 6:21, 427–32, 522–24; *Gukanki*, entry for Enbun 3 (1358)/2/3; *DNS* 6:21, 737).

56. *Sanmon gōsoki*, entry for Ōan 1/8/28, in *DNS* 6:30, 38; Tsuji, *Nihon bukkyō shi: chūsei 3*, 330.

57. Tsuji, *Nihon bukkyō shi: chūsei 3*, 331.

58. *Gukanki*, entries for Ōan 2/7/19, 7/28; *Gogumaiki*, entry for Ōan 2/7/27; *DNS* 3:31, 29–31.

59. Portable shrines were carried to the capital on 1368/8/29 (*Moromoriki*, entry for Ōan 7/6/20, *Hie shin'yō gojūraku kenmon ryakki*, in *Shinkō gunsho ruijū, jingibu 1*, and *Kōdaiki*, entry for Ōan 1/8/29; *DNS* 6:30, 41–42) and then again on 1369/4/20 (*Gogumaiki* and *Gion shaki*, entries for Ōan 2/4/20; *DNS* 6:30, 415–19).

60. *Kaei sandaiki*, entry for Ōan 5 (1372)/7/11 in *DNS* 6:36, 23–24; *Gukanki, Gogumaiki*, entries for Ōan 6 (1373)/8/10 in *DNS* 6:38, 60–61; *Gukanki, Gogumaiki, Moromoriki, Kaei sandaiki*, entries for Ōan 7 (1374)/6/20 in *DNS* 6:41, 22–27; *Gukanki*, entries for Ōan 8 (1375)/7/27, Eiwa 5 (1379)/2/9, 6/8, 6/14; *Kaei sandaiki* (in *Shinkō gunsho ruijū*), entry for Eiwa 5/6/8; *Hie shin'yō gojūraku kenmon ryakki*, entry for Kōryaku 2 (1380)/6/30.

61. Gay, "The Muromachi Bakufu in Medieval Kyoto," 85; Wakita Haruo with Susan B. Hanley, "Dimensions of Development: Cities in Fifteenth and Sixteenth Century Japan," 319; Yamamura, "The Development of *Za* in Medieval Japan," 447–51.

62. Toyoda Takeshi and Sugiyama Hiroshi, "The Growth of Commerce and Trade," 137; Yamamura, "The Development of *Za*," 447–49; *Gion shitsugyō nikki*, entry for 1343/7, in *DNS* 6:7, 757–59.

63. Gay, "The Muromachi Bakufu in Medieval Kyoto," 117; Yamamura, "The Growth of Commerce in Medieval Japan," 389–91; *Kitano tenmangū shiryō: komonjo*, edited by Kitano tenmangū shiryō kankōkai, doc. 3 (Kōryaku 1 (1379)/9/20), p. 3, and doc. 4 (Kakei 1 (1387)/9/16), pp. 3–4.

64. Gay, "The Muromachi Bakufu in Medieval Kyoto," 117–18; *Kitano tenmangū shiryō: komonjo*, docs. 7 and 8 (Ōei 26 (1419)/9/12; 9/14), pp. 5–6.

65. Yamamura, "The Development of *Za*," 449–54; Gay, "The Muromachi Bakufu in Medieval Kyoto," 119.

66. Kenkyū 2 (1191)/3/29–6/20, *DNS* 3:4; Kenpō 1 (1213)/3/29, *DNS* 3:12; Katei 1 (1235)/6/26–Katei 2/8/28, *DNS* 5:10.

67. See *Chūsei hōsei shiryō shū 2*, Satō Shin'ichi and Ikeuchi Yoshisuke, eds., doc. 1, Kenmu 4 (1337)/10/7; doc. 6, Ryakuō 3 (1340)/4/15; doc. 55, Kannō 2 (1351)/6/13; doc. 56, Kannō 3 (1352)/7/24; doc. 57, Kannō 3/8/21; docs. 79–

83, Enbun 2 (1357)/9/10; docs. 84–85, Jōji 6 (1368)/6/27; docs. 96–97, Ōan 1 (1368)/6/17. For Enryakuji, there is a specific edict issued for the noble cloister of Nashimoto on Enbun 1 (1356)/9/13, in *DNS* 6:20, 795–96.

68. Satō Shin'ichi, "Kyōto sōdatsusen," 270–72.

69. *Ashikaga shogun daidai gechijō*, Kannō 2/1/8, in *DNS* 6:14, 386; *Entairyaku*, entry for Kannō 2/1/9, in ibid., 385.

70. *Kachō yōryaku*, Bunna 1 (1352)/3/18, 4/2, in *DNS* 6:16, 370, 412–13; *Kyoto teikoku daigaku shozō monjo*, Enbun 5 (1360)/3/18 in *DNS* 6:23, 82; *Gogumaiki*, entry for Jōji 2 (1363)/4/13 in *DNS* 6:25, 56–57.

71. Bunna 1 (1352)/4/2 in *DNS* 6:16, 412–13; *Gogumaiki*, entry for Jōji 2 (1363)/4/13 in *DNS* 6:25, 56–57.

72. Gay, "The Muromachi Bakufu in Medieval Kyoto," 92–93.

73. There is no exact information on the toll gates during the fourteenth century. However, seven toll stations (Honzeki, Dōmuseki, Kōdōseki, Yokawaseki, Chūdōseki, Taniseki, and Saitōseki) are mentioned in a document of 1448/9 (Shimosaka Mamoru, "Sanmon shisetsu seido no seiritsu to tenkai," 106, 110, 112; *Nanzenji monjo*, cited in Imatani Akira, *Sengoku ki no Muromachi bakufu*, 92–93).

74. Jōji 2/*uru* 1/24, in *Moromoriki*, vol. 6, 236, entry for *uru* 1/26.

75. Jōji 5 (1366)/8/11, in *DNS* 6:27, 360–61; Jōji 6 (1366)/8/21, in *DNS* 6:28, 305–6. See also, Shimosaka Mamoru, "Sanmon shisetsu seido," 106.

76. *Chūsei hōsei shiryō shū 2*, entries for Ōan 3 (1370)/12/16, doc. 105, and Shitoku 3 (1386)/8/25, doc. 145.

77. In 1268, Hōjō Tokimune issued an edict threatening to punish the monks, who were fighting among themselves, if they did not make peace. See Hisano Shūgi, "Sanmon-jimon no sōkoku," 91–95. Edicts proclaiming the restriction of arms were issued on 1188/2/22, 1189/2, 1212/3/22, and 1265/8/21.

78. All 34 head abbots appointed from 1336 to 1400 were aristocrats or imperial princes who were brought up in Kyoto (*Tendai zasuki*, 339–404).

79. Shimosaka, "Sanmon shisetsu seido," 82, 90–92, citing *Hie shin'yo gojūraku kenmon ryakki*. The term *daimyō* was usually reserved for warriors of magnate status.

80. *Entairyaku*, entry for Jōwa 1 (1345)/8/8; *DNS* 6:9, entry for Jōwa 1/8/14, 199.

81. *Gukanki*, entry for Ōan 2 (1369)/7/4; Shimosaki, "Sanmon shisetsu seido," 89.

82. According to Shimosaka, the envoys were in part a measure to weaken the power of the Rokkaku family and its vassals in Ōmi Province. See Tonomura, *Community and Commerce in Late Medieval Japan*, 31, citing an article by Shimosaka in *Yōkaichi-shi shi*, vol. 2.

83. Shimosaka, "Sanmon Shishetsu seido," 91–92. Imatani Akira believes that Yoshimitsu's involvement in the coup was limited (*Sengoku ki no Muromachi bakufu*, 67–68). However, as Shimosaka points out, the sources reveal that Yoshi-

mitsu was in close contact with the new magistrates in the fifth month of that year (Shimosaka, 91). There should be no real doubt as to his personal involvement in the new policies.

84. Shimosaka, 87.

85. Ibid., 94, 113.

86. I have found only two forceful protests (*gōso*)—in 1415 and 1428—and one appeal (1427) for the whole of the period 1378–1433. Clearly, this lack of disturbances indicates that the temple had been effectively contained for the first time. The Eikyō incident of 1433 marked the beginning of the end of the Bakufu's successful intervention. An uprising by temple constables was easily suppressed by Ashikaga Yoshinori, but it also resulted in a substantial loss of influence by the Bakufu within the temple. Our principal source for this incident is in *Mansai jugō nikki*. See also the article by Shimosaka.

Chapter 12

1. On Daitō, see Kraft, *Eloquent Zen: Daitō and Early Japanese Zen.*

2. Tamamura Takeji, *Musō kokushi.*

3. This biography is based on the *Chronology* of Musō's life provided by his leading disciple, Shun'oku Myōha, the "Tenryū kaizan Musō shōgaku shinsō fuzai kokushi nenpu," in *Zoku gunsho ruijū,* 9:496–523. This is more commonly known as *Musō kokushi nenpu.* I shall refer to it simply as *Nenpu.* I am also indebted to the detailed biography by Tamamura, *Musō kokushi.*

4. *Nenpu,* 496. The entry relating to Musō's birth also includes the hagiographic legend that his mother, hoping for a son, made devotions to Kannon. One evening in her dream a ray of light from the west entered her mouth and she conceived a son. Musō may have spread this story. He certainly maintained a lifelong devotion to Kannon.

5. Ibid.

6. Ibid., 497.

7. Ibid., 498.

8. On Muhon, the eclectic nature of his Zen, and the reclusive tendency in Japanese Rinzai Zen, see Yampolsky, "Hatto Kokushi's *Dharma Talks,*" 251–54.

9. *Nenpu,* 498.

10. Ibid.

11. Ibid., 499.

12. On the development of the *gozan* system, see Collcutt. *Five Mountains: The Rinzai Zen Monastic Institution in Medieval Japan.* In Japanese see Imaeda Aishin, *Chūsei zenshū shi no kenkyū,* and Tamamura Takeji, *Nihon zenshū shi ronshū.* The development of Sōtō Zen in medieval Japan is well covered in Boddiford, *Sōtō Zen in Medieval Japan.*

13. The roles of the various Chinese monks in Japanese Zen monasteries are

discussed by Tamamura Takeji in *Rinzai shū shi* and in the same author's *Gozan zensō denki shūsei.*

14. *Nenpu*, 499.

15. Ibid.

16. Ibid.

17. Ibid., 499–500.

18. Ibid., 500.

19. The literary activities of Musō and other fourteenth-century Zen monks are discussed by Pollack in *Zen Poems of the Five Mountains and The Fracture of Meaning: Japan's Synthesis of China from the Eighth Through the Eighteenth Centuries.*

20. *Nenpu*, 501.

21. Ibid.

22. Ibid., 502.

23. Ibid., 503.

24. Tamamura, *Musō kokushi*, 41–42.

25. *Nenpu*, 504.

26. Tamamura, *Musō kokushi*, 42.

27. *Nenpu*, 505.

28. Ibid.

29. Ibid., 506.

30. These moves are recorded in *Nenpu*, 506–7.

31. Ishii Susumu, "Musō Soseki to Nikaidō Dōun—Musō Zen hansei ni okeru gegosha no ichi kōsatsu," cited in Tamamura, *Musō kokushi*, 152.

32. On Daitō Kokushi and Hanazono, see Kraft, *Eloquent Zen: Daitō and Early Japanese Zen*, 126–28. For a discussion of the whole range of Hanazono's religious interests, which were by no means restricted to Zen, see Goble, "Truth, Contradiction, and Harmony in Medieval Japan: Emperor Hanazono (1297–1348) and Buddhism."

33. *Hanazono tennō shinki*, 3:144 (entry for Shōchū 2 (1325)/10/2).

34. Ibid.

35. *Nenpu*, 508.

36. *Musō kokushi goroku*, vol. 1, in *Taishō shinshū daizōkyō*, vol. 80, doc. 2555, p. 449. Also, Yanagida Seizan, ed., *Nihon no zen goroku 7, Musō*, 133.

37. *Nenpu*, 508.

38. Ibid.

39. *Musō kokushi goroku*, vol. 1.

40. *Nenpu*, 508.

41. Ibid., 509.

42. From *Muchū mondō*, dialogue 15. Cited in Kraft, trans., "Musō Kokushi's *Dialogues in a Dream*, 85.

43. These moves are traced in *Nenpu*, 509–10.

44. Ibid., 510.

45. Ibid.

46. Ibid.

47. *Musō kokushi goroku*, vol. 1.

48. Go-Daigo's generosity to Nanzenji can be gauged by the land rights he granted the monastery. See *Nanzenji monjo*, vol. 1, docs. 2–33, and *Nenpu*, 511.

49. In its day Rinsenji was an important monastery. It declined during the Edo period and its documents were lost, scattered, or mingled with those of Tenryūji. This section is based on Tamamura, *Musō kokushi*, 59–60.

50. The important role of subtemples, *tatchū*, in the life and administration of medieval Zen monasteries is discussed in Tamamura Takeji, "Gozan sōrin no tatchū ni tsuite."

51. *Jikusen ossho goroku*, Ryakuō 4 (1341)/3/20.

52. Ibid., 7/2.

53. On Ashikaga Tadayoshi, see Takayanagi, *Ashikaga Takauji*; Satō Shin'ichi, *Nanbokuchō no dōran*; and Kasamatsu, "Ashikaga Tadayoshi."

54. These are discussed and translated in Collcutt, *Five Mountains*.

55. *Nenpu*, 512.

56. Ibid., 512–13.

57. The building of Tenryūji is detailed in *Tenryūji zōei kiroku*, entry for Ryakuō 2 (1339)/10/5. In *Dai Nihon shiryō*, part 6, vol. 5: 752–53.

58. *Tenryūji zōei kiroku*, Ryakuō 2 (1339)/10/5, pp. 752–53.

59. Ibid.

60. Ibid., 10/13, p. 754.

61. On the building of Tenryūji and its role in fourteenth-century church-state relations, see Suga Kikuko, "Gokoku to seijō." On the importance of fund-raising campaigns in the history of medieval Buddhism, see Goodwin, *Alms and Vagabonds*.

62. *Tenryūji zōei kiroku*, Ryakuō 3 (1340)/4/21, *Dai Nihon shiryō*, pt. 6, vol. 6, p. 123.

63. Ibid.

64. Ibid., 4/27, p. 130.

65. Ibid., 6/15, p. 185.

66. Ibid., 7/16, p. 236.

67. Ibid., 8/17, p. 305.

68. Ibid., Ryakuō 4 (1341)/12/23, p. 1000.

69. *Nenpu*, 513.

70. *Tenryūji zōei kiroku*.

71. Ibid.

72. These events are described in detail in Tōin Kinkata's *Entairyaku*.

73. See Imaeda, *Chūsei zenshū shi no kenkyū*, 77–138.

74. Ibid.

75. Ibid.

76. From *Muchū mondō*, cited in Ryusaku Tsunoda et al., eds., *Sources of Japanese Tradition*, 1:255.

77. From *Musō kokushi goroku*, cited in ibid., 1:250.

Chapter 13

1. Interest in such historical writing spans the period from the late Heian through the Nanbokuchō. The "historical tale," for example, is typically represented by the "four mirrors" (*shikyō*) of history that begin to appear in the late Heian with the *Ōkagami* and continue into the Muromachi. "Military tales" begin

with accounts of the Hōgen and Heiji disturbances of the mid-twelfth century and reach their apotheosis in the famous *Heikei monogatari*, thought to have originated in the early Kamakura and to have undergone much textual development thereafter; they continue in works like the *Jōkyūki* and *Taiheiki*, from the fourteenth century. "Tale literature," of course, has a much longer history, but beginning with the late-Heian *Konjaku monogatari*, it received particular attention throughout this period. The first two general histories of Japan frame the Kamakura: the *Gukanshō*, by the Tendai prelate Jien, was composed in the early years (1219–20); the *Jinnō shōtōki*, by Kitabatake Chikafusa, dates from just after its fall (rev. 1343).

2. The centrality of *mappō* thought in late Heian and Kamakura culture is repeated in many studies of this period; a general treatment of the subject can be seen in Ozawa Tomio, *Mappō to masse no shisō*; for a representative statement of its role in historiography, see, e.g., Ichiro Ishida, "Structure and Formation of *Gukanshō* Thought," 420–50. The notion here of a shift from *hakanashi* to *mujō* is taken from Karaki Junzō, *Mujō*. A detailed account of the origins and development of the Buddhist theory of historical decline is given in Nattier, *Once upon a Future Time: Studies in a Buddhist Prophecy of Decline*.

3. Kuroda developed the notion in his *Nihon chūsei no kokka to shūkyō*; for a more recent account of the establishment's interest in history, see his "Kenmitsu bukkyō ni okeru rekishi ishiki."

4. *Kōfukuji sōjō*, in *Kamakura kyū bukkyō*, 312; the text has been translated in Morrell, *Early Kamakura Buddhism: A Minority Report*, 75–88.

5. The eight schools, of course, represent the six scholarly traditions said to have been current in the Nara period, plus the Tendai and Shingon. For some discussion of the genre of doctrinal classification in the Kamakura, see my "Filling the Zen Shū: Notes on the *Jisshū yōdō ki*."

6. The *Jinnō shōtōki* account appears in the entry for Emperor Kenmu; see *Jinnō shōtōki* (1965 ed.), 112–15; Varley, *A Chronicle of Gods and Sovereigns: Jinnō Shōtōki of Kitabatake Chikafusa*, 152–59. The *Hasshū kōyō* can be found in *Dai Nihon bukkyō zensho 3*, 7–40; an English translation by the late Leo Pruden has recently appeared. The importance of the book for modern Japanese Buddhism is discussed in Ketelaar, *Of Heretics and Martyrs in Meiji Japan: Buddhism and Its Persecution*, 174–212.

7. The text can be found in *Nihon kōsōden yōmon shō Genkō shakusho, Kokushi taikei 31*; this edition has a convenient personal name index.

8. In the Western literature, I have come across (admittedly without having made a serious search) almost nothing on this text in the quarter-century since Marian Ury's Berkeley dissertation: "*Genkō Shakusho*, Japan's First Comprehensive History of Buddhism: A Partial Translation with Introduction and Notes" (1970).

9. Much of what is known of Shiren's biography comes from the *Kaizō oshō kinenroku*, by his disciple Ryūsen Reisai (*Zoku gunsho ruijū 9*, 458–95); and *Kokan oshō gyōjō*, by Mugan Soō (in his *Kanrin shū*) (*Zoku gunsho ruijū 12*, 265–67).

For a modern study of Shiren's life and works, see Fukushima Shun'ō, *Kokan*, in *Fukushima Shun'ō chosakushū 2*, 69–311; a convenient and detailed chronology of Shiren's life appears at 290–307.

10. The *Byōgi ron*, together with selections from the *Saihoku shū* and *Genkō shakusho*, has received a modern Japanese translation in Miki Sumito and Yamada Shūzen, eds., *Mujū Kokan, Daijō butten*. The *Hakkai ganzō* (*Dai Nihon bukkyō zensho 3*, 83–86) was only discovered at the beginning of this century; it follows the precedent of Enni's *Jisshō yōdō ki* in expanding Gyōnen's list of schools to include Zen and Pure Land.

11. Tendai resentment of government support for Zen would flare up again in the 1360s, in the ugly Nanzenji Gate incident. The evidence for several of these squabbles is brought together in Tsuji Zennosuke, *Nihon bukkyō shi: chūsei hen*, 2: 373–94.

12. *Zengaku taikei*, 8: 1–7. The *Shūmon jisshō ron* seems to have circulated widely and provoked responses from Tendai, Shingon, and Jōdo authors. The peculiarity of some of Shiren's arguments here is noted by the Edo-period Zen scholar Shōboku Myōtai (or Gitai), whose discussion of the text in his *Zenseki shi* rejects points 2, 4–6, and 8 (*Dai Nihon bukkyō zensho 1*, 318).

13. For such references to Zen in the early Tendai authors, see my "Filling the Zen Shū."

14. See, e.g., Eisai's *Kōzen gokoku ron*, in *Chūsei zenke no shisō*, ed. Ichikawa Hakugen and Yanagida Seizan, *Nihon shisō taikei 16*, 104, 110; and Dōgen's *Bendō wa*, in *Shōbō genzō Shōbō genzō zuimonki*, *Nihon koten bungaku taikei 81*, 84–85.

15. See Michiie's "Letter of Disposition" (*shobunjō*) for the monastery, in *Tōfukuji shi*, 72. As Mikael Adolphson has pointed out to me, the Tendai documents from the Tenryūji affair cite the case of Kagenji as an instance of the court recognizing Tendai authority: in this affair, from 1305, Emperor Go-Uda apparently abandoned under pressure his project to build a monastery of this name in Higashiyama for the Zen master Nanpu Jōmyō. The same document also cites the example of Kenninji as precedent for the claim that Zen monasteries were properly branch temples (*matsuji*) of Enryakuji. (The relevant passage appears in the *Nochi kagami* [*Kokushi taikei 31*, 286] and is discussed in Ogisu Jundō, *Nihon chūsei zenshū shi*, 218.)

16. Though they are, of course, very different works, the *Genkō shakusho's* multifaceted approach to historiography is somewhat reminiscent of an oft-noted feature of the *Ōkagami*. Marian Ury's dissertation (see above, n. 8) translates a selection from the "Biography" section; another selection appears in Japanese translation in Imahama Michitaka, *Genkō shakusho*, Kyōikusha shinsho (Genpon gendaiyaku) 62. The last section (*josetsu*) of the "Records," on the rationale of the book itself, has been rendered into Japanese in Miki and Yamada, eds., *Mujū Kokan*, 267–83.

17. *Kokushi taikei 31*, 378.

18. The attribution of the *Genkō shakusho* to Gyōnen and the evidence against it are discussed in Ōkubo Dōshū, *Nihon bunkashi sōkō*, 144–70.

19. In his *Naiten jinro shō*, Gyōnen notes that the Pure Land faith tended to be nondenominational, without a distinct lineage of its own (*Dai Nihon bukkyō zensho 3*, 64); a few months later, he produced such a lineage in a general history of the faith, the *Jōdo hōmon genru shō*. In the biography of his teacher, the *Enshō shōnin gyōjō*, Gyōnen goes out of his way to note Enshō's dismissal of Zen theology, which he consigns to the status of a "third son" in the Buddhist family (*Zoku zoku gunsho ruijū 3*: 483).

20. *Kokushi taikei 31*, 42–46.

21. Ibid., 399–402.

22. Ibid., 407–11.

23. Ibid., 99–131. For the definition of Zen as the tradition of *zazen*, see Shiren's *Hakkai ganzō* (*Dai Nihon bukkyō zensho 3*, 85). Shiren's decision to identify the Zen masters as specialists in contemplation puts him at odds with those apologists, like Dōgen, who denied that Zen is merely a form of meditation and complained that Tao-hsüan's *Hsü kao-seng chuan* had mistakenly put Bodhidharma's biography in its section on monks who specialized in the "practice of *dhyāna*" (*shūzen*). (See my *Dōgen's Manuals of Zen Meditation*, 134–35.)

24. Funaoka, *Nihon zenshūshi no seiritsu*, 3; Yanagida, "Yōsai to Kōzen gokoku ron no kadai," 443.

25. *Kokushi taikei 31*, 29, 33. In a later section, Shiren also reports on the well-known tradition that the Nara missionary Tao-hsüan (Dōsen, 702–60) taught Zen at Daianji (*Kokushi taikei 31*, 231).

26. Proponents of Sōtō Zen also complain about the absence of their early patriarchs, among whom only Dōgen receives notice.

27. For the legend of Śubhakarasiṃha, see *Kokushi taikei 31*, 30. Ishikawa Rikizan has called attention to Shiren's mixture of Zen sectarianism and *mikkyō* in his "*Genkō shakusho* to Kokan Shiren," 176–77.

28. Chih-p'an's work is a particularly relevant example here, in that, like the *Genkō shakusho*, it combines a general history (employing the biography, annals, and records genres) with a sectarian focus on the author's favorite (Tendai) tradition. For a useful, if somewhat dated, survey of the Sung Buddhist historical literature, see Jan, "Buddhist Historiography in Sung China."

29. *Kokushi taikei 31*, 448. Shiren offers here a novel argument for the term *shakusho* in his title: Śākya refers both to the descendants of the Buddha and the Buddha himself; since the Buddha's body is not different from his spiritual kingdom (*shin do funi*), a history of Śākya is analogous to the histories of the Chinese dynastic kingdoms. Apparently both Shiren and his readers at court chose to overlook the possibility that such an argument could be made to entail a "buddhocracy."

30. See, e.g., the lengthy *ron* passage (*Kokushi taikei 31*, 251–53), portions of which are translated in Andrew Goble's essay in the present volume.

31. Pollack, *The Fracture of Meaning: Japan's Synthesis of China from the Eighth Through the Eighteenth Centuries*, 110–32.

32. *Kokushi taikei 31*, 448–49.

33. The legend was well known in Shiren's day; see, e.g., Mujū's version in his *Shaseki shū* (*Nihon koten bungaku taikei 85*, 253–54). Shiren's entry on Bodhidharma appears at *Kokushi taikei 31*, 27.

34. The first celebration of the ritual, the *rōsaku daruma ki*, which became an annual event at Shiren's Sanshōji, took place in 1330. Shiren notes Bodhidharma's advent in his *Hakkai ganzō* (*Dai Nihon bukkyō zensho 3*, 85).

Chapter 14

1. I am indebted to my friend John S. Brownlee (University of Toronto), the scholar who has written most extensively on Japanese pre-Restoration historiography, for a general background to this subject. See his *Political Thought in Japanese Historical Writing: From Kojiki (712) to Tokushi Yoron (1712)*. I have also benefited from reading the draft manuscript of Professor Brownlee's forthcoming companion volume, *Japanese Historians and the National Myths, 1600–1945*. I am also grateful to my brother David McMullen (University of Cambridge), Jeffrey Mass (Stanford University), as editor of this volume, and to the members of the Hertford College Conference for commenting on earlier drafts of this essay.

2. Webb, "What Is the *Dai Nihon shi*?"; Nakai, "Tokugawa Confucian Historiography: The Hayashi, Early Mito School, and Arai Hakuseki"; see also, Nakai, *Shogunal Politics: Arai Hakuseki and the Premises of Tokugawa Rule*, esp. chap. 11 (pp. 265–97), "Redefinition of the Parameters of *buke* Rule"; Brownlee, *Political Thought*, esp. chap. 10 (pp. 116–28), "Secular, Pragmatic History in Tokushi Yoron (1712)."

3. A paradigmatic case is provided by the historiography of the thirteenth-century Yüan invasions of Japan. See Kawazoe Shōji, "Edo jidai ni okeru Genkō kenkyū." A particularly striking instance of the duality is afforded by *Mōko shogunki bengi* (Doubts Dispelled on the Military Records Concerning the Mongols, 1839) of Tachibana Moribe (1781–1849), a nativist scholar who claimed descent from the fourteenth-century Southern Court loyalist general and historian Kitabatake Chikafusa himself. Moribe, who was inspired by fear of a foreign invasion in his own time, argued, for instance, that sections of the *Takesaki Suenaga ekotoba* (Takizaki Suenaga Illustrated Scroll), while a useful source, had been assembled in the wrong order. Alongside this critical rigor, however, went a shrill antiwarrior stance. Moribe professed a belief that the invasion and the weakness of Japanese defense were part of a Hōjō plot, with Buddhist monks as intermediaries, to sell Japan to the Yuan (Kawazoe, 27–29, 33). I am grateful to Thomas Nelson, University of Stirling, for drawing my attention to this article.

4. For this controversy, see Uyenaka, "The Textbook Controversy of 1911: National Needs and Historical Truth."

5. Satō Shin'ichi, *Nanbokuchō no dōran, Nihon no rekishi 9*, 2–4.

6. Morisue Yoshiaki et al., eds., *Kokusho sōmokuroku*, 5: 474–75; 7: 193–94.

7. Hori Isao, *Yamaga Sokō*, 258.

8. In approaching this topic, the following studies have been useful: Nakai, "Tokugawa Confucian Historiography," and Bitō Masahide, "Seimei ron to mei-bun ron."

9. For a general description, see Pulleyblank, "Chinese Historical Criticism: Liu Chih-chi and Ssu-ma Kuang," 151–66.

10. Known in full as the *Tzu chih t'ung chien kang-mu*. For a brief consideration of this work, see Schirokauer, "Chu Hsi's Sense of History," 200. Chu's principles for compiling the work are detailed in the "Fan li" (General Rules) in *Tzu chih t'ung chien kang-mu, chüan 1*, Ming edition, 59 vols., Chiang Hsi: An-ch'a ssu, (1534), 1: 3a–26b. For a partial English translation, see de Bary et al., eds., *Sources of Chinese Tradition*, 507–9. Of Chu Hsi's redaction, Ogyū Sorai (1666–1728), a critic of Chu Hsi Confucianism, wrote: "The *kang* [outlines] are headings (*mokuroku*). The *mu* [details] are the basic text of the *T'ung chien kang-mu*]. Therefore, they exhibit no difference from [Ssu-ma Kuang's original] *T'ung chien kang-mu*. However, the method of writing the *kang* is at variance with [the content of] the *mu*, and because they establish praise and blame through use of particular characters, when you are reading them you will promptly tend to be [over-]rationalistic, and your style of learning will become [over-]rationalistic in the Chu Hsi manner." See *Sorai sensei tōmonsho*, in *Nihon koten bungaku taikei* (hereafter NKBT), 94: 187.

11. Cf. *Mencius VA*, 5, 8; Legge, trans., *The Chinese Classics* (hereafter, *CC*), 2: 357: "'Heaven sees according as my people see; Heaven hears according as my people hear.'"

12. Nakai, "Tokugawa Confucian Historiography," 67.

13. Bol, "Government, Society, and State: On the political visions of Ssu-ma Kuang and Wang An-shih."

14. Ibid., 189.

15. Ibid., 189, 180. The slow dissolution of the Six Dynasties, Sui, and T'ang aristocratic order is the main theme of Ebrey, *The Aristocratic Families of Early Imperial China: A Case Study of the Po-ling Ts'ui Family*.

16. Bol, "Government, Society, and State," 152–53.

17. See Sariti, "Monarchy, Bureaucracy, and Absolutism in the Political Thought of Ssu-ma Kuang."

18. Bitō, "Seimei ron," 13.

19. *Chüan 1*, entry for Wei Lieh Wang 23 (403 B.C.); Ssu-ma Kuang, *Tzu chih t'ung chien*, 1: 2.

20. *Tzu chih t'ung chien*, 6; cf. Nakai, "Tokugawa Confucian Historiography," 64–65.

21. *Tzu chih t'ung chien*, 3.

22. *Mencius IB*, 8; *CC* 2: 167. Ssu-ma Kuang was the author of an essay entitled *Yi Meng* (Casting Doubt Upon the *Mencius*); Bitō, "Seimei ron," 14–15.

23. *Chu Wen-kung wen-chi, chüan* 47, quoted in Schirokauer, "Chu Hsi's Sense of History," 198. Ssu-ma Ch'ien (147–c. 90 B.C.) and Pan Ku (d. A.D. 92) were the authors, respectively, of the *Shih chi* and *Han shu*.

24. Bitō, "Seimei ron," 15.

25. Ssu-ma's discussion of the criteria for legitimacy is to be found in *Tzu chih t'ung chien, chüan 69*, entry for Huang ch'u 2 (A.D. 221), 3:2183–88; English translation in de Bary et al., eds., *Sources of Chinese Tradition*, 504–7. This discussion suggests that what Nakai (p. 68) refers to as his "'realistic' outlook" was a historian's strategy for dealing with the retrospective historiographical problem of periodization as much as advocacy of direct and autocratic imperial control of government.

26. Bitō, "Seimei ron," 7.

27. A summary of the respective claims to legitimacy of the "three states" and the grounds for preferring the Shu Han are given by Asami Keisai in his *Seiken igen kōgi*, in Arima Sukemasa and Kurokawa Mamichi, eds., *Kokumin dōtoku sōsho* 3, 125–29.

28. In Hanawa Hokiichi, comp., *Gunsho ruijū*, 6:1167; cf. Wajima Yoshio, *Nihon Sōgaku shi no kenkyū*, 134–37, 171–72.

29. For the influence of *Tzu chih t'ung chien* on the *Jinnō shōtōki*, see Miyai Yoshio, "*Jinnō shōtōki to Shiji tsugan*," 468–72.

30. Varley, trans., *A Chronicle of Gods and Sovereigns: Jinnō shōtōki of Kitabatake Chikafusa*, intro., 5.

31. For a general discussion of this work, see Brownlee, *Political Thought in Japanese Historical Writing*, chap. 9, "Historical Explanation in *Jinnō shōtōki*," 103–15; also, Varley, trans., 1–41.

32. Varley, trans., 131, 167, 175, 189.

33. Ibid., 231, 225.

34. Ibid., 260.

35. Duke Ch'eng: 2d year; *CC* 5:344; Ssu-ma Kuang, *Tzu-chih t'ung-chien*, Wei-lieh Wang 23, *chüan 1*, vol. 1, p. 4; Varley, trans., *A Chronicle of Gods and Sovereigns*, 251–52.

36. H. C. McCullough, trans., *The Taiheiki: A Chronicle of Medieval Japan*, 9.

37. Varley, trans., intro., 20–22.

38. Asami Keisai, *Seiken igen kōgi*, 155–56.

39. Inaba Mokusai, *Koshō zenkō*, quoted in Maruyama Masao, "Ansai gaku to Ansai gakuha," in *Nihon shisō taikei* (hereafter *NST*), 31: 618.

40. Asami Keisai, *Satsu roku, NST* 31: 397.

41. Ibid., 398.

42. Asami, *Seiken igen kōgi*, 153–54.

43. Ibid., 125, 190–91.

44. Inaba Mokusai, *Bokusui itteki* (preface 1766), in Seki Giichirō, ed., *Nihon jurin sōsho*, 3: 8.

45. Asami, *Satsuroku*, 385.

46. Ibid., 351.

47. Ibid., 385.

48. Ibid., 351; quoted by Keisai from the preface (or, according to a variant reading, postface) by Chu to *T'ung chien chi-shih pen-mo* by the Sung scholar Yuan Chi-chung (Yuan Shu). The modern edition of this work, 12 vols. (Peking: Chung-hua Shu-chū, 1964), does not reproduce Chu's postface, nor have I found it among the prefaces or postfaces in Chu's collected writings, *Chu Wen-kung wen chi, Ssu-pu ts'ung k'an* edition.

49. Asami, *Satsuroku*, 352.

50. Ibid., 351.

51. Ibid.

52. Ibid., 352.

53. Ibid., 351.

54. Bitō, "Seimei ron," 5–6.

55. Varley, trans., *A Chronicle of Gods and Sovereigns*, 264.

56. Asami, *Satsuroku*, 352.

57. Ibid., 354. See *T'ung chien kang-mu*, *chüan 36*; Yang ti's murder of his father Wen ti is recorded by Chu with the verb *shih* [to murder a superior] Jēn-shou 4 [604], 7th month, *chüan 36*, p. 67b.

58. Asami, *Satsuroku*, 353.

59. Keisai's outraged account of Ts'ao Tsao's treatment of Hsien ti is in *Seiken igen kōgi*, 126–27.

60. Asami, *Satsuroku*, 408–9.

61. Ibid., 410–11.

62. Ibid., 411.

63. See Asami Keisai, *Chūkō ruisetsu*, woodblock edition (Nagoya: Eirakuya Tōshirō et al., 1870), p. 14a; for the incident in *Taiheiki*, see *Taiheiki*, *Kan 31*, *NKBT* 36: 174–79. For *Chūkō ruisetsu*, see McMullen, "Rulers or Fathers?: A Casuistical Problem in Early Modern Japanese Thought," 85–88.

64. Asami, *Satsuroku*, 408.

65. Ibid., 354.

66. Ibid., 409.

67. Bitō, "Seimei ron," 7.

68. See McMullen, "Rulers or Fathers?" 95–96.

69. Varley, *Imperial Restoration in Medieval Japan*, 149.

70. Asami, *Seiken igen kōgi*, 123–24.

71. Yamaga Sokō, *Haisho zanpitsu*, in *NST* 32:334–35; English translation in Uenaka, "Last Testament in Exile: Yamaga Soko's *Haisho zampitsu*," 149–50.

72. The text of these chapters, entitled "Kōtō yōryaku" (Essentials of Imperial Government) and "Butō yōryaku" (Essentials of Warrior Government), is in Hirose Yutaka, ed., *Yamaga Sokō zenshū*, 13:383–504.

73. Ibid., 389–90.

74. Ibid., 391.

75. Ibid., 399–400.

76. Ibid., 394–95.

77. Ibid., 431.

78. Ibid., 433.

79. Ibid., 437.

80. Ibid., 433.

81. Ibid., 439.

82. Ibid., 445.

83. Ibid., 448.

84. Ibid., 462.

85. Further research is required to establish Sokō's debt, if any, to historical texts sympathetic to the Ashikaga, such as the *Baishō ron* (c. 1349).

86. Matsumoto Sannosuke, "Kinsei ni okeru rekishi jojutsu to sono shisō," in *NST* 48:578–615.

87. For *meibun* in the Mito school, see, e.g., Bitō, "Seimei ron," esp. 9–10, 19–20.

88. Ogyū Sorai, *Sorai sensei tōmonsho*, in *NKBT* 94:187.

89. Sorai's views on the importance of historical understanding are usefully described in Maruyama Masao, *Studies in the Intellectual History of Tokugawa Japan*, 99–101.

90. Nakai, *Shogunal Politics*, 275–77.

Chapter 15

This paper was translated by Jeffrey P. Mass and Haruko Wakabayashi.

Bibliography

Primary Sources in Japanese and Chinese

(Unless otherwise noted, the city of publication is Tokyo.)

Azuma kagami. Edited by Kuroita Katsumi. In *Shintei zōho kokushi taikei.* 4 vols. Yoshikawa kōbunkan, 1975–77.

Baishōron. Edited by Yashiro Kazuo and Hiroshi Kami. In *Shinsen Nihon koten bunko.* Gendai shichōsha, 1975.

Bendō wa (Dōgen). Edited by Nishio Minoru et al. In *Shōbō genzō zuimonki, Nihon koten bungaku taikei 81,* 69–97. Iwanami shoten, 1965.

Bokusui itteki (Inaba Mokusai). Edited by Seki Giichirō. In *Nihon jurin sōsho 3.* Tōyō tosho kankōkai, 1928.

Chikanaga-kyōki (Kanroji Chikanaga). Edited by Sasagawa Taneo. In *Shiryō taisei 40.* Naigai shoseki, 1941.

Chūkō ruisetsu (Asami Keisai). Woodblock ed. Nagoya: Eirakuya Tōshirō et al., 1870.

Chūsei hōsei shiryōshū, 1–2. Edited by Satō Shin'ichi and Ikeuchi Yoshisuke. Iwanami shoten, 1955–57.

Chūsei seiji shakai shisō, ge. Edited by Kasamatsu Hiroshi, Satō Shin'ichi, and Momose Kesao. *Nihon shisō taikei 22.* Iwanami shoten, 1981.

Chūyūki (Fujiwara no Munetada). In *Zōho shiryō taisei 9–14.* Kyoto: Rinsen shoten, 1965.

Dai Nihon komonjo, iewake 1: Kōyasan monjo. Compiled by Tōkyō teikoku daigaku shiryō hensanjo. 8 vols. 1904–7.

———, *iewake 11: Kobayakawa ke monjo.* 2 vols., 1927.

———, *iewake 14: Kumagai-ke monjo—Miura ke monjo—Hiraga ke monjo.* 1937.

———, *iewake 16: Shimazu-ke monjo.* 3 vols. to date. 1942–.

Dai Nihon shiryō. Compiled by Tōkyō teikoku daigaku shiryō hensanjo. Tōkyō teikoku daigaku shuppan, 1901–.

Daigoji to Ninnaji, Daikakuji. In *Nihon koji bijutsu zenshū 14.* Shūeisha, 1982.

Enshō shōnin gyōjō (Gyōnen). *Zoku zoku gunsho ruijū 3.* Keizai zasshisha, 1904.

Entairyaku (Tōin Kinkata). Edited by Iwahashi Koyata and Saiki Kazuma. 7 vols. Zoku gunsho ruijū kanseikai, 1970–86.

Fuga wakashū. Edited by Tsugita Kasumi and Iwasa Miyoko. Miyai shoten, 1985.

Fukushima kenshi 7, shiryō hen, kodai-chūsei. Compiled by Fukushima ken. Fukushima, 1966.

Geki nikki. Compiled by Kondō Heijō. *Zoku shiseki shūran 1.* Kondō shuppansha, 1918.

Genkō shakusho (Kokan Shiren). Edited by Kuroita Katsumi. In *Shintei zōho kokushi taikei 31.* Yoshikawa kōbunkan, 1932.

Genpei seisuki. Kokumin bunko kankōkai, 1911.

Genshoku han, Kokuhō 11, Nanbokuchō, Muromachi. Edited by Sawada Iwao. Asahi shinbunsha, 1980.

Go-Daigo tennō shinkan haiten mokuroku. Kyoto: Kyōto hakubutsukan, 1938.

Gogumaiki (Sanjō Kimitada). Edited by Tōkyō daigaku shiryō hensanjo. *Dai Nihon kokiroku 19.* Iwanami shoten, 1952–.

Gukanki (Konoe Michitsugu). Edited by Tsuboi Kumezō, Kusaka Hiroshi, and Takeuchi Rizō. *Zōho shiryō taisei 1–4.* Kyoto: Rinsen shoten, 1965.

Gukanshō (Jien). Edited by Ōkami Masao and Akamatsu Toshihide. *Nihon koten bungaku taikei 86.* Iwanami shoten, 1967.

Gunsho ruijū. Compiled by Hanawa Hokiichi. 19 vols. Keizai zasshi-shū, 1893–1902.

Gyokusui. Edited by Imagawa Fumio. Kyoto: Shibunkaku, 1984.

Gyokuyō (Kujō Kanezane). Edited by Kurokawa Masamichi and Yamada Yasue. Kokusho kankōkai, 1970.

Hakkai ganzō (Kokan Shiren). In *Dai Nihon bukkyō zensho 3.* Yūseitō shuppanbu, 1932.

Hanazono Tennō shinki (Hanazono Tennō). In *Shiryō taisei.* 2 vols. Naigaisho, 1938.

Hanazono Tennō shinki (Hanazono Tennō). In *Shiryō sanshū.* 3 vols. Zoku gunsho ruijū kanseikai, 1982–86.

Hasshū kōyō (Gyōnen). In *Dai Nihon bukkyō zensho 3.* Yūseitō shuppanbu, 1932.

Heiji monogatari. In *Nihon koten bungaku taikei.* Iwanami shoten, 1964.

Heike monogatari. In *Nihon koten bungaku taikei.* Iwanami shoten, 1964.

Hennen Ōtomo shiryō. Compiled by Takita Manabu. 2 vols. Fuzanbō, 1942–46.

Hie shin'yō gojūraku kenmon ryakki. In *Shinkō gunsho ruijū, jingibu 1.* Naigaisho, 1938.

Hizen Matsura tō Ariurake monjo. Edited by Fukuda Ikuo and Murai Shōsuke. Osaka: Seibundō shiryō sōsho, 1982.

Hōryūji to Ikaruga no koji. In *Nihon koji bijutsu zenshū 2.* Shūeisha, 1979.

Imabori Hiyoshi jinja monjo shūsei. Compiled by Nakamura Ken. Yūzankaku, 1981.

Iwate ken chūsei monjo 1. Edited by Iwate ken kyōiku iinkai. Morioka, 1960.

"Iyo no kuni Yugenoshima no shō kankei shiryō." In *Nihon engyō taikei, shiryō hen, kodai-chūsei 1.* Edited by Nihon engyō taikei henshū iinkai. Nihon engyō kenkyūkai, 1975.

Jikusen ossho goroku (Jikusen). Edited by Taishō shinshū daizōkyō kankōkai. *Taishō shinshū daizōkyō.* Dōkan kōkai, 1969.

Jinnō shōtōki (Kitabatake Chikafusa). Yūhōdō bunkō, 1915.

Jinnō shōtōki (Kitabatake Chikafusa). Edited by Iwasa Masashi et al. *Nihon koten bungaku taikei 87*. Iwanami shoten, 1965.

Jūyō bunkazai. Edited by Mainichi shinbun sha. Mainichi shinbun sha, 1974.

Kagawa kenshi, kodai-chūsei shiryō. Kagawa: Shikoku shinbunsha, 1986.

Kagoshima ken shiryō, kyūki zatsuroku jūi, iewake 1–2. Kagoshima: Shunendō bunkan, 1987.

Kaizō oshō kinenroku (Ryūsen Reisai). In *Zoku gunsho ruijū 9*. Zoku gunsho ruijū kanseikai, 1974.

Kamakura ibun. Compiled by Takeuchi Rizō. 49 vols. to date. Tōkyōdō shuppan, 1971–.

Kanagawa kenshi, shiryō hen, kodai-chūsei, 1, 3. Yokohama, 1975.

Kanazawa bunko no meihō. Edited by Kanagawa kenritsu Kanazawa bunko. Yokohama, 1994.

Kannō ninen hinami ki. In *Zoku gunsho ruijū*. Zoku gunsho ruijū kanseikai, 1975.

Kenmu shikimoku. Edited by Satō Shin'ichi and Ikeuchi Yoshisuke. In *Chūsei hōsei shiryōshū 2*. Iwanami shoten, 1957.

Kinsei buke shisō, buke shohatto. Edited by Ienaga Saburō. In *Nihon shisō taikei 27*. Iwanami shoten, 1974.

Kitano tenmangū shiryō: komonjo. Edited by Kitano tenmangū shiryō kankōkai. Kyoto: Kitano Tenmangū, 1978.

Kōdaiki. In *Gunsho ruijū*. Naigaisho, 1928–37.

Kōfukuji sōjō (Jōkei). Edited by Kamata Shigeo and Tanaka Hisao. In *Kamakura kyū bukkyō, Nihon shisō taikei 15*. Iwanami shoten, 1971.

Kojiki Norito. Edited by Kurano Kenji and Takeda Yūkichi. In *Nihon koten bungaku taikei 1*. Iwanami shoten, 1993.

Kokan (Fukushima Shun'ō). In *Fukushima Shun'ō chosakushū 2*, 69–311. Mokujisha, 1974.

Kokan oshō gyōjō (Mugan Soō). In *Zoku gunsho ruijū 12*. Zoku gunsho ruijū kanseikai, 1975.

Kokumin dōtoku sōsho. Edited by Arima Sukemasa and Kurokawa Mamichi. 3 vols. Hakubunkan, 1911–12.

Kōzen gokoku ron (Eisai). Edited by Ichikawa Hakugen and Yanagida Seizan. In *Chūsei zenke no shisō, Nihon shisō taikei 16*, 7–122. Iwanami shoten, 1972.

Kutsuki monjo. Edited by Okuno Takahiro. 2 vols. Zoku gunsho ruijū kanseikai, 1978.

Mansai jugō nikki. In *Zoku gunsho ruijū, bui, no. 1*. Zoku gunsho ruijū kanseikai, 1974–75.

Mōko shōgunki bengi (Tachibana Moribe). 1839.

Moromoriki (Nakahara Moromori). In *Shiryō sanshū*. Zoku gunsho ruijū kanseikai, 1968.

Muchū mondo shū (Musō Soseki). Edited by Naramoto Tatsuya. In *Kōsō meichō zenshū 16*. Tenryūji Jisha, 1931.

Mujō (Karaki Junzō). In *Chikuma sōsho 39*. Chikuma shobō, 1965.

Musō kokushi goroku. Edited by Shunoku Myōha. In *Taishō shinshū daizōkyō*. Taishō shinshū daizōkyō, 1960–78.

Myōshinji. In *Nihon koji bijutsu zenshū 24*. Shūeisha, 1982.

Naiten jinro shō (Gyōnen). In *Dai Nihon bukkyō zensho 3*. Yūseitō shuppanbu, 1932.

Nanbokuchō ibun, Chūgoku, Shikoku hen. Edited by Matsuoka Hisatō. 5 vols. to date. Tōkyōdō shuppan, 1987–.

Nanbokuchō ibun, Kyūshū hen. Edited by Seno Seiichirō. 7 vols. Tōkyōdō shuppan, 1985–92.

Nanzenji monjo. Edited by Sakurai Kageo and Fujii Manabu. 3 vols. Kyoto: Nanzenji, 1972–78.

Nara rokudaiji taikan, Hōryūji 4. Edited by Iwanami shoten. Iwanami shoten, 1971.

Nezu bijutsukan meihin shūsei. Edited by Nezu bijutsukan. Kōdansha, 1986.

Nihon emaki taisei, bekkan. Edited by Komatsu Shigemi. Kyoto: Chūō kōronsha, 1979.

Nihon jurin sōsho. Edited by Seki Giichirō. Tōyō tosho kankōkai, 1927–29.

Nihon no shōzō. Edited by Kyōto kokuritsu hakubutsukan. Kyoto: Chūō kōronsha, 1978.

Nihon shisō taikei. Edited by Ienaga Saburō. 67 vols. Iwanami shoten, 1970–82.

Nobutane kyōki (Nakamikado Nobutane). Edited by Sasagawa Taneo. In *Shiryō taisei 41*. Naigaisho, 1943.

Nochi kagami (Narushima Chikuzan). Edited by Kuroita Katsumi. In *Shintei zōho kokushi taikei 34*. Yoshikawa kōbunkan, 1980.

Ōshima jinja-Okutsujima jinja monjo. Compiled by Shiga daigaku keizaigakubu shiryōkan. In *Kenkyū kiyō 1–9*. Nagahama, 1968–75.

Oyudono no ue no nikki. Edited by Hanawa Hokiichi and Ōta Toshirō. In *Zoku gunsho ruijū, bui*. Zoku gunsho ruijū kanseikai, 1980.

Sanemi kyōki. Unpublished.

Sata Mirensho. In *Zoku gunsho ruijū 25*. Zoku gunsho ruijū kanseikai, 1975.

Seiken igen kōgi (Asami Keisai). Edited by Arima Sukemasa and Kurokawa Mamichi. In *Kokumin dōtoku sōsho 3*. Hakubunkan, 1912.

Shaseki shū (Mujū Ichien). Edited by Watanabe Tsunaya. In *Shaseki shū, Nihon koten bungaku taikei 85*. Iwanami shoten, 1966.

Shinshū Nihon emakimono zenshū 26. Edited by Miya Tsuguo. Kadokawa shoten, 1978.

Shiryō Nihonshi. Compiled by Ienaga Saburō and Inagaki Yasuhiko. Sanseidō, 1968.

Shitennōji to Kawachi no koji. In *Nihon koji bijutsu zenshū 7*. Shūeisha, 1981.

Shūmon jisshō ron (Kokan Shiren). Edited by Zengaku taikei hensankyoku. In *Zengaku taikei 8*. Ikkatsusha, 1913.

Sōma monjo. Edited by Toyoda Takeshi. Zoku gunsho ruijū kanseikai, 1979.
Sonpi bunmyaku (Tōin Kinsada). In *Shintei zōho kokushi taikei*. 5 vols. Yoshikawa kōbunkan, 1964.
Sorai sensei tōmonsho (Ogyū Sorai). In *Nihon koten bungaku taikei*. Iwanami shoten, 1957–58.
Suganoura monjo. Compiled by Harada Toshimaru. 2 vols. Shiga daigaku keizaigakubu shiryōkan, 1960–67.
Suwa daimyōjin-ekotoba. In *Zoku gunsho ruijū, jingi bu 3*. Zoku gunsho ruijū kanseikai, 1975.
Taiheiki. Edited by Gotō Tanji and Kamada Kisaburō. 3 vols., *Nihon koten bungaku taikei*. Iwanami shoten, 1961–62.
Taiheiki. Edited by Yamashita Hiroaki. 5 vols. Shinchō Nihon koten shūsei, 1980.
Takemukigaki zenshaku (Hino Meishi). Edited by Nakada Norio and Mizukawa Yoshio. Kazama shobō, 1972.
Takemukigaki (Hino Meishi). Edited by Mizukawa Yoshio. Benseisha, 1978.
Takemukigaki (Hino Meishi). Edited by Iwasa Miyoko. In *Chūsei nikki kikōshū, Shin Nihon koten bungaku taikei 51*. Edited by Fukuda Hideichi et al., 271–344. Iwanami shoten, 1990.
Tendai zasuki (Kōtei zōho Tendai zasuki). Compiled by Shibuya Gaiji. Daiichi shobō, 1973.
Tenryū kaizan Musō shōgaku shinsō fuzai kokushi nenpu (Musō kokushi nenpu). Edited by Shunoku Myōha. In *Zoku gunsho ruijū 9*. Zoku gunsho ruiju kanseikai, 1927.
Tenryūji zōei kiroku. Edited by Tōkyō daigaku shiryō hensanjo. In *Dai Nihon shiryō*, part 6, vol. 5. Tōkyō daigaku shiryō hensanjo, 1947.
Tōfukuji shi. Kyoto: Daihonzan Tōfuku zenji, 1930.
Towazugatari zenshaku. Edited by Nakada Norio. Kazama shobō, 1978.
T'ung-chien chi-shih pen-mo (Yuan Chi-chung [Yuan Shu]). 12 vols. Peking: Chung-hua Shu-chū, 1964.
Tzu chih t'ung chien 1 (Ssu-ma Kuang). 10 vols. Peking: Ku-chih Chu-pan, 1956.
Ukyō no daibu. *Kenreimon'in Ukyō no daibu shū*. Edited by Itoga Kimie. Shinchōsha, 1979.
Wakayama kenshi, chūsei shiryō 1. Compiled by Wakayama kenshi hensan iinkai. Wakayama ken, 1975.
Yamaga Sokō zenshū. Edited by Hirose Yutaka. 15 vols. Iwanami shoten, 1940–41.
Yoshisadaki. Edited by Hanawa Hokiichi. In *Gunsho ruijū 23*. Gunsho ruijū kanseikai, 1960.
Zenseki shi (Shōboku Myōtai). In *Dai Nihon bukkyō zensho 1*. Yūseitō shuppanbu, 1930.
Zoku Nihon emaki taisei 1–3, 18. Edited by Komatsu Shigemi. Kyoto: Chūō kōronsha, 1981–83.

Secondary Sources in Japanese

(Unless otherwise noted, the city of publication is Tokyo.)

Amino Yoshihiko. *Chūsei no hinin to yūjo*. Akashi shoten, 1994.
————. *Igyō no ōken*. Heibonsha, 1986.
————. *Nihon chūsei no hinōgyōmin to tennō*. Iwanami shoten, 1984.
————. *Nihon rekishi o yominaosu*. Chikuma, 1991.
————. *Nihonron no shiza: rettō no shakai to kokka*. 2d ed. Shōgakkan, 1992.
————. "Nōson no hattatsu to ryōshu keizai no tenkan." In *Nihon keizaishi taikei 2, chūsei*, Nagahara Keiji, ed., 99–139. Tōkyō daigaku shuppankai, 1965.
————. "Sanjū ban: tachigimi, zushigimi." In *Shichijū-ichiban shokunin uta awase, shokushu ichiran*, Shokunin uta awase kenkyūkai, ed. Iwanami shoten, 1993.
Anonymous. "Go-Daigo tennō no itsushin." *Bessatsu rekishi tokuhon*, no. 10 (1990): 129–35.
Ariyoshi Tamotsu. *Waka bungaku jiten*. Ōfūsha, 1982.
Atsuta Kō, ed. "Nanbokuchō, Muromachi." *Zusetsu Nihon bunka no rekishi 6*. Shōgakkan, 1980.
Bitō Masahide. "Seimei ron to meibun ron." In *Ienaga Saburō kyōju Tōkyō kyōiku daigaku taikan kinen ronshū 2: kindai Nihon no kokka to shisō*, Ienaga Saburō kyōju Tōkyō kyōiku daigaku taikan kinen ronshū kankō iinkai, eds., 2–22. Sanseidō, 1979.
Fuji Naomoto. *Buke jidai no shakai to seishin*. Sōgensha, 1967.
Fujikake Shizuya. "Kenmu gan no nenki aru gokei monjū e ni tsuite." *Kokka* 535 (1935).
————. "Monkan sōjō to Hachiji Monjūshiri bosatsu zu." *Kokka* 352 (1923): 108–14.
Fujikawa Yū. *Nihon shippei shi*. Heibonsha, 1969.
Fujioka Kenjirō. *Nihon rekishi chiri sōsetsu, chūsei hen*. Yoshikawa kōbunkan, 1975.
Fujioka Kenjirō, Yamori Kazuhiko, and Ashikaga Kenryō. *Rekishi no kūkan kōzō*. Daimeidō, 1976.
Fukuda Ajio. *Ajia no naka no Nihonshi*. Tōkyō daigaku shuppankai, 1992.
Fukuda Hideichi. *Chūsei wakashi no kenkyū*. Kadokawa shoten, 1972.
————. "Enkyō ryōkyō sochinjō no seiritsu." *Kokugo to kokubungaku*, July 1957: 32–41.
————. "Enkyō ryōkyō sochinjō no seiritsu ni kansuru shiryō." *Kokugo to kokubungaku*, January 1957: 32–45.
————. "Kaisetsu: chūsei nikki kikō bungaku no tenbō." In *Chūsei nikki kikōshū*, 507–28. Fukuda Hideichi et al., eds. Iwanami shoten, 1990.
Fukuo Takeichirō. *Nihon kazoku seidoshi gaisetsu*. Yoshikawa kōbunkan, 1972.
Fukutō Sanae. "Jun mukotorikon o meggutte." *Rekishi hyōron* 455 (March 1988): 2–11.

————. "Yūkō jofu kara yūjo e." In *Nihon josei seikatsushi, 1*, Joseishi sōgō kenkyūkai, ed., 217–46. Tōkyō daigaku shuppankai, 1991.

Funaoka Makoto. *Nihon zenshūshi no seiritsu.* Yoshikawa kōbunkan, 1987.

Furukawa Tetsushi and Ishida Ichirō, eds. *Nihon shisōshi kōza 2, chūsei no shisō 1.* Yūzankaku, 1976.

Futaki Ken'ichi. *Chūsei buke girei no kenkyū.* Yoshikawa kōbunkan, 1985.

Geinōshi kenkyūkai, ed. *Nihon geinōshi 2.* Hōsei daigaku shuppankyoku, 1981.

Gotō Michiko. "Nanbokuchō, Muromachi no josei no shoryō sōzoku: tandoku sōzoku to no kankei." In *Kazoku to josei no rekishi: kodai, chūsei.* Zenkindai joseishi kenkyūkai, ed., 344–66. Yoshikawa kōbunkan, 1989.

Gotō Ryōji. "Higo Takuma-shi no ryōshu-sei no tenkai ni tsuite." *Seiji keizai shigaku* 189, no. 2 (1982).

Hagihara Tatsuo. *Chūsei saishi soshiki no kenkyū.* Yoshikawa kōbunkan, 1962.

Hamaguchi Hiroaki and Ogawa Michiko. "*Tamekanekyōki* Ryankuchū." *Kōnan daigaku kiyō, bungakuhen 36.* 1979.

Hara Tsunehira. "Sasaki Dōyo." In *Nanchō to Hokuchō*, Toyoda Takeshi et al., eds. Shōgakukan, 1976.

Hayashiya Tatsusaburō. *Nairan no naka no kizoku.* Kadokawa shoten, 1991.

Higo Kazuo. "Ōmi ni okeru miyaza no kenkyū." *Tōkyō bunrika daigaku bunka kiyō 16* (1938).

————. *Rekidai tennō zukan.* Akita shoten, 1975.

Hikoyoshi Kazuta, ed. *Nihon kōsōden yōmon shō Genkō shakusho jinmei sōsakuin.* Yokohama: Seiji keizai shi gakkai, 1982.

Hioki Shōichi. *Sōhei no kenkyū.* Kokusho kankōkai, 1972.

Hirayama Kōzō. *Wayō no kenkyū.* Yoshikawa kōbunkan, 1964.

Hirose Kazuo. "Chūsei e no taidō." In *Iwanami kōza, Nihon kōkogaku 6, Henka to gakki.* Iwanami shoten, 1986.

Hisano Nobuyoshi. "Chūsei Tōdaiji to Shōmu tennō." *Bukkyō shigaku kenkyū* 34, no. 1 (1991): 1–21.

Hisano Shūgi. "Sanmon-jimon no sōkoku." In *Shinshū Ōtsu shishi 2, chūsei*, Ōtsu shiyakusho, ed., 71–98. Ōtsu: Nihon shashin insatsu kabushiki gaisha, 1978.

Hōgetsu Keigo. *Chūsei kangaishi no kenkyū.* Unebi shobō, 1943.

Hori Isao. *Yamaga Sokō.* Yoshikawa kōbunkan, 1959.

Hosokawa Ryōichi. "Kazoku o kōsei shinai josei." In *Kazoku to josei: chūsei o kangaeru*, Minegishi Sumio, ed., 210–40. Yoshikawa kōbunkan, 1992.

Hotate Michihisa. "Chūsei minshū keizai no hatten." In *Kōza Nihon rekishi 3, chūsei 1*, Nihonshi kenkyūkai Rekishigaku kenkyūkai, ed. Tōkyō daigaku shuppankai, 1984.

————. *Chūsei no ai to jūzoku: emaki no naka no nikutai.* Heibonsha, 1987.

Ichikawa Hakugen et al., eds. *Chūsei zenke no shisō.* In *Nihon shisō taikei.* Iwanami shoten, 1972.

Ienaga Saburō. *Nihon dōtoku shisō.* Iwanami zensho, 1967.

Ienaga Saburō kyōju Tōkyō kyōiku daigaku taikan kinen ronshū kankō iinkai, ed. *Ienaga Saburō kyōju Tōkyō kyōiku daigaku taikan kinen ronshū 2: kindai Nihon no kokka to shisō.* Sanseidō, 1979.

Imaeda Aishin. *Chūsei zenshū shi no kenkyū.* Tōkyō daigaku shuppankai, 1970.

———. *Zenshū no rekishi.* Shibundō, 1962.

Imahama Michitaka. *Genkō shakusho*, Kyōikusha shinsho (Genpon gendaiyaku) 62 (1980).

Imai Masaharu. *Chūsei o ikita Nihonjin.* Gakuseisha, 1992.

Imatani Akira. "Jūyon-jūgo seiki no Nihon—Nanbokuchō to Muromachi bakufu." In *Iwanami kōza Nihon tsūshi.* Iwanami shoten, 1994.

———. "Kamakura, Muromachi bakufu to kogun no kikō." In *Nihon shakaishi.* Iwanami shoten, 1994.

———. *Muromachi bakufu kaitei no kenkyū.* Iwanami shoten, 1975.

———. *Muromachi no ōken.* Chūkō shinsho, 1990.

———. *Sengoku ki no Muromachi bakufu.* Kadokawa shoten, 1975.

———. "Wagakuni chūsei shiyō yōsuisha no fukugen." *Kokuritsu rekishi minzoku hakubutsukan kenkyū hōkoku* 4 (1984).

Inagaki Shisei. *Sengoku buke jiten.* Seiabō, 1971.

Inagaki Yasuhiko. "Chūsei no nōgyō keiei to shūshu keitai." In *Iwanami kōza Nihon rekishi 6, chūsei 2.* 167–206. Iwanami shoten, 1975.

———. "Shōen kaihatsu no ato o saguru-Yamato no kuni Ikeda no shō." In *Shōen no sekai*, Inagaki Yasuhiko, ed. Tōkyō daigaku shuppankai, 1973.

———, ed. *Shōen no sekai.* Tōkyō daigaku shuppankai, 1973.

Inagaki Yasuhiko and Toda Yoshimi. *Nihon minshū no rekishi 2, doikki to nairan.* Sanseidō, 1975.

Inoue Muneo. *Chūsei kadanshi no kenkyū: Nanbokuchōki.* Rev. ed. Meiji shoin, 1987.

Inukai Kiyoshi et al., eds. *Waka daijiten.* Meiji shoin, 1986.

Ishida Yoshisada and Satsukawa Shūji. *Minamoto Ienaga no nikki zenchūkai.* Yūseidō, 1968.

Ishii Susumu. *Chūsei o kangaeru: shakairon, shiryōron, toshiron.* Itakura shobō, 1972.

Ishii Susumu et al., eds. *Nihon chūsei seiji shakai shisō.* In *Nihon shisō taikei 21.* Iwanami shoten, 1972.

Ishikawa Rikizan. "*Genkō shakusho* to Kokan Shiren." *Indogaku bukkyōgaku kenkyū* 212 (1973).

Ishike Tadashi. "Muromachi bakufu no seiji shisō." In *Nihon shisōshi kōza 2, chūsei no shisō*, Furukawa Tetsushi and Ishida Ichirō, eds. Yūzankaku, 1976–77.

Ishioka Hisao. "Kyūdō." In *Nihon budō taikei.* Kyoto: Dōbōsha, 1982.

Itō Kiyoshi. *Nambokuchō no dōran.* Shūeisha, 1992.

———. *Nihon chūsei no ōken to ken'i.* Kyoto: Shibunkaku, 1993.

Iwasa Miyoko. *Kyōgokuha waka no kenkyū.* Kasama shoin, 1987.

Iwasaki Kae, ed. *Shokunin uta awase: chūsei no shokunin gunzō.* In *Heibonsha sensho 114.* Heibonsha, 1987.

Iwasaki Kae et al., eds. *Shichijū-ichi ban shokunin uta awase.* In *Shin Nihon koten bungaku taikei 61.* Iwanami shoten, 1993.

Kaji Hiroe. "*Shokugenshō* no shisō teki kiban wo megutte." In *Nihon shi ronshū,* Tokinoya Masaru kyōju taikan kinen kai, ed., 259–74. Osaka: Seibundō shuppan, 1975.

Kakehi Yasuhiko. *Chūsei buke kakun no kenkyū.* Kazama shobō, 1967.

Kakehi Yasuhiko and Osawa Tomio. *Nihonjin no rinri shisō.* Tōsen shuppan, 1972.

Kami Hiroshi. *Taiheiki kyōjushi ronkō.* Ōfūsha, 1985.

Katsuura Noriko. "Josei no hosshin, shukke to kazoku." In *Kazoku to josei: chūsei o kangaeru.* Minegishi Sumio, ed., 241–71. Yoshikawa kōbunkan, 1992.

Kawai Masaharu. *Chūsei buke shakai no kenkyū.* Yoshikawa kōbunkan, 1973.

Kawane Yoshiyasu. *Chūsei hōkensei seiritsushi ron.* Tōkyō daigaku shuppankai, 1971.

Kawauchi Yōsuke. "Nihon chūsei no chōtei, bakufu taisei." *Rekishi hyōron* 500 (1992): 22–39.

Kawazoe Shōji. " 'Chinzei tandai' Ashikaga Tadafuyu: Kyūshū ni okeru Kannō seihen." In *Kyūshū chūsei kenkyū 2:* 187–242. Bunken shuppan, 1980.

———. "Edo jidai ni okeru Genkō kenkyū." *Kyūshū bunka shi kenkyūjo kiyō,* no. 15 (March 1970): 1–44.

———. *Imagawa Ryōshun.* Yoshikawa kōbunkan, 1969.

———. *Kamakura bakufu.* Kyōkikusha, 1978.

———. *Kikuchi Takemitsu.* Jinbutsu ōraisha, 1966.

Kimura Shigemitsu. "Chūsei seiritsuki ni okeru batasaku no seikaku to ryōyū kankei." *Nihonshi kenkyū* 180 (1977): 1–40.

———. "Chūsei zenki no nōgyō seisanryoku to batasaku." *Nihonshi kenkyū* 280, no. 12 (1985): 52–82.

———. "Daikaikon jidai no kaihatsu: sono gijutsu to seikaku." In *Gijutsu no shakaishi 1, kodai-chūsei no gijutsu to shakai,* Miura Keiichi, ed. Yūhikaku, 1982.

———. "Nihon chūsei bungyō-ryūtsu shi kenkyū no ichi shikaku." *Rekishi hyōron* 426, no. 10 (1985): 2–10.

———. *Nihon kodai chūsei batasakushi no kenkyū.* Azekura shobō, 1992.

Kinda Akihiro. *Bichikei to chūsei sonraku.* Yoshikawa kōbunkan, 1993.

———. "Heian ki no Yamato bonchi ni okeru jōri jiwari naibu no tochi riyō." *Shirin* 61 (1978): 75–112.

———. "Nara Heian ki no sonraku keitai ni tsuite." *Shirin* 54, no. 3 (1971): 49–117.

———. "Shōen sonraku no keikan." In *Nihonshi 2, chūsei 1,* Toda Yoshimi, ed., 127–58. Yūhikaku, 1978.

Kōdate Naomi. "Shiryō shōkai 'Ketsubonkyō wakai': kinseiki Jōdoshū ni okeru ketsubonkyō shinkō." *Bukkyō minzoku kenkyū* 6 (1989): 59–91.

Koizumi Yoshiaki. "Nairanki no shakai hendō." In *Iwanami kōza, Nihon rekishi 6, chūsei 2*: 125–66. Iwanami shoten, 1975.

Koyō Hiroshi. "Monjo yori mitaru Ashikaga Yoshiakira no chii to kengen." In *Nihon komonjo ronshū*. Yoshikawa kōbunkan, 1984.

Kuroda Hideo. "Go-Daigo tennō to Shōtoku taishi." *Rekishi wo yominaosu, Tenmu, Go-Shirakawa, Go-Daigo—ōken no henbō* 3, no. 12 (1994).

———. "Kumano kanshin jikkai mandara no uchū." In *Bukkyō to Nihonjin 8: sei to mibun*, Miyata Noboru, ed., 207–72. Shunjūsha, 1989.

———. *Nihon chūsei kaihatsushi no kenkyū*. Azekura shobō, 1984.

———. *Ō no shintai, ō no shōzō*. Heibonsha, 1993.

———. "Sengoku-Shokuhōki no gijutsu to keizai hatten." In *Kōza Nihon rekishi 4, chūsei 2*, Nihonshi kenkyūkai Rekishigaku kenkyūkai, ed., 275–316. Tōkyō daigaku shuppankai, 1985.

Kuroda Hiroko. "Chūsei kōki no mura no onna tachi." In *Nihon josei seikatsushi 2*, Joseishi sōgō kenkyūkai, ed., 187–222. Tōkyō daigaku shuppankai, 1990.

———. *Chūsei sōsonshi no kōzō*. Yoshikawa kōbunkan, 1985.

———. " 'Dayu nari' to nō: chūsei Kokawadera ryō Higashimura." *Kokawachō shi kenkyū* 5, no. 7 (1979): 1–14.

Kuroda Toshio. "Chūsei jisha seiryoku ron." In *Iwanami kōza, Nihon rekishi 6: chūsei 2*, Asao Naohiro et al., eds., 245–95. Iwanami shoten, 1975.

———. "Chūsei kokka to tennō." In *Iwanami kōza, Nihon rekishi 6: chūsei 2*, Ienaga saburō et al., eds., 261–301. Iwanami shoten, 1967.

———. *Jisha seiryoku*. Iwanami shoten, 1980.

———. "Kenmitsu bukkyō ni okeru rekishi ishiki." In *Nihon chūsei no shakai to shūkyō*, Kuroda Toshio, ed., 191–208. Iwanami shoten, 1990.

———. *Nihon chūsei no kokka to shūkyō*. Iwanami shoten, 1975.

———. "Sonraku kyōdōtai to chūseiteki tokushitsu." In *Nihon chūsei hōkensei ron*, Kuroda Toshio, ed. Tōkyō daigaku shuppankai, 1974.

Kurokawa Naonori. "Jūgo, jūroku seiki no nōmin mondai." *Nihonshi kenkyū* 71 (1964).

Kuwata Kazuaki. "Muromachi-jidai ni okeru Munakata-shi no dōkō." *Kyūshū shigaku* 96, no. 10 (1981).

Kuwata Tadachika. *Shinchō kōki*. Jinbutsu ōraisha, 1965.

Maruyama Masao. "Ansai gaku to Ansai gakuha." In *Nihon shisō taikei*. Iwanami shoten, 1970–82.

Maruyama Yoshihiko. "Shōen sonraku ni okeru sōyūchi ni tsuite—Ōmi no kuni Tokuchinho o chūshin ni." In *Chūsei no kenryoku to minshū*, Nihonshi kenkyūkai shiryō kenkyūbukai, ed., 297–323. Sogensha, 1970.

Masaki Shin'ichi. "Kamo no Chōmei to Yoshida Kenkō." In *Nihon no shisō*, Usuda Noboru et al., eds. Shin Nihon shuppansha, 1980.

Matsubara Shigeru. "Shōwa sannen hon Shingon hassō zō." *Kokka*, nos. 1089, 1090 (1985): 35–41; 33–44.

Matsui Teruaki. "Kunijōshi, kunishisetsu ni tsuite no oboegaki." *Hiroshima kenshi kenkyū* 5 (1980).

Matsumoto Shinpachirō. "Nanbokuchō nairan no shozentei." In *Chūsei shakai no kenkyū*. Tōkyō daigaku, 1978.

Miki Sumito and Yamada Shūzen, eds. *Mujū Kokan, Daijō butten 25 (Chūgoku Nihon)*. Kyoto: Chūō kōronsha, 1989.

Minegishi Sumio. "Chūsei shakai no kaikyū kōsei—toku ni 'genin' o chūshin ni." *Rekishigaku kenkyū* 312 (1965): 36–49.

———. "Jūgo seiki kōhan no tochi seido." In *Taikei Nihon shi sōshō 6, Tochi seido shi 1*, Takeuchi Rizō, ed., 395–446. Yamakawa shuppansha, 1973.

———. "Sonraku to dogō." In *Kōza Nihonshi 3, Hōken shakai no tenkai*, Nihonshi kenkyūkai, Rekishigaku kenkyūkai, eds., 139–60. Tōkyō daigaku shuppankai, 1970.

———, ed. *Sōten Nihon no rekishi, chūsei hen*. Shinjinbutsu ōraisha, 1990–91.

Minegishi Sumio and Ikegami Hiroko, eds. *Shinshiten Nihon no rekishi 4, chūsei hen*. Shinjinbutsu ōraisha, 1993.

Miura Keiichi. *Chūsei minshū seikatsushi no kenkyū*. Kyoto: Shibunkaku, 1981.

———, ed. *Gijutsu no shaki shi 1, kodai, chūsei no gijutsu to shakai*. Yūhikaku, 1982.

Miyai Yoshio. "Jinnō shōtōki to Shiji tsugan." *Rekishi kyōiku* 154 (1940): 468–72.

———. *Nihon no chūsei shisō*. Seikōshobō, 1981.

Mizuno Shoji. "Chūsei no kaihatsu to sonraku." *Rekishigaku kenkyū* 65 (1994).

Mori Shigeaki. *Nanbokuchō ki kōbu kankei shi no kenkyū*. Bunken shuppan, 1984.

———. *Ōjitachi no Nanbokuchō*. Kyoto: Chūō kōronsha, 1988.

Mori Tōru. *Kamakura jidai no shōzōga*. Misuzu shobō, 1971.

Morisue Yoshiaki et al., eds. *Kokusho sōmokuroku 5, 7*. Iwanami shoten, 1963–72.

Moriyama Seishin. *Tachikawa jakyō to sono shakaiteki haikei no kenkyū*. Shikanoen, 1965.

Morohashi Tetsuji, comp. *Dai kanwa jiten 4*. 12 vols. Taishūkan, 1960.

Murai Shōsuke. "Tokusei to shite no Ōan hanzeirei." In *Nihon chūsei no shosō*, Yasuda-sensei tainin kinen ronshū kankōkai, ed. Yoshikawa kōbunkan, 1989.

Murai Yasuhiko. *Bungei no sōsei to tenkai*. Kyoto: Dōhōsha, 1991.

Murata Masashi. *Murata Masashi chōsaku shū 4, Chūshō Chin'yōki*. Kyoto: Shibunkaku, 1984.

Murata Masashi and Matsumoto Shūji. *Yoshida Sadafusa jiseki*. Matsushige Yūichi, 1941.

Nabata Takashi. "Ōken to bukkyō—*Genkō shakusho* no naiyō to kōsei." *Bukkyō shigaku kenkyū* 32, no. 2 (1989): 1–23.

Nagahara Keiji. "Chūsei no shakai kosei to hōkensei." In *Kōza Nihon rekishi 4, chūsei 2*, Nihonshi kenkyūkai, Rekishigaku kenkyūkai, eds. Tōkyō daigaku shuppankai, 1985.

———. "Joseishi ni okeru Nanbokuchō, Muromachiki." In *Nihon joseishi 2*, Joseishi sōgō kenkyūkai, ed., 137–71. Tōkyō daigaku shuppankai, 1982.

————. *Nihon chūsei shakai kōzō no kenkyū*. Iwanami shoten, 1973.

————. "Nihon kokka shi no ichi mondai." *Shisō* 47, no. 5 (1964): 42–51.

————. *Shin-momen izen no koto, Choma kara momen e. Chūkō shisho 963*. Kyoto: Chūō kōronsha, 1990.

Nagahara Keiji and Kishi Shōzō. *Zenyaku Azuma kagami*. Vol. 4. Shinjinbutsu ōraisha, 1977.

Nagai Michiko. "Go-Daigo tennō." In *Jinbutsu Nihon no rekishi, 7, Nanbokuchō*. Shōgakkan, 1976.

Nagashima Fukutarō. "Yamato Shimoda Kagoshima-sha Kenchinza monjo to chūsei sonraku." *Nihon rekishi* 176 (1963): 67–82.

Nakabayashi Shinji. "Nihon kobudō ni okeru shintairon." *Risō* 604 (September 1993).

Nakamura Ken. "Chūsei kōki ni okeru Ōmi no kuni Tokuchinho Imabori gō no nōgyō." *Nōgyō keizai kenkyū* 484 (1977).

————. *Chūsei sōsonshi no kenkyū, Ōmi no kuni Tokuchinho Imabori gō*. Hōsei daigaku shuppankyoku, 1984.

Nihon sonrakushi kōza henshū iinkai, ed. *Nihon sonrakushi kōza, keikan 1, seiji 1, seikatsu 1*. Vols. 2, 4, 6. Yūzankaku, 1990–93.

Nihonyanagi Kenji. *Bukkyō igaku gaiyō*. Kyoto: Hōzōkan, 1994.

Niki Ken'ichi. *Chūsei buke girei no kenkyū*. Yoshikawa kōbunkan, 1985.

Nitta Ichirō. "'Taibon sankajō isetsu'—jōshiki no saikentō." *Haruka nara chūsei* 14, no. 3 (1995).

Nomura Ikuyo. "Chūsei ni okeru tennōke: nyoinryō no denryō to yōshi." In *Kazoku to josei no rekishi: kodai, chūsei*. Zenkindai joseishi kenkyūkai, ed., 294–319. Yoshikawa kōbunkan, 1989.

————. "Nyoin kenkyū no genjo." *Rekishi hyōron* 52, no. 5 (January 1994): 44–55.

Ogawa Makoto. *Ashikaga ichimon shugo hattenshi no kenkyū*. Yoshikawa kōbunkan, 1980.

————. "Hosokawa Kiyouji no botsuraku." *Kokugakuin zasshi* 70, no. 8 (1969).

————. "Hosokawa Kiyouji no taitō." *Kokugakuin zasshi* 69, no. 7 (1968).

————. *Hosokawa Yoriyuki*. Yoshikawa kōbunkan, 1972.

Ogisu Jundō. *Nihon chūsei zenshū shi*. Mokujisha, 1965.

Okajima Hatatsu, ed. *Nihon saiishi*. Chijin shokan, 1967.

Okamoto Takenori. "Ōmi no okeru chūsei sonraku no seiritsu to tenkai." In *Nihonshi no okeru shakai to shūkyō*, Katata Osamu, ed. Bun'eidō, 1991.

Ōkubo Dōshu. *Nihon bunkashi sōkō*. Seishin shobō, 1977.

Okutomi Takayuki. *Kamakura Hōjō-shi no kisoteki kenkyū*. Yoshikawa kōbunkan, 1980.

Ōsumi Kazuo. "*Genkō shakusho* no buppō kan." *Kanazawa bunko kenkyū* 271 (1983): 1–21.

————. "*Genkō shakusho* to jingi." Tōkyō joshi daigaku fuzoku hikaku bunka kenkyūjo, eds. *Kiyō* 48 (1987).

————, ed. *Chūsei shintō ron*. In *Nihon shisō taikei*. Iwanami shoten, 1977.

Ōyama Kyōhei. *Nihon chūsei nōsonshi no kenkyū*. Iwanami shoten, 1978.

Ozawa Tomio. *Mappō to masse no shisō*. Yūzankaku shuppan, 1974.

Sagara Tōru. *Nihon shisōshi nyūmon*. Perikan-sha, 1984.

Saiki Kazuma. *Kokiroku no kenkyū*. In *Saiki Kazuma chosakushū 2*. Yoshikawa kōbunkan, 1989.

Sasaki Ginya. "Shōen sonraku to myōshu hyakushō." In idem, *Muromachi bakufu* (*Nihon no rekishi 13*). Shōgakkan, 1975.

Sasaki Kaoru. *Chūsei kokka no shūkyō kōzō: taisei bukkyō to taiseigai bukkyō no sōkoku*. Yoshikawa kōbunkan, 1988.

Satō Kazuhiko. *Nanbokuchō nairan* (*Nihon no rekishi 11*). Shōgakkan, 1974.

————. *Taiheiki no sekai*. Shinjinbutsu ōraisha, 1990.

————. *Taiheiki o yomu*. Gakuseisha, 1991.

Satō Shin'ichi. "Kamakura bakufu seiji no senseika ni tsuite." In *Hōkensei seiritsu no kenkyū*, Takeuchi Rizō, ed. Yoshikawa kōbunkan, 1957.

————. *Komonjogaku nyūmon*. Hōsei daigaku shuppankyoku, 1971.

————. "Kyōto sōdatsusen." In idem, *Nanbokuchō no dōran* (*Nihon rekishi 9*). Kyoto: Chūō kōronsha, 1967.

————. "Muromachi bakufu-ron." In *Iwanami kōza Nihon rekishi*, Iwanami shoten, 1963.

————. *Zōtei Kamakura bakufu shugo seido no kenkyū*. Tōkyō daigaku shuppan-kai, 1971.

Satō Tokiko. "[Masu kagami] no kōi keishō kan—sanshū no jingi wo megutte." In *Kokka to shūkyō*, Minamoto Ryōen and Tamakage Hiroyuki, eds., 163–85. Kyoto: Shibunkaku, 1992.

Sawa Ryūken. *Butsuzō zuten*. Yoshikawa kōbunkan, 1962.

Sekiguchi Hiroko. *Nihon kodai kon'inshi no kenkyū*. 2 vols. Haniwa shobō, 1993.

Sekiguchi Tsuneo. "Chūsei zenki no minshū to sonraku." In *Iwanami kōza, Nihon rekishi 5, chūsei 1*, 121–68. Iwanami shoten, 1975.

Seno Seiichirō. *Chinzei gokenin no kenkyū*. Yoshikawa kōbunkan, 1975.

Shiga Setsuko. "Chūsei kōki shōen sonraku to kendan." *Rekishigaku kenkyū 569* (1989).

Shiga-ken Kyōiku Iinkai, ed. *Biwako no gyorō seikatsu: Biwako sōgō kaihatsu chi-iki minzoku bunkazai tokubetsu chōsa hōkokusho 1*. Shiga-ken bunkazai hōgō kyōkai, 1978.

Shikata Masakazu. "Kikuchi-shi no kigen ni tsuite." *Kumamoto shigaku 15–16* (1959).

Shimokawa Ushio. *Kendō no hattatsu*. Reprint of *Dai Nihon butokukai* edition. Taiiku to supōtsu shuppansha, 1977.

Shimosaka Mamoru. "Sanmon shisetsu seido no seiritsu to tenkai." *Shirin 581* (1975): 67–114.

Shiroyama Hōtarō. *Shokugenshō no kisoteki kenkyū*. Shintōshi gakkai, 1980.

Sōgō joseishi kenkyūkai, ed. *Nihon josei no rekishi: bunka to shisō.* In *Kadokawa sensho 241.* Kadokawa shoten, 1993.

———. *Nihon josei no rekishi: sei, ai, kazoku.* In *Kadokawa sensho 225.* Kadokawa shoten, 1992.

Suga Kikuko. "Gokoku to seijō—Tenryūji sōken to Musō Soseki." In *Kokka to shūkyō,* Minamoto Ryōen and Tamakake Hiroyuki, eds., 185–207. Kyoto: Shibunkaku, 1992.

Sugimoto Hisao. *Kikuchi sandai.* Yoshikawa kōbunkan, 1963.

Sugiyama Hiroshi. *Sengoku daimyō (Nihon no rekishi 11).* Kyoto: Chūō kōronsha, 1971.

Sugiyama Jirō. "Hannyadera Monjū bosatsu zō ni tsuite." *Museum* 133 (1962): 11–15.

Suma Chikai. "Yamashiro no kuni Kii gun ni okeru shōensei to nōmin." In *Chūsei no shakai to keizai, Nihon hōkensei kenkyū 2,* Nagahara Keiji and Inagaki Yasuhiko, eds. Tōkyō daigaku shuppankai, 1962.

Suzuki Kunihiro. "Chūseishi kenkyū to Takamure Itsue: 'kafuchōsei kazoku'ron no saikentō kara." *Rekishi hyōron* 455 (March 1988): 12–24.

Tabata Yasuko. "Chūsei kōki ni okeru ryōshu shihai to sonraku kōzō—sōshō sōgo no kinō to yakuwari." *Nihonshi kenkyū* 187, no. 3 (1978).

———. "Daimyō ryōgoku kihan to sonraku nyōbō za." In *Nihon joseishi 2.* Joseishi sōgō kenkyūkai, ed., 209–50. Tōkyō daigaku shuppankai, 1982.

———. *Nihon chūsei joseishi ron.* Hanawa shobō, 1994.

———. *Nihon chūsei no josei.* Yoshikawa kōbunkan, 1987.

Taira Masayuki. "Chūsei bukkyō to josei." In *Nihon josei seikatsushi 2.* Joseishi sōgō kenkyūkai, ed., 75–108. Tōkyō daigaku shuppankai, 1990.

———. *Nihon chūsei no shakai to bukkyō.* Kōshobō, 1992.

Takahashi Osamu. "Kamakura goki ni okeru chiiki kenryoku to bakufu taisei." *Nihonshi kenkyū* 136, no. 9 (1992).

Takahashi Shōmei. "Nihon chūsei nōgyō seisanryoku suijun saihyōka no isshiten." *Atarashii rekishigaku no tame ni* 148, no. 8 (1977): 1–13.

Takahashi Tomio. *Bushidō no rekishi 1.* Taiyōsha, 1986.

Takamaki Minoru. *Miyaza to matsuri.* In *Kyōikisha rekishi shinsho, Nihonshi 35.* Kyōikusha, 1982.

Takamure Itsue. *Josei no rekishi 1.* Kōdansha, 1977.

———. *Shōseikon no kenkyū,* 1 and 2. In *Takamure Itsue zenshū 3.* Roronsha, 1966.

Takayanagi Mitsutoshi. *Ashikaga Takauji.* Haruakisha, 1966.

Takeda Sachiko. "Igyō no Shōtoku taishi." *Rekishi hyōron* 493 (1991): 23–30.

Takemi Momoko. " 'Ketsubonkyō' no keifu to sono shinkō." *Bukkyō minzoku kenkyū* 3 (September 1976): 1–9.

———. "Nyonin kyūsai to bukkyō." *Rekishi kōron* 6, no. 3 (March 1980): 65–71.

Takemitsu Makoto. "Kenmu nenchū gyōji ni kisareta chōgi no tokushitsu." *Fūzoku* 182 (1980): 55–64.

Takeuchi Naoji. "Zenrin bijutsushi kō—Musō ha kyōdan no bijutsu ni tsuite." *Tōkyō kokuritsu hakubutsukan kiyō* 11 (1975): 37–150.

Tamakake Hiroyuki. "Buke seiken to seiji shisō." In *Nihon shisōshi kōza 2, chūsei no shisō*, Furukawa Tetsushi and Ishida Ichirō, eds. Yūzankaku, 1976.

———. "Musō Soseki to shoki Muromachi seiken." *Tōhoku daigaku bungakubu kenkyū nenpō* 35 (1985): 97–129.

Tamamura Takeji. "Gozan sōrin no tatchū ni tsuite." *Rekishi chiri* 76 (1940).

———. *Gozan zensō denki shūsei*. Kōdansha, 1983.

———. *Musō kokushi*. Kyoto: Heirakuji shoten, 1969.

———. *Nihon zenshū shi ronshū*. Shibunkaku, 1976.

———. *Rinzaishū shi*. Shunchōsha, 1991.

Tanaka Yoshinari. *Nanbokuchō jidaishi*. Kōdansha gakujutsu bunko, 1979.

Toda Yoshimi. "Chūsei shoki nōgyō no ichi tokushitsu." In *Nihon ryōshusei seiritsushi no kenkyū*, Toda Yoshimi, ed. Iwanami shoten, 1967.

———. "Sanya no kizokuteki ryōyū to chūsei shoki no sonraku." In *Nihon ryōshusei seiritsushi no kenkyū*, Toda Yoshimi, ed. Iwanami shoten, 1967.

Tokieda Tsutomu. "Chūsei Tōgoku ni okeru ketsubonkyō shinkō no yōsō: Kusatsu Shiraneyama o chūshin to shite." *Shinano* 36, no. 8 (July 1984).

Toyoda Takeshi, ed. *Buke no shōri 7*. In *Zusetsu Nihon no rekishi*. Sūeisha, 1975.

Tsuchida Naoshige. "Naishi sen ni tsuite." In *Nihon komonjogaku ronshū 4: Kodai II: Nara, Heian jidai no monjo*, Nihon komonjo gakkai, ed., 63–95. Yoshikawa kōbunkan, 1988.

Tsuda Sōkichi. *Bungaku ni arawaretaru kokumin shisō no kenkyū 2*. In *Tsuda Sōkichi Zenshū 5*. Iwanami shoten, 1964.

Tsuji Zennosuke. *Nihon bukkyō shi: chūsei hen*. 3 vols. Iwanami shoten, 1947–49.

Uchida Keiichi. "Hachiji Monjū gazō no zuzōgaku teki kōsatsu." *Nanto bukkyō* 58 (1987): 39–59.

———. "Saidaiji Eizon oyobi Saidaiji ryū no Monjū shinkō to sono zōzō." *Bijutsushi kenkyū* 26 (1988): 42–61.

Uejima Tamotsu. *Kyōkō shōen sonraku no kenkyū*. Hanawa shobō, 1970.

Urushihara Tōru. "Nanbokuchō-jidai ni okeru shugo kengen no ichikōsatsu." *Komonjo kenkyū* 38, no. 3 (1994).

———. "Nanbokuchō shingi ni okeru shugo kengen no ichikōsatsu." *Komonjo kenkyū* 27, no. 7 (1987): 57–72.

Usuda Noboru et al., eds. *Nihon no shisō 1–2*. Shin Nihon shuppansha, 1980.

Wajima Yoshio. *Chūsei no jugaku*. Yoshikawa kōbunkan, 1965.

———. *Nihon Sōgaku shi no kenkyū*. Yoshikawa kōbunkan, 1962.

Wakita Haruko. "Chūsei kōki, machi ni okeru 'onna no isshō'." In *Nihon josei seikatsushi 2*, Joseishi sōgō kenkyūkai, ed., 147–86. Tōkyō daigaku shuppankai, 1990.

———. "Chūsei ni okeru seibetsu yakuwari buntan to joseikan." In *Nihon joseishi 2*, Joseishi sōgō kenkyūkai, ed., 65–102. Tōkyō daigaku shuppankai, 1982.

———. *Nihon chūsei joseishi no kenkyū: seiteki yakuwari buntan to bosei, kaisei, seiai.* Tōkyō daigaku shuppankai, 1992.

Yagi Seiya. "Muromachi shoki no onryō shisō—Tenryūji sōken wo megutte." *Bunka shigaku* 49 (1993): 1–20.

Yamagishi Tokuhei et al., eds. *Kodai seiji shakai shisō.* Iwanami shoten, 1979.

Yamaguchi Takamasa. "Kunijōshi ni tsuite." In *Chūsei Kyūshū no seiji shakai kōzō.* Yoshikawa kōbunkan, 1988.

———. *Nanbokuchōki Kyūshū shugo no kenkyū.* Bunken shuppan, 1989.

Yamamoto Takashi. "Rōnin to chūsei sonraku." *Shichō* Shin 4 go (1979).

Yamamoto Takeo. *Kikō no kataru Nihon no rekishi.* Sōshiete, 1976.

Yanagida Seizan. *Nihon no zen goroku, 7 Musō.* Kodansha, 1977.

———. "Yōsai to *Kōzen gokoku ron* no kadai." In *Chūsei zenke no shisō*, Ichikawa Hakugen and Yanagida Seizan, eds., 439–86. Iwanami shoten, 1972.

Yasuda Motohisa. *Shōen.* Kondō shuppansha, 1977.

Yoshida Toshihiro. "Chūsei sonraku no kōzō to sono henyō katei—shōson='sankyōgata sonraku' ron no rekishi chirigakuteki sankentō." *Shirin* 66, no. 3 (1983).

———. "Sōson no tenkai to tochi riyō—Tokuchinho no Imabori gō no rekishi chirigakuteki monogurafu to shite." *Shirin* 61, no. 6 (1978): 122–49.

Yōkaichi shishi hensan iinkai, ed. *Yōkaichi shishi 2, chūsei.* Yōkaichi shiyakusho, 1983.

Yoshie Akio. "Shoki chūsei sonraku no keisei." In *Kōza Nihonshi 2, Hōken shakai no seiritsu.* Nihonshi kenkyūkai Rekishigaku kenkyūkai, ed. Tōkyō daigaku shuppankai, 1970.

Zusetsu Nihon bunkashi taikei. Edited by Shōgakkan. Vols. 1–13 plus 12 supplements (*bekkan*). Shōgakkan, 1957.

Sources in Western Languages

Arnesen, Peter Judd. "The Provincial Vassals of the Muromachi Shoguns." In *The Bakufu in Japanese History*, Jeffrey P. Mass and William Hauser, eds., 99–128. Stanford, Calif.: Stanford University Press, 1985.

———. "The Struggle for Lordship in Late Heian Japan: The Case of Aki." *Journal of Japanese Studies* 10, no. 1 (winter 1984): 101–41.

Beasley, W. G., and E. G. Pulleyblank, eds. *Historians of China and Japan.* London: Oxford University Press, 1961.

Bielefeldt, Carl. *Dōgen's Manuals of Zen Meditation.* Berkeley: University of California Press, 1988.

———. "Filling the Zen Shū: Notes on the *Jisshū yōdō ki.*" *Cahiers d'Extrême Asie* 7 (1993–94): 221–48.

Bodiford, William M. *Sōtō Zen in Medieval Japan. Studies in East Asian Buddhism: A Kuroda Institute Book.* Honolulu: University of Hawaii Press, 1993.

Bol, Peter K. "Government, Society, and State: On the Political Visions of Ssu-ma Kuang and Wang An-shih." In *Ordering the World: Approaches to State and Society in Sung Dynasty China*, Robert P. Hymes and Conrad Schirokauer, eds., 128–92. Berkeley: University of California Press, 1993.

Boserup, Ester. *Population and Technological Change: A Study of Long-term Trends.* Chicago: University of Chicago Press, 1981.

Boston Art Museum, ed. *Courtly Splendor: Twelve Centuries of Treasures from Japan.* Boston: Boston Art Museum, 1990.

Bourdieu, Pierre. *Outline of a Theory of Practice.* Translated by Richard Nice. Cambridge: Cambridge University Press, 1977.

Brazell, Karen, trans. *The Confessions of Lady Nijō.* Stanford, Calif.: Stanford University Press, 1973.

Brown, Delmer M. "The Japanese Tokusei of 1297." *Harvard Journal of Asiatic Studies* 12 (1949): 188–206.

Brownlee, John S. *Japanese Historians and the National Myths, 1600–1945.* Forthcoming.

————, ed. *History in the Service of the Japanese Nation.* Toronto: University of Toronto–York University Joint Centre on Modern East Asia, 1983.

————. *Political Thought in Japanese Historical Writing: From* Kojiki *(712) to* Tokushi yoron *(1712).* Waterloo, Ont.: Wilfred Laurier University Press, 1991.

Brundage, James A. "Rape and Seduction in the Medieval Canon Law." In *Sexual Practices and the Medieval Church*, Vern L. Bullough and James Brundage, eds., 141–48. Buffalo, N.Y.: Prometheus Books, 1982.

Carter, Steven D. "Ichijō Kaneyoshi and the Literary Arts." In *Literary Patronage in Late Medieval Japan*, Steven D. Carter, ed., 19–44. Ann Arbor: University of Michigan Center for Japanese Studies, 1993.

Cohen, Abner. *Two Dimensional Man: An Essay on the Anthropology of Power and Symbolism in Complex Society.* Berkeley: University of California Press, 1976.

Collcutt, Martin. *Five Mountains: The Rinzai Zen Monastic Institution in Medieval Japan.* Cambridge, Mass.: Harvard University Press, 1981.

Craig, Albert. *Chōshū in the Meiji Restoration, 1853–1868.* Cambridge, Mass.: Harvard University Press, 1961.

de Bary, William Theodore, et al., eds. *Sources of Chinese Tradition.* New York: Columbia University Press, 1960.

de Man, Paul. *Blindness and Insight.* Minneapolis: University of Minnesota Press, 1983.

Ebrey, Patricia. *The Aristocratic Families of Early Imperial China: A Case Study of the Po-ling Ts'ui Family.* Cambridge: Cambridge University Press, 1978.

Fairbank, John King. *China: A New History.* Cambridge, Mass.: Belnap Press, 1992.

Farris, William Wayne. *Heavenly Warriors: The Evolution of Japan's Military, 500 to 1300.* Cambridge, Mass.: Harvard University Press, 1992.

———. *Population, Disease, and Land in Early Japan, 645–900.* Cambridge, Mass.: Harvard University Press, 1985.

Foard, James. "Prefiguration and Narrative in Medieval Hagiography." In *Flowing Traces,* William LaFleur, James Sanford, and Masatoshi Nagatomi, eds., 76–92. Princeton, N.J.: Princeton University Press, 1992.

Foucault, Michel. *The Foucault Reader,* ed. Paul Rabinow. New York: Pantheon Books, 1984.

———. *The Order of Things: An Archaeology of the Human Sciences.* New York: Random House, 1970.

Friday, Karl. *Hired Swords: The Rise of Private Warrior Power in Early Japan.* Stanford, Calif.: Stanford University Press, 1992.

Fuller, Richard E. *Japanese Art in the Seattle Art Museum.* Seattle: Seattle Art Museum, 1960.

Gay, Suzanne. "The Kawashima: Warrior-Peasants of Medieval Japan." *Harvard Journal of Asiatic Studies* 46 (1986): 81–119.

———. "The Muromachi Bakufu in Medieval Kyoto." Ph.D. dissertation, Yale University, 1982.

———. "Muromachi Bakufu Rule in Kyoto: Administrative and Judicial Aspects." In *The Bakufu in Japanese History,* Jeffrey P. Mass and William B. Hauser, eds., 49–65. Stanford, Calif.: Stanford University Press, 1985.

Goble, Andrew. "Go-Daigo and the Kemmu Restoration." Ph.D. dissertation, Stanford University, 1987.

———. *Kenmu: Go-Daigo's Revolution.* Cambridge, Mass.: Harvard University Press, 1997.

———. "Social Change, Knowledge, and History: Hanazono's *Admonitions to the Crown Prince.*" *Harvard Journal of Asiatic Studies* 55, no. 1 (1995): 61–128.

———. "Truth, Contradiction, and Harmony in Medieval Japan: Emperor Hanazono (1297–1348) and Buddhism." *Journal of the International Association of Buddhist Studies* 12, no. 1 (1989): 21–63.

Goddard, Victoria. "Honour and Shame: The Control of Women's Sexuality and Group Identity in Naples." In *The Cultural Construction of Sexuality,* Pat Caplan, ed., 166–92. New York: Routledge, 1989.

Goodwin, Janet. *Alms and Vagabonds: Buddhist Temples and Popular Patronage in Medieval Japan.* Honolulu: University of Hawaii Press, 1994.

The Gossamer Years: The Diary of a Noblewoman of Heian Japan. Translated by Edward Seidensticker. Rutland, Vt.: Tuttle, 1973.

Grapard, Alan. *The Protocol of the Gods.* Berkeley: University of California Press, 1993.

Grossberg, Kenneth A. "From Feudal Chieftan to Secular Monarch: The Development of Shogunal Power in Early Muromachi Japan." *Monumenta Nipponica* 30, no. 1 (1976): 24–49.

Grossberg, Kenneth A., and Kanamoto Nobuhisa, trans. *Laws of the Muromachi*

Bakufu: Kenmu Shikimoku and the Muromachi Tsuika-hō. Tokyo: Monumenta Nipponica and Sophia University Press, 1981.

Hall, John W., and Toyoda Takeshi, eds. *Japan in the Muromachi Age.* Berkeley: University of California Press, 1977.

Hare, Thomas Blenman. *Zeami's Style.* Stanford, Calif.: Stanford University Press, 1986.

Harries, Phillip. *The Poetic Memoirs of Lady Daibu.* Stanford, Calif.: Stanford University Press, 1980.

Harrington, Lorraine F. "Regional Administration Under the Ashikaga Bakufu: Power and Politics Outside the Central Provinces." Ph.D. dissertation, Stanford University, 1983.

————. "Social Control and the Significance of *Akutō.*" In *Court and Bakufu in Japan,* Jeffrey P. Mass, ed., 221–50. New Haven, Conn.: Yale University Press, 1982.

Hori, Kyotsu. "The Mongol Invasions and the Kamakura Bakufu." Ph.D. dissertation, Columbia University, 1967.

Hosokawa Ryōichi. "Medieval Nuns and Nunneries: The Case of Hokkeji." In *Women and Class in Japanese History,* Hitomi Tonomura, Anne Walthal, and Haruko Wakita, eds. Ann Arbor: University of Michigan Center for Japanese Studies, forthcoming.

Huey, Robert. "The Kingyoku Poetry Contest." *Monumenta Nipponica* 42, no. 3 (autumn 1987): 299–330.

————. *Kyōgoku Tamekane: Poetry and Politics in Late Kamakura Japan.* Stanford, Calif.: Stanford University Press, 1989.

————. "The Medievalization of Poetic Practice." *Harvard Journal of Asiatic Studies* 50, no. 2 (December 1990): 651–68.

Hurst, J. Cameron, III. "Death, Honor, and Loyalty: The Bushidō Ideal." *Philosophy East and West* 40, no. 4 (October 1990).

————. "The Good, the Bad, and the Ugly: Personalities in the Founding of the Koryo Dynasty." *Korean Studies Forum,* no. 7 (spring-summer 1979).

————. "The Kōbu Polity: Court-Bakufu Relations in the Kamakura Era." In *Court and Bakufu in Japan,* Jeffrey P. Mass, ed., 3–28. New Haven, Conn.: Yale University Press, 1982.

————. "The Quest for Records: Japanese Archery as Competition." Unpublished paper, 1994.

Hymes, Robert P., and Conrad Schirokauer, eds. *Ordering the World: Approaches to State and Society in Sung Dynasty China.* Berkeley: University of California Press, 1993.

Imatani Akira, with Kozo Yamamura. "Not for Lack of Will or Wile: Yoshimitsu's Failure to Supplant the Imperial Lineage." *Journal of Japanese Studies* 18, no. 1 (1992): 45–76.

Ishida Ichirō. "Structure and Formation of *Gukanshō* Thought." In *The Future* and the Past: A Translation and Interpretation of the Gukanshō, an Interpretive History of Japan Written in 1219, Delmer Brown and Ichirō Ishida, eds. Berkeley: University of California Press, 1979.

Jan, Yün-hua. "Buddhist Historiography in Sung China." *Deutsche Morgenländische Gessellschaft, Zeitschrift* 114, no. 2 (1964): 360–81.

Katō Shūichi. *Geschichte der japanischen Literatur*. Darmstadt: Wissenschafteliche Buchgesellschaft, 1990.

Kauffmann, Laura. "Ippen hijiri e." Ph.D. dissertation, New York University, 1980.

———. "Nature, Courtly Imagery, and Sacred Meaning in the *Ippen Hijiri-e*." In *Flowing Traces*, William LaFleur, Masatoshi Nagatomi, and James Sanford, eds., 47–75. Princeton, N.J.: Princeton University Press, 1992.

Keene, Donald. "The Comic Tradition in Renga." In *Japan in the Muromachi Age*, John W. Hall and Toyoda Takeshi, eds., 241–77. Berkeley: University of California Press, 1977.

———, trans. *Essays in Idleness: The* Tsurezuregusa *of Kenkō*. New York: Columbia University Press, 1967.

Keirstead, Thomas. *The Geography of Power in Medieval Japan*. Princeton, N.J.: Princeton University Press, 1992.

Ketelaar, James E. *Of Heretics and Martyrs in Meiji Japan: Buddhism and Its Persecution*. Princeton, N.J.: Princeton University Press, 1990.

Kiley, Cornelius J. "The Imperial Court as Legal Authority in the Kamakura Age." In *Court and Bakufu in Japan*, Jeffrey P. Mass, ed., 29–44. New Haven, Conn.: Yale University Press, 1982.

Kraft, Kenneth. *Eloquent Zen: Daitō and Early Japanese Zen*. Honolulu: University of Hawaii Press, 1992.

———. "Musō Kokushi's *Dialogues in a Dream*." *Eastern Buddhist (New Series)* 14, no. 1 (1981): 75–93.

LaCapra, Dominick. *Soundings in Critical Theory*. Ithaca, N.Y.: Cornell University Press, 1989.

Legge, James, trans. *The Chinese Classics*. 5 vols. Hong Kong: Hong Kong University Press, 1961.

———. *Li Chi: Book of Rites*. New Hyde Park, N.Y.: University Books, 1967.

Leyser, Karl. *Rule and Conflict in an Early Medieval Society*. Oxford: Basil Blackwell, 1989.

Liu, James T. C. "Yueh Fei (1103–1141) and China's Heritage of Loyalty." *Journal of Asian Studies* 31, no. 2 (1972).

Marra, Michele. *Representations of Power: The Literary Politics of Medieval Japan*. Honolulu: University of Hawaii Press, 1993.

Maruyama Masao. *Studies in the Intellectual History of Tokugawa Japan*. Translated by Mikiso Hane. Tokyo: University of Tokyo Press, 1974.

Mass, Jeffrey P. *Antiquity and Anachronism in Japanese History*. Stanford, Calif.: Stanford University Press, 1992.

————. *The Development of Kamakura Rule, 1180–1250: A History with Documents.* Stanford, Calif.: Stanford University Press, 1979.

————. "*Jitō* Land Possession in the Thirteenth Century: The Case of Shitaji Chūbun." In *Medieval Japan: Essays in Institutional History*, John W. Hall and Jeffrey P. Mass, eds., 157–83. Stanford, Calif.: Stanford University Press, 1974.

————. "The Kamakura Bakufu." In *The Cambridge History of Japan*, vol. 3, *Medieval Japan*, Kozo Yamamura, ed., 46–88. Cambridge: Cambridge University Press, 1990.

————. *The Kamakura Bakufu: A Study in Documents.* Stanford, Calif.: Stanford University Press, 1976.

————. *Lordship and Inheritance in Early Medieval Japan: A Study of the Kamakura Soryō System.* Stanford, Calif.: Stanford University Press, 1989.

————. "The Missing Minamoto in the Twelfth-Century Kanto." *Journal of Japanese Studies* 19, no. 1 (winter 1993): 121–46.

————. "Patterns of Provincial Inheritance in Late Heian Japan." *Journal of Japanese Studies* 9, no. 1 (winter 1983): 67–95.

————. *Warrior Government in Early Medieval Japan: A Study of the Kamakura Bakufu, Shugo, and Jitō.* New Haven, Conn.: Yale University Press, 1974.

————, ed. *Court and Bakufu in Japan: Essays in Kamakura History.* New Haven, Conn.: Yale University Press, 1982.

Mauss, Marcel. *The Gift.* Translated by W. D. Hall. New York: W. W. Norton, 1990.

McCullough, Helen Craig, trans. *The Taiheiki: A Chronicle of Medieval Japan.* New York: Columbia University Press, 1959.

————. *The Tale of the Heike.* Stanford, Calif.: Stanford University Press, 1988.

McCullough, William H. "Japanese Marriage Institutions in the Heian Period." *Harvard Journal of Asiatic Studies* 27 (1967): 103–67.

McKean, Margaret A. "Japanese Experience with Scarcity: Management of Traditional Common Lands." *Environmental Review* 6 (1982): 63–88.

————. "Management of Traditional Common Lands (*iriaichi*) in Japan." Paper presented at the Proceedings of the Conference on Common Property Resource Management, April 21–26, 1985, Annapolis, Md.

————. "A Success on the Commons: A Comparative Examination of Institutions for Common Property Resource Management." *Journal of Theoretical Politics* 4.3 (1992): 247–81.

McMullen, I. J. "Rulers or Fathers? A Casuistical Problem in Early Modern Japanese Thought." *Past and Present*, no. 116 (August 1987).

McMullin, Neil. *Buddhism and the State in Sixteenth-Century Japan.* Princeton, N.J.: Princeton University Press, 1984.

————. "Historical and Historiographical Issues in the Study of Pre-Modern Japanese Religions." *Japanese Journal of Religions Studies* 16, no. 1 (1989): 3–40.

McNamara, Jo Ann. "Chaste Marriage and Clerical Celibacy." In *Sexual Practices and the Medieval Church*, Vern L. Bullough and James Brundage, eds., 22–33. Buffalo, N.Y.: Prometheus Books, 1982.

Miner, Earl, Hiroko Odagiri, and Robert E. Morell, eds. *The Princeton Companion to Classical Japanese Literature*. Princeton, N.J.: Princeton University Press, 1985.

Morrell, Robert. *Early Kamakura Buddhism: A Minority Report*. Berkeley, Calif.: Asian Humanities Press, 1987.

Murai Yasuhiko. "The Development of *Chanoyu*: Before Rikyū." In *Tea in Japan: Essays on the History of Chanoyu*, H. Paul Varley and Kumakura Isao, eds. Honolulu: University of Hawaii Press, 1989.

Murdoch, James. *A History of Japan*, vol. 1. Kobe: "The Chronicle," 1910.

Nagahara Keiji. "Village Communities and Daimyo Power." In *Japan in the Muromachi Age*, John W. Hall and Toyoda Takeshi, eds., 107–23. Berkeley: University of California Press, 1977.

Nakai, Kate Wildman. *Shogunal Politics: Arai Hakuseki and the Premises of Tokugawa Rule*. Cambridge, Mass.: Harvard University Press, 1988.

———. "Tokugawa Confucian Historiography: The Hayashi, Early Mito School, and Arai Hakuseki." In *Confucianism and Tokugawa Culture*, Peter Nosco, ed., 62–91. Princeton, N.J.: Princeton University Press, 1984.

Nattier, Jan. *Once upon a Future Time: Studies in a Buddhist Prophecy of Decline. Nanzan Studies in Asian Religions 1*. Berkeley, Calif.: Asian Humanities Press, 1991.

Nickerson, Peter. "The Meaning of Matrilocality: Kinship, Property, and Politics in Mid-Heian." *Monumenta Nipponica* 48, no. 4 (winter 1993): 429–67.

Philippi, Donald L., trans. *Kojiki*. Tokyo: Tokyo University Press, 1968.

Piggott, Joan. "Tōdaiji and the Nara Imperium." Ph.D. dissertation, Stanford University, 1987.

Pollack, David. *The Fracture of Meaning: Japan's Synthesis of China from the Eighth Through the Eighteenth Centuries*. Princeton, N.J.: Princeton University Press, 1986.

———. *Zen Poems of the Five Mountains*. Edited by American Academy of Religion. "Studies in Religion 37." New York: Crossroad, 1985.

Popkin, Samuel L. *The Rational Peasant: The Political Economy of Rural Society in Vietnam*. Berkeley: University of California Press, 1979.

Pruden, Leo. "The *Hasshū kōyō* by the Scholar-Monk Gyōnen (1240–1321)." *The Pacific World* (journal of the Institute of Buddhist Studies, Berkeley, Calif.), New Series 7, 8, 9 (1991, 1992, 1993): 53–67; 61–83; 106–36.

Pulleyblank, E. G. "Chinese Historical Criticism: Liu Chih-chi and Ssu-ma Kuang." In *Historians of China and Japan*, W. G. Beasley and E. G. Pulleyblank, eds. London: Oxford University Press, 1961.

Raybin, David. "Aesthetics, Romance, and Turner." In *Victor Turner and the Construction of Cultural Criticism: Between Literature and Anthropology*, Kathleen M. Ashley, ed., 21–41. Bloomington: Indiana University Press, 1990.

Reischauer, Edwin O., and Albert Craig. *Japan: Tradition and Transformation.* Boston: Houghton Mifflin, 1989.

Rimer, Thomas, and Yamazaki Masakazu, eds. *On the Art of the Nō Drama.* Princeton, N.J.: Princeton University Press, 1984.

Rogers, Michael C. "The Chinese World Order in Its Transmural Extension: The Case of Chin and Koryo." *Korean Studies Forum,* no. 4 (spring–summer 1978).

Rosenfield, John. "The Unity of the Three Creeds." In *Japan in the Muromachi Age,* John W. Hall and Toyoda Takeshi, eds. Berkeley: University of California Press, 1977.

Ruch, Barbara. "Coping with Death: Paradigms of Heaven and Hell and the Six Realms in Early Literature and Painting." In *Flowing Traces: Buddhism in the Literary and Visual Arts of Japan,* William R. LaFleur, Masatoshi Nagatomi, and James H. Sanford, eds., 91–130. Princeton, N.J.: Princeton University Press, 1992.

———. "The Other Side of Culture." In *The Cambridge History of Japan,* vol. 3, *Medieval Japan,* Kozo Yamamura, ed., 500–543. Cambridge: Cambridge University Press, 1990.

Ryavec, Carole Ann. "Political Jurisdiction in the Sengoku Daimyō Domain: Japan, 1477–1573." Ph.D. dissertation, Columbia University, 1978.

Ryusaku Tsunoda et al., eds. *Sources of Japanese Tradition.* Vol. 1. New York: Columbia University Press, 1958.

Sanford, James. "The Abominable Tachikawa Skull Ritual." *Monumenta Nipponica* 46 (1991): 1–20.

Sansom, George. *A History of Japan, 1334–1615.* Stanford, Calif.: Stanford University Press, 1961.

Sariti, Anthony William. "Monarchy, Bureaucracy, and Absolutism in the Political Thought of Ssu-ma Kuang." *Journal of Asian Studies* 32, no. 1 (November 1972): 53–76.

Schirokauer, Conrad. "Chu Hsi's Sense of History." In *Ordering the World: Approaches to State and Society in Sung Dynasty China,* Robert P. Hymes and Conrad Schirokauer, eds. Berkeley: University of California Press, 1993.

Schlesinger, Walter. "Lord and Follower in Germanic Institutional History." In *Lordship and Community in Medieval Europe,* Fredric L. Cheyette, ed., 65–99. New York: Holt, Rinehart, and Winston, 1968.

Smith, Thomas C. *Agrarian Origins of Modern Japan.* Stanford, Calif.: Stanford University Press, 1959.

Smyers, Karen A. "Women and Shinto: The Relation Between Purity and Pollution." *Japanese Religions* 12, no. 4 (July 1983): 7–19.

Steenstrup, Carl. *Hōjō Shigetoki (1198–1261) and His Role in the History of Political and Ethical Ideas in Japan.* London: Curzon Press, 1979.

———. "*Sata Mirensho*: A Fourteenth-Century Law Primer." *Monumenta Nipponica* 35 (1980): 405–35.

Takemi Momoko. " 'Menstruation Sutra' Belief in Japan." *Journal of Japanese Religious Studies* 10 (June–September 1983): 229–46.

Teeuwen, Mark. "Attaining Union with the Gods: The Secret Books of Watari Shinto." *Monumenta Nipponica* 48 (1993): 225–45.

Tonomura, Hitomi. "Black Hair and Red Trousers: Gendering the Flesh in Medieval Japan." *American Historical Review* 99, no. 1 (February 1994): 129–54.

————. *Community and Commerce in Late Medieval Japan: The Corporate Villages of Tokuchin-ho*. Stanford, Calif.: Stanford University Press, 1992.

————. "Sexual Violence Against Women: Legal and Extralegal Treatment in Premodern Japan." In *Women and Class in Japanese History*, Hitomi Tonomura, Anne Walthall, and Haruko Wakita, eds. Ann Arbor: University of Michigan Center for Japanese Studies, forthcoming.

————. "Women and Inheritance in Japan's Early Warrior Society." *Comparative Studies in Society and History* 32, no. 3 (1990): 592–623.

Toyoda Takeshi and Sugiyama Hiroshi. "The Growth of Commerce and Trade." In *Japan in the Muromachi Age*, John W. Hall and Toyoda Takeshi, eds., 129–44. Berkeley: University of California Press, 1972.

Troost, Kristina Kade. "Common Property and Community Formation: Self-Governing Villages in Late Medieval Japan, 1300–1600." Ph.D. dissertation, Harvard University, 1990.

————. "The Evolution of Self-Governing Villages: From Festivals to Common Land." Presented at the 47th Annual Meeting of the Association for Asian Studies, 1995.

Turner, Victor. *Dramas, Fields, and Metaphors*. Ithaca, N.Y.: Cornell University Press, 1974.

Twitchett, Denis, and John K. Fairbank, eds. *The Cambridge History of China*, vol. 3, *Sui and T'ang China, 589–906*. Cambridge: Cambridge University Press, 1979.

Tyler, Royall. *Miracles of the Kasuga Deity*. New York: Columbia University Press, 1990.

Ury, Marian. "*Genkō Shakusho*, Japan's First Comprehensive History of Buddhism: A Partial Translation with Introduction and Notes." Ph.D. dissertation, University of California, Berkeley, 1970.

Uyenaka, Shuzo. "Last Testament in Exile: Yamaga Sokō's *Haisho zampitsu*." *Monumenta Nipponica* 32, no. 2 (summer 1977).

————. "A Study of *Baishōron*: A Source for the Ideology of Imperial Loyalty in Medieval Japan." Ph.D. dissertation, University of Toronto, 1979.

————. "The Textbook Controversy of 1911: National Needs and Historical Truth." In *History in the Service of the Japanese Nation*, John S. Brownlee, ed., 94–123. Toronto: University of Toronto–York University Joint Centre on Modern East Asia, 1983.

Varley, H. Paul. "Ashikaga Yoshimitsu and the World of Kitayama." In *Japan in the Muromachi Age*, John W. Hall and Toyoda Takeshi, eds. Berkeley: University of California Press, 1977.

———. *A Chronicle of Gods and Sovereigns: Jinnō Shōtōki of Kitabatake Chikafusa.* New York: Columbia University Press, 1980.

———. *Imperial Restoration in Medieval Japan.* New York: Columbia University Press, 1971.

———. *The Ōnin War.* New York: Columbia University Press, 1967.

———. *Warriors of Japan as Portrayed in the War Tales.* Honolulu: University of Hawaii Press, 1994.

Wade, Robert. *Village Republics: Economic Conditions for Collective Action in South India.* Cambridge: Cambridge University Press, 1988.

Wakita Haruo, with Susan B. Hanley. "Dimensions of Development: Cities in Fifteenth- and Sixteenth-Century Japan." In *Japan Before Tokugawa: Political Consolidation and Economic Growth*, John W. Hall, Nagahara Keiji, and Kozo Yamamura, eds., 295–326. Princeton, N.J.: Princeton University Press, 1981.

Watson, Burton, trans. *Records of the Grand Historian of China.* New York: Columbia University Press, 1961.

Webb, Herschel. "What Is the *Dai Nihon shi*?" *Journal of Asian Studies* 19, no. 2 (1960): 135–49.

Wechsler, Howard J. *Offerings of Jade and Silk: Ritual and Symbol in the Legitimation of the T'ang Dynasty.* New Haven, Conn.: Yale University Press, 1985.

———. "T'ai-tsung the Consolidator." In *The Cambridge History of China*, vol. 3, *Sui and T'ang China*, 589–906, Denis Twitchett and John K. Fairbank, eds. Cambridge: Cambridge University Press, 1979.

Weir, Alison. *The Princes in the Tower.* London: Bodley Head, 1992.

Wilson, William S. *The Ideals of the Samurai: Writings of Japanese Warriors.* Burbank, Calif.: Ohara Publications, 1982.

Wintersteen, Prescott B. "The Early Muromachi *Bakufu* in Kyoto." In *Medieval Japan: Essays in Institutional History*, John W. Hall and Jeffrey P. Mass, eds. Stanford, Calif.: Stanford University Press, 1988.

———. "The Muromachi *Shugo* and *Hanzei*." In *Medieval Japan: Essays in Institutional History*, John W. Hall and Jeffrey P. Mass, eds. Stanford, Calif.: Stanford University Press, 1988.

Wrigley, Edward Anthony. *Population and History.* New York: McGraw-Hill, 1969.

Yamamura, Kozo. "The Development of Za in Medieval Japan." *Business History Review* 47, no. 4 (1973): 438–65.

———. "The Growth of Commerce in Medieval Japan." In *The Cambridge History of Japan*, vol. 3, Kozo Yamamura, ed., 344–95. Cambridge: Cambridge University Press, 1990.

———. "Tara in Transition: A Study of Kamakura Shoen." *Journal of Japanese Studies* 7, no. 2 (1981): 349–91.

———, ed. *The Cambridge History of Japan*, vol. 3, *Medieval Japan*. Cambridge: Cambridge University Press, 1990.

Yampolsky, Philip. "Hattō Kokushi's *Dharma Talks.*" *Cahiers d'Extrême-Asie* 7 (1993–94): 249–65.

Yanagisako, Sylvia J., and Jane F. Collier. "The Mode of Reproduction in Anthropology." In *Theoretical Perspectives on Sexual Difference*, Deborah L. Rhode, ed., 131–41. New Haven, Conn.: Yale University Press, 1990.

Index

Abutsu (Abutsu-ni), 182, 276–77
"Admonitions to the Crown Prince"
   (*Kaitaishi sho*, Hanazono), 133–34
Adolphson, Mikael, 4, 10–12, 443n15
Adultery, 155–57, 417nn69,71,75
Advice manuals (*kakun*): on civil/military
   balance, 10, 216–17, 220–21; of
   Takauji, 10, 214–17, 369n7; on
   Sovereign-subject relationship, 215;
   on training of the mind, 218–19;
   Yoshisadaki compared to, 221–22
Age of the Northern and Southern
   Courts, *see* Nanbokuchō period
Agriculture: intensified technology
   in, 6, 90–91, 93–94, 95–96, 108,
   392n2, 393nn19,22,24, 394nn25,33,34;
   increased productivity in, 46, 97,
   395nn41,42, 395–96n47; and irriga-
   tion methods, 94–95, 394n30; and
   rise of smallholders, 97–98, 395n40,
   396nn49,50; historiographical empha-
   sis on, 361f
Aida Nirō, 351
Aizen myō/ō, 126, 407n59
Ajia no naka no chūsei Nihon (Medieval
   Japan Within East Asia, Murai), 363
Akamatsu family, 80, 84
Akiie (Kitabatake), 43, 58, 225
Akinori (Isshiki), 86
Akitsura (Betsugi), 232–33
Akiuji (Hosokawa), 50, 56, 383n89
Akugyō (iniquitous deeds), 27
Aku-kuchi (bad-mouthing), 27
Akusō (evil priests), 42, 245

Akutō (bandit gangs), 26–27, 356, 358–59,
   372nn35,36,38, 372–73n43, 373n44
"Akutō to sono jidai" (*Akutō* and Its
   Period, Kuroda), 358–59
Amagasaki (Settsu), 94
Amaterasu ōmikami (progenitress of the
   imperial family), 125, 126–27
Amida worship, 299
Amino Yoshihiko, 93, 161, 345–46, 358,
   361–62, 364, 392n10, 418n92
Ancient practices, *see Kojitsu*
Andō family, 119, 403n28
Andō of Tsugaru, 45
Ankokuji (Temples for Peace in the
   Realm), 287–89
Annen, 307
Ansai (Yamazaki), 331–32, 335
Anthologies, *see* Imperial anthologies
Antoku, Emperor, 404n33
Arai Hakuseki, 321, 339, 344
Archery, *see* Mounted archery
Aristocratic women: public documents
   by, 142–43, 144, 412n17; diminished
   property rights of, 146, 148, 150–51. *See
   also* Women; Women's writing
Arnesen, Peter, 40
Artistic production, 118, 201, 402nn21,22.
   See also Go-Daigo, Emperor, portraits
   of
Asaka Tanpaku, 342
Asakawa Kan'ichi, 371n12
Ashikaga Bakufu: *shugo* policies of, 6,
   79–81, 84–88, 89–90, 390nn21,27;
   Keisai on, 13, 335–36; in Nanbokuchō

Wars, 70–77 *passim*; factional feuds
within, 83–84; *shisetsu* system of, 89–
90; Go-Daigo's antipathy toward, 115–
16, 127, 135, 407n63; Musō on, 116–17;
Shōtoku taishi and, 124; Hino wives
of, 139; intervention in anthologies
by, 185, 188–91, 426n56, 426–27n59;
and Nanzenji Gate incident, 237, 250f,
437n59; as Zen patrons, 248–52, 259,
281, 282–83, 284–85, 291; toll gate authority of, 250, 256; control of guilds
by, 253–54, 256–57; confirmation
of temple land by, 255–56; maintenance of *kenmon* system by, 255–56;
containment of Enryakuji by, 257–59,
286, 438nn79,82, 438–39n83; Ankokuji and Rishōtō network of, 287–89.
See also Kenmu shikimoku; Tadayoshi
(Ashikaga); Takauji (Ashikaga)
Ashikaga collaterals, 6; regional lordships
vs., 42, 52; mobilization success of, 49–
50; symbolic capital of, 52f, 61, 63; use
of rewards by, 52–55, 56–57, 62, 87,
381–82n71, 382n72, 390n26; as agents
of Bakufu, 81–82; Kannō Disturbance
and, 83–84, 388–89n11, 389nn13,14; in
Kamakura period, 389n12
*Ashikaga ichimon shugo hatten-shi no
kenkyū* (The Study of Shugo Develop-
ment, Ogawa), 364–65
Aso Koresumi, 379n28
Asukai family, 172
Atsuta Shrine, 360
Awa Province, 31
Azuma kagami, 152, 227

Baishōron, 53–54, 56, 72ff, 75, 378n16
Bajutsu (equestrian skills), 233, 433n80.
See also Mounted archery
Ban Biao, 133
Basara (extravagance), 9, 194–96, 211–12,
429n9. *See also* Dōyo (Sasaki)
Bendō wa (Dōgen), 304
Ben'en Enni, *see* Shōichi Kokushi
Bielefeldt, Carl, 4, 12
Bingo Province, 80, 89
Birth process, 163, 164–65

Bitō family, 82
Bitō Masahide, 337
Blood Bowl Sutra (*ketsubonkyō*), 164–65,
419n98, 420nn105,106
Bodhidharma: lineage tradition of, 303,
305–7, 316–17, 445nn33,34
Bol, Peter, 325
Boserup, Ester, 95–96
Bōshonin (forgers), 27
Bourdieu, Pierre, 420–21n114
Brower, Robert, 171
Brownlee, John, 321
Buddhas: Go-Daigo as, 130; mothers of,
162
Buddhism: Gyōnen's historiography of, 12, 299–300, 311, 444n19;
Shiren's revisioning of, 12, 311f, 313–
17, 444nn26,28; Go-Daigo's sovereign
ties to, 116, 125, 126–27, 130f; and warrior preparedness, 218; Musō's early
training in, 263, 267, 269, 292–93;
mappō doctrine of, 296–97, 442n2;
eight orthodox forms of, 297–98, 311–
12, 317, 442n5; Bodhidharma lineage
of, 307, 316–17, 445n33. *See also* Buddhist establishment temples; Buddhist
schools; Zen; Zen monastery system
Buddhist establishment temples: Zen's
competition with, 11f, 244, 248–52,
303–4, 309, 433–34n1, 443n15; and
warrior status, 34, 35–36, 376n98; role
of, in *kenmon* system, 238, 241–42,
243, 359f; court's interdependence
with, 241–43, 245–46; in multidoctrinal system, 246–48; in hierarchical
arrangement, 248–52, 259; and Rishōtō
network of, 287–89; *kenmitsu* term for,
435n18; conflict between, 436n40. *See
also* Enryakuji temple
Buddhist schools: doctrinal classification of, 297–98, 311–12, 317, 442n5;
lineage tradition of, 299–300, 305–
6, 444n19. *See also Genkō shakusho*;
Shiren (Kokan)
Buke jiki (Encyclopedia of the Warrior
Houses, Sokō), 323, 339
Buke kojitsu (warrior customs): manuals

on, 10, 209, 213, 232f; Kamakura regard for, 226–27, 431–32n51, 432n54; Yoshimitsu's cultivation of, 228–29, 432nn58,61; nostalgic dimension of, 230, 233; to legitimize military regime, 230–31

Buke shohatto (1615), 210, 212, 222, 428–29n3

Bunbu ryōdo (civil and military arts): advice manuals on, 10, 209, 216–17, 220–21; Tokugawa code of, 210, 428–29n3; Kenmu codes of, 211–12; as separated functions, 222; Chinese source of, 223–24; courtiers' notion of, 224–25. *See also Buke kojitsu*; Warrior legislation

Bungo Province, 89

Bungun shugo (split *shugo* posts), 80, 86, 388n6. *See also Shugo*

Bunpō era, 183–84, 425n41

Bushi, see Warrior elite; Warrior poets

Bushidan (warrior league), 66

Bushidō (warrior codes), 214. *See also* Advice manuals; *Bunbu ryōdo*

Busshin shū ("Buddha Mind" school), 305

Butsugoshin ron (Shiren), 303

Byōgi ron (Shiren), 302–3, 443n10

Carter, Steven D., 410n5

Central Police Office (Kebiishi-chō), 20

Chan kuo tsē (Intrigues of the Warring States), 333

Ch'an monastic rule, 273

Chidon Kūjō, 265

Chih-p'an, 314, 444n28

"Chiikishi kenkyū no ichishiten" (One Perspective on the Study of Regional History, Amino), 362

Chikafusa (Kitabatake): on warriors, 52–53, 329; and Ishikawa homelands, 58–59; on aristocracy's role, 121; on regalia, 131; *bunbu* ideal of, 225; Confucian influence on, 225, 329, 431n47; on legitimacy, 328–29, 331, 335

Chikanaga (Kanroji), 150

Chikanaga kyōki (Chikanaga), 150

Chikatomo (Yūki), 59f, 384n106

Chikubashō (Shiba Yoshimasa), 214, 217–19

Chinese influence: on sovereignty/legitimacy notion, 131–33, 325–27; Blood Bowl Sutra, 164, 419n98; on cultural production, 201, 203; on fourteenth-century governance, 212, 225; on warriors' advice manuals, 216, 217–18, 220–21; on *bunbu* ideal, 223–25; on war tales, 224; of Zen émigré masters, 266–67, 308, 311; and Japanese Buddhism, 305–7, 312–15, 316–17; on historiographical style, 314–15, 324f, 444n28

Chinese language, 142, 412n15

Ch'ing-cho Cheng-ch'eng (Seisetsu Shōchō), 272–73

Ching ti, 327

Chinso, see Zen teachers

Chinzei Tandai, 67f, 69–70

Chisei no kimi (ruler of the land), 181, 423–24n30

Chokusenshū, see Imperial anthologies

Chou dynasty, 115, 132, 223, 326

Chu Hsi, 324f, 327, 331–38 *passim*, 343, 448n57

Chu-hsien Fan-hsien (Jikusen Bonsen), 273, 281f

Chūjō family, 79

Chūkō ruisetsu (Classified Views on Loyalty and Filial Piety, Keisai), 336

Chūkyō, Emperor, 404n33

Ch'un ch'iu (Confucius), 326, 332f

Chūsei nikki kikōshū (Iwasa Miyoko, ed.), 410n7

Chūsei ni okeru seishin seikatsu (The Spiritual Life in Medieval Japan, Hiraizumi), 349

Chūsei ni okeru shaji to shakai to no kankei (The Relationships Between Shrines and Temples, Hiraizumi), 349

"Chūsei no kokka to tennō" (The State and Emperor in Medieval Japan, Kuroda), 359

Chūsei shakai no kenkyū (Studies on Medieval Society, Matsumoto), 357

Chūseiteki sekai no keisei (The Formation

of the Medieval World, Ishimoda), 356

Chūsetsu (loyalty or service): as service for sale, 5, 41, 53; fourteenth-century versions of, 40–41, 377nn5,6, 378n7; landholding's relation to, 42, 44, 47–48; of *miuchi*, 43–45, 378nn14,16; of *tozama*, 47; of Motoharu, 52; and warriors' misguided alliances, 66–77 *passim*; in *Taiheiki*, 330. *See also* Rewards

Chūshōshi (Master of the Centered and Correct, Engetsu), 133

Collcutt, Martin, 11–12

Commoners, *see* Peasants

Common property, 96, 102, 394n36. *See also* Villages

Compromise of 1317 (Bunpō Wadan), 183f

Confucian influence: on Kenmu code, 211, 213–14; on advice manuals, 215–17 *passim*; on *bunbu ryōdō* ideal, 223–24; on Chikafusa, 225, 329, 431n47; of *jusō* (monks), 225, 431n46; on Keisai's historiography, 324–32 *passim*; decline of, 431n45

Conlan, Thomas, 3, 5

Courtiers, 3; as military leaders, 33–34; portraits of warriors as, 119, 403n29; female entertainers of, 159–60, 418n87; on *basara* behavior, 195; warrior elite's ties to, 204–5, 208, 213, 228–30; *yūgen* aesthetic of, 205–6; as separate from warriors, 222, 228; *bunbu* notion of, 224–25; *kojitsu* ceremonials of, 226, 431n50

Court nobility (*kuge*): *See also* Aristocratic women; importance of continuity to, 120–21; patrilocal marriages of, 146–52; role of, in *kenmon* system, 238, 240; in dual polity with Bakufu, 240–41, 434n16, 435n17; Buddhist sects' ties to, 241–43, 245–46

Criminal acts: village prosecution of, 106–8, 400nn103–6, 400n112. *See also* Akutō

Crown: Go-Daigo and the, 125–26, 406n55

Daigo, Emperor, 124, 130, 406n50, 408n75, 408–9n77

Daijōkan kaigi (The Assembly of the Great Council), 350f

Daikakuji line, 274–75

Daikōmyōji temple, 285

Daimyō, 257, 438n79

Dainichibō Nōnin, 304

Dainichi nyōrai, 126–27

Dai Nihon hennen-shi (The Chronological History of Japan), 347f

Dai Nihon-shi (History of Great Japan, 1657), 321, 342, 347

Dainihon Shiryō, 189

Daiō Kokushi, 273

Daisō Shōbō of Zuishin'in, 55, 383n80

Daitō Kokushi, *see* Shūhō Myōchō

Daitokuji monastery (Kyoto): Go-Daigo's portraits in, 122, 123–24, 273, 275, 283, 404–5n44

Dannoura, battle of, 66

Dazai Shōni (title), 74

Dengaku performance, 203

Denjō nikki (Palace Diary), 142, 412n15

Dharma of the Buddha (*buppō*), 116

Dharma of the Sovereign (*ōbō*), 116

Diamond Bell (*Kongō goko rei*), 125f

Diamond Pestle (*Kongō goko sho*), 125f

Diaries (*nikki*), 8, 139, 410n2. *See also* Women's writing

Die Aufgaben der Kulturgeschichte (Gothein), 352

Divine descent, *see* Legitimacy

Dōbōshū (companions), 201

Dōgen, 304, 308, 444n23

Dōkei (Nejime), 380n39

Dōshō (Nara monk), 313

Double-cropping, 94f, 393nn22,24, 394n25. *See also* Agriculture

Dōun (Nikaidō), 272, 274, 277f, 280

Doxa (deep-level social structure), 420–21n114

Dōyo (Sasaki): extravagance of, 9, 50, 83, 84, 86, 194, 200–201, 429n9; military career of, 197; exile of, 198–99; and Kiyouji, 199; cultural contributions of, 201, 203–4; Ōharano party of, 202–3

Dōyū (Isshiki), 57–58, 76, 383n95
Dual polity, 3, 19, 228, 240–41, 370n2,
    434n16, 435n17. *See also* Kamakura
    period
Duolocal marriage, 148. *See also* Marriage

Eastern Barbarians, 34–35
Edo period, *see* Tokugawa period
Eifukumon'in, 183ff
Eight Shingon Patriarchs, 118
Eihōji hermitage (Mino), 270
Eikyō incident (1433), 439n86
Eisai (Yōsai), 244, 266, 293, 304, 308–13
    passim
Eison (head of Saidaiji), 166, 420n107
Enchin, 307
Engakuji monastery (Kamakura), 265,
    268, 278
Engetsu (Chūgan), 132–33
Enjo's diary, 410n2
Enni, *see* Shōichi Kokushi
Enryakuji constables (*sanmon shisetsu*),
    258–59, 438n82, 438–39n83, 439n86
Enryakuji magistrate (*sanmon bugyō*), 258
Enryakuji temple, 11, 12, 103, 198; and
    Nanzenji Gate incident, 237, 250f,
    437n59; court's interdependence with,
    245–46; as protector of the state, 246,
    249, 251, 436nn52,53; in temple con-
    flicts, 246–48, 304, 435n32, 436n40;
    Tenryūji's struggle with, 249–50, 284–
    85, 286, 309; Bakufu containment
    of, 251, 257–59, 286, 436nn54,55,
    438nn79,82, 438–39n83, 439n86; Jōzan
    on monks of, 251, 436n51; growth
    of guilds and, 252–54; confirmation
    of estates of, 254–56; toll gate rights
    of, 256, 438n73; head abbots of, 257,
    438n78; immunity status of, 257,
    438n77. *See also* Buddhist establish-
    ment temples; Tendai sect
Enshin (Akamatsu), 54, 80, 83
Enshō, 444n19
Enshō shōnin gyōjō (Gyōnen), 444n19
Entairyaku (diary of Tōin Kinkata), 56,
    151, 185, 188, 286, 415n52
Epidemics, 92

Extravagance, *see* Basara

Fairbank, John King, 223
Famines, 92, 392n5
Farris, William Wayne, 433n74
Female body: spatial organization of
    marriage and, 146–49; warrior-class'
    commodification of, 152f, 155–57,
    416n59, 417nn71,74; commercializa-
    tion of, 160–61, 418n91; renounced
    sexuality of, 165–66. *See also* Women;
    Women's writing
Flower Garland Dharma-realm (*Kegon
    hokkai*), 117
Flower imagery, 186, 426n52
Formularies, *see* Warrior legislation
Fo-tsu t'ung-chi (Chih-p'an), 314, 444n28
Foucault, Michel, 8, 165, 420n106
The Fracture of Meaning (Pollack), 316
Fūgashū (Kōgon), 171, 425n44, 426n53;
    innovations of, 185–87, 425–26n51,
    426n52
Fujimoto Ryōtai, 348
Fuji Naomoto, 432n61
Fujitani Mitsue, 321
Fujiwara Akisue, 432n52
Fujiwara no Fubito, 339
Fujiwara no Teika, 193
Fujiwara Onshi, 410n2
Fujiwara regents, 144, 150, 329, 350; in-
    heritance practices of, 151, 415n51; in
    kenmon system, 239, 242–43
Fujiwara Yorinaga, 413n35
Fukkanjō (service documents), 29,
    374n62
Fukuda Ajio, 99
Fukuda Hideichi, 183
Fukuda Toyohiko, 389n14
Fukuma no Saburō, 232
Fukuo Takeichirō, 154
Funaoka Makoto, 312
Fushimi, Emperor, 180, 182, 184–85, 248
Fuyunori (Takatsukasa), 350
Fuyusuke (Shōni), 39, 52, 63

Gakukai Enjō, 270f, 273
Gakuonji monastery (Iga Province), 288

Gambling, 194–95

Gay, Suzanne, 196, 244, 369n9, 401n119

Gekokujō (overthrowing one's superiors), 40, 196, 252–53

Gen'e, 328

Genealogies, *see Keizu*

Genji monogatari (The Tale of Genji), 204f

Genkō shakusho (Shiren), 131, 442n8; composition and printing of, 300–301, 309; Gyōnen's style vs., 310–11, 317; Zen-transmission accounts in, 311, 313; sectarian leanings in, 312, 313–14, 444n26; Chinese historiographical style of, 314–15, 444n28; Bodhidharma biography of, 316–17, 445nn33,34; title of, 444n29

Gennō Hongen, 270, 277, 280

Genpei War (1180–85), 17, 425–26n51

Genshō (Tameie's son), 177f, 422n17

Genshō Waka Kuden (Genshō), 177f

Gi (duty), 378n14. *See also Chūsetsu*

Gidō Shūshin, 291

Giō (female entertainer), 159

Gion Shrine, 253

Goble, Andrew, 3, 7, 89

Go-Daigo, Emperor, 3, 7, 65, 409n80; and collapse of *shiki* system, 35, 36–37, 129, 136, 354, 360, 376n105, 376nn110,111, 377n113, 377–78n114; elimination of *gokenin* by, 46–47; rewards to warriors from, 54, 70, 381–82n71; use of military force by, 67, 71, 123, 135–36, 405n47; Kikuchi's loyalty to, 74–75, 76–77; Ashikaga Bakufu and, 79–80, 115–16, 127, 135, 197, 211, 407n63; misleading interpretations of, 113–14; pacification of spirit of, 114–16, 117, 284–85, 290–91; Musō's ties to, 116, 273–80 *passim*, 292; sovereign-Buddhism vision of, 116, 125, 126–27, 130f; Shōtoku taishi's ties to, 124, 125–26, 405–6n49, 406nn50,55; origins/legitimacy vision of, 128–29, 407–8n68; Buddhahood claims of, 130; posthumous name of, 130, 408n75;

privilege restructured by, 134–35, 136, 167, 420–21n114; control of regionalism by, 136–37; Saionji's treachery against, 140–41, 411n10; in Meishi's memoir, 143, 167; anthology commissioned by, 183–84; Kenmu code's indictment of, 213; as Zen patron, 273–74, 275; and Rinsenji temple, 280–81, 374–75n75, 375n77; as author of *Nenjū gyōgi*, 349–50; Satō's analysis of, 350–51, 360; Kuroda Toshio on, 360

Go-Daigo, Emperor, portraits of: in *Tenshi sekkan miei* scrolls, 119–20, 122, 404n41, 404–5n44; in Daitokuji, 122, 123–24, 404n43, 404–5n44; in Shōjō-kōji, 122, 125–27, 404n43; at Rozanji and Yoshino jingū, 403–4n31

Go-Enyū, Emperor, 189

Go-Fukakusa, Emperor, 151, 159, 176, 178f, 412n18

Go-Fushimi, Emperor, 143, 145, 185

Go-Hanazono, Emperor, 189

Go-Horikawa, Emperor, 173, 175

Go-Kameyama, Emperor, 341

Goke ben (Shiren), 302

Gokenin: Yoritomo's introduction of, 17–18, 21; warrior's identity as, 29, 46f, 374nn62,64, 379n35; continued currency of term, 37, 46–47, 377n116; elimination of, 46–47, 391n33. *See also Tozama*

Go-Kōgon, Emperor, 120, 188f, 404n34

Go-Komatsu, Emperor, 166

Go-Murakami, Emperor, 120, 274, 404n35

Gonchūnagon (Provisional Middle Counselor), 140

Gondainagon (Provisional Major Counselor), 140

Go-Nijō, Emperor, 404n34

Gorō Tarō (Kabata Ishikawa), 58f, 61

Goryō Shrines, 165

Go-Saga, Emperor: anthologies commissioned by, 175, 176–77, 179, 181, 274, 422n20

Goseibai shikimoku (or *Jōei shikimoku*,

Kamakura law code), 85, 155–56, 417n71
Gōshin (court painter), 404–5n44
Goshūishū (Shirakawa), 421n3, 425n40
Go-Takakura, Emperor, 120, 404n34
Gothein, 352
Go-Toba, Emperor, 66, 151, 422n20; anthology compilation and, 172, 174, 176, 184, 421n5; poetry devotion of, 172, 417–18n81, 421n4; *Shokukokinshū's* ties to, 178
Go-Uda, Emperor: portraits of, 122, 179, 180, 372–73n43, 405n45, 409n80; anthologies commissioned by, 181, 183; Rensho committee of, 182, 424n35; in temple conflict, 247–48, 304, 443n15; Zen interest of, 274–75
Gozan, see Zen monastery system
Gozan bungaku (Literature of the Five Mountains), 267, 302
Grand Master (*daishi*), 247, 436n37
Guilds (*za*), 252–54, 256–57, 353
Gukanki (Konoe Michitsugu), 189
Gukanshō (Jien), 162, 295, 441–42n1
Gunki monogatari (war tales), 197, 224, 295, 441–42n1. *See also Genji monogatari; Heike monogatari; Taiheiki*
Gunzei saisokujō (recruitment order), 71, 87
Gusoku Nakaaki seishi (Ryōshun), 214, 219–21
Gyokuyō (Kujō Kanezane), 159, 162
Gyokuyōshū (Tamekane, comp.), 182–83, 191, 424–25n37
Gyōnen, 12, 299–300, 305–11 *passim*, 317, 444n19

Hachijō'in (daughter of Emperor Toba), 151
Hachiman *daibosatsu* (tutelary deity), 125f
Haga hyōe nyūmon Zenka, 44
Hakanashi (ephemeral): shift to *mujō* from, 296, 442n2
Hakata, 67–68, 265, 363–64
Hakata Nikki, 67–69, 385n4

Hakkai ganzō (Shiren), 303, 443n10
Hakone Takenoshita, battle of (1335), 71
Hakozaki Shrine, 74
Hakozaki Temple, 74
Hakusen'an hermitage (Miura peninsula), 271
Hall, John, 10
Hana no moto entertainment, 195, 202
Hanazono, Emperor: portraits of, 122, 130, 405n46; on divine descent, 133–34; in Miushi's memoir, 143, 145; and anthology compilations, 179–80, 184–87, 225, 417–18n81, 423n26, 425–26n51, 426n53; on Musō, 275–76, 277
Hand paintings, 118
Han dynasty, 327
Han Fei Tzu, 223
Hangan (Enya), 196
Han shu (History of the [Former] Han), 223, 333
Hanzei (half-rights), 87f, 255
Hara Katsurō, 345, 351–52, 359
Hare, Thomas, 428n38
Harima Province, 89
Haruda family, 66
Harunobu (Takeda), 153
Hasshū kōyō (Gyōnen), 299, 310f. *See also* Gyōnen
Hata Estate (Yamato Province), 375n77
Hatakeyama family, 76, 82, 161, 389n13
Hatsukura-no-shō (Tōtōmi), 97
Hayami Shirō, 44
Hayashi Gahō, 321, 339
Hayashi Razan, 210, 321, 339
Hayashiya Tatsusaburō, 345
Hearth taboo, 149f, 415n44
Heian period, 3f, 103; marriage patterns of, 147, 149, 414n39, 417n69; emperor-scholar ideal of, 224; *kenmon* system of, 242–43; Buddhism of, 298; the "mass" in, 352; female writing in, 410n2
Heiji monogatari (The Tale of Heiji), 197, 224
Heike monogatari (The Tale of the Heike), 159, 197; Kakuichi version of,

193; Zeami's *nō* and, 206f; *bunbu* concept of, 224; swords in, 232, 433n76; Tokugawa interest in, 323; monograph style of, 334
Hekizan nichiroku, 310
Hells (bloody incidents): pictorial representations of, 164–65, 411n13, 419n101
Hennen (chronological annals), 333–34
Hidetoki (Hōjō), 67, 69f, 154, 375–76n96
Hidetsuna (Sasaki), 198
Hiei, Mount, 58, 384n102
Hie Shrine, 198
Higashimura (Kokawa-no-shō), 101f, 107, 157–58, 398nn71,72,77
Higashi to nishi no kataru Nihon no rekishi (Japanese History as Told by East and West, Amino), 362
Higo (poetess), 175
Higo Kazuo, 406n50
Higo Province, 66
Hikobe family, 389n14
Hine-no-shō (Izumi), 92f, 104, 399n86
Hino family, 139, 410n5
Hiraizumi Kiyoshi, 345–50 *passim*, 356
Hirakana (Japanese syllabary), 139, 142
Hiroda Shinsaemon no jō Hisayoshi, 68
Hirose Kazuo, 396n51
Hiroyo (Ōuchi), 51, 390–91n32
Hisatsune (Shimazu), 89
Historical doctrine: Buddhist concern for, 296–97, 298; tied to lineages, 299–300
Historiographical Institute (Shiryō Hensan Gakari), 347–48
Historiography: of Gyōnen, 12, 299–300, 311, 444n19; of twentieth century, on fourteenth century, 13–14, 345–46; of Shiren, 309–12, 313–17, 443n16, 444nn26,28; Chinese influence on, 314–15, 324f, 444n28; of Tokugawa period, 321–24, 445n2; realism of Sokō's, 324, 339–42, 343; Keisai's ahistorical approach to, 332–33, 338–39, 342; *hennen* method of, 333–34; positivism of Sorai's, 343–44; chronicle type of, 346–47, 348–49; European

movements in, 349; archival method of, 351; cultural trends in, 352–54; Marxist influence on, 355, 356–57; revival of *Taiheiki* in, 358–59; role of religious institutions in, 359f; ethnographic distinctions of, 361–62; East Asian international perspective of, 363–64
Hitomi Tonomura, 397n61
Hōgen monogatari (The Tale of the Hōgen), 197, 334
Hōjō family, 6; military recruitment by, 34; *ichimon shugo* of, 79; clan enterprise of, 82–83, 90; as Zen patrons, 265–66, 271, 272–73, 278–79; legitimacy of, 330; Sokō on, 340–41
Hōjō kudaiki (Record of the Nine reigns [under] the Hōjō), 336
Hokkeji nunnery (Nara), 166, 420n107
Homosexual relationships, 413n35
Honchō Tsugan (Comprehensive Mirror of This Court, 1670), 171, 177, 321
Hōnen: Pure Land school of, 297–98, 299
Honke (patron), 31f, 375n77
Honryō (hereditary homelands): inviolability of, 55–56, 57; of the Ishikawa, 58–59; "law of surrender" on, 60–61, 384n108, 385n113
Hosokawa family, 49f, 62, 80, 82, 217
Hotoke (female entertainer), 159
Houses, village, 98
Hsiao hsueh (Lesser Learning, Chu Hsi), 332–33
Hsien ti, 335
Huey, Robert, 8–9
Hui-ssu, 316
Hurst, G. Cameron, 3–4, 9–10, 369n7
Hyakurenshō, 174
Hyōrōmai (commissariat rice), 87

Ichijō Kanera, 328
Ichimon (kinsmen), 79
Iehira (Ryūzōji), 384n99
Iemasa (Ryūzōji), 57
Ietaka (Fujiwara), 175

Ietane (Ryūzōji), 57
Ieuji (Shiba), 389n13
Ieyasu (Ryūzōji), 382n78
Ieyasu (Tokugawa), 40
Ieyoshi (Fujiwara), 177, 422n15
Igyō no ōken (Amino), 361
Ikki (military units), 45
Ikō Dōnen, 265
Imabori village (Ōmi Province): migra-
   tion rules of, 93, 392–93n14, 393n15;
   houseland of, 99, 396n54; land owner-
   ship by, 102, 398nn74,76; dues collec-
   tion by, 102–3, 398n77; warriors' ties
   to, 104–5; judicial functions of, 106f,
   400n106; shrine association of, 157f
Imaeda Aishin, 287f
Imagawa family, 39, 49f, 80, 389n12;
   advice manual for, 214, 219–21
Imagawa Ryōshun gusoku Nakaaki seishi,
   214, 219–21
Imakumano Shrine (Kyoto), 204
Imatani Akira, 114, 390n21, 438–39n83
Imazaike village, 102, 105, 398n75
Imperial anthologies: politics of inclusion
   in, 8–9, 173f; as canonical form, 170f,
   176; evolution of *waka* and, 171, 421n3;
   Kamakura Bakufu's intervention in,
   171, 182–83, 424n36; warrior poets'
   inclusion in, 171, 175, 179, 189, 421–
   22n12, 423n25, 426–27n59; the last of,
   171–72; Michiie's compilation of, 172–
   75; commissioned by Go-Saga, 175–77,
   179; Munetaka's literary intervention
   in, 177–78; court rivalries over, 178–
   80, 181–83, 423nn26,27, 424–25n37;
   Go-Uda's commissioning of, 181, 183;
   Rensho's role in, 182, 424n35; commissioned by sitting emperors, 183–84,
   425n40; marking legitimacy, 184, 187,
   188–89; Hanazono's commissioning of,
   184–87, 425–26n51, 426n53; Ashikaga
   Bakufu's intervention in, 185, 188–91,
   426n56, 426–27n59; and *Fūgashū's*
   innovations, 185–86, 190, 425–26n51,
   426n52; Southern Court's sponsorship of, 187–88; Nijō designations of,
   426n54
Imperial Army (*kanpei*), 34
Imperial rule (*Tennō shinsei*), *see* Legitimacy; Sovereignty
Inheritance: partible vs. single, 29f,
   374n60; patrilineal, 146, 148, 150–51; as
   lifetime bequest, 151, 415n51; warriors'
   practice of, 153–54, 416n62
Inoue Muneo, 181
Insei system, 128, 350
Inuoumono (form of archery), 218, 231–32,
   430n23. *See also* Mounted archery
Iron tools, 97, 395n46, 395–96n47
Irrigation methods, 94–95, 394n30. *See
   also* Agriculture
Ise family, 231, 433n72
Ise Province, 85
Ise Sadataka, 430n30
Ise Taira family, *see* Taira family
I-shan I-ning (Issan Ichinei), 266ff, 274,
   301, 308, 314
Ishibashi, 50
Ishidō Uma no Kami, 336
Ishii Susumu, 272
Ishikawa family, 58–59, 60f, 384n106
Ishimoda Shō, 345, 356–57
Issan kokushi gyōki (Shiren, comp.), 302
Isshikiden fields, 396n50
Isshiki family, 49, 57
Itai family, 66
Itō family, 76
Itō Kiyoshi, 114, 346, 363–64
Iwasa Miyoko, 186, 410n7, 412n29
Iwashimizu Hachiman Shrine, 76
Iyo Province, 48–49, 85
Izumi Province, 31

Jibi Estate (Yamanouchi), 55
Jien (Kujō), 162, 175, 418–19n93
Jikan (Ritsu master), 263
Jiki (monographs), 333
Jikkinshō, 224
Jimyōin line, 128, 139, 151, 181, 274,
   275–76
Jinin (hunting people), 361

Jinmu, Emperor, 30
Jinnō shōtōki (Chikafusa): on aristocracy's role in, 121; ideal warrior of, 225, 295, 299, 324, 441–42n1; on legitimacy, 328–29, 331, 335; chronological framework of, 334
Jisha (temples and shrines), see Buddhist establishment temples
Jisshū yōdō ki (Shōichi Kokushi), 304
Jitō (managerial authorities): as class-specific, 18; judicial governance of, 18–19; expanded eligibility and, 20; fractional, 21, 28, 370nn9,10, 373nn57,58; commenders as, 25; in bandit gangs (akutō), 26–27, 372n40; documents of appointment to, 29, 374n65; gokenin status of, 29; in Rinsenji petition-document, 31–33, 375n76; as proprietors, 32, 36; Go-Daigo's control of, 35f; Marxist analysis of, 355, 377n1
Jitōdai (deputy jitō), 28, 373nn56–58
Jitō gokenin, 26, 29, 48–49, 52, 372n40, 374n64, 378n11. See also Gokenin
Jitō shiki: commendations of, 18, 25, 45, 51, 285, 288, 372n30, 379n28, 381–82n71, 383n95; of warrior-class women, 154
Jiyū rōzeki (unchecked confusion), 195f
Jōchiji monastery, 278
Jōdo hōmon genru shō (Gyōnen), 313, 444n19
Jōdo Shinshū sect, 435n26
Jōei shikimoku, see Goseibai shikimoku
Jōkei, 297–98, 299, 305
Jōkyoji hermitage (Kai), 272
Jōkyū War (1221), 66, 165, 172
Jōshō, 304
Jōtatsu, 269
Jōzan Sozen, 250–51, 436n51
Ju-chiang (scholar-official) ideal, 223–24. See also Bunbu ryōdo
Judicial system: of dual polity, 18–19; new evil language of, 19–20, 27, 370n3; patronage goal of, 20; banditry's pressures on, 26–27, 372n38; warrior genealogies in, 29–30, 374nn67–69; and

compromise accords, 30–31; villages' role in, 106–8, 400nn103–6, 400n111; confirmation of temple estates by, 254–56
Jūdo (ten perfections), 316
Jufukuji monastery (Kamakura), 278
Junbo (associate mother), 151, 162, 415n50
Juntoku, Emperor, 174, 176
Junzen (pure Zen), 308
Jūzenshi roku (Shiren), 302

Kabata Ishikawa family, 58f, 61
Kadochigai ikki, 45
Kaga Province, 31, 89
Kagari pun, 423n25. See also Warrior poets
Kagetsuna (Bitō), 82
Kaisho (banquet chamber), 201
Kajishi (surtax on land), 97, 395nn43,44
Kakumei (priest), 224–25
Kakushin, 308
Kakushō (Kikuchi), 68
Kakyō (Zeami), 205
Kamakura: Musō in, 266f, 271, 278; Hōjō's Zen patronage in, 271, 272–73, 278–79
Kamakura Bakufu, 8; institutional innovations for, 17–18, 82, 340; judicial system of, 18–19, 254–55; collapse of shiki and, 21, 29, 35, 36–37, 371n11; debt-cancellation decrees of, 21–22, 371nn14,15; establishment of, 66; fall of, 67–70, 279; artistic representation of, 118–19; marriage practices of, 152, 155–56, 417n71; female-authored documents of, 154–55; motherhood codes of, 163; and imperial anthologies, 171, 182–83, 424n36; court culture's influence on, 193–94; warrior codes of, 210; warrior ceremonial of, 226–27, 431–32n51, 432n54; role of, in kenmon system, 242–43; and religious conflict, 247–48; Rensho commission and, 424n35
Kamakura period (1185–1333): dual polity of, 3, 19, 228, 240–41, 370n2, 434n16,

435n17; role of *shugo* in, 78–79, 85, 87; jurisdictional boundaries in, 80; dues collection in, 103; warrior-class inheritance practices of, 153–54, 416n62; numbers of warriors in, 232, 433n74; Buddhist establishment temples of, 254–55, 257, 303–4, 438n77; representations of hells in, 411n13

Kameyama, Emperor, 151, 176–81 *passim*, 274, 304

Kami (native gods), 131ff

Kamikuze-no-shō, 101–2, 103, 397n68

Kamikuze village, 104

Kan'ami, 203f

Kaneie (Fujiwara), 150

Kanemitsu (Fujiwara), 361–62

Kanemitsu (Iga), 118

Kaneshige (Kimotsuki), 71

Kaneyoshi, Prince, 67, 137

Kanezane (Kujō), 151, 159, 162, 172, 418–19n93

Kangen Incident (1246), 83

Kanjō (testament of valor), 87, 390n26

Kannō Disturbance (1350–51), 50f, 63, 83, 388–89n11

Kannō era (1350–52), 56

Kannon, 268, 270, 439n4

Kannondō (Buddhist chapel), 397n66

Kanrei (Ashikaga Bakufu post), 82, 84

Kantō Kubō (Ashikaga Bakufu post), 81

Kanzan Egen, 275, 283

Kao-seng chuan, 314, 315–16

Karei (house administrator), 82

Karita rōzeki (illegal harvesting of crops), 85

Karon (poetic treatises), 171

Kasagake (form of archery), 218, 430n23. *See also* Mounted archery

Kasuga *daimyōjin* (tutelary deity), 125f

Katari (extended narratives), 206

Kawane Yoshiyasu, 94

Kawazoe Shōji, 346

Kazuhito, Prince (*later* Emperor Kōgon), 133, 140, 143–44. *See also* Kōgon, Emperor

Kazunari (Ōtsuka), 154

Kazuyoshi (Ishibashi), 80

Keirstead, Thomas, 391n1

Keisai (Asami), 13, 323; Confucian influences on, 324f, 327–28; Japanese historical sources for, 328–31; hierarchical moral imperatives of, 331–33, 337–38; ahistorical perspective of, 332–33, 342; *hennen*-style of, 333–34; on *Taikeiki*, 334–35; on Takauji, 335–36; on Nitta family, 336–37; influence of, on Mito school, 342–43

Keizan Jōkin, 292

Keizu (genealogies), 29–30, 46, 121, 374nn67–69

Kenchōji monastery (Kamakura), 266

Kenkō (Yoshida), 195f

Kenmitsu temples, *see* Buddhist establishment temples

Kenmon system, 10–11; as tripartite ruling system, 238, 240–41, 359, 434n7; criteria of members of, 239; development of, 239–40; flaws in concept of, 241–42; and *kenmon* theory's impact, 242–43; fourteenth-century decline of, 243–45, 252–53, 259–60, 369n9; Ashikaga Bakufu's maintenance of, 255–56; use of term, 434n6

Kenmu chūkō no hongi (The True Meaning of the Kenmu Restoration, Hiraizumi), 349

Kenmu nenchū gyōji (Go-Daigo), 128

Kenmu Restoration (1333–36), 1; *kunijōshi* of, 88–89; misleading interpretations of, 113–14; policy initiatives of, 134–36; Kyoto-based *buke* of, 194, 427n3; *hana no moto* entertainment of, 195, 202; Tokugawa interest in, 322–23; Sokō on, 341; Satō on, 350–51; Shimizu on, 355; Matsumoto on, 357. *See also* Go-Daigo, Emperor

"Kenmu seiken no shoryō ando seisaku" (The Land Rights Confirmation Policy of the Kenmu Regime, Kuroda), 360

"Kenmu seiken no shūkyō seisaku" (The Religious Policies of the Kenmu Regime, Kuroda), 360

Kenmu shikimoku (Kenmu Code), 124, 231; on female sphere, 156, 163; against *basara*, 194, 211–12, 429n9; compilers of, 197, 211, 429n5; Confucian influence on, 211, 213–14; justifying military regime, 212–13, 228

Kenninji Temple and monastery (Kyoto), 198, 264f, 309, 443n15

Kenshū (joint practice), 308

Kessho claims, 55

Kian Soen, 301

Ki band, 43, 45, 227, 379n29

Kiden (biographies), 333

Kii Province, 88f

Kikuchi Castle, 71, 75

Kikuchi family, 6, 39, 66–77 *passim*, 386n18

Kimon school, 342

Kimotsuki family, 76

Kim Pu-sik, 224

Kinda Akihiro, 94, 99

Kinkata (Tōin): diary of, 56, 151, 185, 188, 286, 415n52; granddaughter of, 149–50

Kinkazu (Tōin), 151, 415n52

Kinmune (Saionji, Lord Kitayama), 140; *Taiheiki's* account of, 140–41, 161, 163, 411nn10,12; poem of, to Meishi, 141, 411n11; Meishi's marriage to, 145–46, 148–49, 414–15n41, 415n43

Ki no Tsurayuki, 175

Kinsada (Tōin), 121

Kinshige (Saionji), 140, 161

Kintada (Tōin), 160, 418n88

Kintsuna (Utsunomiya), 43

Kintsune (Saionji), 175, 411n9

Kira family, 49, 389nn12,13

Kiroku (monographs), 333

Kishin (commendations), 21; expanded donor-base for, 23, 371n24; to religious institutions, 23–24; motivation for endowment of, 24–25, 371n25, 372n28; types of, 25, 372n30; of property to villages, 102, 397–98n70, 398n71. *See also* Rewards

Kishinjō (commendation deeds), 23–24, 371n24

Kitabatake family, 85

Kitano Shrine, 254

Kitayama epoch, 201; *nō* theater of, 203–7

Kitayama Mansion (home of Saionji), 141, 146, 410n4, 411n9

Kiyomori (Taira), 159, 240

Kiyonari (Nejime), 47, 76, 380n39

Kiyosuke, 178

Kiyotake (Nejime), 380n39

Kiyotane (Nejime), 47, 380n39

Kiyouji (Hosokawa), 44, 82, 84, 199–200

Kiyoyoshi (Nejime), 380n39

Kobayakawa family, 36, 89–90, 154

Kōbō daishi, 126, 406n58; document of *826* of, 129, 407–8n68

Kō brothers, 56, 383n90

Kōdate Naomi, 165, 419n98

Kō family, 83, 388–89n11, 389n14

Kōfukuji petition (1205), 297–98

Kōfukuji temple, 246, 250

Koga family, 161

Kōgon, Emperor (Kōgen): Go-Daigo and, 72, 115, 117, 145, 249, 282; *Fūgashū* anthology of, 185–87, 425n44, 425–26n51, 426nn52,53; Yoritō and, 199; Zen interest of, 276; and Tenryūji temple, 284, 285–86. *See also* Kazuhito, Prince

Kōgyoku, Empress, 162

Kōhō Kennichi, 268–74 *passim*, 281

Koji (Hisa), 272

Kojitsu (ancient practices), 10, 219, 226, 431n50. *See also* Buke kojitsu

Kokawadera village, 103

Kōken, Empress, 162, 225

Kokinshū, 205

Kokin waka rokujō, 422n18

Kōkoku shikan (imperial land view of history), *see* "Name and status" ideology

Kokubo (mother of the country), 151, 162

Kokujin (men of the province), 32

Kokushigaku no kotsuzui (The Heart of National History, Hiraizumi), 349

Koma inu, 125f

Kōmyō, Emperor, 211, 276, 282, 285

Kōmyōin shinki, 286
Kongō satta, 126f, 406n58
Konoe, Emperor, 404n33
Kōno family, 48–49, 380nn43,47
Koresumi (Aso), 60, 384n110
Koretoki (Aso), 60, 384n110
Koreyoshi (Ogata), 66
Kōsan no hō (law of surrender), 60, 384n108
Kōsen Ingen, 281, 284, 287
Kotani Toshihiko, 389n12
Kōyasan monastery (Kii), 30
Kōzen gokoku ron (Eisai), 304
Kōzen ki (Jōshō), 304
Kōzuma-gun (Chikugo), 73
Kūa (Zen monk), 263
Kuge (court nobility), *see* Court nobility
Kuge daimyō, 85
Kugonin (fishing people), 361f
Kujō estate (Harima Province), 36, 376n110
Kūkai, 311
Kumagai family, 375n83
Kume Kunitake, 345, 346–47
Kunijōshi (enforcement officer), 88–89
Kunitaishō (supraprovincial military commanders), 80
Kuo yü (Narratives of the states), 333
Kuriyama Sempō, 342
Kuroda Hideo, 97, 122, 125, 404–5n44, 406n58, 419n101
Kuroda Toshio: *kenmon* theory of, 10–11, 238, 369n9, 434nn5–7; on *kenmon* system, 239–40, 244–45; flaws in theory of, 241–42; continuity notion of, 297, 345, 442n3; feudal revolution analysis of, 358; revival of *Taiheiki* by, 358–59; on Go-Daigo's religious policies, 360. *See also Kenmon* system
Kusome of Hizen Province, 154, 416n64
Kusu Castle (Bungo Province), 75f, 387n21
Kusunoki family, 71, 337
Kutsuki Yoriuji, 50
Kyōgoku family, 84, 86f

Kyōgoku school of poetry, 181, 185, 426n53
Kyoso (mendacious charges), 27
Kyōsō hanjaku (doctrinal classification), 298, 442n5
Kyoto, 8; judicial system of, 18–19; warrior-courtier fusion in, 33–34, 228; warrior elite in, 192–93, 194, 196, 207–8, 427n3; Southern Court's attacks on, 200; Kenmu code on, 211; as Zen center, 265–66, 274, 279, 292; Musoō in, 276f, 292
Kyūba mondō (Dialogue on Mounted Archery, Nagahide), 231
Kyūsei, 203
Kyushu, 65–77 *passim*

Lamprecht, Karl, 352–53
Lan-ch'i Tao-lung (Rankei Dōryu), 264f, 267, 274, 308
Landholdings: as village-owned common property, 7, 96, 102, 394n36, 395n39, 397–98n70, 398nn71,75,76; of *miuchi* organizations, 45; *kessho* claims on, 55; inviolable hereditary, 55–56, 57, 58–60; mistaken identifications of, 57, 383n91; of smallholders, 97–98, 395n40, 396nn49,50; diminution of women's, 150–51, 153–55, 416n62; of shrine associations, 158. *See also Kishin*; Rewards; *Shiki*; *Shōen*
Land rights, *see Shiki*
Language, evil, 19–20, 27
Lankāvatārasūtra, 303
Late Kamakura (Kamakura *makki*), 1
Later Han dynasty, 128
Legal formularies, *see* Warrior legislation
Legitimacy: continuity issues of, 120–22, 128, 133–34; of religious tradition, 129, 407–8n68; imperial anthology as mark of, 184, 187, 188–89; Ssu-ma's criteria for, 325–27, 447n25; Chu Hsi on, 327; Chikafusa on, 328–29; *Taiheiki*'s view of, 329–30, 331; Keisai's criteria for, 332; Sokō's criteria for, 339–41; Hakuseki on, 344. *See also* Sovereignty

Lineage: to legitimate Buddhist schools, 299–300, 305–6, 444n19
Liu Pei, 327
Lordships: regional vs. hegemonic, 42, 48–52; *miuchi's* allegiances to, 43–44, 378nn14,16. *See also* Ashikaga collaterals; *Tozama*
Loyalist Force (Kantō *gunsei*), 34
Loyalty: Confucian imperative to, 325, 329, 332. *See also Chūsetsu*
Lung-hsing t'ung-lung (Tsu-hsiu), 314

McCullough, William H., 147, 414n39, 415n47
McKean, Margaret, 394n36
McMullen, I. J., 13
Mahāprajñāpāramitā-sūtra, 316
Mahāyāna, 299, 316–17
Maihime (dancing maidens), 159–60, 418n87
Makashikan, 267
Mandate of Kings (Ban Biao), 133
Manjushri, statue of, 361
Man'yōshū chūshaku (Sengaku), 422n19
Man'yōshū poems, 178, 422nn18,19
Mappō doctrine, 12, 296f, 442n2
Marra, Michele, 426nn53,56
Marriage, 8; transition to patrilocal, 146–51, 155, 168, 415n47; residential patterns of, 147, 150, 414nn38,39, 415n47; duo-local, 148; as public ceremony, 149, 152–53; rice cake ceremony of, 149, 415n44; hearth taboo of matrilineal, 149f, 415n44; of warriors, 152–53
Maruyama Yoshihiko, 398n75
Marxist historiography, 355f
Masakado rebellion (935–40), 339
Masamoto (Kujō), 399n86
Masanori (Kusunoki), 200
Masashige (Kusunoki), 11, 34, 65, 372–73n43, 375n83
Masatsune (Fujiwara Asukai), 172, 175
Masayo (Asukai), 189
Masayuki (Taira), 166, 241–42
Mashido family, 76
Mass, Jeffrey, 180, 435n17

Masukagami, 171, 177f, 183, 422n24
Mato (form of archery), 218, 430n23. *See also* Mounted archery
Matoharu (Mōri), 40
Matsui Teruaki, 89
Matsumoto Shinpachirō, 14, 79, 345, 357f, 362
Mauss, Marcel, 382n75
Medieval period: periodization debate on, 2, 3–4, 91, 354, 369n4, 391n1; Kenmu Revolution's ties to, 113–14; sovereignty issue of, 114, 135–36. *See also* Nanbokuchō period
Meigetsuki (Teika), 173
Meishi (Hino), 8; family background of, 139; Kinmune and, 141, 145–46, 148–49, 411n11, 415n43; motherhood role of, 161; in childbirth, 163. *See also Takemukigaki*
Meishō ryakuden (Shōchō), 313
Mencian argument, 327, 330
Menstrual blood, 165, 420n103
Michichika (Minamoto), 421n5
Michihide (Miyoshi), 55
Michiie (Kujō), 130f, 172–73, 174–75, 274, 406n58, 408n72
Michimori (Kōno family), 49
Michinaga (Fujiwara), 150
Michitada (Yamanouchi), 55
Michitsugu (Konoe), 149, 189, 228, 432n58, 436n54
Migration rules, 93
Mikkyō tradition, 313
Mikohidara school of poetry, 175–81 *passim*, 426n53
Military estate, *see* Warrior elite
Minami family, 389n14
Minamoto family, 18, 37, 82, 192–93
Minamoto Ienaga nikki, 421n4
Minatogawa, battle of (1336), 58, 65
Miner, Earl, 171
Ming-chi Ch'u-chun (Minki Soshun), 273f
Mingji Chujun (Minki Shoshun), 119, 403n28
Mino Disturbance (1390), 86

Mito family, 389n14
Mito school, 342–43, 347
Mitsufusa (Sugiwara), 89, 390–91n32
Mitsutada (Ise), 231
Mitsuyori (Toki), 86
Miuchi ("insider" warriors): *tozama's* distinction from, 42–43, 44, 62, 378n12; allegiances of, 43–44, 378nn14,16; corporate membership of, 45–46, 379n28; as landholder, 47–48; of the Hosokawa, 50
Miyabi (courtliness), 206
Miyake Kanran, 342
Mizukawa Yoshio, 410nn4,7, 412n29
Moaku (ferocious evil), 27
Moats, 99
Mōko shogunki bengi (Doubts Dispelled on the Military Records Concerning the Mongols, Tachibana Moribe), 445n3
Mokuren (priest), 164
Momonoi family, 49
Monastic Affairs, Office of, 245
Mongol invasions, 29, 266
Monjusri, 118
Monkan (priest/painter), 118, 129f, 361–62, 404–5n44, 407–8n68
Monzeki (noble cloisters), 245
Moribe (Tachibana), 445n3
Mōri family, 416n59
Morinaga, Prince (Moriyoshi), 34–35, 225, 375n83
Mori Shigeaki, 364–65
Moritomo (Matsuda), 80
Moronao (Kō), 194–95, 286, 388–89n11, 427–28n21
Morotoshi (Minamoto), 175
Motherhood: categories of, 151, 162, 415n50; Meishi's role of, 161; essentialized biological nature of, 162–63, 168–69, 418–19n93
Motoharu (Mōri), 40, 52
Motoie (Kujō), 177–78
Mōto (newcomers without land), 93, 392–93n14

Motonaga (adopted son of Chikanaga), 150
Motoori Norinaga, 321
Mototada (Takatsukasa), 181
Mototsugu (Konoe), 149
Mountain hut imagery, 186, 426n52
Mounted archery (*kyūba*), 218, 227, 231–33, 430nn22,23, 431–32n51, 433n72
Muchū mondō (Dialogues in a Dream, Musō), 116, 278–79, 283, 289–90
Muen, kugai, raku (Amino), 345–46, 361
Mugen (ghostly dream) plays, 205–6, 428n38
Muhon Kakushin, 264
Muin Enpan, 264f
Mujō (impermanence): shift from *hakanashi* to, 296, 442n2
Mukotori (taking a groom or son-in-law), 146–52 *passim*, 413–14n36, 414nn38,39, 415n44
Mukyoku Shigen, 280, 283, 291
Mukyū Tokusen, 265
Munakata family, 375–76n96
Munehiro (Yūki), 35, 58
Munenaga Shinnō, 187
Munetaka, Prince (Munetaka Shinnō), 152, 176ff, 179, 416n56
Murai Shōsuke, 88, 346, 363–64
Murdoch, James, 40, 52, 369n5, 377n3
"Murodomari no gungi," 79ff, 86, 387–88n4
Muromachi Bakufu, *see* Ashikaga Bakufu
Muromachi period, 1; Blood Bowl hells of, 101, 164–65, 411n13, 419n98; female-authored documents of, 142–43, 412n17; extravagance of, 196; courtier-warrior fusion of, 228–30; increased warfare of, 232–33. *See also* Nanbokuchō period
Musō kokushi nenpu (Shun'oku Myōha, ed.), 268, 439n3
Musō Soseki: ubiquitous ties of, 11, 261–62; and pacification of Go-Daigo's spirit, 115–16, 117, 284–85, 290–91, 292; on imperial-military relationship, 116–17; and Tenryūji temple,

117, 249f, 284–85, 286f; artistic representation of, 118, 402n21; and Yoritō's execution, 199; negative views on, 262; birth/parents of, 263, 439nn3,4; esoteric Buddhist training of, 263, 267, 269, 292–93; Zen inclinations of, 264, 268–69, 289–90, 293; wanderings of, 264–65, 269–70; I-shan and, 267, 268–69; Kōhō and, 269f; building hermitages, 270, 271–72; Go-Daigo's invitations to, 273–80 passim; Hanazono on, 275–76, 277; on Hōjō's Zen patronage, 278–79; and Rinsenji temple, 280–81; Ashikaga's patronage of, 282–83; pagoda/temple proposal of, 287–88; disciples/lineage of, 291
Myōe, 165
Myō fields, 396n50
Myōhōin Temple (Kyoto), 198
Myōhōjiki, 153
Myō no Shimotsuke, 43
Myōshinji monastery (Kyoto), 275, 283
Myōshu (farmer-managers), 96f, 101–2, 397n68

Nagahara Keiji, 2, 244, 345
Nagahide (Ogasawara), 231
Nagahiro (Ōuchi), 80
Nagatoshi (Nawa), 141, 351
Nagoya (Nagoe) family, 83
Naikyōbō (Female Dancers' and Musicians' Office), 418n87
Naiten jinro shō (Gyōnen), 300, 444n19
Nakaaki (Imagawa), 220f
Nakada Norio, 410nn4,7, 412n29
Nakai, Kate Wildman, 321, 447n25
Nakajima Kumakichi, 322
Nakamura Naokatsu, 345, 353–54, 356, 362
"Name and status" ideology (taigi meibun), 322, 326, 329, 332–37 passim, 342–43
Nanbokuchō jidai-shi (Kume), 346f
Nanbokuchō jidai-shi (Tanaka), 348–49, 353
Nanbokuchō kōbu kankei-shi no ken-

kyū (The Study of Court-Warrior Relationships, Mori), 364–65
"Nanbokuchō nairan no shakaiteki igi" (The Social Significance of the Nanbokuchō Disturbance, Amino), 361
Nanbokuchō no dōran (The Nanbokuchō Disturbance, Itō), 363
Nanbokuchō no dōran (The Nanbokuchō Disturbance, Satō), 350
Nanbokuchō period (1336–92): various names for, 1; as medieval turning point, 2, 3–4, 91, 354, 369n4, 391n1; scholarly interest in, 2; kenmon system's decline in, 10–11, 243–45, 252–53, 259–60, 369n9; twentieth century historiography of, 13–14, 344–45; versions of chūsetsu in, 40–41, 377nn5,6, 378n7; role of shugo in, 78–79, 85f; transformed marriage practices of, 146–53; sectarian conflicts of, 244, 435n26; Tokugawa interest in, 322–23; new professional groups of, 353–54; feudal revolution of, 357f; ethnographic transition of, 361
Nanbokuchō Wars: origins of, 68–69, 68–77, 73, 77; battle of Tatarahama, 73–75
Nanpō'an hermitage (Kamakura), 278
Nanpu Jōmyō, 443n15
Nan-Taiheiki (Ryōshun), 220
Nanzenji Gate incident, 237, 250f, 437n59
Nanzenji temple (Kyoto), 274, 276–81 passim
Nara period, 2, 298
Nejime tozama, 47, 380n39
Nelson, Thomas, 6
Nenbun dosha (scholarship monks), 298
Nenjū gyōgi (Go-Daigo), 349–50
Nenpu (Shun'oku Myōha, ed.), 439n3
Nichiren sect, 435n26
Nigatsu-no-Ran (1272), 83
Nihon bunka-shi josetsu (A Prelude to the Cultural History of Japan, Nishida), 352

Nihon bunka-shi—Nanbokuchō jidai
(The Cultural History of Japan—
The Nanbukuchō Period, Nakamura),
353–54
Nihon chūsei no minshū-zō (Images of the
Common People in Medieval Japan,
Amino), 361
Nihon chūsei no sonraku (The Villages of
Medieval Japan, Shimizu), 355
Nihon chūsei-shi (The History of Medi-
eval Japan, Hara), 351–52
Nihon Kōki (Later Chronicle of Japan),
334
Nihon sandai jitsuroku, 346
*Nihon shakai saikō—kaimin to rettō
bunka* (Rethinking Japanese Society,
Amino), 362
Nihon shoki (Chronicles of Japan), 316,
333–34
Nijō, Emperor, 404n34
Nijō, Lady, 139, 143, 159, 412n18, 417n69
Nijō family, 175; in poetry disputes, 178–
79, 180, 423n26; Tsumori family and,
182, 424n34; anthological inclusion
of, 188f; anthology designations by,
426n54
Nijō-Kawara Rakusho (Nijō-Kawara
Lampoons), 194–95, 427n3
Nijō rakusho, 212
Niki family, 49, 389n12
Nishida Naojirō, 345, 352–53, 356
Nishioka Toranosuke, 348
Nishitani Saku, 410n2
Nitchū gyōji (Go-Daigo), 128
Nitobe Inazō, 214
Nitta family, 43, 71, 336–37
Nitta-no-shō (Kōzuke), 92
*Nitta sachūshō Yoshisada kyōkunsho, see
Yoshisadaki*
Nobunaga (Oda), 207
Nobushi (those who lie in the fields), 42
Nomoto Tsujūmaru, 41
Nō plays, 192f, 196, 203–7, 428n38
Norikuni (Imagawa), 220
Norisada (a Sahyōe guard), 423n25
Noritoki (Nagoya), 83

Northern Court, 85, 115, 120
Nunneries, 165–66, 420n111
Nyōbō hōsho (female palace official's
pronouncements), 142, 412n25
Nyōirin Kannon, 126

Ōbō-buppō (the Imperial Law and the
Buddhist Law) concept, 241, 244
"Ochō no shōmin kaikyū" (Nishida), 352
Ōe Hiromoto, 373n52
Ogasawara family, 231f, 433n72
Ogawa Makoto, 364–65
Ogawamiya, Prince, 166
Ōgimachi Machiko, 410n2
Okamoto Takenori, 93, 98
Okehazama, Battle of (1560), 207
Okinohama (Hakata), 70
Okujima village, 101–7 *passim*, 397–
98n70, 398n77
Okuma Shigenobu, 347
Okushima-no-shō (Ōmi Province), 158
Okutsushima Jinja, 101
Ōmi Province, 86–87, 98
Onari (shogunal processions), 208
Ōnin War (1467–77), 142, 244, 413–14n36
Onjōji temple, 247, 250, 435n32
Onryō (vengeful spirit): of Go-Daigo,
114–16, 117, 401n6
Ontokusei (debt-cancellation decrees),
21–23, 88, 371nn14,15
Ontsukai (enforcement officers), 88f
Ōryō (shrine lands), 51. *See also* Shrine
associations
Ōshima Jinja (shrine association), 101f
Ōta Estate (Bingo Province), 373n58
Ōta Gyūichi, 336
Otogi-no-shō (Yamato), 99
Ōtomo family: commendations to,
39, 67, 87, 377n1, 390n24; Kikuchi's
conflict with, 68–69, 70f, 75ff
Ōtomoki, 232
Ōuchi family, 51, 87, 381n61
Ōura village, 399–400n94
Owari Province, 86
Ōyama Estate (Tanba Province), 36,
376n106

Ōyama Kyōhei, 13–14, 397n62
Oyudono no ue no nikki (Daily Records of the Honorable Lady of the Imperial Office of Housekeeping), 142, 167

Pagodas of the Buddha's Favor, 287–89
Pai-chang Huai-hai, 273
Paintings, 118. See also Go-Daigo, Emperor, portraits of
Pan-China Sea region, 362f
Pan-Japan Sea region, 362f
Parturition, 163, 164–65
Patriarchy (kafuchōsei): periodization debate on, 146–47, 413–14n36
Patrilineal descent/inheritance, 146, 148, 150–51. See also Inheritance
Patrilocal marriage: transition to, 146–51, 155, 168, 415nn44,47. See also Marriage
Peasants (sōbyakusho): assuming proprietary powers, 6–7, 103–4, 105–6, 399nn86,92; in bandit gangs, 26, 372n36; as petitioners, 101–2, 104, 397nn67,68, 417–18n81, 418n87; women's roles, 157–60, 417–18n81, 418n87. See also Agriculture; Villages
Philippi, Donald L., 420n103
Po-chang, 306
Pollack, David, 316
Ponds, irrigation, 94–95, 394n30
Popkin, Samuel L., 400n105
Population, 92–93, 392nn5,10
Prajñātāra, 306
Prelude to the Cultural History of Japan (Nishida), 353
"Procedures of the Engi Era" (Engishiki), 165
Property rights, see Landholdings
Proprietors (ryōke): expanded eligibility for, 20, 23, 30–31, 371n24; jitō as, 32, 36; patron as, 32; peasants' interaction with, 103–4, 105–6, 399nn86,92
Public sphere: female-authored documents of, 142–43, 144, 154–55, 412n17; private sphere and, 144–45, 412n25; of marriage ceremony, 149, 152–53; shrine-association documents of, 158

Pure Land school: petition against, 297–98, 299, 311, 444n19

"Queen Srimala" painting, 124f

Raijun (Nejime), 380n39
Ran'aku (widespread and wanton), 27
Ranchin (spurious defense), 27
Records Office (Kirokujo), 20
Reischauer, Edwin, 428–29n3
Reizei line, 180, 189f
Rekishi kōron (Kuroda), 359
Rekishi monogatari (historical tales), 295, 441–42n1. See also Gunki monogatari
Religious figures: artistic representation of, 118, 402nn21,22
Religious institutions: as commendation recipients, 24f, 372n30; warrior elite's disrespect for, 198–99; role of, in kenmon system, 238, 241, 243, 359f. See also Buddhism; Buddhist establishment temples; Zen; Zen monastery system
Renga (linked verse), 170, 192, 194–95, 203
Renga anthologies, 190f, 427n60. See also Imperial anthologies
Rensho committee, 182, 424n35
Revenge custom, 156–57
Rewards (on): from hegemonic lordships, 42, 52–55, 56–57, 62, 381–82n71, 382n72; different forms of, 53, 381–82n71; for encampment, 54, 382n78; promises of, 54–55; and inviolable hereditary lands, 55–56, 57, 58–60; for Tatarahama warriors, 75–76; issued by shugo, 87, 390n26. See also Kishin
Rikka (flower arrangement), 201f
Rikka Kuden Daiji (Dōyo), 202
Rinji (imperial edict), 412n25
Rinsan Dōin (Ling-shan Tao-yiu), 271
Rinsenji (Musō), 284
Rinsenji temple (Kyoto), 12, 280–81, 441n49; petition-inventory of, 31–33, 374–75n75, 375n77
Rinzai Zen, see Zen

Rishōtō (Pagodas of the Buddhas's Favor), 287–89
Risshū kōyō (Gyōnen), 313
Ritsuryō (Fujiwara no Fubito), 339
Ritsu school, 165
Rokkaku family, 86–87
Rokuhara (Kyoto headquarters of Bakufu), 143ff
Rokujō poetry line, 177
Rokujō, Emperor, 404n33
Rokuonindono gogempukuki, 229
Rokuonindono on'naoihajimeki, 229
Rozanji (Kyoto), 403–4n31
Ruijū jingi hongen (Watarai Ieyuki), 132, 409n80
Ryakuōji temple, *see* Tenryūji
Ryavec, Carole Ann, 104
Ryōhen, 305
Ryōke, see Proprietors
Ryōke shiki (titles of ownership), 18, 381–82n71. *See also* Proprietors
Ryōkoku (semiindependent domains), 78
Ryōshi (enforcement officers), 88, 391n33
Ryōshun (Imagawa Sadayo), 39, 52, 55, 63, 87, 209, 390n24, 390–91n32; advice manual of, 214, 219–21
Ryūzan'an hermitage (Kai), 270
Ryūzōji family, 57

Sadahira, 141
Sadahisa (Shimazu), 70f, 75f
Sadako (Saionji), 118
Sadamasa (Takuma), 71
Sadamoto (Aki), 71
Sadamune (Ogasawara), 232, 433n73
Sadamune (Ōtomo), 68, 70f, 375–76n96, 416n64
Sadanori (Ōtomo), 71
Sadatoki (Hōjō), 266–67, 340–41
Sadatsune (Shōni), 41, 68–73 *passim*, 386n17, 416n64
Sadatsura (Miura), 272
Sadayoshi (Itoda), 70
Sagami, 175
Sagari Castle (Nagato Province), 71

Saichō (founder of Enryakuji), 245, 307, 311, 313
Saihoku shū (Shiren), 302
Saiki Kazuma, 142
Saionji family, 140–41, 161, 411n10
Saisokujō (orders of mobilization), 47
Sake brewers, 253f
Sakume nikki (Nishitani Saku), 410n2
Sakunin shiki (right to cultivate), 24
Śākyamuni, 296, 305f
Sale deeds: invalidation of, 21–23, 371nn14,15, 371nn17,19
San'ein ikai (Musō), 284
San'ein monastery, 283–84
Sanekane (Saionji), 181–82
Sanemoto (Tokudaiji), 160
Sanetomo (Minamoto), 175, 193, 421–22n12
Sanetoshi (son of Hino Meishi), 140f, 161, 163, 410n7
Sangi ittō ōsōji (Outline of the Unified Three Teachings), 231
Sangoku buppō denzū engi (Gyōnen), 300
Sanjō, Emperor, 150, 415n49
Sankajō duties, 85
Sanoyama, battle of (1335), 71
Sansom, George, 209, 369n8, 371n12, 377n3
Sarugaku performance, 203–4
Sasaki family, 86, 263
Sasaki Ginya, 395n44
Sata Mirensho, 42f, 46, 378n11
Satō Shin'ichi, 78–79, 81, 345, 350–51, 358, 360, 387–88n4, 388n6
Satsuroku (Collected Notes, Keisai), 333
Scroll paintings, 118
Seiashō (Ton'a), 174–75, 178
Sei band, 43, 45, 379n29
Seiken igen (Last Testaments of Calm Self-Sacrifice, Keisai), 323, 332–33
Sekiguchi Hiroko, 414n38
Sekiguchi Tsuneo, 395nn39,40
Sekiso shōsoku (Letters and Correspondence, Ichijō Kanera), 328
Sekito (Chinese monastery), 264

Senchaku bukkyō (selective Buddhism), 299. *See also* Pure Land school
Senchaku shū (Hōnen), 299
Sengaku, 178, 422n19
Sengoku age, 207
Seno Seiichirō, 1, 5–6
Senshūmon'in (daughter of Kujō Kanezane), 151
Sera, Prince (son of Go-Daigo), 280
Sesson Yūbai, 302
Seta family, 161
Setsuwa bungaku (tale literature), 295, 441–42n1
Seventeen Article Code (Prince Shōtoku), 212, 429n10
Shiba family, 49, 82f, 389n13; advice manual for, 217–19
Shiba Yoshimasa, 10
Shibukawa family, 49
Shibuya family, 63
Shigekage (Kobayakawa), 155
Shigemori (Heiki), 115
Shigenari (Otaka), 85–86
Shigetada (Hatakeyama), 389n13
Shigetoki (Hōjō), 214, 224
Shigetsuna (Sasaki), 227
Shih-chi (Ssu-ma), 314, 333
Shijō, Emperor, 404n34
Shiki (estate rights): expanded eligibility and, 4, 20–21; social hierarchy of, 18–19, 31; fractional *jitō* and, 21, 370nn9,10; as infinitely divisible, 21, 371n12; debt-cancellation decrees and, 21–23, 371nn14,15,19; unregulated commendations and, 23–25; banditry's impact on, 26–27; pretensions to holding of, 27–28, 373n52; as anachronism, in Rinsenji petition, 31–33; Go-Daigo's control of, 35, 36–37, 129, 136, 354, 360, 376nn105,110, 376nn111,113, 376–77n114; of warrior-class women, 154; and *kenmon* system, 239
Shikimoku, see Warrior legislation
Shikoku island, 80
Shikoku warriors, 50
Shimada Toranosuke, 218

Shimahata (raised fields), 93–94, 393n20
Shimazu family, 35, 39, 63, 70
Shimazu Suō Gorō Saburō Tadakane, 55
Shimizu Mitsuo, 345, 354–56, 357–58, 362
Shimosaka Mamoru, 438n82, 438–39n83
Shinchō Kōki (Record of Nobunaga), 207, 336
Shinchokusenshū (Teika, comp.), 171, 172–73, 174–75, 421–22n12
Shin'e (Nakahara), 211
Shingon monasteries, *see* Buddhist establishment temples
Shingosenshū (Tameyo, comp.), 181–82
Shin go shikimoku (New Formulary for the Palace, 1284), 340
Shingoshūishū (Tametō and Tameshige, comp.), 189, 190
Shin goshūi wakashū, 217
Shinjin yōketsu (Ryōhen), 305
Shinkan (Hamuro Mitsutoshi), 176ff, 422nn14,17
Shinkokinshū (Go-Toba, comp.), 171–72, 176, 184
Shinkoku (Japan as a divine country) theory, 354
Shinrokujōdai waka, 175–76
Shinsei (Kenmu), 70f
Shinsenzaishū (Tamesada), 188
Shinshokukokinshū (Asukai Masayo, comp.), 188–89
Shinshūishū (Tameaki and Ton'a, comp.), 189
Shin'yōshū (Munenaga Shinnō), 187–88, 426n54
Shirabyōshi (female entertainers), 159f
Shirakawa, Emperor, 171, 193, 246–47, 421n3, 425n40
Shiren (Kokan), 12, 118, 402n22; on Japan's sovereignty, 131–32; writings of, 300–301, 302–3, 443n20; religious training of, 301–2; on Zen's superiority, 306–7, 443n12; Chinese-style Zen of, 308–9; and Bodhidharma ritual, 316–17, 445n34. *See also Genkō shakusho*

Shiryō Henshū Kokushi Kōsei-kyoku, 346
Shiryō (private holdings), 23
Shisetsu system, 85, 88–90
Shitsuji (chief administrator), 82
Shōboku Myōtai, 443n12
Shōchō, 313
Shōdenji monastery (Kyoto), 304
Shōen (estates): fourteenth-century undermining of, 4, 26–27, 243–44; *jitō's* management of, 18; as commended property, 23f; and lack of house codes, 214; *kenmon* system and, 239, 255–56, 359; Nakamura's study of, 353–54. *See also* Landholdings; *Shiki*
Shōen-sei shakai (Society Under the Shōen System, Kuroda), 359
Shōichi Kokushi (Ben'en Enni), 266, 274, 288, 293, 301–80 *passim*, 312
Shōichi kokushi goroku (Shiren, comp.), 302
Shōin nikki (Ōgimachi Machiko), 410n2
Shoin-style rooms, 201, 208
Shōjō, 305
Shōjōkōji (Fujisawa): Go-Daigo's portraits in, 122, 125–27, 404n43
Shōkeibō Jizen, 166
Shokugenshō (Treatise on the Origins of Posts, Chikafusa), 121
Shokugosenshū (Tameie, comp.), 175–76
Shokugoshūishū (Tamefuji), 183–84
Shokukokinshū (1235), 171, 177–79
Shoku-Nihongi (Chronicle of Japan Continued), 333–34
Shokunin uta awase (Poetic contests in the voice of artisans and merchants), 158, 417–18n81
Shokusenzaishū (Tameyo, comp.), 183
Shokushūishū, 179, 422n24, 423n25
Shōmu, Emperor, 30, 128
Shōmyōji temple, 372n30
Shōni family, 43; dominance of, 67, 74; Kikuchi family and, 68–69, 72–73, 75ff; and Chinzei Tandai, 70; divided *shugo* post of, 87, 390n24

Shoshi (collateral branches), 81. *See also* Ashikaga collaterals
Shōshi (daughter of Go-Toba), 166
Shōshū ron (Shiren), 302
Shōtoku, Prince: Seventeen Article Code of, 212, 316f, 339, 429n10
Shōtoku taishi: Go-Daigo's ties to, 124, 125–26, 130, 405–6n49, 406nn50,55
Shrine associations (*miyaza*), 93, 100–101, 103, 157–58, 397nn63,66
Shūbun inryaku (Shiren), 302
Shu ching (Book of documents), 223, 333
Shūgi no jo (as a group), 102
Shugo (provincial military governor): Ashikaga's division of, 6, 20, 80, 86–87, 390nn21,27; in bandit gangs (*akutō*), 26, 372n35; *gokenin* appointments by, 29, 374n62; *taishō* status of, 49–50; dominant Kyushu families as, 67, 73–74; as intermediary figure, 78–79; family members as, 79; Takauji's initial placements of, 79–80, 387–88n4; *sankajō* duties of, 85; duties/powers of, in Nanbokuchō era, 85f, 87–88; *shisetsu* system and, 88–90, 390n30, 390–91n32; as Ankokuji and Rishōtō patrons, 288f
Shugo-daimyō, 78
Shugo ryōgoku, 358
Shu Han dynasty, 327
Shūhō Myōchō (Daitō Kokushi), 118, 262, 273, 275ff, 283, 402n22
Shūmon (essential gate), 306
Shūmon jisshō ron (Shiren), 303f, 306f, 443n12
Shun'oku Myōha, 277, 291, 439n3
Shunzei (Teika's father), 175
Shunzei no Musume (Teika's niece), 174, 176, 421n11
Shura (warrior) plays, 206–7
Smallholders, 6, 92, 97–98, 100–101, 395n40, 396nn49,50, 397n63
Smith, Thomas, 100, 397n63
Sō (community of the whole), 102, 397–98n70
Sokō (Yamaga), 13, 323; empirical/realist

approach of, 324, 339–42; on legitimacy, 339–41, 343
Sonkei (sister of Lady Nijō), 166
Sonpi bunmyaku (Bloodlines of Noble and Base, Kinsada), 121
Sorai (Ogyū), 343–44, 446n10
Sōryō system, 357
Southern Court: Shimazu's defection to, 39; confirmation of homelands by, 58–59, 60, 384nn108,110; Yoshiakira's defection to, 84; Shōni's defection to, 87, 390n24; anthology sponsorship by, 187–88; Kiyouji's defection to, 199–200; occupation of Kyoto by, 200, 255; *Taiheiki's* treatment of, 334–35; *Jinnō shōtōki's* view of, 335
Sovereignty: military force's ties to, 67, 116–17, 123, 135–36, 405n47; medieval views of, 114; Buddhism's ties to, 116, 125, 126–27, 130f; Chinese models of, 131–33; Go-Daigo's assertion of, 136–37. *See also* Legitimacy
Sozan (Chinese monastery), 264
Ssu-ma Ch'ien, 314
Ssu-ma Kuang: on legitimacy, 324–27, 328, 331, 333, 337, 447n25
Steenstrup, Carl, 224, 230
Śubhakarasimha, 313
Suganoura village (Ōni Province): land purchased by, 102, 104; dues/tax collection role of, 103, 398n77, 398–99n79, 399n85; warrior rivalries and, 104, 105, 397n66, 399–400n94; judicial functions of, 107f, 400n103; documentary records on, 401n119
Sui Yang ti, 335, 448n57
Sukehiro (Ito), 71
Sukemori (Taira), 410–11n8
Sukena (Hino), 139, 145
Suketomo (Hino), 139
Sukō, Emperor, 276
Suma Chikai, 395n43
Sumitomo rebellion (939), 339
Sung dynasty, 223, 225
Sung kao-seng chuan (Tsan-ning), 314
Sutoku, Emperor, 115, 401n5

Swords, 123f, 143, 232–33, 405n47, 405–6n49

Tachikawa sect, 130, 361–62
Tadafuyu (Ashikaga), 43, 56–58, 62, 378n13, 383n91
Tadayoshi (Ashikaga), 11, 116; and Kōno mobilization order, 48–49, 380nn43,45; rewards from, 54–55; Takauji's feud with, 56, 83–84, 90, 115, 197, 291, 383nn87,90, 388–89n11; in battle of Tatarahama, 73–75; Go-Daigo's vengeful spirit and, 114–15, 401n6; anthology approval by, 185; and Dōyo's exile, 198; and Yoritō's execution, 199; and Tenryūji temple, 249, 284f; Zen commitment of, 281, 282–83; Ankokuji and Rishōtō network of, 287–89; and Kenmu codes, 429n5
Taigi (the greater righteousness), 332
Taigi meibun, see "Name and status" ideology
Taiheiki (The Chronicle of the Grand Pacification): Dōyo in, 9, 198–203, 429n9; on rewards, 53–54; on Nanbokuchō wars, 68–74 *passim*; on Ashikaga clan divisions, 82; Go-Daigo's spirit in, 114ff, 401nn3,6; on Lord Kitayama's treachery, 140–41, 161, 163, 411nn10,12; on *basara* in Kyoto, 194, 195–96; historical value of, 197–98; *bunbu* concept in, 225; swords in, 232–33; Tokugawa interest in, 322–33; view of legitimacy in, 329–30, 331; "name and status" deficiencies of, 334–35; Kume on, 347; Kuroda's revival of, 358–59; international perspective on, 363–64, 378n16; Meishi and, 411n13
"*Taiheiki* to Nanbokuchō nairan" (The *Taiheiki* and the Nanbokuchō Disturbance, Kuroda), 358
"*Taiheiki* wa shigaku ni eki nashi" (Kume), 346
Taikō gyoki (Fujiwara Onshi), 410n2
Taira family, 66, 192f, 263

Taishō (military commanders), 49–50, 51, 86

Taizanji (Harima), 36

Takaie (Fujiwara), 66

Takamasa (Kiku), 70

Takama Yukihide, 36

Takamure Itsue, 8, 415n43; on marriage residence patterns, 146–47, 413–14n36, 414nn37,38; on commodified female body, 148f, 416n57; on warrior-class marriage, 152; on female roles, 160, 418n91; on rice cake ceremony, 415n44

Takanaga (Sasaki), 258

Takanao (Kikuchi), 66

Takatoki (Hōjō): lost legitimacy of, 35, 330, 341; mocked status of, 37, 197, 377n115; as Zen patron, 271, 272–73; Musō and, 277ff

Takatsuna (Ōi Kishirō), 55, 383n80

Takatsuna (Sasaki), 227

Takatsune (Shiba), 82, 202

Takauji (Ashikaga), 3, 145, 279, 369n5; rewards generosity of, 5, 45, 54–55, 56, 58f, 75–76, 381–82n71, 383n87, 384n106; *shugo* placements of, 6, 79–80, 387–88n4; imperial anthology production and, 8, 185, 188–89, 426n56, 426–27n59; advice manuals of, 10, 214–17, 369n7; Keisai on, 13, 335–36; Sokō's praise of, 13, 341; as new military patron, 35f, 376n98; defeat of Yoshisada by, 43, 65, 71; Tadayoshi's feud with, 56, 83–84, 90, 115, 197, 291, 383nn87,90, 388–89n11; Kōgon's legitimation of, 72; in Battle of Tatarahama, 73–75; Kyushu warriors of, 75, 386nn18,19; Kenmu codes of, 194, 211f; Dōyo and, 197f; as Zen patron, 249, 255, 281f, 284f; and Shōni lands, 390n24; warrior portrait of, 403n30

Takeda family, 79

Takegosho, 152, 416n55

Takemi Momoko, 164–65

Takemuki (Facing the Bamboo), 139, 410n4. *See also* Meishi (Hino)

Takemukigaki (memoir of Hino Meishi), 139, 140–44, 159, 161, 163, 410n7, 411n13

Takemukigaki zenshaku (Nakada and Mizukawa), 410n7

Takeo Shrine (Hizen), 76

Takesaki Suenaga ekotoba (Takizaki Suenaga Illustrated Scroll), 445n3

Takeshige (Kikuchi), 71

Taketoki (Kikuchi), 67–69, 70

Taketoshi (Kikuchi), 71–73, 76

Takeuchi Rizō, 356

The Tales of Ise, 205

Tamamura Takeji, 262, 270f, 278, 283

Tameaki (Nijō), 189

Tamefuji (Nijō), 184

Tameie (Mikohidari), 175–76, 177f, 181

Tamekane (Kyōgoku), 180–85 *passim*, 191

Tameko (Kyōgoku), 180

Tamenori, 180

Tamesada (Nijō), 188

Tameshige (Nijō), 189

Tamesuke (Reizei), 180, 274, 276–77

Tametō (Nijō), 189

Tameuji (Mikohidari), 179ff

Tameyo (Nijō), 180f, 182–83, 423n26, 424–25n37

Tanaka Yoshinari, 345, 347–49

Tanba Province, 86

Tanehira (Sōma), 60–61

Tanenao (Haruda), 66

T'angshu, 223

T'ang T'ai-tsung, 223f, 231

Tao-hsüan, 444n23

Tara Estate (Wakasa Province), 36, 376n106

Tatarahama, battle of (1336), 65, 73–75, 232

Tatchū (subtemple), 281

Tax system, 253f, 256, 357

Tea ceremony (*chanoyu*), 201, 203, 208

Tea competitions, 194, 196

Teika (anthology compiler): *Shinchokusenshū* anthology of, 171, 172–73, 174–75, 181, 421–22n12

"Temple for Pacification and Protection of the State" (*chingo kokka no dōjo*), 246. *See also* Enryakuji temple

Temples, *see* Buddhist establishment temples; Zen monastery system

Tendai sect, 244f; in multidoctrinal system, 246–47, 435n32; Zen patronage as threat to, 249–50, 251, 304, 436n54, 443n11; Jōzan's polemic against, 250–51, 436n51; Bodhidharma's ties to, 307, 316–17, 334n33; recognized authority of, 309, 443n15. *See also* Enryakuji temple

Tenmu, Emperor, 224f

Tenryūji (Temple of the Heavenly Dragon), 11; to honor Go-Daigo, 115–16, 117, 284, 290–91; Enryakuji's conflict with, 249–50, 257–58, 286, 309; land commendations to, 285; Zen documents on, 304

Tenryūji's Chronicle of Construction (*Tenryūji zōei kiroku*), 116

Tenshi sekkan miei scrolls, 119–22, 404nn33–35

Ti-fan (Plan for an Emperor, T'ang Tai-tsung), 223

Toba, Emperor, 120

Tōdaiji temple, 30, 33, 246, 250, 373n52

Toduko (tonsure), 263

Tōfukuji temple, 301, 376n98

Tōji (Shingon temple), 24, 397n62; petitions to, 101, 104f, 397n68; in temple conflicts, 246–47, 248, 436n40

Tōjiin goisho (Takauji), 214–17

Tōjiji temple, 287

Tokashi family, 89

Tōkei Tokugo, 265

Toki family, 86

Tokifusa (Madenokōji), 420n111

Tokimune (Hōjō), 83, 263, 278–79, 341, 438n77

Tokisuke (Hōjō), 83

Tokiuji (Yamana), 85–86, 286

Tokiyori (Hōjō), 83, 278, 340

Tokiyuki (Hōjō), 197

Tokoro arawashi (*mukotori* marriage ceremony), 152

Tokuchinho (Ōmi), 92

Tokugawa Bakufu, 210, 336–37

Tokugawa (Edo) period: *See also* Keisai (Asami); Sokō (Yamaga), 100; Blood Bowl hell of, 165; Buddhist organizations of, 298; historiography of, 321–24, 343–44, 445n3; female writing of, 410n2

Tokusei edicts, *see* Ontokusei

Tokushi yoron (A Reading of History, 1712), 321

Tokushō Zennin, 264

Tokusō (Hōjō chief), 83

Tōkyō Daigaku Shiryō Hensanjo, 346

Toll dues, 250, 256, 438n73

Tomiko (Hino), 139

Tomo family, 227

Tomomasa (Oyama), 227

Tomosada (Uesugi), 86

Ton'a (a waka scholar), 174–75, 178, 182, 189, 423n25

Tonomura, Hitomi, 3, 7–8, 105

Tosa family, 404–5n44

Tosa Province, 363–64

Toshimoto (Hino), 139

Toshiyori (Minamoto), 175

Towazugatari (The Confessions of Lady Nijō), 139, 143, 159, 412n18

Tozama: *miuchi's* distinction from, 42–48 *passim*, 62, 378n12; *gokenin* status of, 46f, 379n35; mobilization activity of, 48–51; as source of hegemonic power, 52, 53, 61, 63; Chikafusa on, 52–53; hereditary lands of, 55–56, 57, 58–60; surrendered autonomy of, 63–64, 86. *See also* Gokenin; Miuchi

Tōzan Tanshō, 301

Troost, Kristina Kade, 3, 6–7

Tsan-ning, 314

Ts'ao P'i, 327

Ts'ao Ts'ao, 335

Tso chuan (Commentary of Tso), 326, 329

Tsuchimikado, Emperor, 174, 176

Tsugita, 186
Tsugufusa (Madenokōji), 420n111
Tsu-hsiu, 314
Tsuji Zennosuke, 288
Tsukubashū, 203, 427n60
Tsumadoi (visiting a wife), 146
Tsumori family, 182, 424n34
Tsuneyori (Imagawa), 57
Tsung-ching lu (Yen-shou), 305
Tsung-mi, 305
Tsurezuregusa (Essays in Idleness, Kenkō), 195
Tsutsui no Jōmyō Meishū, 423n25
T'ung-chien kang-mu (Outline and Details of the *Comprehensive Mirror*, Chu Hsi), 325, 327, 332, 344, 446n10
Turner, Victor, 167
Tzu chih t'ung chien (Comprehensive Mirror for Aid in Government, Ssu-ma Kuang), 324–25, 331, 344

Uchikanrei (office of Bitō family), 82–83
Uchiyama Castle (Dazaifu), 72–73
Uchiyama Myōchin, 263
Uejima Tamotsu, 395n41
Uesugi family, 281, 388–89n11, 389n14
Ujihira (Kobayakawa family), 49
Ujimasa (Hōjō), 153
Ujimitsu (Hino), 411n12
Ujinori (chief priest of Munakata Shrine), 73
Ujiyasu (Ōtomo), 71, 75
Ujiyori (Imagawa), 231
Ujiyori (Shiba), 82
Ukyō no daibu, 410–11n8
Unganji monastery (Shimotsuke Province), 263, 268, 271
Unsui (wandering monks), 265, 268–69
Ury, Marian, 442n8
Ushio (Shimokawa), 232
Utsunomiya warriors, 43, 45, 423n25
Uwa Estate (Iyo), 85

Varley, H. Paul, 9–10, 225, 338, 429–30n20

Villages: permanent features of, 6–7; self-government of, 7, 99–100, 397n61, 397n62; confirmation of, 92–93, 392–93n14, 393n15, 396n51; communally owned resources of, 96, 102, 394n36, 395n39, 397–98n70, 398nn71,75,76; houseland of, 98–99, 396nn54,56,57; shrine associations of, 100–101, 157–58, 397n63, 397n66; commendation of property to, 102, 397–98n70, 398n71; dues/tax collection role of, 102–4, 398n77, 398–99n79, 399n85; assuming proprietary powers, 103–4, 105–6, 243–44, 399n92; judicial functions of, 106–8, 400nn103–6, 400n111; documentary records on, 109, 401n119; Marxist historiography of, 355, 357. *See also* Agriculture

Wade, Robert, 107
Wajima Yoshio, 431nn45–47
Wakadokoro (Bureau of Poetry), 182
Waka poetry, 170f, 192f, 195, 204. *See also* Imperial anthologies
Wakatsuki-no-shō, 99
Wakita Haruko, 144, 412n25
Wakō (pirates), 363
Wang Kŏn, 223–24
Warrior ceremonial, *see Buke kojitsu*
Warrior-class women, 8, 153–57, 416nn62, 64, 417n71
Warrior elite (*buke*): extravagance of, 9, 194–96; *jitō* role of, 18; *gokenin* status of, 29, 46f, 374nn62,64, 379n35; intervention in anthologies by, 171, 182–83, 185, 188–91; Kyoto presence of, 192–93, 194, 196, 207–8; disrespectful of authority, 198–99, 427–28n21; cultural contributions of, 201, 202–4; courtiers' ties to, 204–5, 208, 213, 228–30; role of, in *kenmon* system, 238, 240–41, 242–43; legitimacy of, 330f, 340, 343. *See also* Advice manuals; *Buke kojitsu*; *Bunbu ryōdo*
Warrior legislation (*buke-hō*), 9–10;

of Kamakura Bakufu, 85, 155–56, 210, 417n71; of Muromachi Bakufu, 194, 210–14, 429nn5,9; of Tokugawa Bakufu, 210, 428–28n3. *See also Kenmu shikimoku*

Warrior manuals, *see* Advice manuals

Warrior plays, *see Nō* plays

Warrior poets: imperial anthologies' inclusion of, 171, 175, 179, 189, 421–22n12, 423n25, 426–27n59; courtier style of, 190f. *See also* Warrior elite

Warriors: compensation of, for services, 5, 41, 43, 53–54, 381–82n71, 382n72; misguided military alliances of, 5–6, 66–67, 68–69, 70, 74–75; genealogies of, 29–30, 46, 121, 374nn67–69; competition for patronage of, 33–36, 375n95, 375–76n96; turncoat phenomenon of, 40, 377n3; *miuchi* vs. *tozama*, 42–43, 44, 47–48, 62, 378n12; Chikafusa on, 52–53, 329; hereditary lands of, 55–56, 57, 58–59; and "law of surrender," 60–61, 384n110, 385n113; Go-Daigo's sovereign ties to, 67, 116–17, 123, 135–36, 405n47; collateral branches of, 81; peasants' manipulation of, 104–5, 399–400n94; absented from villages, 109; artistic representation of, 118–19, 403nn28–30; marriage practices of, 152–53; inheritance practices of, 153–55, 416n62; adultery codes of, 155–57, 168; motherhood codes of, 163; martial skills of, 231–33, 433nn72,76,80. *See also* Advice manuals; *Miuchi*; *Tozama*; Warrior elite; Warrior legislation; Warrior poets

Was ist Kulturgeschichte? (Lamprecht), 352–53

Watarai Ieyuki, 132, 409n80

Waterwheels, 96, 394nn33,34

Wayo (compromise accords), 28, 30–31, 373n56

Webb, Herschel, 321

Wechsler, Howard, 223

Wei chih, 223

Wei dynasty, 327

Wenwu, 223–24. *See also Bunbu ryōdo*

Western culture: adultery laws of, 157, 417n75; duality model of, 163

Widows (*goke*), 161, 163, 165–66, 420n111

Wintersteen, Prescott, 87–88, 196

Women: diminished property rights of, 150–51, 153–55; roles of peasant, 157–60, 417–18n81, 418n87; as "dancing maidens," 159–60, 418n87; domestic vs. sexual roles of, 160–61; motherhood categories of, 161–63; birthing role of, 163–64; Blood Bowl hells of, 164–65, 419n98, 419n101. *See also* Female body; Women's writing

Women's writing: of diaries, 8, 139, 410n2; end of female subjectivity in, 139, 144, 167; descriptive categories of, 140, 410–11n8; strategy of concealment in, 140, 141–42, 411n13; of imperial public documents, 142–43, 144, 154–55; diminished property rights and, 154–55; of shrine-association documents, 158; revived palace diary and, 167f

Wrigley, E. A., 392n5

Wu-hsüeh Tsu-yuan (Mugaku Sogen), 265ff, 268, 270, 283, 308

Yagi Seiya, 401n6

Yakushin, 247–48

Yamaguchi Takamasa, 89

Yamana family, 83, 86

Yamanouchi family, 55

Yamato, 98, 396n52

Yamato Hannya-ji temple, 362

Yanagida Seizan, 312f

Yano-no-shō (Harima), 92f

Yasumori (Adachi), 83

Yasutoki (Hōjō), 82

Yen-shou, 305

Yi Sŏnggye, 224

Yometori (taking a bride or daughter-in-law), 146–47, 152, 416n57. *See also* Patrilocal marriage

Yonekura Michio, 403n29

Yoriharu (Hosokawa), 49, 380n47

Yorihisa (Shōni), 71f, 73–74, 75

Yoritaka (Kikuchi), 68
Yoritomo (Minamoto): institutional
 innovations of, 17–18, 66, 82, 115,
 152, 340; painting of, 119, 403n29; on
 bun and *bu*, 224; *buke kojitsu* of, 227,
 432n54
Yoritō (Toki), 194, 199
Yoritsune (Kujō), 152, 173, 416n55
Yoriyuki (Hosokawa), 44, 82, 84, 90, 217,
 251
Yoriyuki (Isshiki), 76, 387n21
Yoshiakira (Ashikaga), 43, 84, 189, 220,
 250; Dōyo and, 199, 200, 202; as
 Enryakuji patron, 255–56
Yoshida Toshihiro, 396n54
Yoshihiro (Ōuchi), 217, 220
Yoshiie (Minamoto), 192–93, 240
Yoshimasa (Ashikaga), 139
Yoshimasa (Oshima), 80
Yoshimasa (Shiba), 82, 202, 429–30n20;
 advice manual of, 214, 217–19
Yoshimi (Ashikaga), 139
Yoshimitsu (Ashikaga), 45, 189, 217, 250;
 tozama mobilization by, 49, 52; at *saru-
 gaku* performance, 203–4; *buke kojitsu*
 of, 228–29, 432n61; Enryakuji con-
 stables of, 258–59, 438n82, 438–39n83;
 and *gozan* system, 289
Yoshimitsu (Ishikawa), 384n102
Yoshimochi (Ashikaga), 139, 217
Yoshimoto (Imagawa), 207
Yoshimoto (Nijō), 203f, 228, 432n58
Yoshinaga (Niki), 75, 84
Yoshinao (Niki), 288
Yoshinobu (Ōnakatomi), 175
Yoshino chō-shi (The History of Yoshino-
 chō, Nakamura), 354
Yoshino jingū, 403–4n31
Yoshinori (Ashikaga), 139, 189, 439n86
Yoshisada (Nitta): advice manual of,
 10, 11, 58, 197, 214, 221–22, 279, 375–
 76n96, 430nn30,31; Takauji's defeat of,
 43, 65, 71
Yoshisadaki (Yoshisada), 214, 221–22,
 382n72, 430nn30,31
Yoshitoki (Hōjō), 82

Yoshitsune (Kujō), 152, 172, 175
Yoshiuji (Shiba), 389n13
Yoshiyasu (Ichijō), 173
Yuasa family, 88f
Yūgen aesthetic, 205–6
Yugenoshima village, 101, 104f, 397n67
Yūki family, 58–59, 61
Yukiie (Fujiwara Rokujō), 177
Yumiya no ie (warrior house), 42

Zasu (head abbot), 245
Zazen (meditation), 275, 312, 444n23
Zazen ron (Enni), 304
Zeami, 203, 204–6
Zeen (Nakahara), 211f
Zekkai Chūshin, 291
Zen: Buddhist establishment's competition with, 11–12, 244, 249–52,
 303–4, 309, 443n15; Ashikaga Bakufu's
 patronage of, 248–52, 259, 281, 282–
 83, 284–85, 291; Musō's commitment
 to, 264, 268–69, 289–90, 293; *sōrin*
 monasteries of, 264; Hōjō patronage of, 265–66, 271, 272–73, 278–79;
 Kyoto center of, 265–66, 274, 279,
 292; Kamakura center of, 266f; Chinese source of, 266–67, 273, 308,
 311, 312–15; Go-Daigo's patronage of,
 273–74, 275; Hanazono's interest in,
 275–76; doctrinal disadvantage of,
 305; Bodhidharma lineage of, 305–7,
 316–17, 445nn33,34; historical views
 of, 307–8; joint practice vs. pure, 308;
 standard transmission accounts of,
 311, 313; meditation component of,
 312, 444n23. *See also Genkō shakusho*;
 Musō Soseki; Shiren (Kokan); Zen
 monastery system
Zengi gemon shū (Shiren), 302
Zen monastery system (*gozan*): development of, 265–66; public temples of,
 280f; Tenryūji's rank in, 286; Tōjiji's
 rank in, 287; and Ashikaga Ankokuji
 network, 287–89; "medieval" component of, 293–94; Tōfukuji's rank in,

301; Chinese-style Zen of, 308. *See also* Zen

Zen *mondō* (encounter), 265

Zenmon ju bosatsu kaiki (Shiren), 302

Zenmyōji institutions, 165–66

Zenshū kōmoku (Shōjō), 305

Zen teachers (*chinso*): artistic representation of, 118, 402nn21,22

Zoku jūzenshi roku (Shiren), 302

Zoku shōbōron (Jōzan Sozen), 250–51

Zōta-no-shō (Sanuki Province), 55

Library of Congress Cataloging-in-Publication Data
The origins of Japan's medieval world : courtiers, clerics, warriors,
    and peasants in the fourteenth century / edited by Jeffrey P. Mass.
        p.   cm.
    Includes bibliographical references and index.
    ISBN 0-8047-2894-1 (cloth : alk. paper)
    1. Japan—History—Period of northern and southern courts,
1336–1392.   2. Japan—History—Kamakura period, 1185–1333.
3. Japan—Court and courtiers.   I. Mass, Jeffrey P.
DS865.5.O75   1997
952′.02—dc21   97-2475
                                                      CIP

♾ This book is printed on acid-free, recycled paper.
Original printing 1997
Last figure below indicates year of this printing:
06   05   04   03   02   01   00   99   98   97